ENCYCLOPAE

Not since the publi[...]
CALENDAR (1828), LIVES OF THE CRIMINALS (1735),
and PELHAM'S NEW NEWGATE CALENDAR (1886)
has a compilation of this kind been attempted.
Succinct but intensely readable accounts are given
of murders going back in time from the Hounslow
footpath case in 1960 to the case of the legendary
Sawney Bean who preyed on his victims from a
cave-dwelling in fifteenth century Scotland. The
scope is worldwide too, and the classic cases –
Crippen, Lizzie Borden, Christie, Heath, and the
rest – are given especially detailed treatment: but
there are hundreds of other murderers whose
names even addicts of murder cases will read here
for the first time; names such as Robert James, the
Californian barber who, before drowning his wife,
attempted to kill her by thrusting her leg into a box
of rattlesnakes. In addition to murder cases,
articles on fingerprints, assassination, the death
penalty, etc., are included under the various letters
of the alphabet.

Each of the joint authors contributes a preface:
Colin Wilson, in a brilliant essay, relating the
subject of murder to his Outsider thesis; Patricia
Pitman presenting an entirely opposing viewpoint
in which she adds the reservation – 'this
encyclopedia does not intend to be inclusive, nor
indeed could it be. In the last hour two murders
will have been committed in Mexico alone'.

ENCYCLOPAEDIA OF MURDER

COLIN WILSON
and
PATRICIA PITMAN

PAN BOOKS
LONDON, SYDNEY AND AUCKLAND

First published 1961 by Arthur Barker Ltd
First Pan Books edition published 1964
This edition published 1984 by Pan Books Ltd,
Cavaye Place, London SW10 9PG
9 8 7 6 5
© Colin Wilson and Patricia Pitman 1961, 1984
ISBN 0 330 28300 6
Printed and bound in Great Britain by
Cox & Wyman Ltd, Reading

ILLUSTRATIONS
IN PHOTOGRAVURE

We are indebted to Radio Times Hulton Picture Library for permission to use illustrations Nos. 8, 12, 15, 16, 17, 24, 28, 31, and 37. To Mirrorpic for permission to use illustrations Nos. 2, 4, 6, 7, 10, 14, 18, 20, 22, 23, 26, 29, and 34. To Keystone Press Agency Ltd for permission to use Nos. 1, 3, 5, 9, 11, 19, 21, 25, 27, 32, 33, and 36. To P.A. Reuter Photos Ltd for permission to use illustration No. 30 and to Paul Popper Ltd, for permission to use illustration No. 13.

CONTENTS

(See also the index at end of volume)

PREFATORY NOTE

Several articles in this volume were written by Jeffrey Gibian, including the sections on German war crimes and Japanese war crimes. All Mr Gibian's articles are signed with his initials; otherwise the compilers have made no attempt to indicate the authorship of various articles, although their differing views on subjects as capital punishment may offer an indication!

The compilers wish to offer their warmest thanks to Frank Lynder, who has supplied them with many details on German murder cases that they would otherwise have found unobtainable.

Indirect responsibility for this volume must go to Mr John Braine, who introduced the compilers. Within a few minutes, a mutual interest in crime and criminals had been discovered, and the present volume was planned and begun almost immediately.

Mr Philip Stephens has offered much advice on various points, as well as assisting in the detail of certain cases. The help of Dr Francis Camps has also been invaluable. Mr Peter Vane had been extremely helpful in the compiling of details concerning American murders.

It is impossible to list the number of people who have written to the compilers offering help or information. We would like, however, to offer our thanks to the correspondent who sent us C. H. Norman's note on Capital Punishment which we have used as an appendix, although we are no longer able to discover his name. We offer him our apologies for this carelessness.

It is hoped to publish a second volume in due course. This one makes, of course, no kind of claim to completeness, but is intended as a preliminary attempt at the task of classifying crime and criminals.

C. W. – P. P.

TO FRANK LYNDER

THE STUDY OF MURDER

For every minute that ticks past on your watch, a murder is committed in some part of the world. New York has a murder a day; Paris had (up till recently) two murders a day. London is law-abiding; it has only a murder a fortnight. In tropical countries, the murder rate is very high indeed, and in Mexico, murder accounts for more people than most diseases.

With murders multiplying at this rate, it would obviously be impossible to produce a volume that could honestly be called 'encyclopaedic'. Within six hours of my writing these words, more murders will have taken place than there are in this volume.

What, then, is its purpose? Can one learn anything from the study of murder?

In the scientific sense, I doubt it. The sort of 'facts' I have learned in compiling my half of this book are of no particular interest. You will observe that the names of most murderers fall in the first half of the alphabet, from A to M. I do not know why this should be; the fact, if it *is* a fact, is wholly useless. And so are most facts about murder. Sherlock Holmes once told Doctor Watson that one of his great advantages over the police was his wide knowledge of criminal cases of the past. 'Crime, like history, repeats itself.' Since I have been working on this book, I have found no evidence for the truth of his statement. This being so, I can think of no sound, scientific reason for an encyclopaedia of murder. Although its cases are arranged from A to Z, it is not intended primarily as a reference book; it is for casual reading, like any one of the innumerable volumes on murder that appear every year. Its cases have been selected because of some peculiar interest in the method of murder or circumstances surrounding the crime, or occasionally because some unusual legal point arose in connexion with the case. Ninety-nine per cent of murders are unpremeditated: brawls in pubs, family quarrels, the sudden violent impulse. There are very few of these in this book. Of the murder cases that remain, the ones that I personally have found most interesting are those in which it is possible to gain some insight into the murderer's mind. For this reason, the Kürten case must always remain a kind of classic, like that of Lacenaire. If, in fact, there is anything to be learned from the study of murder, it is from such cases as these.

There was a time when murder was purely a moral issue. In recent years, it has been the fashion to treat it as a purely sociological or psychological problem. But even modern psychology is learning that there is a point at which it becomes impossible to avoid asking 'ultimate' questions. Progoff's book, *The Death and Rebirth of Psychology*, begins with the sentence: 'Although it began as a part of the protest against religion, the net result of modern psychology has been to reaffirm man's experience of himself as a spiritual being.'

This expresses my own conviction. No doubt it is true that the time has gone past when man could accept the ready-made answers of religion to his questions about ultimates. But this does not mean that it is now useless to ask the questions. On the contrary, it is time that men began to repeat the questions in a new tone – in a spirit of caution and empiricism. Generalizations must always be regarded with suspicion, but there is no way of finally avoiding them. The subject of philosophy is not Mr Smith's relations with his boss and 'the hidden persuaders'; it is not Professor X's criticisms of Hegel and Bradley either. There is still the universe, which is an alien and empty place; there are still human beings; some of them living strangely meaningless lives in dirty wooden huts with less than enough to eat, others suffering from dyspepsia in central-heated apartments. The poets continue to assure us that man is the master of his fate, is a thinking reed, is a creature who will one day become a god. Taken at its surface value, the world offers no support for these views.

But how do we go about investigating the problem? If human beings ever acted with freedom, we might have a chance to judge man's spiritual stature. As it is, all man's most important activities – from writing a symphony to committing a murder – are mixed up with all kinds of urges and ties that comprise ninety-nine per cent of his identity.

The problem must be approached as if we were analytical chemists confronted with a strange powder. As far as possible, the element we are looking for must be separated from the rest.

So, for me, this volume represents three hundred or so watchglasses containing unknown powders, each one a challenge in analysis. Shaw said that we judge an artist by his highest moments and a criminal by his lowest. If we are to accept the word of the artists about what man can attain in his highest moments, then we should counterbalance it with an examination of his lowest moments. The analysis of crime is unpleasant; it is not unlike the pathologist's task in dissecting a year-old body. Of necessity, it cannot be accompanied by the same pleasure we might take in analysing Mozart or Beethoven; but it has to be undertaken. Many murderers are spiritual corpses; but we can learn as much from dissecting a corpse as from a living body. There *are* other ways of learning about human free will – for example, from the works of Dostoievsky and Strindberg and Wedekind. But this volume is the raw material of Dostoievsky and Wedekind. After spending a year compiling it, my final feeling is not revulsion, but a sense of tragedy, of pity. This is a human rubbish dump. If man can ever become a god, this is what he has to surmount.

Since this is a book for the general reader, it might be as well to offer some preliminary account of the background of existentialism against which my own study of murder has taken place. Readers of my previous books are advised to skip several pages.

Existentialism

Existentialism is preoccupied with the same basic questions as all the religions: What is man? Why are we alive? What is the purpose of human existence? A school of modern thought regards these questions as nonsensical in the sense that they are unanswerable, and that therefore there is no point in asking them. Existentialism ignores the possibility that they are unanswerable, and concentrates on the problem of the most logical and 'scientific' method of studying them. Inevitably, it removes the emphasis from 'philosophical speculation' in the manner of Hegel or the British empiricists, and transfers it to the study of human psychology. In this sense, Pascal is the most important forerunner of modern existentialism. Nietzsche and Kierkegaard may be regarded as its joint founders. In the twentieth century, the greatest single contribution to existential thought has been made by George Gurdjieff, and can be studied in the works of his disciple, P. D. Ouspensky.

An inevitable preliminary to speaking of the study of murder is to attempt to give a brief exposition of the 'position of man' in our time according to existential philosophy. Within its context can be seen the meaning of the 'raw material' offered elsewhere in this volume.

The starting point of existentialism is a denial that the values by which most civilized men think they live have any reality or meaning. It holds that civilized man has a false picture of himself, and that its falseness has led to the dangerous position in which man finds himself today, sitting on a world that is like an enormous powder-barrel waiting to be detonated by an atomic explosion.

There is in human beings an automatic tendency to assume that man lives by values, that 'what we are' is an outcome of our free will, directed by our sense of values. Hence we live in a civilization, which is a result of our need for peace; we live in houses, which are the result of our need for security, etc. Everything about our existence demonstrates some aspect of our sense of values. Values are what distinguishes a man from an animal; they are also the most essential difference between one human being and another. They give a man what is most essential to his self-respect: the right to judge other human beings. This does not depend on intellectual brilliance or athletic prowess; his values permit him to pass judgement on a scientist, a poet, a film star or the world boxing champion. They make him unique.

The existential view is pessimistic by comparison with this one. Man lives entirely on the biological level; he has no need whatever of values, or of free will. He is alive; that is the primary fact, and the life in him responds to the pressures of everyday living. His stomach is kept filled with food and his mind with activity. Men are propelled through life by the gentle pressure of physical events, and the amount of free will called upon is infinitesimal. 'When his café empties, his head empties too', says Sartre of one of his characters. There is another French novel that describes a number of men trapped in a dugout, with food and drink enough for years; it tells the story of their complete moral disintegration with 'nothing to do'. (Peter Kürten, the Düsseldorf sadist, attributed his 'moral breakdown' and the development of his sadism to long periods of solitary confinement in jail.) This is the 'pointless freedom', dealt with by Camus in the early pages of *L'Étranger*, and by Samuel Beckett in a series of works whose aim is to make the reader aware that his own life is totally devoid of values.

In earlier ages, this lack of free will in human beings was hardly important. Life was busier and harsher than in the twentieth century, and, without leisure, belief is irrelevant. Although the Middle Ages are called 'The Ages of Faith', faith was, in fact, more dispensable than it is today. A few men – saints and ascetics – felt the indignity of living under the inexorable authority of events, and retired into solitude to confront the problem of boredom. They had more dramatic names for this problem – like 'The dark night of the soul', 'The cloud of unknowing' – but it amounted to the same thing. The pressure of events is man's chief ally against boredom; the saints and ascetics declined the help of this ally and sought to develop an inner strength capable of propelling them from day to day. Many such men completely mistook the nature of the problem, and transferred it to the lower physical level; instead of the mind declining the help of physical distractions, the body was made to reject the help of food and drink, and was goaded with unpleasant stimuli – hair shirts, self-flagellation, etc. These exercises were naturally effective up to a point, since they developed strength of will; but they were bound to fail in their main purpose: to produce an interior power, a concentration.

The development of science and mathematics in the hands of men like Galileo and Newton produced the greatest revolution in Western civilization since the advent of Christianity. 'Nature's great book is written in mathematical symbols', said Galileo; and Darwin added, some centuries later: 'Mathematics seems to endow one with something like a new sense.' New senses, new freedom, man raised to the possibility of the understanding of a god, all knowledge at his disposal: this was the scientific vision. And there can be no doubt that science was a new dimension of freedom for human beings, as momentous, perhaps, as the step that Nietzsche imagined between man and superman.

But a movement towards freedom does not mean the achievement of ultimate freedom. The mathematician who can sit at his desk for ten hours at a stretch, working out equations, has progressed beyond the peasant, whose incentive to work is the feeding of his family. But he cannot be said to be exercising free will. His mind limps forward, using the crutches of logic. The dawn of scientific knowledge is not the dawn of the final emancipation of the human spirit. In some ways, the Christian Church was wiser; the saints and ascetics at least knew how little free will man possesses, and that his evolution depends on the development of this minute spark of will. The humanists also knew that freedom is subjectivity; but they made the mistake of supposing that, since knowledge has widened man's inner world and made him more 'subjective', he needed only to keep on increasing his knowledge to achieve complete freedom. The Church further muddied the issue by treating the humanists as heretics and burning them. It was a great many centuries before a healthy revolt against humanism took place, a revolt that attacked its real weaknesses, and did not raise false issues of 'heresy'. Men like Blake, Law, Kierkegaard, Dostoievsky, recognized that man does not necessarily develop an atom of free will even if he devotes his whole life to abstract thought. The philosopher or scientific thinker can be propelled forward by the logic of abstraction as will-lessly and effortlessly as the ploughman is propelled by the logic of events. Such a life requires no values. Real values are insights into the meaning of free will. The man who knows himself well enough to recognize his lack of free will, comes also to recognize that man's evolution is the development of free will, and that the step from ape to man, from ploughman to philosopher, is simply a gain in freedom. The sense of the real meaning of freedom is the religious sense.

Dostoievsky possessed this insight in a powerful degree, and it is significant that his mind was obsessed by atheism and murder. These two have an important characteristic in common: they clearly imply the values they contradict. Atheism is a distillation of all that is negative about humanism. The mediaeval Christian believed he possessed 'truth' when all he possessed was a number of religious dogmas. The atheist makes the opposite mistake of supposing he possesses truth because he is clever enough to reject these dogmas. The result is a system of 'values' that are really not values at all, but negations.

Dostoievsky's work is largely an attempt to dramatize this failure of values. Perhaps his most typical character, in this sense, is Kirilov (in *The Devils*) who declares that since there is no God, it is necessary to kill himself to prove his own godhead. The other major character in that novel, Stavrogin, is driven to commit crimes to prove to himself that he possesses free will even if he has no beliefs. Hence murder is the meaninglessness of life become dynamic, a dramatization of the hidden futility of life. It is the human act, with all its inherent values, placed upon the microscope slide where it cannot dissolve into the featureless landscape of all other human acts. The study of murder is not the study of abnormal human nature; it is the study of human nature stained by an act that makes it visible on the microscope slide.

In an over-simplified form, the problem might be stated in this way: If everyday life is futile and trivial, we can find no reason in our 'everyday values' why it should not be so. To become aware of such reasons, we would need a standpoint outside our day-to-day existence, the standpoint of an intenser state of consciousness. All art is an attempt to provide such a standpoint. Unfortunately, because of a peculiarity of human consciousness,[1] it is easier for the artist to communicate this intensity by evoking negative rather than positive values, i.e. the artist finds it easier to provide his contrast to the 'everyday world' by writing of human suffering and misery rather than of human happiness.

Duerrenmatt's The Pledge

In art, then – especially the kind of art that is concerned with moral values – the reader's disposition to reflect is aroused by presenting him with negative values, i.e. with a proposition designed to provoke his resistance. Dostoievsky's art depends almost entirely on producing this kind of effect; Raskolnikov is an example, with his: 'Murder is lawful', or Kirilov: 'Suicide is the only logical reaction to the death of God'.

An interesting example of the use of 'negative values' is presented in Friedrich Duerrenmatt's book The Pledge (Das Versprechen), which has an additional relevance here because of its use of the theme of sexual murder. The story is narrated by 'Herr M.', a Zürich chief of police, who takes the narrator to a garage where a drunken old man serves them with petrol. Herr M. reveals that the old man was once one of his best detectives, a man named Mätthai. Mätthai was about to fly to Jordan to take up an appointment when he was appointed to a case in which a small girl had been murdered by a sex maniac with a razor. An old pedlar was arrested for the murder, and grilled until he 'confessed'; he later committed suicide in his cell. The case is apparently closed. But Mätthai has promised the parents of the

[1] For my own convenience, I have always referred to this peculiarity as 'the St Neot margin' or 'threshold', since the idea first clearly presented itself to me when I happened to be travelling through St Neots in Huntingdonshire. There is a certain margin of boredom or indifference when the human mind ceases to be stimulated by pleasure, but can still be stimulated by pain or discomfort. Its cause is usually mental exhaustion (or inactivity), and it is the chief subject of a great deal of nineteenth-century literature, including Goncharov's Oblomov and many stories of Tchekov.

murdered girl that he will find the murderer, and he is convinced that it was not the pedlar. He decides not to fly to Jordan, and continues to work on the case as a 'freelance'. The girl is the third to have been murdered in the same area over a period of several years. From clues he discovers, Matthäi decides that the killer is a man who drives an American car with the symbol of a nearby Canton on its number plate. He buys a garage on the main road, takes as his housekeeper a prostitute with a small daughter who resembles the three murdered girls, and settles down to wait for the murderer to fall into his trap.

The morality of the matter is plainly somewhat dubious. The prostitute has no idea that her daughter is being used as bait for a sex-murderer.

One day, Matthäi phones his ex-colleagues in Zürich; he is almost sure that the bait is about to be taken. A strange man has started to meet his adopted daughter out of school and give her sweets. The police lie in wait in a wood near the child, and watch for the killer. But no one appears. Matthäi continues his wait at the service station, certain one day that the killer will fall into the trap. The prostitute now knows that her daughter is merely 'bait', and becomes sluttish; the daughter grows up and follows in her mother's footsteps; Matthäi becomes a drunk.

But the real point of the story occurs in the last chapter. By complete chance, Herr M. discovers that Matthäi was right. The killer, a moronic youth, *had* selected Matthäi's adopted daughter as his next victim. But on the day he set out to murder her – and while the detectives lay in wait – he was killed in a car crash.

The story is an existentialist parable. At one point, Herr M. comments that, if this were a film, the murderer would have been caught just as he was about to kill the child, and Matthäi would have been a hero.[1] The end would have 'justified' the means. But although Matthäi was right, there was no 'happy ending' to distort the meaning. By being rendered negative, Matthäi's act can be seen clearly.

The Hollywood film at which Herr M. jeers is the perfect symbol for our curious way of passing value judgements. The end justifies everything; the end is the 'meaning', the summary. One of the favourite Hollywood film plots is the story of the genius who preserves his faith against all odds and is finally

[1] I believe that a film with such an ending has been made of the book.

justified. But this type of reasoning is not confined to Hollywood. We bring it to bear, for example, on the lives of men like Keats, Shelley, Rupert Brooke. (An example can be found in Sir Edward Marsh's introduction to Brooke's poems, which ends by describing Brooke's grave with the sunset behind it and 'a crimson halo'. 'Every colour had come into the sea and sky to do him honour.') The early death neatly rounds off the life, allows it to be interpreted and invested with meaning – usually romantic. (The extraordinary cults that sprang up after the deaths of Rudolph Valentino and James Dean demonstrate the same point.)

By introducing his 'banal' ending, Duerrenmatt has suspended this activity of *interpreting in the light of the end,* and left the problem exposed, naked.

This is precisely the function of the existential study of murder. By its negative nature, the act creates a resistance in the reader; when the cause of this resistance is analysed, the result is an insight into positive values. The method might be compared to the mathematical system of 'negative proof'; in order to prove that a theorem must be true, this method begins by stating: 'Let us suppose for a moment that it is not true . . .', and then demonstrates that the consequences would be self-contradictory.

The Lonely Inn Murder

A typical and simple example is provided by the murder of Mrs Collinson at Little Hayfield in 1927. The murderer, George Hayward, was a traveller for a firm of soap manufacturers, and lived close to the New Inn, run by Arthur Collinson. In October 1927, he was dismissed from his firm and asked to return £70 of the firm's money that he held. He also owed money for rent, and for furniture bought on the hire-purchase system.

The New Inn itself does not seem to have been a paying proposition; its owner went to work every day, leaving his wife in charge. On November 11th, Hayward bludgeoned her to death and stole about £40. He immediately travelled to Manchester and paid off two instalments of £2 each on the furniture (the second was not quite due). The police had no difficulty in tracing the crime to Hayward; the bludgeon, a piece of lead pipe, was found to fit a sawn-off waste-pipe outside Hayward's cottage. In due course, Hayward was executed; it was an 'open and shut' case, with no interesting aspects. But the most pathetic feature of the case is the hire purchase on the furniture. Hayward was a married man; he had the usual longing for security. This was the only 'value' underlying the crime – security, domestic peace. One becomes aware of his complete under-estimate of the value of life – his victim's and his own. Two lives were sold for £40 and the hire purchase on some furniture.

There are no doubt millions of lives in every civilized country today whose underlying values are equally trivial and pathetic and, by our present standards, these are the lives of decent and socially desirable human beings. And nothing is more difficult to speak about than these values. Physical facts, lives 'taken for granted', are disconcertingly self-contained; by their very factuality they deaden the reaction that would be an assessment of their value. When Zola sets out to condemn the lives of his Parisian bourgeoisie in *Pot Bouille*, he is forced to turn them into adulterers, liars, and hypocrites.[1] But this kind of condemnation defeats its own purpose, for it is not the true objection to the values of the 'bourgeois'; in order to attack them, it is forced to transform them into something else. It is the *essential triviality* of George Hayward's values that is dramatized by his crisis, and which thus becomes assessable.

One of the favourite methods of existentialism is to reassess values in the face of the 'absolute' value of life, as revealed by death. Dostoievsky speaks of this absolute value in *Crime and Punishment*, when Raskolnikov meditates:

> ... someone condemned to death says, or thinks an hour before his death, that if he had to live on a high rock, on such a narrow ledge that he'd only have room to stand, and the ocean, everlasting darkness, everlasting solitude, everlasting tempest around him, if he had to remain standing on a square yard of space all his life, a thousand years, eternity, it were better to live so than die at once.

It is precisely this knowledge of the value of life that the murderer lacks. But we all lack it to some extent. Only a few saints and mystics break through the hedge of daily trivialities to some partial awareness of the reality. Murder is a mani-festation of the *universal* failure of values. As such, its study has for the existentialist the same kind of message that the lives of the saints have for the devout Christian.

---

[1] Grace Metalious, of course, goes even further in *Peyton Place*, where the American bourgeois become murderers and sexual perverts.

The 'Abnormality' of Murder

Belief in the abnormality of the murderer is a part of the delusion of normality on which society is based. The murderer is different from other human beings in degree, not in kind. *All our values are makeshift;* the murderer simply goes further than most people in substituting his own convenience for absolute values.

But it is interesting to note how society prefers to regard the murderer as a being of alien species. Consider, for example, the case of the murder of Wanda May Wheatley in the United States a few years ago. The murderer was a taxi-driver who strangled the girl to silence her outcry after raping her. He was traced through her wrist-watch, which he had made the mistake of pawning.

In his confession, the taxi-driver – who knew the girl slightly – told how he had offered her a lift home in his taxi, and had stopped in a dark lane and tried to kiss her. She slapped his face, and he hit her back. The blow knocked her half-unconscious and, in the taxi-driver's own words, 'I had to have her'. The next evening, he returned to the scene of the crime and stole her wrist-watch.

Sentencing the murderer, the judge described the crime as 'one of the most callous and cold-blooded in my experience'. In view of the facts of the case, his words seem almost laughably inapplicable. The taxi-driver was a bachelor who lived alone; he had an inferiority complex where women were concerned. It is almost certain that he did not intend to murder the girl when he stopped his taxi in the dark lane; his confession gives the impression that he thought about rape only when the girl was half-unconscious. The words 'callous and cold-blooded' are, under the circumstances, absurd, but they serve the important function of placing the murderer in the category of the abnormal, the inhuman, the 'monsters'.

The Crime of Boredom

Existentialism is the attempt to evaluate human existence pragmatically, to create a system of values 'without appeal' – without appeal, that is, to religion or scripture or supernatural authority. Its methods may be those of a logical positivist, but its field is the field of day-to-day human existence. It finds a washerwoman's quarrel with her husband as interesting as Kant's speculations about time and space. It could be defined as the method of the scientist applied to the material of the novelist.

But the two cases cited above provide only the simplest kind of example of the existential approach to the study of murder, the attempt to study values. A great number of similar cases could be cited and labelled 'murder for insufficient reason' (for example, the cases of Albert Burrows, Patrick Higgins or Frederick Seddon, cited in this book). But there are other crimes that lead into deeper waters. Take, for example, the strange case of Edgar Edwards, the Camberwell murderer. In December 1902, Edwards was an unemployed clerk, a slender, adenoidal young man with a receding chin. He saw in a newspaper an advertisement for the sale of a grocery business in Camberwell, owned by a man named Darby. Armed with a sash weight on the end of a length of cord, Edward visited Mr Darby and asked to see the business; he then murdered Mr and Mrs Darby and their baby, and put the bodies in packing cases, which he buried in the garden of a house which he rented in Leyton. He also transferred from the shop all the furniture and goods. He told some of Mr Darby's customers that the family had moved 'up north', and the explanation was accepted, except by those to whom the Darbys owed money.

For the next few months, Edwards lived quietly and decorously in his Leyton house, spending the contents of the cash box taken from the shop. When this was empty, he tried the same method a second time, inviting to his house a man named Garland who had a business to sell. Garland proved to have a harder skull than the Darbys, and gave the alarm. Discovery of the bodies followed. At his trial, Edwards seemed bored by the formalities, and objected several times to the length of speeches. He even found the demand whether he plead guilty or not guilty an absurd waste of time. Later, as he approached the scaffold, he commented: 'I've been looking forward to this a lot.'

The case has some resemblances to Camus' *L'Étranger*, written forty years later. Like Meursault, Edwards was indifferent to the usual values of life. Living was mostly boring formalities. One can imagine his attitude on being reprimanded by one of his seniors for being late at the office. For such a man, life is a farce in dubious taste. After the murder, he lived quietly; all he asked was to be left alone. It is unlikely that the crime troubled his conscience; in committing it, he had been taking his revenge on 'life' – or perhaps only on society (two abstractions that play a considerable part in the minds of most murderers).

But the trial, again, was a ridiculous and meaningless ritual, another proof of the malevolence, the grotesque irony, of life. It could only confirm his feeling that life is absurd.

The case of Edwards goes closer to the heart of the existentialist dilemma because his values had collapsed so much more completely than those of George Hayward. It brings to mind an autobiographical essay by Graham Greene, 'The Revolver in the Corner Cupboard', where this state of mind is expressed with great clarity. Greene tells how he used to play Russian roulette with his brother's revolver on Berkhamsted Common after a course of psycho-analysis had left him 'correctly oriented' and able to take an 'extrovert interest' in his fellows, but totally bored with life.

> I think the boredom was far deeper than the love. It had always been a feature of childhood. . . . For years . . . I could take no aesthetic interest in any visual thing at all; staring at a sight that others assured me was beautiful, I would feel nothing. I was fixed in my boredom.

He took the revolver on to Berkhamsted Common, loaded one chamber, pointed it at his head, and pulled the trigger. When the hammer clicked on an empty chamber, he experienced a sense of release from the tension.[1]

This episode reflects some light on the case of Edwards. In Edwards, the boredom led to an act of violence against society; in Greene, to an act of violence against himself. In Stavrogin, Dostoievsky showed the same state of mind leading to both kinds of violence.

It is interesting to study Greene's account of how his positive values developed out of the state of boredom; it occurs in the preface to *The Lawless Roads*:

> And so faith came to one – shapelessly, without dogma, a presence above a croquet lawn, *something associated with violence, cruelty, evil across the way*. One began to believe in heaven because one believed in hell, but for a long time, it was only hell one could picture with a certain intimacy. [My italics.]

[1] Greene was living within the 'St Neot Margin'. This episode could serve as the perfect ostensive definition of this mental state: complete insensitiveness to beauty, but ability to find release through danger or discomfort.

He goes on to speak of the kind of episodes that were able to convey a sense of values across the indifference threshold:

A boy of twenty and a girl of fifteen had been found headless on a railway line. They had lain down together with their necks on the rails. She was expecting a child – her second. Her first had been born when she was thirteen, and . . . her parents had been unable to fix responsibility among fourteen youths.

The father said that when they spoke to the girl about the baby, 'she dropped her head and started crying'.

It has sometimes been objected that Greene's work, like Camus', possesses a sense of hell without the sense of heaven. This cannot be said of Dostoievsky, whose imagination returns repeatedly to the idea of some perfect harmony in the world, a vision of the final happiness of all human beings. But Dostoievsky's vision, like Greene's, began with hell, and it is difficult to see how it could have begun otherwise.

The Psychology of Motiveless Crime

The twentieth century is notable for the increase in sexual murder and sadistic murder. The question of why this should be so deserves study. The 'typical' murder of the mid-nineteenth century was the domestic poisoning case, or various crimes of passion. (We think of Dr Pritchard, Madeleine Smith, Constance Kent, the Charles Bravo case.) Half a century earlier, it was robbery with violence (Thurtell and Hunt, the Ratcliffe Highway murders, Burke and Hare). But to find a parallel with the crimes of the twentieth century, we have to go to an altogether earlier age, and read of witchcraft, and the crimes of men and women who thought themselves vampires or werewolves. It is difficult to understand why this should be so, except that in our time, as in the Middle Ages, many crimes are an expression of revolt against society. One might say (borrowing David Riesman's terminology) that both ages were 'other directed'; in the Middle Ages, it was the Church that represented the beliefs of society; in our own time, the machinery of government and business dominates the individual. The age of reason and scepticism was also the age of reasonable crimes. But we have only to compare the celebrated cases of the past – the Red Barn murder, Lacenaire, Crippen, Charley Peace – with those of our own day – Christie, Haigh, Heath, Kürten, Fish – to see that a strangeness has come into murder. Jack the Ripper

(1888) inaugurated the era of twentieth-century crime, together with his contemporaries, Neill Cream and George Chapman. The twentieth-century murderer tends to be insane; but this should not be made an excuse for declining to try to understand the complex pressures and strains that lead to his apparently 'motiveless crime'. They throw some interesting light on the relation of the individual to society in our time.

Does 'motiveless crime' exist? There are certain crimes whose only motive seems to be a desire to break beyond the 'indifference threshold'. For example, the case of Norman Smith, who in April 1959, was charged with the shooting of Mrs Hazel Woodard. Smith was a bachelor who lived alone in his caravan in Sarasota County, Florida. On the evening of the murder, in March, he had been watching a television programme called 'The Sniper' about a man with a psychopathic hatred of women. At the end of the play, he took his pistol and went out with the intention of shooting someone. The victim happened to be Mrs Woodard, who was sitting alone in front of her TV set. Smith was unacquainted with her. Apparently he killed out of boredom.

The same might be said of the Leopold and Loeb murder case; the two teen-age students who killed Bobby Franks were bored rich boys who found life dull; students of Nietzsche, they felt immeasurably superior to their fellow students at the University of Chicago. But something had to be done to prove it to themselves, something to confirm them in their sense of being lone wolves, supermen in a society of pygmies. As most men only feel confident to label themselves 'authors' when they have published a book, so Leopold and Loeb needed to commit a 'definitive act' to assure them of their status as 'outsiders', as men to be clearly distinguished from the surrounding mediocrity. In another ten years' time, the act of violence would have been unnecessary; both would have been sufficiently certain of superiority not to have to go through with the 'dare'; but the teens is a period of uncertainty, when the authority of society seems overwhelming, and an act of violent revolt seems the only satisfactory form of self-assertion.

The murder, of course, was stupid and appalling; but the judgement of society was barbaric. In Sweden today, they would have been sentenced to a maximum of ten years' imprisonment, with a possibility of parole after five, and undoubtedly this sentence would have met the case. In spite of its horrifying nature, the crime was essentially a piece of juvenile delinquency; it is almost certain that neither Leopold nor Loeb would have committed another murder on their release from jail. Instead, both were sentenced to ninety-nine years imprisonment, avoiding the death sentence only because of the impassioned plea of their attorney, Clarence Darrow, who declared his certainty that they were insane (which they were not). Richard Loeb was murdered in jail by another prisoner to whom he had allegedly made homosexual advances; Leopold was released after serving more than a quarter of a century in jail.

But the point I wish to emphasize is not the stupidity of the sentence, but the strangeness of the motive. I have tried to show elsewhere that 'outsider psychology' – the need of the man of potential genius to thrust himself outside society – has developed steadily in our civilization since the mid-nineteenth century, until it has become an overwhelmingly important factor in our cultural life. It is plainly as much a comment on society as on the men and women who need to dissociate themselves from society. The Leopold and Loeb case should be studied as an example of the interaction between two rich, spoiled, but undeniably intelligent and sensitive young men, and the 'affluent society' that formed them; it can also serve, indirectly, as a revelation of the nature of civilization in the twentieth century.

The Problem of Sex Crime

Crime statistics are notoriously unreliable, but it is undoubtedly true that the number of crimes of violence and sexual offences has risen steadily and alarmingly since the beginning of the war. The number of offences against the person in 1939 was approximately seven thousand in England and Wales; in 1959, this had risen to thirty thousand.

It would be dangerous to try to generalize too much about these figures. We do not know the statistics for offences against the person for 1759 and 1859, but they may have been higher, since a very large proportion of eighteenth- and nineteenth-century crimes were burglaries and robbery with violence, and footpads and highway robbers were common.

On the other hand, there seems to have been very little sex crime, in the sense we know it today, in these earlier centuries. In the memoirs of Vidocq, the notorious criminal-turned-policeman and founder of the Paris Sûreté, hundreds of crimes are detailed, but (as far as I can recall) there is not a sex crime among them. Mr John Gordon has told me of a press cutting in his possession, dating from the early nineteenth century; it

30

mentions a man who was sentenced to death for stealing a loaf of bread, and a man who received a fortnight in jail for raping a servant girl. The lightness of the sentence in the latter case indicates that rape was not a crime that was taken very seriously. Today, in many parts of the United States, rape carries a death sentence.[1] In a recent case in Arizona, a habitual drunk named Wayne Vance Taylor was sentenced to life imprisonment without parole for dragging a 7-year-old girl into his car and beating her, although the child was not raped. The crime, admittedly, was serious enough (the girl was in hospital for ten days afterwards), but the punishment may still be regarded as excessive, since the man was known as a dipsomaniac.

The conclusion to be drawn, surely, is that robbery was one of the most serious social problems in the early nineteenth century, and the crime that excited most fear in the minds of legislators and guardians of the law. Today, sex crime is the major social problem. Increased wages and improved living conditions have made robbery less of a menace. But the enormous complexity of our civilization produces all kinds of frustrations and strains that manifest themselves as neuroses; and an increase in sex crime is one of the inevitable consequences. Our increased leisure challenges the capacity for freedom which, unfortunately, has not kept pace with social improvements. In the moral vacuum that results, the sexual urge is one of the few positive drives.

The 'crime of boredom' increases as the 'leisured class' increases. The most infamous perverts of history were men of leisure – Gilles de Rais, Ivan the Terrible, De Sade himself. In Nicholas Stavrogin, Dostoievsky tried to show the relation between boredom and crime. The crime of poverty proves nothing, but the crime of boredom is closely related to the problem of human free will.

Consider, for example, the strange aftermath of the 'Black Dahlia' case. Elizabeth Short, the 'Black Dahlia', was murdered by an unknown sadist in Hollywood in 1947; her body had been cut into halves, and there was evidence that she had been suspended upside down and tortured before death. The horrible nature of the crime made it front page news for a long time. During the next year, six more murders of the same type were

[1] Although of course it carried the death sentence, even in the eighteenth century. (See *Chronicle of Crime* by Camden Pelham, 2 volumes, Reeve & Turner, 1886.) This sentence only applied in practice to the socially underprivileged.

committed in the Los Angeles area. The police had no reason to connect any of these murders with the Black Dahlia case; in fact, some of the murderers were caught. Still more interesting is the fact that the police were deluged with confessions to the killing – including one from a Lesbian. The twenty-eighth came nine years after the murder. All proved to be false.

The urge that produces the fake confession is obviously closely related to the urge that produces the 'imitative crime': a certain envy of the murderer's experience. It also has some relation to the irrational desire for self-destruction that Poe analysed in *The Imp of the Perverse*, as well as to Stavrogin's criminal psychology. It is due to a lack of sense of purpose, which produces a self-disgust. Without motive or purpose, Stavrogin has no spiritual pressure to resist the necessity of the physical world. With nothing happening 'inside him', he is aware mainly of the logical sequence of natural events. His crimes are an attempt to 'sin', to prove that he exists spiritually. In existential terms, they are an attempt to assert the reality of the subject, to overcome the nausea that springs from the meaningless pressure of objects. The same is true of the self-betrayal of Poe's murderer; his confession springs from shame in the face of a meaningless future, dominated by the logic of mere physical needs. Both are revolts against 'rationality', as De Sade's perversions were partly a revolt against eighteenth-century rationalism.

There is a remarkable study in this type of revolt in a story by Valeri Briussov that has some bearing on the problem of crime and twentieth-century society. *The Republic of the Southern Cross* can be regarded as an extension of certain ideas propounded by Dostoievsky in *Notes from Underground*. Dostoievsky's 'beetle man' had asserted that man would rather go mad than become the slave of an ultimately rational and logical universe. Briussov (1873–1924) writes about some date in the future when a great city is built at the South Pole; it is covered by an enormous dome of glass, has a population of two million, and is the perfect welfare state, the ultimate realization of democracy. But although the workers live in a condition approaching luxury, their houses are all exactly alike; internal decorations never vary; clothes and food have the same monotony. It is a dictatorship, but a completely benevolent dictatorship, with well-fed and contented workers.

But a disease called 'contradiction mania' begins to appear. Its victims contradict their wishes by their actions; when they want to say yes, they say no; when they want to say something pleasant, they feel compelled to be abusive. As the disease becomes more serious, its victims go insane from frustration and psychic turmoil; some commit suicide; others die from a form of apoplexy. Finally, the majority of the population of 'Star City' suffers from '*mania contradicens*', and the city is half-destroyed. The final pages of the story describe the burning city, and its insane survivors tearing at one another among the ruins.

The story requires very little commentary. The 'irrational' has taken its revenge. In *Man and Superman*, Don Juan remarked that if a man is given a sense of purpose, he can be inspired to do almost anything. Briussov's story is the necessary corollary to this remark: if man's purpose is taken away, he will react by becoming insane and murderously destructive.

Is this partly the key to the rise in crimes of violence? In the records of American crime, the psychopath who 'runs amok' and kills anyone in his path, has become more common in recent years. (In one typical case, a teen-age boy and girl drove around the country killing people 'for fun'; their only motive was that their parents refused to allow them to marry.)

It seems possible, then, that crimes of violence and sex crimes are one of the prices we pay for our high level of civilization. Few people feel 'at home' in a complex society, but most people manage to bear it with the help of psychiatrists or alcohol, or some other means of periodic 'escape'. The men who manage to bear it best are those with a sense of social purpose and an enthusiasm for organization. But the sub-normal men, the weaklings, find it impossible to accept on any terms, and become social problems; they can only be said to live 'in' society in the sense that a maggot lives in cheese; their rôle is wholly parasitic. Many such men are not even habitual criminals; they simply possess no sense of social responsibility, and will take whatever offers itself.

The bigger and more centralized a society becomes, the more of these socially irresponsible individuals it creates. The impersonality of society produces either revolt or contemptuous indifference. Hence the age of centralization is also the age of the juvenile delinquent and the sex maniac.

The Psychology of Sexual Murder

The revolt against society explains partly, but not altogether, the increase in violence and sex crime. The psychology of sexual perversion must also be taken into account. Increased

33

sexual activity has always been associated with the final stages of a decadent civilization. Why should this be so? A number of answers suggest themselves. One of the most obvious is proposed by Tolstoy in *The Kreutzer Sonata*. Intense sexual activity, he argues, is associated with people who have nothing better to do. A man who labours for sixteen hours a day on his land is too tired to take much interest in sex; his wife soon finds the burden of a family absorbing all her energies. This, Tolstoy asserts, is as it should be. Social inequality, which creates so many rich and brainless idlers, also creates an abnormal interest in sex; this leads to endless adulteries, whose basis is not the natural urge to reproduce the species, but boredom and pampered nerves. Tolstoy's conclusion is that the only definition of 'normal sexual activity' would be 'activity aimed at producing children'. All other sex is 'abnormal' or perverse. This is one of the few logically satisfying attempts to define the boundary of 'normality'.

The more leisure afforded by the society, the more emphasis is placed upon sex, and the more sexual perversion develops. This in any case, without committing oneself to Tolstoy's assumptions, is a reasonable argument. De Sade himself admitted that sexual perversions are inspired by satiety. 'One grows tired of the commonplace. . . .'[1]

Like boredom, the problem of sexuality is related to human freedom. It requires very little analysis to recognize that the sexual urge is not a physical urge on a level with the need to eat and sleep. Food is necessary to the well-being of the physical organism; sex is not. In animals, sex is connected with a distinctive smell that acts as an aphrodisiac; in human beings, the process would appear to be largely psychological. The development of the human sexual impulse usually begins in childhood with talk about sex, and possibly some rudimentary sexual experience. The appetite feeds and grows on these imaginative experiences, and the whole later sexual orientation may depend on their nature. For example, slum areas are not frequently

[1] I have heard it argued, by a man who knew Neville Heath, that Heath's sadism was the outcome of boredom. It was suggested that Heath was a vain and not particularly intelligent man, whose sexual conquests were the basis of his self-esteem. His charm and good looks made conquest easy. 'When he walked into a party, he usually felt that he could have pretty well any woman in the room.' 'Normal sex' became so easily obtainable that it began to bore him, and his perversions developed.

productive of homosexuality, because in such areas, hetero-sexual experience often begins at an early age. But they *are* productive of various forms of sexual violence connected with sadism, and this is undoubtedly due to the component of brutality in the environment. Public schools are notorious incu-bators of homosexuality because the sexual urge is again coloured by its environment before it possesses much power of differentia-tion. The imagination becomes hypnotized by some aspect of sex, and can never free itself from its influence.

These factors are worth taking into account in an examination of the causes of the basic violence in modern society. Peter Kürten, the Düsseldorf sadist, told Professor Berg that he had known a sadistic dog-catcher when a child, and had been taught to masturbate the dogs. Madame de Brinvilliers, the poisoner, admitted that she had had sexual experience with all her brothers before she entered her teens. William Heirens, the Chicago murderer, was only 17 when arrested for the killing of two women and a child; he killed in the process of burgling women's flats to steal underwear, and admitted that he had been stealing underwear from an early age. Dozens of cases could be cited to illustrate the importance of early sexual experiences on the imagination. (Paul de River even cites a case of a young girl who had relations with an Alsatian dog and, as a consequence, became fixated on dogs, and was horrified at the idea of having intercourse with a man.) In the case of fetichists, the objects that 'hypnotize' the imagination in childhood often seem absurdly arbitrary, ranging from nightcaps and wigs to crutches.[1]

One might say, then, that the sexually normal person is lucky that his imagination had been hypnotized by the usual object – the opposite sex. There may be many Casanovas among crutch fetichists who will never dare to write the history of their sexual conquests.

Bearing in mind, then, the close connexion between sex and the imagination, it becomes easier to understand the alarming increase in sexual offences in our time. Nietzsche pointed out that the basic need of the higher animals is to discharge their energy. When a civilization increases the leisure of the individual without providing a substitute purpose, men are thrown back upon their physical urges. The realm of the body provides an escape; stimulated by alcohol, or sex, or drugs, it can produce an illusion of meaningful living.

[1] See Stekel: *Sexual Aberrations*. 2 vols. Vision Press.

35

The Criminal Mentality

De Sade and Lautreamont tried hard to convince themselves and their readers that crime can be the expression of a kind of 'noble vitality'. The idea had been current since Byron's 'Childe Harold'; but it should be noted that Byron never actually shows Childe Harold committing any of the crimes that 'weigh on his soul'. And John Millington Synge later made this difference between imagined crime and real crime the subject of *The Playboy of the Western World*; the villagers all admire the man who is supposed to have killed his father, until they actually see him attempting to kill his father.

Is it possible for crime to be an expression of a higher vitality? Shaw makes Mendoza say that his brigands are made up of two types of men: those who are not good enough for bourgeois society, and those who are too good for it: the scum and the dregs. And his long analysis of the mentality of the tramps of the Sierra Nevada (in *Man and Superman*) might be taken as a defence of a certain type of criminal. One can even imagine Shaw, in a spirit of paradox, defending Sawney Bean (whose history will be found in the present volume). Unfortunately, the facts are against this view. Jesse James may be a popular hero in the estimation of Hollywood scriptwriters, but a study of his life reveals the same stupidity and insensitivity that characterizes most criminals. This is generally true of outlaws, even the ones – like Dillinger – of whom some good can be spoken. Reading their life stories produces a terrifying sense of futility. If life can be compared to a roundabout with a still centre, then the Jameses, the Barker mob, the Dillinger gang, lived on the circumference in a futile whirl of activity that ended in death.

The nearest approach to the 'noble criminal' that I have discovered in compiling this volume was Lacenaire, who produced memoirs that show considerable honesty and intellect. But Lacenaire's crimes were not 'noble'; he was a weak man and an unlucky man, caught up in a habit of petty crime. The same is true of the anarchist Charrier, who told the court that he was an implacable enemy of society.

I am inclined to doubt whether such a thing as the 'subjective' or 'inner-directed' criminal exists. Criminality is essentially a socially immature attitude. In reading through this volume, it will be noticed how many murderers were habitual liars and petty criminals. Now lying is something that most of us do in childhood – pointless lying for the sake of lying. It springs from the child's lack of responsibility and lack of purpose. Paradoxically, the most truthful man is likely to be the most anti-social man; a person with a thorough contempt for his fellow human beings (such as Swift possessed) cannot see the point in lying. Honesty is an outcome of certainty of superiority. Dishonesty is usually united to a desire to impress. The confidence-swindler type of murderer is usually a bully and a braggart; one has to agree that a sadist like Kürten is in every way a better type of character than Deeming, Heath, or Manuel.

While on this subject, it is also worth noting that almost everything connected with the criminal tends to make for criminality, and that even the most conscientious police officers often get involved in issues of doubtful morality. Shaw pointed out in his masterly 'Imprisonment' preface that prison degrades the warders as much as the criminals. But the same might be said of the police. Was Samuel Furnace's brother-in-law justified in betraying his confidence and spending a whole morning with the hunted man, while the police waited outside? Such cases are common, and no one questions their morality; and yet Sophocles posed exactly this problem in his *Philoctetes* twenty-five centuries ago. Moreover, there are many cases in the present volume where evidence was obtained against a criminal by getting a detective to pose as a fellow criminal in jail and draw the accused man into making admissions. Admittedly, there are few cases of policemen as dishonest as the infamous Bony,[1] executed finally by the French resistance after the war, but there are enough cases of minor acts of betrayal and immorality on the part of the police to justify the assumption that crime breeds crime, even in those who fight against it.

Capital Punishment

While on this subject, it may be as well to make clear my own attitude on capital punishment, which emerges indirectly in many of my entries. Since, however, these entries are unsigned, and since my collaborator takes the opposite view about the death penalty, this may not be easily apparent.

Many reputable persons have advanced to me the view that society cannot do without the death penalty. I emphatically disagree. It seems to me obvious and axiomatic that a point will come where the human race will regard all killing as a remnant of the dark ages, and that, if human evolution means anything

[1] See under 'Seznec'.

at all, it means an increased love of life – of all life. The word 'evil' has almost no meaning in modern psychological terms. Human acts are stupid or misguided; but there are no super-Mephistopheles, enemies of God. If evil has a meaning in modern terms, it is insensitivity to the sufferings of others. This kind of insensitivity is the opposite of what we mean by civilization and evolution.

Most defenders of capital punishment would agree with this, but go on to argue that executing murderers is a way of defending the values of civilization and evolution. This kind of statement seems to me to be based on exactly the same kind of lack of imagination that characterizes the murderer. Albert Camus, in an article against capital punishment, described how his father had been strongly in favour of it until he went to see a murderer executed; the sight of a man being decapitated made him vomit. (Shaw shows the same kind of reaction on the part of Stogumber; who had shouted 'To the fire with her' at the end of Joan's trial, but was revolted by the actual sight of her being burnt alive.)

Mr Jack Smith-Hughes, in what he evidently imagines to be a passage of great wit, suggests that the abolitionists should be allowed to specify that anyone murdering themselves or members of their families should not be executed.[1] But this is completely to miss the point. It is not a question of whether a murderer *deserves* to die, but of the effect on a society that is based on violence. There is a parallel here to the puritan who objected to bear-baiting, not because it gave pain to the bear, but because it gave pleasure to the men.

In his Imprisonment preface, Shaw suggests that all prisons should be done away with, since they imprison the warders as well as the criminals, and are a useless expense to society. Instead, he suggests, all criminals except the incorrigible ones should be allowed to go free, while the incurable criminals should be executed as nuisances, even if they are only pickpockets.

This is impractical, but there is much to be said for it all the same. Crime is the outcome of social irresponsibility; the final answer to civilization is anarchism. Passing judgement degrades men as much as crime, just as giving orders degrades men as much as obeying them. Our increased crime-rate is an increase in other-direction, in lack of purpose, a characteristic of the

[1] *Nine Verdicts on Violence*, by Jack Smith-Hughes, Barrister at Law, Cassell & Co.

age of centralization. The only answer to it will be a society of men who take full responsibility for their own existence.

It might be objected that this kind of anarchism will not appear until the millennium, and that, in the meantime, society is full of brutalized, socially irresponsible individuals who will continue to live by crime. This is no excuse for murdering these individuals. Otherwise, we may as well be logical and murder the lot of them, whether they have committed a murder or not. In this way, we might breed a 'free society' sooner. The argument is not dissimilar to that employed by Hitler to justify the massacre of the Jews.

The arguments against capital punishment may be summarized: (a) most murderers do not deserve to be executed, and (b) we brutalize ourselves by executing even the murderers who deserve it. It is my own conviction that, if the human race has any future, it must lie through the total abolition of capital punishment.

A Personal Postscript

Summarized briefly, the argument of this preface has been: we must study criminals in order to know ourselves. But unless it is related to a system of ideas, such a statement means nothing. And such a system of ideas cannot be argued briefly. I therefore prefer to take the simple way out, and speak from personal conviction. The grounds for these convictions can be found, at least partly, in such books as my *Outsider*, *Religion and the Rebel*, and *Age of Defeat*.

I am not personally fascinated by murder, and I regard the man who feels a *frisson* when he goes into a room where a crime was committed as a fool. Most murderers are bores, and nearly all strike me as stupid. When I was a child, murder held a morbid fascination for me, as if evil vapours would rise over a spot where a corpse had been buried. Later, I came to regard murder as an unpleasant irrelevance, a back-sliding of the human spirit on its road towards godhead. But at the time, science seemed to me the symbol of this advance. Eventually, I came to mistrust science, since logic takes place against a background of our total nescience. There are no irrefutable premises, no footholds for belief; our only ground for taking life calmly is this predictability of everyday experience. The scientific view of life is this predictability projected on to a universal canvas by men of little imagination.

The collapse of my belief in a humanist millennium led me to

39

a re-examination of murder (inspired mainly by Dostoievsky's anti-rationalist logic), almost, one might say, in the hope of discovering that murder is a logical response to the meaninglessness of life. There was still a basic craving for logic and meaning. At this time, the views I have expressed above on capital punishment, and the view that 'evil' is insensitivity to the pain of others, would have struck me as nonsense. Arguing from subjectivist – almost solipsist – premises, there was no possible way of reaching Portia's views on 'the quality of mercy'. But at the same time, it is easy for the solipsist to reach the conclusion that life is not worth living. This produces a logical absurdity, since one *is* alive, and even the conclusion that life is not worth living has been 'subsidized' by life. (There is a similar illogicality in the view expressed by Charrier, the 'implacable enemy of society'.) The only logical alternative is to accept as a basic premise that, even if one does not feel it to be obvious, life is nevertheless worth living, and therefore worth living *more*. In the same way, if one is a member of society, then the logical aim should be to become a totally responsible member of that society.

All this led me to the development of what seems to me (as far as I understand it myself) a wholly optimistic vision of human life and human society. It now seemed clear to me that my earlier picture of human society was inaccurate. I had assumed that men fell into two classes: rational men, like Bertrand Russell, and emotional and unthinking men, who make up the larger part of society. It now seemed to me that the dividing line ran in a different direction. There were men who lived comfortably within the compass of their everyday experience, and took it for granted that somehow 'life' meant something because their personal lives were orderly; these included most of the scientists and rationalists. And there were a few men – like Van Gogh and Nijinsky – who wanted to know if the defeat and suffering of human existence really outweighed the achievement – taking into account the ultimate mystery of death and the human capacity for self-delusion.

If these men – the Nijinskys – were the *élite*, then the problem was to persuade most men to consider what lies beyond the narrow range of their personal experience.

Dostoievsky understood that, while most men lack the inclination to talk philosophy, almost everyone can be persuaded to stop and listen when the talk is of violence. And Dostoievsky's own life – like those of Van Gogh and Nijinsky – contained enough violence to enable one to 'dramatize' the problems implicit in it. It was at this point that the problem of murder came to re-engage my interest.

There are, it seems to me, three types of murder. The first is the rarest – the murder that springs from frustrated vitality, in the same way that some juvenile delinquency springs from the frustrated adventurousness of youth. A few sexual murderers, a few political assassins, may fall under this heading. (Charlotte Corday, perhaps?) Then there are a number of murders that arise out of sheer brutality, insensitivity to suffering. Such murderers feel no more pity for the victim than a cat feels for the mouse it tortures. They are the opposite of all that we mean by civilization, which is essentially learning to feel for other people. They are found mainly in the gangster class, and it might be argued that, if any criminals deserve the death sentence, it is these men.

Luckily, they do not form a very large proportion of murderers. By far the largest class of murderers kill out of the narrowness of their lives and lack of imagination. Hayward is an example, and so are most of the criminals in this volume. Consider, for example, George Townley, who stabbed the girl who threatened to jilt him, and escaped the death penalty with a plea of insanity. Two years after the murder, Townley committed suicide in Pentonville by jumping over a staircase, head first on to a stone floor. The prison chaplain made a penetrating statement: he said that he had not considered Townley insane to begin with, but that after his suicide, he was convinced that Townley was *morally* insane. There is some justification for this view; Townley had weighed his whole life, his future career, in the scales against his emotional turmoil caused by Bessie Goodwin; later, he threw away his own life in the same careless way. Could it be said that such a man had any idea of what his own life was worth, what he might have done with it? But then, if Townley was morally insane, where is the dividing line? By the same criterion, are not we all morally insane?

In *Crime and Punishment*, Svidrigailov has a sudden horrible idea that perhaps eternity might be like a small room with spiders in the corners. In a single symbol, Dostoievsky had caught all that is worst about human life. Freedom is unlimitedness; the worst things about life are justified by the possibility of something beyond them, and all 'beyonds' are summarized in the word eternity. It is in this sense that Nietzsche uses it when he makes Zarathustra say, 'For I love thee, oh eternity'. Svidrigailov has destroyed man's final hope in destroying eternity and turning it into a narrow room.

But Svidrigailov's room is the symbol for human existence; we are all trapped, to a lesser or greater extent, in personality, the world of other people. All our art, philosophy, and science has been an attempt at a jailbreak on the part of the human spirit. The aim is not to destroy the room (as Socrates cunningly argued in the 'Phaedo)' but to make it limitlessly big.

We grow more 'civilized' by humanizing our environment, by imposing order where there was chaos. In this sense, art and science have the same purpose. But the sole purpose of creating order is to bring freedom. And of what use is this kind of freedom to ninety per cent of the murderers in this volume? The kind of freeing of the human spirit that comes to all men of genius when they begin to feel their own powers is completely alien to most murderers. In a sense, any man of spiritual greatness, from Newton to Beethoven (to take two extremes), is the diametrical opposite of George Townley. Dante had a quatrain in the Purgatorio (14th canto) about the envious: 'The heavens call to you and wheel round you, displaying for you their eternal splendours, and your eyes see only the ground; wherefore he who discerns all punishes you.' The murderer is aware only of the ground. But how far is he to be blamed for this?

This, surely, is one of the very greatest problems of the century we live in, as it has been (in a sense) in all ages. 'The ground' here means society, other people. And as society becomes centralized, more people orient their lives according to other people; as Riesman says, society is becoming steadily more 'other-directed'. And what I have elsewhere called 'the fallacy of insignificance' develops. Men live contentedly in narrow lives, certain enough of their own insignificance not to question the unfulfilment. Nietzsche brutally referred to the type as 'the ground fleas' and remarked that they are inexterminable.

The difficulty is to persuade such people that they have an act of choice. They might be compared to men who sit in a chair convinced that they are paralysed from the waist down.

The problem, it seems to me, is that we have no psychology to deal with this state. If the mental state of the 'ground flea' could be summarized verbally, it would express itself 'Man is man is man is man . . .' *ad infinitum*. Human life is what it is. Things are what they are. Human life is like a game of chess in which only a certain number of moves are possible; but the alternative would be to throw away the chess board, and nobody wants to do that. . . . Our increasing centralization pushes men steadily and inexorably into this mental state; but what alternative pressure could goad them out of it?

Let us be clear about this. There is *nothing*, short of a conscious assessment of the value of human life, and a conscious effort to increase its intensity, that could make any difference to our present state. And this is the reason that I attach such importance to existentialism. Existentialism is not merely a limited philosophy developed by a few highbrows; it is a conscious attempt to create a system for dealing with certain problems of modern man, just as much as Freudian psychology or the invention of penicillin. While the individual 'accepts' life and drifts will-lessly from mood to mood, he cannot be considered to be 'living'. Husserl's 'phenomenalism', which became the basis of all later existentialism, asserted that, while man thinks he is merely perceiving, he is actually unconsciously *choosing* his perceptions by imposing a form on them. The patterns you see in the fire are an example. You may think you see a face, but if you were staring at the fire quite *blankly* (i.e. making no act of will-to-perceive) you will not notice a face. An even more striking example occurs if you rub your eyes until great purple spots appear on the inside of your eyelids. By 'looking' at these spots (an impossibility, of course, since your eyes are closed) you can see them change form, swelling or contracting, and changing colour. If you make an effort of will, you can change these 'spots' into almost anything – a man riding a motor-bike, a pink elephant. . . . The form-imposing element of your perception is working.

Existentialism went on to state that not merely does man interpret the series of geometrical lines and curves that are his perceptions; he also selects every element of his perception of the external world, including his basic notion of whether life is worth living, whether he is a timid or an aggressive person, etc. Sartre points out that even a man dying of cancer can make an act of choice; he can choose the moment when he surrenders to the pain and abandons himself.

All great art is the bringing-to-consciousness of new areas of existence. Existentialism is an attempt to persuade men to focus their attention on their *power of choice*, and to understand the relation of this power of choice to the changes they can make in their environment. And these changes are not merely physical changes, but changes in the way of seeing. Ruskin's pathetic fallacy (to regard an inanimate object as alive) is the companion of the fallacy of insignificance (which is the pathetic fallacy applied to society). Sartre's 'nausea' is the extreme of the pathetic fallacy: physical objects appear to be *too real*, to be imposing themselves. This is a stage of mental disease. (For certain paranoiacs, the whole physical world is actively menacing; a chair is as horrible as a crouched tarantula spider.) The limit of this fallacy would be to regard everything else as alive and yourself as dead.

But this form-imposing element of consciousness is of more importance than is generally realized. We tend to think of the world as governed by laws which impose a form on our perceptions; and because the act of choice remains unconscious, we are unaware of the choice that governs the form under which the perceptions present themselves. (Expressed in this way, the relation between Husserl and Kant can be clearly seen.) For example, our modern literary criticism neglects this instinctive element of perception, and insists on an intellectual justification for literary preferences that usually manages to miss the point completely. Our intellectual methods are still too clumsy to catch the shape of an instinctive perception, but we still insist on trying to form writers into 'hierarchies' according to what they 'say', instead of identifying our perceptions with theirs and concentrating on the way they *see* things. For example, I personally find the work of Shaw and Wells invigorating, not because of what they say, but because they obviously *felt* that life was worth living. In the same way, I feel an instinctive detestation of the work of men like D. H. Lawrence, Graham Greene, William Golding, William Faulkner, Jean Paul Sartre, because I feel that their basic feeling about life is so much duller than my own – so much more gloomy and unexciting. The *facts* they write about are the same as the facts that Shaw and Wells write about; but the fallacy of insignificance appears plainly in the interpretation they impose on these facts.

The consequence is that any critic could prove to me that I am wrong to prefer Shaw to Lawrence, explaining that Lawrence is in favour of the deepest vital urges while Shaw is a superficial intellectual. If I refused to trust my own instinctive perceptions, I would allow myself to be convinced. As it is, I feel that both Lawrence and Shaw had an act of choice to make, a decision about the interpretation of the world they both saw quite clearly; Shaw, being a born optimist, chose the high-handed way, treating the universe as if it were a financial empire and he a business tycoon; Lawrence, while remaining true to a certain subjective perception, allowed 'facts' to depress him. It is therefore natural that his work contains more 'conflict' than Shaw's – conflict between his natural certainty and the fallacy of insignificance that he allowed to bulk so large. What 'counts' for me in reading Lawrence is not Lawrence's 'message', as a don might expound it, but the way he obviously saw and felt about the world in a book like *Lady Chatterley*. The same is true of Sartre, and here, where I am concerned, the dichotomy is even more obvious. If I wrote an essay about Sartre, I would find myself expounding his ideas about 'bad faith', etc., with a certain agreement, not to say enthusiasm. When I actually try reading one of Sartre's *Roads to Freedom* trilogy, I am plunged first into gloom, then into a feeling of total rejection. The intellectual vitality of what he 'says', and the deadening boredom of the way he seems to *see* the physical world, seem to me in complete opposition.

There is a long essay to be written some time on this problem of ways of seeing the world, and the techniques certain writers use to present ideas tinged with pessimism by imposing their own despair on the world in their novels.[1] It is truer that the writer has at all times presented the world 'as he sees it himself' to argue his own view of life; but the novel is a relatively modern invention, and it seems to me that many modern novelists take an unfair advantage in imposing their system of perceptions on the reader, who is not fully conscious of what is going on, and feels vaguely uncomfortable without finding anything to actually disagree with. A system of existential criticism would try to analyse the system of perception of the novelist in the same way that phenomenalism tries to analyse the forms of physical perception, and restore some of the advantage to the reader, who would thus cease to be the passive target of various forms of 'propaganda'.

At this point, it might be possible to see the way in which an encyclopaedia of murder could be regarded as a series of exhibits in a lecture on the meaning of existentialism. Each case presents fairly clearly, by implication, the way in which a murderer 'sees' the world. It is almost as if you could fire at every murderer the question: What is the value of life?, and get from him the answer in quite precise physical terms: ten pounds, a snub, my wife's infidelity, a broken engagement, etc. And no doubt

[1] I have touched on the matter in a section headed 'Literary Faking' in *The Age of Defeat*.

many murderers in the death cell changed their estimate radically, and felt, like Raskolnikov, that they would prefer to live on a narrow ledge for ever rather than die at once.

Murder confronts us with this act of decision about the value of life more directly than most human acts. But of course, it must be admitted that every minute of a man's life bears witness to the value he attaches to life just as clearly as the act of murder, and every minute is as unreversible as that final unreversible act. To a reader with deep enough perceptions, James Joyce's *Ulysses* would serve as well as a book on murder to illustrate the act of human choice. But until men have reached that stage, a volume like the present one might be regarded as the nursery textbook on existentialism. It might even be regarded as a kind of modern counterpart of De Sade's meditations on hell, designed to awake in the reader a perception of the meaning of heaven.

All this follows logically from my basic beliefs about life, the certainty that man *can* eventually become superman, and that the greatest moment will be when he has the audacity to believe that the change might come about in his own lifetime. It seems to me that our intellectual life has reached a point of stagnation; intellectual adventure has disappeared from our world. I have only to open any Sunday newspaper to be irritated by the stuff that is being peddled as the latest word in Western culture. But the thought does not dismay me, since I am certain that existentialism is the most powerful instrument that has so far been developed for the evolution of the human race. The word may disappear (it is too long anyway, and sounds like some new discovery in atomic physics), but the concept has already passed the embryo stage, and if it can be freed from the mumbo-jumbo of traditional philosophy, should prove an instrument of extraordinary power. (Gurdjieff preferred to use simply the word 'psychology' – which, however, is likely to create some confusion, especially in the minds of American readers.)

Ultimately, human life is a mystery, possibly even a tragedy. At the basis of all knowledge is the problem of solipsism. How can the world be judged and evaluated, when any judgement must be based on the obviously untrue notion that what is true for me is true for all men? And yet, unless a man regards himself as a member of the human race, sanity and meaning are impossible. For this reason, man's sanity is balanced on a knife-edge. Ultimately he cannot allow others to judge for him; but, if he judges for himself, he may be faced abruptly with the sense of absurdity that comes from suddenly realizing how limited is the context in which we make any judgement; we are suspended in total unknowledge; we know nothing *outside* life; we do not even know if human life is an escape from some inevitable horror beyond existence. Under such circumstances, it might almost be regarded as insane presumption to claim to know anything; it might be better to be grateful for life and try to cling on to it as long as possible. There are no standards; we know nothing.

And yet a volume like this indicates that, even in the midst of total ignorance, there are certain clearly marked 'directions'. There is, as it were, a kind of grain in the wood of the universe, even if both the ideas of its limitedness and of its limitlessness are equally unthinkable. Life may be absurd, but death is even more absurd. And although a lifetime of inner-directedness and effort may seem futile to an Ecclesiastes, there can be no earthly doubt that the self-deceiving life of a man like Guiteau[1] – the assassin of President Garfield – is futile in a far deeper sense.

It may be true that the time for asking 'ultimate questions' about the universe and human destiny has passed; modern philosophy shows a healthy tendency to regard metaphysics as nonsense and organized religion as a form of mild insanity accompanied by delusions. The effect has been to bring philosophy down to earth. But now we are back on the earth again, it is time to reconsider the problem of values from the standpoint of human psychology. We debate again the meaning of meaning; its context: human life.

COLIN WILSON

[1] See article on assassination.

WHY AN ENCYCLOPAEDIA OF MURDER?

Why should anyone want an encyclopaedia of murder? Or why –
to ask first things first – should anyone want to read about
murder at all? In earlier times it was a question which simply
did not occur. There was never any sophisticated pretence that
murder could be anything but extremely interesting. When
Cain used a heavy blunt instrument on Abel or when Uriah
was placed by murderous conspiracy in the forefront of the
battle or when Agamemnon, a returning soldier of a type so
common in 1945, was stabbed – in each case it was assumed that
every normal person would wish to know how and when and
for what motive. Macbeth, Julius Caesar, and Hamlet are all
murder cases, related with much the same documentary detail
that we expect from modern masters such as Mr Edgar Lustgarten. Other plays of the period – such as *Arden of Feversham*
and *A Yorkshire Tragedy* (parts of which have sometimes been
ascribed to Shakespeare) – are based on actual contemporary
murders. Two centuries later, when John Williams murdered
two almost entire households in Wapping, no one accused
Charles Lamb and his friends of being warped or morbid for
spending hours discussing the circumstances. Stendhal, Dickens,
Zola, and Dostoievsky each made an intense and detailed study
of murder for the purposes of their art. It was taken for granted
that any situation in which one of our fellow beings decides to
take away the life of another must be of concern to all who are
concerned with life itself.

A glance at any of the records on which the encyclopaedia is
based will provide one excellent reason for taking this for
granted. Today the sociologists and the mass observers have
taken on most of the research into human habits which Dickens
and Zola used to carry out for themselves. Yet a year's modern
research in depth into the social habits of a class or neighbourhood could never yield as much vivid and accurate information
as a single murder case. Suddenly, within the covers of one
murder-file, an entire way of life is illuminated. The social precision of a Jane Austen novel – the precision which records in-
comes, fashions, habits, peculiarities of speech, and which
unravels every subtle strand in a nexus of family and class rela-

tionships – is applied automatically in any murder trial to any mode of life. From *Northanger Abbey* and *Persuasion* we can reconstruct an accurate picture of middle-class life in Bath at the beginning of the nineteenth century. But for the life of a Warren Street car-dealer in 1949 we had best turn not to a novel but to the Setty case; for the social background of a suburban commercial traveller in 1930 to the case of Arthur Rouse; for the relationship between brothers in the East End in the 1870's to the trial of Henry and Thomas Wainwright. Recently there has been a good deal of academic research into the changes which took place in the East End in the years which immediately followed. There have, for example, been several studies of the conditions of Jewish immigrants – but none which is so informative as the court records of the trial of Steinie Morrison, whose victim, Leon Beron, never carried fewer than twenty sovereigns in a wash-leather purse fastened to his waistcoat pocket by a safety-pin – and spent most of his time in the Warsaw Restaurant off the Whitechapel Road, where, with other Jewish immigrants, for eighteen pence he could buy both lunch and dinner and a place at the table for the whole day.

And so it is with case after case. When Marr, the poor haberdasher, shortly before being bludgeoned by John Williams, sends out his servant girl to buy oysters at midnight on Saturday; when Haigh listens to Mrs Durand-Deacon discussing theosophy over their rationed breakfast at the Onslow Court Hotel in South Kensington; when John Christie sits drinking tea at night with one of his future victims and her man-friend in a darkened room (because the electricity bill has not been paid and the current is cut off), on furniture which consists of a deck-chair, a wooden box, and a plank across a coal-scuttle (because Christie, desperate for cash, has sold everything else); when, in short, a murderer or his victim or anyone connected with them does almost anything – the court shorthand-reporter is instantly transformed into an Aubrey or a Pepys. A way of life has been put on film for ever.

Such is the sort of answer which I give when asked to account for my own interest in murder. Yet clearly it is not a universal answer. For example, it is not the answer given by my co-author, Colin Wilson, who prefers to link the subject with his *Outsider* thesis. Yet, is it possible that there is an underlying compulsion shared, not only by Mr Wilson and myself, but by all the millions who have ever reached eagerly for the headlines about the latest murder case? Is it that we are all morbid-minded? Or, to put our interest in an even more sinister light, is it that we relish the courtroom details about bludgeonings and mutilations because unconsciously we wish we had been doing the bludgeoning and the mutilating? Is it that we are all murderers under the skin? That is certainly a fashionable view today – and not only today. Years ago Alexander Woolcott admitted that he always read of a murderer going to execution with the thought, 'There, but for the grace of God, go I.' It is widely supposed that murder is the non-criminal's crime, the sort of crime that anyone could commit – a belief which naturally has played a powerful part in the campaign against capital punishment. Yet does this explain our interest in murder too? I say no. I believe that we are fascinated by murderers not because they are so like the rest of us but because they are so utterly different. I believe that most people are born with an instinct against cold-blooded killing and that murderers lack this instinct.

To justify this view I begin with the nursery. In their first months and years of life young human beings have to learn all the social attitudes which are not actually inborn. They have to learn not to steal, not to kick and punch, not to soil clothes and carpets. Ceaselessly the admonitions are rapped out: 'Don't touch the cake. Don't take things which aren't yours. Don't wet your pants. Don't pull little Johnnie's hair.' All necessary; all repeated every minute in every country in the world. Yet – if we are to believe Alexander Woolcott's 'There, but for the grace of God . . .' theory – isn't it striking that no mother has to say: 'Don't kill little Johnnie'? Murder, by children, of children, should be remarkably easy. But – despite all the jungle horridness of children in every other respect – it is also remarkably rare.

Cold-blooded killing within a species is rare among most higher animals too. True, there is no instinct which prevents animals of the same species fighting and perhaps killing each other in the fight. Yet, even in the midst of fighting – as Dr Konrad Lorenz points out – a submission gesture made by a defeated animal will produce a reflex response in its rival which makes it physically incapable of carrying on the fight to the death. If you own a small dog, watch its behaviour when a larger dog comes bounding along growling viciously. Your dog will grovel with tail wagging and muzzle submissively touching the ground – and the larger dog is automatically rendered powerless. Is it too fanciful to believe that similar instinctive chivalry may be found in human beings too – except, that is, in the rare and dangerous freaks who become murderers?

For further evidence I turn from Lorenz, a writer on animal behaviour, to writers on murder itself. I used to be surprised that even the most sophisticated of them, such as Mr Lustgarten or the late Mr Edmund Pearson, took a comparatively unsophisticated attitude towards the actual murderer. 'Here was an evil man,' their books would tell me again and again, 'a grim and pitiless killer who thoroughly deserved to be hanged.' Indeed, Edmund Pearson went beyond even this. He rarely credited a murderer with any redeeming qualities at all. He contemptuously rejected the belief that the nineteenth-century American multi-murderer Edward Ruloff was a man of great learning:

> We know how some writers described the alleged profound learning of Loeb and Leopold, and in the light of their exaggerations, I am disposed to question Ruloff's erudition. Professor Goldwin Smith called him a 'great philologist' which means, probably, a great philologist – for a murderer. . . .

Pearson continued:

> The opponents of capital punishment signed a petition to save his valuable life. They did this on two grounds: first, that he was insane; and second, that his was a matchless intellect. . . . It was of no interest to them how many other lives, really valuable, might have been sacrificed if this savage were again spared.

The same simple and unrelenting attitude is taken by expert after expert – ranging from such tireless collectors of crime cases as Mr Rupert Furneaux and Mr Leonard Gribble to analysts of the courtroom such as Mr Bechofer Roberts. None of them ever seems to imagine that there but for grace of God goes he. They all – and now having studied perhaps even more cases than any of them I fully understand why – regard the average murderer as a creature utterly different from themselves, a creature for whom there can be no redemption. Yet they go on studying murder. Why? Clearly not from any desire to identify themselves with murderers – but rather from an entirely opposite motive. They watch the murderer with horror and fascination as men gaze at a high-wire artist – precisely because he lacks a basic instinct which the rest of us possess.

I began this preface by asking two questions: 'Why an interest in murder?' and 'Why an encyclopaedia of murder?' In answering the first I have already begun to answer the second. For, you see, it is the sheer number of cases studied by the murder writers that gives them a special insight into what makes a murderer. The experts in forensic medicine base their science in the same way, on the records of a vast number of slashed throats and indented skull fractures. But the psychologists who study the murderer's mind have gone about things differently. They either have made an intense study of a particular criminal such as Peter Kürten – or else they have studied a particular criminal group, such as the sexual murderers. Yet an encyclopaedia of murder, assembling in one volume the experience of a large number of murder writers, soon begins to throw up patterns which run through murder cases of every kind. For example, the reader who browses at leisure through this dictionary may suddenly note the remarkable number of times some such phrases as, 'He fancied himself as a poet' or 'During his trial he composed various verses . . .' will occur in accounts of even unlettered and brutish murderers. Peter Manuel, the Glasgow mass-murderer, who would kill for any reason or none at all, spent his time before execution writing a sonnet. Thomas Griffiths Wainwright, the nineteenth-century poisoner for gain, was also a very minor poet. Leonard Mills in 1951 claimed to have found the body of a woman (whom he had himself strangled) while searching for a quiet spot where he could write a sonnet. Percy Mapleton wrote verse and short stories, though he made his name by killing and robbing a fellow-passenger on a train to Brighton in 1881. Lacenaire, convicted in 1835 of running a murder gang for gain, was a verse writer; so, nearly a century later, was Landru.

Now it is true that the relationship between the poetic urge and the urge to commit sadistic murder has already been noted by such criminologists as Dr Paul de River, who devotes a chapter of *The Sexual Criminal* to a selection from the work of a sado-masochistic patient who was able to sublimate his tendencies entirely in verse. Yet, so far as I know, it has required this dictionary to trace how far among murderers of all types the verse urge makes itself known.

The same is true of music. In the following pages you will learn that Charles Peace played the violin; that George Joseph

Smith, the bath-killer, and Arnold Walder, who committed a sensational murder in a Paris chemist's shop in 1879, were both proficient on the harmonica; that Alfred Arthur Rouse was an amateur baritone; and that even the shambling Joseph Vacher, who roamed south-east France from 1894 to 1897 murdering and disembowelling young farm-workers of both sexes, entertained the peasants, who finally caught him, with a gay accordian medley until the police arrived. Perhaps the most telling piece of evidence against William Herbert Wallace is that in his last years, before Mrs Wallace was mysteriously killed but while his own kidney trouble was probably already stimulating his mental powers, he unexpectedly taught himself the violin – and played it well.

Such are just two new facts about murder which the encyclopaedia method can provide – quite apart from providing plots for novels, questions for quizzes, and innocent entertainment for eerie winter evenings. Yet there has been no previous encyclopaedia of murder ranging over all the centuries and over all the continents. Even Mr E. Spencer Shew's excellent *A Companion to Murder* – of which only one volume has so far been published – is limited to notable British murders from 1900 to 1950. Our encyclopaedia, then, is a pioneering work and as such we hope it will be judged – as a work of enthusiasm and fun and as the rough framework for more meticulous and fully documented successors. In particular, we hope that the present NATO bias towards British, French, and American murder, may be corrected in other dictionaries. Our encyclopaedia, in short, does not claim to be comprehensive – indeed it could not be. During the last hour two more murders will have been committed in Mexico alone.

PATRICIA PITMAN

A

ALLAWAY, Thomas
Chauffeur, hanged for the murder of Irene Wilkins in 1922.

On December 22nd, 1921, Irene Wilkins, an unmarried cook of Streatham, advertised in the *Morning Post* for employment in a school. She received a misspelt telegram a few hours later, urging her to come at once to Bournemouth, where she would be met by a car. A Mr Frank Humphris, who happened to be travelling on the same train, noticed Miss Wilkins, and saw her get into a greenish-grey touring car, driven by a chauffeur.

The following morning, her body was found in a field near Ilford Lane, a few miles to the north-east of Boscombe. Although her clothes were disarranged, rape had not been completed. Death was due to shock and blows on the head from a hammer or some similar instrument. Near the scene of the murder was found the track of a Dunlop-Magnum tyre.

Thomas Henry Allaway, chauffeur to a Mr Sutton, was among those interviewed, but seemed to have a sound alibi. Although three tyres of Mr Sutton's car were Dunlop-Magnums, the fourth – the near hind wheel – was a worn Michelin.

Inquiries at nearby post offices revealed that three telegrams had been sent within a few days of one another, all to young women advertising for jobs. Two of the clerks remembered a chauffeur as the sender.

On January 4th, 1922, Mr Humphris again saw the grey touring car and took its number, which he passed on to the police. Due to some inexplicable inefficiency, this was not followed up. And a month later, a clerk in the Boscombe post office recognized Allaway as the sender of one of the telegrams, and noted the number of his car. Incredible as it may seem, this was also ignored by the police. A few days later, Allaway was followed to his home by the post office officer, again on identification by the same clerk; still no arrest was made.

On April 20th, Allaway took his master's cheque book and absconded; he then proceeded to forge Mr Sutton's signature. He was arrested in Reading on April 29th. The suspicions of the police were at last aroused. (For comparable slow-wittedness on the part of the police, one has to look to the three murders

54

committed by Earle Nelson in Portland, Oregon.) Allaway's handwriting was now found to match the writing on the three telegrams.

On the day after the murder, Allaway had driven Mrs Sutton to tea with her sister, and had to wait for an hour and a half; later, Irene Wilkins' attaché case was found close to the spot.

Allaway was identified by the clerks as the man who sent the telegram, and by Mr Humphris and the railway signalman who had seen him waiting for the train on the night of the murder. It was also pointed out that although Allaway had been authorized to buy four new tyres for the car before the murder, he had changed one of them for the worn Michelin.

He was tried at Winchester Assizes in July 1922, before Mr Justice Avory. Mr Thomas Inskip prosecuted.

The defence attempted to prove an alibi, without success. Allaway was sentenced to death after the jury had been absent for an hour.

The motive for the murder was obviously rape; which, as noted above, was not completed.

ALLEN, John Edward

Twenty-five-year-old assistant chef of the Lamb Hotel at Burford, Oxfordshire, was found guilty before Mr Justice Finlay at Oxford Assizes on October 21st, 1937, of the murder of 17-month-old Kathleen Diana Lucy Woodward and sentenced to death. Allen had, some months before the killing, been befriended by the child's parents, Mr and Mrs Frederick Woodward, who were also employed at the Lamb Hotel. According to the child's mother, Allen had appeared devoted to the child, and often played with her and took her for rides on his cycle. On June 19th, 1937, Allen went to Mrs Woodward saying, 'Fred has sent me up to take the kiddy for an airing.' He gave the baby two pennies, and carried her outside, Mrs Woodward instructing him, 'Be careful, John, don't hurt her. . . .' Later that day Allen was missing, and the infant Woodward (still clutching the two pennies) was found dead by the roadside at Fulbrook, Oxfordshire, strangled by part of a hempen clothes-line. On June 21st, Allen surrendered to the Southwark (London) police, and the following day was charged with the murder. On his clothing were still traces of hemp. At his trial it was revealed that the defendant had twice been in a mental institution, and when giving their verdict the jury recommended that an inquiry be made into Allen's mental state. Mrs Woodward maintained that Allen had murdered her daughter through jealousy: '. . . he was jealous of me. . . . I was put in charge of the making of the cakes for a banquet. . . . He hated that, I know, and was jealous. . . .'

On November 6th, 1937, the death sentence was respited and John Allen committed to Broadmoor Criminal Lunatic Asylum, where he would seem to have settled down happily, becoming a regular performer for the inmates' concert party – the 'Broadhumoorists'. On July 20th, 1947, he escaped from Broadmoor wearing a parson's collar, a stage 'prop' he had worn in the 'Broadhumoorists'. Until his recapture on May 19th, 1949 he was referred to as the 'Mad Parson' by the Press, and there were periodic reports throughout this period from excited citizens who claimed to have seen the wanted man. Allen was to write a book on Broadmoor (*Inside Broadmoor*, W. H. Allen), in which he described his escape as being 'incredibly simple, and about as risky as walking carefully across Piccadilly during the rush hour'. He had obtained employment during his two years of freedom, and upon returning to Broadmoor applied for a rebate of income tax, since he was no longer earning; he received £16 10s. Allen was released from Broadmoor on September 18th, 1951.

ALLEN, Margaret
Forty-two-year-old ex-bus conductress, social misfit, frustrated Lesbian who went around with cropped hair and male clothing claiming she had undergone a sex-change operation, convicted of the murder of Nancy Ellen Chadwick, aged 68.

The battered corpse of Mrs Chadwick, a somewhat disagreeable eccentric with a miserly reputation, was found on August 29th, 1949, by the main road at Rawtenstall, Lancashire. At first sight she seemed to be the victim of a 'hit and run' car, but it was found later that the old lady's scalp wounds and fractured skull were the result of hammer blows. Margaret Allen's small, ill-kept house was situated a few yards away from where the body was found by a bus driver, and Mrs Chadwick had last been seen the previous morning walking towards this house. Margaret Allen herself spent the two days after the murder being over-voluble with reporters in a local public house, drinking stout and advancing theories on the crime to anyone who was interested. ('She was an old fool to sit on a roadside bench counting her money.') Allen found time, however, to point out to a constable Mrs Chadwick's missing handbag, just visible in the water of the River Irwell behind her [Allen's] home; the murdered woman was known to carry about large sums of money but the handbag was empty. Allen's curious and obvious relish of the crime caused suspicion, and on August 31st she was questioned by police officers; on September 1st her home was searched, and recent bloodstains seen near the cellar. Either from bravado or intimidation, Margaret Allen suddenly blurted out, 'Come on, I'll tell you all about it . . . that (pointing to the coal cellar) is where I put her.' More bloodstains were found in the cellar, of both Allen's and the victim's groups, and one of Mrs Chadwick's hairs retrieved from a pile of cinders. Coal-dust and ash found on Mrs Chadwick's clothing corresponded to that in Allen's coal-hole. Margaret Allen's subsequent confession told how she had come across Mrs Chadwick outside her home: '. . . I was in a funny mood . . . she seemed to insist on coming in. I just happened to look around and saw a hammer in the kitchen . . . on the spur of the moment I hit her . . . she gave a shout and that seemed to start me off more and I hit her a few times – I don't know how many . . .'

At Allen's trial the woman reputed to be her only friend, a Mrs Annie Cook, spoke of the defendant's frequent bouts of depression and headaches and of how on one occasion she had attempted to gas herself. Questioned about a holiday she and Allen had taken together, Mrs Cook mentioned a 'certain suggestion' put to her by her companion, one which she had, apparently, unhesitatingly rejected. Whatever the effects the irascible Allen had on the other inhabitants of Rawtenstall (only a hundred out of the twenty-eight thousand inhabitants would afterwards sign the reprieve petition organized by Mrs Cook) there is no doubt that Mrs Cook's family were genuinely fond of her, and she had, up to the time of the crime, enjoyed much hospitality in this home. The defence tried to prove Allen's insanity, but she was found guilty and subsequently hanged – the first woman for twelve years to undergo capital punishment in Britain; the wretched woman remained ill-tempered to the end, kicking over the last breakfast tray (for which she had, understandably, little appetite) with a remark to the effect that at any rate no one else would enjoy it.

ARAM, Eugene

Profligate scholar born in 1704, publicly hanged in 1759 at
Tyburn Field outside the gates of York for the murder of Daniel
Clark, shoemaker, in Knaresborough fourteen years before.
Aram's father was a gardener employed by Sir Edward Blackett
at Newby in Yorkshire. From him the son inherited poetical
inclinations. Self-taught, Eugene became a schoolmaster at
Gouthwaite in the West Riding of Yorkshire and married
Anna Spence, by whom he had seven children. According to his
pupils a 'rigid disciplinarian', stern in his adherence to scholarship and the Christian faith, Aram's out-of-school activities
were petty thieving and the professional receiving of stolen
goods. His crony was William Houseman, a flax-dresser, and on
February 7th, 1744, they extended their business to include
murder, by braining with a pick Daniel Clark ('pockmarked,
stammering, and weedy'), who was foolishly carrying £200 of
his wife's dowry. They put the corpse, doubled up, beneath a
rock in St Robert's Cave in Knaresborough, through which
flowed the River Nidd. As he and Houseman had been seen in
Clark's company on the night of his disappearance, Aram
thought it wiser to leave the district, and he deserted his family;
he went first to Nottingham and then to London in 1745, where
he caroused until 1757, when a desire for the academic life – or
need of money – drove him to seek a post at the Grammar
School, King's Lynn, Norfolk. Here, for £20 a year, he taught
Latin, one of his pupils being authoress Fanny Burney's brother.

In June 1758 Aram was recognized by a Knaresborough visitor
to King's Lynn, but Aram denied the identity. Two months
later William Houseman, under interrogation over the finding of
a skeleton mistakenly believed to be that of Daniel Clark, confessed to the Justices his and Aram's killing of Clark, and led
them to the remains at St Robert's Well. Informed by the King's
Lynn visitor of Aram's whereabouts, two constables brought
Aram back in a chaise to Knaresborough, crowds meeting them
as they entered the town. Alighting from the chaise and seeing
his wife and children for the first time since his departure
fourteen years before, Aram walked up and said, 'Well, and how
do you do?'

Houseman had become a witness for the Crown, but Aram was
kept in a York jail for almost a year before his trial; he spent his
time preparing his defence, studying in particular the book
Monasticon Eboracense, which dealt with the relics of saints –

claiming, at his trial, that the remains at St Robert's Well might well be the bones of a saint or hermit interred hundreds of years before.

Found guilty of murder, he attempted suicide by slashing his wrists the night before the execution, and was dragged along half-dead to his hanging. His bones were left dangling in a nearby forest, and his skull given to the College of Physicians.

Seventy years afterwards he was eulogized in a poem by Thomas Hood, 'The Dream of Eugene Aram', stanzas from which were often recited at Victorian musical evenings by that other callous criminal, Charley Peace.

ARMSTRONG, Herbert Rowse
Fifty-two-year-old solicitor, Cambridge MA, clerk to the Justices of the Peace in the Welsh town of Hay in Brecknock, tried for the murder of his wife, Katherine Mary.

Married in 1907 the Armstrongs appeared to enjoy a comfortable middle-class existence with their three children at their house called Mayfield in Cusop Dingle, a valley on the Wales–England border. It was observed that Mrs Armstrong was inclined to 'bully' her diminutive (7-stone) husband, who clung somewhat wistfully to his 1914–18 rank of Major; he was frequently admonished in public for some trifling offence (smoking or drinking for other than health reasons), all of which wifely rebukes Major Armstrong bore with a charming good-humour. (It was to be found later that he had not been without other distractions, and indeed one of the added aggravations at the time of his trial was a bout of venereal disease.) In July 1920, however, Armstrong was able to influence his wife into making a will leaving him all she possessed; whether this action was, in itself, a symptom of her mental deterioration is uncertain, but the following month she was committed to a lunatic asylum suffering from delusions, leaving the Major free to imbibe as he would wish, to make frequent week-end trips to London and, of course, to pursue his hobby of weed-killing, for which he invariably concocted his own weed-eradicator mixture from pure arsenic. By January 1921, Mrs Armstrong's condition had improved so much that she was allowed to return home; to her death, as it turned out, on February 22nd, which was attributed to heart disease, although the symptoms indicated stomach disease.

Later that year Mr Oswald Norman Martin, the head of a rival firm of solicitors in Hay, received through the post a box of chocolates from an unnamed donor; Mr Martin himself did not eat any of the chocolates, but a dinner-guest accepted some, and was taken violently ill shortly afterwards. Arsenic was later found to have been injected into the bases of some of these chocolates. On October 26th Mr Martin went to Armstrong's house in response to a tea invitation; the Major selected a buttered scone from a plate, and, in a somewhat unorthodox fashion, handed it to his guest, saying as he did so: 'Excuse my fingers.' Within a few hours Mr Martin became violently ill; the local physician, Dr Thomas Hincks (who had tended the dying Mrs Armstrong), was puzzled at the erratic pulse, not usually associated with biliousness, and sent a specimen of the invalid's urine to the Clinical Research Association for analysis. Dr Hincks learnt that 1/33rd of a grain of arsenic had been found in the specimen; this information, plus the knowledge of the Armstrong tea-invitation and his own uneasy recollection of certain of Mrs Armstrong's symptoms, caused Dr Hincks to report his suspicions to the Home Office. The Director of Public Prosecutions decided to start inquiries on the spot, all to be conducted, however, with the utmost secrecy; there followed for the wretched Mr Martin, a month of torture, because he was now bombarded with both tea and dinner invitations from the hospitable Major Armstrong. When all these invitations were refused the Major began to take afternoon tea in his office, requesting that Mr Martin should join him in a few delectable work-breaks; Mr Martin's frantic reluctance to do so was understandable, but his ordeal was increased by police insistence that he should never, ever, behave with the timidity of a prospective murder victim, so putting the wily little major on his guard. Mr Martin's trying period ended on December 31st, 1921, when (after exhaustive police inquiries) Armstrong was arrested on a charge of attempted murder; on his arrest, a small packet of arsenic was discovered in one of the major's pockets – the twentieth part, said the accused, of 1 oz. of arsenic bought to destroy nineteen dandelion roots in his garden; later a packet containing 2 oz. of arsenic was found in this conscientious gardener's office bureau. While the major was in custody, Mrs Armstrong's body was exhumed and examined by Home Office pathologist Dr Bernard Spilsbury, 3½ grains of arsenic being found in certain organs, and on January 19th, 1922, Armstrong was charged with the murder of his wife, the trial at Hereford Assizes (which lasted ten days) commencing on April 3rd.

The Attorney-General, Sir Ernest Pollock, conducted the prosecution, Sir Henry Curtis-Bennett defended, and the presiding judge was Mr Justice Darling. The defence line was that Mrs Armstrong had committed suicide, but the prosecution produced evidence that on the day she died the unfortunate woman had murmured to her nurse: 'I am not going to die, am I? Because I have everything to live for – my husband and my children.' Even so, the demeanour of Herbert Rowse Armstrong in the dock was impressive; his old job as clerk to the Justices of the Peace probably gave him confidence, and in Hereford they were betting five to one on his acquittal. There was a dramatic and decisive moment, however, when at the end of Armstrong's evidence, Mr Justice Darling said, 'Wait a minute, Major Armstrong', and proceeded to question the accused in a more stringent fashion about the arsenic found in his possession. Why, for example, had he taken the trouble to divide one supply of arsenic into twenty packets instead of merely sprinkling this drastic weedkiller directly around each dandelion root? 'I really do not know,' Armstrong feebly replied, 'at the time it seemed the most convenient way of doing it.'

Found guilty, Armstrong was subsequently hanged at Gloucester Prison on May 31st, 1922.

ASSASSINATION of Public Men

Assassination and attempted assassination have played a considerable part in modern history. In 1589, a fanatical Dominican friar named Jacques Clement took some letters to Henry III of France at his headquarters at St Cloud (he was storming Paris) and stabbed him to death. He believed that the King intended to allow concessions to the Protestants. Twenty-one years later, Henry IV was murdered by François Ravaillac, who believed he was plotting to make war on the Pope.

In 1800 there was an attempt on the life of George III of England, when he was attending a performance in Drury Lane Theatre. A former soldier, James Hadfield, who had received severe head wounds in battle, suffered from the delusion that the end of the world was at hand and that he was a messenger of Christ. He wanted to commit suicide, and resolved to do it by assassinating the King. On May 15th, 1800, he fired a pistol at the King, but missed. A jury acquitted Hadfield on grounds of insanity.

On Monday, May 11th, 1812, John Bellingham, a lunatic, shot

the Prime Minister, Spencer Perceval, as he was leaving the House of Commons. Bellingham, who was 41, had lost all his money when his business failed in Russia, and had been petitioning the government for recompense, which he did not receive. After the Prime Minister's death, Bellingham was tried and sentenced to death, although it was fairly plain to everyone that he was insane. He read the court a long, rambling statement that no one understood.

In 1843, another lunatic, Daniel McNaghten, set out to shoot the Prime Minister of England, Sir Robert Peel. He shot the wrong man – Edward Drummond, Sir Robert's secretary, who died from the wound. McNaghten was tried, and his defence pleaded that he suffered from an acute persecution mania. The judges acquitted him and he was committed to an insane asylum. The House of Lords put certain questions to the judges, as a result of which the 'McNaghten Rules' were formulated; these declared that a man could not be condemned if, at the time of the crime, he was suffering from a defect of reason such as to make him unaware of the nature of the act, or that he was doing wrong. Undoubtedly Bellingham would have been acquitted under these rules.

Three presidents of the United States have died by the assassin's pistol, and four others have had attempts made on their lives. The first attempt on a president was made by a lunatic named Richard Lawrence, who fired two pistols at Andrew Jackson on Friday, January 30th, 1835, when the President was attending the funeral of a former representative of South Carolina. Both pistols misfired (an extraordinary chance that has never been explained). At Lawrence's trial, it emerged that he believed himself to be Richard III of England, and that he had large estates in England. His delusions had begun (for no known cause) two years earlier. He was acquitted and sent to an asylum.

The next attempt was the most famous in American history, and resulted in the death of Abraham Lincoln. John Wilkes Booth, an actor, at first contemplated kidnapping the President and handing him over to the South, who would use him to bargain with the North for Confederate prisoners. This was in 1864. The end of the war only determined Booth to assassinate the President. (A kidnapping attempt on March 20th had collapsed because of a change of plan on Lincoln's part.) Booth was well known at Ford's Theatre in Washington, and had no difficulty in getting in on the evening of April 14th, 1865.

Lincoln was watching a third-rate comedy called *Our American Cousin*, when Booth entered his box and shot him in the back of the head. Another man tried to stop him but was slashed with a dagger; then, shouting 'Revenge for the South', Booth jumped on to the stage. His spur caught in a flat, and he fell eleven feet, breaking his shin.

At the same time Booth was killing Lincoln, another conspirator, Lewis Paine – a 20-year-old giant who was completely under Booth's sway – attempted to stab the Secretary of State, William H. Seward, who was in bed with a broken jaw following a carriage accident. Although he wounded Seward and four other men, the attempt was unsuccessful. George Atzerodt, another conspirator who was scheduled to kill Andrew Johnson, the Vice-President (and Lincoln's successor), funked it and got drunk on the evening of the murder. (He was later executed, together with Paine and two other conspirators, Mrs Suratt and David Herold, on July 7th; another conspirator, John Suratt, escaped to Egypt, but was finally captured and tried; he was acquitted.) Booth lived like a hunted animal for twelve days after the murder; he was on the run with Herold, but his broken leg was a handicap. Finally, they were surrounded in a barn in Virginia; Herold surrendered, but Booth was shot by a Sergeant Corbett, who said he had had orders from the Almighty.

Lincoln had dreamed of assassination several times shortly before his death; in one dream he saw his own murdered corpse in the White House. On the afternoon of his death he actually said that he expected to be killed.

It is amusing to note that many people believed that the man who died in the blazing barn on Garrett Farm was not Booth. Francis Wilson wrote a book on the subject. And there is still on display at carnivals in America the mummified body of a man named John St Helen (or Daniel George) who, shortly before he committed suicide in 1903 at Enid, Oklahoma, 'confessed' that he was Booth. The mummy undoubtedly bears a close resemblance to Booth. (There is a photograph of it in Curtis Macdougal's book of hoaxes.) About forty people 'confessed' to being Booth before they died; it was almost as fashionable as confessing to being Jack the Ripper.

In 1881, a crank named Charles J. Guiteau shot President James Garfield as he was walking to a train in Washington. Guiteau is worth study as illustrating how a man who completely lacks direction can murder out of sheer need to commit a 'definitive act'. Guiteau was a very short man – barely five feet tall – who was one of the few assassins of presidents who was a habitual petty crook. He was born in Freeport, Illinois, in 1841. His father, Luther Guiteau, was also a crank, a believer in the divine mission of the Rev John Noyes, founded of the Oneida Community (which believed in free love); Luther Guiteau also held the belief that he would never die.

Guiteau eventually joined this Oneida Community when he was 16, as a manual worker. The community supported itself competently with various trades. It practised 'Bible communism', and its main source of inspiration was Noyes' book *The Berean*. Noyes regarded monogamy as pernicious, and the Oneida women were communal. Guiteau remained here for five years. On his walls, he had such signs as this: 'Charles J. Guiteau, Premier of England, will deliver a lecture in St James's Hall, London'. At the age of 23, he grew tired of communal life and went to live in New York. He had an idea that he thought would make his fortune: a string of newspapers called *The Theocrat*, that would be published 'under the power and magnetism of God', and would replace all secular dailies. He wrote to his father that he was working for 'the very ablest and strongest firm in the universe – Jesus Christ and Co'. Nothing much came of this venture, and Guiteau returned to the Oneida Community in a dejected frame of mind, convinced that 'the world' was still in the devil's power. However, he grew bored after a year, and left for a second time without telling anyone of his intention. He married a 16-year-old girl named Annie Bunn in Chicago, and they had a child. Guiteau had expensive tastes, and he and his wife made a habit of sneaking out of their hotels by night. Guiteau now decided that his career was in politics, and used to pose in front of a mirror, asking his wife, 'Don't you think I look like a good foreign minister?' He began campaigning for Horace Greeley. Greeley's defeat was a great blow to Guiteau, and his death twenty-four days later was an even greater one. Guiteau's wife now left him, and divorced him on grounds of adultery with prostitutes. (He had contracted syphilis.) Guiteau was by now working as a lawyer – with his usual lack of moral scruples – and the *New York Herald* ran an article exposing his methods; this did more damage to his professional career. He served a short period in jail for fraud. He went to Chicago and tried to start a newspaper – without success – and became a devoted follower of the 'hot gospel evangelists' Moody and Sankey, at whose meetings he served as an unpaid usher. This decided him to become a preacher himself, and for the next three years he toured America lecturing on Christ's second coming. He also published a book called *The Truth*, much of it plagiarized from *The Berean*.

It was in 1880 that his ill-fated interest in politics began. He decided to join in the presidential campaign, and wrote a pamphlet called 'Garfield Against Hancock'. When Garfield won, Guiteau supposed this to be largely due to his own support, and went to see Garfield to demand his reward – the Austrian ambassadorship. Later, he lowered his sights and demanded the Paris consulship. Still he was ignored. Then, a few months later, the President's nomination of a collector of customs in New York caused strife within the Republican party, and Guiteau began to feel that the man he had 'made' was causing the downfall of Republicanism. On June 6th, 1881, Guiteau bought a large revolver. On July 2nd, he shot the President as he was walking to board the train at the Baltimore and Potomac depot. He was immediately arrested. The President was rushed to the White House. He lingered on for two months, until September 19th, when he died as a result of the breaking of the aneurysm.

Guiteau entered a plea of insanity at his trial; he also told the jury that the assassination of the President was an act of God. When he was sentenced to death, he shouted 'God will avenge this outrage'. He was hanged on June 30th, 1882.

Leon Czolgosz (pronounced Cholgosh), who murdered President McKinley, was an entirely different type from Guiteau (although he shared with Guiteau and all other would-be assassins the feature of small stature). He was a young anarchist, with his head full of notions of assassination. He was born in the United States a few months after his family – Polish Jews – arrived in America. The family were Roman Catholics, but Czolgosz eventually became a dissenter through reading pamphlets on free-thought. In 1893, when he was 20, the workers in the mill near Pittsburgh went on strike, and Czolgosz did a certain amount of agitating. When he was 21, he joined a socialist and anarchist circle, and decided that the American system of government was all wrong. But it was not until he was 25 that he had a serious illness that seemed to have a strong effect on his nervous system; he ceased to be sturdy and hard-working, and became sickly and abnormal. In 1900, he read an account of the assassination of King Humbert I of Italy by an American weaver named Gaetano Bresci. Bresci was an anarchist who travelled to Italy especially to kill the King. Newspaper accounts of the killing fascinated Czolgosz, who re-read them endlessly. He joined an anarchist club in Cleveland, but was thought to be a spy. The anarchists were suspicious of his strange manner and ignorance of anarchism.

In July 1901, his family returned seventy dollars of the money that Czolgosz had put into a farm, and he went to Buffalo. And it was in Buffalo, on September 6th, 1901, that he shot President McKinley, who was visiting the Pan-American Exposition. Czolgosz joined a row of people who were queuing to shake hands with the President, his revolver concealed beneath a handkerchief in his hand, and shot the President in the chest and the abdomen. Czolgosz was badly beaten by soldiers who stood by. McKinley died eight days later, singing a hymn. Czolgosz was tried under peculiar circumstances; he did not believe in courts or lawyers, and refused to speak to anyone or to take the stand. He was sentenced and executed (by electrocution) on October 29th, 1901. There was no attempt of any kind to determine his mental state. Sulphuric acid was poured into his coffin after his death, and the body dissolved (anticipating the method employed by John George Haigh!).

There have been three more attempts on the lives of presidents. John Schrank, a boastful New York saloon keeper, managed to shoot Theodore Roosevelt on October 14th, 1912, hitting him in the chest. (Roosevelt was then no longer president.) Schrank was confined in an insane asylum, after psychiatrists testified that he was a paranoiac with constant delusions. Roosevelt, who recovered, carried the bullet in his chest until his death.

On February 15th, 1933, Guiseppe Zangara attempted to shoot Franklin D. Roosevelt, the president elect, at Miami. As the President was speaking under floodlights at Biscayne Bay, Zangara fired five times, and hit five men and women near the President. One of them, the mayor, Anton Cermak, died with the words, 'I'm glad it was me instead of you'. Although psychiatrists testified that Zangara was a psychopath, he was sentenced to death, and electrocuted in Florida on March 20th, 1933.

Finally, two Puerto Rican nationalists tried to get into Blair House to shoot Harry S. Truman on November 1st, 1950, and killed two men and seriously wounded three others. They were Oscar Collazo and Griselio Torresola. Torresola was shot and killed, while Collazo recovered from a bullet wound to be sentenced to death, and later to have his sentence commuted to life imprisonment by the President.

On March 1st, 1954, four Puerto Ricans fired off revolvers in the House of Representatives and wounded five members, all of whom recovered. They were three men and a woman; all received long prison sentences.

AXE MAN of New Orleans, The
Remarkable unsolved American murder case, which has some features in common with the Jack the Ripper crimes of 1888. It took place in New Orleans in 1918.

On the night of May 23rd, 1918, someone chiselled out a panel in the door of the grocery shop of Mr and Mrs Joseph Maggio. The assailant struck the sleeping couple with an axe and then cut their throats with a razor, which was left on the scene of the crime. Since more than $100 was found beneath the blood-soaked pillow, it seemed fairly clear that robbery was not the motive. On the pavement, a block away, someone chalked the words, 'Mrs Maggio is going to sit up tonight, just like Mrs Toney'.

In 1911, there had been three axe murders of similar type, one of a certain Tony Schiambras and his wife. All victims were Italian grocers. (The other two were named Cruti and Rosetti.)

Joseph Maggio's brothers were arrested for the murder, but released a few days later.

Detective Theodore Obitz, in charge of the case, was murdered by a negro whom he had arrested for burglary. Then several weeks passed with no further development.

In the early hours of June 28th, the Axe man again chiselled his way into the grocery store of Louis Besumer, and attacked the grocer and his wife with a hatchet he found in the store. Mrs Besumer (who subsequently proved to be a wife only at common law) died of her wounds some days later. There was confused talk of Besumer being a German spy, and he was later arrested for his 'wife's' murder. This was on August 5th. On the same night, the Axe man attacked Mrs Edward Scheider, and left her unconscious, to be found by her husband when he returned late from work. A week later, Mrs Scheider was delivered of a baby girl, and she made a perfect recovery.

On August 10th, the Axe man visited to home of Joseph Romano. His two nieces heard noises and investigated. A tall white man rushed out of the room, and left Romano dying of head wounds. A panel had been chiselled out of the door. Unlike the other victims, Romano was a barber, not a grocer.

World War I ended, and there were no more attacks. But on March 10th, 1919, the Axe man chiselled his way into the home of Charles Cortimiglia and injured the husband and wife, while killing the baby. Subsequently, Mrs Cortimiglia accused an Italian family who lived opposite, of the attack; their name was Jordano. Charles Cortimiglia stated emphatically that the assailant had not been either of the Jordanos; nevertheless, Frank Jordano and his father were arrested.

Louis Besumer was tried for the murder of his 'wife', but found not guilty.

The citizens of New Orleans were by no means as electrified by the mysterious crimes as the citizens of London had been by the Ripper murders, or by the earlier Ratcliffe Highway murders. Someone even composed a 'Mysterious Axeman's Jazz', which became popular. On March 13th, 1919, the editor of the *Times Picayune* printed a letter, dated from 'Hell'. Unlike the 'Ripper's' correspondence, this letter *was* literate, and it declared that the writer was a demon, and that on Tuesday next he intended to pay a visit to New Orleans. But, he added, he was very fond of jazz, and he would pass by all houses in which a jazz band was playing. Tuesday, March 19th, was St Joseph's night, usually an occasion for celebration in New Orleans; on this particular St Joseph's night, the whole city rocked with jazz. But the Axe man failed to appear.

On May 21st, 1919, the Jordanos went on trial for murder. After five days they were found guilty, and Frank was sentenced to be hanged, while his father was sentenced to life imprisonment. The courtroom audience shouted their disapproval.

On August 10th, the Axe man attacked Steve Boca in the usual way. Boca recovered, and had to defend one of his friends, Frank Genusa, who was accused of the murder. Genusa was released.

On September 2nd, William Carlson, a chemist, disturbed the Axe man in the act of chiselling out his door panel, by firing through the door. The Axe man made off. On September 3rd, a 19-year-old girl, Sarah Laumann, was attacked in her bed by the Axe man; she also recovered later from head injuries, but could tell nothing.

On October 27th, 1919, came the last attack. This time, it was a grocer named Mike Pepitone, and his wife saw the Axe man running away when she rushed into the room. Her husband was dead, and the door panel had been chiselled out.

Rosie Cortimiglia, the woman who had accused the Jordanos, made headlines by bursting into the office of the *Times Picayune* and confessing that she had made the accusation out of spite. 'God has punished me. . . . I have lost everything. My baby is dead, my husband has left me, I have had smallpox. . . .' The Jordanos were set free.

The Axe man murders were over, but the case has a curious aftermath. On December 2nd, 1920, a woman shot a New Orleanian named Joseph Mumfre in a Los Angeles street; he died instantly. The woman declared that she was the wife of Mike Pepitone, the last victim, and that Mumfre was the Axe man. Mrs Pepitone received ten years in jail, but was released after three.

Mumfre's case history makes him the most likely suspect for the Axe man. He had a criminal record, and his dates in jail were the dates on which no murders occurred. He had been released in 1911, just before the murder of the Schiambras, Cruti, and Rosetti. He had then been sent back to jail, where he had remained until a few weeks before the Maggio attacks in 1918. In the lull between August 1918 and March 1919, he had been in jail on a burglary charge.

But, as in so many other cases of the same nature,[1] the murders ceased abruptly, and the identity of the killer remains a mystery.

AXILROD, Dr Asher Arnold
Dentist, sentenced to five to twenty years in prison for man-slaughter in Minneapolis in 1955.

On April 23rd, 1955, the body of a 21-year-old girl, Mary Moonen of East 17th Street, Minneapolis, was discovered by a motorist lying in the road in the fashionable Lake of the Isles district of the city. She had been strangled, but not sexually assaulted, and her purse had not been touched. The autopsy also revealed that she had had sexual relations with a man shortly before her death, and was three months pregnant. This threw some fresh light on the case. Her husband was a soldier in Korea, and had been shipped overseas more than three months before. And yet Mrs Moonen was known as a virtuous girl, and no one in her family suspected a lover. The victim's sister, Mrs Newton, found out that the girl had an appointment with her dentist, Dr Axilrod, on the previous evening. Checking up, the police now discovered that Dr Axilrod's methods were some-what peculiar. He had given Mrs Newton a pill that had knocked her out for several hours on one occasion, and had later talked

[1] See 'Moonlight Murderer'.

suggestively to her. 'I thought he was kidding.' On another occasion he had 'made a pass' at her, and she walked out of his office and stopped going there. But this did not prevent her from recommending Dr Axilrod to her sister.

A 17-year-old girl now phoned the police department to complain that Dr Axilrod had given her a pill that had knocked her out for several hours. And Mrs Moonen's doctor stated that Mrs Moonen had claimed that Dr Axilrod was the father of her child, and that he had assaulted her while she was under the influence of a knock-out pill.

Dr Axilrod was arrested, and it was later alleged by the police that he confessed to the murder. He indignantly denied that he had raped Mrs Moonen under the influence of a drug. He also stated that the pills were not intended to render the patient unconscious, but only to deaden the reflexes, and that cases in which the patient was knocked out were rare. He refused to sign a statement admitting to the murder, and when asked if he had had sexual relations with Mrs Moonen on the night of the murder, said he did not know because he had had 'a black-out'. He admitted that she had come to see him to talk to him about her pregnancy, and that they had quarrelled.

In the course of the investigation the police discovered about twenty young women who had been 'put to sleep' for five or six hours by one of Dr Axilrod's pills, and that no nurse had been present on these occasions. Newspapers were not slow to run headlines about the doctor's 'love pills'.

The trial began in September; three weeks were spent calling a jury; testimony started on October 10th, 1955, and the County Attorney, George M. Scott, lost no time in describing the dentist as an amorous philanderer who repeatedly drugged his pretty victims so they could not resist his sexual advances.

Dr Axilrod maintained that he had not killed Mary Moonen and that he had never had sexual relations with her. He was sentenced on November 3rd, 1955.

B

BALL, Joe

Forty-year-old Texan alligator breeder and owner of the Sociable Inn, near Elmendorf, Texas; a man of intemperate sex life, whose mistresses (when their presence became tedious) provided regular nourishment for his five alligator pets. In September 1937 yet another of his ever-changing retinue of barmaids disappeared; 22-year-old Hazel Brown had, like the others, unaccountably left behind all her clothes and personal possessions. Her mother, uneasy, took her suspicions to Deputy Sheriff John Klevenhagen who had for some time been hearing hostile reports from neighbours living near the inaptly named tavern: one man, apparently terrified of Ball's violence, had, overnight, moved his entire family and belongings to a neighbouring state. Another neighbour, Policeman Elton Cude, spoke of a foul smell coming from the alligator pool at the edge of the Ball property, and of how, when he complained, Ball had pulled out a gun and threatened to shoot him. Cude, surreptitiously investigating the source of the stench some time later, saw what appeared to be hunks of flesh floating about in a rain-barrel adjoining the alligator pool; when questioned by the sheriff, Ball explained that they were bits of 'spoiled meat' for his pets. The police learnt that Hazel Brown had opened a bank account only two days before disappearing, and that none of this money had been withdrawn; many other barmaids and Ball's second and third wives had similarly vanished from Elmendorf. Confronted with the sheriff's persistent questioning, Ball said he knew nothing of the women's whereabouts. When deceived into thinking that his loyal but weak-minded hired hand had betrayed him ('he has spilled', claimed the sheriff) Ball strode behind the tavern-bar, produced a revolver and shot himself, the method of killing he had apparently used on his victims. Ball's one-time neighbour who had fled the area now revealed that he had, one night in 1936, come across the innkeeper hacking up the body of a woman and feeding chunks of the corpse to the alligators: '... he shoved a gun in my face ... said he would let me go because I had a big family ...'

The five alligators subsequently found a permanent home at the San Antonio Zoo.

BARLOW, Kenneth
Thirty-eight-year-old male nurse, found guilty at Leeds Assizes in 1957 of the murder of his wife Elizabeth.

At Thornbury Crescent, Bradford, on the night of May 3rd, 1957, Elizabeth Barlow was found dead in her bath. Her husband said that he had found her submerged and apparently unconscious; he had unsuccessfully applied artificial respiration before the doctor's arrival. The pupils of the eyes were dilated, and there were no signs of maltreatment. The doctor noticed, however, that there were many recent hypodermic punctures on the buttocks; substances were taken from the corpse and injected into mice, who produced insulin reaction. Barlow denied using a syringe on his wife, but later retracted his statement, saying that at her own request he had injected her six times with ergometrine in order to produce an abortion. Barlow was charged with murder, the trial not taking place until the following December, to facilitate the collecting of medical data. Mr Justice Diplock presided, with Sir Harry Hylton-Foster, Solicitor-General, prosecuting, and Mr Bernard Gillis, QC, defending. Mr Harry Stork, of Northfield Sanatorium, Driffield, Yorkshire, with whom the accused had worked two years before, recalled a conversation in which Barlow had mentioned insulin-injection as being the only perfect method of murder, for the drug soon dissolved into the bloodstream where it was untraceable. A similar conversation had taken place with another workmate, a Nurse Waterhouse, at East Riding General Hospital; even a patient, Mr Arthur Evans, had been tactlessly regaled at Driffield Sanatorium with Barlow's homicidal theories. The male nurse said to him of insulin; 'Anybody get a load of this, and it's the quickest way out'. Evidence was given that Barlow's hospital work involved the injection of diabetic patients with insulin; three ampoules of ergometrine were missing from this hospital (St Lukes, Huddersfield), but a pathologist's report on Mrs Barlow stated that her death could not have been facilitated by this drug. Barlow, indignantly pleading not guilty, said he had been deeply in love with his wife, and had had no reason to kill her. (It was not revealed in court that his first wife had died eighteen months before, at age 33, the doctors then being unable to determine the cause of death, although believing it to be from natural causes.) The defence asserted somewhat vaguely that although the experimental mice had shown insulin reaction, it was by no means certain that the body had contained insulin; moreover, if Barlow had intended to carry out murder by insulin, would he have publicized this method in the past to various colleagues? After a short deliberation, the jury found Barlow guilty of murder; he was sentenced to life imprisonment.

BARNES, Peter

Thirty-two-year-old Irish labourer and IRA agent, convicted with 29-year-old Irishman James Richards of the murder of 21-year-old Elsie Ansell, fatally injured during a time-bomb explosion.

In 1939, the leaders of the Irish Republican Army had formulated the 'S Plan', a campaign of systematic terrorism and sabotage, designed to draw attention to the Republican aims, namely, the withdrawal of all British armed forces from Northern Ireland, and the inclusion of the six northern counties in the Irish Free State. The 'S Plan' was condemned by Mr de Valera, the Irish president '. . . no one can think that this Government has any sympathy with it . . .' In May, Richards was sent by the IRA to Coventry, to work there as 'operating officer' and contact man. He found lodgings with an Irish family at 25 Clara Street: Joseph Hewitt, a tinsmith's mate, his wife Mary, their baby aged 15 months and Hewitt's mother-in-law, Mrs Brigid O'Hara, aged 49. Richards' bedroom at Clara Street became the HQ of Irish terrorists in Coventry; at first he kept a store of the explosive potassium chlorate in a suitcase, but presently he dug a hole under the stairs, lined it with cement and used it as a dump for explosives. Mrs O'Hara, at the trial, was asked: '. . . That is a peculiar thing for a lodger to start to do . . . did you not say "What on earth are you breaking up our hall for?"'

'I did ask Jim Richards that. He said he was making a dump.'

'A dump for what?'

'He would not tell me.'

'It was a nice pattern on the tiles, and there he was shattering the nice tiles and you could not get any reason from him?'

'He would not tell me what his business was.'

'Was he assisted by somebody in that work?'

'Yes . . . Joseph Hewitt, my son-in-law.'

On August 21st, Peter Barnes, hitherto a stranger to Clara Street, called on Richards. Mrs O'Hara was sent out by the two men to buy a suitcase, and her daughter asked to fetch two flour bags from a nearby confectioner. The flour bags were rejected as unsuitable by Barnes and Richards (the mesh being too coarse to hold explosive powder) and were taken back to the shop. The receipt was retained, however, as was the receipt for the suitcase, and these documents were later found in the possession of Barnes' fiancée in London. On August 22nd, Richards and an unidentified man purchased a bicycle from the Halford Cycle

Company in Coventry. On August 24th, another unidentified man (referred to throughout the subsequent trial as 'the strange man') called at Clara Street, and commenced to make a bomb in the Hewitts' front sitting-room, Mrs O'Hara and the young Mrs Hewitt walking the baby out in the perambulator until almost midnight. On Friday, August 25th, the 'strange man' returned and completed his task shortly after noon, setting the bomb (by means of an alarm clock mechanism) for 2.30 pm: the bomb was placed in the carrier of the new bicycle, the 'strange man' then riding the bicycle with its lethal burden to Broadgate, a busy thoroughfare in Coventry, leaving the bike in front of a parked car. At 2.32 pm the bomb exploded, causing widespread devastation and the loss of five lives, including that of Elsie Ansell. The number of the shattered carrier cycle was just perceptible, and through this the plotters Barnes and Richards, together with the Hewitts and Mrs O'Hara, were traced. Traces of potassium chlorate were found at 25 Clara Street and eagerly given testimonies from angry and long-suspicious neighbours taken. An unposted letter (dated August 24th) to one Jim Kelly in Dublin, found in Barnes' pocket at the time of his arrest, left no doubt of Barnes' participation in the Coventry bomb plot.

First charged with offences under the 1883 Explosive Sub-stances Act, the defendants were later charged with the murder of Elsie Ansell and the trial started at Birmingham Assizes on December 11th, 1939, all five prisoners pleading not guilty. Barnes and Richards were found guilty as charged, and executed at Winson Green Prison on February 7th, 1940. The Hewitts and Mrs O'Hara, found not guilty of the murder of Elsie Ansell, faced, on December 15th, 1939, a charge of murdering the other four victims of the bomb explosion; the prosecution offered no evidence on this indictment, and the judge directed the jury to return a verdict of not guilty.

BARNEY, Elvira Dolores
Twenty-seven-year-old 'Society' woman, tried at the Old Bailey, London, in July 1932 for the murder of her lover, 24-year-old Scott Stephen.

Mrs Barney lived at No. 21 William's Mews, Knightsbridge; there police were summoned in the early morning of May 31st, 1932. Mrs Barney was hysterical, and Stephen lay dead from a gunshot wound in his lung. Despite her condition, Mrs Barney made a statement in which she described a quarrel ('about a woman he was fond of') which culminated in her and Stephen struggling in the spare room, each seeking possession of Mrs Barney's revolver: 'As we were struggling together – he wanted to take it away, and I wanted to get it back – it went off. Our hands were together – his hands and mine . . .' For a period Mrs Barney was allowed to return to her wealthy and distressed parents at their town house in Belgrave Square; on June 3rd she was arrested and charged with the murder of Scott Stephen. The judge at the trial was Travers Humphreys: Sir Percival Clarke prosecuted, and Patrick Hastings defended. Neighbours from William's Mews gave evidence of frequent quarrels between victim and accused; one, a chauffeur's wife, told of an earlier incident when Mrs Barney had leant out of the window and fired at Stephen in the mews below. Sir Bernard Spilsbury, pathologist, who had examined Stephen's body shortly after death, stressed how the fatal wound could not have been suicidal; he had himself experimented on a skeleton to prove this theory. Hastings' interrogation of Spilsbury was brief, and, as he remarked afterwards to the jury: '. . . Sir Bernard Spilsbury gave no shred of evidence to suggest that the young man's death could not have been caused in the way that Mrs Barney has always said it was. . . . He did not affect my case.' Mr Robert Churchill, firearms expert, gave evidence that Mrs Barney's revolver, a five-chambered ·32 American weapon, was one of the safest types made; considerable pressure was needed to fire it. Hastings indicated the absence of a safety device, and, holding the revolver aloft in court proceeded to press the trigger several times, observing as he did so: 'It doesn't seem to require any terrific muscular strength.' During Hastings' questioning of Mrs Barney, great dramatic effect was registered when, after requesting that the revolver be placed on the edge of the witness-box, defence counsel suddenly shouted, 'Pick up that revolver, Mrs Barney!' and the accused, jerking with genuine shock, automatically picked up the revolver with her right hand, thus casting doubt on the testimony of the chauffeur's wife, who had asserted that Mrs Barney, during the earlier shooting, had fired with her left hand. During his summing-up, Mr Justice Humphreys referred to the 'remarkable forensic effort' of the counsel for the defence. Found not guilty of murder, Mrs Barney was cheered by an enthusiastic crowd.

BARTLETT, Adelaide

Thirty-year-old Anglo-Frenchwoman, accused of murdering her 40-year-old husband Edwin, found dead in bed at their Pimlico lodgings on New Year's Day, 1886, having, according to the post-mortem, swallowed chloroform. They seemed a contented couple throughout their eleven years together, but Edwin's views on matrimony, said Adelaide, were eccentric. He believed that a man should be entitled to two wives, one for companionship, and one 'for use'. Her rôle was that of companion, but Edwin showed no particular desire – according to Adelaide – to acquire a second partner. Male contraceptives found in Edwin Bartlett's clothes-cupboard lend an ambiguous note to all this, but Adelaide's story was borne out by the Rev George Dyson, a young Wesleyan minister, known to the couple for about a year, who had enjoyed many a friendly chat with Edwin on matrimony and other topics. In these sessions Edwin had stated that in the event of his death he wished to 'give' Adelaide to George, and during his last months he derived much unhusbandly pleasure from the sight of Adelaide and the Rev Dyson dutifully kissing each other in anticipation of his dearest wish. The bewildered but undismayed Dyson wrote poems to Adelaide throughout this period:

> Who is it that hath burst the door
> Unclosed the heart that shut before
> And set her queenlike on its throne
> And made its homage all her own – My Birdie.

Adelaide Bartlett's trial at the Old Bailey opened on April 12th, 1886. The Attorney General (Sir Charles Russell) led for the prosecution, and she was defended by Mr Edward Clarke, QC.

It was proved in court that Dyson had bought varying amounts of chloroform from chemists at Putney and Wimbledon three days before Bartlett's death, but Adelaide insisted that she had required it as a nightly anaesthetic for Edwin, who had suddenly and inexplicably become enthusiastic about the delights of the bedchamber. But instead of a few drops sprinkled on a handkerchief and wafted delicately under nostrils dilated with passion, the contents of an entire bottle were found in Edwin Bartlett's stomach after death. Assuming murder, suicide, or even accidental swallowing, it is one of the biggest mysteries in the history of violent death as to how so much searing fluid found its way inside Edwin Bartlett without roars of agony resounding through that Pimlico lodging, and without any trace of burning around the mouth and windpipe tissues.

The jury were obviously suspicious of Adelaide, but the foreman, delivering their verdict on April 17th, stated that there was insufficient evidence to show how or by whom the chloroform was administered, and Adelaide Bartlett was acquitted.

Attributed to Sir James Paget, the surgeon, is the remark, made after the trial: 'Now she's acquitted, she should tell us, in the interests of science, how she did it.'

BATEMAN, Mary ('The Yorkshire Witch')

An unscrupulous swindler of the early nineteenth century who seemed to take a sadistic pleasure in reducing her victims to destitution. She was executed on March 20th, 1809, at the age of 41, for murder by poisoning.

She was born Mary Harker, daughter of a farmer near Thirsk, and showed a thieving disposition very early in life. She lived in York and Leeds, working as a domestic, and being dismissed for pilfering. Finally she married a wheelwright, John Bateman, and soon caused him embarrassment by thieving. Her thefts, like her later swindles, were always petty, and she was frequently caught. She soon began to practise as a fortune-teller, and showed a sadistic intentness when once she had fixed on her prey; she was completely without pity. For example, a pregnant girl consulted her, and for a few guineas, Mary Bateman sold her a charm to make her lover marry her. Over a period of time she extorted a great deal of money from the girl, and finally performed an illegal operation which almost cost the girl her life. Her lover was now smitten with conscience and married her, but she was already dying: she is quoted as saying: 'Had I never known Mary Bateman my child would now have been in my arms and I should have been a healthy woman. . . .' On another occasion, a man named Stead consulted her about his debtors, and was advised to leave his wife and join the army. He refused, but Mary Bateman used various ruses and charms to persuade him; she also told his wife that he was about to elope with a rival, and took money from her to avert this by magic. Finally, the husband being in the army, the wife was reduced to living off the charity of the Leeds Benevolent Society, which Mary usually managed to intercept. The baby died.

That she was a pathological criminal is certain, a woman who thought of herself habitually as a criminal and took every opportunity to rob or swindle. On one occasion, she happened to overhear a man ordering a pig from a butcher and giving his address; she met the butcher's boy near the man's home, pretending to be the cook, and boxed his ears for being late. The man returned to the butcher to complain about the non-delivery of the pig, and happened to know something of Mary Bateman, whom he had noticed listening when he gave his address; he called at her house and found the pig roasting! But she was lucky; he allowed her to make restitution, and did not pursue the case.

Her husband joined the army, and she followed him around the country, pursuing her trade as fortune-teller, and swindling and robbing whenever she could. One of her favourite tricks was to convince someone that gold pieces or paper money had to be sewn into a bed (or skirt) as a charm; some sleight of hand made sure that whatever was sewn into the bed was worthless.

She invented a 'Miss Blythe', a wise woman who lived in Scarborough, possessing an immense knowledge of magic and astrology; in this way she could escape embarrassing questions on subjects she knew nothing about. 'Miss Blythe' sent her instructions by letter.

It was 'Miss Blythe' who became the family adviser of a couple named Perigo. Mrs Perigo was the aunt of the unfortunate Stead woman whose baby had died. Mrs Perigo complained of a pain, and thought someone had put the evil eye on her; Miss Blythe's help was requested. Then began a long series of swindles that, in six months (from December 1806 to April 1807) extracted from the Perigos £70 in gold, and an impressive list of goods, including sixty pounds of butter and large quantities of other foodstuffs, bed linen, clothes, and bottles of spirits. Finally, for reasons of her own, she decided to poison the Perigos. For this purpose, 'Miss Blythe' was made to send from Scarborough various letters warning them of immense misfortunes that were about to descend on the gullible couple. These could only be averted by staying indoors for a week and eating every day a pudding mixed with certain powders that 'Miss Blythe' would send: a powder for each separate day. In case they felt sick (due to the workings of unseen enemies) a pot of honey would provide an antidote. They began to eat the pudding on Monday, May 11th, 1807, and experienced no ill effects until they reached the Saturday's powder, which contained mercuric chloride. Both were sick, and both tried the 'antidote', which contained arsenic. Perigo had the sense to leave off after a mouthful; even so, his lips turned black and he was ill for days; Mrs Perigo died. Mary Bateman explained that no doubt Mrs Perigo had touched something she should not, and that she had thereby endangered not only her own life but those of 'Miss Blythe' and Mary Bateman. She followed this up with a request for some of the late Mrs Perigo's clothes. Perigo was gullible enough to hand them over.

Perigo finally lost faith in her when he opened some bags into which Mary Bateman had sewed guineas as charms, and found that they contained waste paper. Mary Bateman was denounced and arrested; her trial caused a sensation and attracted great crowds. Even in the death cell she continued to swindle fellow prisoners. She was nursing a baby in arms when she was taken out to be executed. She protested her innocence to the end. After death, her body was exhibited to make money for charity, and drew many thousands of morbid sightseers. Finally, the skin was stripped from her body and sold in pieces for charms.

BAYLY, William Alfred
Forty-two-year-old farmer of Ruawaro, New Zealand (seventy-five miles from Auckland), who murdered his neighbours, dairy farmer Samuel Pender Lakey and his wife Christobel.

There had been disagreement in the past between Bayly and the Lakeys over sheep-grazing and land boundaries, with threats and grim prophecies on both sides (Mrs Lakey: 'You murdered Elsie Walker and we can expect the same . . .' Mr Bayly: 'You won't see the next season out, Lakey!') When, on Sunday, October 15th, 1933, Mrs Lakey's drowned body, with head wounds, was recovered from the Lakey duckpond, Bayly maintained that Lakey had panicked on finding his wife's body, and, thinking he would fall under suspicion of murder, had fled. Police discovered, however, that Lakey must have fled wearing a pair of boots belonging to Mr Gilmour, a neighbour who always kept a spare pair at the Lakeys' because of the muddy approaches; suspicion grew that Lakey had been murdered, and that his killer had taken the wrong boots to give an impression of sudden flight.

Police commenced a search of neighbour Bayly's farm, and nearby land. A pair of old cart wheels was found by the boundary fence; some of the wood looked new, and it was evident that parts of the woodwork had been recently pared. Human blood was found on the axle and wheel framework, and, as the grass underneath the wheels was fresh, it was obvious that the apparatus had been in recent use. There were no wheel-marks by the duckpond, so police became convinced that the wheels had been used to convey the body of Mr Lakey. Human blood was found in great quantity inside Bayly's tool-shed, which the suspect attributed to a cut finger, a recent calving, and a hare he had shot two days before. Search was intensified for Lakey's body. In the cowshed a shovelful of ash was found, analysed as bone-ash; a neighbouring farmer spoke of thick smoke coming out of the cowshed on the day the Lakeys disappeared, and several people said that Bayly's eyes had been red and sore around that time. Buried near the Bayly farmhouse were bone-fragments, two false teeth, a bracer stud, part of a cigarette-lighter, and the stem of a cherrywood pipe, similar to one Lakey owned. A sheep-dip vat was tipped, and revealed more burned bones, a tuft of grey hair, and the cigarette-lighter case which contained, as a wick, white wool identical with some in Mrs Lakey's work basket. Buried around the farm were hundreds of fragments of human bone, all of which had been recently subjected to intense heat; found with the bones were minute pieces of shot-lead. A rifle shell discovered in Bayly's dungarees was proved to come from Lakey's pea-rifle, retrieved earlier from a water-hole on Bayly's land. Police experimented by burning a sheep, then a ram and a calf, in a benzine drum like the one owned by the suspect; in all cases the carcase was reduced to crumbling bone in a few hours.

Police now charged William Bayly with the murder of Samuel Lakey. The trial, in Auckland, lasted twenty-nine days; on June 23rd, 1934, Bayly was found guilty and was executed at Mount Eden Jail on July 30th, 1934.

BEAN, Sawney (Legendary)
Bandit and highway robber during the reign of James I of Scotland (who came to the throne in 1424). The exploits of Sawney Bean and his family are so horrible that an encyclo-paedia of murder would be incomplete without some reference to him. The present account is taken from Traditional Tales of the Lowlands, *by John Nicholson of Kirkcudbright.*

Sawney Bean was born in East Lothian sometime in the sixties of the fourteenth century. He lived in the country eight or nine miles east of Edinburgh, and followed his father's trade, that of a hedger and ditcher. However, he disliked working for a living, and, together with a woman 'as viciously inclined as himself' he went to live in a cave on the seashore in Galloway. There they lived for twenty-five years without going into towns or villages, and produced many children. Through incest, the family finally swelled to eight sons, six daughters, eighteen grandsons, and fourteen granddaughters. They lived by highway robbery, and ate the bodies of their victims, which they pickled in sea water.

The high mortality rate among travellers in that area was a matter for some conjecture; but since none escaped, the existence of the family remained a secret. When a band of travellers was attacked (never more than six on foot or two on horse), members of the family waited around in ambush to make sure that any who fled should be cut off. In spite of the size of the family, they had such a plenitude of their meat that odd arms and legs were frequently cast into the sea, causing 'astonishment and terror' wherever they were washed ashore.

In the usual hit-and-miss method of that time, all suspects were executed including innkeepers in whose house the missing travellers had last lodged. But this produced no obvious effect. Finally, the region became almost depopulated.

The family was caught by an accident. They attacked a man and his wife on their way home from a fair, and managed to cut the throat of the woman, 'and fell to sucking her blood with as great a gusto as if it had been wine; this done, they ripped up her belly and pulled out all her entrails'. But while the husband, on horseback, was fighting for his life, six more travellers from the same fair came along, and the Bean family fled.

The man was the first to live to tell of the horde. He related his experience to the magistrates in Glasgow; the King was told, and he set out with 400 men and bloodhounds.

The men would have passed by the cave – as many previous searchers had done – but the dogs ran in and bayed. The men ventured in with torches, and after 'intricate turnings and windings', found themselves in the main cave, a huge charnel house, with pickled limbs and lumps of human meat hung up. Sawney Bean and his family of forty-seven were taken alive, and the human flesh was buried in the sand. They were taken to Edinburgh, where they were committed to the Tolbooth, and then to Leith. There they were executed 'without any process'; the men were allowed to bleed to death after their hands and legs had been chopped off; the women watched this, and then were burnt alive in three fires. 'They all in general died without the least sign of repentance, but continued cursing . . . to the very last gasp of life.' Under the circumstances, this is not surprising. One wonders which was more barbarous, the crime or its punishment.

BENDER Family, The

One of German extraction, with thieving and murderous tendencies, consisting of Father Bender, 60 years of age, his ten-years-younger wife, 27-year-old son John, and 24-year-old Kate. In 1871 they came to live in Labette County, Kansas, at an isolated spot in the prairieland fourteen miles east of Independence. Here they were reputed to offer board and refreshment to travellers riding through those regions. Miss Kate Bender (calling herself 'Professor') enjoyed fame as a psychic, and regularly lectured in the nearby towns of Oswego, Labette, Parsons, and Chetopa; a newspaper advertisement of June 18th, 1872, reads: 'Professor Miss Kate Bender can heal disease, cure blindness, fits and deafness', and a contemporary print shows a handsome wasp-waisted young woman declaiming on table-tapping to an admiring throng.

On March 9th, 1873, Dr William H. York, who had been visiting his brother Colonel York at Fort Scott, left for his home at Independence, carrying a fair amount of money; when last seen he was riding near the Bender house, and told friends of his intention to stop there for his midday meal. Dr York never arrived home, and after three weeks had elapsed with no trace of his brother, Colonel York began an intensive search. Uneasy at rumours of ambiguous hospitality at the Bender hostelry (two travellers had left hurriedly, instinctively sensing impending violence) the Colonel, with a posse of twelve men, called on the Bender family on April 24th to inquire after his brother. Mother Bender was hostile, but father and son (muttering about murderous outlaws in the vicinity) helped the search-party drag a nearby creek, after admitting that Dr York had stopped by that day for his lunch. On May 5th, Colonel York called at the Bender homestead with a larger posse to find the family had fled five days before. Traces of recently spilled blood were found on the cellar floor, and presently Colonel York made what has become one of the classic phrases in the annals of criminology:

'Boys, I see graves yonder in the orchard!'

The Colonel's observation was a true one, and not only was his brother found, but also the bodies of eleven other people – nine men, a woman, and a small girl; all bore severe head injuries, except the child, who appeared to have been buried whilst alive, under the body of her father. All save two were identified, and most were known to have been carrying money while travelling in that area. From the testimony of surviving travellers, it is believed the killings actually occurred at meal-times, the killer (presumably either father or son) concealed by a curtain behind the diner's head; Professor Kate Bender was known to serve the meals, and it has been suggested that she also employed her psychic powers to lull the victim into a state of ease.

There are many theories about the fate of the Bender family – that they were overtaken while journeying through Oklahoma and hanged, that the Vigilantes of Independence shot them 'out of hand'; that they joined a gang of desperadoes operating in the Indian Territory, but there has yet to be a satisfactory explanation of their whereabouts after April 1873 or of what became of their stolen hoard, estimated at seven thousand dollars.

BENNETT, John Herbert
Hanged for the murder of his wife, Bennett was undoubtedly a scoundrel, but there are many who believe he was innocent of the murder.

On Sunday morning, September 22nd, 1900, a boy walking on Yarmouth beach found the body of a young woman; she had been strangled with a mohair bootlace and her disarranged clothing suggested rape. She had, in fact, been criminally assaulted. The only clue to her identity was a laundry mark, 599, on her clothes. A Yarmouth landlady, Mrs Rudrum, soon identified the woman as a lodger named 'Mrs Hood' who had been with her for a week, since September 15th. But 'Mrs Hood' remained unidentified until a Bexleyheath laundry came forward to say that they marked the clothes of a certain Mary Bennett with the number 599; they identified a photograph of 'Mrs Hood' as Mrs Bennett.

Mrs Bennett's husband was now sought by the police, and he was finally arrested on November 6th, 1900 in Woolwich.

The most damning evidence against him was a long gold chain with a silver watch on it, which was found in his lodgings. A photograph of 'Mrs Hood' taken by a beach photographer a few days before her death showed that she was wearing this chain. The landlady declared positively that Mrs Bennett had been wearing it on the Saturday evening when she left the house for the last time. Also among Bennett's possessions was a false moustache and wig. Mrs Bennett had been seen with a man with a large moustache in a public house on the Saturday evening of her death.

It was soon revealed that Bennett's career had been punctuated by encounters with the law. He had met his wife at Northfleet, Kent, when she was only 18. She was Bennett's music teacher, and he, at that time, was a grocer's assistant. They married and immediately searched for easy ways of making a living. They bought old violins very cheaply; Mrs Bennett was then sent from door to door, dressed respectably, telling a hard-luck story about her husband's recent tragic death and trying to sell his 'last possession' to avoid starvation. In this way they made £400 in a year and set up in a grocery business; this was soon burnt down when the Bennetts (together with their baby daughter) were out of the house, and the insurance paid up. They took another shop, stocked it up on credit, and Bennett left hastily when the goods were sold, leaving his creditors behind. He went to South Africa, where he was suspected of being a spy for the Boers, and deported back to England. He worked at Woolwich Arsenal, and seemed always to have a great deal of money; it was suspected that he was a spy on the Arsenal for some foreign power. He was also frequently unfaithful to his wife, and finally established a permanent liaison with a pretty parlourmaid, Alice Meadows, who accompanied him to Yarmouth and Ireland.

It was Alice Meadows who recommended to Mrs Bennett the lodgings in Yarmouth where she went for a holiday on September 15th, 1900. Mrs Bennett appears to have told the landlady a great many lies; she declared herself a widow, and said that her brother-in-law was madly in love with her. (She had no brother-in-law.) On her first night at Mrs Rudrum's, she went out and got a little drunk; on her return, she told her landlady that she had been out with her brother-in-law.

The landlord of the South Quay Distillery pub in Yarmouth said that Bennett and his wife had been drinking there until closing time on the Saturday night, and had then gone off in the direction of the beach. A booking-clerk at Yarmouth Station swore that Bennett had travelled back to London on the seven-twenty train on the following morning. When arrested, he was about to move into a house with Alice Meadows. He still had a great deal more money than he could have obtained from his employment at the Arsenal, but he refused to say where it came from, and this has never been revealed since. It was also established that he had spent the Saturday night of the murder in a Yarmouth hotel. Altogether, the evidence against him was overwhelming.

He was tried in March 1901 at the Old Bailey before Lord Alverstone, the Lord Chief Justice, with Sir Charles Gill prosecuting and Marshall Hall defending. This was the first case that brought Marshall Hall into the limelight he enjoyed for the rest of his life. He believed completely in the innocence of his client, although he admitted that Bennett's was a 'worthless life'; he felt that Bennett was too clever a scoundrel to murder in such a bungling manner. A man was produced who said that Bennett had been with him on the Saturday of the murder, but under cross-examination it became obvious that he was mistaken. Bennett was sentenced to death. Marshall Hall continued to believe the murder was the work of a sex maniac.

Strangely enough, in 1912, a girl named Dora Grey was found strangled with a bootlace on the very same spot on the beach; her murderer was never discovered.

BENTLEY, Derek
Petty criminal aged 19, convicted and hanged for the murder of policeman Sydney George Miles.

At 9 pm on November 2nd, 1952, two men were seen clambering over the locked main gates of a confectioners' warehouse in Tamworth Road, Croydon, Surrey; the police were summoned, and a fracas developed on the roof of the factory, during which one of the intruders, Derek Bentley, was taken into custody. The other would-be burglar, 16-year-old Christopher Craig, a Camberwell garage-hand, skulking behind a lift-shaft, was ordered to surrender. According to police testimony, Bentley then shouted to his confederate, 'Let him have it, Chris,' referring to Detective-Constable Frederick Fairfax who was holding him. Craig, in possession of a gun, started to fire, wounding Fairfax in the shoulder. While other policemen clambered on to the roof, Craig continued firing, Bentley at one point saying: 'He's got a Colt ·45 and plenty of bloody ammunition too.' In the meantime, police reinforcements had broken into the factory by a ground-floor entrance, but as PC Miles, having climbed the inside staircase leading to a roof, climbed on to the flat roof he was shot dead between the eyes. Craig shouted out: 'I am Craig. You've just given my brother twelve years. Come on, you coppers. I'm only sixteen.' (Niven Scott Craig, aged 26, had been sentenced at the Old Bailey three days before for armed robbery.) After twenty minutes, with sporadic bursts of firing from Craig, pistols arrived for the police. Craig, when informed of this fact, jeered: 'So you're going to make a shooting match of it, are you? It's just what I like. . . . Come on, brave coppers, think of your wives.' A few seconds later Craig dived off the roof, injuring his spine and breastbone; before becoming unconscious he said, 'I hope I've killed the bloody lot.' Taken to the police station, Derek Bentley said he knew Craig was in possession of a gun, but had not thought he would use it.

The trial of Bentley and Craig for the murder of PC Miles commenced at the Old Bailey on December 9th, 1952, before the Lord Chief Justice, Lord Goddard. Prosecuting Counsel were Mr Christmas Humphreys and Mr J. T. Bass, and for the defence Mr E. J. Parris for Craig and Mr F. H. Cassels for Bentley.

Craig's father, a bank cashier, told how his son Christopher suffered from 'word blindness', and how the boy's favourite books were Enid Blyton's fairy tales, read aloud to him by members of the family, he remarked the gentleness of his son's nature, how Christopher had regularly attended Bible classes at a Streatham church, although he admitted a family interest in firearms (Mr Craig himself possessed a revolver) and that he had taught his sons to shoot with air-guns and air-pistols. Mr Parris, defending, maintained that Craig was guilty of manslaughter, that in defying arrest he had accidentally caused a fatal injury.

In Bentley's defence it was stressed that at the time of the shootings he was under arrest. A knife and knuckleduster were found in his possession on the night of the murder, and when asked by the Lord Chief Justice what had been his purpose that evening, Bentley replied: 'Just to go to Croydon for a ride, sir, an ordinary ride. Just to walk around.'

Bentley denied inciting Craig to use the gun, but in his summing-up Lord Goddard said, referring to the testimony of the police: '. . . are you going to say that they are conspicuous liars? Because, if their evidence is untrue, that Bentley called out, "Let them have it, Chris," those officers are doing their best to swear away the life of that boy. If it is true, it is, of course, the most deadly piece of evidence against him. . . .'

Both Craig and Bentley were found guilty of murder. Craig, because of his age, was sentenced to be detained, and Bentley was condemned to death, although the jury added a recommendation to mercy. Bentley's subsequent application to the Court of Criminal Appeal was rejected, and despite protests and petitions from many quarters he was executed at Wandsworth Prison on January 28th, 1953.

BENTON, Wallace
Sentenced to death for the murder of Thomas Herbert Williamson in June 1929, but reprieved.

The story of this case is rather pathetic. Benton lived on his small estate at Tilney St Lawrence, near King's Lynn in Norfolk, for twenty-five years, making a living by fruit-farming. As he grew older, he also grew deaf, short-sighted, and cantankerous, and had difficulty running the business efficiently. He mortgaged the estate, but never paid interest on the mortgage, and the mortgagees finally had to have recourse to the law. The property went up for auction but was not sold. An order of ejection was made against the 70-year-old Benton, and a man named Williamson, who lived nearby, was asked to rescue the land from the state of neglect into which Benton had allowed it to fall. Benton had moved out most of his property, but continued to sleep on a mattress in the farm, together with his wife.

A short time before the order of ejection was due to be put into force, Benton fetched his shotgun from the place where he was storing it, and shot Williamson in the stable. This was at six-fifteen in the evening of Thursday, March 21st, 1929. Benton then fetched the local constable and claimed that he had quarrelled with Williamson and the gun had gone off accidentally. The constable accompanied him back to the stable, where Williamson was found to be dead.

The evidence at the trial showed a certain premeditation; he had wrapped the gun in brown paper, and told someone who saw him with it that it was a roller-blind. It was also revealed that the trigger of the gun required great pressure to fire it. Mr Justice Humphreys tried the case; Benton was found guilty, with a strong recommendation to mercy.

BERNARDY, Sigoyer de

Thirty-nine-year-old French criminal and self-styled Marquis (police records in most European countries, including Germany, Austria, Hungary, Rumania, Bulgaria, Italy, and Spain, mainly for assault and financial frauds), who added wife-murder to his list of crimes in March 1944.

Twice, in the 1930's, he was committed to a lunatic asylum. On his first discharge, in 1937, he acquired a large house, La Maison Rouge, at Hautvillers in the Chevreuse Valley, which he ran with the help of two former asylum inmates. Here he indulged his hobby, black magic (he had founded 'schools of magic' in Barcelona and Lisbon years before), and was to be accused of abduction by a man called Petroff Gautcheff, who claimed that the Marquis had lured him to the house. Some peasants found the exhausted Gautcheff naked, with chains on his wrists and ankles, a mile from La Maison Rouge; he had escaped, he said, after being tortured into giving Bernardy information about 'rich, solitary friends'. The authorities, checking Gautcheff's story, found the papers and passport of a missing American at La Maison Rouge, and, suspecting Bernardy of murder, began to search for a corpse. The Marquis reacted by saying he had eaten the American, and was placed, for the second time, in a lunatic asylum. Within a few months an ex-mistress intervened on Bernardy's behalf, securing his release.

During the war the Marquis de Bernardy was running a restaurant on the avenue de la Grande Armée and an 'Esoteric Centre' at 27 rue Bleu; he sold wholesale brandy to the German Army of Occupation, and became a wealthy man. He married Janine Kergot (described as 'cheerful and sports-loving'), who bore him two children; the children's nursemaid, Irène Lebeau, bore him one, in 1943, and in 1944 the Marquise de Bernardy, exasperated, achieved a court order for 10,000 francs a month from her husband, and went to live with her mother, leaving Irène Lebeau in charge of the Bernardy residence at 7 Boulevard de Bercy. On March 28th Bernardy was late in paying the monthly settlement, so his wife decided to call on him; she was last seen alive entering her old home. Her mother, frantic, and suspicious of Bernardy, called on the French police and even the Gestapo to help trace her daughter, but Bernardy withstood the questioning – and Gestapo 'interrogation', saying that his wife had left his house within half an hour of her arrival.

With the liberation of Paris in 1945, Bernardy was imprisoned for his collaborationist activities, and letters he had smuggled out of Fresnes Jail provided the first clues to his wife's fate. In one, he instructed a friend to contact Irène Lebeau (who, much to Bernardy's fury had become engaged to be married) and 'remind' her of the 'red armchair'. In another, to Irène herself, he advised a safer hiding place for a cask 'containing confidential papers' which was at Boulevard de Bercy; she handed the cask to her inquisitive brother-in-law who, upon seeing that it contained clothing and trinkets identifiable as those belonging to the Marquise, went to the police. Shown the contents, Irène Lebeau gave information that resulted in the police digging up the wine cellar in Bernardy's warehouse in the Rue de Nuits. The Marquis expressed mournful satisfaction upon hearing that his wife had been found: 'One always wishes to know where the dead are resting.' Irène Lebeau told how she had seen Bernardy strangle Janine as she sat in a red armchair during that fatal visit to the Boulevard de Bercy. Bernardy asserted that Irène had shot his wife in a moment of jealousy, and he had merely helped conceal the body; but no evidence of a bullet wound was found. The Marquis and Irène Lebeau were tried jointly for the murder of Janine Sigoyer de Bernardy; on December 23rd, 1946, Irène was acquitted, and Bernardy was sentenced to death. He was guillotined the following June.

BESSARABO Case, The

Hera Myrtel was born in 1868 at Lyon, France, daughter of a wealthy tradesman. She was interested in literature and wrote poetry and stories. Until she was 26 she assisted her father in his business (he had gone bankrupt) and then went out to Mexico, where she married a wealthy husband, Paul Jacques. A daughter, Paule, was born. They returned to Paris, and Mme Jacques set up a literary salon, and began to take lovers. Her husband seems to have been complaisant. The marriage appears to have lasted precariously for about twenty years when, in 1914, a maidservant saw Mme Jacques slip a white powder into her husband's soup. She warned the husband, who took the soup to be analysed; it turned out to contain bichloride of mercury. M. Jacques did nothing about it, and continued to live with his wife. But shortly afterwards, he was found dead with a revolver at his feet; a verdict of suicide was returned.

In 1915, Mme Jacques returned to Mexico to handle her husband's estate. As Hera Myrtel, the poet and mystical novelist, she soon had her salon in Mexico City. And here she met a man named Weissmann (who preferred to call himself Bessarabo), a Rumanian whose means of income were probably criminal. She married him and they returned to France. Again, Hera Myrtel — now Mme Bessarabo — set up her salon and behaved outrageously; she had now become a drug taker. Her new husband seems to have been as complaisant as the old one. But he soon suspected that his wife wanted to be rid of him; she made an attempt to strangle him one night in bed, and on another occasion, fired at him with a revolver, fortunately missing. He recalled how a certain rancher in Mexico had been shot dead when alone at his ranch with Hera Myrtel and her daughter, and how his wife had told a strange story of a gang of masked men riding up and shooting him. No charge had been made against her.

M. Bessarabo felt, with reason, that his own life was not safe. He sought consolation in the arms of other women, in particular his secretary. In March 1920, Mme Bessarabo received a mysterious letter from Mexico which caused her a fit of hysterics; the same evening, she and her husband had a violent quarrel, and he remained shut in his own room for three days and, for several weeks after this, hired a car to take him everywhere. Obviously, he was afraid of assassins. A few weeks later, on July 30th, 1920, another letter arrived, and husband and wife again quarrelled. The next morning, Mme Bessarabo told the concierge she was moving to the country, and requested her help in bringing down a large trunk. This was taken away in a cab, together with Mme Bessarabo and her daughter, Paule. But that evening, the ladies returned and declared they had changed their minds. There seemed to be no sign of M. Bessarabo, and a chauffeur who came to collect him that morning was told he was away on business and would be back on August 2nd. He was suspicious, and when M. Bessarabo failed to show up on that date, he notified the police. They called at the Bessarabos' address — 3 Place Bruyère — and asked what had become of M. Bessarabo since the night of July 30th; she told a confused story about Bessarabo asking her to meet him at the Gare du Nord on the morning of Saturday, July 31st, of how she had taken the trunk there, but the husband failed to show up.

The story was suspicious; the police finally traced the trunk to Nancy and had it opened. Inside was a man, his face battered out of recognition. He had been shot in the back of the head.

The police found a further clue. On August 1st a boatman on the lake at Enghien had seen two women behave in a most suspicious manner. They had hired his boat, rowed out alone, and apparently dumped something heavy in the lake. The lake was dragged, but nothing came to light.

Mother and daughter were arrested, and now Mme Bessarabo changed her story and claimed that she had shot her husband accidentally. The daughter, Paule, she said, had only been an accessory after the murder.

Mother and daughter were tried before the Paris Assize Court on February 15th, 1921; the Corsican Maître Moro-Giafferi, who had defended Landru, defended them. He did so with the same tremendous ability he had shown in the Landru case, and so ridiculed all the evidence against his clients that there seemed to be a fair chance of their being acquitted. However, just as the jury were about to retire, Paule jumped to her feet and shouted, 'I must and will tell the truth'. She then went on to say that she had been wakened by a shot on the night of the murder, and had found her mother in the room with a bloodstained corpse on the bed. However, Mme Bessarabo had declared that it was not her husband's body, and hinted at secret societies (as she frequently had during the course of the case). She told Paule that Bessarabo had gone off with his secretary, and made the girl sign a forged power of attorney in Bessarabo's name. Paule, according to herself, had had no part in the crime or in handling the body.

As a result of this confession, Paule was acquitted, while her mother received twenty years in prison.

There are still many curious aspects to the case. Was it Bessarabo's body in the trunk? It was never definitely identified. What were the letters from Mexico that caused both the husband and wife such terror? And was there actually a secret society somewhere in the background of the case? This seems at least plausible in the light of the evidence.

Whatever the answer, it seems certain that, in the light of her earlier career, Mme Bessarabo's sentence was not unjust. But was she guilty of murdering her husband? The problem is still unsolved.

BICHEL, Andrew

Among the earliest known cases of a mass-murderer for profit. Bichel was apparently born around 1770 at Regendorf in Bavaria.

Little is known of Bichel's history, except that he was happily married, with children 'esteemed for their piety'. According to his own confession, his first murder was committed when a girl named Barbara Reisinger came seeking a position as a maid-servant in 1807; he was tempted by her clothes. Apparently one of his trades was fortune-telling, and he told the girl he would show her her future husband in a glass. He tied her hands and bandaged her eyes, then stabbed her in the neck. He dis-membered her body and buried it underneath a heap of straw and litter. He then tried to entrap three more girls, but failed; his next success was with a girl named Catherine Seidel. This was in 1808. A sister of Catherine Seidel actually saw a tailor making up a waistcoat from a piece of dimity that she recognized as being from her sister's petticoat. She remembered that Bichel had asked her sister to come to him in her best clothes to have her fortune told, and so suspicion was finally aroused against Bichel. His house was searched, and a chest of women's clothes was found in his room. Finally, a dog so persistently ran around the woodshed that the police dug in there and found two dis-membered bodies.

The number of Bichel's victims is not known; it is thought that they were not very many. He certainly tried to lure many girls to come to see him, without success.

Bichel was sentenced to be broken on the wheel, but the sentence was commuted to beheading. The motive of stealing the girls' clothes seems hardly adequate, yet it may have been more so in 1807. Or possibly Bichel had a psychopathic hatred of women, or may even have been a transvestite; no further details of the case are known.

BLANDY, Mary

Executed in 1752 for the murder by poisoning of her father. The case has many pathetic aspects.

Mary Blandy was born at Henley-on-Thames in 1720. Her father was a prosperous lawyer, and Mary herself was an attractive and good-natured girl. There seemed to be no reason why she should not contract a good marriage, especially since her personal fortune was around £10,000.

But her father was too ambitious for her, and choked off so many suitors that finally Mary reached the age of 26 and was still unmarried. At this point, the Honourable William Henry Cranstoun entered her life. He was the fifth son of a Scottish peer, and his relations were many and aristocratic. He was not a handsome man; small, freckled, and ungainly. But Mary fell in love with him, her mother conceived an immense liking for him, and he lived with the Blandys at Henley for six months – no doubt a satisfying arrangement for a penniless bachelor with heavy debts and no prospects.

Unfortunately, he was married already, although his wife was a Jacobite lady who was out of favour since the rising of 1745, and her husband chose to declare that she had only been his mistress, never his wife. She took an action against him, and it was decided in her favour. When Mr Blandy finally learned of this obstacle to his daughter's marriage he was enraged, but the mother and daughter did not lose faith in Cranstoun, and he continued to be Mary's suitor. Mrs Blandy fell ill, and insisted on Cranstoun being near her all the time, so that he stayed at Henley for another six months. Finally, in 1749, Mrs Blandy died (it seems certain that her death was due to natural causes), and Mr Blandy now began to show his dislike of Cranstoun (who was now in the hands of bailiffs).

Cranstoun now told Mary of a love powder which a Scottish herbalist concocted, which should have the effect of making her father feel less hostile to his daughter's lover. Some of this was introduced into Mr Blandy's tea, and seemed to make him altogether more amiable to Cranstoun. But the change of temper did not last long.

It was at about this time that Mary discovered that Cranstoun kept a mistress in London. She appears to have been a singularly placid girl, who forgave her lover without effort. Cranstoun, however, was upset by these continual setbacks, and began to set about persuading Mary to poison her father. It is possible that he began by telling her that the poison he sent her was more 'love powder'. It arrived with a box of Scotch pebbles (an ornament fashionable in 1750), and was labelled 'powder to clean Scotch pebbles'. This was in June 1751, and soon Mr Blandy began to feel ill.

Unfortunately for Mary, the poisoning did not go smoothly; mainly, one suspects, because she was an inefficient poisoner.

When Mr Blandy left some of his poisoned tea untouched, a servant drank it and was seriously ill. A poisoner who knew her business would have seen that such misadventures were avoided. There was the even more careless episode of the oatmeal soup. Mr Blandy was ill after eating a cupful of the soup; but again, Mary did not take the obvious precaution of throwing it away; the cook ate some and was ill. The housemaid Susan was suspicious that the gruel was poisoned, and tasted it; she was ill for two days. She took the gruel to the chemist for analysis. Then she told Mr Blandy that his daughter was poisoning him – she had actually seen Mary tampering with the gruel.

Mr Blandy took the news remarkably well, but he quickly let his daughter know that he suspected, and Mary was panic-stricken. She threw a pile of letters and some powder on the kitchen fire, but the cook rescued the powder as soon as the hopelessly inefficient Mary left the room.

A doctor from Reading was sent for, to examine Mr Blandy who was sinking. He declared his opinion that Mr Blandy had been poisoned. He also warned Mary that if he died her position would be very serious. Mary now panicked and wrote Cranstoun a letter warning him to burn all letters that had passed between them and thoroughly incriminating herself. Her stupidity is almost unbelievable, but what is even more incredible is that she then gave the letter to someone else to post. The clerk who took it knew what was going on and handed it to the chemist who had examined the powder (which the Reading doctor found to be arsenic).

Although Mr Blandy's relations with his daughter reveal a selfish and stupid man, his end does him much credit; he told her that he knew about the poison, and forgave her, warning her to beware of Cranstoun. Then, on Wednesday, August 14th, 1751, he died.

Mary Blandy was arrested and charged with causing his death by administering arsenic. She now tried to throw the blame on Cranstoun, but without success. There were many who believed her innocent. She was tried at Oxford Assizes, and the prosecution was weakened by the obvious malevolence of the two servants. Many persons testified to her kindness and affectionate relations with her father. The defence declared that she had believed the powder to be a love potion. But the jury had no hesitation, and in five minutes returned a verdict of guilty. The trial took place in the Divinity School.

Cranstoun escaped abroad, but died soon afterwards in great poverty and suffering. A touch of irony was added when it transpired that Mr Blandy's total fortune was only £4,000, and the £10,000 that Mary was to receive on her marriage was a figment of his imagination – or an invention to tempt a husband.

BLAZEK, Frank
Dark, puny, Austrian-born water-works clerk, resident in New York City, electrocuted on September 11th, 1940 for the murder of his ex-fiancée.

In June 1934 Blazek (then 28) met 16-year-old Virginia Bender, a collegiate who was impressed by the sophisticated-seeming Viennese who read poetry and collected gramophone records of symphonies and who had shown, until now, little interest in women. Mutual infatuation followed, and they announced their official engagement in January 1936, although the girl's mother stipulated that her daughter finish her schooling before the marriage. Continual friction caused by Blazek's possessiveness and jealousy prompted Virginia Bender, early in 1938, to break off the engagement; she got employment away from home and did not see Blazek for a year. On June 5th, 1939, after reading in a paper the announcement of her forthcoming marriage, Blazek rang up Virginia at her office:
'I wish you all the luck in the world,' he said.
'Do you mean that?'
'You bet I do. You're going to need luck.'
During the afternoon of June 19th at an Army and Navy Store down 125th Street, Blazek purchased a hunting knife, then went to Virginia Bender's apartment on 137th Street where he awaited her return from work. He half-strangled the girl, and dropped her unconscious on to a bed; he covered her with a blanket and stabbed her to death with the hunting knife. His victim's fiancé, inquiring at the apartment some minutes later, was told through a narrowly opened door: 'Come back in an hour. She'll be here then.' Afterwards, to police officers, the fiancé said of the voice: 'It sounded kind of guttural.' Learning of the belligerent Viennese, Detective-Captain Glen Armstrong of the Bronx Police went to Blazek's bed-sitting-room, and in face of the suspect's denials of the killing confronted him with police photographs taken hours earlier of the mutilated girl. Blazek collapsed, screaming, 'I can't stand the sight of blood,' thus confirming Armstrong's suspicions that the blanket had been used as a

psychological 'buffer' for a squeamish murderer. The next day Blazek confessed the crime to Assistant District Attorney Martin Klaus.

BOLAM, Archibald (Manager of Newcastle Savings Bank)

On the night of November 7th, 1839, an alarm was raised that the Newcastle Savings Bank was on fire. The clerk of the bank was found dead, with a smashed skull, and Mr Bolam, the manager, was unconscious in the next room with throat wounds. The latter claimed they had been attacked by a man with a blackened face as they were doing accounts, but he was not believed; the wounds were obviously self-inflicted, and blood had run down his jacket, proving that he had sat up to cut his throat and then lain down. Three account books and a sum of gold were missing; these were subsequently found in Bolam's house. The clerk's body had coal stuffed into the pockets, obviously to encourage it to burn once the fire was well started.

Bolam was tried for his life, but the judge suggested to the jury that Bolam had killed the clerk in a quarrel and had assaulted him with the poker. A verdict of manslaughter was returned. Either view is plausible – that Bolam thought out the murder as deliberately as Arthur Rouse, for motives of gain, or that he killed the clerk in a rage, and staged the robbery to hide it. Major Arthur Griffiths, who tells the story, does not mention Bolam's sentence, but the *New Newgate Calendar* states he was sentenced to life transportation and allowed to leave the country.

BONAFOUS, Louis (Frère Léotade)
French lay-brother found guilty in April 1848 of the murder of 14-year-old apprentice bookbinder Cécile Combettes and sentenced to hard labour.

At 9 am on April 10th, 1847, Toulouse bookbinder Bertrand Conte and his slightly built girl apprentice delivered two baskets of newly bound books to the Institute of Christian Brethren. Conte, handing her his umbrella, told Cécile to await him in the vestibule while he went to chat to the director; on his return he found his umbrella propped against a wall, but Cécile had vanished. At 6.30 am the following day her body was found in kneeling posture by a corner of St Aubin cemetery, an angle formed by two high walls, one facing on to the Rue Riquet, the

96

other on to the garden of the Christian Brethren Institute. The girl's head was battered (cause of death) and she had been raped; there were no footprints in the damp earth around the corpse, so the body must have been thrown over the wall, either from the street or institute. From the curious posture it was assumed that rigor mortis had set in before the body was deposited. Leaves of cypress were found in the girl's hair, presumably from a tree flanking the street wall, and about the girl's person were shreds of twine identical with a length of rope in the institute garden. A sentry in the Rue Riquet had not seen any curious happening on the night before the body was discovered, but it had been a rainy night and so he had spent most of it in the sentry-box.

Baffled, the police arrested Conte, the girl's employer, on a suspicion of murder; he was by repute a lecherous individual, and Cécile Combettes had been known to complain of his behaviour. The police theory was that he had, on leaving the institute, taken the girl to some nearby building where he had assaulted and killed her, returning by night to the cemetery. Conte, protesting his innocence, mentioned to a magistrate that when he left his apprentice, two of the religious brotherhood had been talking together in the vestibule. The brethren concerned, Frère Jubrien and Frère Léotade, were immediately arrested and Conte released; eventually Frère Jubrien was also released, and proceedings instigated against Frère Léotade, who denied guilt and indeed any knowledge of Cécile Combettes. Conte asserted that Frère Léotade had previously promised him some rabbits, and insinuated that the brother might have lured her to the hayloft on the pretext of giving her the rabbits. (Deposits of hay, clover, and wheat, similar to those in the institute hayloft, were found adhering to the girl's dress.) Grains of fig were in the folds of the victim's clothing, and on a shirt found concealed in the Noviciat, one of the institute buildings; the shirt, numbered 562, was never proved to have belonged to Frère Léotade.

BOOHER Case, The

Curious Canadian murder case whose main interest lies in the use of a thought reader to produce evidence against the murderer. Such cases as these – in which an element of the near-supernatural enters – are not rare, but they are seldom so well authenticated as this. (Other examples are: the Red Barn murder, the Nodder case, when Estelle Roberts is reputed to have predicted the finding of Mona Tinsley's body in the river, and the Van Buuren case.)

On July 9th, 1928, the police at Mannville, near Edmonton, Alberta, were notified that there had been a multiple murder out at the Booher ranch. Mrs Booher was found shot in the kitchen, a son, Fred, was in the next room, a hired hand, Gabriel Cromby, was found in the bunkhouse. Finally, a cowhand named Rosyk was found dead in one of the outhouses. Vernon Booher had found the bodies. Robbery did not seem to be the motive; Mrs Booher's diamond ring was not taken. The murder weapon, a ·303 rifle, was nowhere to be found. It had been stolen from a neighbour of the Boohers, Charles Stephenson, the Sunday before the murder.

Dr Maximilien Langsner of Vienna was called into the case. He had already helped the police in Vancouver to find some stolen jewellery by 'reading the mind' of a suspect, and then describing the room in which the jewellery was hidden. Langsner attended the inquest, and told the police afterwards that Vernon Booher was the murderer, and that he could take them to the place where the ·303 rifle was hidden. The police went to the Booher farm, and Dr Langsner led them to the clump of prairie grass where the rifle was hidden.

Back in Edmonton, Police Chief Gier booked Vernon as a material witness, and Langsner sat outside his cell for about an hour. At the end of the hour, he was able to describe to the police exactly how the murders had been committed, and to advise them to find a small woman in a poke bonnet who had seen Vernon leave the church on Sunday when the rifle was stolen. The woman, Erma Higgins, was found, and was made to confront Vernon with the words, 'I saw you leave the church the day Charlie's rifle was stolen'. Booher broke down and confessed to the four murders, describing them to the police exactly as Langsner had already done. He had murdered his mother because she had opposed his marriage to the daughter of a local farmer. After killing her, he was forced to kill his brother Fred and the two hired men, fearing that they had seen him enter the farmhouse.

He was hanged on April 26th, 1929.

Dr Langsner died in a small hut near Fairbanks, Alaska, when he was continuing his research into 'brain waves'.

BOOST, Werner

Sexual murderer, who killed five people around Düsseldorf in the early part of 1956. Boost's first victim was a business man, Dr Servé, who was shot while sitting in his car on the banks of the Rhine. A young man who was in the car with him was only knocked unconscious, and testified that the attack was committed by two men. Shortly afterwards, the charred bodies of a Herr Falkenberg and Fräulein Wissing were found under the ashes of a pile of straw. Falkenberg had been shot while the girl had been given an injection of cyanide. The next victims were a Herr Behre and Fräulein Kuessmann, who were battered unconscious and then the car was pushed into a deep pool, where they drowned.

On June 6th a forester named Spath saw a man spying on a courting couple, gripping a revolver. Spath managed to capture the man. He turned out to be Werner Boost, who had a bad criminal record. He had begun stealing at the age of six, and had spent many years in an institution for delinquents near Magdeburg. Before the end of the war he was released for military service, and taken prisoner by the British. In 1951 he was sentenced for stealing metal parts from tombs in cemeteries.

Boost was cross-questioned by Chief Inspector Mattias Eynck, but refused to admit to murder. He declared that he wanted to scare the courting couple, because the sight of men and women in cars made him 'see red'. 'These sex horrors are the curse of Germany.'

At this point, Boost's accomplice, Franz Lorbach, gave himself up. Lorbach, a timid, frail-looking man, declared that he was completely dominated by Boost, and had been 'hypnotized' into committing crimes with him. Their association had begun when they went out shooting together. Soon, Lorbach became aware of Boost's obsession about courting couples; he would creep up on them and demand money. Later, Boost prepared a drug by which he was able to stupefy the couples; after robbing the men, Boost would then rape the women, and persuaded Lorbach to do the same.

On the evening of the Servé murder, Boost had devised a new means of killing the couples: to fill toy balloons with cyanide gas, which he would release into the car. Boost evidently assumed that the stationary car containing Dr Servé and his friend concealed another courting couple; he wrenched open the door and killed Servé without looking further. Boost ordered

99

Lorbach to kill the other man, but Lorbach was unable to do so; instead, he whispered to the man to lean forward, and then hit him with the pistol, telling Boost, 'He won't wake up again.'

Lorbach's confession led to Boost's being charged with the murders. His revolver was identified by a ballistics expert as the one that shot Servé. Further investigations were opened into a series of murders around Helmstedt in Lower Saxony in 1945, when many people trying to cross the border between the Russian and the British zones were shot. Boost was living in Helmstedt at this time. 'The indictment,' stated Inspector Eynck, 'will be one of the longest on record.'

Because of the length of the indictment, the case drifted on for several years: when the present writer last inquired about it, sentence had still not been passed. Since there is no death sentence in West Germany, Boost can only receive life imprisonment.

BORDEN, Lizzie

Thirty-two-year-old Massachusetts spinster, a frequent visitor to the Corcoran Art Gallery in Washington, a secretary of the Christian Endeavour Society, Sunday School teacher, member of a Fruit and Flower Mission, a supporter of the Women's Christian Temperance Union, and a keen painter of decorative pictures on porcelain, accused of the hatchet murders of her father and stepmother.

Andrew Jackson Borden, 69-year-old banker, lived with his second wife Abby, aged 63, and his two daughters Emma, 41, and Lizzie, 32, on Second Street, Fall River, a small Massachusetts town; it was a modest, narrow, two-storied house (counting the attic floor) flanked on either side by similar dwellings, and in 1892 the Bordens had lived there for twenty years. For a long time there had been a poor relationship between Abby Borden and her two stepdaughters; differences about money and an exaggerated devotion towards the memory of their dead mother resulted in a situation whereby the Misses Emma and Lizzie invariably referred to their stepmother as 'Mrs Borden' instead of using a more affectionate epithet. On Wednesday, August 3rd, 1892, a brother of the first Mrs Borden, Uncle John Vinnicum Morse, came to stay, and found the two elder Bordens suffering from severe stomachic pains and vomiting. (It was afterwards established that on August 2nd Miss Lizzie had made a purchase of prussic acid, which may or may not have been relevant to their indisposition.) At 9 am on August 4th, Lizzie Borden breakfasted alone in the kitchen (sister Emma was with friends at Fairhaven, fifteen miles away), requesting only a cup of coffee, telling the maid Bridget Sullivan that the oppressive heat had taken away her appetite; Mr Borden had left for a round of business calls, Mr Morse had departed to take a morning walk and Mrs Borden was employed on household tasks, calling out to Bridget that the windows needed cleaning. Accordingly, the maid busied herself with bucket and wash-leather, pausing at 10.45 am to open the locked and bolted front door for the returning Mr Borden (Bridget Sullivan said afterwards that as her master entered the hallway, Lizzie Borden, standing on the upper landing, uttered a short, cackling laugh). Inquiring after the whereabouts of Mrs Borden, the old man was told by his daughter that she had gone out, having received a note requesting help from a sick friend, whereupon Mr Borden, hot and tired, retired to the ground-floor sitting-room to lie down. At 11.45 am the maid, taking a nap in her attic room, was woken by a shriek from Miss Lizzie: 'Bridget! Come down quick! Someone's killed father!' The maid, dispatched for Dr Bowen who lived across the way, returned with that physician and a Mrs Churchill, the Bordens' next-door neighbour, who was to discover, within a few minutes, the presence of yet another corpse in the house – that of Mrs Borden, in the first-floor guest-room. Both old people had been slain (presumably as they slept) by savage blows to the head from a hatchet-like instrument; their faces were literally hacked to pieces and almost unrecognizable. It was medically established that the murders had occurred an hour to an hour and a half apart, and that the doomed Mr Borden had, therefore, been unwittingly a widower upon his return to the house that morning. On August 11th Miss Lizzie Borden was arrested on the charge of murder; apart from the well-known fact of her hostility towards her parents, there were many divergences in her story. No one had come forward as the writer of the 'sick-note'; she had given varying answers to queries as to her whereabouts just before the murders were discovered – 'in the barn looking for a piece of iron', 'in the barn getting lead sinkers for a fishing line', 'in the barn resting', 'in the barn for twenty minutes', 'in the barn for half an hour', 'in the barn when I heard strange scraping noises' . . . after this last statement inferring that the noises had caused her to enter the house, and so discover the murders, although in another statement she said she had quite accidentally come across the body of her father. Nor had any of the neighbours seen any strangers entering or coming that morning from the Borden house, which had been, in any case, securely bolted and barred. Miss Lizzie had, it transpired, burnt one of her gowns on the Sunday following the disaster, it being suggested and thought probable that the garment was stained with blood. Perhaps the most sinister truth was that only twenty-four hours before the crime Miss Lizzie had suddenly acquired powers of clairvoyance, forecasting violence and disaster for her unfortunate family, half of which were already then in the throes of the mysterious bilious attack.

The trial of Lizzie Borden commenced on June 1st, 1893, at New Bedford, Massachusetts, under Judges Mason (Chief Justice), Blodgett, and Dewey. The District Attorney, prosecuting, was Mr Hosea Knowlton; Mr George D. Robinson, former Governor of the State, was defending counsel, who elicited from Bridget Sullivan the admission that the Borden side door might, on the fatal morning, have been unbolted, thus giving support to the 'murderous intruder' theory. No weapon had been found on the premises, although the head of a hatchet, the shaft burned off, was found on the kitchen chimney shelf, where, of course, it might have lain for years. Mr Robinson accounted for Miss Borden's curious premonitions by breezily attributing them to a mind unbalanced by the event of menstruation; he ended his address to the jury by saying that if his client was guilty, then she must indeed be a fiend: '. . . Gentlemen, does she look it?' On June 13th the jury brought in an acquittal, and Miss Lizzie Borden, chubby and ladylike, with her pince-nez and long capable fingers, was free to join the outside world where she lived with her sister Emma in fairly affluent fashion, the two women having inherited, through their father, an estate worth half a million dollars. Some Fall River inhabitants suspected Dr Bowen of the crime, and some even questioned the eccentric behaviour of Uncle Vinnicum Morse, who, returning from his jaunt on the morning of the crime, had happily picked and munched pears in the Borden back garden, oblivious, apparently, of the uproarious post-murder scenes then being enacted by police and neighbours in and around the Borden house. Most students of this crime, however, subscribe to the sentiments expressed in the rhyme (authorship unknown):

> Lizzie Borden took an axe
> And gave her mother forty whacks
> When she saw what she had done
> She gave her father forty-one.

Miss Lizzie Borden died in Fall River in 1944, preferring, during the second half of her life, to be known by the more decorous derivative 'Lisbeth'.

BOUVIER, Léone
Twenty-three-year-old French peasant girl, sentenced to life imprisonment on December 10th, 1953, for the murder of her lover.

Léone Bouvier and her older sister Georgette were brought up in sordid circumstances in the village of Saint-Macaire-en-Mauges, Western France; their parents were alcoholic through the constant drinking of gniole, a rough cider (the father having frequently to be strapped down on his bed to curb fits of violence,) all four existing in two small filthy rooms. Both sisters, when old enough, sought means to escape the horror of their environment, Georgette by entering Holy Orders, Léone by a pathetic pursuit of love, pathetic because she was ugly and her desire to be cherished merely benefited the unscrupulous males of that region. In 1951, however, she met at a dance hall 22-year-old car mechanic, Émile Clenet, who by some strange alchemy was then sufficiently attracted to Léone Bouvier to request a second, then even a third meeting. The two established a regular Sunday rendezvous in a hotel bedroom, Émile being sufficiently transported on these occasions to murmur endearments which Léone Bouvier accepted as tokens of an eternal love, a love which must surely result in marriage. Soon Clenet became indifferent, then physically revolted, by Léone Bouvier, seeking every opportunity to humiliate her. Learning she was pregnant, Clenet ordered her to procure an abortion, an undertaking resulting in a prolonged illness and the girl's ultimate dismissal from her factory job during which time she did not hear from Clenet. On Wednesday, January 15th, 1952, she cycled over to Nantes, where Clenet worked in a garage; he expressed both fury and amazement that she should have chosen a mid-week day instead of the customary Sunday to contact him. Reproached for this effrontery, Léone Bouvier was dismissed, no arrangement having been made for a further meeting. From then on she became preoccupied with gunsmiths' windows, and on Monday, February 17th (having left home for Nantes the previous Saturday, her 23rd birthday) she purchased, with her savings, a ·22 automatic pistol. That week she existed by prostitution; on Sunday she waited hopefully and, as it turned out, futilely, at the old rendezvous. By chance she saw Clenet coming out of a cinema, and exacted from him the promise that he would take her to the Mid Lent Carnival at Cholet, a neighbouring town. On February 27th, during the carnival activities, Clenet casually mentioned that he would shortly be leaving to make a permanent home for himself in North Africa; questioned by the distraught girl, he emphasised that never had marriage been further from his mind. That night, in the middle of a farewell embrace (more endured than indulged in by Clenet) Léone Bouvier shot her one-time lover through the head, afterwards journeying to the convent where she was tended by her sister who, though aware of the other's wild distress, was ignorant of the killing. Inquiries following the finding of Clenet's body inevitably led police to the convent, and as Léone Bouvier was led away, the Mother Superior made the comment: 'Poor child.'

Léone Bouvier's trial on the charge of murdering Émile Clenet began at the Assizes of Maine-et-Loire at Angers on December 10th, 1953. The prosecuting counsel, Advocate General Maître Lécrivain, demanded the death penalty; the defending counsel, Maître Claude Fournier, spoke of the accused's appalling home life, even calling her drunken father into the witness-box, where his inarticulateness was perhaps more eloquent than a psychiatrist's report. Léone Bouvier's mother was also called, and managed to convey the fact that her other daughter was a nun, which caused Judge Diousidon to observe to the prisoner: 'You see! There was no need for you to go wrong! Why did you go wrong?' and later, referring to the actual killing: 'Your gesture ... was atrocious ... you kissed him, you kissed Émile Clenet and at the same time with your right hand you drew your pistol from under your coat. You placed it behind the head of this unfortunate man, you rested it on his coat collar. Then you pressed the trigger! Atrocious, I repeat, atrocious ... why did you kill him?'

'I loved him.'

The jury, returning after a quarter of an hour, found the accused guilty of murder, but not of premeditation, which, under French law, automatically excluded the death sentence; Léone was sentenced to penal servitude for life.

BOWER, Elliot

Victorian murder scandal in which an enraged husband stabbed his rival.

Bower was a journalist on the *Morning Advertiser*, a highly popular newspaper of its day, a Victorian *Daily Mirror*. Bower was its Paris correspondent in 1852. He had been married for ten years to a young widow, Fanny Vickers, who had one child; he was not a faithful husband. Mrs Bower bore him two children.

In a visit to London in 1849, Bower ran across an old Cambridge friend, Saville Morton, another journalist, who had known his wife since childhood. Morton worked for Dickens' newspaper the *Daily News*.

In 1850, Mrs Bower received a letter from a Mrs Isabella Laurie, whom Bower had seduced and then discarded; the letter was written for revenge, and told of Bower's affair – which had begun shortly after his marriage – with Mrs Laurie. Fanny Bower was upset; she found her husband's violent temper trying; she turned for comfort to Morton, who was also in Paris as a correspondent. Morton fell in love with her and tried to arrange a divorce; this, however, was difficult in 1850.

Finally, in 1852, Fanny Bower had another child, and – no doubt due to the mental strain of her domestic disagreements – became a victim of a puerperal insanity. She was so ill that Bower sent for Morton – of whom he was jealous – and Morton spent many days with Mrs Bower, trying to calm her, and sleeping on a settee in her room. Mrs Bower became a Roman Catholic during this illness. But even the priest who received her into the Church thought she was insane.

Finally, Fanny Bower called her husband to her room and told him that the child was Morton's. He refused to believe her, and she summoned the housekeeper, who confirmed that Morton had spent a night with Mrs Bower exactly nine months earlier while her husband was away. Bower rushed downstairs in a passion and found Morton sitting at the table; he seized a knife and tried to attack him. Bower's mother, who was also sitting at supper, seized her son's coat, and enabled Morton to reach the door; however, Bower tore himself free and ran after Morton, stabbing him in the neck. The blow severed the carotid artery, and Morton fell dead.

Bower fled to London, but eventually returned to France and surrendered to justice; he was brought to trial at the Seine Court of Assize on December 28th, 1852, less than three months after his crime. His wife had recovered from her insanity and was now healthy; however, she refused to be reconciled to Bower, and went to London with her children, going into mourning for Morton. The prosecution – which, in the French manner, took the form of a cross-examination of Bower by the judge – depended largely upon the notion that Bower had murdered a man solely on the evidence of an insane woman. Bower's defence – conducted by M. Chaix D'Estange – submitted that there was no doubt whatever of Mrs Bower's infidelity and that Bower had every right to kill Morton.

Bower was acquitted. It is not recorded whether he was ever reconciled to his wife. However, it is certain that the scandal ruined them both socially, since Victorian society was merciless towards such open breaches of its code. *The Times* declared primly, 'It seems as though we are reading the history of three maniacs bent on mutual destruction, who had been reduced to so pitiable a condition by their own immorality . . .'

It is difficult to feel a great deal of sympathy for Bower, who had become completely demoralized by living in France and was violently jealous of his wife at the same time that he was unfaithful to her.

BOWERS, Dr J. Milton

This case of poisoning has some interesting legal aspects. Dr Bowers, born in Baltimore in 1843, had lost two wives: the first, Fannie Hammet, in Chicago in 1865, and the second, an actress named Theresa Shirk (whom he met in Brooklyn), in 1881 in San Francisco. His third wife, Mrs Cecilia Benhayon-Levy, married him six months after the death of the second wife, although her family opposed the match because of some suspicion attaching to the death of Theresa Shirk. The third Mrs Bowers fell ill in the late summer of 1885, and died in convulsions, with her body swollen. She was found to have been poisoned by phosphorus. Bowers was arrested, tried, and found guilty. There was some suspicion that his nurse and housekeeper had been accessories after the fact.

However, before he was executed, the brother of the third Mrs Bowers was found dead in a rented room, poisoned by cyanide, with a confession to the murder of his sister beside him. This was on October 23rd, 1887. However, it was discovered that he was not the man who had rented the room, and this man was finally discovered to be John Dimming, the husband of

Bowers' housekeeper. He was also found to have purchased cyanide. The police decided that Bowers had blackmailed Dimming into killing and framing Benhayon and that the 'confession' was a forgery. Accordingly, Dimming was tried for the murder of Benhayon; at his first trial in February 1888, the jury disagreed; at his second, he was acquitted. This now meant that the murder confession was not a forgery. Accordingly, Bowers was re-tried and this time the charge against him was dismissed. He married a girl whom he had been courting prior to the death of the third Mrs Bowers, and lived with her happily until his death in 1905.

BOZZELI, Peter

When the naked, battered body of 24-year-old Gloria Bozzeli, missing for a fortnight, in 1953, was found floating in a duffel-bag along Iron Ore Creek in New Jersey, sympathy was felt for father Bozzeli. Of all his eight children he loved Gloria most, and since his wife's death three years before Gloria had been a little mother to the Bozzeli household. Bozzeli had tended to be over-protective; one of Gloria's boy-friends described him as 'like one of those Spanish duennas ... a chaperone': and yet another told of Bozzeli's reluctance to leave his daughter alone with any man. Checking on Bozzeli's story that he and Gloria had eaten a restaurant meal at around 9.30 pm, shortly before her disappearance, it was discovered that the chef at this establishment had, that night, become uncontrollably drunk and no meals were served after 7.30 pm. Suspicious now, the police examined the Bozzeli home, and many traces of blood were found. Confronted with these facts Bozzeli broke down and confessed to killing his daughter. Jealousy of her possible marriage had maddened him: '... I loved my daughter. ... I didn't want her to leave. ...' Sentenced to life imprisonment, he died after a hunger strike in 1954.

BRAIN, George
Executed for the murder of a prostitute in 1938.

In the early hours of Thursday, July 14th, 1938, the body of a woman was found lying in Somerset Road, Wimbledon, a lonely road opposite the Common. She had head injuries that were later found to be inflicted with a car starting-handle, and had been stabbed. There were tyre marks on the body, indicating that a car had been driven over it.

She was identified as Rose Atkins, a prostitute known locally as the 'Irish Rose'. She had been last seen by an acquaintance the evening before the murder talking to a man in a green van. Inspector Cherrill, examining the tyre marks on her body, managed to ascertain the make of the tyres – an Austin 7 or Morris 8. This narrowed the field of search.

Two days after the murder, the proprietor of a wholesale boot repairing business in St Pancras reported that one of his drivers was missing with £32 of the firm's money. The driver was George Brain, who lived with his parents at Richmond; he drove a green Morris 8 van. The van was in the firm's garage. The police examined it and found signs of blood. A blood-stained cobbler's knife was also found in the garage.

A nation wide police search lasted for nine days, but Brain was finally seen on the Isle of Sheppey by a Richmond schoolboy, dodging around in some undergrowth. The police arrested him as he lay reading a paper-back novel. He confessed to the murder, but claimed the 'Irish Rose' had tried to blackmail him and that he had 'blacked out' and killed her. This did not explain the tyre marks on the body.

He was tried at the Old Bailey and sentenced to death. The motive of the murder was assumed to be robbery, although the prostitute only had four shillings on her at the time of her death. If Brain had not panicked and left the country, he might never have been detected. He was due to be married the week after he committed the murder. He had no previous criminal record.

BRANSON, Edith May Olive
Victim of a curious and unsolved murder in France in 1929.

Olive Branson was one of those uninhibited and artistically talented women who somehow emerge from time to time despite the shackles of their English upper middle class rearing; during the 1914–18 War she volunteered for the Women's Army Corps, and married a colonel who saved her life when the Germans bombed her depot. The marriage, however, was not a success, but Miss Branson, undeterred and undismayed, continued a joyous march through life. She enjoyed dabbling in painting (gipsies, mainly) and exhibited at both the Royal Academy in London and the Paris Salon; she was also able to combine her artistic sensitivity with an almost masculine detachment, so that she revelled in numerous love affairs. ('Frenchmen make the best lovers in the world', she excitedly wrote to a friend shortly before her death.)

In 1928, at the age of 43, Olive Branson went to live at Les Baux, in the South of France, where she bought the Hôtel de Monte Carlo, living herself in a cottage some yards away. She employed 26-year-old François Pinet as a manager of the hotel, and employed Pinet's brother-in-law, Joseph Girard, and Girard's wife as her non-resident housekeepers. Olive Branson's constant companions were four enormous Great Danes; down the road, in a converted ruin lived a middle-aged poverty-stricken Englishman, Vernon Bernard Blake, also an artist and one-time sculptor and writer, whose relations with Olive Branson were (for some unknown reason) slightly strained, so that the two, just before her death, were no longer speaking to each other.

On the morning of April 29th, 1929, the corpse of Miss Branson was found propped upright in a large water-filled cistern thirty yards away from her cottage, clad only in a nightgown and socks; a bullet wound in the head was obviously the cause of death, the revolver being found at the bottom of the cistern. Police at first considered that Miss Branson had committed suicide, although it must have appeared a peculiar method, even for an eccentric Englishwoman, especially as the water tank was only accessible from the cottage through a mesh of barbed wire, a six-foot-high wall, and a craggy pathway. During the post-mortem, however, no water was found in the lungs, so establishing the fact that Olive Branson was dead before immersion in the cistern and quashing the theory of her extraordinary obstacle-walk to a self-imposed death. Examining the dead woman's cottage more closely, police headed by Inspector Alexandre Guibal, OBE (he had worked for British Intelligence during the 1914–18 War), found traces of recently spilled blood in all the rooms; neighbours spoke of hearing a gunshot on the night of the killing about 9 pm. No sound, though, had been heard from the victim's watchdogs, which implied that the murderer was known to them, a frequent visitor to the cottage. Joseph Girard (who had found the body) was now held as a material witness, and Vernon Blake (clad in his customary attire, white trousers and pink jumper) came to the police and hinted that he had seen François Pinet in the vicinity of the cottage on the night of April 28th; it had previously been ascertained, through the testimonies of a Marseilles chambermaid and Olive Branson's chauffeur, Louis Vigne, that young Pinet and the durable matron had been lovers. Two wills were found in Pinet's room; in the earlier one Miss Branson had left him everything, but in the more recent will she had bequeathed her property to a niece who had, incidentally, stayed at Les Baux and been friendly with François Pinet. Bemused by the crime, the police eagerly grilled this obvious suspect for hours, but Pinet steadfastly denied all knowledge of her death. He admitted (in face of Blake's evidence) going to Miss Branson's cottage on the night of the killing, but only to deliver some petrol; he recalled that all the doors had been open, and anyone could have broken in. 'As for me,' said Pinet, 'she was worth more to me alive than dead.' Nevertheless, François Pinet was charged on May 8th, 1929, with the murder of Olive Branson; facing trial the following January his status as a gigolo was established, but the possibility of his being the murderer was always in doubt. Found not guilty, Pinet returned, amid local festivity, to Les Baux. Speculation continued about the killer's identity, and (perhaps inevitably) when artist Blake died shortly after Pinet's acquittal, a journalist called Eugène Blanc wrote an impassioned and accusing leaflet that prompted Blake's relations into bringing an action for libel, from which they were granted the sum of £40. There was wild speculation among the French (which would doubtless have amazed both Miss Branson and Mr Blake) that the two artist neighbours had been members of the British Secret Service, and their deaths merely part of some vast international scheme. There is an appealing Agatha Christie-like air about this murder, but it seems unlikely now that the truth of the story will ever be told.

BRAVO, Florence

One of the most famous of Victorian murders. Charles Bravo, a 30-year-old barrister, died on Friday, April 21st, 1876, after being in constant agony since the previous Tuesday, when he collapsed shortly after consuming a dinner of whiting, roast lamb, and anchovy eggs on toast. He lived in opulence at The Priory, Bedford Hill Road, Balham, with his wife Florence whom he had married five months before, on December 7th, 1875. At the time of meeting Charles Bravo, Florence had been the widow of Captain Alexander Ricardo, Grenadier Guardsman, who had died in 1871 of alcoholism, leaving his attractive 25-year-old wife the sum of £40,000; she had also been, since

Ricardo's death, the mistress of 64-year-old James Manby Gully, a well-known Malvern doctor, pioneer of the Water Cure, phrenologist, playwright, and medical adviser to Tennyson, Dickens, Bulwer Lytton, Disraeli, and Carlyle, although, after Bravo's proposal of marriage, Florence promised to break off the relationship, writing to Charles on October 21st, 1875: '. . . need I tell you that I have written to the Dr to say I must never see his face again; it is the right thing to do in every respect, whatever happens, whether we marry or whether we do not . . .' Charles, who sounds a pompous, conceited young man ('My chief jewel, my modesty' he once wrote, apparently without facetiousness), had had a mistress at Maidenhead, so could perhaps be tolerant about his future bride's lapse: 'I am quite satisfied to make you my wife' he is recorded as saying, a trifle magnanimously. Cynics might have said that he had good cause to be satisfied, since (as the law of those days decreed) he would automatically, upon marriage, take over Florence's property and money; indeed, during part of the honeymoon at his parents' home at Palace Green, Kensington, he received a lewd anonymous letter accusing him of marrying Gully's mistress for her money.

With somewhat less tolerance perhaps, he viewed Florence's maid and constant companion, Mrs Jane Cannon Cox, a physically unattractive, bespectacled 43-year-old Anglo-Indian widow, the mother of three boys, who had been obliged, upon the death of her husband in 1867, to become a governess. By a coincidence, Mrs Cox knew Joseph Bravo, Charles' father, long before she met Florence; the elder Bravo, a Jamaican, had been friendly with Mr Cox in the late 1850's in Jamaica, where the Cox family had settled, and it was to the Bravo family Mrs Cox turned when she arrived in London years later to earn a living for herself and her sons. Mrs Cox subsequently found a position with a Mrs Brooks of Tooting and it was there, in 1871, she met and was engaged by the young Mrs Ricardo who was staying with the Brooks family. The curious associations with Jamaica of the various people involved in this affair (Dr Gully was born in Kingston, Jamaica) have led many into suspecting that some form of black magic was responsible for the subsequent sinister event – a romantic thought, but unlikely.

Upon returning, after their marriage, to The Priory, life for the Bravos seemed fairly smooth, marred perhaps by Florence's tendencies to miscarry and drink rather too liberally for a Victorian matron, and Charles Bravo's meanness: 'My own darling wife' (he once wrote in a Pooter-ish letter), 'I miss you dreadfully, and I would willingly give £100 – if times were not so hard – to have you here now . . .' Shortly before Easter, in April 1876, Florence had her third miscarriage, and throughout the Easter week-end, Charles – probably because of psychological reasons – suffered from toothache and neuralgia, for which complaints he rubbed laudanum on his gums. The following Tuesday, April 18th, both husband and wife felt recovered enough to depart in the landau, with coachman and footman in attendance, for a day in London, Florence returning separately to The Priory, leaving Charles to have a 'jolly lunch' (as he afterwards described it) in town. About 7.40 pm the Bravos and Mrs Cox sat down to dinner; Charles helped himself from the burgundy decanter, and it is with horror and admiration one notes that Florence and Jane Cox drank almost two bottles of sherry between them. At 10 pm, from the bedroom he had occupied himself since his wife's illness, Charles Bravo was stricken with the pains and vomiting that assailed him until his death three days later. Throughout his illness Florence and Mrs Cox behaved with the utmost solicitude, the wife summoning many specialists, all of whom seemed nonplussed but disturbed by Charles Bravo's obviously desperate condition:

Mr Bravo, what have you taken?
I rubbed my gums with laudanum . . .
Laudanum won't explain your symptoms, Mr Bravo . . .

On Saturday, April 22nd, a post-mortem was held at St Thomas's Hospital; no sign of natural disease was found, but ulceration of the large intestine was detected, which signified an irritant poison. An inquest was held privately at The Priory on April 25th, when Mrs Cox testified that Charles Bravo had admitted to her, although to no one else, that he had taken poison deliberately: 'Mrs Cox, I have taken poison. . . . Don't tell Florence!' A pathologist, Professor Redwood, said that he had discovered the presence of antimony in the matter Charles Bravo had vomited: 'There is one form in which alone antimony could have been administered, and that is emetic tartar. It is soluble in water and tasteless. . . .' An open verdict was returned by the jury (replenished by refreshments provided at The Priory by Florence Bravo), which found that the deceased had died from antimony, but with insufficient evidence to show how it came to be in his body.

After weeks of growing suspicion and rumour, the Lord Chief Justice was prompted to quash the findings of the jury, and instigate another inquiry which opened on July 11th at the Bedford Hotel, Balham, and was, in effect, the trial by inquest of Florence Bravo – or the enigmatic Mrs Cox, depending upon one's opinion. First the jury was called upon to witness the remains of Charles Bravo, the gruesome trip to Lower Norwood Cemetery culminating in the appalled jurymen peering through a glass aperture inserted into the coffin-lid: '... the face had acquired the dark hue of a mummy, and the teeth were almost entirely black. ...' At this second inquest the earlier relationship between Dr Gully and Mrs Bravo was revealed to a fascinated populace, the wretched physician being actually called to testify; a servant of his, George Griffith (who had also been employed as a coachman by Mrs Bravo before her second marriage), had given evidence that he had bought 2 oz. of emetic tartar in 1869 on behalf of Dr Gully for the purpose of horse-medicine. Now the unhappy doctor ('I feel my position most bitterly') shrilly denied any participation in engineering Charles Bravo's death. Earlier Mrs Cox repeated how Bravo had told her of taking poison, now adding that he said he had taken it 'for Dr Gully': 'I thought of Mrs Bravo,' the witness asserted. 'It was thinking of her that I withheld the words "for Dr Gully" in my statement to the Coroner.' Mrs Cox spoke of Charles Bravo's jealousy over his wife, which Florence Bravo was to confirm, adding that on one occasion he even struck her in a rage. Mr Brooks (whose wife had employed Mrs Cox) gave interesting evidence when he revealed that, after congratulating Charles Bravo on his engagement the previous November, that gentleman had replied: 'Damn your congratulations. I only want the money.'

This time the jury found that Charles Bravo had been wilfully murdered 'but there is insufficient evidence to fix the guilt upon any person or persons'. Florence Bravo herself died on September 13th, 1878, in Southsea, of alcoholism; there have been suggestions that she murdered her first husband, as well as the second. She certainly inherited a fortune at Ricardo's death, and the realization that perhaps Bravo had been prompted to marry her for similar motives might have induced her to kill yet again; it has also been hinted that the succession of miscarriages (not to mention Bravo's sexual intemperance) unhinged her mind. Mrs Cox departed for Jamaica shortly after the second inquest, where she lived for many years; some think she murdered Charles Bravo because she believed her penurious employer to be a menace to her livelihood and that he was plotting her departure from The Priory. Dr Gully's professional career was ruined (as he had gloomily forecast at the second inquest), but it is hard to imagine that he connived at the killing of the husband of his ex-mistress.

BRENNAN, William Theodore
Sentenced for the murder of farmer John Rowlands in 1925, and sent to Broadmoor Criminal Lunatic Asylum.

A farm labourer named Evans on Rowlands' farm, Model Farm, Penyffordd, near Mold, saw a man whom he supposed to be a poacher on the afternoon of March 5th, 1925, and told the farmer. The farmer went off to look into it, and a report of a shotgun was heard. Evans went out over the fields and saw a man in a light coat running away. He gave chase, and at one point the man turned round and pointed his gun at him. However, Evans felt sick with the violent exertion and gave up the chase. The farmer was found shot dead in a field.

Suspicion centred on a 27-year-old Irishman, William Brennan, who had recently come to live in Penyffordd with his parents. Brennan claimed he had been at home all day, and no gun could be found in his house. His white macintosh looked as if it had been recently scrubbed.

But the villagers of Penyffordd obviously believed that Brennan was the killer, and a few days later his nerve broke, and he told a story of how the farmer had approached him and tried to confiscate the gun. He had offered to pay for the rabbits but refused to give up the gun. He and the farmer struggled; the gun went off without hurting the farmer; Brennan, in a fury, reloaded and shot the farmer in a further struggle. He hid the gun down a drain.

Inquiries into Brennan's history showed mental abnormality; he was easily provoked to fits of insane rage, and had been in various kinds of trouble since he left school; his parents decided to let him live an open air life in a quiet place. There was a strain of hereditary insanity in the family.

The jury at Mold Assizes found him guilty but insane. Brennan's story of the murder has the ring of truth, and the farmer was certainly at fault in trying to confiscate the shotgun.

BRINKLEY, Richard

His trial in 1907 for the murder-by-mistake of a Mr and Mrs Beck is the first time scientific evidence was admitted in a law court. Brinkley's intended victim was one Parker, tricked some time before into witnessing a bogus will by which Brinkley later claimed property and money. Others questioned the will's validity, and Brinkley, needing Parker's reference, found him rightly reluctant to perjure himself, reminding Brinkley that he had signed a blank fold of paper in a public house under the impression that it was a petition for an outing. Fearing exposure by Parker, Brinkley placed some poisoned stout in his lodgings: sight of the bottle proved irresistible to Parker's landlady, Mrs Beck, and her husband, and they died shortly afterwards. The crime and real intention were traced to Brinkley (who carelessly mentioned the poisoned stout to the police before they mentioned it to him) and to substantiate both Parker's deception story and the motive, micro-chemical tests were taken of the inks on the will-form. It was found that the ink in use at the public house and the ink from Parker's signature on the form were identical: Brinkley's explanations for the different inks were inadequate, and after a four-day trial at Guildford Assizes he was found guilty of murder.

BRINVILLIERS, Marie Madeleine de
Noted poisoner in seventeenth-century France.

Mme de Brinvilliers was born Marie Madeleine d'Aubray, on July 22nd, 1630, eldest of five children of Antoine Dreux d'Aubray of Offémont and Villiers, Civil Lieutenant of the City, Mayoralty, and Viscounty of Paris, Councillor of State, Maître de Requêtes; her father was the son of a Treasurer of France.

Marie d'Aubray received some education, although apparently this did not include religion. Little is known about her home background, but it appears that she was allowed to do whatever she liked. Before she reached her teens she had had sexual intercourse with her brothers, and other admissions which she made in her confession indicate that she was something of a nymphomaniac from the beginning.

At 21, she married the son of the president of the Audit office, Antoine Gobelin de Brinvilliers, Baron of Nourar, officer of the Norman regiment. Marie was extremely beautiful at the time of her marriage, with chestnut hair and blue eyes. She brought her husband a dowry of 200,000 livres (which would be equivalent to £60,000 by present-day standards).

The Baron was a gambler, and soon spent Marie's dowry. Eight years passed, during which husband and wife appeared to get along well enough. Then the Baron met the man who was to have a fateful effect on the course of his life, a young libertine named Godin, known generally as Ste Croix. Godin was a man of considerable intelligence and talent, but a gambler and debauchee. But his immense charm and vitality were felt by many. Marie de Brinvilliers lost no time in becoming his mistress. The Baron appeared not to mind; his own love affairs were numerous. The lovers made no secret of their affair and paraded it in public. But Marie was indiscreet enough to tell her father, who had Ste Croix seized as he was driving with his mistress and thrown into the Bastille. Here he met a noted Italian poisoner named Eggidi or Exili, who had been in the service of Queen Christina of Sweden.

Ste Croix was in the Bastille from March 19th to May 2nd, 1663. Exili was released on June 27th and was deported to England; however, he soon returned to Paris and went to live at the house of Ste Croix. He was there for six months, during which time Ste Croix became his pupil in the art of poisoning. He passed on this knowledge to his mistress, who had returned to her lover with renewed ardour.

Ste Croix was a considerable drain on Marie's resources; she was also a gambler who lost heavily. The clash with her father had developed in her a violent hatred of him. The lovers decided to hasten the hour when Marie should inherit her father's wealth.

For some reason, they decided not to use one of the 'succession powders' that Ste Croix was an expert in concocting; instead they approached a Swiss chemist named Glaser, Apothecary-in-ordinary to the King. Glaser provided a powder, and the next step was to test it. So Marie visited hospitals, bearing food for the patients, and administered some of Glaser's powder in wine and fruit. Her purpose was to find out whether the poison could be detected at an autopsy. She also tried it out on some of her servants, causing one of them to become a chronic invalid.

At Whitsun, 1666, her father asked her to go with her children to stay with him on his estate at Offémont. There he fell ill and was carefully nursed by Marie; he returned to Paris for expert medical attention, his devoted daughter continuing to attend him; it took eight months; her father finally succumbed on September 10th.

Marie now launched again into debauchery. A dominating personality, she expected her lover to remain faithful while she took a series of lovers. She was involved with her husband's cousin, the Marquis de Nadaillac, and had a child by her own cousin. (She had two children by Ste Croix.) She also became the mistress of a young man named Briancourt, a tutor of her children. Mme de Brinvilliers spent a great deal of money on this male harem. Her dislike of being crossed is revealed by an incident that took place in 1670. A creditor caused a house belonging to Marie and her husband to be sold to repay a debt; she immediately tried to set fire to the house.

She decided that the next victims were to be her brothers, who lived in the same house. Ste Croix agreed to help her, for a consideration of 55,000 livres. (A livre would be five or six shillings by current standards.) An attempt to have one brother murdered by assassins had failed; so a poisoner was introduced into their house, a man called Jean Hamelin, known as La Chaussée.

The poisoning of the elder brother, the Civil Lieutenant, went on throughout a great deal of 1667; he succumbed finally on 17th June. The second brother followed him to the grave in September. An autopsy revealed that the latter had died by poisoning, but no accusations were made, and La Chaussée received an honorarium of 100 crowns for his devoted service.

However, Mme de Brinvilliers' tendency to talk was one of the causes of her downfall; the other was the unworthiness of the men she trusted. La Chaussée blackmailed her and became her lover. (It is not known whether this was a part of his exactions, or whether Marie took him of her own accord.) And Ste Croix blackmailed her unceasingly. He had many of her letters, and the two promissory notes she had signed (for 55,000 livres) on the day he agreed to help poison her brothers. Marie became panic-stricken and threatened to poison herself; Ste Croix called her bluff, and when she took a small quantity of the poison, she was forced to drink warm milk to make her sick; she was ill for several months after.

Marie had decided that her sister and sister-in-law should be the next victims. But she made the mistake of confiding in Briancourt, the tutor, who was terrified, but tried hard to dissuade her. He even sent Marie's maid with a message to warn Mlle D'Aubray. Marie decided that Briancourt should be the next to go, but the tutor was expecting something of the kind, and assaulted the man who had been sent to ply him with food and drink. Two more unsuccessful attempts were made on Briancourt's life; Ste Croix came into his bedroom through a secret door in the chimney-piece, but the tutor was fully dressed, and Ste Croix (who was disguised) had to make off. Briancourt consulted a professor of law named Bocager and told him all he knew, but for some reason, Bocager urged him to silence. After this, there was an attempt to shoot Briancourt, who retaliated by going to Ste Croix's house and telling him he was a murderer and a scoundrel.

A touch of comedy is provided by the next incident. Marie decided to poison her husband so that she could marry Ste Croix; Ste Croix had no desire to marry her, and kept administering counter-poisons. The resulting disturbances did the Baron's health no good. He suspected his wife's intentions, and engaged a personal valet, who had to prepare his food. At about this time, Briancourt managed to escape, and fled to Aubervilliers, where he taught in the establishment of the Fathers of the Oratory.

Then Ste Croix died. When Marie heard the news, she cried: 'The little box!' Her concern was not misplaced. It was this that brought her to the headsman.

A legend has it that Ste Croix accidentally gassed himself while seeking the elixir of life in his laboratory, but the truth seems to be that he died from natural causes.

Ste Croix's widow, from whom he had been separated for a long time, took charge of his effects, and Mme de Brinvilliers' box was discovered. With it was a 'Confession' of Ste Croix, and a note asking that the box should be returned unopened to Mme de Brinvilliers. For some odd reason, the confession was burnt unread, but the box was opened.

Ste Croix died in late July 1672; during August, Marie de Brinvilliers made frantic efforts to regain the box. Even Briancourt was persuaded to intervene, but to no effect. La Chaussée gave himself away by bolting for the door when told that the box had been opened; he was arrested on September 4th and tortured. Mme de Brinvilliers decided to flee to England, taking a kitchen-maid with her. The following February, 1673, La Chaussée confessed and was sentenced to be broken alive on the wheel. Application was made to extradite Marie, but she anticipated it by fleeing to the Netherlands. From there she proceeded to Cambrai and Valenciennes, where she entered a convent (which she had to leave on account of the war), then to Antwerp and Liége, where she entered another convent. Altogether, she was at large for over three years, until she was arrested on March 25th, 1676. She was arrested the day before the city of Liége was handed over to the Spaniards – after which the French King's jurisdiction would have come to an end. A confession was found on her, which is so frank and detailed that it had to be printed finally in Latin.

The court, presided over by Lamoignon, had twenty-two sittings between April 29th and July 16th, 1676. She was sentenced to death. Before the execution, she was taken in a cart to the principal door of the Church of Paris, there to make public confession of her sins. She was tortured by having large quantities of water poured into her mouth through a funnel and into her stomach. A priest named Edmé Pirot was with her in her last days and seems to have brought her much consolation. She made her public confession at Notre Dame, and was then taken to the scaffold in the Place de Grève. The executioner, Guillaume, severed her head with one stroke. The body was burnt and the ashes scattered. Some of her relics were sold as charms. The story of her contrition and the dignity of her death made many consider her a saint. An excellent account of the case is given by Hoffmann in his tale *Madame de Scudéry*.

BROWN, Eric (The Rayleigh Bath-chair Murder Case)
Murdered his invalid father on July 23rd, 1943, by placing a grenade mine under the cushion of the elder Brown's bath-chair.

The Browns (father, mother, and sons, Eric 19, and Colin 16) lived at Summerfield, London Road, Rayleigh, in Essex; in 1938 the father's legs had become paralysed, the result of an accident years before, and he took regular outings in a velveteen-seated invalid chair. Although ailing, Father Brown was a tyrant to his household, most of his wrath being aimed at Eric (at this time serving in the army), who from his boyhood had been subject to paternal persecution.

At 1.45 pm on July 23rd the Browns' resident help, Nurse Mitchell, helped Mr Brown into his bath-chair, wrapping him up for the afternoon's walk. Nurse and patient had not gone far when – after some readjusting of the chair blankets – there was a tremendous explosion. The nurse survived, but very little remained of her charge, who was almost literally blown to the winds. The explosion was caused by a British Hawkins No. 75 Grenade Mine, used in warfare against tanks, and, in this case, detonated two feet above ground level. This convinced police that someone had placed it beneath the velveteen cushion. Nurse Mitchell recalled that Eric Brown (on leave from his battalion) had spent much time on the day of the tragedy in the air-raid shelter where the bath-chair was kept. When inquiries into his army life were made, it was found that he had attended lectures on the Hawkins 75 Grenade Mine, and there was a store of these mines at his Company HQ. Interrogated, Eric Brown soon confessed to the killing of his father: 'My father is now out of his suffering, and I earnestly hope that my mother will now live a much happier and normal life.'

Arrested and committed for trial, Eric Brown attempted suicide while in custody. He was tried at Essex Assizes on November 4th, 1944. A nerve specialist, Dr Rowland Hill, called by the defence, referred to the suicide bid, stating that Brown was a typical schizophrenic: '. . . he came to prison in a happy buoyant frame of mind . . . he suddenly realized for the first time that by what he had done people might call him a murderer.'

The jury found Eric Brown guilty but insane.

BROWNE and KENNEDY (The Gutteridge Murder)
Two desperadoes who were executed on May 31st, 1928, for the murder of Police Constable Gutteridge.

Frederick Guy Browne was the more interesting of the two. Born at Catford in 1891, he was a man of powerful personality and enormous physical strength. (One of his photographs makes him look comically like Nietzsche – this may be the effect of the walrus moustache.) Like many murderers, he might have achieved eminence – or at least riches – if he had attempted to turn his considerable strength of mind and mechanical ingenuity towards legitimate ends. But at the age of 18, he moved to Oxford and became head of a gang of bicycle thieves. In 1912 he was tried for burglary at Bletchley and sentenced to twelve months in prison. His violent disposition was here revealed by a threat to shoot the detective who arrested him if he ever met him again. It was revealed that he had equipped the room in which he changed the appearance of bicycles with an electrical device for locking the door and electrifying the handle when a switch on the bench was pressed. On his release, he returned to bicycle stealing and received another twelve months in jail. He married in 1915, and joined the army. In 1918, he was in jail for ten months for stealing a motor cycle. He then set up in a garage in Clapham, moving later to Southend. Three years later, he was sentenced with three other men to four years in prison for insurance frauds. A prison official later offered a revealing comment on his character: 'He was a complex sort of character, and would respond to human treatment. A pleasant word was sufficient to move him, but at the very whisper of a command, his prickles would go up like a hedgehog's. . . . He suffered from a sense of wrong.' Apparently Browne again demonstrated his remarkable powers as a mechanic when he was offered work in the prison toolshop.

One of the mainsprings of Browne's character was a sense of resentment; and this pushed him further and further beyond the law.

He was transferred to Dartmoor prison as a result of being found in possession of a skeleton key (a fellow prisoner had 'peached' on him), and here behaved so badly that he lost all remission of sentence and served his four years to the full. Here he also met his future confederate, William Kennedy, with whom he joined forces on being released from jail in 1927. On his release, he declared that he would never be taken alive again.

Kennedy was a Scotsman, born in 1884, and was in every way less remarkable than Browne; he was a commonplace habitual criminal who came under Browne's powerful sway rather as Franz Lorbach came under that of Werner Boost.

Browne joined Kennedy in the Clapham garage shortly after he was released from Dartmoor, and a few months later, they committed together the murder of Constable Gutteridge.

On the night of September 26th, 1927, Browne and Kennedy set out with the intention of stealing a car. They went by train to Billericay in Essex to steal a Riley car garaged in the High Street, but a dog frightened them off, and they walked through the village to the bungalow of a Dr Lovell. They waited until his lights went out, and then Browne forced the garage door, and they pushed the car out on to the main road. It was a Morris Cowley. They then proceeded to drive through the back lanes, avoiding Brentwood, where a constable was known to be stationed night and day. In one of these lanes, PC Gutteridge saw the car approaching and signalled it to stop with his torch. Browne drove on, and the police whistle blew. Browne now stopped, and the constable proceeded to question them about the car. As he drew out his notebook to write down particulars, Browne shot him, and then got out of the car and shot him at close range through both eyes. He may have been influenced by the notion that the eyes of a dead man photograph the murderers, or he may simply have been expressing his rage at the interference of the law. They then drove off, Browne damaging the car's front bumper by driving it into a tree.

The car was abandoned in Foxley Road, Brixton, where it was found at 7.30 the next morning by a clerk on his way to work. Browne and Kennedy returned to Clapham by tram, taking the doctor's instruments, which they destroyed.

The loss of the car was reported early the next morning; the police connected it with the murder of Gutteridge, and hastened to examine it. Blood was found on the driver's side, and an empty cartridge case was found on the floor. This proved to have been fired from a Webley revolver – the gun that had killed Gutteridge.

Police inquiries came to a standstill after several months, until an incident in Sheffield. Browne was driving a car at high speed, and forced a van driver into the wall. The indignant driver took his number and reported the incident to the police, who traced the car, found Browne, and demanded to see his licence. Later, a summons was served on him in London; the police then discovered that the address on the licence was false, as also was the licence plate on the car. At this point, an 'old lag' who had been sitting beside Browne when the van incident occurred, approached the police and told them the true identity of the man who was driving the car. It turned out that the car was a stolen Vauxhall, and that Browne had since changed it for an Angus Sanderson with a man in Sheffield. The police kept watch on the Globe Garage, Northcote Road, Clapham Junction, until Browne drove in with the Angus Sanderson. At this point they had no evidence to connect Browne with the murder of PC Gutteridge, but there was always the possibility. They also remembered that Browne had once threatened never to be taken alive again. So when Browne entered the garage (he had been to Dartmoor to fetch a friend on his release), they waited until he was clear of the car, and then arrested him in the inner office. The precaution proved to be wise; Browne later confessed that if he had been in the car when the six police officers came in, he would have shot them with the revolver in his side pocket and then killed himself.

Inspector Barker charged Browne with stealing the Vauxhall in Tooting, and Browne seemed relieved. Then the discovery of Webley cartridges in his pocket and of four revolvers on his premises strengthened their suspicion that perhaps they were dealing with the Gutteridge killer.

After Browne's arrest, Kennedy left his lodgings with his wife; he was traced to Liverpool. When a detective tried to arrest him, he turned round with a loaded revolver, and pulled the trigger.

Fortunately, the safety catch was on. This action certainly destroyed his only chance of escaping the gallows.

Kennedy asked to be allowed to see his wife (whom he had only recently married) and told her that he was involved in the Gutţeridge murder; he then made a full confession, inculpating Browne and (as far as possible) excusing himself.

Browne and Kennedy were put on trial at the Central Criminal Court on Monday, April 23rd, 1928, before Mr Justice Avory. The Solicitor General (Sir Boyd Merriman) led for the Crown; E. F. Lever defended Browne, and F. J. Powell defended Kennedy.

Browne damaged his own case by his bullying and overbearing demeanour in the witness-box. Certain of his statements to the police who arrested him were remembered against him: his comment that he would have shot six of them if they had taken him while he was in the car, and his later comment: 'What I can see of it, I shall have to get a machine-gun for you bastards next time.'

Both were found guilty. Browne was executed at Pentonville and Kennedy at Wandsworth.

BROWNRIGG, Elizabeth
Sadistic wife of a wealthy plumber, hanged at Tyburn on September 14th, 1767, for causing the death of a servant girl through ill-treatment.

The date of Elizabeth Brownrigg's birth is not mentioned in the Newgate Calendar, but it is stated that she was the mother of sixteen children, and that her husband, James Brownrigg, made himself rich enough as a plumber in Greenwich to move to Fleur de Lis Court, Fleet Street, and keep a house at Islington for occasional retreat.

Elizabeth Brownrigg was a midwife who was appointed by the overseers of St Dunstan's Parish to take care of poor women in labour in the workhouse; no evidence of her sadism appears at this period.

In 1755, Mary Mitchell, a poor girl of the precinct of White Friars, was made apprentice to Mrs Brownrigg, together with Mary Jones, one of the children from the Foundling Hospital. Mrs Brownrigg still practised as a midwife and found the free help useful.

Both girls were treated with the kind of sadism which Ivan Bloch declares to be characteristic of the English: they were stripped and whipped on the buttocks at every opportunity, and subjected to various other indignities and cruelties. Finally, Mary Jones escaped and returned to the Foundling Hospital, where her wounds and bruises were so appalling that the governors wrote to James Brownrigg, threatening to prosecute him unless he explained why she had been treated so badly. Brownrigg did not reply and the matter was dropped.

The escape of Mary Jones seemed to enrage Mrs Brownrigg, so that her cruelties became more atrocious. Mary Mitchell tried to escape but was caught and beaten. Another girl was obtained from the precinct of White Friars, Mary Clifford. The girl was not healthy, and Mrs Brownrigg made her sleep on a mat in the coal cellar, starved her, and often forced her to remain naked for twenty-four hours at a time, beating her with a whip handle.

Mary Clifford in particular seems to have aroused Mrs Brownrigg's sadism. One day, when the girl complained to a Frenchwoman living in the house, and the Frenchwoman had spoken to Mrs Brownrigg, there was a terrifying scene in which Mrs Brownrigg tried to cut out the girl's tongue with scissors and succeeded in cutting it in two places. Their son John appears to have inherited his mother's love of inflicting pain and often beat the girls himself.

Mary Clifford's mother-in-law now came to look for the girl, and was turned away from the house by Mrs Brownrigg. But a Mrs Deacon, the next-door neighbour, called in the mother-in-law and told her that she suspected that the girls were being badly treated. Watch was kept on the house, and Mary Clifford was finally seen through an open skylight; but she was so badly wounded that she could not be induced to speak. The St Dunstan's overseers were now called in, and they called on Mrs Brownrigg. James Brownrigg told them he did not know anyone called Mary Clifford, and offered to let them see Mary Mitchell. They immediately took Mary Mitchell away, and when she tried to remove her clothes at the workhouse, the cloth stuck to the dried blood and made her scream. A Mr Grundy, one of the overseers, now returned to the house, where James Brownrigg flew into a passion and threatened him with lawyers; Mr Grundy refused to be intimidated, and in turn sent for a coach to take Brownrigg off to the Compter. This had the effect of making Brownrigg produce Mary Clifford from a cupboard. The girl was covered with ulcers. A few days later she died in hospital. Brownrigg was taken to the Wood Street Compter, who sent him before Alderman Crossby, who committed him. Mrs Brownrigg and her son John escaped – in time to avoid being arrested for the murder of Mary Clifford.

The mother and son disguised themselves with clothes bought at the Rag Fair and moved to Wandsworth, where they took a lodging. Their landlord, a chandler named Dunbar, recognized them from the description in a newspaper, and went up to London, where he informed the overseers of St Dunstan's. Elizabeth and John Brownrigg were arrested.

They were tried for murder at the Old Bailey. Elizabeth Brownrigg was found guilty and sentenced to death; the husband and son each received six months in prison.

Before her death, Elizabeth Brownrigg made public confession of her misdemeanours and acknowledged the justice of her sentence. The public were extremely hostile. After her execution, her body was dissected at the Royal College of Surgeons and her skeleton hung up.

It seems arguable that midwifery may have been a profession that led to sadism, or at least extreme carelessness of human life. Dickens' portrait of Mrs Gamp will be recalled; Mrs Pearcey was also a midwife. William Stewart, a student of the Jack the Ripper murders, even produced a plausible theory that the Ripper was a woman and a midwife by profession.

BRUNEAU, Abbé Albert
Executed in 1894 for the murder of the Abbé Fricot, rector of the parish of Entrammes, in Mayenne, France.

Mayenne is the province that lies inland between Normandy and Brittany; its capital is Laval. The Abbé Albert Bruneau came to Entrammes, six miles from Laval, in November 1892. He was 31 at the time, of peasant origin, and his past was hardly suitable for a priest. At 13, he had been suspected of stealing 1,400 francs from the rector of Voutré, from whom he was learning Latin. He then went to a seminary, but left when he was caught stealing money from a fellow student. In 1886 he was ordained and sent to Astillé, near Laval, as a curate. Here, an old lady left him 16,000 francs in her will, which he was intended to spend on charity; he paid off his parents' debts with it (the franc was then worth about tenpence), and spent the rest on himself, mostly in the brothels of Laval. In the last two years of his curacy, the rectory was burgled four times and burnt twice. The latter incidents caused Bruneau to benefit from the insurance companies. Desirous of supplanting the priest of Astillé,

Abbé Pointeau, Bruneau spread stories about his sexual immorality; the mayor of Astillé persuaded the Bishop of Laval to remove Pointeau; but the Bishop also sent Bruneau to be the Abbé Fricot's curate. Perhaps rumours of Bruneau's escapades had reached his ears, for at this time Bruneau had contracted gonorrhoea. Soon after Bruneau's arrival in Entrammes, a strong-box was broken into, and 500 francs stolen. There is reason to believe that Fricot knew Bruneau to be the thief.

On January 2nd, 1894, Fricot gave a lunch party at the rectory. At half past six, the only people in the rectory were the two priests, the 62-year-old housekeeper, Jeanette, and a 9-year-old boy, Joseph, the odd-job man's son. At this time, Joseph went to tell the two clergymen that the choir had arrived for practice; Bruneau said he was tired, and sent the choir away. Fricot was doing his accounts. This was the last time Fricot was seen alive by anyone but Bruneau. When Joseph came in at seven, to say supper was ready, Bruneau told him that Fricot was out. Bruneau then began to play the organ. Finally, Bruneau came in, looking shaken, and said he would take his supper alone since the rector was not back. He ate a hearty meal.

That night, nobody went to bed; neighbours were called in to help search for Fricot. The next morning, Bruneau suggested that the Abbé might have committed suicide, and mentioned the well in the garden; he went out to look, and returned claiming that his nose was bleeding, and holding a handkerchief to it. The housekeeper said later that she noticed no blood. He and the neighbour, Chelle, then went to look in the well; the rector's body was found under thirty-odd feet of water and a number of logs; there were also three laundry poles protruding from the top. A nun and local headmistress, Louise Bouvier, called at the rectory, and the Abbé took her into a private room and confided that the rector had committed suicide in the well, and that logs had been thrown down on top of him to make it look like murder (suicide being a serious matter for a Catholic).

The edge of the well was stained with blood, and when the rector's body was recovered, it was seen that he had been murdered with some heavy instrument that had battered in his head. Bruneau's hand was cut, and he claimed this had been done as he looked into the well at three o'clock that morning; keys of the organ were found to be bloodstained, as was the lamp on top of the organ.

The curate was immediately arrested. In his desk were found 1,300 francs in large notes, and he admitted to hiding some bonds

126

in the attic. In a strong-box belonging to Fricot were found several hundred francs and another bond. It looked as if Bruneau might have helped himself from the strong-box; he certainly possessed a key.

The police, for some reason, decided to try to hang another murder on Bruneau, that of an old flower-seller in Laval, Marie Bourdais, who had been murdered and robbed in February 1893. A coachman declared that he had driven Bruneau back to Entrammes from Laval on the night of the murder.

Bruneau was tried on Monday, July 9th, 1894, before Judge Francis Giron. Several prostitutes testified that he was a frequent customer, and one brothel madame commented that he was not the only priest to turn up in his cassock.

Bruneau was found guilty of the murder of Fricot (not of the flower-seller) and sentenced to death. Sixteen thousand people attended his execution on August 29th, 1894; Bruneau died with dignity, still protesting his innocence.

Some years after his death, a rumour started that Fricot had been murdered by a woman whom he had caught stealing; the woman had sealed Bruneau's lips by confessing her crime to him. This story, which was supposed to be a death-bed confession, made many people think of Bruneau as a saint, and a Madrid newspaper declared he was a sacred martyr. People brought sick children to his grave to be healed. However, there is no evidence for the 'death-bed confession' story.

Bruneau's guilt seems fairly certain. As well as being a thief, he seems to have been a pathological liar. On one occasion, he preached a good sermon in which he told the story of a close friend who had gone to the gallows, and had written him a letter from the death cell. The rector of Forcé asked him afterwards if all this was true, and Bruneau declared solemnly that he still had the letter, which was almost in pieces from continual use. Later, Bruneau admitted that he had made the story up. This kind of childish lying is a familiar characteristic of certain criminals.

It should not be forgotten that the Abbé Fricot was doing his accounts at the time of the murder. According to a friend of Fricot's, he was in the habit of asking his curates out to the well in the garden if he had something special to say to them. He may have decided to speak firmly to Bruneau about his criminal habits. (But since it was a cold January evening, and the Abbé went out without a coat, it is not likely that he anticipated a long discussion with Bruneau.) We may suppose that Bruneau attacked him and pushed him into the well between six-thirty and seven. The Abbé, although a slight man, succeeded in crawling to the top, and was knocked down again with logs thrown on top of him. Bruneau then played the organ to drown the noise of splashing. (Some neighbours claim they heard groans coming from the garden at about eight o'clock.) The nose-bleeding story was probably fabricated as an excuse in case blood was found on his clothes.

The execution of clergymen was not uncommon in France in the nineteenth century. In 1822 the Abbé Mingrat was guillotined at Grenoble for the rape and murder of a young married woman. In 1836, the Abbé Delacollongue was sentenced to hard labour for the murder of his mistress; in 1848, Father Léotade was sentenced to hard labour for the rape and murder of a child; in 1882, the Abbé Auriol poisoned two elderly lady parishioners.

BRYANT, Charlotte (The Sherborne Case)
Thirty-three-year-old Irishwoman, slut and illiterate, convicted in 1936 of the murder of her husband.

The Bryants met and married in Londonderry during the 'Troubles', when Frederick Bryant was serving with the British Military Police, settling afterwards in a small cottage at Coombe in Dorset, an isolated hamlet. Bryant, a docile man, worked as a farm labourer, and Charlotte bore him five children, the paternity of which must have been dubious to both husband and wife. Charlotte had decided nymphomaniac tendencies and since she could not read (and therefore, through reading paper-back romances, satisfy her desires by proxy) her reputation in Dorset public houses was, justifiably, notorious. There is no evidence of Bryant objecting to his wife's sexual adventures, and he did not complain when, in 1933, a gipsy named Leonard Parsons came to the already crowded cottage as a lodger, sleeping on a couch in the kitchen and sharing not only Bryant's razor but, very soon, Bryant's wife. Parsons continued to stay with the Bryants spasmodically, at other times pursuing his peddling occupation and visiting his 'natural wife', gipsy Priscilla Loveridge, and their four children; Charlotte looked forward to his arrivals, when her behaviour would become even more abandoned and her home even more dirty and neglected. It was during one of these visits, in May 1935, that Bryant had the first of a series of agonizing stomachic bouts, diagnosed by the local physician, Dr MacCarthy, as gastro-enteritis. On December 19th, 1935 Charlotte Bryant, doubtless feeling a compulsive desire for Parsons, unsuccessfully searched for him at a gipsy encampment near Weston-super-Mare, receiving much abuse not only from the jealous Priscilla, but from Mrs Loveridge's fierce pipe-smoking old mother, Mrs Penfold. On December 20th Bryant became ill once again; on doctor's orders he was removed to hospital where he died at 3 pm on December 22nd. Told there would be an inquest and enlightened as to its meaning ('What is an inquest?' she had asked), Mrs Bryant appeared indignant; 4 grains of arsenic were found in the body of Bryant, and while police made an examination of the Coombe cottage and its contents, Charlotte Bryant and her children lived at the 'workhouse', Sturminster Newton Institution. On February 10th, 1936, she was charged with the murder of Frederick Bryant, and in May was tried at Dorchester Assizes under Mr Justice Mackinnon, with Sir Terence O'Connor, Solicitor General, leading for the Crown and Mr David Casswell for the defence. A much-battered empty tin had been recovered from a pile of garbage at the back of the cottage, scrapings from which contained arsenic, and identified by a firm manufacturing weed-killer as one of their containers. Charlotte Bryant, asked by her counsel whether she had ever possessed any kind of poison, stared uncomprehendingly and replied, 'I can't tell you poison', although admitting the ownership of a coat (trying it on in court), the pockets of which contained traces of arsenic. Gipsies Loveridge and Penfold made a literally colourful appearance at the trial, the aged Mrs Penfold wearing a man's trilby hat and full of violent oaths against the accused; Parsons seemed unaffected by Mrs Bryant's fate (as indeed did that lady herself, chewing caramels in court) and bewildered by expressions such as 'intimate with' when relations with his former landlady were being discussed. Unkempt and unshaven, it was difficult to imagine him arousing female passion, although the embittered Priscilla Loveridge had described him as 'a woman's fancy man, the kind of man who would break up any man's home'.

Charlotte Bryant was found guilty of murder, and executed on July 15th, 1936. It is still surprising that she should have thought it necessary to destroy a husband who for so long had tolerated her dissipations.

BUCKFIELD, Reginald Sidney

Nicknamed 'Smiler' because of his usual sunny demeanour, Gunner Buckfield of the Royal Artillery was tried at the Old

Bailey in 1943 for the murder of Mrs Ellen Symes, stabbed three months before as she wheeled her young son down Brompton Farm Road near Gravesend in Kent. The son, aged four, mentioned a soldier attacking his mother, and Buckfield had been absent without leave at that time, eking out a living by farmwork; apprehended by a suspicious-minded constable, he spent his first hours in a prison cell smilingly composing a twelve-page literary work entitled: 'The Mystery of the Brompton Road Murders'. The writing and grammar were execrable, but the meaning clear: Gunner Buckfield knew more than anyone else about the circumstances of Mrs Symes' death, and his subsequent protestations that he had meant Brompton Road in London were futile. Still smiling he was condemned to death but was subsequently found insane and sent to Broadmoor.

BUISSON, Émile
French gangster and Chicago-style killer executed in February 1956 at Santé Prison.

Buisson's heredity seems to have been extremely bad. His father was a drunkard, a builder of bakers' ovens, addicted to absinthe. Only four of his nine children survived, and one of them was a weak-minded deaf-mute girl. The two criminals of the family, Jean-Baptiste and Émile, were its only two healthy members; a third brother died of tuberculosis at the age of 20. The mother, worn out by overwork, starvation, and continual brutal beatings from her husband, was taken to an asylum. The father took to exhibiting his deaf-mute daughter in cafés for money; he was sent to jail for carnal knowledge of minors – including his daughter – and died in an asylum.

Émile was born at Paray-le-Monial, in the Sâone-et-Loire department of southern France, on August 19th, 1902. His elder brother fought in the war, deserted, and was sent to a penal battalion in Algeria. Released in 1921, he promptly became a pimp in Paris.

Émile served his first term in jail at the age of 16, and then twenty months' imprisonment for theft. He was due for military service, and so sent out to a penal battalion in North Africa. The brutality of these battalions was unspeakable – and still is, according to many writers. However, Émile managed to distinguish himself in the fighting, and got the Croix de Guerre. Back in France, he took up a life of petty crime and served many short terms in jail.

In 1932, he helped to rescue his brother from jail. The plan was bold. Jean-Baptiste got himself transferred to Strasbourg model prison at Ensisheim by confessing to a crime in Strasbourg and getting three years added to his eight-year sentence. He there broke his leg by smashing it with a table leg. He was transferred into the hospital, and the same night jumped from a first-floor window, breaking it again. However, with the help of Émile he made a clean getaway.

Émile Buisson committed his first big robbery on December 27th, 1937, and got himself the nickname 'Mimile le Dingue' – Crazy Mimile. He was driving a 'traction avant' Citröen – front-wheel drive (known generally simply as 'tractions'), and he and a gangster named Charles Desgrandchamps (known as 'Big-footed Charlie') robbed two bank messengers outside the Banque de France in Troyes. Émile fired at one messenger, wounding him in the thigh, and then, to the surprise of Big-footed Charlie, began to fire at random down the street and into the bank.

He was arrested a month later. French justice is slow, and in 1940, at the time of the invasion, he was still awaiting trial in Troyes Prison. He escaped. In early 1941, he robbed the Credit Lyonnais bank in Rue Notre Dame des Victoires, Paris, killing two bank messengers in cold blood.

Shortly after this he was caught by the Gestapo carrying arms and sent to a military prison; he was then sentenced for the Troyes hold-up in 1937. He escaped by simulating lunacy until he was transferred to the asylum. In 1947, with four associates, he robbed a café in the Rue Lesueur (site of Petiot's crimes), and later executed one of his associates who kept back a brooch. This gave him such a terrible reputation in the underworld that he was not betrayed by professional informers in the usual way, and stayed at liberty a great deal longer than he might otherwise have done.

Over the next few years he took part in many hold-ups, always using sten-guns and Citröen 'tractions'. After the war, Paris had become a great deal more dangerous than Chicago in the Prohibition era, and gang killings were commonplace. (Paris still has a higher murder rate than New York – and the latter city has a murder a day.) Finally, the police were armed with sub-machine-guns, but after accidentally shooting up an old gentleman who was drunk and a bus full of passengers, they were forced by public opinion to be a little more cautious. Finally, a special bandit squad was formed, adequately financed, and run by Charles Chenevier of the Sûreté, who had arrested Buisson in 1937. There was one unsuccessful attempt to arrest Buisson, when a whole convoy of heavily armed police cars rushed out of Paris towards a hotel at Arpajon; but their spectacular exit from Paris excited attention, and someone phoned Buisson, who escaped. However, he was finally arrested in 1955, and tried for the murder of the gangster whom he had 'executed'. He was guillotined in 1956.

His brother, Jean-Baptiste, nicknamed 'Fatalitas' because of his fatalism, shot a restaurant proprietor, Jean Cardeur, when the latter cast aspersions on his dead brother's memory. Maître Carboni, who defended him, turned to the jury as they filed out and said pathetically: 'Do not let me have two heads from the same family on my conscience for the rest of my life'. (He had defended Émile.) The appeal was successful; Jean-Baptiste was found guilty with a recommendation to mercy, and sentenced to a life sentence of hard labour in Melun Prison.

BURDETT, Brian

Twenty-four-year-old poisoner, convicted at the Old Bailey in February 1957 of the murder of his wife Moira, aged 21.

The Burdetts and their child lived at Appleford Road, North Kensington, London. On November 27th, 1956, a few minutes after an early morning shopping expedition (she was seen to leave her flat at 7.25 am) Mrs Burdett collapsed over the breakfast things and died. A post-mortem was performed, and the exact fatal dose of cyanide was found in tea inside the stomach contents; it was also established that the woman had been dead over an hour before her husband summoned help. Burdett, charged with murder, admitted he had stolen cyanide from his work, intending to kill himself; he spoke of marital discord: 'I felt they would be better off without me. I felt I was responsible for my wife's listless and tired condition.' He said how he had found the bottle of cyanide, empty, by the body of his wife; not wishing her to be thought a suicide he had concealed the bottle.

Sir Harry Hylton-Foster, QC, prosecuting, asserted that the poison was taken with the tea, and constituted murder. Mr Ryder Richardson, QC, defending, spoke of suicide: '. . . was it possible she could have thought she was drinking ordinary tea? . . . the cyanide would discolour the tea and give it a peculiar taste.'

Mr Justice Pearson, in his summing up, referred to Burdett's constant lying: the accused was either trying to conceal the fact of murder or the fact of suicide. The jury preferred the former surmise; Brian Burdett was sentenced to death, but eventually reprieved.

BURKE and HARE
One of the most celebrated cases of mass murder in British criminal history; it occurred in Edinburgh in the late 1820's.

William Burke was born about 1792 in County Tyrone, Ireland, son of a farmer. He was in turn baker, cobbler, weaver, and militiaman. After a quarrel with his family he moved to Scotland. Here he joined forces with a prostitute named Helen McDougal and took her on a tramp of southern Scotland. Finally, they settled at the Beggar's Hotel, Edinburgh, where they earned a precarious living patching up old shoes and selling them. Burke was a short, thick-set man with round shoulders; he is sometimes described as a dancing master.

Nothing is known of William Hare's life before he joined forces with Burke. Hare was long and thin, and physically in every way Burke's opposite.

In 1826, Burke and Hare met and moved to Log's Boarding House in Tanners Close. On the death of Log, Hare joined forces with his 'wife', Maggie Laird.

Their trade of murder started accidentally. A Highlander known as Old Donald died in his room in the house, owing rent. Hare now bethought himself that a medical school would probably be willing to pay for the body, since the dissection of corpses was illegal and they were consequently hard to come by. A lucrative trade of body-snatching flourished in Edinburgh, and newly buried corpses were likely to be on the dissection table within twenty-four hours unless the relatives of the deceased kept careful watch.

So Donald's coffin was filled with tan bark, and his body was sold to an unofficial anatomist, Dr Knox, of 10 Surgeon's Square, for £7 10s. – a profit of £4 over and above the rent Donald owed them.

Burke and Hare decided that selling corpses was an ideal way of making a living; but body-snatching was a more dangerous occupation than cobbling. While they brooded on this, another tenant, Joe the Mumper, fell ill. His fever was a serious inconvenience; it kept away other lodgers. Burke and Hare hastened his death with the aid of a pillow pressed over his face, and obtained another £10 in gold for the corpse.

In February 1828, Burke and Hare and their 'wives' decided that this was a business worth pursuing, and on the 11th of that month, lured Abigail Simpson, a hawker of hearthstone and salt, into their house and plied her with whisky. It may have been that they had not definitely decided on murder, or that this first deliberate murder took some screwing up of courage; however, Abigail lived overnight, and was made drunk again the next day, and dispatched, with Hare suffocating and Burke holding the kicking legs. Dr Knox asked no questions, and paid £10. The next victim was another worn-out strumpet named Mary Haldane. Then, on April 9th, 1828, an attractive little harlot, Mary Paterson, was drinking with Janey Brown, one of her associates, after an overnight arrest. The two women were approached by Burke, who persuaded them to return with him to the house of his brother, Constantine Burke, in Gibbs Close, Canongate. But while Burke was tending the prostrate Mary, Helen McDougal burst in and made a scene, which resulted in Janey leaving the house in fright and leaving her friend behind. Hare now arrived, Helen was pacified, and Mary suffocated. Janey Brown called several times for her friend, but was told she had left. But one of the students at Surgeon's Square recognized the body as that of a lady he had once patronized. However, if Dr Knox suspected the methods by which the 'body-snatchers' obtained their corpses, he said nothing.

The next victim was an unidentified female derelict, and Mr and Mrs Hare dispatched her without the help of Burke. Another of the same type followed, this time with Burke and Hare in collaboration, and an Englishman suffering from jaundice.

Mary Haldane, their second victim, had a half-witted daughter; one day she met Hare and asked where her mother was. Hare offered to take her to join her. And, in fact, the daughter followed her mother to Surgeon's Square.

The next crime was a double murder. Burke had selected an old drunkard as his victim, but on his way back to the boarding house, he was accosted by an Irish beggar woman and her dumb grandson. He strangled the grandmother, and broke the back of the boy over his knee.

This murder was followed by a piece of grim comedy. An aged horse was hired to pull the bodies, in their large herring-box, to Surgeon's Square. In the middle of the Grassmarket, it stopped immovable; neither blows nor threats would drive it on. A porter was found who helped them to get the box to Surgeon's Square on his barrow, and Burke and Hare received £16. In a fury, they slit the throat of the horse.

Mrs Hare apparently mistrusted Helen McDougal, and proposed that they sell her to Dr Knox. Burke took her away to stay with friends at Falkirk. But on their return, the hostility flared up again. Hare had murdered a cinder woman in their absence and refused to share the proceeds. Burke and Helen McDougal now left Log's, and moved to Gibbs Close with a cousin of Helen's named Groggan.

Anne McDougal, Helen's cousin, was invited to Edinburgh to stay with them. She never returned to Falkirk. But Burke took no part in this killing; possibly he liked the girl.

It is not known how many killings followed, since there are no accurate records of the case, and contemporary accounts differ; but Groggan was bribed to leave Edinburgh, and Burke and Helen McDougal carried on the business at Gibbs Close, while Hare and Maggie Laird presumably conducted a rival branch at Log's.

The next victim to be lured to Gibbs Close was an idiot known as Daft Jamie, who was known all over Edinburgh. Apparently he put up a considerable struggle before he succumbed. Dr Knox's suspicions were now a certainty, but he preferred to close his eyes to what was going on, and denied it when his students identified Jamie.

The last murder took place on the night of October 31st, 1828. Burke met a beggar woman, a widow named Docherty, in a grocer's shop, and claimed that his mother's maiden name had been Docherty. He invited her back with him. Later that day she was already very drunk. Finally, the Hares turned up. The widow Docherty was dispatched in the night. For this purpose Burke had to persuade two beggars who were lodging with him to go to Log's for the night. When the beggar couple – named Grey – returned the next day, they found Burke sprinkling whisky around the room, and scattering straw. For some extraordinary reason, the Greys were then left alone in the house, and soon located the corpse of the widow. They rushed off to tell the police, but luckily met Helen McDougal *en route*; Helen saw from their faces that they knew, and fell on her knees. Mrs Hare wandered up, and the Greys were persuaded to go to a public house, where the pleas were continued by both ladies.

In the meantime, David Patterson, Dr Knox's assistant,

arrived with a tea chest to collect the widow; he paid only £5 for the body.

Finally the Greys told their story to the police, and an officer named Ferguson called at Gibbs Close, where the quartet were deep in drink. At first he thought the accusation was nonsense; but Burke said that Mrs Docherty had left at seven that morning and Helen McDougal said seven the previous evening. Ferguson's suspicions were aroused and he searched the premises; he found old clothes and blood.

The trial opened on December 24th, 1828, in the High Court of Justiciary in Edinburgh, before the Lord Justice Clerk and Lords Pitmilly, Meadowbank, and Mackenzie.

Burke had already confessed, and his confession was published by the *Edinburgh Courant*. Hare turned King's evidence and was thus not tried. Burke and Helen McDougal were the only two who were brought to trial. Helen McDougal protested that she knew nothing of the goings on, and the case against her was 'not proven'. Burke was sentenced to death. Dr Knox was not even asked to give evidence.

In the condemned cell Burke ranted about being swindled over the body of the widow Docherty, and charged sixpence to people who wanted to sketch him. He was hanged on January 28th, 1829. The crowd was of record size, and apparently record prices were charged by people who had windows overlooking the scene of execution.

It is not known what happened to Hare. There is a story that he went to the Midlands, and worked in a lime-kiln. When his identity was discovered, his fellow workers blinded him with quicklime. Whether this is true or not, it seems reasonably certain that he died as a blind old beggar in London, and one contemporary writes of seeing him outside the British Museum.

It seems a curious injustice that Hare should have escaped. It is said that when he gave evidence, his delight in his crimes was so evident that people struggled to reach him and attack him.

It is not known what happened to Maggie Laird and Helen McDougal.

A contemporary rhyme ends:

> Burke's the murderer, Hare's the thief,
> And Knox the boy who buys the beef.

BURNS, Alfred

Manchester labourer in his twenties, tried at Liverpool Assizes with Edward Francis Devlin, for the murder of Beatrice Alice Rimmer.

Fifty-four-year-old widow Mrs Rimmer was found dead, battered about the head, in the passage-way of her home in Cranborne Road, Liverpool, on the night of August 20th, 1951; entry had been forced through a kitchen window. The victim's blood grouping was A, and blood of this type was spattered everywhere, on walls, doors, and – pathetically – on the widow's neat straw hat, umbrella, gloves, and a bunch of flowers, all lying nearby. On the evidence of Liverpool underworld characters, Burns and Devlin were arrested in October for this crime, both protesting that at the time of Mrs Rimmer's death they were 'on a job' in Manchester, breaking into the premises of Messrs Sunblinds Limited in Great Jackson Street. It was true that these premises had been robbed of goods worth hundreds of pounds during the week-end of the Rimmer killing. The entire clothing belonging to the two men was tested for blood; some stains were too old to determine the group, some (on Devlin's clothing) was animal blood, and some (on Burns' trousers and a pair of shoes) belonging to Group B. Chief witness for the prosecution was 17-year-old waitress Marie Milne, an associate of both the accused, who spoke of hearing Burns and Devlin discussing a 'job'; this discussion occurred on a train, and although Marie Milne was vague as to details (she had been seated by the train window singing to herself), she had ascertained that the plan involved the robbing of a house in Cranborne Road, Liverpool, and that her own allotted task was to 'stand between the old lady and the door'. Apparently not called upon to fulfil this sinister rôle, she had heard Devlin ask Burns, 'Will the old lady live?', shortly after the murder, although they had previously denied carrying out the Cranborne Road project. Sir Noel Goldie, QC, defending Burns (Miss Rose Heilbron, QC, appeared for Devlin), tried to show that a hole in his client's trousers was the result of contact with the glass-jabbed wall surrounding the factory premises in Manchester, but it was proved that the material had been deliberately snipped out during the scientific tests on the men's clothing to determine (unsuccessfully) the exact nature of a minute stain on that portion of material.

Convicted largely on the evidence of their underworld

associates, they were condemned to death by Mr Justice Finnemore and subsequently hanged.

BURROWS, Albert Edward

Sixty-two-year-old labourer, hanged for the murder of his mistress, Hannah Calladine, and her two children, near Glossop in 1923. Three years after the murder, which occurred in January 1920, Burrows killed and sexually assaulted a 4-year-old boy, flinging his body into the same airshaft of a disused coal mine into which he had earlier flung the bodies of his mistress and her children.

Hannah Calladine was a native of Nantwich, Cheshire, and was 28 years old in 1918. She had an illegitimate daughter who was two and a half in 1918. In October 1918 she gave birth to a son, whose father was Burrows, a married farm labourer of Glossop. Burrows 'married' his mistress, and was subsequently jailed for six months for bigamy. When he left jail, Hannah Calladine applied for a bastardy order against him. Burrows failed to pay and was jailed for twenty-one days. His mistress then left her home in Nantwich and went to live at Burrows' home in Glossop. Mrs Burrows walked out and went to stay with a Mrs Streets, who lived nearby. Mrs Burrows now applied for a maintenance order against him.

Burrows was in arrears with his rent; he had the alternative of paying his mistress seven shillings a week, or paying his wife whatever sum the local justices should decide to award her.

On January 11th, 1920, Burrows took his 'wife' and son out on to the moors and murdered them. The following morning, at six-forty, he left Glossop with Hannah Calladine's daughter, whom he also murdered and flung down the airshaft. He probably strangled his three victims, although the condition of the bodies, when discovered three years later, made it impossible to tell with any certainty.

Burrows told a neighbour that 'Nance' had left, but would not say where she had gone. Later he told the same neighbour that 'Nance' was working in a bacon shop with a relative of his in Stretford.

Burrows had written to Hannah Calladine's sister, asking her to send his mistress' clothes on to him. When these arrived, the Thursday after the murder, he immediately proceeded to sell them. Later he sold her wedding ring too. In all, he received only a few pounds for all the goods. Mrs Burrows obtained an order for £1 a week against him, but returned to live with him on the Friday after the murder.

During the next three years, Burrows wrote five letters, all with the aim of supporting his story that 'Nance' was still alive. These included a photograph of a little boy named Williamson, which Burrows sent to Hannah Calladine's mother with an inscription claiming this was his son Ernest.

On March 4th, 1923, Thomas Wood, a 4-year-old boy, disappeared from his home in Glossop; Burrows volunteered the information that he had been with the child on the moors just before he disappeared. The spot to which he led the police was near a disused mine shaft on the Symmondley Moor, and the police tried to search the shaft with the aid of grappling irons, which finally broke. The police then tried a shaft known as the Dinting Shaft, about 150 yards away from the first one, and found the outraged body of the child. It took a further fortnight to clear the inside of the shaft and uncover the remains of Hannah Calladine and her two children.

Burrows was arrested and sent to Manchester Jail. Here, he begged a fellow prisoner to write him a letter signed Hannah Calladine and saying, 'I am still alive'. This prisoner later gave evidence against him.

The trial took place before Mr Justice Shearman, with Sir Henry Maddocks prosecuting and Mr Winning defending. The defence suggested that Hannah Calladine had committed suicide in a moment of depression; but the result of the trial was a foregone conclusion when Mr Winning decided to call no witnesses for the defence, and Burrows was sentenced to death.

BUTLER, Robert
One of the most remarkable criminals of the nineteenth century, whose name should be remembered with those of Lacenaire and Henry Wainwright as that of a man who might have done better things but for a criminal streak.

Butler's career of crime came to an end somewhat ignominiously on the evening of March 23rd, 1905, in Tooringa, Queensland. He tried to hold up an old gentleman between Tooringa and Toowong; the old man – a Mr William Munday – resisted, and Butler shot him in the stomach. Later in the same evening Mr Munday died in a hospital, but not before he had described Butler. Late the same night, a man corresponding to Butler's description was seen by Constable Hennessy, who challenged him. The man tried to draw a revolver, but the constable was too quick for him and grappled. Butler was arrested and eventually tried and executed for the murder of Mr Munday.

Butler was about 60 in 1905. He was born in Kilkenny, Ireland, but went to Australia when he was 14. He spent sixteen years in Australia, thirteen of them in jail for various crimes, including highway robbery and burglary. (His first period in prison was for vagrancy, which may have embittered him and started him on a career of crime.)

In prison, Butler did a great deal of reading – particularly of the lives of Napoleon and Frederick of Prussia. He also developed a philosophy of crime somewhat similar to De Sade's – 'A man's life is of no more importance than a dog's; Nature respects one no more than the other; a volcanic eruption kills mice and men. . . . The divine command, "Kill, kill, and spare not", was intended not only for Joshua but for all men of all time; it is the example of our rulers, our Fredericks and Napoleons.'

Butler left Australia about 1875 and went to New Zealand, where he decided to start a school; his prospectus included algebra, book-keeping, geography, logic, French, and Latin. Unfortunately he was suspected of theft and moved hastily from Cromwell to Dunedin. There, after two weeks, he was sentenced to four years' hard labour for several burglaries. He was released on February 18th, 1880, with money and a suit of clothes from the Governor of Dunedin Jail. A detective named Bain found him employment as a journalist on the *Dunedin Evening Star*. Butler gave satisfaction in this job. But he tried writing some 'Prison Sketches' for another newspaper and the creative labour was too much for him, and he protested that it made him feel like committing suicide. Bain, tired of playing the good Samaritan, commented acidly that he wished he would. Bain now got Butler a job as a manual labourer, but three hours of it were enough, and Butler walked off the job. This was on March 10th. At about this time, Butler remarked to Inspector Mallard of the Dunedin police how easy it would be to destroy all traces of a crime by fire. On March 13th, the house of a Mr Stamper, a solicitor, was broken into and burnt to the ground. On the morning of the next day, March 14th, 1880, a far more horrifying crime was discovered. A young married couple and their baby had been murdered and an attempt made to set fire to the house.

A neighbour discovered the crime at six-thirty on Sunday morning. He saw smoke coming from a house in Cumberland

Avenue, the home of a couple named Dewar. Inside, he found Dewar and his wife; the husband dead and the wife dying. They had been attacked with a hatchet. The baby had died of suffocation, but the man who had committed the crime had obviously intended it to be burnt to death.

Bain was placed in charge of the case, and almost immediately was told by the chambermaid of the Scotia Hotel that Butler had arrived back in the early hours of Sunday morning in a state of alarm and excitement. He had then left hastily with his luggage.

Butler was arrested the following morning near Dunedin. He told Inspector Mallard that he was guilty of the Stamper burglary (he had some opera glasses, stolen from Stamper's house, on him) but not of the treble murder. Some days later some clothes were found under a bush outside Dunedin and identified as Butler's; they had many small blood splashes on them, but no large stains.

Butler decided to defend himself, and did so competently and convincingly. The least convincing part of his defence was the explanation of the bloodstains, which he claimed came from some scratches on his hands which he had when arrested. His examination of the medical witnesses was expert, and he suc-ceeded in casting doubt on their explanation of the bloodstains – that they came from the blood that sprayed as the hatchet struck. Butler made much of the ferocity of the crime, of the relative poverty of the victims (Dewar was a journeyman butcher), con-cluding that a criminal lunatic had been responsible. He received extremely fair treatment by the prosecution during the trial – the result of being without a counsel (although he was in constant touch with one of the ablest lawyers in New Zealand). Butler was found not guilty after the jury had been out for three hours.

Some years later, a man who claimed to have been a fellow-prisoner of Butler's declared in an article that Butler had known Mrs Dewar, and had entrusted some stolen jewellery to her when he first came to New Zealand; he had murdered her family when she refused to give it up. There are many reasons for doubting this story, however.

For his burning of Mr Stamper's house, Butler received eighteen years' imprisonment. He served sixteen of them, until 1896. His fellow-prisoners found him bitter, destructive, and treacherous. The effect of a lifetime in prison on Robert Butler was similar to its effect on Peter Kürten in Düsseldorf. Butler was 50 when he was released from jail; he had spent thirty-two of those years in prison; a total hardly calculated to turn a man into a good citizen.

Butler went to Australia on his release; but the police shadowed him, and soon arrested him, charging him with the offence of entering Victoria within three years of release from prison; for this he was given a year in jail. He was also charged with highway robbery and burglary. He again defended himself so ably that he was found not guilty of the charge of highway robbery. But the judge sentenced him to fifteen years in prison for the burglary – a brutal sentence, since Butler had stolen only a few worthless articles. It was later reduced to ten years. Later, Butler admitted that he had actually committed the highway robbery of which he was found not guilty.

Although Butler was a habitual criminal, it is impossible not to feel some sympathy for him. On leaving jail in 1904, he made another attempt to earn a living by his pen in Melbourne. He then set out as a tramp, tired – he was 60 years old – bewildered, penniless, and often sick. So came the murder of Mr Munday in March 1905, and his death sentence. Before his execution, he wrote a confession of faith that shows him to have been a curiously honest, if otherwise unworthy old man. Declaring that he could not die with the consolations of religion, he wrote:

> In these matters, I have for many years carried an exempt flag. . . . There is an impassable bar of . . . the inexorable logic of philosophy and facts, history and experience . . . between me and . . . any religious organization. So instead of the 'depart Christian soul' of the priest, I only hope for the comfort . . . of the last friendly goodbye of anyone who cares to give it.

BYRNE, Patrick

The Birmingham YWCA hostel murder was one of the criminal sensations of late 1959. The manhunt that followed is a matter of great credit to the British police, and deserves to be compared with the mass finger-printing in the Griffiths case. It is, of course, true that when the police finally interviewed Byrne, they had no more reason to suspect him of the murder than the thousands of other suspects who had been interviewed, and that if Byrne had seriously wanted to evade justice, he could have done so with ease.

Byrne was a 28-year-old labourer who, according to his own admission, had been indulging in sadistic sexual fantasies since he was 17. These included cutting a woman in half with a circular saw. Dr Percy M. Coates of Birmingham Prison said that Byrne was below average intelligence and that his sexual development was immature.

On December 23rd, 1959, Burne was working as a labourer on a building site in Hagley Road, Birmingham (Edgbaston). In the lunch hour he went to the Ivy Bush public house and returned to work drunk. The foreman told him to return to the yard. Towards six in the evening he saw a girl enter the hostel; he followed her, hoping to peep at girls undressing – a thing he had done before. He could see only one light in the hostel, on the ground floor in the Queen's Wing; he peered through the window and saw a girl – Stephanie Baird – in her underskirt, wearing a red pullover. He found an unlocked window and climbed into the corridor, then went and looked through the skylight of Stephanie Baird's room, standing on a chair. The girl did not take any more clothes off, and as he was about to go away, she came to the door. She asked Byrne what he wanted and he told her he was looking for someone; she offered to go and get the warden, and Byrne tried to kiss her. She screamed, and Byrne put his hands round her throat and pushed her back into the room, strangling her as he lay on her. When she was unconscious, he undressed her, removed his own clothes, and raped her. He then cut off her head with a table knife, breaking the blade off as he did so, and then committed further acts of assault on the body. He scrawled a note: 'This was what I thought would never happen', and left it near the body, then dressed and went out. The sight of another lighted window excited him, and he decided he ought to terrorize all the women 'to get my own back on them for causing my nervous tension through sex'. He saw a girl who was not pretty and decided that she would not be a suitable victim; he wanted to kill beautiful women. He picked up a stone from the garden and wrapped round it a brassière from the clothes-line, and went to the wash-house in the main block, where he saw another girl washing; he pushed open the door to attract her attention, but she ignored it. He then switched off the light, and struck the girl with the stone. As she screamed, he ran out of the YWCA and went back to his lodgings.

The police were summoned by the girl who had been struck, and the body was found in the Queen's Wing. In the meantime, Byrne had returned to his lodgings and wrote a note to his land-lady and 'the boys' living in the house, in which he said that

'Like Jock', he had two personalities, and that one was bad and the other was the 'real him'. But he did not send the note; instead he went out for a drink with a cousin and then spent the night with him, being afraid to be alone. Although he tore up the note, he still contemplated suicide like the 'Jock' he mentioned. Early the next day he went to his mother's home in Warrington, Lancashire. The police hunt went on for many weeks. By a curious coincidence, a drunken young man, covered with blood, had been seen near the hostel at about seven on the evening of the murder, and had travelled into the centre of Birmingham on a bus without anyone asking him where the blood had come from! The police appealed for this man to come forward and for any other passengers on the bus to help, but no one volunteered information. It was pointed out that a film called *Jack the Ripper* had recently been shown in Birmingham, and that Donald McCormick's book on Jack the Ripper had also been published. The police interviewed certain people who had borrowed the book from public libraries.

Finally, in the course of routine investigation into everyone who had lived in Birmingham at the time of the murder and subsequently left, Byrne was interviewed. He almost immediately confessed his guilt, saying that the thought of the murder had tormented him for the past two months. (This was on February 7th, seven weeks after the murder.) The police soon established that he was the man who had written the note. He was even able to point out to them a fingerprint which he had left on a ledge above the window, and which they had missed!

He was tried at Birmingham Assizes before Mr Justice Stable; Mr John Hobson, QC, prosecuted and Mr R. K. Brown defended. There was a great deal of question about his sanity, but the three doctors who had examined him agreed that, while sexually abnormal, he was not insane. Byrne claimed that while he committed the murder, he was under the delusion that he was being watched by the police and public. Dr Tetlow declared that in his opinion, this was the result of abnormal sexual excitement, not insanity. Byrne was found guilty of murder and sentenced to life imprisonment; however, he appealed, and the verdict was altered to one of manslaughter. This changed verdict made no difference to the sentence.

BYRON, Lord

The great-uncle of the poet was tried for murder, but claimed 'benefit of clergy' and escaped. Byron got into an argument with a friend, Mr Chaworth, in the Star and Garter Tavern in Pall Mall. The argument was about the amount of game on their estates. This was in January 1765. The argument was dropped and the rest of the company assumed it was forgotten. But, as everyone was leaving later in the evening, the two men met on the stairs and continued the argument, and Byron invited Chaworth into a small room lit by a candle. As Chaworth started to close the door, Byron drew his sword and ordered Chaworth to defend himself. Chaworth did so, and a few moments later was run through, the sword coming out on the other side of him.

Byron was tried in the House of Lords; his account of the crime laid half the blame on Chaworth's doorstep, but witnesses disagreed. The trial took place on April 16th and 17th. He was convicted of manslaughter; but when the Lord High Steward asked if he had any reason to give why the sentence for manslaughter should not be passed, he claimed benefit of clergy, and so escaped scot-free.

It is worth commenting that the poet Byron fell in love with the great-niece of Mr Chaworth, Mary Chaworth; she preferred to marry another man.

C

CAILLAUX Affaire, The

Henriette Caillaux, 36-year-old second wife of the French Finance Minister, M. Joseph Caillaux, swept into the headquarters of the Paris newspaper *Le Figaro* on Friday, March 13th, 1914, where she shot dead its chief columnist, Gaston Calmette. For two months, 138 articles and cartoons deriding Caillaux had appeared in *Le Figaro*; but when Calmette published a letter Caillaux had written, in 1901, to his first wife ('I have crushed the Income Tax Bill while appearing to defend it, thereby pleasing the Centre and Right without too much upsetting the Left...') the Finance Minister and his wife were frantic, knowing that the first Madame Caillaux also possessed copies of their own pre-marital correspondence. In 1909, during a separation from his mistress (who became, in 1911, the second

Madame Caillaux) the Finance Minister had written her letters – on paper headed Chambre des Députés – which were both politically and amorously indiscreet. Realizing their inflammatory nature, M. Caillaux had asked Henriette to return the letters and his first wife had discovered them. Now, Henriette Caillaux, distraught, sought the advice of a judge, President Monier, who told her that in France there was no law to protect individuals against newspaper libels. She left a note for her husband ('I will see that justice is done. . . . France and the Republic have need of you . . . I will carry out the task. . . .') and called at a gunsmith's, where she tested weapons in the firm's shooting gallery before making a purchase. Soon afterwards she fired four bullets at Calmette in his office and he died in hospital that night.

M. Caillaux handed in his resignation, an English newspaper stated that the wife of a British Cabinet Minister would never behave in such a way, and Le Figaro printed a list of people who deplored the killing – including Saint-Saëns and Sarah Bernhardt.

Henriette Caillaux was tried the following July: she pleaded great provocation and said the gun had gone off accidentally – 'the bullets seemed to follow one another automatically'. The jury found her not guilty of murder, or premeditation to murder. Caillaux resumed his political life, although after the First World War he was imprisoned by Clemenceau for 'correspondence with the enemy'. Henriette Caillaux died in 1943.

CAMB, James
Thirty-one-year-old deck-steward on board a Union Castle liner, convicted of the murder on the high seas, of 21-year-old actress Eileen Isabella Ronnie Gibson (stage name Gay Gibson) whose body was never found.

Gay Gibson, who during the war had served with the Women's Auxiliary Territorial Service, had been appearing in a Johannesburg stage production of *Golden Boy* (a play about boxing by Clifford Odets, in which one of her co-players was ex-welterweight boxing champion, Eric Boon) and embarked from Cape Town on the liner *Durban Castle* for England on October 10th, 1947. On the morning of October 18th (when the liner was 147 miles off the West Coast of Africa), Gay Gibson was found to be missing; assuming that she might have accidentally fallen overboard Captain Arthur Patey ordered the ship to turn about in the vain hope that the girl could be rescued alive from the shark-infested waters. A watchman, Frederick Steer, gave information that the bell-pushes in Gay Gibson's Cabin 126 (summoning both steward and stewardess) had been pressed for several seconds that morning at 2.58 am and upon responding to this call he had been intercepted by a man, whom he recognized as Camb, standing in the doorway of cabin 126, who had muttered 'All right'. Communicating with officials of the Union Castle Line in London, Captain Patey received the radio message: 'Padlock and seal the cabin – disturb nothing – CID officers will come aboard at Cowes Roads (Southampton).' Meanwhile, Camb denied that he had ever been in Gay Gibson's cabin; it was noticed, however, that he now wore a jacket with long sleeves when working (as opposed to a singlet, the usual wear in tropical climes) and it transpired that he had a number of long scratches down the right wrist – 'a heat rash', said Camb.

Interviewed by detectives at Cowes Roads, James Camb (who had a reputation as a nautical Lothario) now admitted going to the missing girl's cabin at 11 pm, but only to ask if she wanted a lemonade. Police Sergeant Quinlan, acting as Inspector, told Camb that he had been seen inside Cabin 126 in the early hours of October 18th, and hinted that if he had any reasonable explanation of the girl's fate, this was the opportune moment to divulge it. Camb (somewhat eagerly, one senses) replied: 'You mean that Miss Gibson might have died from a cause other than being murdered, she might have had a heart attack or something?' Camb then made a statement in which he said that Gay Gibson had invited him to her cabin on the night of October 17th; while in the act of sexual intercourse she had suddenly thrown a fit, had foamed at the mouth, and died: '. . . I tried artificial respiration on her. While doing this, the night-watchman knocked at the door and attempted to open it. I shut the door . . . I panicked . . . I did not want to be found in such a compromising position . . . I could not find any sign of life. . . . After a struggle with the limp body [by the way, she was still wearing her dressing-gown] I managed to lift her to the porthole and push her through . . . I cannot offer any explanation as to how the bells came to be rung as I most definitely did not touch them myself.'

Charged with the murder of Miss Gibson, Camb's trial began at Winchester Assizes on March 20th, 1948, before Mr Justice Hilbery; leading counsel for the Crown was Mr G. D. Roberts, defence counsel being Mr J. D. Casswell. Camb persisted in his story that he had gone to Cabin 126 at 2 am at the young actress's invitation, and that she had greeted him wearing nothing but her yellow dressing-gown, which, if Camb's statement were true, indicated a ready promiscuity on the girl's part. Suspicion, however, was aroused by the fact that Gay Gibson's black pyjamas were also missing, which would certainly imply a curious lack of abandonment, if not, indeed, a downright reluctance during the sexual act, and which cast doubt on the whole of James Camb's story, particularly when the urgent ringing of the night-bells was considered. Pathologist Dr Teare, called by the Crown, gave evidence that blood, saliva, and urine stains on the bed-sheets were indicative of strangulation, although defence pathologists Dr Hocking and Professor Webster claimed that these stains were equally indicative of a fit. Dr Griffiths, the ship's surgeon, spoke of examining Camb's arm scratches on October 19th, and said they were consistent with intentional fingernail-scratching – the efforts of a woman trying to defend herself, rather than caused by the berserk graspings of a person in a convulsion. Camb could give no satisfactory reason why he had not brought medical assistance to the wretched girl; moreover why, if his story of accidental death was true, had he disposed so hurriedly of the only evidence which could have substantiated that story. It is now thought that Camb reasoned under the false supposition that a murder prosecution was impossible without the corpse.

Found guilty on March 23rd, Camb escaped capital punishment because the 'no-hanging' clause was then under discussion in Parliament as part of the Criminal Justice Bill (it was to be thrown out later by the House of Lords), and he was eventually released from prison in September 1959.

CAMPBELL, Henry Colin (alias Ross)
Sixty-year-old self-styled doctor, executed in 1931 at New Jersey State Prison, Trenton, for the murder of 50-year-old widow, Mildred Mowry.

Campbell (already married, and living spasmodically with his legal wife at 471 Madison Avenue, Elizabeth, New Jersey) met wealthy Mrs Mowry through a Detroit matrimonial agency, going through a form of marriage with her, and persuading her to deposit several thousands of dollars into a joint bank account. Uneasy at her supposed husband's continual absences, and the

148

unsatisfactory predominance of correspondence in their marriage, Mrs Mowry Campbell traced the elusive doctor by haunting the vicinity of the address he had given – Room 404, Mirel Secretarial Service, inside a building on West 42nd Street, New York. Campbell drove her to a rural spot near Cranford, New Jersey, shot her through the crown of the head, and, after pouring petrol over the body, set it alight, intending to destroy all evidence of identification.

On finding the charred corpse the Public Prosecutor enlisted the help of the Pinkerton National Detective Agency. The approximate age of the victim being determined, William A. Wagner of Pinkerton's studied the bone structure and concluded the woman had been of Polish extraction; there were many Polish settlements in Pennsylvania, and the chief of police in Greenville, Pennsylvania, wired Wagner suggesting the probable identity of the woman. Two of Mrs Mowry's friends, Mrs Straub and Mrs Dodds, had called on him, worried about her disappearance; almost a year before, Mildred Mowry told them of her marriage to a surgeon, Dr Richard M. Campbell (who had been obliged to desert his bride shortly after the nuptials in order to perform 'special operations' in California), but now the two ladies were agitated since they had not heard from Mildred for two months. The shoes of the murder victim had not been wholly destroyed by the fire, and each had contained a metal arch support. The two women confirmed that Mrs Mowry had worn such shoes, and, in viewing other salvage, a pair of distinctive rhinestone ear-rings, remembered that their fellow-matron had worn such a pair. Mildred Mowry's Greenville apartment was searched, and letters from the often-absent 'Dick' found, some giving the Mirel Service accommodation address, but the agency, although recalling the uncommunicative Dr Campbell, knew nothing of his present whereabouts. The Pinkerton detective went to Elkton, Maryland, where the Mowry–Campbell marriage was believed to have taken place. In the marriage records the doctor's address was given as 3707 Yosemite Street, Baltimore, which was a stretch of waste ground. The tenants of 3505, however, disclosed that their landlord's name was Henry Colin Campbell, and so, the murderer (and the bewildered, lawful Mrs Campbell) was located, very soon signing a confession to the murder, for gain, of Mildred Mowry. Yet another victim had been middle-aged Margaret Brown who had gambled for happiness through a matrimonial agency a year before, so meeting a prepossessing Dr Ross and suffering a death identical with that of Mrs Mowry.

CAPONE, Al

Most notorious of America's vice- and murder-gang leaders. Of Neapolitan parentage, born in 1899, Capone lived a life of lawlessness from infancy; theft, gang fights, suspected murder, young Capone was familiar with most facets of New York street-corner crime by the time he was summoned to Chicago in his 21st year by the city's vice-king (see TORRIO, Johnny) to act as that uneasy monarch's bodyguard. Stockily built, squat-nosed, and thick-lipped, Capone had a scar (the result of a knifing brawl) across his left cheek, which gave him the nickname 'Scarface', the epithet by which he was to become world-famous.

Capone's zest for work earned him from an appreciative employer the job of supervising activities at the Torrio Syndicate's headquarters on South Wabash Avenue, the Four Deuces Café, an ambitious establishment which sought to cater for all the physical needs of its customers, with gambling (on the second and third floors) thrown in. Further promotion followed in 1923, when Capone was put in charge of the Syndicate's affairs at the neighbouring town of Cicero, an elevated position for a 24-year-old when the Torrio organization controlled virtually all civic authority in the Chicago province, not excepting the police, who, like the politicians, willingly disregarded all iniquity sponsored by racketeers providing they themselves could share a percentage of the not inconsiderable profits. In 1927, two years after Capone had taken over the entire Syndicate (Torrio fled to Italy after an attempt on his life by a rival vice organization), the profits soared to 105 million dollars; the Syndicate this year demonstrated its political consciousness by belligerently patrolling Chicago polling booths to ensure the election as mayor of Republican 'Big Bill' Thompson, long suspected of an active benevolence towards Syndicate affairs – a previous mayor, Joseph Z. Klenha, unfavoured by the mobsters, had on one occasion been pushed down the Town Hall steps by Capone, who was never indicted for this assault. Capone eventually set up his office at the Lexington Hotel in Chicago, where a gigantic portrait of George Washington – Capone's hero – graced the wall; the estimated private earnings of the Neapolitan were over 30 million dollars a year. Many of the Syndicate's would-be rivals and rebels were murdered, usually by machine-gun fire, including Hymie Weiss, part-inheritor of Chicago's North Side bootlegging gang (see O'BANION, Dion), after whose violent demise Capone ruefully remarked: 'Forty times I've tried to arrange things so we'd have peace and life would be worth living, but Hymie couldn't be told anything.' On St Valentine's Day, February 14th, 1929, came one of the worst mass gang-executions, when five members of the rival North Side organization were slain in a red brick-walled garage on Clark Street, where they had gone one morning to collect instructions concerning a consignment of whisky; the killers (who were never caught), disguised as policemen, had followed the North Side mobsters (plus two unfortunate 'hangers-on', a doctor and a newspaper reporter) and, after swiftly lining them up against the garage wall, apparently in the name of the law, had slaughtered them with machine-guns. The real target is believed to have been 'Bugs' Moran, who had taken over the North Side organization after the killing of Weiss, and who, incidentally, was one of the few racketeers of the 20's ever to survive the gangland massacres, dying in a more orthodox fashion in 1957. The real culprit is believed by some to have been Al Capone, who at the time of the actual murders was staying on his Florida estate, but who was known to suspect and resent Moran's complicity in the shooting of Pasqualino Lolardo and Anthony Lombardo, who had been presidents of the Unione Siciliana (Mafia), an organization devoted to the welfare of Sicilians in the United States, which, because of the turbulent natures of most immigrants, could be now described as a sort of criminal brotherhood or trade union rather than a harmless freemasonry. Another story is that the killers, supposedly John Scalisi, Albert Anselmi, and Joseph Guinta, although members of the Capone gang, had acted without their chief's foreknowledge and incurred his wrath. Years later an eyewitness spoke of how, at a Unione Siciliana banquet soon after the garage killing, the doomed trio suddenly realized that the amiable chat over food and wine was but part of a Mafia ritual murder, and they the prospective victims; Capone is said to have suddenly substituted a savage snarl for his amiable host's beam, and brained all three with a baseball bat. In all, 227 would-be rivals and challengers to the Capone administration were murdered in the 1920's; Capone's dictum, 'I want peace and I will live and let live', was true only up to a point. After the St Valentine's Day massacre, warned that he was now certain of extinction from vengeance-bound North Siders, Capone contrived to get himself arrested in Philadelphia on a charge of illegally possessing firearms, thus ensuring for himself a safe berth for a year in jail, where he spent the time ruminating on the misfortunes of being a racket leader ('you fear death every moment . . . and the rats of the game who would run around and tell the police if you don't constantly satisfy them with money and favours'), reading copies of *Country Life*, and supervising his 'vice-empire' over the Warden's phone. Eventually, soon after a delegation of long-horrified Chicago citizens had approached President Hoover about corruption in their city, Al Capone was indicted once again – this time for income-tax evasion during the years 1924–29 – and sentenced to eleven year's imprisonment, which he served at Atlanta's Federal Jail and later at Alcatraz. With a sentence deduction he was released in 1939, all his former power gone, and a sick man; an old case of syphilis had affected his brain, but he lived in comparative obscurity and peace until 1947.

CARROLL, Francis M.

A curious case of double murder which, it seems, may have involved a miscarriage of justice.

On October 16th, 1937, two policemen noticed a youth asleep in a car in North Arlington, N.J., and took him to the police station to check whether the car was stolen. The youth was 19-year-old Paul Nathaniel Dwyer, and the car was found to have two bodies concealed in it, a man and a woman, both battered and strangled. They were identified as Mrs Lydia Littlefield and her husband, James Littlefield, who was a doctor. Dwyer confessed to both murders. He claimed that he suspected he had contracted veneral disease from a waitress in his home town of South Paris, Maine, and had consulted the doctor. Dr Littlefield had upbraided him for immorality; a quarrel had started, and he had finally killed Dr Littlefield with a hammer. He had put his body in the boot of the car, and told the doctor's wife that her husband had killed two men in a road accident, and wanted to meet her secretly in Concord, New Hampshire. The next day, as they waited in the car near New Gloucester, she became suspicious and accused him of killing her husband; he then strangled and battered her, and then began a wild drive southward, that ended when the police arrested him.

He was tried on November 15th, 1937, and sentenced to life imprisonment.

But when he was in prison at Thomaston, a deputy, Sidney Verrill, began to ponder the case, and certain strange features. Dwyer was a puny youth who weighed less than eight stones; how had he carried the heavy body of the doctor to the car? A cigarette-lighter had been found on the driveway of Paul Dwyer's home, and the deputy thought he recognized it as one he had bought for Francis M. Carroll, a police officer. Dwyer had made some comment about Carroll when arrested. And Carroll had been drinking heavily since the murder trial.

Carroll's movements on the murder night were checked. For a year past he had not missed a meeting of the American Legion; but on the murder night he had not been present. An interview with Dwyer in jail produced a seventh confession which involved Carroll and revealed him as the real murderer.

Dwyer had seduced Carroll's 17-year-old daughter Barbara, and Barbara had one day confided in him that her father had been the first to seduce her, and that she hated him for it. She wrote Dwyer certain letters alluding to this. One night when he was drunk, Dwyer met Carroll and made a reference to the seduction, and said that if Carroll seduced his other daughter, he would see that the letters from Barbara got to Carroll's wife. Carroll wrote to Dwyer ordering him to destroy the letters. Then, a few days later, someone fired at Dwyer in the dark, and a car drove off. Dwyer accused Carroll of trying to murder him, and Carroll told him that Barbara was pregnant and that Dwyer was responsible. Dwyer thought this impossible, and invited Carroll to bring Barbara to the house where he lived with his widowed mother to discuss the matter. Dwyer arranged that Dr Littlefield should be present, to call Carroll's bluff (or confirm Barbara's pregnancy). Carroll, however, came alone; it was October 13th, the night of the murder. The doctor apparently made some threatening statement about incest, and Dwyer went outside to see if Barbara was really in the car; while he was out, Carroll attacked the doctor, and ended by knocking him unconscious with a hammer, and then killing him with a gun-butt. Carroll now made Dwyer hand over the letters, and made him help in carrying the body to the boot of the car. He ordered Dwyer to get rid of the body. Dwyer drove to the doctor's home and told Mrs Littlefield that her husband had killed two men in a road accident and wanted to meet her at Concord. However, as they drove there, he told her the truth, omitting, however, to mention that the doctor's body was in the boot. Mrs Littlefield told him to drive back to Carroll's house, which he did. There he called to Carroll that Mrs Littlefield wanted to speak to him; Carroll burst out and clubbed the woman with the same gun that had killed the doctor, and then ordered Dwyer to drive off and get rid of the bodies. Dwyer found money on the two corpses, and drove around for three days until his arrest.

This was Dwyer's confession. Carroll was arrested on June 24th, 1938, and brought up before the Oxford County Superior Court, South Paris, on August 1st, with Justice William H. Fisher presiding. Ralph M. Ingalls, the State Attorney, prosecuted, and Clyde R. Chapman defended. The prosecution had a strong case, and many witnesses testified to seeing Carroll's car parked outside Dwyer's home on the night of the murder, as well as Dr Littlefield's. Barbara Carroll talked and laughed with her father throughout the trial, but was not called into the witness-box. Finally, Carroll was found guilty of murder in the first degree and sentenced to life imprisonment.

He was finally released from prison on September 20th, 1950, on a writ of habeas corpus based on the contention he did not receive a fair trial. He returned to South Paris, where he worked as a carpenter until his death on October 3rd, 1956. His wife had divorced him and taken his two daughters away.

But Dwyer, who, by implication of the verdict, was guilty only of being an accessory, was kept in prison. His applications for a pardon were refused. He was still in jail at the time of Carroll's death. Carroll had been 62 when he died, but Dwyer has spent the greater part of his life – from the age of 19 – in prison for a crime he apparently did not commit. His motive in concealing Carroll's guilt at his trial may have been a misguided chivalry towards Barbara Carroll (he agreed to make his first confession only on condition that the name of a girl was kept out of it – the girl about whom he and Dr Littlefield had quarrelled). The vagaries of American law appear to be incomprehensible.

CARTER, George
Twenty-nine-year-old labourer, ex-RAF, murdered his pregnant 33-year-old wife, Ruby May, at their home, Pear Tree Cottage, Penllyn, Cowbridge, Glamorganshire.

At lunch-time on Saturday, January 2nd, 1960, Carter returned home from work; his wife was dead in bed upstairs, her skull fractured from three heavy blows, and his 6-year-old son Alun, barely alive, lay nearby, similarly injured. A bureau in the cottage was smashed in – a trademark, presumably, of the murderous intruder. Carter sought medical assistance for his son, whose brain was to be permanently affected by the attack. Carter said he had had some presentiment of the tragedy when, leaving work at the Asbestos Works, Rhoose, at 12.15 pm he drove, as usual, round to his wife's place of employment, Cowbridge High School for Girls, where he had sounded the car's hooter without success; he claimed that £25 was missing from the house. During the immediate investigations into what was obviously a murder case Carter displayed a perhaps understandable reluctance to view the body of his wife – 'a horrifying, terrible sight', said one doctor. Ruby Carter had been dead about six hours, therefore the intruder had struck near the time Carter left for work at 5.15 am. Fingerprints other than those made by the Carter family were not found in the cottage; police, however, on January 3rd, discovered a 6-lb circular metal object in a field half a mile from the house, about which it was established that (a) it was the weapon employed in the attack on Ruby Carter and (b) it came from the factory where George Carter worked. Meanwhile the bereaved husband appeared on television asking for the public's assistance in finding his wife's killer. On January 16th George Carter was charged with the murder of his wife, replying, 'I did not do it. . . .'

He stood trial at Glamorgan Assizes, Cardiff, on March 21st, before Mr Justice Barry; prosecuting counsel was Mr W. L. Mars-Jones, QC, defence counsel Mr Norman Richards, QC. Carter's jacket was produced, upon the right-hand sleeve of which were twenty-three minute spots of blood, invisible except in strong sunlight. Evidence was given by Carter's workmates that on the morning of January 2nd the accused had produced a bundle of banknotes (although the police were to find only 3s. 6d. in his possession later that day), the prosecution's inference being that Carter had secreted this money in order to support the homicidal burglar theory. Workmate Paul Galton testified that Carter had asked him if he knew how to end a pregnancy, as he and his wife could not afford another child: '. . . so I told him to see a druggist.' Carter, examined, admitted that he was fairly heavily in debt, but continued to reiterate the intruder theory:

Mars-Jones: This is becoming a fantastic story.

Carter: No, sir.

Although the evidence against Carter was circumstantial, the jury took only thirty-five minutes to find him guilty of wife-murder, and he was sentenced to life imprisonment. Motive for the killing here is uncertain, although it was suggested that his hire-purchase commitments had produced in the debt-ridden labourer (who was known to take an inordinate pride in his new car) a murderous resentment against his family and a compulsive desire to be rid of his financial obligations towards them.

CASTAING, Dr Edmé

Twenty-seven-year-old French doctor, the first (known) murderer to use morphine. In 1823 Castaing entered into a contract with one, Auguste Ballet, whose wealthy elder brother Hippolyte was too-slowly dying from tuberculosis. Auguste knew that his brother had made a will excluding himself, so he persuaded Castaing to gain possession of this will before destroying both it and Hippolyte, so that he, Auguste, would speedily and automatically gain the family fortune. The doctor complied, then persuaded the strangely trustful Auguste to draw up a will of his own, leaving the fortune to Edmé Castaing. Some time later the couple drove out to a tavern, the Blackamoor's Head at St Cloud, where Castaing liberally sugared some mulled wine for Auguste Ballet, who was soon taken violently ill. In his agony he asked Castaing to fetch another doctor: Pigache, the local physician, promptly sent for Dr Pellatan, a professor at the Paris School of Medicine. Pigache and Pellatan both noticed the 'pinpoint' condition of Auguste's eyes, now one of the recognized symptoms of morphine poisoning. Auguste expired, and Dr Pellatan, being told by Castaing of the will's contents, naturally advised an autopsy as a safeguard against the inevitable gossip. Castaing, gambling on the fact that little was known of the drug morphine, agreed to this step, and eventually the bodies of both brothers Ballet were examined. Unmistakable signs of morphine poisoning were discovered in Auguste's body; there was disagreement as to whether Hippolyte had died from an overdose of morphine, although the majority of doctors suspected this form of poisoning. (In 1823 between 10 and 100 grains were palpable proof of foul play, whereas nowadays 1/5,000th of a grain can be located by post-mortem.)

Castaing, acquitted of the murder of Hippolyte Ballet, was convicted of the younger brother's death and guillotined.

CAWLEY, Brian (Shortest Murder Trial)

The trial of Brian Cawley at Winchester Assizes on December 14th, 1959, for the murder of Rupert Steed was the shortest murder trial on record. Cawley, 30-year-old unemployed wireless technician killed 67-year-old Steed, a retired bachelor who had befriended Cawley, his wife, and their three children. Steed bought a house in New Road, Basingstoke, where the Cawleys lived rent free; a lonely man, he found pleasure in being the benefactor of this young family, lavishing gifts upon them. But Cawley took to drink, and his wife left him, taking the children. Cawley, returning home one night, unaccountably battered Steed to death. At his trial he pleaded guilty and was sentenced to life imprisonment, the whole procedure lasting only thirty seconds.

CHANTRELLE, Eugène-Marie

Convicted in 1878 of the murder of his wife, Elizabeth. The couple had met in 1867, when she was fourteen and a pupil at the Edinburgh Academy, where Chantrelle taught French; by 1868 Elizabeth Callen Dyer was pregnant, and prevailed upon by her Presbyterian parents to marry the licentious instructor, although Elizabeth herself had become disenchanted. The day after her marriage she wrote in a letter: 'I know I shall not be happy. He is not a kind man, and I can't trust him.' Her prediction proved correct; Eugène-Marie Chantrelle was brutal, a dipsomaniac, and, eventually, jobless. By 1877 she had four children and a life-insurance for one thousand pounds, taken out by her husband and costing thirty shillings; uneasy, she wrote her mother: 'Come and see me at once if you want to see me alive. E. has a revolver.' Eugène had a revolver, unaccountably a toy one: Mrs Dyer, hurriedly summoned, retired abashed. At the end of December, Elizabeth Chantrelle had developed an insurance-neurosis: '. . . is it foolish to wonder why my life has been insured against accidents? I seldom go out . . . I'm almost always at home. Why should my life be insured?' On January 1st, 1878, she became fatally ill, dying in Edinburgh Royal Infirmary after much diarrhoea and vomiting; Chantrelle blamed a leaking gas-pipe, but no trace of carbon monoxide poisoning was found in the body. Organically the woman was healthy, but Dr Littlejohn, Medical Officer of Health to the City of Edinburgh, analysed the vomit on the woman's bedlinen, finding the presence of opium. Chantrelle, charged with wife-murder, was tried the following April in Edinburgh before the Lord Justice Clerk, Lord Moncrieff (see SMITH, Madeleine). The maid, Mary Byrne, stated how the dying woman had murmured about lemonade brewed by Chantrelle, and how, after his wife's death, Chantrelle had persisted in his allegations of leaking gas.

The jury found Chantrelle guilty; he behaved hysterically

when sentenced to death, admitting the presence of opium on the linen, but claiming it had been administered to his wife by 'an enemy'. Chantrelle was hanged three weeks later.

CHAPIN, Kenneth R.
Eighteen-year-old technical student, active churchworker and Boy Scout, convicted of the murder of 14-year-old Lynn Ann Smith in Springfield, Massachusetts.

During the early evening of September 25th, 1954, 'baby-sitter' Lynn Ann Smith sprawled in a chair inside a ground-floor room at the home of Mr and Mrs Bernard Goldberg; she read *Gone With The Wind* while her charges, 6-year-old Robert and 4-year-old Stephen Goldberg, slept in nearby adjoining bedrooms. At 11.30 pm the Goldbergs returned and found their baby-sitter dead on the living-room floor from thirty-eight stab wounds, and son Stephen dead in his bedroom, bludgeoned about the head and stabbed twenty-four times; the girl had not been sexually assaulted, and was a nervous type who had been instructed by the Goldbergs not to open the door to anyone during their absence. Robert Goldberg was found unharmed in his bedroom; he had remained concealed under the blankets upon hearing inexplicable sounds of violence a few hours earlier. The younger boy's bedroom door was always left open, and it was assumed that Stephen had been slain because the killer feared identification from the awakened, horrified child. A six-inch length of crocheting yarn was found on a rug near the girl's body; it was sent to the American Thread Company, who identified it as one of their own types, dispatched to many shops and stores in Springfield. Police embarked on a house-to-house canvass of Springfield, checking on households having this kind of thread. At No. 63 Daviston Street, only a hundred yards from the Goldberg residence, a ball of yarn was produced identical with the thread found near the baby-sitter's body; here lived the Chapin family, the daughter of which had been Lynn Smith's great friend, the son Kenneth having acted as one of the pall-bearers ('solemn, white-gloved') at the girl's funeral, the only student to sign the mourning register. On October 8th Kenneth Chapin was brought from school to police headquarters; he denied knowledge of the crime, but seemed uneasy, finally admitting guilt when confronted with the crocheting yarn; 'I used it to tie a piece of paper around the handle of the knife.' He had, on the night of Sptember 25th, looked through a window of the Goldberg apartment and noticed the pretty baby-sitter with whom he was friendly: 'I got my knife at home and came back ... I knocked at the window ... she let me in ...' Chapin said he had 'gone beserk' when the girl resisted his advances: '... the boy woke up and began to cry ... I was afraid he saw me, so I killed him too.'

Tried in March 1955, Chapin's counsel contended that the boy was insane; the jury, however, found him guilty of murder in the first degree and he was sentenced to death. Many ineffectual attempts were made by the defence lawyers to quash this sentence, but eventually, twenty-four hours before his execution, Chapin's sentence was commuted to life imprisonment because of the intervention of prominent psychiatrist, Dr Frederic Wertham, who pronounced Chapin a schizophrenic and therefore not responsible for his actions.

CHAPMAN, George (real name, Severin Klosovski)
Polish poisoner, executed in 1903 for the murder of three of his 'wives'.

Chapman is one of those criminals about whom we know too little – H. H. Holmes is another example. We know absolutely nothing of his character, or the state of mind that made him poison three women – although this is no doubt due to the foreign language difficulty. H. L. Adam speaks of 'his *idée fixe*, the pursuit, capture, and destruction of women', but this can be regarded as only one of the possibilities. Another chronicler declares positively that Chapman had decapitated a woman before he left Poland; but there appears to be not a shred of evidence for this statement.

Severin Antoniovitch Klosovski was born on December 14th, 1865, in Nargornak, in the district of Kolo, Poland, son of a carpenter. At the age of 15 he was apprenticed to a surgeon in Zvolen; although he remained there for six years, he failed to obtain a degree as junior surgeon. He travelled around Poland as a *feldscher*, a barber combining the office of 'surgeon' (probably for blood-letting and other simple operations).[1] He married in Poland, and was employed in a hospital in Prague. He also spent eighteen months in the Russian army, then journeyed to England.

This was probably early in 1888. He went to Whitechapel and

[1] This used to be a commonplace in England, and explains the use of red and white poles outside barbers' shops.

took a job as a barber in the High Street. Mr Donald McCormick has it that Klosovski had a barber's shop in the basement of George Yard Buildings at the time when Jack the Ripper murdered Emma Smith there (August 1888).

From Whitechapel he moved to West Green Road, South Tottenham, and even tried setting up in his own business there. He was unsuccessful and had to return to being an assistant.

He 'married' a Polish woman, Lucy Baderski, and was then embarrassed by the arrival of his first Polish wife. For a while, the two women even lived in the same house. Finally, the legal wife left. Klosovski and Lucy Baderski lived together in Cable Street, then Greenfield Street. In 1890, they went to America, and Mrs Klosovski returned alone in 1891, having quarrelled with her husband. Chapman returned in 1892 (although a document later found in his possession gives the date as 1893). His wife returned to him, but apparently Chapman had become a confirmed philanderer, and she left him again. For a while, he lived with a girl named Annie Chapman (curiously enough, the name of the Ripper's third victim). After a year, she also left him. Lucy Baderski retained custody of two children.

Klosovski now decided to call himself George Chapman, and thereafter kept his Polish name a secret.

In 1895, while working in Leytonstone, Chapman met his first victim, Mary Spinks. She was a married woman whose husband left her because she drank too much. Chapman and she lived openly together, claiming to be married. She had private means, which may have been an additional attraction to Chapman. In 1897, the 'Chapmans' moved to Hastings, where Chapman used some of her money to set himself up in a hairdresser's shop. He even improved business by installing a piano in the shop, which his 'wife' played while he worked; the 'musical shaves' became very popular. Chapman purchased a sailing boat which, on one occasion, capsized; the Chapmans were rescued by fishermen. (H. L. Adam seems to regard this as Chapman's first attempt to murder Mrs Spinks.)

After six months, the shop at Hastings was sold and they moved back to London, taking the lease of the Prince of Wales Tavern in Bartholomew Square, off City Road. There, Mrs Spinks became ill, suffering from severe vomiting attacks. A doctor was called in, but Chapman continued to nurse the patient, who finally died on Christmas Day, 1897. (On April 2nd of the same year, Chapman had bought tartar emetic from a chemist in Hastings.) Mrs Spinks' death was attributed to consumption.

Mrs Spinks was buried in a common grave at Leyton. A few months later, Chapman advertised for a barmaid, and finally accepted a farmer's daughter and domestic servant named Bessie Taylor. Some time during the following year, he 'married' her. And after her marriage, Bessie Taylor's health began to fail. For some reason, Chapman gave up the Prince of Wales and took a pub called The Grapes at Bishop's Stortford. Bessie Taylor had to go into hospital for some kind of an operation; when she came out, Chapman treated her harshly, on one occasion threatening her with a revolver.

Soon they moved yet again—this time to the Monument Tavern in Union Street, Borough. Chapman continued to treat his wife very badly, in spite of her failing health; she finally died on February 13th, 1901. This time, the death was attributed to 'exhaustion from vomiting and diarrhoea'.

Chapman's third victim, Maud Marsh, also became a barmaid at the Monument Tavern. She was the daughter of a Croydon labourer, and her mother 'vetted' the premises before she took the job. Soon, Chapman gave her a gold watch and chain. Apparently he had some trouble in persuading the girl to become his mistress, because she wrote to her mother that unless she gave Chapman 'what he wants' he had threatened to pack her off home. She added that since they were engaged, it would not matter if she did. So no doubt Chapman soon had a new sleeping partner. Her parents were extremely anxious about her and did a great deal of interfering, all to no effect, since she eventually told them she had gone through a marriage ceremony with Chapman at some 'Roman Catholic Rooms' (Chapman was RC). But Maud Marsh's parents never ceased to mistrust Chapman, and this mistrust led to his downfall.

In 1902, Maud Marsh began to suffer from the same symptoms as Bessie Taylor. She recovered for a spell in Guy's Hospital, but became worse on returning home. Meanwhile, Chapman had changed addresses yet again, moving this time to the Crown Public House, also in Union Street, the Borough. Although Maud Marsh's mother came to nurse her daughter, the girl became steadily weaker. A glass of brandy and soda that Chapman prepared for his wife was drunk by Mrs Marsh and the nurse, who were both ill with vomiting and diarrhoea. Mrs Marsh thereafter became suspicious. Chapman's own doctor seemed to have no suspicion, so she called in her Croydon doctor, a Dr Grapel. He decided that Maud Marsh was being poisoned with arsenic. Chapman got alarmed at the doctor's visit and finished off his patient with a stronger dose than usual; she died on October 22nd, 1902. Dr Stoker, alerted by a message from Dr Grapel, refused this time to sign a death certificate. He also performed a private (and unauthorized) autopsy, and discovered arsenic in Maud Marsh's body. Chapman was arrested on October 25th, 1902, on the day of the coronation procession of Edward VII. He was charged with the murder of Maud Marsh; a second inquest on her body revealed that the poison which had killed her was antimony, not arsenic.

It is worth mentioning that Chapman, while in custody, provided a gratuitous testimonial to his fellow-murderer Edgar Edwards, remarking 'Edwards is a hot 'un'.[1]

He was tried at the Central Criminal Court on March 16th, 1903, before Mr Justice Grantham.

Sir Edward Carson led for the prosecution, and Mr George Elliot, KC, defended. The defence knew it was fighting a losing battle, and the judge's summing up was almost a continuation of the speech for the prosecution. The trial lasted for four days. The jury was out only for eleven minutes, and found Chapman guilty. He seemed terror-stricken by the sentence, and was hissed. (There was a strong feeling against aliens in England at the time, and Chapman was extremely unpopular throughout his trial.) He was executed on April 7th, 1903.

From the foregoing account, it will be obvious that there is much about Chapman that is unknown. Many writers have suggested that his motive was simply sexual lust, but if so, he went to a great deal of trouble to sleep with three women. On the available evidence, one might just as easily guess that he was motivated by a craving for money and security (hence his frequent changes of business – to try to improve his prospects) and killed his wives when overcome by a neurotic feeling that they were not improving his financial position. There is no final evidence that he was a sadist who had to make women suffer. The murder of Mrs Spink was almost certainly motivated by his increasing dislike of her drinking. He may simply have grown tired of Bessie Taylor. Only the murder of Maud Marsh is wanton and inexplicable enough to justify a suspicion that Chapman was a homicidal maniac.

Chapman is one of the most frequent candidates for the identity of Jack the Ripper. He was actually under suspicion in 1888, the year of the Ripper murders, and Chief Inspector Abberline, who was in charge of the investigation, later remarked on the

[1] See Preface, 'The Study of Murder'.

arrest of Chapman: 'You've caught the Ripper, then?' Facts in favour of Chapman being the Ripper are: his presence in Whitechapel in 1888, his profession as a surgeon, the evidence of Lucy Baderski that, at the time of the murders, he was often out all night, and his physical resemblance to descriptions of the Ripper. The chief fact against it: that a sadistic 'ripper' would content himself with the relatively tame method of poisoning. This is surely the most conclusive objection.

CHARRIER, Mecislas
Poseur and anarchist, bastard son of a Russian philosopher, executed for train robbery in 1922.

On July 23rd, 1922, two officers, Captain Morel and Lieutenant Carabelli, were travelling by the night train from Paris to Lyons. They were awakened by a man who held a gun to Captain Morel's forehead, and told to produce their money. Lieutenant Carabelli leapt from his upper bunk on to the man and got his revolver away from him; at this moment, another bandit appeared in the door of the train and shot the Lieutenant in the head, killing him instantly. The communication cord of the train was pulled, and three men were seen to drop off. Many passengers had been robbed by the three, who wore black, but not particularly well-fitting, masks, for one had dropped off and a passenger had seen the robber's face.

Police found traces of the robbers at various stations, and discovered that they seemed to have doubled back and forth around Nevers, Nolay, and Étang.

The trail was picked up by sheer good fortune some days after the robbery. A man had been heard boasting about it in a bar. The police were able to discover that this man, who was known as something of a character, was 27-year-old Jacques Mecislas Charrier, known as a medical student, who regarded himself as an anarchist. The man to whom he had been boasting was identified as a sculptor who called himself Marcel Bréger, who had been staying with Charrier at the Hotel Excelsior in the Rue Cujas for a time. In his vacated room, an old letter was found addressed to someone named Dujardin. The police had reason to suspect that Dujardin was Charrier's alias, so they consulted the Service des Garnis, the police service that keeps a check on every hotel room occupied, even for a night. They discovered that a Dujardin had taken a room at the St Jacques Hotel on the same day Charrier had left the Hotel Excelsior. It was soon confirmed that Dujardin was Charrier, and he was arrested as he left his hotel. Under examination, he quickly broke down and implicated two other men named Thomas and Bertrand, habitual criminals whom he had met in jail at Grenoble. (Charrier had served four terms for robbery with violence.) Bertrand was Bréger. Charrier told of how he had gone to Marseilles with his two accomplices, and how the three had robbed a wealthy woman who had once been Charrier's mistress. (Charrier, it appeared, was something of a lady's man.) But they had only gained five hundred francs (£25), and soon were running short of money again. On July 23rd they decided to rob the Paris–Lyon express. They boarded the train at the Gare de Lyon. Charrier claimed that his job was only to watch at the entrance to the sleeping-car, and that he did not know of the murder until they were running away from the train. However, he took his share of four thousand francs.

On information from Charrier, the police waited near a café in the Rue des Ternes, and on July 30th, at midnight, saw the wanted men. They attempted to arrest them, but the men pulled out guns. There was a fight in the Avenue Wagram that ended with the two men being killed, and Police Inspector Curlier was seriously wounded; he died later in hospital.

Charrier was tried alone. He was well-dressed, and spent much of his trial posing, declaring, 'I am a desperate enemy of society and my hatred will only finish with my life. I defy you, gentlemen of the jury, to take my head.'

The jury obliged, and he was guillotined on August 22nd, 1922; the bravado had now gone and he died pleading for mercy.

CHEVALLIER, Yvonne

Plain, homely, 40-year-old wife of Dr Pierre Chevallier, French Cabinet member, whom she was, in 1951, accused of murdering. Five heavy-calibre bullets were removed from the corpse (which had been found at the Chevallier residence in Orleans) and it was established that between shooting the fourth and fifth bullets, Madame Chevallier had requested a maid to 'look after' Mathieu, the Chevalliers' 4-year-old son, who was showing a natural curiosity about the firing fracas in papa's room. Such parental solicitude was impressive, but hardly squared with the Gallic notion of a true, impulsive 'crime passionnel', and feeling against Madame Chevallier ran so high in the Orleans area (where the victim had been a popular mayor) that the trial was

transferred to Rheims. Jealousy against Madame Jeanette Perreau, Chevallier's mistress, appeared to be the motive. Monsieur
Perreau, interviewed in court, showed himself a more tolerant
soul than Madame Chevallier when he admitted a liking for his
dead rival: 'I got on with him very well.' But the spectators'
guffaws changed to hisses when attractive Jeanette Perreau
walked to the witness-stand and her defiance when questioned
about her love affair with Chevallier did much to swing public
opinion towards the accused. When the jury finally acquitted
Madame Chevallier there was great rejoicing in the court-room,
but male writers in the national press appeared uneasy at the
verdict: 'Astonishing' said one, while another openly called
Madame Chevallier 'a murderess'. Women writers, however,
were pleased by the jury's decision, apparently regarding it as a
moral victory for their sex.

CHRISTIE, John Reginald Halliday
*Multiple sex murderer and psychopathic personality responsible
for the deaths of at least six women, at 10 Rillington Place, London W.11 (now Rustyn Close), off St Mark's Road.*

On March 24th, 1953, a Jamaican tenant of 10 Rillington Place
was sounding the walls in the kitchen on the ground floor, previously occupied by Christie. One wall sounded hollow and the
Jamaican pulled off a corner of wallpaper. He discovered that the
paper covered a cupboard, one corner of which was missing. He
was able to peer into the cupboard with the help of a torch and saw
the naked back of a woman. Hastily summoned policemen discovered that the cupboard contained three female bodies. The
first was naked except for a brassière and suspender belt; the
other two were wrapped in blankets and secured with electric
wire. There was very little smell, which was due to atmospheric
conditions causing dehydration. (Some of the more sensational
accounts of the case state inaccurately that the tenant was led to
the discovery by the smell of decomposition.) Floorboards in the
front room appeared to have been disturbed, and they were
taken up to reveal a fourth body, also wrapped in a blanket.
    Christie had left on March 20th, sub-letting to a Mr and Mrs
Reilly, who had paid him £7 13s. in advance. The Reillys had
been turned out almost immediately by the owner, a Jamaican,
Charles Brown, since Christie had no right to sub-let, and had,
in fact, left owing rent.
    The back garden was dug up, and revealed human bones – the

skeletons of two more bodies. A human femur was being used to prop up the fence.

It was now remembered that in 1949, two other bodies – those of Mrs Evans and her baby daughter Geraldine – had been discovered at the same address. Both had been strangled, and the husband, Timothy Evans, was hanged for the double murder. Evans was a near-mental defective, and it seemed conceivable that the murders for which he was hanged were the work of the man who had killed the women in the downstairs flat.

On March 31st, Christie was recognized by PC Ledger on the embankment near Putney Bridge and was taken to Putney Bridge Police Station. In the week since the discovery of the bodies, the hue and cry had been extraordinary, and newspapers ran pictures of the back garden of 10 Rillington Place and endless speculations about the murders and whether the murderer would commit another sex crime before his arrest. (Mr Alexie Surkov, the secretary of the Soviet league of writers, happened to be in England at the time, and later commented with irony on the Press furore.)

Christie made a statement admitting to the murders of the four women in the house. In it he claimed that his wife had been getting into an increasingly nervous condition because of attacks from the coloured people in the house, and that on the morning of December 14th, 1952, he had been awakened by his wife's convulsive movements; she was having some kind of a fit; Christie 'could not bear to see her', and strangled her with a stocking. His account of the other three murders – Rita Nelson, aged 25, Kathleen Maloney, aged 26, Hectorina McLennan, aged 26 – described quarrels with the women (who were prostitutes) during the course of which Christie strangled them. Later, he also confessed to the murders of the two women in the garden. One was an Austrian girl, Ruth Fuerst, whom Christie claimed he had murdered during sexual intercourse; and Muriel Eady, a fellow employee at the Ultra Radio factory in Park Royal where Christie had worked in late 1944.

A tobacco tin containing four lots of pubic hair was also found in the house.

There were many curious features in the murders. Carbon monoxide was found in the blood of the three women in the cupboard, although not in Mrs Christie's. The three had semen in the vagina; none was wearing knickers, but all had a piece of white material between the legs in the form of a diaper. This has never been satisfactorily explained.

Christie admitted at his trial that his method of murder had been to invite women to his house and to get them partly drunk. They were persuaded to sit in a deck-chair with a canopy, and a gas pipe was placed near the floor and turned on. When the girl lost consciousness from coal-gas poisoning, Christie would strangle her and then rape her. But since the women were prostitutes, it would hardly seem necessary to render them unconscious to have sexual intercourse. One theory to explain this has been advanced by Dr Francis Camps, the pathologist who examined the bodies. He suggested that Christie had reached a stage of sexual incapability where the woman needed to be unconscious before he could possess her. (In Halifax, as a young man, Christie had earned from some girl the derogatory nicknames, 'Can't Do It Christie' and 'Reggie-No-Dick'.)

The body of Rita Nelson was found to be six months' pregnant.

Christie was tried only for the murder of his wife; his trial opened at the Central Criminal Court on Monday, June 22nd, 1953, before Mr Justice Finnemore; the Attorney-General, Sir Lionel Heald, led for the Crown; Mr Derek Curtis-Bennett, QC, defended.

Christie's case history, as it emerged at his trial, was as follows: He was 55 years old at the time of his arrest. He was born in Chester Street, Boothtown, Yorkshire, in April 1898, son of Ernest Christie, a carpet designer. The father was a harsh man who treated his seven children with Victorian sternness and offered no affection. Christie was a weak child, myopic, introverted, and jeered at by his fellow pupils as a 'cissy'. He had many minor illnesses in his childhood – possibly to compensate for lack of attention. He was in trouble with the police for trivial offences, and was beaten by his father whenever this occurred.

At the age of fifteen (this would be in about 1913) he left school and got a post as a clerk to the Halifax Borough Police. Petty pilfering lost him the job. He then worked in his father's carpet factory; when he was dismissed from there for petty theft, his father threw him out of the house.

Christie was a chronic hypochondriac, a man who enjoyed being ill and talking about his past illnesses. (His first confession starts with an account of his poor health.) In 1915 he suffered from pneumonia. He then went to war, and was mustard-gassed and blown up. He claimed that he was blind for five months and lost his voice for three and a half years. The loss of voice was the psychological effect of hysteria, for there was no physical abnormality to account for it. His voice returned spontaneously at a time of emotional excitement.

Christie claimed that one of the most important events in his childhood was seeing his grandfather's body when he was 8.

In 1920, Christie met his wife Ethel, and they were married in the same year. They had no children. Christie claimed he had no sexual relations with his wife for about two years – which, if true, supports the view of his sexual inadequacy and the inferiority neurosis that afflicted his relations with women. In 1923, he quarrelled with his wife and they separated; he also lost his voice for three months. Details of the life of the Christies between the two wars are not available, except that he was knocked down by a car which did not stop, in 1934, and sustained injuries to the head, the knee, and collar-bone. (Christie seems to have been one of those unfortunate people who are born unlucky.) And when he worked for the post office, it was found that he was stealing money and postal orders from letters; for this he received seven months in prison. His longest term of employment was with a transport firm; this lasted for five years.

Duncan Webb, who was not the most reliable of crime-writers, declared that Christie claimed to be a rich man when he married his wife, and that he joined the Conservative Association (presumably in Halifax) and tried to play the man about town. On separating from his wife in 1923 (after a second term in prison for false pretences), he came to London, and lodged in Brixton and Battersea. He struck a woman over the head with a cricket bat, and went to jail again. His wife was induced to visit him, and started to live with him again when he came out.

In 1939, Christie joined the War Reserve Police, and became known as an officious constable who enjoyed showing his authority and 'running in' people for minor blackout offences. His wife often went to visit her family in Sheffield, and it was during one of her visits there that Christie brought Ruth Fuerst back to the house and strangled her. Although in his second confession he mentions strangling her during the act of intercourse, it is almost certain that he somehow persuaded her to inhale gas – perhaps from the square jar of Friar's Balsam, which he covered with a towel, claiming that it was a cure for nose and throat infections: while the victim's head was hidden under the towel, Christie inserted a tube leading from the gas tap. It may be that he only wanted to render the girl unconscious in order to have sexual intercourse, and decided to kill her later to cover up the assault. In his confession he told of hiding Ruth Fuerst's body under the floorboards when his wife returned with her brother. The next day, when they were out, he moved the body to the wash-house and later buried it in the back garden under cover of darkness.

At his trial, Christie declared that he was not sure whether Ruth Fuerst was his first victim. However, unless he had some other place in which to dispose of bodies, it seems probable that his 'vagueness' was intended to impress the jury that his mind was wandering.

In December 1943, Christie was released from the War Reserve and went to work at Ultra Radio. Here he became friendly with Muriel Eady, who often came to visit the Christies. On one occasion she came alone when Christie's wife was on holiday, and complained of catarrh. She buried her face in Christie's jar of Friar's Balsam, and later ended, like Ruth Fuerst, buried in the tiny garden.

Whether the Evans' murders were committed by Christie or by Timothy Evans will now never be known, but it seems almost certain that Christie committed them. In his third confession from Brixton Prison, he declares that in August 1949, Timothy Evans and his young wife (who lived above the Christies) quarrelled violently about a blonde woman. Christie claimed that he found Mrs Evans lying on the floor in front of the gas fire, having attempted suicide, and that he gave her a cup of tea. The next day he found her there once again, and she asked his help in killing herself, offering to let him have sexual intercourse. He strangled her with a stocking, and (in view of the later cases) probably had intercourse with her.[1] When Timothy Evans came home, Christie told him that his wife had gassed herself and that no doubt Evans would be suspected of her murder. What happened then is not certain. It is possible that Evans then murdered the baby, Geraldine, who was later found with her mother in the wash-house. Within a few days he sold his furniture and disappeared. But he then walked into the Merthyr Tydfil police station and claimed that he had killed his wife and put her body down a drain. The bodies were discovered in the wash-house, and Evans was charged with murder. At one point, he claimed that Christie was the murderer, but when told that the child's

[1] Ludovic Kennedy states that Christie offered to perform an abortion on Mrs Evans, who was pregnant at the time of her death. Mrs Evans panicked when Christie tried to persuade her to inhale gas, and was strangled. Kennedy believes Christie told Evans that his wife had died of the abortion, and persuaded him to keep silence.

body had also been found, he withdrew this allegation. Evans was of low mentality and illiterate; it is impossible to know what went on in his mind before his execution, or whether he murdered his daughter. What is most surprising is that he did not inform on Christie when he found that his wife was strangled; this makes it seem possible that he had murdered his daughter, and saw no point in involving Christie too.

In December 1952 came the murder of his wife. The motive for this is not clear, although it may well have been a desire to have the house to himself for further murders. Whether or not this was his intention, Christie killed again a few weeks later. Rita Nelson had last been seen alive on January 2nd, 1953. Hers was the second body in the cupboard. Christie claimed she had accosted him and demanded money, finally forcing herself into his house and starting a fight. What seems more likely is that she came back to the house by his invitation and was gassed as she sat in the deck-chair.

The next victim was Kathleen Maloney, last seen alive on January 12th, 1953. Again, Christie claims she started a fight, but this seems unlikely.

Christie had no money at this time, and sold his furniture for £11 and his wife's wedding ring. He had written to his wife's bank in Sheffield, forging her signature, and asked for her money to be sent. (He had also sent a postcard to his wife's sister before Christmas claiming that she had rheumatism in her fingers and could not write.)

Some time in February, Christie claims that he met a couple who told him they had nowhere to stay. The man was out of work. They came and stayed with Christie for a few days, and then left. Later, the woman – Hectorina McLennan – returned alone, and was murdered by Christie around March 3rd. After this, Christie claims he lost his memory and wandered around London (subsequent to March 20th, when he left Rillington Place) sleeping in a Rowton House part of the time. When caught, he was unshaven and shabby, with no money.

The defence was of insanity, but the jury rejected it, following several medical opinions that Christie was sane, and he was sentenced to death and executed on July 15th, 1953.

There are many peculiar features about the case. Christie was certainly a hysteric and a hypochondriac (he claimed, for example, that he could not have intercourse with Mrs Evans because of his fibrositis). Apart from the murders, his sexual activity consisted largely of masturbation; he may have masturbated standing over the bodies, for semen was found in the seams of his shoes, as well as on his clothes. For two and a half years before his wife's death, they had not had sexual intercourse.

The pubic hairs in the box were never explained. Christie claimed they came from the girls in the cupboard, but they did not, in fact, correspond. Only one lot resembled the pubic hair of Mrs Evans, but if it was from Mrs Evans, it must have been taken six months before her death, which seems unlikely. Two lots might have come from the two bodies buried in the garden, but this still leaves two lots unaccounted for.

Finally, Christie made a bad impression on practically everyone connected with the case; he seemed to be a habitual liar (unlike, for example, Peter Kürten) and a weakling, whining about his illness, vague about many of the facts, although trying to give an impression of eagerness to help, and of a detached interest in an intriguing case. But it is almost certain that his state of mind after the death of his wife was completely vague; he killed compulsively, and would have gone on killing, given the opportunity, because it was his only way of satisfying his emasculated sex impulse. A lady who met Christie in a café near his home tells how she was invited back to have her 'catarrh cured' on two occasions; luckily for her, she was prevented by accidental circumstances. The Christie who committed the last three murders was a man completely at the end of his tether, who had lost all impulse to avoid detection; possibly he felt it was only a matter of time before his wife's relatives investigated her disappearance (since she was such a frequent visitor to Sheffield), and allowed himself to sink into a mental twilight in which the only remaining impulse was the urge to satisfy his enfeebled sexual appetite. (Considering the absence of knickers on the three bodies in the cupboard and the curious fact of the 'diapers', it may be that some strange element of fetichism also entered into his abnormality.) It has not been established what effect the sight of his grandfather's body had on the development of a morbid attitude towards death and sex.

CHRISTOFI, Mrs Styllou
Executed for the murder of her daughter-in-law in Hampstead in 1954.

In 1925, Mrs Christofi, a Cypriot, was tried for the murder of her mother-in-law by ramming a burning torch down her throat, and acquitted. In 1953 she came to live with her son and his

German wife in South Hill Park, Hampstead. The son was a waiter in a West End restaurant. But Mrs Christofi and Hella did not get on well together. Hella (who had béen married for fifteen years) returned to Germany for a holiday with the children, and it was agreed that Mrs Christofi should return to Cyprus when she returned.

At 1 am on the night of July 29th, 1954, a Mr and Mrs Burstoff, sitting in a car near Hampstead Station, were spoken to by Mrs Christofi (who had almost no English), who talked about a fire. The body of Hella Christofi was found on the floor near the french windows. Parts of the body were charred and smelt of paraffin. The skull was fractured, and death had been caused by strangling with a ligature. The body was naked except for briefs.

A neighbour, John Young, testified that he had looked into the Christofis' garden at eleven-forty-five and seen the body (which he thought was a tailor's dummy) surrounded by flames, and then saw Mrs Christofi stirring the fire.

Mrs Christofi was tried before Mr Justice Devlin, Mr Christmas Humphreys prosecuting, and Mr David Weitzman defending. The doctor of Holloway prison had stated his conviction that she was insane, but Mrs Christofi refused to allow her defence to plead insanity. She was sentenced to death in October 1954. An appeal was dismissed, and after being examined by three doctors who declared her sane, she was executed. Possibly her earlier murder was taken into account in the decision not to reprieve her. The motive was certainly jealousy of her daughter-in-law.

CHUNG YI MIAO
Hanged at Strangeways Jail, Manchester, on December 6th, 1928, for the murder of his wife near the village of Grange-in-Borrowdale in the Lake District.

The chief difficulty presented by the case is the apparent lack of motive.

The bride's maiden name was Wai Sheung Siu, daughter of a wealthy merchant prince of the Mandarin class, resident in Macao, the Portuguese island near Hong Kong. An extremely clever and capable girl, she ran her father's household from the age of 11 (after the death of her mother). In 1922, she graduated from Boston University, USA, and returned home. On her father's death, she opened an art shop in Hong Kong, and travelled to America with a consignment of *objets d'art* in 1927. Here she met her future husband, who told her that he was a law student and son of a wealthy couple living in Shanghai. Their meeting in New York was followed by a 'whirlwind courtship'; they were married in May 1928. The bride was a small, plain woman of 29; her husband gave his own age as 28. There seems to be some doubt about the 'wealth' that the husband claimed he possessed; in New York, he had paid $1,500 into a bank, and two days later, had drawn it out again. In Buffalo, on his honeymoon, he had told his host that he had lost his traveller's cheques, but had subsequently made no effort to recover them. In Albany, the bride had a minor operation to make sexual intercourse possible, and there was a suggestion at the trial that she was told that she would be unable to bear children.

They arrived in England on June 18th, 1928, having drawn money from a bank in Glasgow. They went to the village of Grange, at the lower end of Derwentwater, for a holiday on the same day. On the following day, they went for a walk in the morning, returning for lunch, and at two o'clock, went out again. At four o'clock, the husband returned alone, and told someone in the hotel that his wife had gone to Keswick to buy some warmer underwear. At six o'clock, he commented that he was worried because his wife had not yet returned, and continued to express anxiety throughout the evening. The body was found at seven-thirty by a farmer, lying near a bathing pool. She had been strangled with three separate pieces of cord; the clothes were bunched around her waist, and the knickers were torn; the body was lying in a position that indicated rape. A police inspector went to the hotel and told the husband of his wife's murder at eleven that night. The prisoner is said to have asked a constable, 'Had she knickers on?', although he later claimed that what he had asked was, 'Had she necklace on?' The next morning, when interviewed by the police at the police station, Miao remarked, 'It is terrible – my wife assaulted, robbed, and murdered'. No one at that point had mentioned assault or robbery. The rings were missing from his wife's fingers, suggesting robbery, but they later fell out of a camera when the police examined it to develop the films. Miao was also reported to have asked a maid at the hotel: 'Did she go to the place where they bathe?', indicating knowledge of the murder spot, and his curiosity as to whether a Miss Crossley (to whom he was referring) might have discovered the body. Later, Miao's counsel suggested that he had really asked whether Miss Crossley had gone to look for his wife 'at the place where people take the bus'.

The trial took place at Carlisle Assizes on November 22nd, 1928, and lasted for three days. Mr Justice Humphreys was on the bench; Mr J. E. Singleton, KC, prosecuted, and Mr J. C. Jackson defended.

The Crown based its case largely on circumstantial evidence. The husband seemed to show knowledge of the murder before he knew the details; there was the matter of the rings, which were found in the camera in his room, and the appearance of rape that was not substantiated by a medical examination. The husband had gone to bed when the police brought news of the murder, which was hardly the action of a newly married man whose wife was out alone after dark.

The defence called the prisoner to testify. It was claimed that Mrs Chung had removed the rings herself before they left the hotel and had put them into the camera to save time. Miao declared that he had been followed by two Orientals, whom he had seen at various times on his honeymoon. Some witnesses were called to testify that they had seen two Orientals around Keswick and in the area of the murder on the 19th, the day of the murder.

The jury returned with a verdict of guilty; the prisoner seemed to be annoyed by their stupidity. There was an appeal that was dismissed, but right to the end, Miao seemed to believe that he would be reprieved.

The evidence in the case is completely circumstantial, and the lack of motive is disturbing. It has been suggested that Miao murdered his wife for her money; but since he was legally the possessor of all her goods in any case, this seems unlikely. More likely is the explanation that his wife's suggested sterility may have been a powerful factor in wanting to be rid of her. An article which appeared in the *Sunday Express* for March 24th, 1929, quotes Miao as saying that his wife died willingly to allow him to remarry and beget heirs.

CLARK, Joseph Reginald Victor (alias Kennedy)
Twenty-one-year-old, British-born amateur hypnotist and libertine ('The Boy with the Hundred Sweethearts'), ex-pantry-boy at Princeton University, USA, convicted of the murder of Mrs Alice Fontaine.

Brought up by relations in America, Clark worked his passage back to England in 1927. This was the last time he submitted to the dire necessity of honest work; upon arrival at Southampton he straight away embarked on a series of parasitical schemes for extorting money from gullible girl-friends. A little shop assistant gave him all her earnings, so that when escorting her he might be impeccably attired (he had told her: 'Only the best is good enough when I am with you'). Another victim referred to his so-called 'hypnotic' powers: 'I used to find myself tired . . . when he looked into my eyes . . . I could not resist him and would do anything he suggested . . . I gave him money whenever he wanted it . . .' A girl in Nova Scotia sent him a regular remittance, but whenever he thought himself impoverished he would employ the guile of his pen, as in this letter to the shop assistant:

> Oh girl! Can you imagine wearing the same underclothes for six weeks with never a change? Of not having a bath for three weeks? If you could help me out again this week, I should be eternally and truly grateful. . . . Will you try and write me a letter? And let me always remain . . . Your loving and devoted boy, R.K.

He became the devoted suitor of four sisters in Liverpool, each girl being unaware of his amorous entanglements with the other three. Clark stole a ring from their mother, with which to plight his dubious troth with the youngest daughter, and presented the birth certificate of the eldest daughter (aged 22) at Birkenhead Registrar's Office when giving notice of his intention to wed the younger girl. This project discovered, in a fit of fury he attempted to strangle with a pyjama cord the sister of his choice, screaming out, 'If I can't have you nobody else shall.' Fearing publicity, the girl did not bring a charge against her former swain.

Clark (who was now using the name Kennedy) then met Alice Fontaine, and went to lodge at her mother's house in Northbrook Street, Liverpool. He ingratiated himself with both mother and daughter, although he never paid for his keep; he constantly borrowed money, on one occasion exacting £20 from the trusting Mrs Fontaine with which to make a wireless set 'to sell at a profit'. Upon discovering letters from one of Clark's sadly credulous 'fiancées', Alice Fontaine realized his villainy, and Clark was told to leave the house. He retaliated by sending mother and daughter obscene notes.

One Sunday morning in October 1928, shortly after Clark's

expulsion from Northbrook Street, Alice Fontaine was in her bedroom getting dressed for church: '. . . Clark appeared. He came
towards me and placed his hands on my shoulders. . . .' He attempted to strangle the girl with a pyjama cord, and she lost
consciousness: '. . . when I came to, I found that he had tried to
cut my throat. I wondered why my mother did not come to my
aid, for the noise we made in our struggle was terrific . . .' Mrs
Fontaine lay downstairs, strangled.

Arrested on the murder charge, Clark made a statement concerning the killing of his former landlady and benefactor:

> After I had pressed Mrs Fontaine's throat . . . I relaxed my
> grip . . . she recovered sufficiently to murmur some words . . .
> 'Teddy Bear' (Clark's pet name while in the Fontaine house),
> 'I am dying. You must always take care of your "Boofie"'
> (Alice Fontaine's pet name). 'The deceased lady smiled at me
> in her last moment . . .'

The trial of Clark took place at Liverpool Assize Court on
February 3rd, 1929. His counsel, Mr Basil Nield, advanced a plea
of insanity, but Clark pleaded guilty and was sentenced to death,
being duly executed. His trial had lasted four and a half minutes,
and is one of the shortest murder trials on record.

CLARK, Lorraine
*Twenty-eight-year-old Massachusetts housewife, convicted of
husband-murder in 1954.*

Married for ten years to assiduous electronics foreman, 29-year-
old Melvin Clark, Lorraine Clark lived with her family in a well-
appointed 'cottage' on the banks of Lake Attitach in Amesbury,
a Boston suburb. To relieve the tedium of her husband's frequent
absences from home (he also ran his own boat rental service on
Lake Attitach), Mrs Clark took to attending licentious levees
held by some of Amesbury's married couples. One of the 'sports'
indulged in was the Housekey Game, when husbands would
throw down their housekeys for the scrabbling wives, each
woman taking as that night's mate the owner of the key she had
procured.

On the night of April 10th, 1954, Melvin Clark arrived home
unexpectedly to find his wife entertaining a man; in the quarrel
following, Lorraine Clark stabbed her husband twice in the
chest with a darning-needle and shot him dead with two shots in
the head from a ·32-calibre pistol. In her subsequent confession

she stated that for three hours she pondered on how to dispose of the body; finally she trussed it chicken-wise with wire, rolled and pushed it out to the car, and drove to a bridge over the Merrimack River, six miles away. She secured three 15 lb. anchors to the body and heaved it over the bridge rail into the river below, hoping that tides would carry the corpse out to sea. Lorraine Clark explained her husband's absence as due to a quarrel, and on April 17th filed a suit for divorce, charging him with 'cruel and abusive treatment'; for weeks she scrubbed at the Lake Attitach cottage, removing bloodstains. Owing to river flooding, Melvin Clark's body drifted into marshlands, where it was found in a badly decomposed condition by a birdwatcher on June 2nd, but identifiable by thumbprints. Evidently a case of murder, the widow was interrogated by the police and on June 26th wrote out a confession not only of the killing but of the eccentric social customs of certain Amesbury residents, so causing local apprehension.

On September 17th, 1954, at Salem, Massachusetts, Lorraine Clark was indicted for first-degree murder, but Superior Court Judge Charles Fairhurst found her guilty of second-degree murder, sentencing her to life imprisonment in the Women's Reformatory at Framingham, where she will be eligible for parole after fifteen years. District Attorney Clegg accepted the second-degree murder plea: 'It will save the cost of a trial and save the defendant's parents and children the shame ... of further notoriety.'

CLARKE, Morris Arthur

Twenty-seven-year-old lorry driver, convicted in 1957 of the murder of his wife's employer, 53-year-old Huntingdonshire bachelor, farmer Arthur Johnson. On October 15th, 1956, Johnson disappeared from his home, Crowtree Farm, where formerly Mrs Clarke had worked as housekeeper. On October 25th, Johnson's body was recovered from a canal; the head was battered, and one leg broken. Police interviewed Clarke, and found over £700 in his possession: 'It is Johnson's money; I killed him. I may as well tell you now.' During the trial, presided over by Mr Justice Donovan, Clarke mentioned his jealousy of Arthur Johnson, having suspected for years that his wife was having an affair with her employer. After a quarrel with his wife concerning Johnson, he had gone to see the farmer: 'I wanted to know the truth.' Clarke asserted that Johnson had attacked him; 'I broke

away from him and picked up a piece of wood from the ground
. . . I hit him on the head . . . he never got up any more.' Clarke
hid the farmer's body in a drainage dyke; having found on his
victim's clothing the safe key, he had stolen money with which
to pay his many debts. Found guilty of murder, the judge, when
passing sentence of death said '. . . the circumstances of your
crime are so dreadful that you should not count on some other
sentence being substituted. . . .'

Clarke was eventually reprieved.

CLEMENTS, Robert George

*Fifty-seven-year-old Ulsterman, Fellow of the Royal College of
Surgeons, who murdered his fourth wife, heiress Amy Victoria
Burnett Clements, by the administration of morphine, and is
thought to have killed his previous wives for monetary gain.*

The third Mrs Clements had died eight years before in Southport, ostensibly from cancer, although until her death she had
appeared robust, despite her husband's predictions of an
imminent decease; a doctor friend, suspicious, had influenced
the Chief Constable into ordering a post-mortem, but the body
had already been cremated. The first and second wives, both
wealthy women, had died from sleeping sickness and endo-
carditis respectively. In all three cases Dr Clements had signed
the death certificate.

On May 27th, 1947, the fourth Mrs Clements (whom Dr
Clements had married at fashionable St George's, Hanover
Square, London, in 1939) died at the Astley Nursing Home, Southport, Lancashire. There was some discrepancy about the cause of
death; at Dr Clements' instigation, a pathologist, Dr James
Houston, had diagnosed myeloid leukaemia, but Dr Andrew
Brown, the Staff Surgeon at the nursing home, suspected poisoning, having noticed, upon Mrs Clements' entry into hospital,
that 'pin-point' condition of the pupils which is a symptom of
morphine poisoning. Dr Brown consulted the Southport
Coroner, who contacted the Chief Constable, Mr Harold Mig-
hall; widower Clements, interviewed by the Chief Constable, declared himself satisfied with Dr Houston's findings: 'there is no
cure for myeloid leukaemia'. Police learnt from neighbours how
Dr Clements had seemed to have fore-knowledge of his wife's
recent 'dizzy spells', and how one devoted friend of the dead
woman had been barred from the Clements' flat for months. The
theory that Dr Clements had turned his wife into a morphine

addict was strengthened when it was learnt that the doctor had been prescribing enormous doses of morphine for a patient who never, in fact, received this drug. (During his wife's illness Dr Clements had frequently escorted a wealthy widow, although he was to be full of husbandly grief when recording his fourth matrimonial bereavement in a diary: 'Adorable wife. She was good and devoted, never fair to herself.') Mrs Clements' funeral was stopped and a second autopsy ordered. The autopsy showed that death was due to morphine poisoning. Police, calling upon Drs Houston and Clements, found them dead. Dr Houston, appalled by his earlier precipitate and inaccurate diagnosis, had taken cyanide; Dr Clements, realizing his fate, had taken morphine. Both had left notes. Houston's read: 'I have for some time been aware that I have been making mistakes. . . . I have not profited by experience . . .' Clements' read: 'To whom it may concern . . . I can no longer tolerate the diabolical insults to which I have been recently exposed.'

COKE, Arundel

This is not a murder case – the intended victim recovered – but is interesting as the only trial that took place under the Coventry Act, which states that a man can be executed for lying in wait and slitting someone's nose! This act was brought into force when Sir John Coventry was attacked in Covent Garden in 1671 by footpads and was badly mutilated – the slitting of his nose being among the mutilations.

Arundel Coke lived in Bury St Edmunds; he was a barrister, and he expected to inherit some money on the death of his wife's brother, Edward Crispe, who was not in the best of health. On January 1st, 1722, Coke arranged a supper party and invited Crispe. After supper, the ladies went upstairs, and Coke suggested a visit to a certain Mistress Monke. (It does not appear in the evidence whether her profession was what one might suppose.) Shortly afterwards Coke returned alone, and somewhat later, Crispe came in, streaming with blood from wounds on his face.

A tailor named Moon told the police that Coke had approached him three years before and invited him to murder Crispe. So Coke was arrested. Coke immediately admitted that he had hired a man named John Woodburne to attack Crispe, saying that he had told Woodburne to cut Crispe's 'weasend or windpipe' 'and that if Woodburne had not been a cow-hearted dog, he would have done so and secured Crispe from telling tales'. Woodburne admitted to causing Crispe's injuries with a billhook. They were tried at Bury St Edmunds on March 13th, 1722, before Sir Peter King. Since Crispe had a cut on his nose, the prosecution produced the Coventry Act, which stated that a man could be convicted for putting out an eye, disabling the tongue or slitting the nose, if he had lain in wait with intention to disfigure.

Both were found guilty and executed on March 31st, 1722.

COLOSIMO, Jim
Known as 'Big Jim', a Chicago racketeer and 'bootlegger', whose unsolved shooting was one of the first of many gang-killings of the twenties.

Born of an Italian immigrant family on Chicago's slum-ridden South Side in 1871, Colosimo began work as a 'shoe-shiner', then worked his way through paper-selling and street-cleaning, to local politics and the entertainment-saloon business – these two latter activities being, seemingly, inextricably linked in the American scene of that period. His sponsoring of vice with the solicited approval of Chicago politicians proved highly remunerative to Big Jim, who sported diamonds even on his sock-suspenders and whose main restaurant at the junction of Wabash Avenue and Twenty-second Street was patronized by such celebrities as Amelita Galli-Curci the opera star, Gentleman Jim Corbett the boxer, Florenz Ziegfeld the theatrical promoter, Tetrazzini and Caruso. His penchant for opera and opera stars was well known, and he was eventually, in March 1920, to desert his wife Victoria and elope with a protégée of Caruso's, an Ohio girl named Dale Winter, who years after Colosimo's death scored a success in Jerome Kern's musical comedy, *Irene*. On May 11th, 1920, Colosimo was lured to his death by a 'business appointment'; some believed that his first wife's wrath at being discarded had motivated the killing, some stuck to the theory that the police department itself was responsible, frustrated at being unable to indict Colosimo for many of Chicago's gang murders. Many, however, looked uneasily in the direction of Colosimo's own ambitious aide-de-camp, Johnny Torrio, who now automatically took over his master's ambiguous business concerns, employing as his own bodyguard a scarfaced young mobster named Al Capone. Big Jim's funeral was one of the most spectacular Chicago had seen for years, with Torrio's demonstrative grief much in evidence: 'We wuz like brothers.'

CONRAD, Fritz

Thirty-five-year-old Berlin carter, who murdered his wife and five children in 1881.

The bodies, all hanging in a stranglehold from hooks in a shabbily furnished room were found when police, summoned by an agitated and seemingly apprehensive Conrad (who said he was unable to enter his bolted apartment) had levered the outside door from its hinges. It appeared as if Frau Conrad, depressed by her poverty, had killed her children and then committed suicide. Police Commissioner Hollman felt instinctively the case was not so straightforward, and that Conrad was being evasive. He discovered the carter was infatuated with a young servant girl; searching the Conrad apartment for love-letters (without success), he came upon a book, a well-thumbed translation of an English novel, *Nena Sahib*, by John Ratcliffe. Idly reading the narrative, Hollman was intrigued at a description of a 'perfect murder'; the victim was found dead behind a bolted door – an apparent suicide, but a wary detective found a tiny hole (camouflaged with putty) that had been drilled through the door, adjacent to the bolt. By passing wire through the door, the bolt could be manipulated from the outside. Examining the Conrad apartment door, Hollman discovered a similar hole, now sealed with sealing-wax to which adhered strands of horsehair; the commissioner experimented by pushing strands of horsehair through the hole, and found he could control the bolt on the other side. Confronted, Conrad confessed to the multiple murder, committed through a compulsive desire to marry his mistress; he was subsequently executed.

CONROY, Teresa Miriam (The 'Ritual Burial' Case)

On or about September 23rd, 1953, Mrs Teresa Miriam Conroy, aged 44, murdered her 13-year-old epileptic son, John Michael. The body was found on September 26th by the father, Michael Oliver Conroy, pressed into a ripped-open divan base (upon which Mr Conroy had slept the previous night), with the hands crossed on the breast and the divan-lining surmounting the face neatly folded back like coat lapels. A bed had been made up on the divan, and Mr Conroy had discovered the corpse when searching for a two-shilling piece he thought he might have tucked under the divan mattress in a moment of aberration the night before. Mrs Conroy had telephoned her husband at work on September 25th to say she was going to stay with her cousin at Muswell Hill for a few days and was taking John Michael with her. When interviewed by the police she at first said her son was in hospital, then admitted she knew he was dead. Mrs Conroy explained that after a severe epileptic attack on Tuesday, September 22nd, John Michael had been found on the Wednesday morning 'drooping' by the gas oven; she had put him back to bed, where after a choking attack he died and was buried by her in the divan before her departure to Muswell Hill.

The post-mortem showed a 55 per cent concentration of coal gas, but also 60 grains of methyl-pheno-barbitone. (Normal dose 3 grains, fatal dose 30 grains.) It amounted to murder twice over.

Charged with the murder of her son, Mrs Conroy pleaded not guilty at the Old Bailey on December 8th, 1953. Mr Christmas Humphreys, prosecuting, referred to the 'ritual' and 'ceremonial' nature of the divan burial. Dr Thomas Christie, principal medical officer at Holloway Prison, said of Mrs Conroy: 'She is of low intelligence. Anything requiring deep thought leaves her at a loss.' Detective-Superintendent Leslie Watts said: '. . . throughout the inquiry she has shown no emotion about the death of her son – not even a tear.'

Mr Elliot Gorst, QC, defending, said he did not propose to call the prisoner. Mrs Conroy was found guilty but insane on the charge of murder, and ordered by Mr Justice Havers to be detained.

COOK, DeWitt Clinton
Sexual murderer and 'moon maniac' of Los Angeles.

Ruth Alderman, a student at Los Angeles City College, was attacked by a man in October 1939, but succeeded in fighting him off. On February 24th, 1940, Anya Sosoyeva, a young Russian-born student, was attacked on the campus by a man who battered her with a length of 'two by four'.[1] The girl managed to escape, but died later from head injuries. Curiously enough, the girl had been indirectly involved already in a murder case; her husband, a young radio writer, had shot his mistress, a divorcée. He had been acquitted finally, and had died 'of natural causes' some time before his wife's murder.

One month later, on a moonlit night, Delia Bogard, a 17-year-old actress, who had been a child film star, was attacked as she walked home. Her cries roused neighbours, and a woman hurled

[1] Short piece of wood, 2 inches deep by 4 inches wide.

herself on the attacker wielding a golf club; he ran away. Miss
Bogard later recovered. Again, a piece of 'two by four' was used.

On August 23rd, another moonlit night, a young maidservant
who was baby-sitting was knocked unconscious and raped. A
piece of 'two by four' was found near her unconscious body. The
following night, a man was seen in the back yard of a couple on
Oakwood Avenue; they phoned the police, and DeWitt Clinton
Cook was taken in charge. He was 20 years of age.

He was married, and his wife denied all knowledge of his night
jaunts. Large quantities of loot were found in his home, and he
confessed to three hundred burglaries. Finally, he admitted to
the attacks on women, claiming that it was an irresistible
impulse.

Paul de River, the police psychiatrist, has given some interesting details of the case in his book *The Sexual Criminal* (omitting
names). He mentions that Cook had a sexual inferiority feeling,
that may have been induced by the smallness of his sexual member, and that the piece of timber which he invariably used as a
weapon may have been for him a kind of symbol of sexual
potency. Cook's photograph shows a young man with weak
mouth and receding chin, and the 'dreamy' eyes that often seem
to go with a certain type of psychotic personality (although, of
course, it does not follow that this is a sign of the sex maniac:
the eyes of Nijinsky the ballet dancer had the same appearance).

Cook re-enacted the attack on Anya Sosoyeva in front of a
film camera, and the film was shown to the jury. He died in St
Quentin Jail on January 31st, 1941.

COOK (James)
Bookbinder of Leicester who murdered a manufacturer in 1832.

Apparently Cook must have been in financial difficulties. Mr
Paas, who supplied him with materials of his trade, came from
London – probably to collect some money due to him. Cook went
to a public house that night and was obviously affluent. The following evening, the neighbours suspected the premises were on
fire – although it is more probable that they were curious about
the huge fire that had burned in Cook's workshop for two days,
and perhaps smelt burning flesh. At all events, they broke in and
found flesh burning on the fire. Cook was fetched, and declared
it was horseflesh, but when bits of Mr Paas's body were found in
the workshop, as well as his trousers and a gaiter, Cook was
arrested. But he was released on bail, and made off. The police

system was imperfect in those days and the relatives of the deceased had to take on the responsibility of the pursuit. They did this with the help of two Bow Street Runners, and Cook was finally taken at Liverpool as he was actually on his way to a ship in an open boat; he would have fled to America.

He was executed in front of Leicester jail and his body exposed in chains – one of the last occasions this happened.

CORDAY, Charlotte
Guillotined on July 17, 1793, for the murder of Marat.

The French Revolution provides a great many stories of murder; four thousand people were executed during the 'terror', until the murder of Robespierre, St Just, Couthon, and Robespierre's brother at the Hôtel de Ville brought the terror to an end. But its only notable case of an 'unofficial' murder is that of Marat by Charlotte Corday.

Charlotte Corday was born in 1768 near Sées in Normandy, a descendant of Corneille; her family were noble but impoverished. She was educated at the Convent of the Holy Trinity at Caen. On the downfall of the Girondins in 1793, many Girondist leaders took refuge in Normandy; she attended their meetings and heard them speak. She decided to go to Paris to assassinate Marat, whom she conceived as a tyrant and the cause of a great deal of the suffering of the Revolution.

Jean-Paul Marat was one of the most intelligent and clear-sighted of the leaders of the Revolution; a doctor and experimental physicist, he had lived a life of poverty and idealism. Carlyle's portrait of him is particularly biased and unfair.

Marat, who was 50 at the time of his death, had published many remarkable works, including a *Philosophical Essay on Man*, various works on light, and a translation of Newton's *Optics*. He was, for a time, physician to the guards of the Comte D'Artois (afterwards Charles X) but resigned this appointment in 1786. On plunging into political life, he wrote a paper on the *Vices of the English Constitution*, and composed a suggested constitution for France. He then edited a revolutionary newspaper, *The Friend of the People*.

Far from being a tyrant or a sadist with a lust for power, he tended to distrust whoever was in power (with the true temperament of an anarchist) and always stood alone and completely independent. In 1789 he was imprisoned for a month for attacking the Constituent Assembly, and in 1790 was forced to flee to

England after a campaign against Lafayette. Returning in May 1790, to Paris, he was forced to hide in the sewers, where he contracted the painful skin disease that later forced him to stay in his bath.

The trial of Louis XVI showed the amazing justice so deeply ingrained in Marat's temperament; he refused to allow Malesherbes, the King's counsel, to be attacked in his newspaper, and declared that it was unfair to accuse Louis of any 'crimes' anterior to his acceptance of the constitution. After the execution of the King, Marat engaged in a struggle with the Girondists, a party made up largely of brilliant orators from the Gironde in Bordeaux, who despised Marat as a rough, red Republican who distrusted their fine sentiments and talk of a Roman constitution. When the Girondists conquered in the Convention they ordered Marat to be tried, but the result was his acquittal and a steep rise in his popularity with the common people. The fall of the Girondists on May 31st, 1793, was a triumph for Marat.

Charlotte Corday came to Paris with very little money. She bought a kitchen knife with a six-inch blade and an ivory handle, and tried to see Marat at his address at 20 Rue des Cordeliers, but was refused admittance by the two sisters who looked after Marat, Simone, and Catherine Evrard. She returned to her hotel – the Hôtel de la Providence – and wrote Marat two letters. A second visit was also unsuccessful, but finally, on July 13th, she managed to gain admittance. Marat heard her voice in the hall, and was curious to see what the letter-writer looked like.

If Charlotte Corday felt any doubt about her mission to kill Marat, they were probably stilled by an item in the newspaper that day: nine of the twenty-six citizens of Orleans accused of the attempted murder of Bourdon de la Crosnière, Marat's drunken lieutenant in Orleans, were to mount the guillotine that day. Bourdon had refused to answer a sentry when drunk, and the sentry had given him a flesh wound with his bayonet; Bourdon used this excuse to arrest the twenty-six citizens, men who had shown themselves particularly opposed to his debaucheries and cruelties.

Marat was in his bath when Charlotte Corday was admitted; this was the only place where he could sooth the horrible sores on his body and manage to read and write. Charlotte Corday proceeded to give him the names of various citizens of Caen who, she claimed, were planning to betray the Revolution; then, as Marat's attention was directed to making a note of them, she stabbed him above the heart, plunging the knife in to its hilt and pulling it out again. At Marat's cry, the two sisters and the cook rushed into the room, and Charlotte Corday tried to walk out to the carriage she had waiting. However, the concierge barred her way and knocked her down with a chair (perhaps in case she still had the knife) and hit her as she lay on the ground. They then tied her hands with a handkerchief.

At her trial before the Revolutionary Tribunal, her advocate put forward a plea of insanity, but she was sentenced to death. Her execution took place a great deal quicker than that of most murderers. She was guillotined on July 17th, four days after the murder. She was 25 years old, and is described by many contemporary chronicles as beautiful.

CORDER, William (The Red Barn Murder)

Twenty-four-year-old farmer turned schoolmaster, sentenced to death in 1828 at the Shire Hall, Bury St Edmunds, for the murder of mole-catcher's daughter, Maria Marten.

The previous year William Corder and Maria Marten had become lovers in the Suffolk village of Polstead; Corder procured lodgings for Maria in Plough Lane, Sudbury, where a son was born. The child died, and Maria returned to her father's Polstead cottage where the parent repeatedly prevailed upon reluctant Corder to marry his daughter. On the morning of May 18th, 1827, Corder informed Maria he had obtained a marriage licence at Ipswich and that the wedding would take place later that very day; he stressed that Maria must not be seen (police and his own mother would raise objections to his marrying a woman who had mothered two bastards) and so she must disguise herself as a man, meeting him for the marriage journey at the Red Barn, a red-tiled outhouse on Corder's farmland. The simple girl complied with this obscurely involved arrangement, putting her own feminine garb in a bag; about noon Maria's stepbrother saw Corder striding towards the Red Barn carrying a shovel and pickaxe. Days later Corder informed Maria's father that his daughter was enjoying a holiday on the Isle of Wight; other inquirers were told of the absent Maria holidaying in Yarmouth or the Continent. Seemingly restless, Corder borrowed £400 from his mother, and departed to London, staying at the Bull Inn in Leadenhall Street. Here he composed a letter to the *Sunday Times*, advertising for a wife: 'Matrimony: a private gentleman of 24 . . . to any female of respectability who would study for domestic comforts . . . who feels desirous of meeting with a sociable, tender, kind, and sympathizing companion, they will find this advertisement worthy of notice. . . .' (this advertisement appeared on November 25th, 1827). Through this medium Corder met and married a young woman who proposed starting a girls' school, a project which greatly appealed to him; the school opened in Ealing and Corder acquired spectacles and became honorary headmaster. Meanwhile, Maria's stepmother, who possessed psychic propensities, had a series of dreams in which she saw William Corder shoot and bury Maria in the Red Barn. Mr Marten, remembering how Corder had been seen with pick and shovel, went to the barn, and there dug up the corpse of his daughter. A warrant for Corder's arrest was issued, and he was apprehended by police-constable James Lea at Ealing. (Lea afterwards unsuccessfully tried to keep Corder's gun as a souvenir.) At his trial, which started on August 8th, the accused said that Maria had shot herself during a quarrel; found guilty on August 10th, Corder was publicly hanged in front of the jail at Bury St Edmunds, after confessing his guilt the previous evening to Prison Governor Orridge.

The Maria Marten murder has been the subject of ballads and stage melodramas, and romanticized versions of it still appear in the more lurid of women's journals.

CORNWELL, Gerry
Jealous lover, of Oakland, California, who, ten days before Christmas, 1955, poured petrol over the bedroom of his ex-mistress, Alice Franklin, and her lover, Robert Hand, a steel-worker, and then set it alight. The two victims were rushed to hospital immediately, but Hand died six hours, and Alice Franklin twelve hours, later.

Police soon discovered that the 35-year-old ex-waitress had lived at 5955 Telegraph Avenue (the scene of the fire) with her lover Gerry Cornwell, a 32-year-old mechanic, until three months before the murder. Then the waitress had transferred her affections to Hand, who was eight years her junior, and Cornwell had moved out. He had continued to be on good terms with the couple, and had been at a party with them on the night of the fire.

A garage attendant recollected selling three gallons of petrol to a man whose description fitted Cornwell. Confronted with this, Cornwell confessed that he had followed his ex-mistress and her lover back to the apartment, and had watched them climb into bed and make love without turning off the light. This enraged him and he went off to buy petrol. The lovers were asleep and probably a little drunk when Cornwell poured petrol over the bedroom. However, before Cornwell had time to strike a light, a trickle of petrol ran over to the pilot light and a tremendous explosion followed, which shattered the windows and startled the arsonist. He escaped in his car, and neighbours rushed to try to rescue Hand and his mistress. The fact that he had not struck the light that ignited the explosion led to some speculation as to whether he was guilty of murder, until the Alameda County District Attorney pointed out that Cornwell's intention had certainly been to murder his mistress and her lover.

CRAWFORD, Annie

Acquitted of the murder of her sister Elise in New Orleans in March 1912.

The three Crawford sisters lived with their uncle and aunt at Peters Avenue, New Orleans, in September 1911. They were Gertrude, 19, Elise, 25, and Annie, 28. Annie was plain and had no suitors; both Elise and Gertrude had gentlemen friends (in fact, it was revealed at the trial that Elise was not a virgin). The year before – in June 1910 – the eldest girl of the family, Mamie, had died suddenly, and in July, both their parents died within a few days of one another.

On Monday, September 18th, 1911, Elise came home from her office in a taxi-cab, feeling ill. She had been having attacks of vomiting for some days. All week she hovered in a semi-conscious condition, her sister Annie tending her (as she had earlier tended her parents and elder sister), but the following Friday she went into a coma, and on Saturday morning she died in hospital. Liquid taken from her stomach and bladder revealed that she had died of morphine poisoning. Annie was arrested and charged with her murder. After being interviewed, she finally admitted that she was a morphine addict, and may have given Elise morphine 'by mistake'. (She had been employed for six years at the New Orleans Sanatorium, where she had access to drugs.)

Strangely enough, the bodies of her parents and elder sister were not exhumed. It appeared, however, that although all the deceased had been insured, it had been for extremely small sums.

The trial opened on March 12th, 1912, and on the 26th, the

jury failed to agree, nine being for acquittal and three for the prisoner's guilt. She was released, and left for Port Arthur, Texas, with another married sister. Her acquittal may have been largely due to lack of motive for the crime.

CREAM, Thomas Neill

Victorian mass-murderer, born in Glasgow, 1850; his parents, both Scots, emigrated to Canada in 1863, where (at McGill University) Cream was to obtain a medical degree. From his early adulthood, however, most of Neill Cream's activities were of the criminal type: insurance company frauds, arson, abortions, blackmail, and petty thieving, although his first conviction, in 1881, was for murder. Cream had moved to Chicago, where he formed an adulterous association with a Mrs Stott, the young wife of an elderly epileptic who seems to have had a pathetic faith in Dr Cream's prescriptions, not to mention his own wife, whose invariable job it was to collect the remedies personally from the doctor. One day, twenty minutes after partaking of a dose of Cream's physic, Mr Stott died – not before Dr Cream had insured his life for a considerable sum; suspicion of foul play might not have arisen if Cream himself had not written letters first to the Coroner, then to the District Attorney, hinting at the advisability of an exhumation. (This curious 'capture-wish' was typical of Neill Cream, and one can only assume that it was an integral factor in his undoubted enjoyment of murder and its aftermath.) The autopsy on Stott revealed strychnine; Cream had fled, with Mrs Stott, who, however, turned State's evidence. Sentenced to life imprisonment for (unaccountably) second-degree murder, Cream was confined to Joliet Prison where (again unaccountably) he was released in July 1891 shortly after his father had left him £5,000.

Dr Neill Cream arrived in London on October 1st, 1891. On October 13th Ellen Donworth, a 19-year-old prostitute, fell writhing with pain on the pavement of Waterloo Road; she died on the way to hospital, saying only that 'a tall gentleman' had handed her a bottle 'with white stuff in it'; a post-mortem revealed that the girl had received a fatal dose of strychnine. One letter was received by the coroner signed 'A. O'Brien, detective', offering to name the killer in exchange for £300,000, and another by the firm of stationers W. H. Smith, in the Strand, naming one of their employees as the murderer, but offering superlative legal aid from 'H. Bayne, barrister'.

On October 20th another prostitute, 27-year-old Matilda Clover, was found dying in extreme agony in her room down the Lambeth Road; she spoke of a man called 'Fred' who had given her some pills. A friend of Clover's, Lucy Rose, had had a glimpse of the mysterious Fred, who was tall and wore a cap and high hat. Matilda Clover's death was certified as being due to alcoholism, but some weeks later a Dr Broadbent, who enjoyed a fashionable practice in Portman Square and had doubtless never heard of Matilda Clover, received a letter signed 'M. Malone' accusing him of the strychnine murder of that unfortunate creature and threatening his exposure unless he paid the writer £2,500; invited to visit Portman Square, 'M. Malone' proved anti-social. The Countess Russell staying at London's Savoy Hotel also received a similar letter accusing Lord Russell of the murder of Clover.

In November Neill Cream returned to the United States, and paid a visit to Canada before his return to London in April 1892. He had commissioned, in Quebec, the printing of five hundred circulars, which for some reason were never circulated:

ELLEN DONWORTH'S DEATH
To the Guests of the Metropole Hotel:
Ladies and Gentlemen,
    I hereby notify you that the person who poisoned Ellen Donworth on the 13th last October is today in the employ of the Metropole Hotel and that your lives are in danger as long as you remain in this Hotel.
                                        Yours Respectfully,
                                            W. H. MURRAY
London, *April 1892.*

At the end of this month two more prostitutes, 18-year-old Emma Shrivell and 20-year-old Alice Marsh, were transported to hospital from their Waterloo Road lodging in the most violent convulsions, both dying shortly afterwards, and both jabbering about a doctor called 'Fred' who had given each of them three 'long thin pills'. These two girls were found to have died from strychnine poisoning. Suspicious, the authorities exhumed Matilda Clover's body, and found that she, also, had been a victim of this maniac poisoner who never waited to view the results of his handiwork.

Cream was eventually caught, chiefly through his own brand of exhibitionism. He had even bitterly complained, quite unjustly, to a Sergeant McIntyre of Scotland Yard, that he was being followed by police anxious to interview him about the murders; he also mentioned a certain diabolical Dr Harper, about whom victims Matilda Clover and Louise Harvey had been warned by letter shortly before their deaths. It is indicative of Cream's confused mental state that 'Lou' Harvey, albeit an intended victim, had remained very much alive, and whose demise, although assumed by the pill-proffering doctor ('I pretended to take them, putting my hand to my mouth and pretending to swallow them'), had never, naturally enough, appeared in the Press. It is to 'Lou' Harvey that we are indebted for a description of the homicidal physician, given in a letter to the Bow Street magistrate. She, too, was a prostitute, and had been 'picked up' by Cream at the Alhambra Theatre, spending the night of October 26th with him at an hotel in Berwick Street, near Oxford Street; the following evening she met him again, and it was on this occasion she pretended to swallow the capsules:

> ... I threw them over the Embankment ... he left me ... gave me five shillings to go to the Oxford Music Hall, promising to meet me outside at 11 o'clock. But he never came ... He wore gold-rimmed Glasses ... he had a dress suit on ... spoke with a foreign twang ... I noticed he was a very hairy man ...

Describing him in court later, Louise Harvey said: '... he had no beard, he had a moustache ... the top of his head was bald. He was cross-eyed.'

Charged and found guilty of the murder of Matilda Clover, Cream was hanged on November 15th, 1892; he never confessed to the killings. Cream's brand of remote-control sadism was unique, and his preoccupation with melodramatic missives so intense, one can be permitted the facetious thought that perhaps these crimes were merely the corollary of a frustrated pamphleteer.

CRIPPEN, Hawley Harvey

Known as 'Peter' Crippen, an American doctor (medical degree from the Hospital College of Cleveland) aged 50, who was hanged on November 23rd, 1910, for the murder of his wife (also American) the previous January.

The Crippens lived in disharmony at 39 Hilldrop Crescent, North London. Timid-seeming Dr Crippen worked on commission for the Munyon Patent Medicine Company and had a partnership in another firm, the Yale Tooth Specialists, that rented offices at Albion House, Oxford Street; flamboyant Mrs Crippen aspired to the stage, without any success – her one professional appearance was during an 'artistes' strike, for which she received abuse from Marie Lloyd. Mrs Crippen had used several names – Cora Turner, Cora Marsangar, and, in London, Belle Elmore – but her real name was Kunigunde Mackamotzki; she was last seen alive on January 31st, 1910, when she and her husband entertained some retired stage performers, the Martinettis, to dinner. Two days after, the Music Hall Ladies Guild, of which Belle Elmore was treasurer, received notice of her resignation – she had been obliged to return to America because of a relative's illness; at the Ladies' Benevolent Fund ball some weeks later, Peter Crippen escorted a young woman, noticed to be wearing Mrs Crippen's jewellery. In March this woman, Ethel Le Neve, aged 27, whom Crippen employed as a typist in his office, moved into Hilldrop Crescent and Peter Crippen was informing inquirers that his wife had perished of pneumonia 'up in the high mountains of California'. A suspicious friend of Belle Elmore's informed the police and Crippen was questioned by Chief Inspector Dew, who searched the house at Hilldrop Crescent. Finding nothing, he was about to drop the investigation, when he heard that Dr Crippen and Ethel Le Neve had disappeared. Probing the house more thoroughly, police unearthed portions of a body (the head, skeleton, and limbs were never found) in the cellar. A warrant was issued for the arrest of the doctor and his mistress. 'Wanted for Murder and Mutilation'. Eight days later, Captain Kendall, the commander of the SS *Montrose*, making for Quebec from Antwerp, observed that two of his passengers, a Mr Robinson and son, were curiously affectionate towards each other, and that the 'son's' trousers, owing to unmasculine proportions, were adjusted by safety-pins. ('All the boy's manners at table were most ladylike . . . his father kept cracking nuts for him, and giving him half of his own salad . . .') Captain Kendall had read the Metropolitan Police circular concerning Crippen and Le Neve, and doubts about the Robinson couple prompted him to send a wireless message to London – the first time wireless was employed in a murder hunt. (Mr Robinson would often sit on deck, looking aloft at the wireless aerial saying, 'What a wonderful invention it is!') Inspector Dew was dispatched on a quicker ship bound for Quebec, and at Father Point on July 31st he confronted the fugitives.

Meanwhile Dr Spilsbury (who was to become the famous

Home Office pathologist) had, with others, examined the remains dug up from Crippen's cellar, finding they contained the narcotic poison, hyoscine. Crippen, a fortnight before his wife's disappearance, had bought five grains of this poison from Lewis and Burrows, the wholesale chemists – although hyoscine was never used in any medicine such as he would prescribe. An operation scar was found on one piece of skin tissue, and Mrs Crippen was known to have undergone abdominal surgery; wrapped around the remains was underclothing belonging to Belle Elmore and a portion of a pyjama jacket whose sale was traced to Crippen. The identity of the corpse was obvious.

Crippen was tried for murder at the Old Bailey on October 18th, and after a four days' trial was found guilty. From the time of his arrest his only concern had been for his mistress, Ethel Le Neve (found not guilty of being an accessory), and he asked if a photograph of her might be buried with him.

Sympathy has been felt for Crippen, considered by many to be a figure of pathos. Beerbohm Tree went about London on the day of the execution muttering 'Poor old Crippen', but criminologist William Le Queux, who claimed to have met Crippen in 1908 (the doctor was seeking information on untraceable poisons for a novel he proposed to write), held a less charitable view: 'Hawley Harvey Crippen was certainly one of the most dangerous criminals of his century.'

CROSS, Philip
Sixty-two-year-old retired Army surgeon who murdered his 40-year-old wife Laura, at Shandy Hall, Dipsey, County Cork, Ireland, in 1887.

The Crosses lived at Shandy Hall with their four children and Aunt Henrietta, a sister of Dr Cross. In June 1886, a 20-year-old girl, Mary Skinner, took over the post as governess to the Cross children, but was soon ordered from the house by Mrs Cross, who had noticed the amorous dalliance between her husband and the governess. Dr Cross, under pretext of business, also left Shandy Hall and followed Miss Skinner to Dublin, where for a short while they stayed together at hotels. From January 1887 the health of Mrs Cross deteriorated; she was subject to attacks of vomiting and diarrhoea, also an abnormal thirst. 'Phil tells me that I have a disease of the heart,' she told a friend. For five months Dr Cross forecast his wife's imminent death, which took place on the night of June 1st. On June 9th, Dr Cross sailed for

England, marrying Mary Skinner at St James' Church, Piccadilly, on June 17th, before sailing back to Ireland on June 21st.
Local gossip caused the exhumation of the first Mrs Cross, and
both arsenic (3·2 grains) and strychnine were found in the body.
Charged with the murder of his wife, Dr Cross was heard to inquire of his sister if she had destroyed two bottles 'with the
white powder inside'; these bottles were never found, nor was
any trace of heart disease in the deceased Mrs Cross. Dr Cross
was known to have purchased a large amount of arsenic 'for
sheep-dipping'.

The trial of Dr Cross lasted four days; he was found guilty of
the murder of Laura Cross and hanged.

CROYDON Murders, The
*Inexplicable series of poisonings in South Croydon in 1928 and
1929, involving two interrelated families, the Sydneys and the
Duffs.*

The first victim was Mr Edmund Creighton Duff, age 59, retired
British Resident in Northern Nigeria, who lived in South Park
Hill Road, near South Croydon Station, and was married to
Grace, younger daughter of Mrs Violet Emelia Sydney, aged 68,
who lived with her other daughter, Vera, aged 40, at Birdhurst
Rise, Croydon. On the evening of April 26th, 1928, Edmund
Duff returned from a Hampshire fishing holiday. His wife had
prepared a meal of chicken and vegetables, and he drank two
bottles of beer; shortly afterwards he felt unwell, and went to
bed complaining of cramp in his leg muscles, and nausea. Mr
Duff's condition deteriorated, and he died the following night;
certain of his organs were sent to Harrow Hospital for analysis
by the pathologist, Dr Robert Brontë, whose findings were
negative. At the Coroner's inquest a verdict of 'Death from
natural causes' was returned.

The second victim was Miss Vera Sydney. On February 14th,
1929, soon after lunch she complained of feeling 'seedy'; her
aunt and the cook who had also partaken of the lunch were similarly afflicted, as was the family cat. Two days later Vera Sydney
died, after hours of cramp and vomiting, and her death was
registered as due to gastric influenza.

The third victim was Mrs Sydney. Under medical care after
the shock of her sudden bereavement, she became violently sick
after lunch on March 5th, 1929, blaming her condition on a tonic
prescribed by her physician, Dr Binning; she insisted the medi-

cine had poisoned her, saying that it had a 'gritty' feel. The remains of the bottle, however (which contained a proprietary product), were never analysed. After a few hours Mrs Sydney died in agony.

Thomas Duff, aged 45, who also lived in South Park Hill Road with his wife and children, expressed unease at the deaths. 'This must be seen into', and eventually, on March 22nd, the bodies of mother and daughter were exhumed from Croydon Cemetery. Sir Bernard Spilsbury conducted the post-mortems, and expressed the opinion that both deaths were due to arsenic poisoning. On May 18th, despite Dr Brontë's previous findings and the protests of the widow (who wrote an indignant letter to *The Times*), Edmund Duff's body was exhumed, and arsenic was found in the internal organs. (It was suggested that at the previous post-mortem, organs from another corpse were accidentally fused with the Duff remains.)

A verdict of murder against some person or persons unknown was returned at the inquest on Edmund Duff and Vera Sydney. At the inquest on Mrs Sydney the verdict was that there was insufficient evidence to show whether she had committed suicide or had been murdered.

CUMMINS, Gordon Frederick
Young airman, who murdered four women in four days in 1942

In the early hours of February 9th, 1942, a 40-year-old schoolmistress, Miss Evelyn Hamilton, was found strangled in an air-raid shelter in Montagu Place, Marylebone. Her handbag was missing; she had not been sexually assaulted. On February 10th, Mrs Evelyn Oatley, known as Nita Ward, a 35 year-old ex-revue actress, was found dead in her Wardour Street flat. She was found naked on the bed; her throat had been cut and the lower part of her body mutilated with a tin-opener. Fingerprints were found on the tin-opener and a mirror.

On February 11th, a Tuesday, another woman was murdered, although the police did not find out about it until three days later. She was Mrs Margaret Lowe, aged 43; she lived alone in a flat in Gosfield Street in the West End. She had been strangled with a silk stocking, and mutilated with a razor blade in the same way as Mrs Oatley. She was discovered on Friday by her 14-year-old evacuee daughter who came to pay a visit.

Some hours after Mrs Lowe's body was found, the fourth victim was also discovered. She was Mrs Doris Jouannet, whose husband was the night manager of a Paddington Hotel. When he returned home on Friday evening he noticed that the milk had not been taken in. Mrs Jouannet had been strangled with a stocking and mutilated with a razor blade. It soon transpired that Mrs Jouannet had been in the habit of picking up soldiers in Leicester Square pubs while her husband was on night duty; he had last seen her alive at ten o'clock on the previous evening.

Shortly after Mrs Jouannet's body was discovered, a young airman tried to accost a Mrs Heywood in a pub near Piccadilly. She refused, and he followed her out into the blacked-out street, saying, 'You must at least kiss me good night.' He dragged her into a doorway and throttled her into unconsciousness. A passer-by heard the scuffle, and investigated; the man ran away, leaving behind his gas-mask. This had his service number stencilled on it.

The young airman immediately picked up another woman and drove with her in a taxi to her flat in Southwark Street, Paddington. She was Mrs Mulcahy, known as Kathleen King. In her room, the light failed, and the airman seized her by the throat. Her terror of the 'ripper' who had already killed four women made her fight violently and scream. The airman fled, leaving behind his belt.

From the gas-mask case, the attacker was identified as Gordon Frederick Cummins, a 28-year-old RAF cadet, married and living in North London. He was arrested within twelve hours of the attack on Kathleen King, on returning to his billet in St John's Wood.

Cummins had a curious record. Although he came from a good family and was well educated, he had been dismissed from a series of jobs as unreliable and dishonest. He had married in 1936 the private secretary of a theatrical producer. One of his companions declared he was a 'phoney', that he spoke with a fake Oxford accent and claimed he had a right to use 'honourable' before his name because he was the illegitimate son of a member of the House of Lords. He was known as 'the Duke' to his companions.

His fingerprints corresponded with those on the mirror and tin-opener; also, like the killer, he was left-handed. It appeared later that another prostitute had had a narrow escape from death; Cummins had accompanied her home on the night he killed Mrs Oatley, but she had mentioned that she had no money, and Cummins, who killed for cash, left her alone.

He was sentenced to death at the Old Bailey, and executed on

June 25th, 1942, during an air raid. Sir Bernard Spilsbury, who had performed the post-mortem on Mrs Oatley, also performed one on Cummins.

D

DAVIES, John Michael (The Clapham Common Murder)

Twenty-year-old labourer of Turret Grove, Clapham, convicted of the murder of John Beckley, 17-year-old apprentice electrical engineer.

On July 2nd, 1953, Beckley was found with fatal stab wounds near a bus stop on the north side of Clapham Common, London. Beckley and his friend, bank clerk Matthew Chandler, had earlier made depreciatory remarks to a gang of 'Teddy Boys' (unknown to either of them) by the bandstand at Clapham Common. Unduly sensitive, the gang kicked and punched the derisive pair, and there was a cry of 'Get the knives out.' Beckley and Chandler attempted to escape by jumping on a 137 bus travelling along Clapham Common. At a 'request' stop they were dragged from the platform of the bus by members of the gang and further assaulted. Chandler managed to mount the bus again, bleeding from stab wounds in the groin and stomach. Beckley, surrounded by attackers, was heard to cry, 'Go on then, stab me', before he fell dying.

Police questioned South London gangs, and six youths were finally apprehended and charged with being concerned in the murder of Beckley. Four of these youths were to be acquitted of the murder charge, facing a second indictment concerning common assault, to which they were found guilty and imprisoned. Sixteen-year-old shop assistant Ronald Coleman and John Michael Davies, both pleading not guilty, were tried at the Old Bailey for the murder of Beckley; the jury were unable to agree on a verdict, and the Crown stated that it did not propose putting Coleman on trial for murder again.

On October 19th, 1953, the retrial of Davies began. Mary Frayling, a secretary, was one of the few out of fifty passengers on the 137 bus to volunteer evidence. ('The true shame of Clapham Common,' said one newspaper.) She identified Davies as the chief attacker of Beckley, mentioning a 'green-handled object' he afterwards placed in his inside breast pocket. ('I said to my friend at the time, "Supposing this is murder in the morning." ') Davies was alleged, as he left the Common, to have remarked to a boy named 'Splinter Wood', in reference to the knife, 'There is no claret on it,' and to have demonstrated at a coffee bar how he used the knife. After his arrest blood was found in Davies' inside breast pocket, but throughout his trial Davies denied using a knife, although admitting assaulting Beckley.

On October 22nd he was found guilty of murder and sentenced to death. Subsequent appeals to the Court of Criminal Appeal and the House of Lords were dismissed, but twelve days before his execution, scheduled for February 2nd, he was reprieved.

The case caused a change in the law of evidence. It established that the evidence of accomplices must be corroborated.

DEATH PENALTY

The death penalty has already been abolished in many countries of the world at the time of writing (1960) including Germany, Sweden, and certain states of America. There is no evidence that violent crime has increased in any country since the abolition of the death penalty.

In England, a violent agitation against the death penalty in 1956 (conducted by Sidney Silverman, MP and Victor Gollancz, the publisher) led finally to the Homicide Act of 1957, a compromise measure, which declared that only the following types of murder would be punishable by death:

1. Murder committed in the course or furtherance of theft.
2. Murder by shooting or causing an explosion.
3. Murder in the course of resisting arrest.
4. Murder of a policeman or prison officer.
5. Two murders committed 'on different occasions'.

Obviously, the act is full of anomalies which must somehow be removed. The case of William Biddick in 1959 brought one of these to light. Biddick had murdered his mistress after a quarrel, and then killed her 15-year-old daughter; the prosecution declared that this constituted two occasions, since medical evidence indicated that an hour had elapsed between the murders, while the defence submitted that less than an hour had elapsed. The defence also declared that Biddick had killed his mistress accidentally in the course of violent sexual activity, and that he was in a state of diminished responsibility due to psychological shock when he killed the girl. Biddick received a prison sentence. But although the judge ruled that the murders had constituted 'one occasion', it is obvious that some murderer will be hanged one day because of half an hour in his timing between the murders.

There were 151 murders in England in 1957, twenty-four of them having been committed before the act came into operation. There were 124 in 1958. Since 1957, about four murders a year have suffered the death penalty – about a third of the anticipated number. A short list may give a cross section of British murder cases:

John Vickers, aged 22. Murdered a woman of 72 in the course of burglary. Executed (the first since August 1955) on July 23rd, 1957.

Dennis Howard, aged 24, who shot a 21-year-old shop-keeper while trying to rob him. Executed November 1957.

Vivian Teed, aged 24, who murdered a 73-year-old post-master with twenty-seven hammer blows, in the course of robbery. Executed May 1958.

Peter Manuel, aged 32. (See below.)

Matthew Kavanagh, aged 32, who murdered a 60-year-old fellow-lodger who caught him stealing in his room. Executed August 1958.

Frank Stokes, aged 44, hotel porter who murdered a 75-year-old widow with hammer blows in the course of robbery. He was also indignant because she had offered him a job as gardener at 6d. an hour less than he was used to. Executed September 1958.

Brian Chandler, aged 20, who murdered an 83-year-old widow while stealing £4. He used a hammer. Executed December 1958.

Ernest Jones, aged 39, who murdered a store manager in the course of stealing £75. Executed February 1959.

Joseph Chrimes, aged 30. Murdered an old woman with a tyre lever in the course of a burglary with an accomplice. Executed April 1959.

Ronald Henry Marwood, aged 24. (See below.)

Michael Tatum, aged 24, who killed an 85-year-old man with a blunt instrument while burgling. Executed May 14th, 1959.

Bernard Walden, aged 33, a lecturer at Rotherham Technical College, who shot a girl student (to whom he had proposed) and her boy-friend out of jealousy. Executed August 1959.

Guenther Fritz Erwin Podola, aged 30. (See below.)

Ernest Fantle, who shot his wife's lover four times with a revolver, pleaded a defence of provocation, and was successful. He received three years' imprisonment. The disparity between this judgement and that on Walden is too obvious to require comment.

Between 1949 and 1953, eighty-five were executed. Fifteen of these were for financial gain, an average of four a year approximately.

DEEMING, Frederick Bailey
Murderer of six people and confidence trickster, executed on May 23rd, 1892.

Little is known of Deeming's early life. He himself claimed that both his mother and father had been in mental homes, and that as a child his own abnormality earned him the nickname, 'Mad Fred'.

His career of crime seems to have started relatively late. In 1883 he was about 30 years of age, and had left his recently married wife in Birkenhead while he went to Australia to seek his fortune. In Sydney he worked as a gasfitter, and very quickly spent some time in jail for stealing fittings. This is the only crime that can be said to be unworthy of Deeming's flamboyant personality; for, like Dr Pritchard, he was a braggart and inventor of tall tales worthy of Munchausen. After a brief term in jail, he made an attempt to earn an honest living, having now been joined by his wife. This failed, owing to his total unreliability, which sent his trade to his more staid rivals. He filed a petition for bankruptcy, and was arrested for fraud. Released on bail, he fled with his wife and children to Port Adelaide. There, under the name of Ward, he stayed in January 1888. It seems that he decided quite definitely on a criminal career at this time. He left there for St Helena, and on the voyage defrauded two brothers named Howe of £60. From St Helena the family moved to Cape Town, where he obtained work from a firm of engineers. He soon tired of this, and moved around to Port Elizabeth, Kimberley, Johannesburg, and Durban, always 'talking big' and managing to support himself with various minor frauds. His chief prey were jewellers, and he was soon wanted for frauds amounting to £1,000 by jewellers in Cape Town, Durban, and Johannesburg. His usual method was to pose as the manager of a diamond mine.

In Johannesburg he offered lavish hospitality to big business men and gained a large sum through a swindle worked on the National Bank.

Next he obtained a post as manager of a gold-mining company at Klerksdorp. Here he devised a new swindle; he offered to sell certain gold mines to a rich financier. When the financier set off for Cape Town to investigate Deeming's claims, his agent, a man named Grice, received a telegram instructing him to pay Deeming 'not more than £2,200'. Grice actually paid up £2,800 for some deeds of property. Soon, Grice received a telegram from Deeming saying he intended to meet a Mr Leevy in Cape Town; soon after that, 'Leevy' himself telegraphed to say that Deeming had died after a brief illness.

Deeming now sent his wife and children (there were now four) to England, and went to Aden on a coal vessel, then to Southampton. Detectives were on his trail, and he went from Hull to Birkenhead, then to Camberwell, Stockton-on-Tees, sailed for Australia, doubled back at Port Said, and returned to England.

At Hull and Beverley in Yorkshire, he was a millionaire and a relative of Sir Wilfred Lawson. He proposed marriage to the landlady of his hotel, who had the sense to refuse him; another woman, a Miss Matheson, accepted him and he married her bigamously. A few months later he deserted her. Shortly before the marriage he was in Antwerp posing as Lord Dunn. After the marriage, he and his 'wife' stayed at Gosport at the Star Hotel under the name of Lawson; he paid the hotel bill with a bogus cheque and returned to Hull.

In Hull, he swindled a jeweller out of £285 worth of jewellery (paid for with a bouncing cheque) and hastily embarked for South America. On this trip he became well known to the passengers as a hospitable and wealthy man, manager of a diamond mine in South Africa; he arranged a concert in aid of the Seamen's Orphanage and headed the subscription list with a generous donation. His fellow passengers were startled when he was arrested at Montevideo. He wrote indignantly to his counsel that the prison fare was doing 'considerable hingery' to his health. (Deeming seems to have been almost illiterate.) On the way back to England he tried all kinds of ruses for escaping; he even told the sceptical detective hair-raising adventure stories in which he had killed men.

At Hull Assizes, on October 16th, 1890, he was sentenced to nine months in jail. On July 16th, 1891, he was released. He now went to the Commercial Hotel, Liverpool, where he posed as

O. A. Williams, who was an inspector of regiments in South Africa (or India – his story varied), who had come to England to take a house for a Colonel Brooks who would be shortly retiring. Deeming was certainly now planning to murder his wife and family, for he found a cottage, Dinham Villa, at Rainhill, and specified that he was to concrete the kitchen floor since the colonel hated uneven floors. His wife came to visit him at Rainhill and had meals with him in the hotel, where she was introduced as his sister. (Deeming was already courting a Miss Mather, daughter of a widow who kept a newsagent's shop.) Towards the end of July 1891, Mrs Deeming and the children moved into Dinham Villa, and were murdered and buried under the kitchen floor. Deeming then cemented the floor himself, getting workmen to help with the finishing touches. Before leaving the hotel, where he had made many friends, he gave a dinner party that was reported in the local papers. This was a month after the murders. He spent two weeks in London, where he wrote to his murdered wife's father, saying that he intended to visit him soon with his wife, and then returned to Rainhill, where he married Miss Mather. He took her to see Dinham Villa, and danced a little jig on the kitchen floor.

They decided to sail for Australia. Before leaving England, Deeming tried one more fraud; he sent a picture by rail, and then tried claiming that it was damaged, and demanded £50 compensation. The railway company called his bluff, and he left England without the money.

Miss Mather appears to have been extremely happy with her lively husband; but by the time they reached Australia – ten days before Christmas, 1891 – she must have had her doubts. A neighbour who saw her described her as a silent woman whose eyes seemed red from weeping. She must have suspected her husband's true character from the fact that he now insisted on an alias of Droven or Drewen. They took a house in Andrew Street, Windsor, Melbourne. In a very short time indeed, Miss Mather found her way under the bedroom floor, where she was cemented in.

On January 5th, Deeming moved out. He applied to a matrimonial agency for a wife, but then left Melbourne suddenly and sailed for Sydney. On the boat he met his next prospective victim, a Miss Katie Rounsfell, who quickly agreed to marry him. She knew him as Baron Swanston. He travelled to Sydney with her, then left her and obtained a job with Fraser's gold mine, Southern Cross. She was actually on her way to join him when chance – in the form of the discovery of Miss Mather – saved her.

Eight weeks after Deeming had moved out of Andrew Street, the agent, a man named Connor, went to look over the place, having heard of an offensive odour in the bedroom. The newly cemented fireplace was crumbling – the heat of an Australian summer had dried it too quickly. Connor kicked away a few lumps of soft concrete and found himself looking at the face of a dead girl.

'Drewen' had left many clues behind him, including a card labelled O. A. Williams, with the Rainhill address on it. This soon led to the discovery of the bodies in Dinham Villa. Detective-Sergeant Considine, of the CID in Melbourne (who was in charge of the case), has declared that three houses in which Deeming had lived in Johannesburg also revealed bodies of women under the hearths. If so, it is not known who these women were. At the time Deeming lived in Johannesburg, his wife was with him.

Considine soon discovered that 'Drewen' was a confidence swindler who had defrauded a Melbourne firm of valuable jewellery, and had tried to swindle another firm of £2,000. He had also tried to blackmail the shipowners whose boat had brought him to Melbourne, declaring that his wife had lost a £1,000 necklace on the trip. (No doubt this accounted for Emily Mather's disillusion, for she must have been called upon to substantiate Deeming's story.)

Deeming was traced to Southern Cross and arrested there. He was taken to Melbourne – great crowds gathering to watch his arrival – and tried there. He suffered from fits (as he had on the voyage back from Montevideo), but detectives suspected these were faked. At one point he narrowly escaped lynching. He wrote to Miss Rounsfell, declaring his innocence and asking her to believe in him; he also asked for money. (Miss Rounsfell was an heiress.)

His defence tried an insanity plea, and Deeming declared that the apparition of his dead mother frequently appeared to him, and had once urged him to kill all his woman friends. He also made a speech declaring that Emily Mather was still alive and that the people in court were the ugliest he had ever seen in his life. He was sentenced to death. In jail he confessed to being Jack the Ripper – an impossibility since he was in jail at the time of the murders.

DE LA POMMERAIS, Dr

In some ways, one of the most revolting of medical murderers.

He was born in Orléans in 1845, and came to Paris to set up as a
doctor in 1859. He was typical of a certain type of murderer –
vain and a pathological liar. He called himself 'Count de la Pommerais' and gambled heavily. His mistress was a beautiful young
widow of an artist named de Pauw, whom Pommerais had attended; she had three small children. But he decided to marry
for money, and secured the hand of the daughter of a widow
who was one of his patients, a Mlle Dabizy. Soon, Mme Dabizy
died after taking a meal with her son-in-law; he certified her
death as due to Asiatic cholera, and her fortune – which came to
Pommerais – saved him from bankruptcy. The unfortunate
Madame de Pauw was starving at this time, and one day Pommerais approached her with a dishonest scheme which, he said,
would secure her an income for life. She was to insure her life
for half a million francs (£20,000) – the premium would be paid
by Pommerais. Pommerais would then give her a drug which
would apparently bring her to death's door. The insurance company, fearful of sustaining a heavy loss, would agree to give her
an annuity for the rest of her life, and Pommerais would produce
the antidote to the drug and make her recover.

It is unnecessary to say that Pommerais had no intention that
his unfortunate ex-mistress should recover. After getting her to
make a will in his favour and to sign a document transferring the
insurance money to himself, the accident was staged, a bad fall
downstairs. Mme de Pauw was badly hurt, and Pommerais'
medicines made her worse. Her aunt, Mme Ritter, was called,
and the patient told her 'in confidence' about the plot. However, she did not get well; she died, and the Paris police received
an anonymous letter urging them to look into Pommerais' affairs.
The insurance company had paid up the half million francs.
Mme de Pauw's body was exhumed, and was found to contain
digitalis. Mme Dabizy's death was now recalled; she was also
exhumed, and found to have died from digitalis poisoning. Mme
Ritter's evidence about the 'plot' which her niece had revealed
to her was conclusive. Pommerais was sentenced to death for the
murder of his mistress. (He was found not guilty of Mme
Dabizy's death, the jury recognizing, no doubt, that this might
be made the grounds for an appeal.) It was expected that the
Empress Eugenie, who had taken an interest in the case, would
secure a reprieve, but this expectation was not fulfilled, and he

was executed, one of the most undeserving murderers of the last century. It is impossible to contemplate a murder like this without being completely baffled about the moral state of the man who could commit it.

DENKE, Karl
German mass murderer, possibly homosexual, and almost certainly guilty of cannibalism. Born at Münsterberg, near Breslau. Because he hanged himself before the trial, fewer details are known of his crimes than might otherwise have come to light.

Denke flourished under the same circumstances as his even more horrible compatriot, Haarmann. He was the landlord of a house in Münsterberg in Silesia, an organ blower at the local church. After 1918, there was a famine in Germany. On December 21st, 1924, a coachman named Gabriel who lived above Herr Denke, heard cries for help. Thinking that his landlord might be in trouble, he rushed downstairs, and found a powerfully built young travelling journeyman with blood streaming from a wound in his head. The journeyman had time to gasp that Denke had attacked him with an axe before he collapsed unconscious. The police were called, and Denke was arrested. His house was searched, and the identity papers of twelve travelling journeymen were found in a sack, together with various articles of clothing. Two tubs of meat pickled in brine were found, as well as pots of fat and bones; these were found to be the remains of thirty victims, both men and women. A ledger was also found which contained the name, date, and weight of every carcass that was pickled. They dated from 1921 – three years before – and applied to tramps, beggarwomen, and journeymen.

Almost nothing is known of Denke's motives or his mental state. He may have been maddened by starvation and the inflation that made his rents worth nothing. Or he may have been a psychopath, like the man who was recently caught in America, whose farm kitchen contained several headless victims hanging upside down.

Denke committed suicide shortly after he was caught, hanging himself with his braces.

DESCHAMPS, Dr Etienne
Executed on May 12th, 1892, for the murder of 12-year-old Juliette Deitsh in New Orleans. It seems fairly plain from the evidence that it was actually a case of manslaughter, and that Deschamps was really executed because he had seduced the child.

Deschamps was born in Rennes in 1830; fought in the Crimean War and was wounded at the Battle of Sevastapol, was apparently involved in revolutionary politics towards 1870, when he was driven from France. He was a skilled dentist, but began to dabble in the occult, and became something of a charlatan. He was highly successful with his 'magnetizing' treatment in New Orleans from his arrival there in 1884.

In 1888, Deschamps became friendly with a carpenter named Jules Deitsh who lived in the Rue Chartres. Deitsh was a widower with two young daughters, Laurence, aged 9, and Juliette, 12. Juliette was a well-developed girl for her age, and Deschamps decided to seduce her. He told the gullible Deitsh that he had decided to locate the buried treasure of the pirate Jean Lafitte, concealed among the swamps of Barataria, and that he needed a young virgin as a medium.

It seems reasonably certain that Juliette did not remain a virgin for long. Like Nabokov's Humbert, Deschamps, it would seem, was in the habit of chloroforming her before sexual intercourse took place, although it also seems certain that the child knew herself to be his mistress and accepted the position.

On January 30th, 1889, Juliette and Laurence paid the doctor a visit at his house at 714 St Peter Street, and an experiment began which involved Juliette stripping naked and climbing into bed. Deschamps also stripped and climbed into bed with her, telling Laurence that this was going to be one of their most successful experiments. He applied a chloroformed handkerchief to her face. He asked Juliette what she saw, and the child replied: 'God, the Holy Virgin, and Jackson Square.' Deschamps now went out, and returned with more chloroform and climbed back into bed. Soon he cried: 'My God, my God, what have I done!' and Laurence began to cry. He told her to run home and tell her father that he (Deschamps) was going to die, and cunningly loaded her with some heavy books, which made her progress slow. When the room was opened again later, the doctor lay naked on the bed, his chest wounded with a dental instrument, and Juliette lay dead beside him. Deschamps' wounds were superficial and he was arrested. A few days later he made a half-hearted attempt to commit suicide in his cell, but allowed his chin to rest on the belt by which he hanged himself from the bars.

The trial began on April 29th, 1889, Deschamps pleading not guilty. He alleged that Juliette was not a virgin when he had first met her (which seems to be untrue). The trial was very brief and Deschamps was found guilty of murder. There was an appeal, on March 28th, 1890, which, like the first trial, lasted only two days. Again Deschamps was found guilty. Between the two trials, Deschamps became a violently unruly prisoner, making insane sprints for freedom whenever he was allowed out of his cell, refusing to be interviewed by reporters, and calling his fellow prisoners criminals. He declared that when he returned to France he would see that war was declared on the United States.

Judge Marr, who passed sentence of death the second time, disappeared mysteriously on April 19th, 1891, and was never seen again. The sentence caused some public scandal and there was widespread protest, including a self-appointed commission of doctors to declare Deschamps insane. (Deschamps spent hours in his cell 'talking' with Juliette and Jean Lafitte.) There were two temporary reprieves. Deschamps was still protesting his innocence when he was hanged.

DEVEUREUX, Arthur
Twenty-four-year-old chemist's assistant, convicted of the murder of his wife Beatrice, aged 25, and his twin sons, Lawrence Rowland and Evelyn Lancelot.

Deveureux was excessively devoted to his eldest child, Stanley, and while living in poverty in a Kilburn, London, back street, determined to dispose of his wife and younger sons so that all his energies could be devoted to the welfare of Stanley. He purchased a large tin trunk and, after poisoning his victims with morphine, stuffed their bodies in the trunk and placed it in a Kensal Rise furniture depository. He then moved to another part of London, taking delight in securing for Stanley, aged 6, a place in a private school. To his mother-in-law's inquiries he was evasive, so evasive that she made further inquiries at her daughter's former address in Kilburn, thus learning about the trunk 'filled with domestic articles' now reposing in the depository. Instinctively apprehensive, the woman went to Kensal Rise, obtaining the authority to have the trunk opened on April 13th, 1905. The contents concerned Scotland Yard, who placed

Inspector Pollard in charge of the case. Deveureux was traced to Coventry, where he had got a job with a chemist; when first approached by Pollard, before even the preliminary introductions were over Deveureux stammered: 'You have made a mistake, I don't know anything about a tin trunk.'

Arrested on a charge of wife-murder, he said his wife had killed the twins, then committed suicide: 'Imagine my terrible position. My wife had poisoned the twins with morphine belonging to me, and had then committed suicide by the same means. I was a chemist's assistant, and in a position to get poison . . .' Deveureux was tried at the Old Bailey before Mr Justice Ridley in July 1905; Sir Charles Matthews prosecuted, and Mr Charles Eliot defended. Deveureux unsuccessfully feigned insanity, and was hanged at Pentonville Prison on August 15th, 1905.

DIBLANC, Marguerite
A cook of Belgian origin who was sentenced to death (but later reprieved) for the murder of her mistress in 1872.

Marguerite Diblanc had been dismissed by the daughter of her mistress, Marie Caroline Riel, with only a week's wages. She had been in the employ of the Frenchwoman since November 1871, and was dismissed in March 1872. She very rightly claimed that since she was paid by the month, she should receive a month's wages. Mme Riel refused, but they compromised by allowing Marguerite to stay another month.

On Sunday, April 7th, 1872, Mme Riel was on her way to take the dog for a walk, and she called into the kitchen. Some kind of a quarrel developed, and the cook ended by strangling her mistress and hiding her body in the cellar. (Marguerite Diblanc was a powerfully built girl of 29.) An hour or so later, having sent out the maid, Eliza Watts, to get some beer, she dragged the body upstairs to the pantry and locked it in, knowing that Eliza had no key. That afternoon she took all the ready cash she could find – some £80 – and left in the evening. The body was not discovered until the next day – Monday – when Mme Riel's daughter Julie returned from France. (She was an actress.) Marguerite Diblanc was by this time in Paris herself; but her demeanour had been so noticeable that the cabman who drove her to Victoria, and a railway clerk, remembered her. She was easily traced, and brought back to England, where she was tried before Baron Channel at the Old Bailey on June 12th. The Attorney General, Sir John Coleridge, led the prosecution, and

Mr Powell, QC, the defence. It was argued by the defence that the prisoner had been so provoked that her crime could not be viewed as murder. The jury found her guilty, with a recommendation to mercy, and she was later reprieved.

DICKMAN, John Alexander

The sixth railway murderer in England. It may be worth listing the other five. The first was Franz Müller, the second, Percy Mapleton (alias Lefroy). The next was unsolved; a Miss Camp was found dead in a second-class compartment on July 12th, 1897, when the Feltham train arrived at Waterloo; a chemist's pestle with blood on it was found on the line. The fourth murder was in 1901, when a Mr Pearson was the victim in a train near Wimbledon; the fifth was the Merstham Tunnel mystery (see 'Moneys').

Dickman murdered John Nisbet on Friday, March 18th, 1910; Nisbet was a cashier who was on his way to pay wages at a colliery near Widdrington Station, 35 miles from Newcastle. Nisbet left Newcastle in company with a man on the 10.27 train; he had £370 in his bag. Dickman was also seen getting into the train with a man, although no witness who knew Dickman also knew Nisbet, and vice versa. Mrs Nisbet came to the platform at Heaton (as was her custom on these pay journeys) and said 'hello' to her husband; she noticed he was travelling with a man. (Although she knew Dickman, she did not recognize him.) At the next station, 2½ miles away, Dickman left the train. When the train arrived at Alnmouth, a porter looked into Nisbet's carriage, and noticed blood running from under the seat; he found Nisbet's body there, shot five times. The bag which had contained the £370 was found on July 9th at the bottom of the Isabella pit, a disused mine shaft near Morpeth, the station where Dickman left the train.

Information of passengers who had seen him led the police to question Dickman, and he was eventually arrested. Nisbet had been shot with two different revolvers; neither of these was ever found, although the police were able to prove that Dickman had owned a revolver recently. None of the £370 was found either.

Dickman was a married man with a son and daughter who lived in Lily Avenue, Jesmond. He had given up the secretaryship of a colliery syndicate in 1907 or 1908, and had since lived precariously by backing horses. He was known to be in financial straits at the time of the murder, and owed several hundreds of pounds to moneylenders.

The case aroused nation-wide interest, and the newspapers were full of it at the time of the trial. Crowds collected to boo as Dickman was taken to court in a Black Maria. He was tried at the Newcastle Summer Assizes on Monday, July 4th, 1910, before Lord Coleridge; Edward Tindal Atkinson prosecuted, and Edward Mitchell-Innes led for the defence.

Dickman was convicted, largely on the weight of circumstantial evidence. He continued to protest his innocence. There were many attempts to get him reprieved by people who felt that the weight of evidence was not sufficiently strong against him, and on the day before the execution London was flooded with handbills begging people to wire the Home Secretary. Dickman was hanged in Newcastle Prison on August 10th, 1910, nearly five months after his crime.[1]

DOBKIN, Harry

Convicted and hanged for wife-murder in 1942, he was arrested through the labours of Home Office pathologist Dr Keith Simpson, who determined that the bones found in a Baptist chapel crypt in Kennington, London, were the remains of Mrs Harry Dobkin, missing for fifteen months. Demolition workers finding the body thought they had unearthed an air-raid victim, but Dr Simpson showed that the head had been severed from the body by hand, not blast, and attempts made to remove all identifiable parts. There were also signs of burning, but despite this it was established that the bones belonged to a woman who had died a year or eighteen months before. The police then remembered both Mrs Dobkin's disappearance and a fire in the crypt which Dobkin, fire-watching in the next-door building, had failed to report. Mrs Dobkin was eventually identified by her teeth fillings and an untreated fibroid growth. A tiny blood-clot, barely discernible on the voice-box, showed that pressure had been exerted on the throat and, after a further examination, Dr Simpson proved that Mrs Dobkin had been strangled.

Although there can be no doubt whatever of Dobkin's guilt, there are, nevertheless, certain circumstances that might be considered extenuating, and that make it seem that the death sentence was in some ways unfair. Dobkin had married Rachel Dubinski

[1] See also Appendix 2.

in 1920. The marriage had been a failure from the start, and they had separated after only three days. However, a baby was born nine months later. Three years later, Mrs Dobkin applied for maintenance, and Harry Dobkin served several periods in jail as a result of her complaints of his irregularity. She was still dunning him for maintenance in 1941 – twenty years later (when surely the child must have been grown up and supporting itself) – and often caused scenes in the street. It is hardly surprising if Dobkin developed a deep sense of grievance. An all-male jury might have felt that it was largely Mrs Dobkin's fault that she was murdered, and added a plea for mercy to the verdict. Or Dobkin might have pleaded manslaughter under extreme provocation, for in addition to dunning him for maintenance, Mrs Dobkin also blackmailed him with something discreditable in his career of which she knew; Dobkin reported her as saying, 'If you don't make peace with me, I'll make trouble for you.'

DOMINICI, Gaston
Seventy-six-year-old Lurs, Provence, peasant farmer, tried at Digne Assize Court in November 1954 for the murder of 61-year-old English biochemist, Sir Jack Drummond and his family on the night of August 4th, 1952.

The bodies of Sir Jack, his wife aged 46, and their 11-year-old daughter Elizabeth (who had been holidaying in France with their shooting-brake) were discovered on some land adjoining La Grande Terre, the Dominici farm-house, near a tributary of the River Durance. Husband and wife were shot, and Elizabeth had been bludgeoned to death; evidently the Drummonds had decided to camp at this spot for the night, and had been attacked. Police soon found the murder weapon, a 'Rock-ola' carbine issued to American war-time troops; it was found in the deepest part of the river tributary, which indicated the killer knew the area. Commissionaire Edmond Sebeille from Marseilles took over the case, and immediately sensed that the Dominici family knew the truth about the murders. Gustave, the 33-year-old son of Gaston Dominici (who had reported the finding of the bodies), was, on September 3rd, severely questioned by the police, with little result. On October 15th he was again grilled; and now admitted that the Drummond child had been alive when he found her; Gustave Dominici was immediately arrested on a charge of failing to aid a person in danger. He was tried at Digne on November 13th, found guilty, and sentenced to two months' imprisonment, which was quashed on submission of appeal. Sebeille, in the year that followed, continued to visit the taciturn Dominicis frequently; a war of nerves developed, chiefly between son Gustave and Sebeille. Finally, on November 13th, 1953, Gustave shouted: 'It was my father!' Another brother, Clovis, aged 49, nodded his head in agreement. Gaston Dominici cursing his sons' treachery, eventually confessed to the murders; in a curious statement he spoke of stealthily watching the Drummonds undress for bed at their improvised encampment. Accosted by an indignant Sir Jack, old Dominici had fired from the American carbine he invariably carried at night; in the resulting pandemonium both adult Drummonds were slaughtered by the fierce patriarch, and the fleeing, terrified Elizabeth Drummond finally collapsed under savage blows from the butt of his carbine. The crime was reconstructed, French-fashion, and during the proceedings Gaston Dominici attempted suicide by trying to jump over the railway bridge. After many confessions and retractions of those confessions, the eldest Dominici was brought to trial; found guilty on a majority vote, he received the death sentence. As he left the courtroom he hissed: 'My sons – what swine!' Later his sentence was changed to one of life imprisonment. He has since (1960) been released.

DOUGAL, Samuel Herbert

A large bearded cockney with an assumed Irish brogue, who after twenty-one years' service in the British Army (during which times he buried two wives, attributing both deaths to oyster poisoning), became steward of the Stroud Green (Essex) Conservative Club, but soon turned his attentions to the more profitable pursuit of 55-year-old Miss Camille Holland, a paying guest at a Bayswater boarding house, with whom he went to live at Moat House Farm, near Audley End in Essex, in 1898. An episode with a frightened servant girl ('I only wanted to wind up the clock in her room') revealed him as a rogue to the once-trusting Miss Holland, who resolved to leave him. Dougal shot her, burying her body in the filled-in moat trench, and proceeded by forgery to derive an income from Miss Holland's bank, informing any inquisitive callers that 'Mrs Dougal' was away on a yachting expedition. For three years Dougal played the jovial squire at Moat House Farm. Hordes of women surrounded him and he was the locality's first motor-car owner; once he was seen in the grounds teaching a naked girl to ride a bicycle. The police became suspicious over the prolonged yachting spree, and when one of Miss Holland's cheques was found to be forged, Dougal was arrested and the search for Miss Holland, dead or alive, began. After many weeks the remains were found, identified as those of Miss Holland by her tiny (size two), specially made boots.

Awaiting his trial, due the following Monday (he pleaded the shooting was accidental), he wrote to a friend concerning the intentions of his various women friends for that day:

> I dare say the girls have received their notices to attend next Monday . . . have they not? there will be several from about there, and it would be a good idea to club together and hire a trap and drive all the way. It is a delightful drive through undulating country and would be a veritable treat for them all. . . .

Convicted of Miss Holland's murder, Dougal eventually admitted his guilt to the chaplain a few seconds before he was hanged.

DREHER, Tom
Louisiana doctor, aged 52, convicted of the murder of Jim Le Boeuf, the husband of his mistress, Ada Le Boeuf.

The Le Boeufs and Dr Dreher, all parents of grown children, lived in Mason City, Louisiana; in 1927 Ada Le Boeuf developed migraine trouble, which necessitated many visits from Dr Tom Dreher, although after-inquiries revealed that no prescriptions for her ailment had ever been deposited with local chemists. Le Boeuf was an enthusiastic fisherman, spending long periods away from home, fishing in the bayou country, usually hiring a canoe from a taciturn individual called James Beadle. One afternoon, after an altercation concerning the hiring of a boat, Beadle spitefully revealed to the husband how people were speculating about Dr Dreher's frequent calls to the Le Boeuf residence, although Ada Le Boeuf, when interrogated, denied the implications, merely stressing the need for her regular course of injections. On July 1st, 1927, Ada and Jim Le Boeuf rowed across nearby Lake Palourde to visit a relation, setting out for home at midnight. On July 6th the body of a man with two bullets in the head was recovered from Lake Palourde; efforts had been made to wire the body down by means of heavy rail-irons, and the stomach had been slashed, presumably to allow for the escape of body gases and so reduce buoyancy in the water. Ada Le Boeuf, whose husband had been missing five days ('on business'), denied that the corpse could be his, but Le Boeuf was identified by his dentist. Under constant questioning the suspect wife began to tell conflicting stories, and when Dreher was questioned he admitted complicity in the plot to kill Jim Le Boeuf, although he said the actual shots were fired by James Beadle: Beadle maintained he had merely rowed Dreher out to a strategic firing position on Lake Palourde. Dreher, Ada Le Boeuf, and Beadle were tried for the killing of Jim Le Boeuf, and all found guilty of murder in the first degree, the elderly lovers being sentenced to hanging.

Numerous anti-hanging petitions were submitted to State Governor Huey Long (no woman had ever been executed in the State of Louisiana) but he declined to order a reprieve, saying such a direction from him would be 'a mockery against decency. . . .'

Dreher and Ada Le Boeuf were hanged jointly on February 1st, 1929.

DUBUISSON, Pauline
Twenty-four-year-old Frenchwoman, convicted in November 1953 of the murder of her ex-lover, Felix Bailly.

From adolescence Pauline Dubuisson had enjoyed a stringent love-life; at 16 she was mistress to 55-year-old Colonel Von Domnick, director of the German Hospital at Dunkirk during the Occupation period, being punished for this misdemeanour after the Liberation by having her hair shorn (along with other 'collaborators') in the main square at Dunkirk. In 1946 she studied medicine at the Medical Faculty of Lille University ('she is well-balanced but haughty, provoking, and a flirt' said one of her reports) also commencing a spare-time study of love-techniques, writing down the names, along with the respective sexual aspirations, of her many lovers; later this eccentric list did much to alienate people's feelings towards Dubuisson. A fellow student was Felix Bailly, with whom Pauline Dubuisson had an affaire which lasted two years, and whose name was duly entered on The List, along with the names of concurrent lovers about whose existence Felix Bailly was unaware. Disillusion followed the realization of Dubuisson's infidelity, and in November 1949 Felix Bailly (despite an abortive attempt by a contrite Dubuisson) transferred his studies from Lille to Paris; there is evidence too, that Bailly had tired of Pauline Dubuisson's attractions. The two were not to meet again until March 1951; in the meantime many more names were added to The List, and Felix Bailly had fallen in love with another, less volatile, girl, Monique Lombard, and received the consent of his parents to their engagement. Pauline Dubuisson subsequently explained her mode of life by saying, 'I wanted to force myself to love other people, in order to persuade myself I was capable of having lasting sentiments for him,' but the fact remains that she never, during the eighteen months spent apart, made any attempt to contact Bailly or visit him in Paris; and Bailly, when seeing a mutual acquaintance, asked after Pauline 'is she still as loose as ever?' Dubuisson learnt of Felix Bailly's engagement, and at the beginning of March 1951 met her ex-lover in Paris; according to her testimony alone, their old relationship was resumed. On March 10th, Dubuisson bought a ·25 calibre automatic pistol, explaining to the police (who had to grant her a certificate of purchase) that she often had to travel late at night alone. On March 15th, Dubuisson left her lodgings after leaving a note for her landlady expressing her intention of shooting Felix Bailly, then herself; the landlady sent telegrams of warning to both the prospective murderee and his parents. That day Dubuisson visited Felix Bailly at his flat and was rebuffed; not, however, without inward consternation, Bailly engaged a few of his student-friends to act as his bodyguards, and slept elsewhere that night. On the evening of March 16th, Bailly returned, with much stealth, to his flat, where he kept the outside door on a chain. On the morning of March 17th he admitted Dubuisson, apparently thinking she was yet another of the friends whose aid he had summoned and whose arrival, in fact, had been delayed by a traffic jam. When this friend, Bernard Mougeot, arrived, he found Felix Bailly dead, shot through the forehead, back and behind one ear; Dubuisson lay unconscious by the stove, a gas-pipe in her mouth.

In custody, awaiting trial on a charge of assassination (this in France means premeditated murder, and carries the death penalty) Dubuisson again attempted suicide by slashing her wrists, but finally stood trial on November 18th, 1953, at the Assizes of the Seine; the Presiding Judge was M. Raymond Jadin, Advocate General Maître Lindon appeared for the prosecution, and Maître Paul Baudet for the defence. Dubuisson's imperturbability earned her the nickname 'Mask of Pride'; she claimed that after sleeping with Bailly one night in March he had unaccountably rejected her: '. . . he kissed me, everything was just as it used to be . . . I felt I was coming out of a nightmare . . . then, in the morning, he threw me out . . . life didn't mean anything any more to me . . . it was at that moment I decided to kill us both.' It is still uncertain whether Dubuisson was motivated by humiliation or jealousy, or even by a grinding and genuine regret for a lost passion; the jury found her guilty of murder, not of assassination, largely, it is believed, through the influence of the only female juror, Mademoiselle Raymonde Gourdeau. The prisoner was sentenced to penal servitude for life.

DUDLEY and STEPHENS (The *Mignonette* Survivors)
Both sentenced to death for the murder of the cabin boy, Richard Parker, whom they afterwards ate. They were later reprieved and sentenced to six months in prison without hard labour.

The *Mignonette*, a 31-ton yacht, was bought by a Mr J. H. Want of Australia in 1884, and he hired a crew of four to sail her to Sydney. Thomas Dudley was appointed captain; he was 31. He chose as crew Edwin Stephens, aged 36, and Edmund Brooks, aged 39. Richard Parker, a youth of 17, was engaged as cabin boy. She left Southampton on May 19th, and on June 17th, crossed the line. Now the storms began, and on July 3rd, the ship finally logged so much water that the small pump could not cope with it. The *Mignonette* was abandoned hurriedly, the four survivors taking no water and no food except two tins of vegetables. After several days at sea they caught a turtle, but this was eaten in eight days. (The captain evidently failed to grasp the situation and to exert his authority to make it last as long as possible.) The cabin boy drank sea water on July 23rd, and his mind wandered. Dudley suggested they should kill him and eat him; Brooks disagreed, but being a single man, he was overborne by his married companions. Parker was killed by a knife thrust in the throat by the captain (who first told him his intention). They then ate the body. On July 28th they were rescued by a German ship, the *Montezuma*, and set down at Falmouth, Cornwall. They made no effort at all to conceal the murder of the cabin boy, and were all three arrested; Brooks, however, was soon released. The other two were tried on November 6th, 1884, before Baron Huddleston at the Cornwall Winter Assizes; the case was later adjourned to the Royal Courts of Justice, the Crown being represented by Sir Henry James and the defence by Mr

Collins, QC. Sentenced to death, the men were reprieved on December 13th. The case aroused widespread sympathy for them.

DUMOLLARD, Martin

A psychopathic criminal, murderer of girls, executed in Montluel (Ain) about 1861. There seems to be some ambiguity about the motive for his crimes; Major Griffiths states that Dumollard and his wife lived off the profits of the murders and bought themselves some land. Other writers state, more plausibly, that his wife was only an accessory after the fact, who accepted her husband's curious pastime of murdering servant girls with peasant calm and fatalism.

Martin Dumollard was a pleasant-faced, reliable-looking peasant who lived in a cottage in the Department of Ain, near Lyon. The case which finally led to his arrest may be taken as typical of his method. A widow named Marie Pichon worked in a house in Lyon. One day, crossing the bridge at Guillotière, a farm labourer in a rough blue smock spoke to her. He was a man of about 45, sturdily built, with a simple and friendly manner; he had a small tumour on his face and a scar on his upper lip. The girl mentioned that she was looking for another situation; the man exclaimed, 'What a coincidence!' He, it appeared, had come to Lyon from the château at Montluel, where he was a gardener, to get a servant girl; the work would be light and the wages good. An hour later they set out from the station of Genève, and alighted at Montluel at dusk. Her companion, who had been attentive and talkative on the journey, now led her across country, claiming it was a short cut. Dumollard carried her trunk, but after a while he left it in the middle of a field, saying he would collect it in the morning. They went on, and re-crossed the railway line, which made her suspicious. After more wandering in the dark, the girl accused him of misleading her, and said she would not go any farther. The man suddenly said, 'We have arrived already,' and tried to put a noose over her head. She dodged away, and the man attacked her. Finally she managed to escape, running wildly in the dark. Following the track, she came to a village named Balan, and knocked at a cottage door. The cottager let her in for the night and in the morning they told the police. She managed to retrace her steps to the field where her trunk had been left, but it was gone. An inquiry began, and finally the police heard rumours about Dumollard, who lived in the district of Dagneux. On interviewing Dumollard, they realized at once that he corresponded with Marie Pichon's description. Dumollard's wife – a grim-faced, silent woman – was asked to say what Dumollard had done on the afternoon of May 26th, 1861. Her story conflicted with his and it was obvious they were both lying. They were arrested and taken to Trévoux, where Dumollard was identified by Marie Pichon and many people who had seen them together. In spite of this, Dumollard denied everything. In his house was found the clothes belonging to Marie Pichon, and whole trunks full of women's clothes, many of which had obviously been washed to remove traces of blood.

Little by little, information was accumulated against the Dumollards. Since it was all of the same nature, it is not worth repeating in detail. On February 28th, 1855, a party of huntsmen had come upon the naked and blood-smeared body of a young girl in the forest of Montaverne (in Tramoyes). She had died from head wounds inflicted with a pointed instrument. She was finally identified as Marie Baday, a servant girl from the Guillotière district of Lyon. Another servant girl, Marie Curt, had much the same experience as Marie Pichon, and ended by taking refuge at a place called 'Farm of the Rages'. Josephe Charlety and Jeanne-Marie Bourgeois also escaped with their lives and gave evidence against Dumollard.

Another girl named Julie Farjat shouted and brought men to her aid; she later recognized Dumollard. An innkeeper named Laborde told of how Dumollard had stayed at his inn with a girl whom he introduced as his niece, in February 1860; he noted her brown check dress, later found in the farm.

As the evidence accumulated, Dumollard decided to admit his guilt, but claimed that he worked with a gang, who did the actual killing.

Madame Dumollard, however, decided to confess. According to her, she had no part in the murders. Dumollard would simply come in and say, 'I've killed a girl in the woods of Montmain. I must go and bury her.' He would then go off with a spade, and usually bring back the girl's trunk, money (if she had any), and bloodstained clothes, for his wife to wash. She was able to lead the police officers to a place where a female skeleton was uncovered; the girl had obviously died of a heavy blow on the head.

Dumollard finally indicated the spots where three bodies were buried, and admitted throwing others into the Rhône. Clothes of at least ten girls were found in his home. Nine others escaped.

The trial caused a nation-wide sensation, and when Dumollard was sentenced to death, a crowd outside was shouting for justice – or lynching. His wife received twenty years' hard labour.

Little is known about Dumollard's character. It seems likely that he was a sadist, like Kürten. (One of his victims was buried while still alive.) He stole from his victims, but then, so did Kürten on some occasions. It is not known whether he sexually assaulted his victims, although he invariably stripped them. That he was extremely mean – with a peasant meanness – is proved by his last words on the scaffold, which were to remind his wife that someone owed them money.

His head was sent to an institute for examination, and the experts declared that, according to its shape, Dumollard should have been a man of the finest character.

E

EDEL, Frederick
Petty criminal, sentenced to death for the murder of Mrs Emmeline Harrington on December 23rd, 1927, at West 190 Street, New York.

Mrs Harrington was a 39-year-old actress who was temporarily 'resting'; her husband was working on the stage in some distant city. On December 29th, a neighbour of Mrs Harrington noticed that the door stood ajar, and looked inside; she found Mrs Harrington dead in the bathroom, her head battered; robbery was obviously the motive. The neighbour now recalled that she had heard a scream at 10 am on December 23rd, and had gone down to investigate; she heard bath water running, and decided she must have been mistaken. The front door of the flat had stood open from the 23rd to the 29th of December. The neighbour also recollected that a man had called on the 22nd, apparently to discuss renting the Harrington flat while she was away; no trace of this man could be found.

The police found themselves baffled, until a lucky chance threw the criminal into their arms. In late January, a man walked out of the Hotel Taft in Hew Haven, Connecticut, leaving behind a suitcase. The manager had refused to cash the man a cheque, and when he had been absent for some days, the suitcase was opened; it proved to contain some bills with Mrs Harrington's name and address on them, and letters addressed to

Frederick Edel. Edel was known to the police, having been acquitted of murder once and involved in another robbery murder since his acquittal. He was wanted for forging cheques, cash-box thefts, and various other petty crimes. Edel was finally arrested at Hopkins, Minnesota, recognized by a post office clerk when he presented a money order for payment. He admitted having had possession of Mrs Harrington's jewellery and fur coat, but claimed he had been her lover. The jury did not believe him, and he was sentenced to the electric chair in 1928.

EICHMANN, Karl Adolf

Born 1906 in Solingen, part of the rapidly expanding German iron and steel region of the Ruhr. His parents were middle class, devoted Protestants and his father, an engineer. At the age of 4 his mother died and his father moved to Linz, a commercial centre in Austria. Adolf's boyhood developed normally in this same town where Adolf Hitler had grown up to manhood and he attended church regularly. Herr Eichmann remarried and as a result of the 1914–18 war became a wealthy man, indulging Adolf's great love of horse riding to the full.

Adolf often visited Vienna with its large Jewish population segregated in its own quarter and with its typically Eastern appearance. These people had long been the target for virulent anti-Semitic propaganda from the nineteenth century onwards, but Adolf, whose own features were by no means un-Jewish, took warmly to them with their strange ways and made many close friends among them. The 1925 inflation, which bankrupted Austria, ruined the Eichmann business among millions of others and Adolf was without work and prospects.

He had read the speeches of Hitler whose National Socialist Workers Party was rapidly expanding and his attitude was changing. 'I began to think these foreign-looking people were the enemy of us all. I wondered about my friendship with Jews and I felt they had always treated me as someone rather inferior. I believed that Hitler was right.' He eventually got a salesman's job, began attending Nazi Party meetings and after hearing Hitler speak joined the Austrian Nazi Party in 1931. 'After hearing the Führer speak I felt a loathing of myself that I had mixed with those Jews who were the enemies of the German people and defilers of our blood.'

At that time the Nazi gangs were well in their stride, terrorizing the streets and savagely attacking any Jew they came across, of whatever sex or age. According to Party records Adolf was soon regarded as a worthy member with just the right spirit. By a profound irony he himself was violently beaten up, doubtless due to his partly Jewish appearance, and failing to produce his Party card was left bloody and almost unconscious. As a result he grew insensate with rage, vengeance, and unquenchable hatred towards the Jews. 'The Jews are responsible for this. I'm not a Jew, I'm a German. If there were no Jewish people I wouldn't be mistaken for a Jew. What the devil are they doing in Germany, anyway?' More ironical still, the Party leaders wondered whether he was a Jewish spy. In order to explain away his knowledge of Jewish ways and Yiddish, which had now become the most guilty aspect of his past, he lied to the effect that he was born in the German colony in Mount Carmel, Palestine. Later the truth about his past was ascertained but the lie that he had concocted could always be used against him in the way that every totalitarian régime deems so necessary.

From then on he was determined to demonstrate his German purity, and with his uniform, armband, gun, whip, and baton, began smashing and beating up with the rest. He rose rapidly, ruthless in his anti-Semitism and highly regarded for his Jewish knowledge which soon proved invaluable to the Party. In 1934 he became an SS man. 'My honour is loyalty.' Within three months he was promoted Sergeant in the Security Service at Berlin Headquarters. There, under Heydrich's wing, he undertook historical research on all Jewish matters, including linguistic studies and in particular the 'destructive' activities of the race. In 1935 he married Veronica Leible. In 1937 Heydrich, who now trusted him as a loyal and conscientious worker, gave him the task of dealing with the Jews in each new country over-run by the Germans, for the SS were to be primarily responsible for the 'solution of the Jewish Problem'. In 1938 a Central Immigration Office for Jews was created in Berlin and Eichmann's main contribution was to have the Jews sent Eastwards by the trainload from all over Germany towards the Russian frontiers and there dumped in freezing desolate areas, to be dealt with at leisure. When Austria was taken over in March, Eichmann immediately entered the country with his henchmen and enthusiastically settled into his new 'work'. The so-called Jewish 'ringleaders' were shot or sent to Dachau and Buchenwald concentration camps, soon to be followed by lorry-loads of men, women, and children, the so-called 'agitators'. As a relief from his hard and painstaking work he spent many of his nights with Heydrich, pub-crawling and fornicating. Hitler was very pleased with his achievements.

In September 1939, soon after the Polish invasion, at a conference led by Heydrich, Eichmann suggested the complete destruction of the huge numbers of Jewish captives, by fire. Instead they were crammed and crushed by the thousand into cattle trucks and deported farther East into Russian-occupied Poland where they died of exposure and hunger. For successfully organizing such work Eichmann was again promoted and now given absolute *carte blanche* over all Jewish deportations. He became chief of the Jewish Office of the Gestapo. In 1940 beginning with Lodz great concentrations of Jews were herded together, combed from the whole of occupied Europe by Eichmann's now vast, complex network controlled from his central office in Berlin. In 1941 he was told that the Final Solution of the Jewish Problem would soon begin. This logically precise statement meant total annihilation. Eichmann thereupon proposed the idea of mass gassing. A comparatively cheap method and one in which much experience had already been gained by the gassing of mental defectives and chronic invalids before the war.

In May, Rudolf Hoess, Commandant of Auschwitz concentration camp, was told by Himmler that the plan would be put into practice in his camp. He too, like Eichmann, was a husband and father and took the matter very seriously. Action Groups had been organized to follow the advance into Russia and they massacred hundreds of thousands of Jews with terrible barbarity behind the invading armies as the Final Solution began. They burnt, raped, mutilated, strangled, shot, and tore their victims to pieces, regardless of age or sex, with unbelievable savagery. Eichmann personally participated in many of these 'actions' and enthused over them. By August the German technicians had materialized Eichmann's gassing ideas in the form of gas lorries in which Jews were crammed shut and gassed by carbon monoxide fumes. But the method was far too slow to deal with the millions of victims. The idea was extended. Into large huts holding 500 people several engine exhausts were run in and the bodies were then thrown into mass graves. Eichmann was still not satisfied. Karl Fritsch, Hoess's deputy, flung some crystals of Cyclone B gas, originally used for exterminating vermin, into a sealed underground cell with several hundred victims. When he entered next day these human 'vermin' were nearly all dead. The method was quickly perfected. Hoess phoned Eichmann who was utterly delighted at the news and ordered Topf and Sons of Erfurt to go into gas chamber production immediately. Crematoria One and Two were completed in the winter with a capacity of 2,000 corpses a day. They were fully equipped with underground dressing-rooms, gas chambers, and electric lifts. Crematoria Three and Four could deal with 1,500 a day. Crematorium Five was the masterpiece and achieved 9,000 a day in the summer of 1944 during the Hungarian 'action'.

The whole of Eichmann's organization was now furiously geared to getting this vast factory of death into rapid production. A teleprinter direct from Auschwitz stuttered its ghastly messages of extermination straight to his desk. As with any modern industrial enterprise, figures are all-important, and continually increasing figures mean delirious success. He and Himmler watched the gassings through peepholes, as did many high officials to whom cigarettes and drinks were afterwards served. Unlike Himmler, who actually admitted that it was a 'hard' job, Eichmann was absolutely indifferent. Conscientiously and efficiently he had the clothes, hair, watches, and gold teeth of the victims sorted, accounted, bundled, and dispatched. In October 1941 he was accordingly promoted to Lieutenant-Colonel SS. Hoess said that he was 'completely obsessed with the idea of destroying every single Jew that he could lay his hands on – without pity and in cold blood – as rapidly as possible'. Closely related to his lust for organizing mass murder was his wild sexual indulgence which occurred during his visits to Paris.

He was utterly devoted to the work which would safeguard the German people for the future and he is never known to have uttered the slightest hint of remorse. In 1944 he said to his aide, Dieter Wisliceny, 'I shall leap into my grave laughing because the feeling that I have the death of five million people on my conscience will be for me a source of extraordinary satisfaction'. Wisliceny further said of him, 'a painstaking bureaucrat – he shunned all personal responsibility and took care to shelter behind his superiors'.

Eichmann killed not only Jews *en masse*, for apparently ideological reasons, but was responsible for the calculated death of twenty-seven RAF prisoners by naked exposure in the snow at his personal orders. By 1943 he was a hated, feared figure throughout Europe and hoped to become Hitler's World Commissioner for Jews. Hirt, Professor of Anatomy at Strasbourg University, asked him to help collect Russo-Jewish skull specimens. Accordingly, proudly seeing himself as a scientific racial expert, he had killed and dispatched 150 victims, who were then skulled for the Herr Professor's 'studies'. Eichmann also organized mass sterilization experiments on Jews and Jewesses, who generally died as a result.

As the Germans were beginning to retreat on all fronts, he speeded up his work. 'If Germany collapses we can at least say that we have achieved something. We will have completely wiped out European Jewry.' At one point near the end he offered to trade one million Jews for cash or army lorries, but the deal fell through. In the final weeks thousands of Jews were being fed daily into the crematoria at Auschwitz. He himself estimated the total of Jews exterminated as six million.

After Germany's defeat he disguised as a labourer, went into hiding, prepared a false past, was taken into a POW camp but escaped unrecognized. He went to Rome, obtained a stateless person's papers and returned into hiding in Germany. Meanwhile a group of Jewish partisans in Poland had pledged themselves to find him and other SS leaders. By 1950 he was aware that people were on his trail and he managed, doubtless with influential help, to reach Buenos Aires with his wife and family. There he was welcomed amid many of his old SS colleagues. In the name of Kurt Steinburg, he obtained a post in a German-Argentine firm staffed by many former SS men. But the search for him was intensifying. The War Crimes Investigators were becoming very clear about the rôle he had played. In Israel, Haganah agents obtained a 1940 photograph of him from a former girl-friend, faded but sufficient. A search began all over Europe and America. In 1957 a Jewish agent in Buenos Aires was alerted and watched a certain house for months without success. Eventually, in 1959, Eichmann's wife returned to Austria to renew her passport and on her return was followed by Israeli agents back to the house and Adolf Eichmann. He was watched for three days, kidnapped, and flown to Israel to await trial.

J. G.

ELLIS, Ruth
Twenty-eight-year-old divorcée and night-club hostess, convicted and hanged for the murder of her lover, 25-year-old racing motorist David Moffat Drummond Blakely.

On April 10th, 1955 (Easter Sunday), Ruth Ellis fired six shots at David Blakely outside a public house in Hampstead, London. Two bullets missed, one piercing the hand of a passer-by; the other four entered Blakely's body, two in the back, one in the thigh, and one in the left arm. Blakely was killed instantly. Passive now, Ruth Ellis was taken to Hampstead Police Station: 'I am guilty. I am rather confused.'

For two years Blakely and Ruth Ellis had been lovers, neither being particularly constant in affection. Ellis entertained other men at her flat above The Little Club, a bottle-club of which she was manageress, but in February 1955 the two of them established domesticity at an apartment in Egerton Gardens, Kensington. Quarrelling was frequent, and soon Blakely departed. At the beginning of April 1955 Ruth Ellis suffered a miscarriage; on April 8th (Good Friday), knowing that Blakely was spending the week-end with friends in North London, she tried to see him, banging on the door of the house in Tanza Road, Hampstead. Refused access, she became obstreperous, and twice the police were summoned to lead her away. On the Sunday evening Ruth Ellis returned; from within the Tanza Road house came sounds of a party. At 9 pm David Blakely, accompanied by a friend, came out and went to a nearby public house, the Magnolia. Alan Thompson, an off-duty policeman, was a Magnolia patron that night, and remembered them: '. . . while they were in the pub I happened to glance at a window and I saw a woman peering in.' As Blakely left the inn he was shot down.

Sent for trial at the Old Bailey Criminal Court, Ruth Ellis showed calm throughout the proceedings, murmuring 'Thanks' as she was sentenced to death on June 21st, 1955.

ELLUL, Philip Louis

Twenty-nine-year-old Maltese gangster, convicted of the murder of fellow-gangster Tommy ('Scarface') Smithson on the night of June 25th, 1956. With two other Maltese, 22-year-old Victor Spampinato and 26-year-old Joseph Zammit, he went to a house in Kilburn, London, owned by gaming-den proprietor George Caruana. There they met Smithson (a part-time croupier) with whom there had been, days earlier, a disagreement when Smithson had demanded money from a reluctant Caruana for the defence of a woman facing a forgery charge; Caruana had been 'cut up', and Ellul threatened. During this second meeting Smithson was shot in the neck, and died on the pavement outside the house. Ellul admitted the shooting to the police: 'Sure, it was me who shot him. He was going to "do" me if I did not get out of London, and I don't stand for that.' Ellul said that Smithson had previously threatened him with a gun, and when he saw Smithson advancing towards him, 'I thought he was going to hit me and I shot him.'

At the Old Bailey trial in September no evidence was offered against Zammit, who was discharged. Marlene Mary Bates, night-club hostess, who had witnessed the incident, described how Smithson moved towards Ellul brandishing a pair of scissors. Ellul (who maintained that Spampinato played no part in the incident) said, 'I thought he was going to stab me.' Asked by Mr Justice Ashworth if he was frightened of Smithson, Ellul replied 'Yes'. Asked why he had not gone to the police when Smithson first threatened him, Ellul said: 'I would have been cut up. I am willing to bring about seven people here and let you see the state of their faces.' Spampinato, when asked by his counsel why he had not interfered when Smithson made to attack Ellul, replied: 'I didn't want to get involved.' The judge, summing up, discounted a verdict of manslaughter on the grounds of provocation. The jury found Spampinato not guilty and Ellul guilty, adding a recommendation to mercy. He was sentenced to death but reprieved.

ELWELL, Joseph, Case

A one-time hardware salesman, whose talent for card-playing hoisted him into New York's upper strata of society. His book, *Elwell on Bridge* is still widely read. Living apart from his wife, he was handsome and young-looking for his forty-five years (with a luxuriant crop of brown hair) and spent the night of June 10th, 1920, dining and watching an entertainment, 'Midnight Frolic', on the roof of the Ritz Hotel, New York. By 2.30 am he was on his way home – alone – in a taxi, only stopping on the way to get a *Morning Telegraph*. He made several phone calls from his bedroom, his last being about 6 am, when he tried to get a Garden City number. At 8 am his housekeeper arrived, and found a shrunken, bald, toothless old man dying from a ·45 calibre pistol bullet in the head. Elwell had preserved his youth by means of wigs (forty were found in a cupboard) and false teeth. A mound of feminine underwear was also found, as was a detailed list of fifty-three women, but it remains uncertain whether this was a file on would-be bridge experts or (as the papers alleged), a 'love index'. A jealous woman or a jealous bridge player, the murderer was never discovered.

EMMETT-DUNNE, Frederick

Thirty-three-year-old British Regular Army sergeant and ex-commando, found guilty of the murder of fellow sergeant Reginald Watters.

At 3 am in the morning of December 1st, 1953, the body of Sergeant Watters was found hanging from banisters at Glamorgan Barracks at Duisburg, Germany. Dr Alan Womack examined the body, and found throat injuries consistent with hanging; at an Army inquest a verdict of suicide was passed. Surprise was felt by friends of Sergeant Watters, as his life had seemed untroubled; there were rumours concerning the friendship of Mia Watters, the dead man's German-born wife, with Sergeant Frederick Emmett-Dunne. When, six months after the death of Sergeant Watters, on June 3rd, 1954, his widow and Sergeant Emmett-Dunne married (after an 'accidental' meeting in Leeds) the gossip so increased that Scotland Yard were informed by the Army authorities and a second post-mortem on Watters' body was arranged, supervised by Dr F. E. Camps. Dr Camps, after the examination, concluded that Watters had been dead before the hanging, and the fatal throat injuries were probably the result of a hand-blow – the kind of injury inflicted in unarmed combat as taught to Commando troops. Emmett-Dunne, now living with his wife at Taunton, Somerset, was seen by the police, and denied knowing anything about the death of Sergeant Watters. ('My only crime was marrying before the proper lapse of time prescribed by Victorian morality.') He was taken to Bow Street and charged with the murder of Sergeant Watters; Emmett-Dunne protested that as he was a citizen of Eire, a British court could not try him for a crime committed in a foreign country. This plea was accepted, but he was handed over to the military police, taken to Germany and there charged on April 15th with murder, the trial commencing in Düsseldorf, on June 27th, 1954. Mr Mervyn Griffith-Jones prosecuted and Mr Derek Curtis-Bennett, QC, was counsel for the defence.

Evidence was given that at 7 pm on the evening of November 30th, 1953, Emmett-Dunne, in response to a telephone call received in the sergeants' mess at Glamorgan Barracks, booked out of the camp at 7.5 pm, leaving in his car; he returned in twenty minutes, although the time of his return, as recorded on the guardroom time-sheet, had been altered to make it appear later. Emmett-Dunne was, in fact, seen cleaning his car outside barrack-block No. 4 at 7.25 pm; just inside the block entrance was a long, bulky bundle, about 5 feet by 2 feet (the height of Sergeant Watters was 5 feet 2 inches) and a Corporal Cane was told by Emmett-Dunne not to use this entrance: 'Sergeant Watters has given orders that this entrance must not be used.' Private Ronald Emmett, Emmett-Dunne's half-brother, told how at 8 pm Emmett-Dunne asked for his help, saying he had fought with and accidentally killed a man and that he wanted to make the death appear like a suicide. Private Emmett, horrified, refused, but at his half-brother's request fetched a bucket; whereupon Emmett-Dunne himself hoisted the body up by a rope from the banisters, leaving the bucket lying on its side, thus simulating suicide. (A week before Sergeant Watters' death, Emmett-Dunne had remarked to a Sergeant Browne that one of their number would be killing himself soon if his wife's behaviour did not improve.) Mr Curtis-Bennett sought to prove that Emmett-Dunne had struck the fatal blow in self-defence, as Sergeant Watters, jealous of the other's association with his wife, had threatened him with a revolver. There was a demonstration by soldiers during the trial (which was a cross between a civil trial and a court martial) of the type of commando-blow which, according to the prosecution, had killed Sergeant Watters. Mr Curtis-Bennett remarked to Dr Camps: 'I quite understand your theory.' Dr Camps replied: 'It is not a theory; this is straightforward mechanics.'

Emmett-Dunne was found guilty of the murder of Sergeant Watters, but, as the killing had occurred in Germany where there is no death penalty, the sentence was one of life imprisonment, to be served in England. A petition was made by Emmett-Dunne to the Queen for a review of his sentence; it was referred to the War Office, who decided there were no grounds for altering the penalty.

EUSTACHY, Dr
Unsuccessful murderer, his intended victim being a Dr Tourna-toire, rival physician in the town of Pertuis, near Vaucluse in France.

In 1884, jealous of newcomer Tournatoire's prosperous and accomplished doctoring, and incensed at being ousted from the Town Council by the man he considered an upstart, Eustachy injected the poison, atrophine (derived from belladonna), into a half-dozen thrush carcases he had won in a raffle, sending this culinary delicacy to the Tournatoire household as 'from a grateful patient'. Madame Tournatoire and her cook devoured one thrush each, both becoming agonized with head pains and beleagured by hallucinations (Madame Tournatoire seeing her husband go forth to fight a duel, and the cook forming a hate-fixation for the family dog, which she tried to throw on the fire). Bemused, Dr Tournatoire analysed the remaining four birds; his findings and subsequent inquiries by the police led to the arrest of Dr Eustachy, who, despite protestations ('It's all a joke') was tried on a charge of attempted murder. At his trial he admitted guilt, and served eight years in jail.

EVANS, Hadyn Evan

Twenty-two-year-old colliery worker, who kicked to death 76-year-old Rachel Allan, washerwoman, of Wattsdown in the Rhondda Valley.

Late on the night of Saturday, October 12th, 1947, the battered body of widowed Mrs Allan was found lying outside her small house in Hillside Terrace. She had spent a sociable evening at the Butchers Arms public house, 200 yards away. The door key was clutched in her hand and the tin of snuff she had bought after leaving the tavern was lying beside the body; nearby walls and doors were bloodstained. Glamorgan County police at once called in Scotland Yard, and Detective Chief Superintendent John Capstick was put in charge of the case. (In his account of the case Capstick recalls with delight the 'bursts of wonderful singing' coming from the chapels as he was driven through the Rhondda Valley towards Wattsdown.) With no clues as to the killer, Capstick asked local police constable Stephen Henton if he could name any possible murderers in the little community, individuals 'who . . . might turn killer, given sufficient provocation'. Uneasily, PC Henton submitted a confidential list to his superior officer some hours later: 'May the Lord forgive me if I am wrong'. On the list was the name of Evan Evans who had been in the singing room of the Butchers Arms with Rachel Allan on the evening she was murdered; he was wearing a new brown suit and there had been a quarrel between him and Mrs Allan.

Capstick went to interview Evans, going up a steep hillside to Heol Llechau, where the suspect lived with his parents and sister. Evans said he had gone straight home from the Butchers Arms on the Saturday night; he denied owning a brown suit, saying that over the week-end he had worn a blue suit. Taken down to the police station Evans repeated his story, but, after persistent questioning, he confessed to the killing; apparently the altercation in the Butchers Arms had continued after 'stop tap', down Hillside Terrace: 'She said to me, "You filthy pig" . . . I had my temper then . . . I hit her . . . kicked her . . . I lit a match and she was all bleeding . . .'

Evans still denied owning a brown suit, although the tailor from whom the suit was purchased was traced, and witnesses who had caroused with him the previous Saturday at the Butchers Arms spoke of how Evans had been teased about the new apparel. Capstick mounted the hillside to Heol Llechau once more, and pleaded with the distraught but uncooperative mother, who disclaimed all knowledge of the brown suit, but said she would have another search for it in her son's bedroom. ('I know there's nothing up there.') In Mrs Evans' absence Capstick prised up the covering fabric of the settee on which she had been sitting, and the brown suit, stiff with dried blood, came to light. Blood was also found on a pair of Evans' socks, and on the shoes he had worn the night of the killing (although attempts had been made, through vigorous cleaning, to remove all blood traces), and fragments of bone and tissue were removed from one trouser turn-up. The blood was of Group A, Rachel Allan's blood-type.

Tried under Mr Justice Byrne at Cardiff Assizes, Evans was found guilty, and executed on February 3rd, 1948.

EYRAUD, Michael
Frenchman convicted in 1890, together with his mistress, Gabrielle Bompard, prostitute, of the murder of Marcel Gouffé Paris solicitor.

Denis Coffy, roadworker, discovered the body of a man, badly decomposed, in a wood near Lyon. Four days later, a man search-ing for snails in the same wood came across a large trunk; from the odour it was apparent that this trunk had contained the corpse. Lyon police, taking over the case, made inquiries about missing persons; solicitor Gouffé was missing from home but his brother-in-law, on being shown the mass of putrefaction, declared it not to be the remains of his relative. The face was in any case unidentifiable, but Gouffé's hair had been auburn and the beard and hair of the corpse were black. Police, however, continuing their investigations into the life of solicitor Gouffé, found his leisure hours to have been largely spent in entertaining a series of mistresses; they also found that two of Gouffé's cronies from this more abandoned side of his life were also missing – the amoral pair Eyraud and Bompard. Meanwhile, Professor Alexandre Lacassagne (1843–1924), prominent French pathologist, was called in to examine the remains further; the hair, when washed clear of dried blood, was found to be auburn, and certain bone malformations proved that the body was that of Gouffé.

The whereabouts of Eyraud and Bompard now intrigued the police, especially when they were revealed as the probable purchasers of the trunk found in the wood; for some indeterminate reason the couple had journeyed to a shop in Euston Road, London, to buy the case, and were clearly recalled by the proprietor, Mrs Schwartizer. Gabrielle Bompard was quickly traced in Paris, and Michael Eyraud apprehended in Cuba; both arrested for the murder of Gouffé, they hurled abuse and accusations at each other, but finally the details of the plot to kill Gouffé were disclosed.

The Eyraud–Bompard alliance had formerly operated to blackmail susceptible members of the *bourgeoisie*, using as bait the wiles of Gabrielle Bompard. In Gouffé's case, however, they resolved to murder, and towards this end the trunk was bought and a highly complicated mesh of ropes and pulleys erected in Gabrielle's bedroom in the Rue Trouson-Ducoudry. The wretched solicitor, invited to partake of amorous delights, journeyed to Gabrielle's apartment in a glory of anticipation; as he caressed on the chaise-longue his desires must have seemed near fruition. Suddenly Bompard whimsically tied her dressing-gown cord round Gouffé's neck, but at a given signal Eyraud (who had been concealed behind a curtain) slipped out and secured by means of a hook, a rope on to the cord; bringing his lethal pulley-work into action he hauled on the rope, thus swinging the amazed Gouffé into a mid-air stranglehold. Gouffé disposed of, Eyraud went home to sleep, Bompard apparently preferring to remain in her own quarters, regardless of the stiffening corpse nearby. Next day they placed Gouffé in the trunk, and travelled with it to the Lyon wood; returning to Paris, Eyraud (having stolen Gouffé's keys) scrabbled unsuccessfully for money in Gouffé's office safe – overlooking, by some irony, a sum of money in a cardboard box on the solicitor's desk. Thwarted and furious, the pair decided to flee across the Atlantic; in America Eyraud deserted his mistress, who returned to Paris where she was to be sought by the police.

At the trial, in December 1890, Eyraud was found guilty of murder, and Bompard guilty of murder 'in extenuating circumstances' – a somewhat bewildering verdict.

Eyraud was guillotined, and Bompard sentenced to twenty years' imprisonment, being released at the turn of the century, when she proceeded to write her memoirs.

F

FAITHFULL, Starr

A New York girl, whose death in the early 1930's is still considered by some to have been self-inflicted, although most students of this case now incline to the view that, however ironical it would appear in the circumstances, Starr Faithfull was a murder victim.

The girl, 25 years old, lived amicably enough with her mother, stepfather, and sister Tucker in an eighty-five-dollar-a-month apartment at 12 St Lukes Place, Greenwich Village; whether this seemingly conventional family was aware of Starr's unconventional mode of life is uncertain. They must, however, have known that she had received treatment from several psychoanalysts, and that a year before her death she had been found naked and 'beaten-up' in a hotel room; people, hearing screams, had rescued her from further assault by a crazed companion, who, clad only in an undershirt, gave his name as Joseph Collins and was then, one gathers, allowed to depart without any more to-do, although Starr Faithfull was removed to, and received treatment at, New York's Bellevue Hospital: 'Brought to hospital by Flower Hospital ambulance. Noisy and unsteady. Acute alcoholism. Contusions face, jaw, and upper lip. . . .' There is evidence to show that Starr Faithfull was, in fact, a nymphomaniac, whose mania was of a somewhat retarded order: 'I'm afraid I've always been a rotten "sleeper",' she wrote to a friend, '. . . it's the preliminaries that count with me.' (One can assume from this that Mr Joseph Collins might well have been frustrated to breaking point.) In the months before her death, however, Starr Faithfull had become infatuated with a young Englishman, George Jameson-Carr, the surgeon on board the British Cunard liner *Franconia*, who, judging from his embarrassed reticence both long before and after Starr's death, had done little to warrant the American girl's amorous attentions. Nostalgic after two trips to England, Starr Faithfull often boarded Europe-bound liners down at the docks and joined in the pre-sailing revelries, in this way meeting Jameson-Carr. On May 29th, 1929, her feelings for the Englishman, together with a flask of 'bootleg' liquor, made her particularly reluctant to leave the *Franconia* as it embarked from New York Bay for England, and she had been forcibly put ashore by tugboat, sobbing hysterically and cursing the entire crew of the *Franconia*, not excepting the unfortunate Jameson-Carr. The following day she wrote a letter to the ship's surgeon, stating her intention of committing suicide:

> . . . I am dead, dead sick of it. . . . I hate everything so . . . life is horrible. I take dope to forget and drink to try and like people, but it is of no use. . . . I am mad and insane over you . . . I have strangely enough, more of a feeling of peace or whatever you call it now that I know it will soon be over. . . .

On 4 June, Starr Faithfull wrote a further letter to Jameson-Carr:

> . . . This is something I am going to put through . . . the only thing I dread is being outwitted and prevented from doing this. . . . If one wants to get away with murder one has to jolly well keep one's wits about one. If I don't watch out I will wake up in a psychopathic ward . . . No ether, allonal, or window jumping. I don't want to be maimed. Nothing makes any difference now. I love to eat and can have one delicious meal with no worry over gaining. I am going to drink slowly, keeping aware every second. I won't worry because men flirt with me in the streets – I shall encourage them – I don't care who they are. It's a great life when one has twenty-four hours to live.

On the night of June 4th, Starr Faithfull did not return home, and the next morning her stepfather reported her absence to the Missing Persons Bureau. On June 8th her body was found, clad only in a silk dress, on Long Beach (a 130-mile length of sand off the coast of New York and Connecticut) by beachcomber Dan Moriarty. Death was diagnosed as due to drowning, she had been in the water at least forty-eight hours; despite her written intentions, Starr Faithfull had consumed two grains of veronal shortly before death, but there was no trace of alcohol in the body. At first it was thought the girl had been raped, but although sexual intercourse had taken place before death, there was no evidence that Starr Faithfull had been forcibly assaulted. There was extensive bruising of the upper part of the body, however, and the lungs were clogged with sand, which disproved the theory that she had leapt overboard from one of the outbound liners (these ships passed within four miles of Long Beach, and it has been established that Starr spent part of Friday, June 5th, on board the *Mauretania*, although the authorities stated that she left it long before sailing time); the sand supported another theory, though, that she had been held head down, in shallow reaches, which would also account for the bruising.

After the discovery of the body many facts about this strange girl were made known: that she had been seduced at the age of eleven by a rich Bostonian, afterwards identified as Andrew J. Peters, an ex-mayor of Boston ('spent night with A. J. P.,' reads one of Starr's diary entries, 'O Horror, Horror!'), that she had a liking for ankle-length skirts (this in the 1920's, when above-knee-length clothes were the vogue) and also, paradoxically enough, for boy's attire, that she was an ether addict (her seduction had been effected, apparently, by this drug), that she thought ladies' swimsuits immoral, that she would spend hours in her room reading obscure philosophical works, and more hours tantalizing thwarted lovers, whose peevish reactions she recorded in a diary packed with unpublishable erotica. It was even hinted that the entire Faithfull household was subsidized by an intimidated Mr Peters and that he had paid them $80,000 in compensation for the harm done to young Starr, who would seem in her youth to have resembled in many ways the central figure of that widely acclaimed novel *Lolita*, published three decades afterwards.

Starr Faithfull's coat, underclothing and shoes were never recovered; their omission seems inexplicable for a suicide, more in keeping as a prelude to one of those curious unconsummated orgies that this time resulted in violence and the death she (albeit) apparently desired. The case has fascinated many, including writer John O'Hara, whose novel *Butterfield 8* was inspired by the character and times of Starr Faithfull, whose true fate, whether as murder victim or suicide, will doubtless never be known.

FERNANDEZ and BECK (The Lonely Hearts Killers)

Raymond Fernandez was a swindler of women of the same type as Landru and Smith; he was a Hawaiian-born Spanish American with gold teeth, who wore a wig to conceal his increasing baldness at the age of 31. He took advantage of the man-shortage in the United States (where, in 1947, there were one and a quarter million more women than men) to seduce lonely middle-aged women, making contact with them through 'Lonely Hearts' clubs – i.e. clubs that, for a fee, would put lonely men and women into contact.

In 1947, Fernandez met Martha Beck, a fat nurse who had been married three times and had been deprived of the custody of her children because she had been found unfit to keep them. For some peculiar reason, they were attracted to one another and formed a partnership. Martha Beck was only 26. As soon as Mrs Beck learned of Fernandez' 'trade' she decided to join him; she would pose as his sister and help him fleece middle-aged women. But she persuaded Fernandez to add a further refinement – murdering the women. This may have been due to a sadism directed against her own sex, or simply to jealousy of the women who shared her lover's bed while they were being swindled. In two years, the couple killed twenty women, and may have murdered more. Finally, the 'brother and sister' moved into the home of 28-year-old Mrs Delphine Dowling, who lived in Grand Rapids, Michigan, with her 2-year-old daughter, Rainelle. Mrs Dowling's husband had been killed in a rail crash. Soon Mrs Dowling disappeared, and the police went to the house to inquire about her. Fernandez and Beck were at the cinema; when they returned, they denied knowing where Mrs Dowling had gone to, and told the police to search the house. The police found a spot of damp cement in the cellar, and soon unearthed the bodies of Mrs Dowling and Rainelle. This was in February 1949, five weeks after the couple had moved into Mrs Dowling's home. Once arrested, Fernandez and Beck talked freely. They admitted to murdering Mrs Dowling by shooting her, and drowning the little girl two days later when she would not stop crying. Martha Beck admitted that it had been she who murdered Mrs Janet Fay, another widow, in late 1948; after they had gained possession of her money, Mrs Beck smashed in her head with a hammer out of jealousy. She was buried in a basement in New York. In 1948, Mrs Beck had been so jealous of a widow named Myrtle Young, who had accompanied them to Chicago, that she had insisted on sharing a bed with her! Myrtle Young was poisoned with barbiturates.

There was no death penalty in Michigan, so the police decided to transfer the trial to New York. The killers naturally objected violently, but after a legal battle, the trial opened in New York. They were charged with the murder of Mrs Fay. The details of their sexual relationship that emerged (both were complete degenerates) were so indecent that they were never published. On August 22nd, 1949, they were sentenced to death.

In Sing Sing, they still caused some commotion; they continued to declare their love for one another and to wave when they had a chance to catch a casual glimpse of one another across the exercise yard. Fernandez' boastfulness about his sex life with Mrs Beck led other prisoners to start a story that she was having an affair with someone in the women's wing, and Fernandez almost went insane with rage and jealousy. But they were still declaring their undying love for one another when they were executed on March 7th, 1951. They were known as 'America's most hated killers'. No full account of their murders has been published, since only the three murders to which they confessed were investigated.

FERRERS, Lord
The last nobleman in England to suffer a felon's death.

Ferrers was almost certainly insane, but his insanity was of the self-induced type. He was born on August 18th, 1720. He matriculated at Oxford. At the age of 20 he went abroad, and plunged into dissipation in Paris. His tendency to sudden bursts of uncontrollable temper and persecution mania was made worse by all kinds of debauchery. The eighteenth century was a time when noblemen had almost absolute power of life and death over their servants, and Ferrers was an exceptionally brutal master. On one occasion, a barrel of oysters arrived and they were found to be bad; one of his servants refused to perjure himself and claim that they had been changed on the road, so Ferrers beat him brutally and then kicked him when he was unconscious so that he was maimed for life. In 1752 he married the daughter of Sir William Meredith, but made a habit of beating her, even, on one occasion, kicking her into unconsciousness in front of the servants. Finally, in 1758, the unfortunate woman left him and obtained a separation order.

Ferrers had long periods of lucidity, but they became rarer, and his fits of maniacal rage more frequent. On Sunday, January 13th, 1760, Ferrers told his steward, John Johnson, that he wanted to see him the following Friday. The management of Ferrers' estate had been left more and more in the hands of this old man, since Ferrers was irresponsible for long periods. Ferrers hated him, and tried to deprive him of his farm; but the trustees stopped this.

On the day he sent the message to Johnson, Ferrers fired a gun at an oak board, and the bullet went through it.

On the following Friday, Ferrers received Johnson in a locked room, shouted accusations at him and ordered him to get on his knees. He then drew the pistol and shot him. Mr Kirkland, a surgeon, was summoned, and ordered to cure Johnson. He also sent for Johnson's son and daughter and promised them money if they would keep silent. They were not to be intimidated or bribed. Later that evening Johnson died, and Kirkland summoned men to help him seize Ferrers; finally, after a six-hour siege of the house, he was caught. He was taken to Leicester Jail in a state of apathy, and later to London, where, after hearing the indictment against him in the House of Lords, he was committed to the Tower. His mistress (apparently one of many, for he was a man who was obsessed by sex) took rooms nearby and they exchanged daily letters.

He was tried at Westminster Hall on April 16th, 1760. His attempted defence was insanity, and many witnesses were called to declare that members of his family had died insane and that he himself had long periods when he was obviously suffering from persecution mania and other delusions. Undoubtedly, Ferrers was as insane as Daniel McNaghten (who assassinated Peel's secretary and caused the McNaghten Rules to be formulated), but, as he himself pointed out in a final speech, it is a little hard to make a man argue his own insanity, since he loses either way – whether he argues lucidly or badly.

Ferrers was found guilty and sentenced to be hanged. He showed some courage and coolness in the fortnight that followed, and insisted on being hanged in the suit in which he was married (an odd sort of sentimentalism when he had treated his wife so badly). He declared he felt the humiliation of dying at Tyburn (where he attracted a record crowd, so much so that it took the cart three hours to get there). The executioner had a wrangle with his assistant on the scaffold – Ferrers accidentally paid the five guineas to the wrong man. He died with complete composure.

FIELD, Frederick Herbert Charles

Thirty-two-year-old British aircraftman, convicted and hanged in 1936 for the murder, by strangling, of prostitute Beatrice Vilna Sutton; now acknowledged as the murderer of Nora Upchurch, found strangled in 1931, for which crime he was tried at the Old Bailey and found not guilty.

On the morning of October 2nd, 1931, the body of Upchurch, a 20-year-old prostitute, was discovered inside empty premises in Shaftesbury Avenue, London. A signfitter's manager and one of his workmen made the discovery; they had had to force the door because the workman, Frederick Field, alleged that earlier he was asked for the key by a 'man in plus fours with gold fillings' who, he said, he assumed was a prospective purchaser of the property. Field even identified this person at the inquest on Upchurch; the Coroner, Mr Ingleby Oddie, wrote afterwards 'I called the man up at the inquest . . . got him to open his mouth whilst the jury and I inspected his teeth . . . there was not a gold tooth in his head . . . it was clear that Field was lying. He was, in fact, the sort of man who could not help lying.' An open verdict on Nora Upchurch was returned. In July 1933 Field (who was now in the Royal Air Force) called at a newspaper office and, in confessing to the Nora Upchurch crime of two years before, bargained that the cost of his defence should be paid by that newspaper. At his subsequent trial at the Old Bailey, however, Field retracted this confession, saying he had desired the trial so that his innocence of the murder charge could be stressed to suspicious members of the public. As Field's account of the killing differed in some respects from the facts, he was found (despite police suspicion) not guilty. In 1936 Field, now a deserter, confessed to the murder, at Clapham, of Beatrice Sutton: 'I was just browned off; I don't even know who the woman was.' He withdrew this confession before the trial but when asked in court how he had been able to describe certain of the victim's injuries so accurately, replied: 'It was pure supposition.' After fifteen minutes the jury returned with their verdict.

FIELD, Jack Alfred
Nineteen-year-old unemployed labourer, convicted with 29-year-old William Thomas Gray of the murder of Scottish-born London typist Irene Munro.

The victim, aged 17, arrived in Eastbourne for a week's holiday on Monday, August 16th, 1920, lodging with a Mrs Wynniatt at 393 Seaside; on August 20th the distressed landlady identified, at the local mortuary, her young boarder's remains. The body of a girl had been found some hours before buried on the Crumbles, a wide stretch of shingle extending from Eastbourne to Wallsend; her head was battered, presumably by a blood-stained stone lying nearby. ('Probably survived for short time – might have been half an hour, but would be deeply unconscious all the time' – wrote pathologist Bernard Spilsbury, who was called in on the case by the Home Office.) Mrs Wynniatt said that Irene Munro left her house wearing a green coat and carrying a handbag stuffed with holiday money at 3 pm the previous day; she had become anxious when hearing of the unidentified murder victim because her lodger had not returned. People remembered seeing, the previous afternoon, a girl in green accompanied by two young men, one wearing a herring-bone-pattern suit. The information resulted in police interviewing every man they saw wearing such a suit. During his investigation Gray (wearing a herring-bone suit) and his 'mate', Field, were questioned, but there appeared no reason then to detain them. Later police learnt that, within an hour of Irene Munro's body being found, both men had gone to a recruiting station and tried to enlist immediately. A barmaid at the Albemarle Hotel told of two men, 'Jack and Bill', who although regular customers up to August 19th, had not been there since; on the morning of that day they were 'broke', asking for credit, but upon returning at 6 pm they appeared affluent. A building labourer, during a house-to-house inquiry, told of seeing 'Bill Gray' with a younger couple, walking in the direction of the Crumbles. Field and Gray were apprehended and committed for trial at Lewes Assizes on a charge of murdering Irene Munro. The trial under Mr Justice Avory was on December 13th; Mr Edward Marshall Hall defended Gray and Mr J. D. Cassels was defence counsel for Field. Both pleaded not guilty; Field said on the day of the murder he had drawn his unemployment pay and had a drink with Gray, after which they had strolled to Pevensey, meeting no one on the way. Marshall Hall advised his client not to submit to cross-examination; apparently bored by court procedure, Gray fell asleep at one point and was reprimanded by the judge. Found guilty, they were hanged at Wandsworth, each, at the end, blaming the other for the actual killing.

FINGERPRINTS

In China and the East the finger- and thumbprint have been used for centuries as a form of signature, to seal official documents, business contracts, and legal claims. A twelfth-century Chinese romance describes the fingerprinting of two women arrested for murder. This already implies an awareness of the relationship of fingerprints to individuality and an awareness of their relative permanence. Regarding the latter, the fingerprints of an early Briton on a pick haft at Brandon, Suffolk, are at least five thousand years old.

In the West a most important early record of the legal awareness of fingerprints is the Major Declamations, the addresses of a Roman lawyer. One of them is a case which centres on the planted evidence of bloody handprints, and this is used by the defending lawyer of the innocent man to break down the real murderer, who then confesses. During the Middle Ages in Europe wax seals were also impressed by the fingerprint as a sign of one's 'act and deed'.

Marcello Malpighi, an Italian physiologist of the seventeenth century, was the first European to consider scientifically the ridge patterns on the skin. His contemporary, Nehemiah Grew, Secretary of the Royal Society, similarly studied the pores of hands and feet. Other scientists followed up these studies over the next two centuries. In 1823 Johann Purkinje, Professor of Anatomy at Breslau, suggested the first system for the classification of fingerprints.

During the 1860's in India, after the Mutiny, the Government were issuing pensions to many natives whose illiteracy and incapability of signing their receipts made the possibility of fraud a crucial issue. William Herschel, an Indian Civil Servant who already had experience of using fingerprints in signing agreements, was inspired to solve the problem by the wholesale and systematic use of them, thus attempting to render impersonation impossible. Having demonstrated the method as a means of identification and prevention of crime on a large and organized scale, Herschel also intuited its possibilities as a detector of crime and recorder of criminals.

Henry Faulds, a Scottish doctor in Tokyo, was also interesting himself in the subject from a similar viewpoint at that time, and in 1880 wrote a detailed article considering the wide variations of ridge patterns, their individuality and persistence. In the 1880's, too, there is evidence that others in the West were becoming very conscious of the significance of fingerprints. In two contemporary detective stories of Mark Twain, *Life on the Mississippi* and *Pudd'nhead Wilson*, fingerprinting plays a crucial rôle. However, the chief system of criminal identification was that devised by Dr Alphonse Bertillon of Paris. It consisted of body measurements, head measurements, limb measurements, full and profile photographs, the recording of detailed skin marks, and a personal history. It marked a great advance in systematic criminal identification and registration, but its descriptive methods were very cumbersome and lengthy, and in particular, unless the subject was fully grown its value was dubious.

In the late 1880's Sir Francis Galton, whilst concerned with the more general question of personal identification, indirectly came across and took up Herschel's achievements in finger-printing. His interest in the subject expanded vastly, resulting in 1895 with *Fingerprint Directories*, dedicated to Herschel, in which is laid the foundation for the police fingerprint system as in use today. With this work he attempted to resolve three issues. (1) Whether the pattern ever changes. (2) Whether their variety is enormous. (3) Whether they can be classified.

In 1892, Juan Vucetich, later Director of the Fingerprint Bureau in Buenos Aires and formulator of a classification system, achieved the first conviction of a murderess on the evidence of fingerprints.

In the 1890's Edward Richard Henry, Inspector-General of Police in Bengal, simplified and made really workable the achievements of Herschel and Galton. His *Classification and Uses of Fingerprints* was published in 1897 and became an official textbook. Within a few years his system had been accepted by many European countries and the United States. Herschel and Galton paid whole-hearted respects to his advance on and transformation of their work. But Faulds spent the rest of his life bitterly resentful at his lack of acknowledgement as the pioneer in this new science.

In 1901 Henry was made Assistant Commissioner at Scotland Yard and in the same year the Central Fingerprint Branch was created. In the early stages the collection of prints grew rapidly,

for every offender was fingerprinted and soon the work of com-
paring and tracing took hours and hours. The other technical
problem which had to be mastered was that of reproduction, in
relation to all the varied materials on which prints can register.
As yet they played a very tentative rôle in criminal inquiries and
for some time were only made *after* the suspect was found.

In 1902, on Derby Day, fifty-four men were arrested on the
Epsom Course and fingerprinted. By next morning an inspector
was ready with the records of twenty-nine old offenders amongst
those charged. In the autumn a burglary at Denmark Hill provided the first trial to accept fingerprint evidence at the Central
Criminal Court. Jackson, the accused, whose prints were already
in the Fingerprint Branch records, received seven years.

In 1905 the Stratton trial was the first murder case in which
fingerprint testimony played a serious rôle. Inspector Collins
discovered eleven points that tallied between the murderer's
thumbprint and that found at the scene of the crime. Justice
Channell accepted this, but nevertheless advised the jury not to
act on this evidence alone.

J. G.

FISH, Albert
Sexual murderer. As described by Dr Frederick Wertham (in
The Show of Violence), *one of the most developed cases of
sexual perversion in the literature of abnormal psychology.*

Fish was tried for the murder of 10-year-old Grace Budd on
June 3rd, 1928. Under the pseudonym of Frank Howard,
58-year-old Fish called on Grace's brother, Edward Budd, saying that he had seen Budd's advertisement for a job on a newspaper, and offering him work. While in the Budds' home, he
offered to take Grace to a party 'given for some children' by
Fish's 'sister'. Reluctantly, the parents allowed the child to go
off with Fish. He took her on the train from New York Central
to the town of Greenburgh. At Greenburgh, he actually left his
'tools' on the train, and was reminded about them by the child.
He took her to an empty house known as Wistaria Cottage, where
he stripped himself in an upstairs room and then called Grace in.
When she screamed, he strangled her, and then cut off her head
and cut the body in two. He took parts of her body home with
him, cooked them with carrots and onions, and ate them over a
period of nine days. During this time he confessed to feeling
great sexual excitement.

The hidden compulsion that had made him leave the 'tools' behind on the train later made him write to the Budds in an envelope that could be traced. This was on November 11th, 1934, six years after the murder. In the letter Fish admitted to killing Grace and eating parts of her, but declared that he made no sexual assault. A month later, on December 13th, Fish was arrested. Frederick Wertham was given the task of probing into his mental condition.

Wertham records that Fish was born in 1870, in a family in which had occurred certain cases of mental abnormality. At 5 he was placed in an orphanage; at 15 he left school and changed his Christian name from Hamilton to Albert. He became a grocer's assistant, then a painter and decorator – his trade for the remainder of his life. In 1898 he married a girl nine years his junior, and they had six children. 'I was always fond of children.' Twenty years later his wife eloped with the lodger. Fish continued to look after the children and 'married' three more times. (He was never divorced.)

'Fish's sexual life was of unparalleled perversity', Wertham says. At 5 years of age, a woman teacher developed in him a taste for being spanked on his bare body. Sadism and masochism were the chief elements in his sexual development. 'Experiences with excreta of every imaginable kind were practised by him. . . . He took bits of cotton, saturated them with alcohol, inserted them in his rectum, and set fire to them. He also did that to his child victims. Finally, he developed a craving (for) . . . cannibalism.' Fish admitted to a lifetime of preying on children, and to seducing at least a hundred. As a painter, often working in basements or empty houses, he had a great deal of opportunity for finding victims. In some cases, he castrated the boys. He developed a habit of sticking needles into himself below the scrotum; an X-ray showed twenty-seven of these needles inside him, some of them eroded into small pieces.[1] He also tried forcing needles under his finger-nails, but found this too painful to continue.

Fish suffered from 'religious insanity'. He had visions of Christ and His angels, as well as of Hell, and believed himself to be a particularly holy man. 'He felt driven to torment and kill children. . . . He felt that he was ordered by God to castrate

---

[1] An interesting account of masochistic perversions can be found in Paul de River's volume, *The Sexual Criminal;* it throws some interesting light on Fish.

little boys.' Fish declared, 'I had to offer a child for sacrifice, to purge myself of iniquities'.

In view of all this, it seems evident that Fish was completely insane, and that the death sentence passed on him expressed the indignation of the jury rather than their considered verdict of his total responsibility. (This was the same situation as in the case of Dr Deschamps.)

Fish had been arrested many times before, on charges including grand larceny. He had also spent ninety days in jail for sending obscene letters (another of his favourite occupations) and received two suspended sentences for passing dud cheques. He was actually sent to a mental hospital for observation in 1930, two and a half years after the Budd murder. The report stated that 'at times he showed signs of mental disturbance'. In hospital a second time, although diagnosed as a sadist (a cat-o'-nine-tails was found in his room), no further investigation was made, and he was released.

Wertham states his belief that Fish was responsible for many child murders over several decades. 'He looked like a meek and innocuous little old man. . . . If you wanted someone to entrust your children to, he would be the one you would choose. A judge of the supreme court . . . had told me he had been reliably informed that Fish was implicated in fifteen child murders.'

FLOYD, Charles
Moronic sexual murderer and 'peeping Tom', arrested in Dallas, Texas on November 22nd, 1949, and sentenced to life imprisonment in an institution.

No full account of Floyd's case history has been given; his first victim may have been Mrs William C. Brown, the 20-year-old wife of a Tulsa truck-driver, strangled and raped in her flat at 825 North Main Street on July 10th, 1942. She was pregnant and only six days away from delivering the child when she was murdered; the unborn baby was also killed.

Less than six months later, 46-year-old Clara Stewart and her daughter, Mrs Georgina Green, were battered to death and raped in their apartment, again on the north side of the city. Mrs Green's husband was in the army. All three victims were redheads.

Two and a half years went by before the next attack, on May 15th, 1945. Panta Lou Liles, the redheaded wife of a sailor, returning to her ground-floor room at 501 Cheyenne Street, undressed without drawing the curtains. The 'peeping Tom' outside watched her undress, waited until she was asleep, and clambered over the windowsill into the room. He knocked the girl unconscious before she woke up, and went on to batter her to death. He then wrapped her head in a sheet, and raped her. Several hours later he was still in the room when Mrs Liles' room-mate, a night nurse, rang up to wake the girl in time to be at her work at a nearby aircraft plant. A man's voice answered; and the nurse called the police.

A man named Henry Owens was arrested on suspicion; he was known to be weak-minded, and had been booked before on a charge of molesting women. A lie-detector test was inconclusive; although the graph jumped when Owens was asked about the murders, it seemed possible that he might be deluding himself by a kind of wishful thinking. The lie-detector operator told of an interesting case, when a lunatic who claimed he was Napoleon was given a test. When asked if he was Napoleon, he denied it, but the detector showed he was lying!

While Owens was still in custody, the murderer had another outburst, this time wounding three girls and killing a fourth. This was on July 1st, 1948. The murderer broke into the flat of a woman on North Cheyenne Street, and attacked the woman and two children who were sleeping in the flat – her daughter and a friend, aged respectively 12 and 14. The woman was knocked unconscious and an 'unnatural sex act' committed on her. The two children were knocked unconscious and partly undressed, but the killer was disturbed by a neighbour who had been roused by screams, and escaped by the back door before he could complete the assault. Two blocks away, at 11 East Cameron Street, the killer found another redhead, Ruth Norton, whom he bludgeoned while she was still asleep and then raped. Ruth Norton died of her injuries. The killer had apparently forced his way in by cutting a hole in the back door – a method reminiscent of the New Orleans Axe Man.

A description of the murderer came from a woman who had been awakened by the barking of a dog on the night of the Ruth Norton murder. She had seen a man standing outside and flashing a torch; he was more than six feet tall and looked like a truck-driver.

The police began a careful check on all trucking companies in Tulsa, and finally discovered that a tall man named Charles Floyd had left his job on the day after the murder of Ruth Norton; Floyd was known to have a passion for redheads. It took some time to find Floyd, but he was finally arrested a year and a half after his last murder. Floyd seemed to be tired and confused, but he was able to supply details that would be known only to the murderer. He admitted to being an inveterate 'peeping Tom' who had killed when the sexual excitement became too over-powering.

In some ways, the case fails to conform to the usual pattern of the sexual murderer, whose crimes tend to become more and more frequent. After the three murders in 1942, two and a half years elapsed before the next, then a period of three years.

It has at least one feature worth commenting on. From Floyd's confession, it emerged that he was in the habit of watching Panta Lou Liles undressing through her window. In a sense, therefore, the girl was partly to blame for not drawing her curtains. One of the causes of the increase in sexual crime is certainly the increase in stimulation. (See also Stacey, William.)

FORSYTH, Francis Robert George
Eighteen-year-old labourer at Hounslow, Middlesex, charged with three companions of the murder 'in the furtherance of theft' (a capital offence) of 23-year-old engineer Alan Jee.

At 11.30 pm on June 25th, 1960, the victim was walking home alone to Isleworth, Middlesex, after having spent the evening with his fiancée, to whom he had become engaged the day before: he chose to walk down an unfrequented alley, leading to a footbridge, and here was waylaid and attacked by Forsyth and his gang (driver Norman James Harris, aged 23, coalman Christopher Louis Darby, aged 23, and 17-year-old labourer Terrence Lutt) receiving such severe injuries, particularly about the face and neck, that he died in hospital on June 27th without ever regaining consciousness. The assailants were traced through the boastful indiscretion of Norman Harris, although when first questioned by the police all four denied being near the alley on the night of the killing. Eventually they admitted complicity, Forsyth confounding his mother's incredulity in the presence of a detective: '. . . I'm sorry, Mum, but I did it, and that is all there is to it. . . .' None of the four was ever to show remorse for the murder and throughout the police proceedings seemed more concerned with forecasting their own fate, Harris with some accuracy ('We'll all dangle together') and Forsyth with some optimism ('I reckon we'll get five years each . . . still, we should be out by the time we are 24 . . .').

Their trial commenced at the Old Bailey on September 20th, 1960, all pleading not guilty. Harris' confession to the police was quoted by prosecuting counsel, Mr Mervyn Griffith-Jones: '. . . I was skint and out of work. I meant to go screwing a shop or a house. . . . Then somebody said "Let's 'jump' somebody" . . . I don't know who said it. Three minutes later Jee came along . . . Lutt "stuck it on him" . . . the chap went down . . . he sort of covered his face . . . he shouted, "What do you want me for?" . . . the lads held him down and I put my hand in his inside pocket to get his wallet, but there was nothing in there at all. Me, Darby and Lutt were holding him down, and Forsyth was standing above us . . . I saw some blood on my hand . . . I realized "Floss" (Forsyth) had put the boot in. . . .' Forsyth's confession was also quoted: 'We decided to go screwing. Lutt suggested rolling (robbing) someone. He likes a fight, come to that we all do when we have had a few shants (drinks). As the fellow came up Lutt struck him . . . he was struggling so I kicked him in the head to shut him up. . . .' (Forsyth's shoes of the sharply pointed Italian type still bore traces of blood when examined by the police.) Darby denied taking part in the attack on Jee although he admitted being present at the time. Lutt admitted knocking Jee to the ground ('he sort of fell against the fence') but denied further assault, a statement which was corroborated by Forsyth: '. . . Lutt only hit him once, he packs a punch, he is a big boy.'

All were found guilty of capital murder; Forsyth and Harris were sentenced to death. Lutt (being a minor) was ordered to be detained During Her Majesty's Pleasure and Darby was sentenced to life imprisonment. On October 24th appeals against these sentences were heard at the Court of Criminal Appeal, and all dismissed. There was an outcry from certain quarters against the proposed hanging of 18-year-old Forsyth; the surprisingly eloquent, yet flowery, pathetic letters he wrote from Wandsworth prison to his girl-friend were published in the Press, but it is interesting to record that no letter expressing regret of his vicious behaviour was ever received by the parents or fiancée of Alan Jee.

Forsyth and Harris were both executed on November 10th, 1960.

FOX, Sidney Harry

Thirty-one-year-old homosexual and petty criminal (stealing, swindling), convicted in March 1930 at Lewes Assizes of the murder of his 63-year-old mother, Rosaline Fox.

Mother and son had received a joint income of 18s. a week, most of it spent on train fares; Sidney claimed 8s. from his country for a questionable 'war-wound', and Mrs Fox got 10s. weekly because her eldest son had been killed in France in 1917. Throughout the twenties the pair, seemingly devoted, had traipsed from hotel to hotel, dispensing worthless cheques (from stolen cheque-books) and of necessity rarely staying in one town longer than a week or two. A temporary break came in 1927 when Sidney was sent to prison and his mother to the workhouse: Sidney, stifling natural instincts, had had an affair with a Mrs Morse (being named as co-respondent in her divorce) prior to stealing her jewellery (for which crime he was imprisoned) and, incidentally, insuring the lady's life for £6,000 shortly before a curious incident when Mrs Morse was to awake in her bedroom, half-asphyxiated, to find a gas tap turned on. On Sidney's release in March 1929, he and his mother resumed their round of hotel-visits. On April 21st he instructed his mother to make a will in his favour; in her impoverished circumstances this seemed a futile move, but ceased to be so when, on May 1st, Sidney insured his mother's life against accidental death, the policy to expire at midnight on October 23rd. (One insurance official said afterwards: 'He asked me what was meant by an accident, and several other questions. . . .')

On October 16th the couple arrived at a hitherto unpatronized hotel, the Metropole at Margate, Kent; they possessed no luggage, although Sidney murmured to the management about their luggage having been sent on ahead and presumably gone astray. On the evening of October 23rd mother and son dined together, Sidney purchasing half a bottle of port for his mother to drink as a 'night-cap'. At 11.40 pm, Fox rushed down the corridor where he and his mother had separate rooms, and charged down the stairs screaming that there was a fire in his mother's room. ('My mummy! My mummy!') A commercial traveller went into the smoke-filled room and emerged dragging out the corpse of Mrs Fox, clad only in a dirty undervest; a burning chair and a patch of smouldering carpet were dealt with. Doctors said that the old lady's death was due to suffocation from the smoke and shock, and she was subsequently buried

248

on October 30th in her home-town of Great Fransham in Norfolk, amid loud lamentations from her son. The insurance authorities were suspicious, and examined the hotel bedroom, finding an inexplicable patch of unburnt carpet between the arm-chair (where Mrs Fox had been sitting) and the gas-stove supposed originally to be the source of the blaze, and discovering that only petrol or some similar inflammable solution could ignite the carpet to a comparable extent. On November 9th Mrs Fox's body was exhumed and pathologist Sir Bernard Spilsbury found the cause of death due to 'Manual Strangulation;' a bruise was found at the back of the larynx and there was no sooty deposit in the lungs, proving that Mrs Fox had been dead before the fire started. Sidney Fox, protesting his innocence, was arrested on a charge of murder. Sir Henry Curtis-Bennett with the Attorney-General Sir William Jowett appeared for the Crown, and Mr J. D. Cassels for the defence. Owing to rapid decomposition, when pathologists called by the defence examined the victim, the bruise on the larynx had disappeared and the jury were obliged to take Sir Bernard's word. The Attorney-General questioned Fox on his somewhat cowardly behaviour after the fire, and asked him why he had not left open the door of his mother's room on his way to give the alarm. Fox replied: 'So that the smoke should not spread into the hotel.'

Sentenced to death, Sidney Fox was hanged at Maidstone Jail in April 1930.

It is interesting to note that Sidney Fox showed the same tendency to deceit and petty fraud as many killers of his type – Heath, Ronald True, Cummins, Deeming, etc. While in the army, he passed himself off as the grandson of Sir John Leslie, and had letters addressed to himself at the Royal Automobile Club (of which he was not a member) under the name 'The Hon. S. H. Fox'. One of these was opened, and proved to be a letter from an elderly officer; it was of such a compromising nature that the writer was dismissed from the army.

Undoubtedly, 'delusions of grandeur' play a large part in the minds of certain criminals, and Fox is as unpleasant an example as any in the history of crime.

FURNACE, Samuel J.

Furnace's murder may have been inspired by the Rouse case. But in Furnace's case, there were no amorous complications, as with Rouse, and he was only £90 in debt. He had a wife and child with whom he lived happily.

On January 3rd, 1933, a Tuesday, Mr Wynne, of 30 Hawley Crescent, Camden Town, noticed that a shed in his yard was on fire. He had let the shed to a builder named Furnace. The shed was broken into, and a charred body was found on a stool. The fire seemed to have been started deliberately, and the next morning a note was found that said 'Goodbye all. No work, no money, Sam J. Furnace'.

But it was soon discovered that the dead man had been shot in the back of the head. An overcoat in the shed contained a Post Office Savings Book with the name Walter Spatchett on it. Spatchett was a rent collector who had been missing since Monday evening; he was supposed to have about £40 on him at the time of his disappearance. He was acquainted with Furnace.

It now became apparent that Furnace had murdered Spatchett, who was roughly his own build, and hoped to 'disappear', assuming that Spatchett's body would be mistaken for his own.

A nation-wide murder hunt began, and on Monday, January 9th, the BBC broadcast a message declaring without any ambiguity that Furnace was wanted for the murder of Spatchett. Furnace's movements were traced to a room in Regent's Park, and then to Southend. There the trail ended.

On January 15th, Furnace's brother-in-law received a letter asking him to come to Southend to see Furnace. It was Furnace's major mistake – as with other men on the run who have betrayed themselves with a letter (Canham Read, and Milsom and Fowler, for example). The following Sunday, the brother-in-law, Charles Tuckfield, went to Southend, as instructed, followed by the police. It was feared that Furnace had a gun and would 'shoot it out'; however, the police managed to take him without violence in his room. This was almost three weeks after the murder.

Furnace made a statement claiming that Spatchett had been shot accidentally.

Furnace managed to poison himself the day after his arrest with a small bottle of hydrochloric acid sewn into the lining of his overcoat. He died 24 hours later.

G

GARDELLE, Theodore
A once celebrated English murder case.

On February 19th, 1761, Gardelle, a Swiss miniature painter, lived at Leicester Fields (now Leicester Square) near Sir Joshua Reynolds' house. His landlady was a Mrs King. Gardelle sent the maid on a message early in the morning, and apparently murdered Mrs King for her money. He later told the housemaid he had been commissioned to dismiss her with her wages. He told callers that Mrs King had gone to Bath or Bristol. A woman came to lodge in the house, and a charlady was engaged. This charlady, ten days after the murder, found the cistern choked with a substance like meat. She drew out a sheet and some blankets. Bow Street Runners were called in, and found that Mrs King's room was heavily bloodstained. Bits of flesh were found about the house and calcined bones. Gardelle had tried to burn the body. And apparently he had sent off some of his landlady's belongings, before the murder, to a friend.

Gardelle's defence was that the crime was unpremeditated; during a quarrel, he had stabbed her with the pointed handle of a comb. But he was condemned to death and executed in the Haymarket. Major Arthur Griffiths mentions that, seventy years after the crime, Theodore Hook makes one of his characters say, 'As dead as Theodore Gardelle'. It is a mystery why Gardelle chose to remain in the house for ten days afterwards, or at least why he did not choose some quicker means of disposing of the body – like dumping it in the river by night.

GARDINER, William

Rose Harsent, aged 23, was the servant at Providence House, Peasenhall, a Suffolk village near Saxmundham. On Sunday, June 1st, 1902, she was found by her father lying murdered in the kitchen; her throat had been cut and attempts made to burn her. She was later found to be pregnant. In her room were several notes from one William Gardiner, a local foreman carpenter and Primitive Methodist choirmaster. Gardiner was 45 and lived with his wife and six children close to Providence House.

Gardiner immediately came under suspicion because a year earlier he had been involved in a scandal with Rose Harsent;

some boys had seen them disappear into a small building known as the Doctor's Chapel and had overheard rustling noises; Rose had then spoken of 'what we are doing now' and quoted verses from the thirty-eighth chapter of Genesis about Onan – from which one might guess the nature of what Gardiner and Rose were doing. But an inquiry among Gardiner's fellow churchmen had acquitted him.

Gardiner was not tried until November 7th, before Mr Justice Grantham – known as a difficult judge, capable of heckling and interrupting the counsel. (He also tried Chapman.) Mr W. F. Dickens prosecuted and Sir Ernest Wild, KC, defended. Gardiner's defence was an alibi, supported by his wife. The jury failed to agree, and Gardiner was tried a second time at Ipswich in January 1903 before Mr Justice Lawrence; again the jury failed to agree. The authorities entered a *nolle prosequi* (similar to the Scottish 'not proven' but meaning proceedings can be re-opened if further evidence appears) and Gardiner was set free. He and his wife opened a shop in a London suburb under their own name. Many people consider that it was a case of suicide, not of murder.

GERMAN WAR CRIMES

During the 1939–45 war it was estimated that the Germans killed twelve million people in a manner which the allied victors considered had made them responsible for the most appalling crime ever against humanity. For these people were 'liquidated', 'given special treatment', or in fact 'murdered *en masse*' by the most unprecedented and unimaginable methods. Total technological resources were called into play, scientists, engineers, doctors, indeed a whole nation, in order to achieve this. At the Nuremberg trial of the twenty-two major German war criminals a competent observer has emphasized that there was seldom a hint of contrition, on the contrary every effort was made to justify these deeds. There seemed no consciousness of responsibility and in fact given the chance 'they would go through it all again'.

The four charges were (1) The Common Plan or Conspiracy, (2) Crimes against Peace, (3) War Crimes, (4) Crimes against Humanity. The first two charges were generally concerned with the planning and waging of wars of aggression in violation of international treaties. Charges three and four concerned systematic murder, torture, and forced labour; death marches, the endless trains 'of thousands of hollow spectres in rags'; gas chambers, crematoria, and concentration camps where the victims were informed, 'Germany needs your arms. You are therefore going to work, but I want to tell you that never again will you see your families. Who enters this camp will leave it only by the chimney of the crematorium'; the 'action groups' and the medical 'experiments'. Four million people were exterminated at Auschwitz; one and a half million at Majdenek. Entire villages were shot or burned alive. In Russia entire folk populations were annihilated. Thousands of tons of fertilizer were made from the crushed bones of the burnt corpses.

The crime of the scientifically planned murder of national, racial, and religious groups was at Nuremberg called *genocide*. It was a new conception for international law. The theoretical framework of Nazi genocide was provided by the teachings and writings of the learned 'geopolitician', Professor Karl Haushofer, who at the age of 76 committed suicide with his wife in 1946 on a lonely Bavarian hillside. 'Lebensraum' and many other Nazi concepts were coined by Haushofer. For him legality was a geographical concept. 'Justice is whatever benefits the German people and injustice whatever harms them', said Hans Frank.

Himmler was the leading Nazi man of action most responsible for seeing genocide put into practice. For him Jews and other inferior races were 'vermin' and 'human animals', who must be treated accordingly. He declared:

Whether 10,000 Russian females fall down from exhaustion while digging an anti-tank ditch interests me only in so far as the ditch for Germany is finished. . . . We will assume a decent attitude towards these human animals . . . the extermination of the Jewish race is easy to talk about – but when 1,000 corpses are lying side by side, to have stuck it out and at the same time to have remained decent fellows, that is what has made us hard. Anti-Semitism is exactly the same as delousing. Getting rid of lice is not a matter of ideology, it is a matter of cleanliness. . . . This is a page of glory in our history – we must be mindful of our principle, blood, selection, austerity – and in twenty to thirty years we must be able to present the whole of Europe with its leading class. . . . It would be an evil day if the Germanic people did not survive. It would be the end of beauty and culture, and of the creative power of this earth.

The chief genocide methods were, as for instance applied to Poland; mass extermination of the Polish intelligentsia, gipsies, and Jews by gassing, shooting, working them to death, sterilization, abortion, castration, and the enforced separation of husbands and wives. A third of the population were thus murdered, and further millions were physically weakened and maimed. The experts apparently differed in their plans for dealing with Russia, the country where the German soldier was reminded 'human life has no value whatsoever'. Russia, of course, was *the* degenerate Slav mass whose fertility the Germans greatly feared, and who would have been the next to endure the full weight of genocide after the Jewish 'action' had ended. Professor Abel recommended total extermination, others thought this a little impractical for various reasons.

As a people the Jews were subject to the greatest genocidal action of all. Six million were exterminated. Attested Mme Lingens-Reiner, a Dutch woman doctor, survivor of the concentration camps, 'Any word of respect and awe sounds trite in the face of the physical and spiritual tortures suffered by the Jews'. Those who actually survived had to become 'strong, hardened, ruthless, armoured against a compassion which might otherwise have destroyed them'. Anti-Semitism was the axis around which Nazism revolved. 'If the Jew did not exist we should have to invent him.' The Jew symbolized evil, impurity, the Devil, and around the race a sacred taboo was created, underlaid with a sense of atavistic horror. 'Race defilement is worse than murder.' This final calculated blood carnage for 'solving the Jewish problem' was the culmination of one hundred years of the Pan-type race theories, which in the hands of Hitler had been made into the centre of a new religious faith. It would unite indissolubly 'master and servant in a destructive and insatiable communion'. It would strengthen irrevocably the bond between all those, leaders and led, who attempted to throw down the barriers and create a total reversal of human values.

Negation of the Jew provided the positive impetus, the motivation, the goal. It was the necessary counter-image for a group madness built on hatred, inferiority, and insecurity. The Enemy, the Gegenreich or Anti-Reich, performed the necessary and invaluable task of cohering the 'Reich', as an inseparable polarity. Poliakov considers that, apart from the outbursts of Streicher and Goebbels ('Death to the Jews has been our war cry for 14 years') in the early years, Hitler and his chiefs certainly did not dream of total extermination in the beginning. For the

Image of the Jew was a necessity in building up the régime. Yet, apart from the inner circle, it was in the air, in the mind of Heydrich too. And it came about.

In Zamosc, mounted SS attacked the Jewish quarter in typical fashion to grab deportees for the extermination centres. 'The spectacle which the ghetto presented after the attack literally drove the survivors mad. Bodies everywhere, in the streets, in the houses. Babies thrown from the third and fourth floors lay crushed on the sidewalks.'

The method of the 'action groups' was quite straightforward. 'The Jews were crowded into trucks – taken to some ravine or anti-tank ditch – stripped of everything – and then men, women, and children were shot on the spot.' From August to November 1942, 363,211 Jews were thus murdered. Eichmann put the total number of Russian Jews murdered at two million. Of the men who did this work day in day out, murdering in tens of thousands, Poliakov comments that their letters and their testimonies on trial convey a mixture of uneasiness and cynicism. 'All the pity of which they were capable they reserved for themselves or their subordinates. Not a word, not a thought for their victims.' 'Many men (i.e. SS men) suffered terribly and had to be sent home for all sorts of reasons, either because their nervous systems were shattered or because they were not able to stand it morally' (General Ohlendorff).

There is evidence that some of the men who carried out this work experienced *the loss of their own humanity*, in what they were doing. In general the Action Commandos worked in an alcoholic stupor and one officer endured the 'most terrifying nightmares'. Poliakov acutely asks, 'Was not the self-pity and persistent uneasiness of the murderers (evidenced in letters, diaries, and court statements) an indication of a secret inner protest of a confused realization that they were destroying *something of themselves* in the death and destruction that they spread'. 'Even amidst the worst excesses of these bestial natures certain mental barriers still remained.' Himmler only mentioned the subject of extermination in *one* speech, earlier quoted. At the trial of the leaders of these 'action groups', who included a professor, architect, lawyers, a former theologian, and a dental surgeon, none pleaded guilty, none showed the slightest remorse. All pleaded the defence of 'superior orders', whilst witnesses testified to their Christianity, their gentleness and their love of family. After 1942, the tens of thousands of corpses left beneath a light covering of earth were felt to be a little inconvenient and

Colonel Blobel, SS, was ordered to lead a special group all over occupied Russia, unearth the corpses and burn them. In true German fashion he took the job very seriously and perfected a technique on which he actually lectured in Berlin to other interested parties.

From Auschwitz thousands of bales of hair shorn from Jewish corpses were dispatched to stuff German mattresses. Tons of their clothing, toys, and spectacles were worn and used by the German people. Seventy-two transports of the gold from their teeth went to the Reichbank, and fat from their corpses made millions of bars of soap to help cleanse the German people. Hitler had explained with his fundamental simplicity, 'They had to be treated like tuberculosis bacilli. This was not cruel if one remembered that even innocent creatures of nature such as hares and deer had to be killed so that no harm is caused by them.' Strange how they cleaned themselves with these dead 'bacilli'.

This crime of genocide and its whole background in the growth of Nazi Germany is related to something far deeper than 'politics' as normally understood. For Hitler the 'political' realm was merely the means of entry. He grasped quite clearly that the vast majority of Germans were not ready for spiritual freedom, for individuality, for personal responsibility and choice, in fact were afraid of freedom and hated it. Within the given circumstances of economic and social chaos, he attempted with his undoubtedly great but sinister powers to halt the evolution of men and force the self-conscious personality back into the dark, warm womb of the national group consciousness.

A close and keen observer said of him, 'Self-surrender to the uncontrollable impulse to wreak destruction seems to be the essence of his spirit. He is incapable of spiritual development – confined in his own tragic nature that shuts out every creative influence that ripens a man.' His so-called 'political' programme was concerned in fact with the depths of man's nature.

I am freeing men from the restraints of . . . the dirty and degrading self-mortification of a chimera called conscience and morality, and from the demands of a freedom and personal independence which only a very few can bear. . . . To the Christian, I oppose the saving doctrine of the nothingness of the individual human being and of his continued existence in the visible immortality of the nation. . . . National Socialism . . . is the will to create mankind anew. . . . A violently active, dominating, intrepid, brutal youth – that is what I am after –

in its eyes the gleam of pride and independence of the beast of prey. . . . The will to power is for us literally the whole meaning of this life – I am restoring to force its original dignity, that of the source of all greatness and the creatrix of order.

It is interesting that some of the chief mass-murderers, Himmler, Goebbels, Eichmann, and Hoess, who was seriously intended for the Catholic priesthood, all came from strict religious families and surrendered completely to this frenzied destruction of Judeo-Christian values.

In Hitler's presence doubts, questions and anxieties dissolved before the simplicity of his actions, that primal simplicity of destruction and annihilation. Like a wizard he was everyone's answer – industrialists, economists, diplomats, generals, teachers, clergy, and the 'masses'. Yet behind his strength, his fanatical, violent, obsessed outer façade was an ego, 'excessively sensitive, sentimental, hopelessly immature. . . . It was an illusion that this man had any freedom of choice left. He followed a course which brought him to the summit of power and an ever more helpless dependence.' In the war years skulking in deep retreat, and in the early march with Hindenburg, one of the first to run. And at the end in the Berlin bunker not even Germany meant anything to him. Only death, destruction, the whole world in flames and the saving of his own ego.

The testimony of the surviving victims is the dark text of our times which demands the intensest imaginative participation in order to pay due tribute to their experience of what is possible for man. Lingens-Reiner declares, 'We had to survive in order to tell the world what we had seen and endured'. Often she looked around in a daze amid the hell of meaningless violence and brutality, asking herself, 'Was it possible that this was not a dream?' A dream indeed, but one which shadows the whole of our contemporary existence.

Nowhere to be found in this concentration-camp world of Hitler's new man was there a genuinely human I, responsible, faithful, unambiguous. Instead a lunatic grimace of irresponsibility and arbitrary judgement played havoc with human morality. Heydrich's slogan was, 'It's all right if you know about it – but you've got to know'. How reminiscent of Kafka's world. At Buchenwald a Polish child of three and a half was listed as a 'partisan'. 'People' were lost on the files for months and years, and the files were left unattended and crumbled away. 'If I rescued one woman I pushed another to her doom – was there any sense in trying to behave decently — You had to pass through all this like a sleepwalker and yet try somehow to arrange things so that you could justify it before your conscience.' This system made it 'impossible to ascertain the final responsibility for any act'. A schizoid path that often began with self-deception and compromise on the part of the SS. These camp guards, of whom there were 3,000 at Auschwitz, were in general men of 'absolute amorality'. The Ten Commandments had absolutely no meaning for them. 'A Jew was human to them in exceptional cases only.'

The victims too experienced a schism in their efforts to survive. Elie Cohen emphasized that, 'one could not have survived without lack of compassion', just as Rudolf Hoess, commandant of Auschwitz, declared that Hitler's orders could not be carried out without the stifling of all human emotions. 'Many kept their bearings only by a kind of split personality. They surrendered their bodies resistlessly to the terror while their inner being withdrew and held aloof. In spite of the conceptions formed, the reality was too terrible for the ego to realize its immediate import . . . were we truly there or was it our shadows that we saw playing their parts?' The 'Kapo' class were the prisoner overseers who adapted themselves by identification. Often they far outdid their SS masters in savagery, in their attempt to attain status and a feeling of *human* existence, *human* reality. But behind the mad flurry of violence and brutality, they too were weak and lost creatures.

Even so, in such unendurable conditions heroic deeds were performed. A British RA sergeant, Charles Coward, a confirmed escapee, had been sent as a difficult prisoner to the small British compound at Auschwitz. He worked there as a slave labourer for I. G. Farben while the four huge chimneys were smoking day and night with the thousands of corpses rolling into them on the conveyor belt from the gas chambers. He not only disguised himself to enter the hell of the Jewish compound but by subterfuge, Cockney cheek, and great courage managed to save at least 400 Jews from the gas chambers.

Beyond all else the ultimate ruler was death, physical and spiritual. An old image arises in modern dress. Not the ferrying boatman but the selection officer at the gas chamber. 'An elegant, well-groomed man, very aloof towards us miserable creatures – in a nonchalant posture, his right elbow cupped in his left hand, his right hand raised and motioning ever so slightly with the forefinger – now left, now right.' The crematorium waiting huts were five deep with corpses, dying and half-dead. A mound of writhing human compost. Yet for a few there was this possibility, 'Death was near and concrete – one struggled against him but one was no longer afraid of him, and to anyone who has ceased to fear death, life belongs truly, completely and without any restriction'.

Lingens-Reiner tells how, when first witnessing a gassing, hearing the screams, smelling the acrid stench, instead of crying out, her 'brain refused to function'. Paralysis overcame her. Instead of calling out to the Jews who passively lined up, and imploring them to escape, 'I only stood helpless, and mumbled, how can this ever be expiated. Slowly we all grew blunted and saw the mass murder of Jews as something which was horrifying but *immutable*.'

Hoess, who spoke quite dispassionately at Nuremberg of his activities, told Gilbert, the American psychologist, in his apathetic way, 'You could dispose of two thousand *head* in half an hour, but it was the burning that took all the time'. He insisted to Gilbert that he was quite 'normal', and of course for that he had only to compare himself with the others about him. A committee of exalted German authorities from Berlin had come to watch the first gassing and subsequent cremation. Through the small Judas holes it was easy for them to watch the process of asphyxiation inside without running any personal risk. These gentlemen expressed their great satisfaction. When it was all over, cigarettes, tobacco, and drink were served — Said Dr X, 'There was beautiful material among those brains; beautiful mental defectives, malformations and early infantile diseases. Where they came from and how, was really *none of my business*.' Dr Hoven 'had finished off a whole row of persons with sodium evipan. He strolled from the operating room, a cigarette in his hand, merrily whistling, "The end of a perfect day".' Dr Kremer, Professor of Münster University, wrote in his diary, 'Excellent lunch, tomato soup, half a hen, marvellous vanilla ice . . . 8 pm outside for a special action.' (Special action is of course typically German double-talk for the murderous gassing of innocent victims.) And there is the sanitary orderly, who quickly scattered his little pile of Cyclone B crystals down the shaft heads, joking, 'Now let 'em eat it', as below him the victims, 'would feel the gas, crowd together away from the menacing column and pile up in one blue clammy blood-spattered pyramid against the huge metal door, clawing and mauling each other even in death'.

Here we are concerned with something prevalent in the inner situation of man since the beginning of our technological era. Mumford's characterization of the early factory, 'Its brutal contempt for life only equalled by the almost priestly ritual it developed in preparation for inflicting death – the ultimate abysses of a quantitative conception of life, stimulated by the will to power', and General Booth's description of the London proletariat as 'that perfect quagmire of human sludge', both sound like early sketches for the camps and the gas chambers. Booth speaks of the dispossessed London poor as men whose 'manhood is crushed out – a reckless despairing spirit – a broken creature – covered with vermin and filth, sinking ever lower and lower, until at last he is hurried out of sight in the rough shell which carries him to a pauper's grave'. This is not far removed from the typical Belsen or Auschwitz victim. In many respects the early English factory and the attitude implied to the slaves who were crippled, mutilated, tyrannized, and murdered to early death in it, is the precursor of the concentration camp.

The SS early acquired the technique of turning a man into something '*no longer human*', mainly through terrorization and degradation. Theirs was a system meant to break all human self-respect. 'Man was beaten back to his most animal basis – the instinct of self-preservation blotted out all other instincts.' From 1936 onwards their camps were developed as self-contained units, with mess, laundry, hospital, brothel, and crematorium. 'Everyone had to appear at roll-call, alive or dead, whether shaken by fever or beaten to a bloody pulp. Often dozens of dead and dying were laid out neatly to answer to their number. Sometimes the NCOs had to rest from the sheer effort of beating – Koch used to say, "There are no sick men in my camp. They are either well or dead." In one camp the Jews committed suicide in groups, joining hands and jumping together into a deep quarry where they were working. They were nicknamed 'parachute troops'. At another, over the camp speaker was announced, 'If any more Jews hang themselves, will they kindly put a slip of paper with their names in their pocket so we know who it is.' Dostoievsky said that man can get used to anything. These infernos had their own quite peculiar idiom 'That must be a Jehovah's Witness snaking up like that – you'll be hitting the grate – you'll be going up the stack', were the kind of remarks passed in regard to the crematorium chimney. They discussed the day's gassings with 'the calmness of a citizen reading his newspaper'.

In the camps, 'obedience reached the point of automatism'. One man was ordered by his Kapo to hang himself at midnight, and at the appointed time he quietly tiptoed away and did so. Obedience even overcame the need for self-preservation. The law of obedience that had moulded the SS did the same for their victims. After two months in Auschwitz, 'When they could still walk they moved like automatons; once stopped they were capable of no further movement. They fell prostrate on the ground; nothing mattered any more to them. You could step right on them and they wouldn't draw back their arms or legs an inch. No protest, no cry of pain came from their half-open mouths. They were men without thoughts, without reactions, without souls, one might say. Sometimes under the blows, they would suddenly start moving like cattle jostling against each other.'

In the camps every feature of human beings in normal life was obliterated. 'One had become a cipher and it was a long time before one became "somebody" again.' The camps and the attitude of Dr Hoven, Dr Kremer, the exalted authorities, and men like Hoess and Eichmann so representative of the whole situation, indicate two quite split poles of being without any real human centre. The *in*human pole of abstraction, ideologies, sentimentality, and technological procedure, and the *sub*human pole of the human-brute, given over to the instinctual, brutality, sadism, and violence. Himmler 'exhibited two essential German qualities quite dissociated from each other, brutality and a romantic streak'. A distorted spirituality, not of this world and the sub-earthly will of the animal. But the truly human centre, the ability to create and maintain real human relationship is lacking. 'Having known men I prefer *dogs*,' said Hitler near the end.

What had the great generality of surviving victims gained from their experiences? At the liberation of Dachau the tendency was to cohere into national groups. 'It was *certainly not* an international fraternity among people who had suffered together.'

'Of the thousands who took part in the Jewish massacres', very few have been tried since the Germans themselves became responsible for the trials. In fact, the great majority of technicians, medical experts, draughtsmen, and real organizers of the extermination programme have simply vanished, let alone been tried. Only a few names even exist among the obviously large number of people directly concerned in this vast industry of murder. Names like Hoess, Eichmann, Globocnik, Blobel,

Heydrich, Ohlendorff, and the firm of Tesch and Stabenow from Hamburg, who made a gross profit of 128,000 marks in 1943 for the supply of Cyclone B gas. Nobody would accept responsibility as an individual. 'My conscience is the Führer', Göring had said. Consequently all of those involved either through silent assent or positive deed, which must have been almost the entire adult population, were in some way guilty. 'The grizzly world of Eichmann's Commando – a world of men without pity or responsibility, because "respectable" Germans in high office chose to condone them and yet deny their existence.' SS General Ohlendorff in charge of the Ukrainian massacres predicted, 'The future would find his firing squads no worse than the press-button killers of the atom bomb'. Many observers are still pessimistic as to whether this whole terrible period has really been a kind of cathartic to purge the corruptions of German social existence; especially as anti-Semitism, regarded as a barometer, has by no means vanished.

Apart from the Warsaw uprising, in which Jews fought to the death in sewers before their annihilation, there was in general no resistance from these millions of people in the face of their murderer-guards' relatively tiny numbers. Many reasons have been put forward for this. As an oppressed minority for twenty centuries they, like all such groups, had come to rely on cunning and compromise for paying far greater dividends than armed resistance. The Warsaw fighters like rats in underground burrows with their home-made weapons, surrounded by the closing ring of the mighty German Army, were impelled to make the first Jewish stand since the revolt of Bar Kochba, 'solely to preserve their human dignity and die fighting'.

For most of them the simple fact was that their fate, their end of straightforward, mechanical, inhuman extermination was unimaginable. *Such things did not and could not happen.* From the very rise to power of the Nazis, most of the German Jews, for instance, quite failed to grasp the situation. They had thought that the whole matter was a temporary misunderstanding, and some even praised Hitler's new government for its 'moderation and wisdom'. Colonel Blobel in charge of many 'actions', by continual machine-gunning into vast mass graves which the victims had to dig and then fill up layer by layer with their own corpses, said, 'They did not know their own human value'. That was why screaming, begging for mercy, or attempted escapes were almost unknown. A witness of the Ukrainian massacres stated, 'I was surprised to see how calm they were, almost too calm. The tranquillity with which these people had accepted their fate seemed horrible to me.' They stripped and waited quietly in their rows, in temperatures well below zero, for the shot in the neck; 'it was the normal resignation of the *condemned*', says Reitlinger. Which means that these innocent people had become convinced of their own 'guilt' by their 'accusers'. Kogon explained, 'Collective death mercifully paralysed its victims, froze them to the bone and marrow – *Death had become normal* – this will account for the quietness with which prisoners who knew they were going to the gas chamber met their fate.' Lingens-Reiner, the woman doctor whose professional status 'protected' her, cannot understand to this day why she never shouted out to the slowly shuffling queue of Jews, 'Get out – run – resist!' A new world indeed had been created with its own overwhelming, paralysing reality. A new man, too, with his new values, for whom death was in fact the norm, and murder the only positive deed.

J. G.

GIBBS, Edward Lester

Outwardly amiable college student from Pitman, New Jersey (slogan: Everybody Likes Pitman), who bore a secret resentment against all women. In January 1950 on the outskirts of Lancaster, Pennsylvania, he worked out this resentment on 21-year-old college secretary Marion Louise Baker. He had arranged to accompany a man friend to see the Gene Kelly–Frank Sinatra film *On the Town* but instead drove Marion Baker into the countryside ('I said . . . as we went over the bridge . . . the tyres sound good, they are singing') and, in a secluded spot, brained her with a lug wrench. Before the murder's discovery he indiscreetly courted police attention by querying an undertaker's son on the length of time it took for a body to decompose. He confessed to the crime shortly after Marion Baker's remains were found. Gibbs was electrocuted in April 1951.

GIFFARD, Miles
Twenty-six-year-old son of the Clerk to the St Austell Magistrates (Cornwall) who murdered his father and mother.

A personable-looking young man, Giffard had always been a difficulty to his parents: in 1940 (twelve years before the crime) he was removed from Rugby public school, his teachers finding him extremely odd, without emotion and impossible to instruct; sent to a psychiatrist in Devon, Dr Roy Neville Craig, his state was diagnosed as a form of schizophrenia, believed caused by a sadistic 'nannie', who had repeatedly locked the infant Miles in a dark cupboard. Failing at law-study and a course in estate management, Giffard became a wastrel, a 'remittance man', subsidized by his parents. From the Giffard home (Carrickowl, Carlyon Bay, Porthpean) he made frequent trips to London and became infatuated with Gabrielle Vallance, aged 19, living at 40 Tite Street, Chelsea. On November 3rd, 1952, Giffard wrote from Porthpean: '. . . the old man . . . has forbidden me to return to London. I am dreadfully fed up as I was looking forward to seeing you. . . . Short of doing him in, I see no future in the world at all. I love you terribly, and it really is breaking my heart to leave you in that den of wolves there.' On Friday, November 7th, at 5.30 pm, Giffard telephoned Gabrielle Vallance from Carrickowl, informing her that he was probably coming up to London in a few hours to conduct some business for his father; he said he would ring her again at 8.30 pm confirming the arrangement. At 7.30 pm Giffard, accosting his father in the garage, hit him on the head with an iron pipe, rendering him unconscious; seeking out his mother in the kitchen, he felled her with a series of blows, then returned to each parent, raining more blows down on their heads. At 8.15 pm he rang Gabrielle Vallance, telling her he was definitely coming up to London in his father's car. '. . . I did not know what to do. There was blood everywhere.' He deposited his fifteen-stone father in a wheelbarrow and tipped him over the cliff edge, a considerable distance from the house, disposing of his mother's body in the same way. After washing bloodstains from the garage and kitchen, Miles Giffard took some of his mother's jewellery and drove up to London, giving a lift to two hitch-hikers on the way. One of the hitch-hikers said afterwards: 'He seemed preoccupied and chainsmoked . . . he had a good suit on and seemed a very decent sort. . . .' He saw Gabrielle Vallance on the morning of November 8th, and after pawning his mother's jewellery took the girl to the Odeon Cinema, Leicester Square, where they saw the Charles Chaplin film *Limelight*. During the evening, at the Star public house, Chelsea Mews, he confessed to her about the killings: '. . . it upset her, and we just moved on to further public houses, drinking'.

Meanwhile the bodies had been found, and the Cornwall Constabulary, believing that Miles Giffard might be in London, had telephoned relevant details (including the conspicuous number of the missing car, ERL 1) to the Metropolitan Police, who apprehended Miles Giffard late on the Saturday night. The following day he was taken back to Cornwall, where he was charged with the murder of his father; Giffard, pleading not guilty, came up for trial at Bodmin Assizes in February 1953. Mr Justice Oliver presided, with Mr Scott Henderson leading for the Crown, and Mr John Maude, QC, for the defence, which was chiefly concerned with proving Giffard's insanity.

Dr Craig, called by the defence, was questioned by Mr Scott Henderson, who asserted that Giffard was a waster: 'As a doctor,' replied Dr Craig, 'I cannot subscribe to that.' Dr Rossiter Lewis, a psychiatrist, agreed with Dr Craig concerning Giffard's lack of reasoning power as a schizophrenic, but Dr Hood of Truro, who had been the Giffards' doctor, asked by the defence why he had not, years earlier, subscribed to the view that mental treatment was necessary for Miles Giffard, replied:

'The picture . . . was of just an idle little waster.'

'Is that what you feel about him now?'

'As a non-expert, I am afraid it is.'

Dr Hood was a close personal friend of Mr and Mrs Giffard, and made no secret of his opinion of Miles. His view of the early history contrasts strangely with that of Dr Craig, the eminent psychiatrist, who wrote in 1941, 'The door is slowly closing on this boy's sanity,' in a letter of advice to Mr Giffard. This letter was discovered after the murders – eleven years after the warning Dr Craig gave the parents in it.

The jury found Giffard guilty of murder, and he was eventually executed.

GILLETTE, Chester

Found guilty in 1906 of the murder of Grace Brown at Herkimer County, New York. Aged 25, handsome and engaging, he worked at his uncle's shirt factory where he was attracted by employee Grace Brown; the attraction was mutual and Gillette was a frequent visitor to Grace's lodging. One morning an upturned boat was found on Big Moose Lake, a vacation resort in upstate New York, and soon the pregnant body of Grace Brown was washed ashore; her escort at the resort hotel had been a 'Carl Graham', but investigations showed a physical similarity between Carl Graham and Chester Gillette. When someone swore to having seen Carl Graham after the boating mishap, the hunt for Gillette began. Within a few hours, wearing a gay straw boater, he was found and questioned. His replies were contradictory and evasive.

He was brought to trial for murder and eventually electrocuted. Apparently he panicked when informed of the pregnancy, believing his career prospects blighted. Pathos, undeservedly perhaps, has surrounded this case. Theodore Dreiser, who was a spectator at the trial, was inspired by Chester Gillette's story to write the famous novel *An American Tragedy*.

GILLIGAN, Nurse

Nurse Gilligan ran an old people's home in Hartford, Connecticut. Early in June 1914, a woman came to the offices of Lucien Sherman, the editor of the *Hartford Courant*, and said that she suspected her brother had been murdered at the Old People's Home. His name was Franklin Andrews, and he had died suddenly, although he had been seen painting a fence on the morning of his death, apparently in the best of health. Nurse Gilligan would not let the sister see his body, claiming it was already being embalmed.

The editor sent a reporter to the home; Nurse Gilligan was a pleasant, motherly-looking woman of 45 who had buried two husbands. But for the past four years there had been an average of twelve deaths a year at the home, although there were fourteen inmates. This was just six and a half times too many, when compared with the other Old People's Home in Hartford. The police were told, and a woman detective was entered in the home, paying $1,500 for 'life care'.

There were no more deaths for nearly six months. Then, on November 11th, 1914, Mrs Amy Hosmer died suddenly. The home's doctor, Dr Wiley, certified cause of death as apoplexy. Twenty-three days later, Dr Emma Thompson was called to one of her own patients in the home, Mrs Alice Gowdy, but Mrs Gowdy, who had taken ill after a Thanksgiving Day dinner, died in the night. Dr Thompson thought her limbs were oddly stiff, and told the police. Mrs Gowdy was buried, but a secret exhumation took place, and arsenic was found in the remains. Four more old people were exhumed, including the nurse's previous husband, Michael Gilligan; all had died of arsenic poison. It was discovered that the nurse sent the aged patients out to buy arsenic 'to kill rats'.

Nurse Gilligan was convicted of murder and sentenced to life imprisonment; a second trial brought the same result. In 1923 she was found to be insane. But it had been revealed at the trial that the murders had been carefully planned; Nurse Gilligan had written to Mrs Gowdy a few days before Franklin Andrews died: 'There will be a vacancy very soon'.

GIRARD, Henri

Wax-moustachioed boulevardier and amateur toxicologist, who, upon his dishonourable discharge from the French 10th Hussars in 1897 (at the age of 22), embarked on a series of financial swindles, fifteen years later turning to murder as a means of increasing his income. Girard kept three mistresses – each unaware of the other two, and their upkeep, combined with his own extravagant tastes in food and dress (he owned innumerable suits), called for money. His own fraudulent insurance company, Crédit Général de France, formed in 1909, brought him a 1,000 franc fine and a suspended prison sentence; but through the company he met Louis Pernotte, a simple-minded insurance dealer who was impressed by the sophisticated Monsieur Girard and flattered by his friendship. At 64 Avenue de Neuilly in Paris, where Girard kept one of his mistresses and a chemical laboratory, his eyes gleamed with a pioneering fervour over the test-tubes, before the sad realization that no untraceable poison existed. Undaunted, he prepared a typhoid germ culture, having first insured Pernotte's life with various companies for 316,000 francs. In August 1912, shortly before Pernotte, his wife, and two children left Paris for a trip to Royan, Girard poured bacilli into the water carafe on the lunch table; the entire family, upon arrival at Royan, became ill, Pernotte's rate of recovery being slower than his family's. (An entry in Girard's diary at this time queries: 'If Pernotte returns?') When the convalescent did return to Paris, months later, the solicitous Girard administered a thigh injection to his friend, who died shortly afterwards; the Pernotte family doctor (who, unknowingly, was also insured by Girard) listed 'Embolism, result of typhoid' as one of the causes of death.

In 1917 Girard decided on oafish (and, as it turned out, imperishable) 'Mimiche' Duroux as a victim; crates of poisonous fungi were delivered to the laboratory and Girard, impressing his mistress with tales of a new poison-gas for the Boche, experimented ceaselessly. Then, Mimiche duly insured, three suspicious entries appeared in Girard's diary:

> May 10th – Mushrooms
> May 11th – Mushrooms
> May 14th – Invite Mimiche to dinner

The servant was told not to wash up Mimiche's plates with the rest as he was suffering from a contagious disease; Mimiche, however, kept his rude health despite the mushroom course and (in the days following) dubious offerings of Cinzano and Byrrh-Cassis. After this last drink Girard hopefully recorded, 'Legs swollen, Mimiche' in his diary, but soon, depressed by Mimiche's beaming survival, he was selecting a less robust victim. Another of his mistresses, Jeanne Droubin, posing as a war widow, took out, from the Phénix Insurance Company, a policy on the life of the widow, Madame Monin, making herself the beneficiary. Subsequently offered an aperitif by Girard, Madame Monin proved more co-operative than Mimiche by dying on a train fifteen minutes later. Her death, so soon after the insurance, intrigued the Phénix Company, who started the inquiries that were to result in Girard's arrest on August 21st, 1918. In Fresnes prison Girard now experimented with self-analysis for the benefit of the prison doctors: '... I am good, with a very warm heart ... very affectionate ... always ready to do a good turn – even to strangers ...'

In May 1921, before he came up for trial, he managed to secure a culture of germs and to swallow them, so dying appropriately.

GOEHNER Kidnapping Case
The main interest of this case, which took place in Stuttgart in April 1958, is the use of the tape-recorder attached to the telephone to record the kidnapper's voice, and the later broadcast of the tape after the body of the kidnapped child had been discovered.

The killer was Emil Tillman, a 40-year-old gardener, who wanted money to marry his 46-year-old mistress (who was already married). Tillman, who lived in the Degerloch district of Stuttgart, lured the 7-year-old boy into the heart of some woods, the Haldenwald, near his home, and strangled him. Before killing him, the gardener had asked him his name and address; he now telephoned the house of a Stuttgart manufacturer and demanded money for the return of his son. The bewildered manufacturer replied that all his seven children were present in the room with him. The kidnapped boy had been talking about his best friend, and the murderer – who was carrying the boy on the back of his cycle – had misheard him. But news of Joachim Goehner's disappearance appeared in the newspaper and enabled Tillman to trace the boy's father, from whom he demanded 15,000 marks (about £1,100). The father asked the man to ring back, and notified the police, who immediately had a tape-recorder attached to the telephone, and established wireless contact between the house and the police station. There were two remarkable pieces of incompetence in the case that might have destroyed all hope of an arrest. An excited telephone operator, trying to trace a subsequent call from the kidnapper, cut off the conversation – thus giving him an intimation that something was wrong. And later, when a call was actually traced and a wireless message relayed to a police car in the vicinity of the call-box, an excitable police sergeant automatically switched on his siren as he rushed towards the box. Naturally, the booth was empty when they arrived.

In the meantime, the body had been discovered in the Haldenwald, but its discovery was kept secret, in an effort to keep alive the killer's hope of ransom. However, Tillman returned to the spot a few days later and found the body gone. The few attempts at a liaison between the father of Joachim Goehner and the kidnapper had been unsuccessful, and Tillman now made no further effort to contact Herr Goehner. The police now tried broadcasting the voice on the tape. This brought immediate results – calls poured in, identifying the voice – but Tillman was not among those interviewed. Another young boy told the police of being accosted by a man near the Haldenwald, who promised him two rabbits if he would come into the woods. The child was able to give a description of Tillman, a short man – under five feet – with a wiry shock of hair. Two suspects were held for questioning, and one of them actually confessed to the murder. When an excited mob formed outside his prison cell, he withdrew his confession, explaining that he had wanted to see his name in the papers.

Finally, the broadcast tape was heard by Mrs Marguerite Helmut, an elderly widow, whose radio had been at the repairer's during the first few days when the voice had been relayed. The police treated her assertion that the voice was that of her ex-gardener with routine caution – they had investigated many such

– but finally picked up Tillman for questioning. He denied all knowledge of the crime, and asserted that the voice was completely unlike his. But the similarity was unmistakable. For six days Tillman was moved from prison to prison to escape the rage of angry mobs. At the twelfth interrogation he broke down and confessed to the murder. On May 26th, 1958 – forty-two days after his murder of Joachim Goehner – Tillman committed suicide in his cell by hanging himself with a strip of his bed-sheet.

GOOD, Daniel

Murdered his wife in 1842 in the stables of Granard Lodge, Roehampton. Good was detected by accident. He attempted to steal a pair of trousers in Wandsworth, and was followed back home. The policeman who was searching the stable found a woman's trunk, without arms, legs, or head under some hay. It was then remembered that Good had kept an enormous fire burning in the harness room for the past two weeks.

Good slammed and locked the stable door while the policeman was searching and managed to escape. However, an acquaintance recognized him a fortnight later in Tonbridge, where he was working as a builder's labourer. Major Arthur Griffiths says somewhat curiously that Good kept combing back his hair over a bald spot, 'a constant trick with the fugitive murderer'. He was using some bloodstained cloth to make a pad for his bricklayer's hod.

Information on the case is scanty. His wife was in her early twenties; it is not known why Good killed her. Presumably he was executed.

GORDON, Iain Hay (The Curran Murder Case)

In the early hours of November 13th, 1952, the body of Patricia Curran, 19-year-old daughter of Mr Justice Curran, was found by the wooded drive leading to the Currans' home, Glen House, in the village of Whiteabbey, outside Belfast, Northern Ireland. She was stabbed thirty times about the head and body, and there had been an abortive attempt at sexual assault. Chief Superintendent John Capstick of Scotland Yard was called in by the Royal Ulster Constabulary; he learnt that the girl's portfolio of notes and textbooks (she had attended Queen's University, Belfast, during the day), together with her cap and handbag, were found neatly stacked forty feet from the spot where her body had been dragged. This indicated that Patricia Curran had known and trusted her assailant. During a check of airmen and civilian workers at nearby 67 Group, Fighter Command, the conduct of quiet, religious-minded Leading Aircraftman Iain Hay Gordon aroused the interest of the RAF Special Investigation Officer. Gordon said he knew Desmond Curran, the dead girl's brother, and had often received hospitality at Glen House. He had a black eye, the result, he claimed, of a playful scrap in the camp billet; seeking confirmation of this story the investigating officer learnt from Gordon's comrades how he had sought an alibi for the evening of November 12th. Desmond Curran told of Gordon's obsession with the crime and how the airman had expressed surprise at the number of stabbings 'since the fourth blow killed her'. Capstick felt that Gordon was the murderer, but two months elapsed before he decided on a course of intensive questioning. Over a period of three days he asked Gordon about his childhood, his ambitions, his innermost thoughts – and finally, about the murder: 'You've been telling the police lies ... can't you possibly speak the truth?' Gordon, suddenly cooperative, told how he had met Patricia Curran by accident soon after she alighted from the Belfast bus on the evening of the 12th, and she asked him to escort her up the drive. At an ill-lit bend he wanted to kiss her. ' ... she laid her things on the grass ... she was not keen ... but consented in the end ... I found I could not stop kissing her ...' Gordon then stabbed her with a service knife, throwing this afterwards into the sea. On January 8th a wooden-handled paper-knife similar to one missing from Gordon's office was found on the beach at Kilroot, and Captain James Lyle, Harbour Master at Carrickfergus, maintained that such an object thrown into the sea at Whiteabbey at the time of the murder would be washed ashore two months later in the Kilroot area.

Gordon was tried at Belfast Assize Court on March 1st. The jury returned a verdict of 'guilty but insane'.

GRAHAM, John Gilbert

Strands of yellow wire strewn around the eight-mile debris area when Flight 629 of United Airlines exploded in mid-air near Denver, Colorado, in 1955 were among the first signs that sabotage had occurred. G-men, during their investigation into the lives of the thirty-nine passengers and five crew (all of whom were killed), in an attempt to discover some motive for the crime found their suspicions centred around John Gilbert Graham, whose mother had boarded the plane at Denver eleven minutes before it became (according to an eye-witness) 'a haystack on fire in the sky'. Dissolute and twenty-three, with a police record (forgery and bootlegging), Graham had taken out a travel insurance on his mother's life and was the beneficiary of her £50,000 estate. Graham eventually confessed; he had constructed a time-bomb from fourteen pounds of dynamite and an alarm-clock fitment. He was charged only with his mother's killing. Millions witnessed his trial, which was a television attraction. Although Graham retracted his confession he was found guilty of first-degree murder, and confessed again shortly before his execution by poison-gas in 1957.

'GREEN BICYCLE' Murder, The

On the night of July 5th, 1919, the body of 21-year-old Annie Bella Wright, a rubber factory worker, was found lying in a pool of blood beside her bicycle down a country lane near Stoughton, Leicestershire. It was thought at first to be an accident, until a local constable named Hall found a bullet embedded in the roadway seventeen feet from where the body had lain. The bullet fitted into a wound above the girl's left cheek-bone, and although there had been no sexual assault, it was now clearly a case of murder.

Witnesses spoke of seeing Bella with a man on a green bicycle on the night of the murder; she had ridden with him into the village of Gaulby where her uncle lived and he had waited for her outside this relative's cottage. The uncle, upon his niece's departure, heard the man say: 'Bella, you were a long time', before they rode off together. Two Leicester schoolgirls said they had been accosted by a man wheeling a green bicycle on the day of the murder, but police investigations proved fruitless until, on February 23rd, 1920, the towing rope of a barge on the Leicester Canal dragged up the frame of a green bicycle. Further dredging brought up a revolver holster containing live ammunition of the type that killed Bella Wright. There had been unsuccessful attempts to file off all identification marks on the machine, and it was traced to 34-year-old Ronald Vivien Light, a Leicester man who had been invalided out of the army with shell-shock and who now was employed as mathematics master at Dean Close School, Cheltenham. Eventually he admitted that the bicycle was his and that he had casually met and spoken to

Bella Wright on the evening of July 5th: '. . . she asked me if I could lend her a spanner . . . we rode on together down a steep hill. . . .' Reading, days later, of the fate of his chance acquaintance and the search for the man with the green bicycle had made him panic and resolve to get rid of the bicycle and his old army holster and ammunition.

In the second week of June 1920, Light was tried at Leicester Castle Courthouse for the murder of Bella Wright. Sir Gordon Hewart, MP, then Attorney General, led for the Crown and Sir Edward Marshall Hall was chief defence counsel. The evidence against Light, although overwhelming, was circumstantial. Marshall Hall, in questioning the two schoolgirls, noted that their statements were not made until eight months after the murder, and therefore, he submitted, unreliable; in questioning Henry Clarke, gunsmith, he drew attention to the minute bullet hole above the girl's left cheek, implying that the bullet could have been fired, perhaps accidentally, from a distance.

Light impressed as a witness, repeating that his acquaintance with Bella Wright was of the briefest type, and that until reading the papers he had not known her name; he said that Bella's uncle had heard him say, 'Hello, you were a long time'. Light denied ever meeting the two schoolgirls.

The jury returned a verdict of not guilty.

GREENLEASE Kidnapping Case

On September 28th, 1953, Bobby Greenlease, 6-year-old son of American millionaire Robert Greenlease, aged 71, was taken from his convent school in Kansas City, Missouri, by a red-haired woman who told the nun in charge that the boy's mother had suffered a heart attack. It was soon obvious that the child had been kidnapped, and a ransom note for 600,000 dollars to be paid in ten- and twenty-dollar bills duly arrived, together with Bobby Greenlease's school cloth badge. The kidnappers instructed how the money was to be packed into a duffel-bag and thrown into a culvert between Kansas City and St Joseph, a small railway town. The Greenleases complied with these orders, waiting in vain for news of their son. Two days after the dumping of the ransom money, police in St Louis two hundred miles away were told of a man spending vast sums of money around the Congress Hotel: 'and he doesn't look the part'. This man, with 250,000 dollars in his luggage (which also contained a revolver with three discharged cartridges), was interviewed all night in a hotel room; the following day, acting on his statements, G-men found a red-haired woman – and Bobby Greenlease's grave. The man was Carl Austin Hall, 37-year-old drug addict, the wayward son of a Kansas City lawyer. The woman was 41-year-old Mrs Bonnie Brown Heady, drink-loving widow of a bank robber; in her back-yard at St Joseph was found, buried, the body of Bobby Greenlease with three bullet wounds. Arrested, they eventually confessed to the crime, even admitting digging the child's grave before the kidnapping. They had driven the boy to a lonely spot: 'Bobby was struggling and kicking,' said Hall, 'so I took my revolver . . . and fired . . . at close range.' (Half the ransom money was, and still is, missing. Carl Hall insisted that the bulk of the ransom was in his luggage at the time of his capture, and two of the St Louis policemen who arrested Hall were charged with giving false evidence about the handling of Hall's luggage, and imprisoned.)

Both kidnappers showed little remorse in prison. Hall was fidgety because of his drug addiction, and Mrs Heady looked at *True Romance* magazines, interrupting her readings on one occasion to tell a fellow-prisoner of Hall's ambition to have a circular bed with silk sheets. Shortly before their joint gas-chamber execution in December 1953, however, they wrote letters to the Greenlease family begging their forgiveness.

GREENWOOD, David
A young turner, aged 21, sentenced to death (but later reprieved and sentenced to penal servitude for life) for the murder of Nellie True, a 16-year-old girl.

On February 10th, 1918, Nellie True's body was found on Eltham Common, near the Eltham–Woolwich road. Although her knickers were in place, she was lying on her back in a position indicating rape, and had been strangled manually. She had been returning from the Plumstead Library, where she had changed her book. She had evidently been raped and strangled at about 2 am that morning. A military badge of the Leicestershire Regiment (the 'Tigers') was found on the scene of the murder, and also an overcoat button. A photograph of the badge and button was sent to the newspapers for reproduction.

It was recognized by one of the employees of the Hewson Manufacturing Company, in Newman Street, off Oxford Street, who showed it to David Greenwood, commenting. 'That looks uncommonly like the badge you were wearing'. Greenwood admitted that it did, but said that he had sold his badge over the week-end to a man on a tram. His workmates suggested that he 'clear the matter up' with the police. The button was found to come from his overcoat.

At the trial before Mr Justice Atkin, Sir Travers Humphreys prosecuted, and Mr Slesser defended. Sir Bernard Spilsbury was called to give evidence. It was revealed that Greenwood had an excellent war record, and had been discharged with neurasthenia from shell-shock and disordered action of the heart. There were no buttons on his overcoat (they had been cut off subsequent to the murder) but the button found on the site of the murder fitted exactly. He was found guilty with a recommendation to mercy.

GREENWOOD, Harold (Murder Trial)

On November 9th, 1920, at Carmarthen Assizes in Wales, Harold Greenwood, a solicitor aged 45, was found not guilty of the murder by poisoning of his first wife, Mabel. The case had been closely followed, not only in Britain, but in Europe and America.

The Greenwoods with their four children and domestic staff lived at Rumsey House, Kidwelly, Carmarthenshire. In the early hours of Monday, June 16th, 1919, Mrs Greenwood died of an agonizing bilious-type illness that had commenced, according to her husband, at 3.30 pm the previous afternoon. Her health, before this final illness, had not been good and her medical adviser, Dr Griffiths, certified the death as being due to valvular disease of the heart. Greenwood, unlike his wife, was not popular in the district, and even before his marriage (only four months after Mabel Greenwood's funeral) to 31-year-old Miss Gladys Jones, daughter of the part-proprietor of the *Llanelly Mercury*, there was much gossip about Mrs Greenwood's death. This speculation caused the police, in October 1919, to inform Greenwood of their probable intention to exhume the body of his wife, when Greenwood replied heartily: 'Just the very thing – I am quite agreeable.' Eventually, on April 16th, 1920, the remains were exhumed and examined at Kidwelly Town Hall. No trace of valvular or any other disease was found, but the body (in a good state of preservation) contained between a quarter and half a grain of arsenic. After a two-day inquest on Mabel Greenwood, June 15th–16th, 1920, the foreman of the jury, George Jones, amid tremendous applause, handed in the following verdict:

> We are unanimously of opinion that the death of the deceased, Mabel Greenwood, was caused by acute arsenical poisoning, as certified . . . and that the poison was administered by Harold Greenwood.

Greenwood, when told the verdict, said 'Oh dear!' He was formally charged with the murder of his first wife on June 17th, 1920 (a year after her death), and spent over four months in prison before his trial at Carmarthen Guildhall on November 2nd, 1920, when he pleaded not guilty. Sir Edward Marshall Hall, KC, defended Greenwood, and Sir Edward Marlay Samson, KC, appeared for the Crown.

Greenwood was known to have bought two lots of Coopers' Weedicide (containing 60 per cent arsenic) in June 1917, the suggestion being made by the prosecution that before the 1 pm Sunday lunch on June 15th, 1919, he had placed some of the arsenic in a bottle of burgundy. Much of the evidence was contradictory. Hannah Williams, the Greenwoods' parlour maid, testified that Greenwood spent half an hour by himself (12.30 pm–1 pm) in the china pantry, a unique occurrence, although Irene Greenwood, the eldest daughter, aged 21, swore that her father spent the whole time before 1 pm out-of-doors cleaning his car. Hannah Williams said that during lunch her employer drank whisky, the Greenwood children (including Irene) drank water, while Mrs Greenwood was the only person to drink any burgundy. Irene Greenwood maintained that she also partook of the burgundy, not only at lunch but during supper – although Miss Philips, a supper guest, said she saw no wine on the table, adding somewhat plaintively: 'Had there been any I should have had some.' Dr Griffiths said that he had made up opium pills for Mrs Greenwood, although at the inquest he said they were morphia pills; Marshall Hall, sensing the doctor's vagueness, suggested that perhaps he had accidentally given Mabel Greenwood Fowler's arsenic solution instead of bismuth – the bottles being adjacent in Griffiths' surgery. Nurse Jones, who had been called in when Mrs Greenwood's diarrhoea and vomiting had started on the afternoon of the 15th, spoke of the seeming indifference of Greenwood to his wife's suffering, and went on: 'I had become suspicious that things were not as they should be.' (She had admitted at the inquest that after the funeral she had gone round Kidwelly saying there should have been a post-mortem.)

The jury added a rider to their verdict of not guilty, which was not made public:

'We are satisfied on the evidence in this case that a dangerous dose of arsenic was administered to Mabel Greenwood ... but we are not satisfied that this was the immediate cause of death. The evidence before us is insufficient, and does not satisfy us as to how, and by whom, the arsenic was administered. ...

Greenwood had appeared calm throughout his ordeal, and the day after his acquittal entertained a newspaper reporter to lunch – joking about the absence of burgundy on the table. But he was ruined by the case; his practice, health, and money gone, he died eight years later.

GRESE, Irma

She was born in 1923 and after leaving school worked for some time at farming and nursing before going to Ravensbruck concentration camp in 1942. After a year she went to Auschwitz till early 1945. There she was put in absolute charge of 30,000 women, soon to be gassed, and emphasized her authority with cellophane whip, walking stick, pistol, and heavy top boots. Finally she went to Belsen under Kramer's command where she was arrested.

Her sister stated at her trial that as a young schoolgirl she was a coward and always ran away when there was any fighting. Further that when she came home in 1943, her father, an agricultural worker, beat her fiercely and turned her out of the house for joining the SS and doing concentration-camp work. It is certainly possible that her father's earlier refusal to let her join the Bund Deutscher Mädchen and this beating only strengthened her Nazi convictions and affinities.

In the dock she simply denied most of the charges, insisting that they were downright lies and only admitting to striking prisoners with her hand. In her first written and sworn statement she denied beating or kicking prisoners or acting on the gas selections, concluding, 'Himmler is responsible for all that has happened but I suppose I have as much guilt as the others above me.' In her second statement she 'again reflected', and admitted to beating prisoners with whips and making them kneel for fifteen minutes at a time. She also considered the treatment at Belsen and Auschwitz to be 'murder'. In a third statement she 'Further reflected' and admitted to carrying an unloaded pistol, a walking stick with which she beat the prisoners, though 'unauthorized', and to consistently carrying her whip.

From the depositions of camp victims it is clear that she was a brutal, ruthless torturer and murderess. Her Appelle lasted up to six hours and she made the victims hold stones high above their heads. If their stance failed to satisfy her she beat them unconscious with a rubber truncheon or kicked them senseless. If, on the selections for forced labour she saw relatives trying to segregate, she beat them mercilessly. When a new transport of victims arrived, she shot dead a woman who dared to stand outside her block and watch it. At gas-chamber selections, when some of the naked women tried to escape with the compliance of a certain Block leader, Grese spotted them, kicking and beating them back again into the waiting rooms. Others she dragged out from hiding under their beds and beat. Two girls jumped out of the window and she shot them dead on the ground.

On one occasion, while following behind on her cycle a column of prisoners sent to pick herbs for the kitchen, she set her dog on those too weak to keep pace. While it tore them to pieces she clubbed at them with a wooden stick. They were then carried back to the camp and dispatched to the gas chambers. At Auschwitz, in charge of a working party of 700 women in the sand pits, surrounded by a four foot high wire covered by twelve guards, her particular pleasure was to order some of the Jewish women to get something from behind the wire. They were challenged, failed to understand the challenge as she picked non-Germans, and shot. Through this alone at least thirty women a day were murdered. At Auschwitz too she was seen to attack a woman who spoke to her daughter over the wire in an adjacent camp. She beat her on the face and head with her leather belt and trampled on her.

The prosecution suggested in the light of her sister's remarks that she had found it great fun to hit people who could not hit back, and that her very rapid promotion for one so young was due to her excellent suitability for the task of brutal murder. As with her co-murderers these victims were simply worthless *Dreck*, Himmler's 'human animals', and not in any way to be considered as, or treated as, human beings. 'See what we can make of a man in five days', the SS had boasted in the thirties of their course of profound degradation and humiliation. And here in Belsen was the final product, the Musselmen. Creatures from whom it was 'impossible to extract their names. Kindness had not the power to make them speak – only a long expressionless stare – their tongues could not reach their dried-up palates to make a sound – only a poisonous breath issued from the entrails already in a state of decomposition'.

To the end in this unprecedented inferno of dead and dying, the staff were most concerned with the Commandant's garden, picking flowers and arranging rock gardens around the kitchen, quite indifferent to this human *Dreck*. Grese herself was particularly interested in arranging little white stones in the kitchen garden. Like Göring, she and the rest could affirm, '*I* have no conscience. My conscience is Adolf Hitler.' Hitler had proclaimed that, 'The world can only be ruled by *fear*. *Terror* is the most effective political instrument.' Grese and her like grew up in that atmosphere. Hitler had announced, 'We are barbarians – pitiless', and that he was seeking to raise, 'A violently active, dominating, intrepid, brutal youth with the gleam of pride and independence of the beast of prey – the god-man'. The prisoners in the dock at Belsen looked more like sub-men than god-men. Lingens-Reiner described the SS guards as 'stupid, incompetent, little people, completely obsessed by their social ambitions – intoxicated by their power – uneasy as any adolescents. All that they wanted was power and the riches power ensures.'

J. G.

GRIFFITHS, Peter
Twenty-two-year-old ex-guardsman, hanged in Walton Prison, Liverpool, on November 19th, 1948, for the murder of 4-year-old June Anne Devaney, whom he took from a cot in ward C.H.3 of Queens Park Hospital, Blackburn, Lancashire, on May 15th, 1948, raping her and beating her to death against a wall in the hospital grounds.

Upon discovery of the body, the babies' ward was examined and the marks of stockinged feet coming from the bay window and traversing several of the cots were found; a Winchester bottle containing sterile water by June Devaney's bed had 'an excellent set of dabs', according to Detective-Inspector Colin Campbell, chief of the Lancashire County Fingerprint Bureau. Detective-Inspector John Capstick of Scotland Yard, in charge of the case, resolved that fingerprints be taken of all males in

Blackburn over the age of 16; in addition, wool fibres were removed from the feet impressions.

At last, on August 13th, three months after the murder, the fingerprints of Peter Griffiths of Birley Street, Blackburn, tallied with those on the Winchester bottle. Upon apprehending Griffiths it was found that fibres taken from the child's body and nightgown were identical with Griffiths' suit material, and the fibres from one of his socks corresponded exactly with the footprint fibres removed weeks before from the hospital floor. Bloodstains on the suit (which Griffiths had pawned after the crime) were of the A Group, which was June Devaney's bloodtype.

The arrest of Griffiths (who confessed to the killing) was a great triumph for forensic detection. Many police officers think that Griffiths was responsible for numerous child assaults in Lancashire at that time, including the murder of 11-year-old Quentin Smith of Farnworth, stabbed and beaten to death near a railway embankment two months before the Devaney killing.

A poem, written by Griffiths and found in his bedroom is typical of those conceived by sadistic criminals:

> For lo and behold, when the beast
> Looks down upon the face of beauty
> It staids its hands from killing
> And from that day on
> It were as one dead.

GROSSMANN, Georg Karl
German mass-murderer, born in Neurüppin in 1863, who, like Denke, committed suicide before his execution.

The case has many resemblances to the Denke murders. In August 1921 the owner of a top-storey flat in Berlin near the Silesian railway terminus heard sounds of a struggle coming from the kitchen and called the police. They found on Grossmann's kitchen bed (a camp bed) the trussed-up carcass of a recently killed girl, tied as if ready for butchering.

Grossmann had been in the place since the year before the war. He had stipulated for a separate entrance, and had the use of the kitchen, which he never allowed his landlord to enter. He was a big, surly man who kept himself to himself, and lived by peddling. He was not called up during the war (which led the other tenants to assume – rightly – that he had a police record), and lived in self-chosen retirement. He picked up girls with great regularity (in fact, he seldom spent a night alone). He killed many of these sleeping partners and sold the bodies for meat, disposing of the unsaleable parts in the river. (The case became known as *Die Braut auf der Stulle* – 'the bread and butter brides', since a companion for a night is known as a 'bride' in Germany.) At the time of his arrest, evidence was found which indicated that three women had been killed and dismembered in the past three weeks.

Grossmann was a sexual degenerate and sadist who had served three terms of hard labour for offences against children, one of which had ended fatally. He also indulged in bestiality. It is of interest that Grossmann was indirectly involved in the famous 'Anastasia' case – the Grand Duchess Anastasia who was believed by many to be the last surviving member of the Tsar's family. At one point it was announced that 'Anastasia' was really an impostor named Franziska Schamzkovski, a Polish girl from Bütow in Pomerania. Franziska's family were told that their daughter had been murdered by Grossmann on August 13th, 1920; an entry in his diary on that date bore the name 'Sasnovski'. Anastasia's enemies insisted that this was not true, that Franziska and Anastasia were the same person.

Grossmann laughed when he heard his death sentence, and afterwards had fits of mania. He hanged himself in his cell. The number of his victims will never be known, but they may well have exceeded Haarmann's total of fifty, since he was 'in business' throughout the war until 1921 – several years longer than Haarmann. All his victims were female.

GUAY, Joseph Albert
Thirty-two-year-old French-Canadian jeweller, executed on January 10th, 1951, for the murder of his wife, Rita, fourteen months before.

On September 7th, 1949, Guay bade his wife goodbye at Ancienne Lorette Airport as she boarded a Dakota of Canadian Pacific Airlines. Twenty minutes later the plane exploded in mid-air above forest land near Sault-au-Cochon, forty miles from the airport; all twenty-three people on board were killed. Guay, when informed, appeared inconsolable. Widower with daughter Lise, 5, tottered to the Hotel Château Frontenac, where the airline authorities had provided a room, and also a priest to ease his anguish, which naturally seemed in no way allayed by the prospect of a ten-thousand-dollar insurance claim on Canadian Pacific Airlines. That company, hiring experts to investigate the wreckage, were soon enlightened as to the cause of the disaster – dynamite. Suspicion centred on one article of freight, a twenty-six-pound brown-paper-covered bundle listed as a 'religious statuette'; it was recalled that a woman dressed in black had delivered the parcel to the freight office, but it was not until ten days after the explosion that a taxi-driver came forward who remembered having driven such a woman to the airport. Police called at the given address to find the woman, Marie Petri, had been taken to hospital suffering from an overdose of sleeping tablets. Recovering, but hysterical, Petri admitted that she had been asked by her one-time lover, Joseph Guay, to take a statuette to the airport; an even stranger request had been that of five weeks before, when Guay had asked her to purchase ten pounds of dynamite: '. . . but I didn't know his wife would be on that plane'. After the air explosion and the inquiries for the 'woman in black', Guay had suggested that her best plan was suicide, a course of action she had obligingly attempted. The accommodating Petri, on release from hospital, was nick-named 'Madame Le Corbeau' or 'Mrs Raven', because of her sombre bird-like appearance, accentuated by a black skull-cap. Her crippled brother, Généreux Ruest, a man of talent at manipulating and mending delicate machinery, had been no less helpful to Guay, who had asked him, a few days before the disaster, to affix a time mechanism to the load of dynamite. Marie Petri also told of Guay's infatuation for 19-year-old night-club 'cigarette girl' Marie-Ange Robitaille (who preferred to be known as Angel Mary) and how the Quebec jeweller was obsessed by the desire to marry her. Guay was arrested on a charge of murder; the papers promptly dubbing the affair, 'The Love Bomb Murder'. (At the first hearing, in October 1949, hordes of angry Quebec citizens marched through the streets shouting, 'The dead must be avenged'.) Guay's trial opened in March 1950. The defence asserted the impossibility of con-structing a delayed-action bomb by means of an alarm-clock mechanism attached to dynamite, but Professor Lucien Gravel of Laval University demonstrated, by means of a clock, a fuse, and a dry cell battery, the deadly simplicity of such a contrivance. One witness, Lucien Carreau, said that Guay had once attempted to bribe him into poisoning the unwanted Mrs Guay, and how, after the explosion, Guay had remarked 'good riddance'. 'Angel Mary' spoke of her illicit relationship with Guay; Rita

Guay had found out, and had threatened to have the young girl arrested by laying a charge of immorality against her.

After Guay's conviction, Marie Petri and her brother were arrested and charged with complicity in the murder; both were found guilty and executed.

GUFLER, Max

Austrian 'bluebeard' murderer, born in a small village in the Tyrol in 1910; his mother was unmarried. At the age of 9 he had been struck on the head by a stone, and had then had moods of unpredictable violence. (There is a similarity here to the case of Lock Ah Tam.) He was an ambulance driver in the Wehrmacht during the war, and was again struck on the head, by shell fragments. Between 1945 and 1952 he was a book salesman. In 1952 he moved to the town of St Poelten, near Vienna. In 1951 Gufler met the woman who became his mistress, Hertha Junn, the daughter of a tobacconist in Vienna. Her father had invited Gufler to share in the business; Gufler had extended it by selling pornographic photos; as a result of this, Gufler, Hertha, and her father all spent some time in prison, and the stand was closed down.

Now Gufler apparently embarked upon his career as a Bluebeard, reading the matrimonial advertisements and writing off letters to lonely widows. It is not known for certain when he committed his first murder, but it seems relatively certain that his career as a Bluebeard began with the murder of a prostitute, 50-year-old Émilie Meystrzik, who was found bludgeoned to death in her ransacked room in the red light district of Vienna in 1952. She had advertised for a husband. But Gufler's most favoured method was to assure a woman that he intended to marry her, and to persuade her to draw her savings out of the bank. On the way to the marriage ceremony the victim was given a dose of some barbiturate in coffee, and was then undressed and dumped in a river, lake, or pond, so that it would appear that she might have committed suicide by drowning.

Gufler was finally brought to justice after the murder of Frau Maria Robas, who kept up a correspondence with Gufler throughout the summer of 1958 from the town of Reifnitz in northern Austria. In early September, Gufler collected her, and they drove off for their honeymoon. A few hours later her naked body was dumped into a pond near Pernegg, and Gufler returned to her room in the hotel, which he ransacked. He later wrote a letter to the woman's former husband, signing it 'Edesharter' and declaring that he had seen the wife of Herr Robas killed in a car accident. Herr Robas went to Innsbruck, found a justice of the peace named Edesharter, and produced his letter – which turned out to be a forgery. Herr Robas now went to the police, who were able to find a hotel porter who had noted the number of Gufler's car when he drove off with Maria Robas. Gufler was soon arrested at his lodging in St Poelten. His rooms were found to contain a fantastic assortment of objects – women's clothing, jewellery, portable typewriters, radios, etc. In the garage were found two sewing machines, a massage machine, a dog kennel, a TV set, and several more typewriters. Gufler's rooms were found to contain a filing cabinet with many letters from lonely women with whom he was corresponding. He was on the point of 'marrying' a woman named Marlene Buchner in Vienna. The police found her in tears because Gufler had failed to show up.

After the police had arrested his mistress, Hertha Junn, Gufler decided to confess to three murders – those of Josefine Kammleitner, Maria Robas, and Juliana Nass. He had made about 100,000 schillings (approximately £1,373) from their deaths.

It is difficult to make any definite statement about the precise number of Gufler's victims, but the police have evidence of eight murders, and strong suspicion of another ten. After the war Gufler lived with a 49-year-old woman named Augusta Lindebner, who owned a railway bookstall at Schwaz in the Tyrol. She died suddenly of 'heart failure' after drinking coffee with Gufler. In September 1955, the body of Theresa Offen, a 53-year-old hospital attendant, was found in the river near Hollenbrunn; the circumstances of the death bore close resemblance to those of the other victims. In October 1957, Theresa Anderl, a widow of independent means, was taken out of the Danube near her home in Floridsdorf; she had also died of drowning after being drugged, and had made large withdrawals from her bank before her death.

Josefine Kammleitner, to whose murder Gufler confessed, was a 45-year-old restaurant cook who had advertised in the matrimonial columns; she was drugged and dumped into the Danube on June 3rd, 1958. The murder of Maria Robas followed in September. A month later, on October 15th, Juliana Nass, a 50-year-old war widow of Fohnsdorf, who owned a tobacconist shop, was drugged and drowned in the Danube.

In addition to these three murders, Gufler confessed to killing the prostitute Émilie Meystrzik in her room.

The police also found evidence for the murder of Theresa Wesely in May 1957, and the shooting and robbing of a Viennese jeweller, Karl Kovaricek, at his shop in the Schulgasse on Christmas Eve, 1951. The jeweller later recovered.

The police discovered sufficient evidence to convict in eight cases: Augusta Lindebner, Theresa Wesely, Juliana Emsenhuber, and a prostitute named Josefine Dangl, and the four murders to which he confessed. Gufler is also suspected of murdering the following women between 1946 and 1958: Theresa Anderl, Anni Melchert, Christine Sindl, Maria Eckschlager, Hedwig Eichorn, Caroline Trattnig, Leopoldine Schwanzer, Alosia Scrabos, Anna Meyer, and Theresa Offen.

In May 1961 Gufler was sentenced to life imprisonment.

GUNNESS, Bella Poulsdatter Sorensen

Mass murderess, born Trondhjem, Norway, 1859, she migrated to America in 1876 and married compatriot Max Sorensen in Chicago. The Sorensens settled in Austin, Illinois, where Bella soon became joyfully preoccupied with motherhood; throughout her life she had a genuine love for all children (she taught in several Sunday schools) and her homesteads invariably rang with their happy cries. Soon a young widow (too soon, in the opinion of many) she invested her savings in a Chicago rooming-house; Bella's days as a landlady, however, were numbered, for the premises were shortly afterwards gutted by fire. With the insurance money Bella bought a baker's shop, but her confections hardly tasted by the populace, this establishment was also burnt to the ground. Peeved and (understandably) suspicious, the insurance company grudgingly gave remuneration, but stipulated that Bella must, in future, do business elsewhere.

With her three children Mrs Sorensen settled in an isolated smallholding at La Porte, Indiana, and soon became Mrs Gunness. Mr Gunness shortly expired with a hatchet wound in his head ('it slipped from a shelf' his widow informed a sympathetic jury) and more insurance money was collected. At this stage a psychological block against insurance companies would seem to have formed in the mind of Widow Gunness, and a scheme was evolved whereby cash could be obtained by more direct methods. In newspapers throughout America appeared an advertisement: 'Rich, goodlooking widow, young, owner of a large farm, wishes to get in touch with a gentleman of wealth with cultured tastes. Object, matrimony.' From many replies Bella chose a commercial traveller who conveniently lacked relatives and close friends, and answered his application thus:

... I feel sure you are the one man for me. I feel you will make me and my dear babies happy, and that I can safely entrust you with all that I possess in the world. ... My idea is to take a partner to whom I can trust everything. As we have no acquaintances ourselves, I have decided that every applicant I have considered favourably must make a satisfactory deposit of cash or security. I think that is the best way to keep away grafters who are always looking for an opportunity. I am worth at least twenty thousand dollars, and if you could bring five hundred just to show you are in earnest, we could talk things over. ...

This first recipient of the subtle summons was seen to arrive at La Porte, but never to depart. Subsequently, other candidates for husbandhood appeared at La Porte – and vanished. Bella sometimes varied her literary style, depending upon how she gauged the character of her would-be suitor. To one poor wretch she wrote:

You are my king. ... I know from your letters you have a loving heart. ... Come to me. Your bride awaits you. We shall be as happy here as a king and queen in the most beautiful home in Northern Indiana. ...

And come these gentlemen did, each with his monetary token of good faith which was carefully removed by Bella prior to the burial of the donor – usually under the hog-lot. It is believed she killed with a hatchet probably as her victims slept, and possibly with the same hatchet that 'slipped' on to the unfortunate Mr Gunness.

In 1908 the brother of one Andrew Holdgren (who had left home five months before to become King to Bella's Queen) became anxious through Andrew's failure to contact him, and decided to write himself to Mrs Gunness. He received back a letter suffused with solicitude:

I would do anything in the world to find him ... he left my house seemingly happy and since that time in January I have not seen him. ... I will go to the end of the world to find him.

In fact, as she was well aware, one need only have journeyed to the end of the garden to find Andrew, where he lay alongside some other aspirants for Bella's hand. This victim's brother (whose presence must have come as a shock to Bella) was persuaded to join in a proposed countrywide hunt for Andrew, a hunt which would, no doubt, have started and ended at La Porte, with more diggings in the hog-lot. The live Holdgren and his brother's killer never met, however, because 'the most beautiful home in Northern Indiana' was burnt down on April 28th, 1908, a few hours before he was due to meet the widow. The headless body of a woman found in the debris was identified as Belle Gunness, and the three children were undoubtedly hers. A worker whom Belle had occasionally employed about the farm, Roy Lamphere, was charged with her murder. He was, in fact, acquitted but convicted of setting fire to the Gunness home, and sentenced to 21 years in the State Penitentiary. He died in prison. But before his death, he confessed that he not only knew all about Belle's murders; he had helped her by burning the bodies. He also said that the headless woman found in the ruin was definitely not his employer. She had lured a drunken female tramp from Chicago and killed her with strychnine. Lamphere kept quiet about this for a long time after his imprisonment because he was in love with Belle.

What became of her has never been discovered. But as the result of her murders, she was undoubtedly a rich woman.

H

HAARMANN, Fritz
Homosexual mass-murderer who is believed to have killed fifty youths; he sold the bodies for meat.

After the Armistice in 1918 most of the Germans starved for a while. Hanover in Saxony was one of the cities that was most badly hit. It was in Hanover that Haarmann committed one of the most amazing series of crimes in modern times.

Haarmann was born in Hanover on October 25th, 1879; he was the sixth child of an ill-assorted couple; a morose locomotive stoker known as 'Sulky Olle' and his invalid wife, seven years his senior. Fritz was his mother's pet and hated his father. He liked playing with dolls, and disliked games. At 16 he was sent to a military school (for NCOs) at New Breisach, but soon released when he showed signs of epileptic fits. He went to work

287

in his father's cigar factory but was lazy and inefficient. He was soon accused of indecent behaviour with small children and sent to an asylum for observation; he escaped after six months. He then took to petty crime, as well as indecent assaults on minors. He also had a brief sexually normal period about 1900, when he seduced a girl to whom he was engaged and then deserted her to join the Jäger regiment. The baby was still-born. He served satisfactorily until 1903, then returned to Hanover, where his father tried to have him certified insane again – without success. He served several sentences in jail for burglary, pocket-picking, and confidence trickery. His father tried getting him to do respectable work, setting him up as the keeper of a fish-and-chip shop. Fritz promptly stole all the money he could lay his hands on. In 1914 he was sentenced to five years in jail for theft from a warehouse. Released in 1918, he joined a smuggling ring, and soon became prosperous. With his headquarters at 27 Cellar-strasse, he conducted business as a smuggler, thief, and police spy. (This latter activity guaranteed that his smuggling should not be too closely scrutinized.)

Many refugee trains came into Hanover; Haarmann picked up youths and offered them a night's lodging. One of the first of these was 17-year-old Friedel Rothe. The lad's worried parents found that he had been friendly with 'detective' Haarmann; the police searched his room, but found nothing. (Haarmann later admitted that the boy's head lay wrapped in newspaper behind his stove at the time.) But they caught Haarmann *in flagrante delicto* with another boy, and he received nine months in jail for indecency. Back in Hanover in September 1919, he changed his lodging to the Neuestrasse. He met another homosexual, Hans Grans, a pimp and petty thief, and the two formed an alliance. They used to meet in a café that catered for all kinds of perverts, the Café Kröpcke. Their method was always the same; they enticed a youth from the railway station back to Haarmann's room; Haarmann killed him (according to his own account, by biting his throat), and the boy's body was dismembered and sold as meat through Haarmann's usual channels for smuggled meat. His clothes were sold, and the useless (i.e. uneatable) portions were thrown into the Leine. At the trial, a list of twenty-eight victims was offered, their ages ranging between 13 and 20. One boy was killed only because Grans took a fancy to his trousers. Only one victim, a lad named Kaimes, was found, strangled in the canal. There was a curious incident in connexion with this case; Haarmann called on the missing youth's parents as a 'detective' and assured them he would restore their son in three days; he then went to the police and denounced Grans as the murderer! Grans was in prison at the time, so nothing came of the charge.

Haarmann had some narrow escapes; some of his meat was taken to the police because the buyer thought it was human flesh; the police analyst pronounced it pork! On another occasion, a neighbour stopped to talk to him on the stairs when some paper blew off the bucket he was carrying; it was revealed to contain blood. But Haarmann's trade as a meat smuggler kept him from suspicion.

In May 1924, a skull was discovered on the banks of the river, and some weeks later, another one. People continued to report the disappearance of their sons, and Haarmann was definitely suspected; but months went by, and Haarmann continued to kill. Two detectives from Berlin watched him, and he was arrested for indecency. His lodgings were searched and many articles of clothing taken away. His landlady's son was found to be wearing a coat belonging to one of the missing boys. And boys playing near the river discovered more bones, including a sack stuffed with them. A police pathologist declared they represented the remains of at least twenty-seven bodies.

Haarmann decided to confess. His trial began at the Hanover Assizes on December 4th, 1924. It lasted fourteen days and 130 witnesses were called. The public prosecutor was Ober-staatsanwalt Dr Wilde, assisted by Dr Wagenschiefer; the defence was conducted by Justizrat Philipp Benfey and Recht-sanwalt Oz Lotzen. Haarmann was allowed remarkable free-dom; he was usually gay and irresponsible, frequently interrupt-ing the proceedings. At one point he demanded indignantly why there were so many women in court; the judge answered apologetically that he had no power to keep them out. When a woman witness was too distraught to give her evidence about her son with clarity, Haarmann got bored and asked to be allowed to smoke a cigar; permission was immediately granted.

He persisted to the end in his explanation of how he had killed his victims – biting them through the throat. Some boys he denied killing – for example, a boy named Hermann Wolf, whose photograph showed an ugly and ill-dressed youth; like Oscar Wilde, Haarmann declared that the boy was far too ugly to interest him.

Haarmann was sentenced to death by decapitation; Grans to twelve years in jail. Haarmann later produced a confession which has much in common with that of Mme de Brinvilliers or Gilles de Rais; it is full of accounts of sexual perversion and the pleasure he took in committing murders that were all inspired by his sexual perversion.

HACKMAN, The Rev. James
Executed at Tyburn for the murder of Margaret Reay, the mistress of the Earl of Sandwich, in 1779.

Margaret Reay had been with the Earl of Sandwich since she was 18, and had borne him several children. He was First Lord of the Admiralty. In 1774 she met James Hackman, an officer in the 68th Regiment of Foot, at Lord Sandwich's country seat near Hinchinbrooke. A love affair developed, and they exchanged passionate letters; but she refused to leave the Earl, to whom she felt gratitude. Hackman left the army and became a deacon in the Church of England in February 1779. He still hoped that Margaret Reay would change her mind and marry him. But one day, a close friend of Margaret Reay told him that he was hoping in vain; she never intended to leave the Earl. He decided to commit suicide. On April 7th, 1779, Hackman happened to see her pass through Whitehall on her way to the Covent Garden Theatre. He followed her there, then went home and got two pistols, and went back to the theatre and waited for her; as she came out, he shot her in the brain. Nine days later he appeared at the Old Bailey before Mr Justice Blackstone. He declared that he had no intention of killing her, but of killing himself before her eyes. The two pistols were in case one misfired. But at the last minute he was seized with an irresistible impulse.

He was sentenced to death. While he was in jail awaiting execution, the Earl of Sandwich wrote to say that, if Hackman wanted to live, he would do all in his power to save him. Hackman replied that he wanted to die.

Dr Johnson took a great interest in the case, and the only difference he ever had with his friend Topham Beauclerk arose out of the case, Johnson holding that two pistols pointed to murder as well as suicide.

HAIGH, John George

Thirty-nine-year-old Yorkshire-born petty criminal, organ player of talent, self-described engineer, convicted of the murder, in 1949, of Mrs Henrietta Helen Olivia Robarts Durand-Deacon.

Haigh, whose father was a colliery foreman, received a strict upbringing, both parents being members of the Plymouth Brethren religious sect, to whom all forms of organized pleasure were sinful, and the reading of newspapers undesirable. Young Haigh won a scholarship to Wakefield Grammar School, and later a choral scholarship which necessitated his presence as a choirboy during services at Wakefield Cathedral. After the sparsities of Brethren ritual, Church of England procedure must have seemed voluptuous, and some who studied this murderer – believed this contrast to have had a diabolical effect on his character – certainly Haigh himself subscribed with enthusiasm to this theory; murder-inciting dream-visions of forests spouting blood and even Haigh's supposed vampirish longings, all were claimed to have arisen as a result of the choral scholarship. In 1934 he married one Beatrice Hamer, of whom little is known; Haigh left her soon after serving his first prison sentence (for fraud) in November of that year. In the years before and during the Second World War, Haigh was a persistent criminal, committing theft and fraud for financial gain; he was not particularly successful, much of his time being spent in prison. Soon after serving a sentence in 1943, Haigh settled at the Onslow Court Hotel in South Kensington, a highly respectable establishment, patronized mainly by professional and retired gentlefolk; if his outward appearance was a little too 'flash' his general manner was pleasant and he was popular with the Onslow Court residents. Haigh still managed to contrive a living from various kinds of fraud; he ran several cars on hire-purchase and rented a basement-workroom at No. 79 Gloucester Road, Kensington, where he worked on his 'inventions'. One of Haigh's fellow-guests at the hotel was a well-to-do widow, Mrs Olivia Durand-Deacon. By February 1949 she had interested Haigh in a little scheme she had thought up concerning the manufacture of cosmetic fingernails, the result being that Haigh suggested she accompany him down to his 'factory' at Crawley, in Sussex, these premises consisting of a storeroom in Leopold Road belonging to Hurstlea Products, to which Haigh was allowed occasional access. On the afternoon of February

18th Haigh drove Mrs Durand-Deacon down to the Crawley storeroom, where he shot her through the back of the head; after removing all valuables from the body, he heaved it into a previously prepared vat of sulphuric acid, where it rapidly disintegrated. Haigh, who at this period was desperately short of money, now proceeded that same day to pawn his victim's wristwatch for £10 and deposit the jewellery she had worn for the excursion, with a Horsham jeweller to await valuation; he then consumed a high tea of poached eggs on toast at Ye Old Anciente Prior's Café in Crawley, afterwards dining at the George Hotel. Two days later, over breakfast at the Onslow Court Hotel, he expressed concern for the whereabouts of the missing Mrs Durand-Deacon, explaining that he had arranged to meet her the previous day at the Army and Navy Stores in Victoria but that she had failed to turn up. At the instigation of another guest, Mrs Constance Lane, they went to Chelsea Police Station in Lucan Place ('we will go together', Haigh had said) to report on Mrs Durand-Deacon's disappearance. Policewoman Sergeant Lambourne instinctively distrusted Haigh, doubtless through long experience of tricksters; Haigh's record was checked and his extensive criminal career disclosed. From February 21st to 28th, Haigh paid repeated visits to Leopold Road, once pouring some of the acid solution on to the earth in the yard before refilling the vat; when he was satisfied that all traces of Mrs Durand-Deacon had disappeared, he tipped the acid on to the yard's earthy surface, so forming a sludge. Also during this period he finally realized £100 on Mrs Durand-Deacon's jewellery, and many of his debts were settled – including £50 he owed Mr Jones, the manager of Hurstlea Products. On the afternoon of February 26th, suspicious of Haigh's glib manner and dissatisfied with his repeated statements about the unkept appointment, police searched the Crawley storeroom and found a cleaner's docket dated February 19th in receipt of a Persian lamb coat, later identified as the one Mrs Durand-Deacon had been wearing the day she disappeared. (Soon after this, the sale of her jewellery at Horsham and Putney, South London, was discovered; in both cases the seller had given the Pimlico address where Haigh had been known to firewatch during the war.) Traces of blood were noticed on one of the storeroom walls and a ·38 Webley revolver which showed signs of being recently fired found in a hat-box. Haigh was apprehended on February 28th and taken to Chelsea Police Station, where he appeared unmoved when told that the Crawley premises had been searched; in a sudden burst of uneasiness, however, he said, 'Mrs Durand-Deacon no longer exists. I've destroyed her with acid. ... You can't prove murder without a body,' and inquired of Detective-Inspector Albert Webb what the chances were of getting out of Broadmoor – one of the most revealing remarks ever made by a suspect. Charged with the murder of Mrs Durand-Deacon, Haigh said he had also murdered seven other people, disposing of their bodies in the same way by tipping them into drums of acid; he had been motivated, he said, by an unusual kind of lust, which prompted him to drink the blood of his victims ('it wasn't a bad idea', Haigh said somewhat wryly after his conviction). Of the fate of these alleged victims there was little doubt, for Haigh had reaped financial gain from their demise: documents relating to the McSwann family (father, mother, and son Donald) and Dr Archibald and Mrs Rosalie Henderson had been found in Haigh's room 404 at the Onslow Court Hotel. Haigh said he had bludgeoned to death and eradi-cated by acid Donald McSwann at the Gloucester Road work-shop on September 9th, 1944, and his parents in July of the follow-ing year. He had first met the McSwanns in 1936, when the elder McSwann, in the amusement-arcade business, had em-ployed him as a secretary and chauffeur; the McSwanns were fairly wealthy, owning property in South London, and Haigh must have been delighted to renew the friendship in 1944, assessing their financial worth (correctly, as it turned out) as his prospective victims, when by skilful forgery (as W. D. Mc-Swann) he eventually secured, by a transfer deed, the ownership of properties in Wimbledon Park, Raynes Park, and Beckenham, Kent, and over £4,000 besides. The Hendersons he met in 1947 through transactions over a house in Ladbroke Square, West London, which the Hendersons wished to sell; this deal fell through, but the three became companions. By February 1948 Haigh was again financially embarrassed, and, almost as a matter of course the acid vats were once more refilled, this time at Crawley; on February 12th Dr Henderson (ostensibly on a sightseeing tour of Haigh's 'factory') met his end there by shooting and eventual immersion in sulphuric acid, Mrs Henderson (brought thither on the pretext that her husband was ill) meeting a similar fate within a few hours. From these deaths and his own subsequent ventures into forgery Haigh gained almost £8,000; he was, however, in his admissions to the police, ready to stress his partiality for drinking the blood of his victims and is thought to have invented the identities of his two final victims, 'Max' and 'Mary', from whom, apparently, there was no financial gain, as a subtle means of stressing his insanity.

As it turned out, Haigh was wrong in assuming that no trace of Mrs Durand-Deacon existed. Many dismal remains were sifted from the sludge outside the Crawley workshop: twenty-eight pounds of body fat, parts of a heel-bone, a pelvis, and an ankle, a hairpin, gallstones, false teeth, cosmetic containers and a red plastic handbag, identified as having belonged to the missing woman.

Long before Haigh's trial excitement ran high in the country over the callous series of murders; one newspaper, the *Daily Mirror*, indulged in an extraordinary contempt of court by referring to Haigh as a Vampire, eventually incurring a debt to the newspaper company of £10,000 and a three months' sentence for the editor, Silvester Bolam.

The trial commenced on July 18th, 1948, at Lewes Assizes, Sussex, before Mr Justice Humphreys; Sir David Maxwell Fyfe, KC, appeared for the defence, pleading insanity, and Sir Hartley Shawcross, KC, for the Crown. Dr Henry Yellowlees, called by the defence, was a psychiatrist who supported the theory that Haigh was a paranoiac owing to his early environment and believed that it was 'pretty certain' Haigh drank the blood of his victims; Haigh's drinking of his own urine while in custody at Brixton Prison had been observed and was now noted.

The jury, unimpressed by what they obviously considered to be simulated insanity, took only fifteen minutes to return a verdict of guilty, and Haigh was executed at Wandsworth Prison on August 6th.

HALL/MILLS Murder, The

Also known as the Crabapple Tree murder, because the bodies of chubby, balding, 41-year-old Episcopal minister the Reverend Edward Wheeler Hall of the Church of St John the Evangelist in New Brunswick, New Jersey, and tiny 34-year-old church chorister Mrs Eleanor Mills were found stretched out under a crabapple tree in De Russey's Lane near their homes in September 1922. The rector was shot through the head; Mrs Mills had been shot three times and her vocal cords slashed. Strewn around the bodies were fragments of a correspondence from Mrs Mills to Dr Hall that was to startle America: '. . . I want to look up into your dear face for hours as you touch my body

294

close.' James Mills, the widower, eventually sold to a newspaper for 500 dollars letters from the rector (known as 'Babykins' to his paramour) to Eleanor ('my Gypsy Queen') Mills.

After a casual inquiry the case was closed for four years until, as a result of Press campaigning, the investigation was reopened and plain, elderly Mrs Frances Stevens Hall, the rector's widow (who had been seven years her husband's senior), her brothers Willie and Henry, and her cousin Henry Carpender (a member of the New York Stock Exchange) were accused of the killings. The prosecution's case largely depended upon the testimony of sluttish, middle-aged Mrs Jane Gibson (known as the Pig Woman) who lived near the murder spot raising Poland pigs and who asserted in court from a stretcher (she was suffering from cancer) that she had witnessed the murder one night while astride her mule Jenny looking for corn-thieves. The defence were unimpressed by this story, as was the Pig Woman's ancient mother who muttered continually from the front row in court: 'She's a liar, she's a liar, she's a liar.' All four defendants denied being anywhere near De Russey's Lane at the time of the murders. A diversion was expected when walrus-moustached brother Willie, aged 54, faced questioning, Willie being an eccentric who liked to ride around with the local and indulgent fire brigade in a special home-made uniform: but he gave his replies in a dignified, confident, and convincing manner, proving quite as erudite and unshakeable as sister Frances, who claimed she had never known of her husband's amorous pursuits. Mrs Hall mentioned that she had paid the hospital bill when Eleanor Mills had undergone a kidney operation shortly before the murders. Asked why she had sent a brown coat to a dyer in Philadelphia immediately after the killings (the inference being that it was stained with blood) Mrs Hall replied indignantly that she needed a black coat for the mourning period.

The jury found all four not guilty, and the murders remain unsolved.

HARRIES, Thomas Ronald Lewis
Twenty-four-year-old Welsh farmworker, convicted of the murder of his uncle, farmer John Harries aged 63, and his wife, Phoebe Mary Harries, aged 54.

On the evening of Friday October 16th, 1953, John and Phoebe Harries of Derlwyn Farm, Llanginning, near St Clears, Carmarthenshire, attended a Harvest Thanksgiving service at the local Bryn Chapel. They were never seen again by their neighbours, and three weeks after their disappearance Mr T. Hubert Lewis, Chief Constable of Carmarthenshire, got Scotland Yard to help in the search for the missing couple.

According to Ronald Harries, they had been driven by him on the morning of October 17th to Carmarthen railway station, reaching there about 11 am, their intention being to go to London for a 'secret' holiday, leaving Derlwyn Farm and their saloon car in the care of nephew Ronald. 15-year-old Brian Powell told the police, however, that 'Ronnie' had visited the Powell council home at 8.30 am on October 17th to enlist his aid at Derlwyn Farm, saying that his aunt and uncle had gone to London. After breakfasting at Ronnie's home, Cadno Farm, the young men had driven to John Harries' farm, where they milked cows, fed the chickens and washed out the cowshed. (Later Powell testified that Ronnie had shown him over deserted Derlwyn Farm, fingering various objects: '. . . Ronnie put the paintbrush in his pocket and said, "They won't miss this one" ').

Chief Superintendent John Capstick, in charge of the case, noted that in Phoebe Harries' oven there was an uncooked joint of meat, and thought it an unlikely purchase for a woman about to start a holiday. A cheque, ostensibly made out by John Harries for the sum of £909, payable to J. L. Harries, Ronald's father, and signed for 'Dada' by the accommodating son was found to be fraudulent, having had the original figure of £9-0-0 overwritten to appear as £909-0-0.

Capstick and his helpers were convinced that John and Phoebe Harries had been murdered, but feared that the suspect had buried the bodies somewhere in the vast stretches of Pendine Sands, where there was little chance of recovery. Following a hunch that the remains might be buried near the Cadno farmhouse, Capstick had reels of thread stretched across every exit from the far and every entry into the nearby fields, in the hope that the murderer would feel compelled to visit the burial site of his victims and so leave a trail for the police. The ruse succeeded; on November 16th the bodies of John and Phoebe Harris, their skulls smashed, were found buried in a kale field adjoining Cadno Farm. Ronald Harries was charged with the double murder and protested his innocence: 'I am sorry to hear uncle and auntie are dead, as I was their favourite.'

The accused, who was known to be in need of ready money, had borrowed a hammer from a Mr Lewis on the night of the murders and failed to return it. Four days after his arrest this hammer was accidentally discovered, hidden shaft-first in the undergrowth around Cadno Farm.

The circumstantial evidence was overwhelming. On March 16th, 1954 at Carmarthen Assizes, Ronald Harries was found guilty of murder, and was ultimately hanged in Swansea Prison.

HARRIS, Carlyle
Twenty-three-year-old student, electrocuted for the murder, by poison, of his wife, Helen Potts Harris.

The 18-year-old victim, a pupil at the Comstock School, West 40th Street in New York at the time of her death, had secretly married medical student Carlyle Harris on February 8th, 1890, giving birth to a still-born child shortly afterwards. In January 1891, after an evening spent with the school principal reading aloud from John Brown's *Talks about Dogs*, Helen Potts collapsed after going to bed; she complained of numbness, and when advised to try and sleep, replied: '. . . if I do, it will be the sleep of death.' A Dr Fowler was called in and, finding the girl's pupils symmetrically contracted, suspected narcotic poisoning; an empty pill box was found by the bed, inscribed 'C.W.H. Student. One before retiring.' Helen Potts' schoolfellows were aware of the identity of 'C.W.H.' without realizing his exact relationship with the dying girl, and this medical student, Carlyle Harris, known as 'Carl', was promptly summoned. He admitted prescribing the pills 'for malaria, for headache, for insomnia and the like'; six capsules had been ordered through the druggist, each one to contain $4\frac{1}{2}$ grains of quinine, and $\frac{1}{6}$ grain of morphine. Harris suggested that a tracheotomy (insertion of a tube into the windpipe) be performed on Helen Potts, an operation which would doubtless have hastened her end. After her death was affirmed he shouted: 'My God, what will become of me?' Suspicion mounted against Harris when a newspaper found out about the secret marriage; Helen Potts' remains were exhumed, and morphine (but no quinine) found in the body. The victim was known to have taken three of the prescribed pills with no ill-effects, and as Harris himself had kept two (presumably to demonstrate, if necessary, their innocuous quality) it was assumed that he had substituted a lethal dose of morphine in the remaining capsule. The two chemists (of Ewen McIntyre and Son) who had prepared the prescription were adamant that no mistake had been made, and the pills in Harris' possession were shown to be accurately compounded. A schoolfellow of

Helen Potts recalled that the ailing girl had said, shortly before dying: 'Do you suppose that medicine Carl gave me could do me any harm?' During the subsequent trial, opinion was divided as to the guilt of the prisoner. His mother, an active speaker on religion and temperance (who had frequently, from the public platform, referred to her son as an example of the paragon to be produced by a good religious and abstemious upbringing), worked constantly on his behalf, disregarding rumours of Carl's secretaryship of the Neptune Club – a 'blind pig and poker joint', and accounts of seductions secured by means of rye-whisky and ginger ale. Leading prosecutor at the trial was Francis L. Wellman; one of Harris' defenders was William Travers Jerome. The defence suggested that Helen Potts suffered from a kidney disease, but no such sign had been seen during the autopsy. Suicide was rejected as a theory; Helen Potts, despite her peculiar marital condition, had appeared lively and untroubled to within a few hours of death. A verdict of guilty was reached, and sustained weeks later by the Court of Appeals. Harris protested his innocence to the end; as he stood by the electric chair he said: 'I have no further motive for concealment, and I desire to state that I am absolutely innocent of the crime for which I am to be executed.' His mother had his coffin plate engraved: 'Carlyle Harris. Murdered May 8th, 1893.' Later she wrote a book, *The Judicial Murder of Carlyle Harris*.

HARUZO, SUMIDA AND THE DOUBLE TENTH TRIAL

Lieutenant-Colonel Sumida Haruzo, born 1903, joined the Japanese Army in 1925 and was posted as Captain to the Kempei Tai in 1935. This organization combined the functions of military police and security police and its members were greatly feared by the ordinary soldier. The army command used it as an instrument of terror, torture, and subjugation but took no responsibility for its methods.

After the surrender of Singapore in 1942, the Japanese established an internment camp for Europeans in Changi Prison, outside the city. By spring of 1943 it contained 3,000 men, and 400 women and children. Its administration was largely left to the internees themselves and as a result many illegal activities were soon flourishing. Not only was news being disseminated by the working parties who maintained contact with their old friends outside the prison, but wireless sets were actually in use. As the Japanese advance rapidly slowed down anti-Japanese feeling grew in the occupied territories. In Singapore sabotage broke out and the Japanese encountered suspicious activities on all sides. Much was discovered and much more suspected.

In summer 1943 they were preparing to raid Changi Camp the following Christmas, certain that it was the main centre of conspiracy and only waiting till they had obtained sufficient information with which to confront the ringleaders. In June, Major Sumida paid his first visit to the camp and was present in civilian clothes when Robert Scott, a barrister and one of the camp leaders, was called to the Commandant's office. Thus did the Kempei Tai enter the scene. Near their HQ over the YMCA dungeons they opened a new prison and mingled their men and informers with the Eastern population. Reports began to flow to Sumida. On September 27th, out of the blue, six Japanese oil tankers were blown up in the harbour. The Army Command were convinced that the Changi interness were directly connected and ordered Sumida to act swiftly and forcibly. Within a fortnight, at 9 am the camp was sealed off by soldiers and Kempei Tai men and thoroughly searched while the first important suspects were arrested.

They were taken to the YMCA dungeons and subjected to weeks of torture, brutality, and degradation in order to extract confessions, which, by Japanese law, would be necessary before trial could proceed against them. Like the Gestapo, the OGPU, and all groups of professional torturers, their methods were refined and their techniques masterly at uncovering and playing on the weaknesses of individuals. Sumida, their chief, was described as a man 'with a shrewd cunning, a deep insight into the weaknesses of his fellow men and a powerful personality which he could make pleasant or frightening at will'.

The Kempei Tai were not respecters of persons. After ten hours of torture on his first day, the Bishop of Singapore was carried back to his cell. Next day, 'I was again carried upstairs and tied face upwards on a table and flogged with ropes, receiving more than 200 strokes – I was carried back and remained semi-conscious for three days and unable to stand for more than three weeks'. Eric Hiltermann described how this elderly man's legs 'from his hips to his ankles had been beaten to pulp. They were literally like raw meat. He could not move at all and was just about able to crawl.'

Dr Stanley's treatment and death were typical. After several days of torture including the electric table, he was forced into signing an untrue confession. He jumped from a verandah to commit suicide, broke his pelvis and paralysed his legs. But still the 'investigation' was not finished. Testified Eric Travis, his cell comrade:

> The English-speaking doctor came and looked at him and said he was not ill enough. They continued to take him away – I could hear him screaming up above. The last time they brought him back he had only his vest on. The tender parts of his body were burned, armpits, crutch, back of knees, in between toes — When I lifted him on to the pedestal of the lavatory, from his penis there oozed something that looked like tomato sauce.

Mr and Mrs Choy were tortured together. He was beaten savagely, given water treatment, electric treatment, and burned with cigarette ends. She was then tied to a frame, kneeling on sharp firewood. 'They took out two leads from a generator which were applied to her body for fifteen minutes. She was yelling all the time. The wires were applied on her bare hands and bare legs.'

Mr Middleton had been a man of six feet two inches and thirteen stone in weight. His friend, Herbert Lord, testified of his last days:

> He had all over the body, particularly on the legs, shins, back, and buttocks, large black scars such as one sees from un-healed ulcers – he was so emaciated that the skin over his bones was as if a thin rubber sheet had been pulled right over a skeleton and the bones were easily observable through the skin.

Lionel Goodall described how:

> I received a fracture of the left shoulder blade – I received a blow from the ropes on my testicles which caused them to swell to an enormous size. At the end I was knocked uncon-scious by a direct blow on the head – I was still in a semi-conscious condition when one of the guards with an electric needle jabbed me on either side of the spine from my neck to the small of my back. I was bleeding profusely, and when they found they could get nothing out of me, began to . . . pour iodine over my chest and back.

The tortures and beatings went on night and day. The War Crimes Commission's report described how the buildings resounded with 'the bellowing of the inquisitors and the shrieks of the tortured. From time to time victims of the torture chamber would stagger back, or, if unconscious, would be dragged back to their cells.' Sometimes they died during the night and their bodies were not removed till the following afternoon. But the Kempei Tai were realizing that the evidence amassing was contradictory and unreliable. Sumida planned to force a confession from Scott by confronting him with overwhelming evidence from the confessions of others. At first he tempted him with bully beef and cigarettes but, sensing failure, he turned to force. Scott's next interview 'opened by my being strung up to a window by my two fingers for a period of two hours whilst I was asked questions continuously, being beaten on every part of my body and head and being stamped upon and kicked'. He held firm through three weeks of terrible torture.

Meanwhile conditions in the crammed dungeons were so bad that the victims were dying rapidly. Food was almost uneatable. The only water available for all purposes including drinking came from the lavatory pedestal. Dysentery, beriberi, scabies, ulcers, and oedema were rampant. Men and women were forced together without any privacy. In fact, the guards 'insisted on exposing and making as public as possible any natural function of the kind', especially menstruation, for which the women were allowed no necessities at all. 'We were not allowed to speak to each other but were supposed to sit on the floor with knees drawn up from 8 am to 10 pm.'

Sumida accepted failure and closed the investigations. After several months six prisoners were eventually 'tried'. But, in fact, the sinking of the oil tankers had nothing to do with the Changi internees at all. This had been achieved by Captain Lyon, who with his party had trained specially and sailed from Australia in a small fishing prau for such a purpose. Having reached Singapore harbour they sank the ships with limpet mines from one-man canoes and returned to Australia. But as a result of the Kempei Tai 'investigations' fifteen men were murdered.

One of Sumida's subordinates described him as 'very extreme' and that whenever he attended an interrogation an 'increase of tempo' occurred. He would not even allow the release of prisoners proved to be innocent. In a statement typical of other war criminals Sumida answered his American War Crimes Investigator, 'I was aware of these beatings, mistreatments, and torture, and, since they were being carried out with my knowledge, I admit being responsible for them.' To disentangle its real content would need the dialectic subtlety of a Hegel. Similarly, Hoess of Auschwitz said that he was responsible for what went on in his camp because the regulations declared that he was responsible. The underlying difficulty appears to stem from the fact that at the time of the deeds the accused was either not at all or only dimly conscious of 'personal responsibility' or the moral wrongness of his behaviour. Now his life is at stake before an accuser whose basic assumption is that *all* men are personally responsible for such deeds. In these strangely ambiguous confessions the accused somehow manages to admit what he thinks will placate his accusers, and yet still deny it.

During the trial Sumida had a bland, confident answer for every concrete charge. Mr Cornelius had been beaten to death and a Kempei Tai man had himself testified to Sumida's presence at the beating. Sumida simply denied it and cheerfully asserted, 'When the interrogation was over Cornelius did not look *so very weak* and still *appeared* of good spirit'. Each word is charged with evasive ambiguity. Poor Dr Stanley had simply been suffering from diarrhoea and a weak heart. In fact, Sumida had considerately asked his personal friend Dr Kuge to see him to hospital and give him a camphor injection. This kind of confession, the complete denial or complete lie, is again familiar in War Crimes Trials reaching its apogee in Göring's declaration at Nuremberg that neither Hitler nor himself knew anything about the ill-treatment of Jews. These men are sufficiently intelligent to know that the accuser will not believe them in face of the overwhelming mass of evidence and it seems that they have no other resort than a complete denial of reality in order to try and save their lives. The acts were originally done quite openly and broadcast specifically as part of a master-race principle. In fact, it was part of the same, brutal, aggressive, power-mongering egoism which as quickly discards it and disowns it, now that its own existence is at stake.

Sumida declared that tea was 'served' to the cells three times a day and that he noticed only 'one case' where the inmate had to sit rigidly. What complex nuances underlie that 'one case' which still hesitates on the brink of complete denial. He insisted that the major cause of death was dysentery. 'I should like to take this opportunity to express my deepest *regret* for what happened in spite of unavoidable circumstances.' Regarding torture, 'The order was urgent – time was short – I emphasized that no unduly harsh torture should be applied – I knew that such an instruction was undesirable, but unavoidable. Now there is no doubt that such a method should not have been employed.' Regarding all the witnesses, 'Their memory must have failed', or 'He may be telling a lie, but I rather think he has mistaken me for some one else'. This before the victims with their living scars and wounds in the court.

Q. So that the witnesses who say that there were shrieks and screams going on the whole time are liars?

A. Maybe the witness is mistaking that loud voice which was interrogating.

Q. Are you suggesting that Mr Cornelius died of heart failure as a result of this loud voice in the interrogation and nothing else?

A. I recognize he was beaten.

Q. Do you think it very odd that all these witnesses make mistakes?

A. – the majority of the witnesses have given false evidence – quite a number are Chinese who are liable to tell lies.

Q. No Japanese are capable of telling lies?

A. No.

Q. Do you think if someone drove a nail through your foot you would be likely to forget?

A. I feel that it is more painful to the person who had to administer such torture than to the person who was maimed.

Q. So you think it was more painful to hammer that nail in the foot than receive it?

A. Yes.

In similar fashion his accused subordinates who administered the tortures denied most of the charges. The battery applied to Dr Stanley only gave a small, as it were, corrective shock, 'as when you touch leaking electricity in some metal'. Another prisoner only had his knee-cap electrified 'to administer formal punishment' and not his genitals, as charged. One of them recalled how he had protested against the interrogation of Mr and Mrs Choy together as being 'against our moral code and against humanity'. Monai, Sumida's chief subordinate, admitted a 'certain amount of torture' but, 'I was personally always very sorry, and it is my wish to repay for any such sins if an opportunity be allowed me'. He was questioned.

Q. Do you remember telling the court that you went to visit Dr Stanley in hospital?

A. Yes.

Q. On more than one occasion?

A. I went to see him two days after he was put in hospital and the next time I went he died.

Q. Do you know that Dr Stanley died the night he arrived at the hospital?

A. That is not true.

Or again:

Q. Do you agree that it is very queer these people I have mentioned remember you and you do not remember anything about their sufferings at all?

A. I would call it odd myself, too.

Perhaps the strangest example of all is the following:

Q. When you hit somebody on the head did you feel then that you were doing something that Col Sumida had specifically said you were not to do?

A. No.

Q. But he has told us that his instructions were that the head and the face were not to be touched. Is that right?

A. Yes.

Q. Then you were breaking his orders if he ordered you not to hit somebody on the face or head?

A. From my point of view I did not disobey his orders.

Q. You were not disobeying orders when you gave the electric treatment?

A. No.

The defence insisted that the Kempei Tai was not at all like the usual secret police. 'Much less is it an organization for the purpose of doing evil. It is nothing more than the usual military police.' Thus an 'honest' Kempei Tai man, simply because of his membership, could not be held responsible for the tortures of another Kempei Tai man. There had been nothing unlawful in raiding and imprisoning these suspects and any maltreatment was quite unintentional. The comparatively large number of deaths was due to diseases and the death of Dr Stanley for instance was clearly due to a weak heart. The whole affair was certainly executed under the direction of Sumida and did not constitute a crime — 'To *suggest* that any responsibility lies with the lower ranking members is *incredible*'. The tortures may in fact only be attributed to Sumida's 'neglect in exercising sufficient supervision, and he may as a result be condemned on a charge arising out of responsibility for supervision, which is entirely different from – criminal responsibility'. Sgt Major Shozo 'had to carry out the duty ordered by his superiors and it can easily be imagined that while using force on the suspects he must have felt pity for them — It is very likely that he never realized that such deeds could constitute a crime.' As for W. O. Monai, the chief torturer, 'he personally felt an unbearable emotion against such tortures'. As for the evidence, 'living in the tropics it is not unusual to make mistakes and to take one person for another'.

Finally the defence observed, 'It is true that some Japanese when excited may sometimes resort to rash actions, but essentially Japanese are extremely quiet-mannered and peace-loving people'. They pleaded that the accused 'be granted the opportunity to co-operate in the re-establishment of peace'.

The prosecutor declared that the dungeon conditions, far from being unfortunately unavoidable, were in fact 'part and parcel of a deliberate policy – to make the civilians as ill and wretched as they could; and so by the addition of mental agony and persecution to wear down their steadfastness and powers of resistance'. For him mere membership of this Kempei Tai unit established a strong presumption of guilt. He described Col Sumida as 'smiling seraphically at all around him – smiling upon the court, laughing at me and beaming upon his fellow assassins', and how when he had spoken of his ignorance of the tortures Private Murata's face had lit up with a sardonic smile. 'The Kempei Tai stalked like a scourge throughout Asia, carving its way with fire and sword.' Could there be any other expiation for their fearful crimes than that they too must surely die?

Three men received life sentences, one fifteen years, two eight years. Seven of the worst murderers were sentenced to hang. To them the President declared, 'You – all of you – are mere professional bullies with no sensibility or finer feelings whatever. You must die because you were willing tools – and willing tools of inhuman, of murderous purpose must surely be destroyed.'

Col Sumida was also sentenced to death and to him the President declared, 'You are a man of education, of intelligence, even in a sense, of culture. Yours is the cunning brain under whose direction your instruments of torture performed their evil task. You were well aware of all the moral implications of your policy — To you there is nothing of higher consequence than domination by brute force and fear — You were prepared – to reduce men and women below the level of beasts and to send them without pity or compunction to an agonizing death — Accordingly it is in no spirit of vengeance – that this court has solemnly decided that you must die. Nor is it merely to rid the world – of one man who is a danger to all moral progress. Rather is it a stern example to all who would willingly support the powers of evil and brute force against the rule of law, justice and humanity.'

J. G.

HAUPTMANN, Bruno Richard (Lindberg Kidnapping Case)

Thirty-six-year-old German, resident in the Bronx, New York, convicted of the kidnapping and murder of Charles Lindbergh, jun., 19-month-old son of American aviator Colonel Charles Lindbergh and poetess Anne Morrow Lindbergh.

During the evening of March 1st, 1932 at the Lindbergh estate near Hopewell, in the Sourland Mountains of Hunterdon County, New Jersey, the Lindbergh child was abducted from his cot; a nursemaid, Betty Gow, made the discovery. Outside the bedroom window was a crudely made ladder, and a laboriously scrawled note on the windowsill demanded, as ransom money, $50,000. It was signed by three interlocking circles, each punched through the centre. (A handwriting expert said the writing and phraseology of the note denoted that the sender was a German 'of meagre education'.) No fingerprints were found.

Lindbergh, believing the kidnapping to be the work of an underworld kidnapping ring, was bent on securing the services of an intermediary, someone both he and the kidnappers could trust. Dr John F. Condon, aged 72, a schoolteacher and lecturer, a hearty homespun-philosopher-type who had, through the *Bronx Home News* offered $1,000 dollars for information leading to the safe return of the Lindbergh baby, seemed ideally suited for the task. In time, Condon received a note, embellished with the triple circle, saying that the schoolteacher was acceptable as a go-between, and on April 2nd another three-ringed letter was delivered by a taxi-man to Condon's home in the Bronx, instructing the schoolteacher to look that evening under a stone in front of a certain Bronx flower shop where he would find a note telling him where to take the ransom, which amount the kidnapper had now raised to $70,000. Lindbergh prepared the money at the offices of J. P. Morgan and Company; $50,000 were placed in a wooden box, after their numbers had been noted, and $20,000 wrapped in brown-paper bundles. Lindbergh then drove Condon to the flower shop, where they found the note instructing the schoolteacher to walk to St Raymond's Cemetery, a short distance away. Just within the cemetery gates Condon encountered a man who gave him an envelope, saying it contained information as to where the Lindbergh child would be found; Condon offered the $50,000 as ransom, which was accepted, the other man walked swiftly away. (Condon stated it had been too dark in the cemetery to distinguish the man's features.) The note stated that the child was on the *Nellie*, a boat anchored off Martha's Vineyard, Massachusetts: this area was searched, but no trace of either the Lindbergh child or the *Nellie* found.

On May 12th, 1932, a lorry driver named William Allen walking in a wood four miles from the Lindbergh estate in New Jersey found the decomposed body of a baby, identified by Anne Lindbergh and Betty Gow as Charles Lindbergh, jun.

Police had previously printed a list of the ransom bill numbers and issued it to all banks, theatres, stores, and petrol stations, but it was over a year before ransom notes began to circulate, all within a certain area of the Bronx. In September 1934, a customer at a Bronx petrol station handed over a $10 bill. The garage attendant automatically checked the bill number with the police list, and found he was in possession of a ransom bill. The customer's car licence number was noted, and in this way Bruno Hauptmann, by trade a carpenter, came into police custody; in his Bronx garage was $14,000 of the ransom money, but Hauptmann, seemingly dazed, insisted it belonged to a friend of his, Isadore Fisch: '. . . he's gone back to Germany; he left the money in my care.' Hauptmann had entered the United States illegally in 1923; in Germany, his homeland, he had a criminal record, one of the crimes being a burglary where he used a ladder to enter the house. In Hauptmann's attic a piece of wood flooring was missing; a rung of the ladder found propped against the Lindbergh nursery window was said by experts to be part of this attic flooring. Condon's telephone number was found scrawled on the inside of a cupboard in

Hauptmann's house, and Condon himself said that Hauptmann's voice resembled that of the man in St Raymond's Cemetery.

Hauptmann was charged with the murder and kidnapping of Charles Lindbergh, jun., his trial before Judge Trenchard beginning on January 2nd, 1935, at Flemington, New Jersey. The prosecution was led by State's Attorney, General Wilentz, and Hauptmann was defended by Edward Reilly, who was to insinuate that both Dr Condon and nursemaid Gow were not above suspicion. The trial lasted six weeks, the jury finding Hauptmann guilty on both charges. After much legal delay (including a temporary reprieve by Governor Harold Hoffman of New Jersey to enable 'further inquiries' to be conducted) Hauptmann was electrocuted at Trenton State Prison on April 3rd, 1936. $32,000 of the ransom money has never been found.

HAYDEN, Rev. Mr Anthony
Thirty-three-year-old Methodist minister of Madison, Connecticut, tried for the murder of 22-year-old Mary Stannard.

In 1878 the body of Mary Stannard was found by her farm-labourer father, lying in a rural region known as Whippoorwill Rock near the village of Rockland, near Madison, Connecticut. She appeared at first in repose, with her gown compact and hands folded crosswise on her breast; but her throat was cut and her skull fractured, and during the post-mortem fifty grains of arsenic were found in her stomach. Days before her death Mary Stannard had referred to the amorous habits of the Rev. Mr Hayden in whose house she had been a servant; already (years before) the mother of one illegitimate child, she hinted of a further indiscretion and it was rumoured that on the day of her murder she had arranged to meet the minister at Whippoorwill Rock where he would give her 'quick Medicine' to remedy the mutual catastrophe. Unable to explain satisfactorily his movements that afternoon, the Reverend Hayden was arrested. It was found that he had purchased 1 oz. of arsenic on the day of Mary Stannard's death 'for to kill rats'; doubt was felt when a devoted parishioner discovered a 1 oz. packet of arsenic in the minister's barn which had already been searched by the authorities. The Rev. Hayden was kept in jail for nearly a year while a lengthy comparison of both arsenics (barn and stomach) was made by a Yale teacher, Professor Edward S. Dana; Dana

308

travelled to arsenic factories in England so that his analysis might be thorough. He found that the barn crystals differed from those in the victim's stomach; nor had they come from the shop allegedly patronized by Mr Hayden during his rat-purge, and that the grains found in the stomach were identical with those sold in another part of the town. The trial of Hayden began in October 1879 and lasted three months. Mrs Hayden testified that on the afternoon of the murder her husband had been in the wood-lot (for a period of four hours) piling up the Hayden wood supply; she was asked by the prosecutor if she would tell the truth even if the truth jeopardized her husband, but this query was disallowed by the court. The jury deliberated for two days; all unconvinced by Professor Dana's findings, they were chiefly concerned with Mrs Hayden's integrity as a witness. Many jurors accepted her story of the prolonged wood-piling, but a small faction (headed by a 30-year-old farmer David B. Hotchkiss) were unconvinced. Finally announcing their inability to reach a verdict, they were dismissed the court, the Rev. Hayden being released on bond ten days later.

HAYES, Catherine
One of the first known cases of disposal of the body by dismemberment in English criminal history.

On March 2nd, 1725, a watchman – one of the 'Charlies' of eighteenth century London – found a human head on the fore-shore of the Thames, near the prison (where the Tate Gallery now stands). The head was laid on a tombstone in St Margaret's Churchyard, where thousands flocked to see it. Later it was set on top of a pole, and several people thought they recognized it as a certain Hayes who lived with his wife in the Tyburn Road. Catherine Hayes declared that her husband had absconded to Portugal, but she was arrested, together with two lodgers, Wood and Billings. Other parts of the body were found in Marylebone Fields in a pond.

Mrs Hayes identified the head as that of her 'poor husband' and simulated great grief.

Wood finally confessed to the crimes. Mrs Hayes apparently had reasons for hating her husband, the main one of which was that he was a freethinker ('and therefore it was no more a sin to kill him than a dog'). She also told Wood and Billings that Hayes had murdered his two children and buried them under a pear tree and an apple tree. Hayes was got drunk and murdered with a hatchet. The head was then severed over a pail to catch the blood. Mrs Hayes wanted to boil it to destroy its features, but her accomplices were afraid, and hurried the head off to the lime wharf near Horseferry Passage (now Lambeth Bridge) where they threw it in.

Wood died in Newgate before execution; Billings was hanged; Mrs Hayes was sentenced to be burned as being guilty of petty treason (husband murder); she should have been strangled first, but the executioner did not complete his task and she was burned alive. (This law continued in force until 1793; the last woman to suffer under it was Phoebe Harris in 1788.)

HEARN, Sarah Ann
Middle-aged widow tried for the murder of Alice Maud Thomas.

Since 1925 Mrs Hearn had lived impecuniously with her sister, Miss Lydia Mary Everard at Lewannick, near Launceston, Cornwall; their neighbours were farmer William Henry Thomas and his wife, who, upon the death of delicate Miss Everard in July 1930 (of some vague stomachic complaint), were to become even more friendly with the now lonely widow, taking her for drives and giving her much hospitality. On October 18th, 1931, the trio drove into Bude, where they took 5 pm tea and cakes at Littlejohn's Café on Bellvue Hill, a meal made more substantial by a heap of tinned-salmon sandwiches Mrs Hearn produced from her straw shopping basket. During the car journey back to Lewannick, Mrs Thomas was taken violently ill with stomach pains and vomiting; Mrs Hearn remained at the farm to help during her friend's illness, which proved persistent, and, on November 4th fatal, arsenical poisoning having been diagnosed. By the time of the burial at Lewannick Church on November 8th there were sinister whispers concerning the death of Mrs Thomas, from whose body organs had been removed and were now under examination by the county analyst (·85 grains were found in the remains). The entire locality seemed aware of the tinned-salmon sandwiches and convinced of the lethal qualities of some of them; particularly outspoken was the deceased's brother – ' 'tis that woman!' – although many held uncharitable thoughts about Farmer Thomas. Mrs Hearn fled, leaving a note for Mr Thomas in which she hinted at suicidal intentions: '. . . I am innocent, innocent, but she is dead and it was my lunch she ate. I cannot bear it . . . when I am dead they will be sure I am guilty and you at least will be cleared. . . .' In mid-November clothes belonging to Mrs Hearn were found on a Cornish cliff-top, rumours of a frantic female roaming from farm to farm circulated throughout the county. On December 9th conjecture triumphed, and sister Everard's body was exhumed and found to contain ¾ grain of arsenic.

Meanwhile, Mrs Hearn, under an assumed name, had secured employment in Hesketh Road, Torquay, and as Mrs Faithful supervised the meals of architect Herbert Powell, who was, however, to realize with uneasiness the true identity of his housekeeper one morning in January 1931, when beholding a photograph of the missing Mrs Hearn in his newspaper. Duly arrested, Mrs Hearn eventually faced trial on June 15th, 1931, at Bodmin Assizes before Mr Justice Roche for the murder of Mrs Thomas; she was defended by Mr Norman Birkett, and pleaded not guilty. It was established that Mrs Hearn had purchased weedkiller containing arsenic in 1926, although it was further established that Farmer Thomas had, in his farm-house, worm tablets for sheep that contained copper, a substance also found in the corpse of Mrs Thomas. Asked by prosecuting counsel, Mr Herbert du Parcq, KC, whether she and Mr Thomas might have made 'a match of it', Mrs Hearn replied emphatically, 'No, never'. Evidence concerning the death of Miss Everard had been deemed admissible, although when it was revealed that the soil in Lewannick Churchyard contained arsenic (125 parts per million), a fact which could account for the small amount of arsenic found in Miss Everard's body, this intelligence became void. Birkett emphasized that if the salmon sandwiches had contained the weedkiller arsenic, they would have stained the bread blue. Farmer Thomas unhappily answered Birkett's probing in the witness-box, admitting that he had administered brandy and tea to his ailing wife.

Birkett: Did you say to Mrs Hearn, 'They will blame one of us'?

Thomas: I don't remember saying that.

Birkett: Did you say, 'A detective might be here at any time'?

Thomas: ... I may have said 'detective' ... I do not remember.

Birkett: To say 'a detective' would come was enough to frighten any woman?

Thomas: Yes.

The judge, directing the jury in his summing up, said that if they were not satisfied that the arsenic was put in the salmon sandwiches by Mrs Hearn, they should acquit her. The jury returned a verdict of not guilty; regarding the indictment against Mrs Hearn for the murder of Miss Everard, the Crown forwarded no evidence, and the jury gave a further verdict of not guilty.

HEATH, Neville George Clevely

Twenty-nine-year-old ex-Borstal boy, ex-RAF officer (dismissed the service in December 1945 for conduct prejudicial to good order and for unlawfully wearing military decorations), sentenced to death on September 26th, 1946 for the murder of 32-year-old Mrs Margery Aimée Brownell Gardner.

At 2 pm on June 21st, 1946, the body of Margery Gardner was found on a bed in Room 4 at the Pembridge Court Hotel in the Notting Hill region of London. The room had been booked in the name of 'Colonel' Heath the previous Sunday; Heath had stayed before at this hotel under the name of Armstrong, a pseudonym he had employed when joining the South African Air Force in 1942. Mrs Gardner had evidently been killed by a sexual maniac. Her breasts were almost bitten off, there were seventeen lash-marks on face and body, and much laceration of the vagina passage ('consistent', said pathologist Keith Simpson, 'with a tearing instrument being thrust into the vagina and rotated'). The cause of death was suffocation, probably with gag or pillow. Mrs Gardner, separated from her husband, had lived the unconventional life of an artistic dilettante in the Chelsea area; the evening before her death she spent with Neville Heath drinking and dancing at the Panama Club, South Kensington. Police issued a statement naming Heath and the possible help he could give in the murder inquiry. On Monday June 24th Police Superintendent Thomas Barratt, in charge of the case, received a letter from Heath, postmarked Worthing, Sussex. In it Heath admitted booking in at the hotel a week before, but said he had lent the key of Room 4 to Margery Gardner: '. . . she met an acquaintance with whom she was obliged to sleep . . . I returned . . . and found her in the condition of which you are aware. I realized I was in an invidious position . . . and left.' Heath gave a description of Mrs Gardner's male companion, and informed the police: 'The personal column of the *Daily Telegraph* will find me, but at the moment I have assumed another name.' This latter was Group Captain Rupert Robert Brooke, and under this name Heath, on the evening of June 23rd, booked a room at the sea-front Tollard Royal Hotel, Bournemouth. (No photograph of Heath had been submitted to the Press, and the police authorities, in view of future events, received much criticism over this.)

On July 5th the manager of the Tollard Hotel received a phone call from the manager of the Norfolk Hotel, Bournemouth; a Miss Doreen Marshall, a 21-year-old guest at the Norfolk, had been missing since Wednesday evening, when she had left in a taxi, naming the Tollard Royal Hotel as her destination. The manager of the Tollard Royal Hotel recalled that on Wednesday evening Group Captain Brooke has entertained a young woman to dinner, and accordingly on July 6th at 10.15 am asked the ex-pilot if his dinner-companion might not be the missing girl. Heath laughed: 'Oh no, I have known that lady for a long while . . .' Fifteen minutes after this conversation Heath rang up Bournemouth police station (still using the name Brooke), saying he might be able to assist their inquiries. At 5.15 pm he arrived at the station (where he met the father and sister of Doreen Marshall) and eventually gave an account of Wednesday's dinner date: '. . . at 11.30 pm we left the hotel and sat on a seat overlooking the sea. We walked down the slope towards the Pavilion . . . Miss Marshall did not wish me to accompany her but I insisted upon doing so – at least some of the way . . .' Detective-Constable Souter soon noticed the physical resemblance between Group Captain Brooke and Heath (whose photograph had been sent to all police stations), and the helpful ex-pilot was detained, denying that he was Heath. In his sports coat, retrieved at the Tollard Royal Hotel (the detained man had complained of feeling cold), was found a cloakroom ticket and the return half of a first-class ticket from Bournemouth to London, subsequently proved to have belonged to Doreen Marshall. At 9.45 pm Detective-Inspector Gates of Bournemouth Police informed the detainee that he believed his real name to be Neville George Clevely Heath, and that he was holding him pending the arrival of the Metropolitan Police for the purpose of interview in connexion with the murder of Margery Gardner. On Monday July 8th the body of Doreen Marshall was found concealed under a rhododendron bush in Branksome Dene Chine, Bournemouth, a gorge leading down to the sea, about 1½ miles west of the Tollard Royal Hotel, and 2 miles west of the Norfolk Hotel, just within the boundary of Poole:

a passer-by, Miss Evans, taking her dog for a walk, wondered uneasily at the vast swarm of flies in one part of the chine and had called upon her father, who, recalling the missing Bournemouth visitor, at once contacted the police. The body, lying on its right side, was naked except for one shoe: a black dress and yellow 'swagger' coat were thrown over the remains and pearl beads from the girl's necklace were strewn everywhere. One stocking was found 21 feet away, hanging 7 feet from the ground in a bush, and it is thought the victim was first attacked at this spot, being dragged farther into the chine minutes later. There were indications that the girl had been gagged and her wrists bound (a knotted handkerchief, blood- and earth-marked, was found in Heath's room at the Tollard Royal Hotel a day before the body's discovery), and it is thought the murderer stripped naked in preparation for his onslaught, as none of his clothes bore signs of blood. Death was caused by the cutting of the throat above the larynx, but all the major mutilations had been inflicted after death: the breasts were slashed (the instrument used, probably a knife, was never found) and one nipple bitten off, the genitals were savagely lacerated, and the body virtually ripped open from groin to breastbone.

Heath, now held in custody in London by police who were convinced they not only had the killer of Margery Gardner but also that of Doreen Marshall, was made to attend identification parades, where he was picked out as Mrs Gardner's companion on the night of June 20th by the receptionist at the Panama Club and as Mrs Gardner's escort into the Pembridge Court Hotel by the taxi-driver who had been hailed by Heath outside the Panama Club. Within a short period he had also been identified by the jeweller to whom he had sold Doreen Marshall's watch, and by the pawnbroker to whom he had pledged her ring; numerous guests and employees of the Tollard Royal Hotel identified him as Group Captain Brooke. When police at Bournemouth claimed luggage on the cloakroom ticket found in Heath's hotel room, they had found, inside a suitcase, a riding switch the criss-cross thong marks of which corresponded with the lash-marks on the body of the first victim. At the end of July 1946 Heath was charged with both murders at the West London Police Court, and at the close of the third hearing was committed for trial at the Central Criminal Court, Old Bailey, on a charge of murdering Margery Gardner. He pleaded not guilty. Counsel for the Crown was Mr E. Anthony Hawke with Mr Henry Elam; Defence Counsel was Mr J. D. Casswell, KC, with Mr E. A. Jessel and Mr J. MacGillivray Asher. Heath's guilt was never in question; the main issue was his mental condition at the time of the murder. Dr Hugh Arrowsmith Grierson, Senior Medical Officer at Brixton Prison, and Dr Hubert Turner Penn Young, Senior Medical Officer at Wormwood Scrubs Prison, for the prosecution, both of whom had examined Heath over a period of weeks and reached the conclusion that Heath fully realized, at the time, the enormity of the sadistic acts inflicted upon Margery Gardner; Dr William Henry de Bargue Hubert, psychotherapist of Feltham Prison and Broadmoor Criminal Lunatic Asylum (1945–46), who had also examined Heath, averred that Heath had not realized his behaviour was wrong or criminal. Hubert insisted that Heath thought it right to inflict cruelty because that was the only means by which he could obtain sexual satisfaction:

Mr Hawke: Is that your answer, Dr Hubert? – Well, he was doing what he wished to do.

That inasmuch as he desired to satisfy a perverted lust he thought that it was right to satisfy it? – Yes.

And therefore he did not know that what he was doing was wrong. Is that accurate? – Yes.

Miss Yvonne Marie Symonds, aged 19, gave evidence that she had met Heath at a Chelsea dance on June 15th, and that on the night of June 16th she was persuaded by Heath to spend the night with him in Room 4 at the Pembridge Court Hotel:

Mr Hawke: Had he treated you quite decently, yourself, personally? – Yes.

Miss Symonds said on June 22nd at Worthing, Heath mentioned the murder of Mrs Gardner, that it had happened in the room they had occupied the previous Sunday, and how he had himself been interviewed by an Inspector Barratt.

Mr Hawke: What did he say? – He told me that he was closely connected with the murder.

. . . did he say that he had been sleeping somewhere else in London that night? – Yes.

Did he say where Inspector Barratt took him after he picked him up? – Yes, to the Pembridge Court Hotel.

Was it then that he said he had seen the body? – Yes.

Did he mention any detail to you in connexion with the

body, something that had been done to it? – That a poker had been used on her.

Did he express any idea as to the sort of person who might have done a thing like that? – Yes, a sexual maniac.

The second murder was referred to in court. Mr Harry Brown, head porter at the Tollard Royal Hotel, spoke of Heath's stay at the hotel under the name of Group Captain Brooke. Mr Ivor Relf, joint manager of the Tollard Royal Hotel, told how, on July 4th, Heath had approached him and jokingly mentioned his method of making an unobtrusive entry in the early hours of that morning: i.e. by means of a builder's ladder that went up to his bedroom window.

Heath was not called upon to give evidence. His Defence Counsel said to the jury: you probably would not believe a word he said if he were called. Mr Justice Morris, summing up, stressed: the law of insanity is not to become the refuge of those who cannot challenge a charge which is brought against them. The judge referred to the deliberate concealing of Doreen Marshall's body, Heath's denial of his true identity, the glib explanation that he had found the first-class return railway ticket in the Tollard Royal lounge: is that or is that not the mentality of a man whose mind is working so that he must have known that what he did was wrong? After an hour's deliberation, the jury returned a verdict of guilty. No appeal was lodged, and Neville George Clevely Heath was executed at Pentonville Prison on October 16th, 1946.

HEIRENS, William

Chicago murderer, 18 years old at the time of his arrest. Heirens first came to police attention at the age of 13, when he appeared in a Cook County juvenile court on a dozen charges of burglary. Heirens had burgled 'for kicks', often throwing away the items he had stolen immediately afterwards. He was sent to the Gibault school for boys at Terre Haute, Indiana. His behaviour was exemplary, and he was released after eleven months. A psychiatrist examined him, but the results of the examination have never been made public. Immediately after his release, he committed more burglaries, and was sent to another 'correctional' school at Peru, Illinois, where he spent the next year and a half. Soon after he was released, he committed his first murder, breaking into the apartment of Josephine Ross, a

Chicago widow, whom he stabbed in the throat as she lay in bed, then knotted her nightgown around her neck.

This, in fact, was not his first attack on a woman. On October 1st, 1945, he had been interrupted when burgling the apartment of a nurse; he had fractured her skull with an iron bar and tied her to a chair. Afterwards, he had gone to his classes at the University of Chicago. The woman recovered.

On December 10th, 1945, ex-Wave Frances Brown was found murdered and mutilated in her bed; on the wall above her, in lipstick, was scrawled the words, 'For God's sake catch me before I kill more. I cannot control myself.' But the sincerity of the demand may be in doubt; Heirens made no attempt to give himself up, and the words may have been intended to influence a jury to find him insane in the event of his being caught.

His last murder was of a 6-year-old child, Suzanne Degnan; Heirens entered her room through the window, carried away the sleeping child to a nearby basement, where he raped her, and then killed and dismembered her. He distributed the parts of the body in various sewers and manholes.

Heirens was arrested shortly after this; the police were notified when suspicious noises were heard in the apartment of Leonard Pera, who was out of town, and he was caught before he could escape, putting up tremendous resistance. In his room at the University were found many items from previous burglaries, and Heirens' fingerprints were quickly identified as being those of the attacker of the nurse. In the attic of his home they found between thirty and forty pairs of women's panties. Heirens admitted that he had first obtained sexual satisfaction from stealing these garments and putting them on. Later, when he was 12, he began burgling to obtain them; soon, the act of entering a strange house through the window induced the orgasm. Finally, the sight of an open window could induce an erection. He declared that he struggled against the urge to commit the burglaries, but that if he resisted for long, he experienced violent headaches. He described how he had once put his clothes in the washroom and thrown the key inside in order to make it impossible to leave his bedroom; half-way through the night, the urge became too great, and he crawled along the house gutter and went out. 'When I went out, it would make no difference to me if I had a summer suit on in freezing weather. I could not feel any temperature.' (This brings to mind Sergeant Bertrand's testimony about his complete insensitivity to cold and discomfort when on a grave-robbing expedition – see

C. W's introduction.) Heirens also declared that he was accompanied by an invisible alter-ego named 'George'. 'He was just a realization of mine, but he seemed real to me. When I went out on a burglary, it seemed that George was doing it.' He explained that his murders had followed his being disturbed in the act of burglary, and that it was 'the noise that set him off. I must have been in a high tension.' The child, Suzanne Degnan, had spoken to him, and he had immediately strangled her.

A psychiatrist declared that, in his opinion, Heirens was not suffering from any psychosis, nor was he mentally retarded. Accordingly, he was sentenced to life imprisonment.

Photographs of Heirens show a handsome and well-built youth. He was the son of Roman Catholic parents. Unlike the underwear fetishist 'Rodney Shires' cited by Israel Beckhardt in his volume *The Violaters*,[1] Heirens does not appear to have been an abnormally shy and timid youth, although he was certainly unsociable. It seems almost certain that, had the psychiatrist who examined him at the age of 13 realized that he was an underwear fetishist, he might have received proper treatment instead of being sent to a reformatory; two and a half years among juvenile delinquents turned a sexually excitable boy into a sexual murderer.

HEMMING, Richard
An interesting case in which a hired murderer was murdered in his turn to keep him silent.

In 1806 the Rev. George Parker was rector of Oddingley in Worcestershire, and he was hated by many local farmers (with whom he quarrelled on the question of tithes). He was also a bullying man. A group of farmers decided to have him murdered; they were: Captain Evans (who was a magistrate), John and William Barnett, George Bankes and John Marshall, and finally Thomas Clewes, a young man who was spending his father's inheritance very quickly. They hired Richard Hemming, a carpenter of Droitwich, to commit the murder, and promised him £50. So on June 24th, 1806, Hemming left home and collected the gun from Captain Evans at Oddingley Church Farm. At about five in the afternoon he shot and killed Parker in his garden, thrust the gun into the hedge, and ran away. But he was

---

[1] Harcourt Brace and Co., 1954. 'Rodney Shires' was sentenced to 'induction in the army'. Six weeks after his induction he was taken critically ill and died in hospital.

recognized, and the police were soon looking for him; he took refuge in the house of Captain Evans. Some accounts have it that he told Evans that if he had to die, he would not be the only one, and also that he hoped to be supported for the rest of his life by the six rich conspirators. At all events, on the day after the murder, Evans summoned the other five. (Some versions give the name of one conspirator as James Taylor instead of Marshall.) They met in a barn on Netherwood Farm, Clewes' home, where Hemming was hiding, and there Hemming was killed with a blow on the head struck by an iron-loaded stick. The blow was struck by Marshall (or Taylor). The body was then buried in the corner of the barn, and the conspirators went home.

Twenty-four years passed, during which time Captain Evans and William Barnett died wealthy men. Taylor (or Marshall) also died. (During the last twenty years he had been a popular singer of comic songs!) All prospered except the feckless Clewes (who had accepted £50 or so as blood money for Hemming, and had had the floor levels of all his barns raised with earth). Netherwood Farm changed hands three times, and its fourth owner decided to improve the place. Workmen levelling the floor of a barn discovered a human skeleton; the widow Hemming identified it as her husband's by the teeth (which were prominent), a carpenter's rule and the shoes. Clewes, now a hopeless drunkard, was found and charged; he immediately confessed, implicating the two remaining conspirators. But since Bankes and Barnett were pillars of local society, they were only charged with being accessories after the fact; Clewes himself was charged with the murder. But a jury decided that he was only an accessory, so he was finally discharged. The entire proceedings were then abandoned.

The case holds no mystery, but it would be interesting to know whether the conspirators decided in cold blood to murder their hired assassin who was now 'on the run', or whether it is true that the assassin drove them to it by talk of blackmail.

HENRIOT, Michel

Weak-minded 24-year-old silver-fox breeder of Brittany, found guilty but insane in 1934 of murdering his plain, crippled 19-year-old wife Georgette, whom he had met six months before through a matrimonial journal, *L'Union des Familles*. They lived an isolated existence in a two-storey wooden house among the sand dunes at Kerbennec, Henriot's chief interests being his caged foxes, money, hunting game, and – according to Georgette's diary and letters – the sexual tormenting of his wife. On the afternoon of May 8th, 1934, a telephone operator, receiving a signal from the Henriot house, heard sounds of screaming and shooting; soon after, Henriot dashed up to peasants working near the sand dunes, shouting that some fiend had shot his Georgette. Before total collapse into grief he sobbed that a telegram must be dispatched immediately to the Paris insurance company, 'La Paix', where he had recently insured Georgette's life for 800,000 francs against the eventualities of murder, accident, and cyclone. Georgette Henriot was found lying on a bed, her head and chest blasted with gunshot from her husband's hunting rifle; no tramp had been seen in the vicinity, but police organized a vast manhunt which continued even while Henriot, at the funeral, plodded after the coffin crying, 'my poor darling'. Henriot's father was the local Procureur de la Republique [public attorney] which might explain the seeming reluctance of the police to suspect Henriot straightaway; but finally he was called to the Brigade Mobile at Rennes for interrogation, where he smiled his way through a maze of questions on the timely insurance clause, the complicated mechanism of his foreign-made rifle (which would have baffled an intruder) and the fact that no tramp had been observed in the area at the time of the murder. Meanwhile the dead woman's diary and letters to her sister were traced, unbeknown to Henriot, and these gave an ugly picture of the marriage:

We have now been married for six days ... Michel is exasperating in ... he kisses me all the time because he knows I don't like it ... besides he licks me ... He is evil ... said he would beat me with a dog whip until the blood came ...

Nine days of marriage ... Tonight Michel beat me ... pinched me ... said he was sorry he hadn't got a whip.

Five days before her death she wrote: Michel told me he would kill me.

Confronted with this literature, Henriot's confidence vanished; within a short time he had dictated a confession, saying an argument had started 'over a sexual matter'. Georgette hobbled up the stairs, trying to escape her husband who had attacked her with a poker; on the landing she snatched up the telephone, attempting to summon aid. At the same moment Henriot took aim with his hunting rifle and fired five times: 'I wanted the pleasure of shooting something new.'

HENRY, Philip

Coloured soldier, executed at Leeds for the lust murder of 76-year-old Flora Jane Gilligan in July 1953.

The body of Miss Gilligan, who lived at 30 Diamond Street, York, was found on March 10th, 1953, lying in the yard of her house. She was naked, and had apparently fallen from the bedroom window. In the house, shelves of the stove had been removed. The police decided that a man had attempted to enter the house next door, number 32, and had moved a board in front of the kitchen window. Unable to effect entry, he had climbed in through the window of number 30, leaving a footprint in a laundry basket inside the door, and leaving fingerprints in the house. Miss Gilligan had come downstairs to investigate the noise; the burglar raped her and beat her; he then decided to try and fake a suicide, and removed the shelves from the gas oven; however, he changed his mind, and took Miss Gilligan upstairs and pushed her from the window. Death was due to injuries of the skull. The prime motive of the crime was not robbery, since money had been left around the house.

Police had two clues – the footprint – of recently repaired shoes – and fingerprints. They decided to check on the prints of all soldiers in surrounding camps, and the Wakefield Fingerprint Department was called in to help. As it happened, the first camp chosen was a lucky choice. They had selected it because its population was frequently shifted overseas. Five hundred men were fingerprinted, and almost immediately the police found that Philip Henry, of the King's Own Yorkshire Light Infantry, was the man they wanted. Although he claimed he had returned on the 11 pm bus on the night of the murder, it was established that he had not returned to camp until reveille the next day. He had carefully washed all his underwear, and cleaned his clothes. A cobbler was found who remembered repairing Henry's shoes with the distinctive heel and sole found in the footprint, although Henry had disposed of them when arrested. He was due to be posted overseas on March 19th; instead, he was executed on July 30th, 1953.

HEPPER, William Sanchez

Sixty-two-year-old Chelsea artist, former native of Gibraltar, convicted of the murder of 11-year-old Margaret Rose Louise Spevick at Hove, Sussex.

Hepper, one-time BBC news typist and translator in the Latin-American section, reputed to have been an agent of the British Secret Service in Spain, was an eccentric, a wanderer who rarely saw his family; head injuries received in a car accident (which caused him to resign from the BBC) were said to bring on amnesia. His wife was friendly with the Spevick family, and when little Margaret Spevick broke her arm it was suggested that she recuperate at Hove, near Brighton, where the Heppers owned a flat; according to William Hepper, given charge of the child (for whom he professed a fondness) there was a resident nurse in the block of flats who would tend Margaret's arm. The child departed for Brighton on February 2nd, 1954. On February 3rd her mother received a postcard; 'Enjoying myself. Having a splendid time. Love.' On February 4th she attended Brighton Hospital, accompanied by an elderly man. On February 6th Mrs Spevick went to Brighton to see her daughter and possibly bring her back: the child was not at the railway station (as arranged) and, the mother, not knowing the flat's address, returned to London. In the evening, having learnt the address, Mrs Spevick journeyed to the flat (which consisted of one room at Western Avenue, Hove). There she found the strangled and raped body of her daughter lying on a divan; on an easel was an unfinished portrait of the child.

The search for Hepper began; his portrait was flashed on television screens, but it was thought he had left the country. He was discovered at the Pension España in the Spanish frontier town of Irun, and eventually extradited to Britain, where he appeared at Hove Magistrates' Court on March 24th. Charged with the murder of Margaret Spevick, he replied, 'All I say at this stage is that I did not do it,' and it was noticed that his usual impeccable English accent was now heavily accented.

He appeared before Mr Justice Jones at Lewes Assizes on July 19th, 1954. The prosecution read letters written by Hepper in which he referred to 'wife-attacks' in the Hove flat. ('You may come to the conclusion,' said Mr R. F. Levy, QC, 'that he did think ... he was attacking his wife and not this little girl. ...') Hepper, in the witness-box for three hours, talked of loss of memory, dreams and hallucinations, and stressed that he

322

had been impotent for over a year. Asked why he went abroad without telling the child's parents he replied: 'I did not do things properly because I was not in a normal condition.'

The defence (led by Mr Derek Curtis-Bennett, QC) pleaded insanity, and produced seven doctors. One, Dr A. W. Watt, a Hove psychiatrist, admitted: 'I cannot give ... an explanation of this', when asked by the Judge the reason for Hepper's flight if, as asserted, the prisoner looked upon his 'wife attack' as an hallucination or dream.

William Hepper was found guilty of the murder of Margaret Spevick and executed.

HEYS, Arthur
Hanged for the murder of 27-year-old Winifred Evans, a WAAF radio operator stationed near Beccles, Suffolk. The main interest of the case lies in the way in which the accused man condemned himself in an attempt to avert suspicion.

On the evening of November 8th, 1944, WAAF Evans attended a dance at an American camp, and returned late with a friend, Corporal Margaret Johns. She then went off to do a late-night stint of duty. Corporal Johns found an airman in the ablutions a few minutes after Winifred Evans had gone, who declared he had lost his way to his own camp. Corporal Johns directed him, and he set off down the same road that Winifred Evans had taken.

What seems to have happened next is that the man overtook Winifred Evans, and made advances to her which ended with his raping her in a ditch, asphyxiating her in the process (by kneeling on her chest). He then went back to his hut, three-quarters of a mile away, arriving there an hour after he left the ablutions in the WAAF camp. He undressed in the dark, although he spoke to some of his companions. The next day he was seen brushing heavy mud off his trousers and shoes.

The body was found early in the next morning by a policeman. Corporal Johns spoke of the Leading Aircraftman she had seen in the ablutions, and she picked out Arthur Heys at a pay parade. Heys' clothing was examined; Dr Eric Biddle, the pathologist, found bloodstains on Heys' tunic, and brickdust and mud on his trousers, as well as rabbit hairs of the same kind that had been found on the dead girl's clothes. Heys was lodged in Norwich Prison; the evidence against him was strong enough to convict him.

323

However, he tried a ruse to divert suspicion from himself. On January 9th, 1945 the Commanding Officer of Heys' squadron received an anonymous letter, printed in blue crayon, which purported to come from the murderer. The writer claimed that he had met Winifred Evans by appointment some time after midnight. He said that he saw an airman go past, and then 'Winnie' came. Winnie told him that the RAF man was drunk, and that a WAAF friend of hers (presumably Corporal Johns) had offered to come with her to escort her.

Heys was in prison, but it was possible to smuggle a letter out of the prison. It had a Norwich postmark. A blue pencil was available in the prison for prisoners who wanted to write letters. The letter bore no fingerprints, but Superintendent Cherrill, a handwriting as well as a fingerprint expert, obtained samples of Heys' printing and declared that the letter had been written by Heys. He gave evidence to this effect at the trial, which took place before Mr Justice Macnaghten at the Bury St Edmunds Assizes in January 1945. Mr John Flowers prosecuted, and Mr F. T. Alpe defended. But the really damning evidence against Heys was the anonymous letter. Mr Flowers pointed out that Winifred Evans could not have told the anonymous writer about the drunken airman, for she had left the camp before Heys was discovered in the ablutions. Only Heys could have had the information about the drunken airman.

The only alternative theory, if one chooses to believe in Heys' innocence, is that the anonymous writer had heard that Heys had been found in the ablutions by Corporal Johns, and was deliberately inventing a lie to try to clear Heys. This hardly seems likely.

Heys was sentenced to death and hanged. But the most striking feature of the case, presuming his guilt, is his stupidity. If he was hiding in the WAAF camp hoping to find a sexual adventure (and, one presumes, drunk) he surely must have realized the likelihood of detection if he committed rape after Corporal Johns had seen him in the light.

Heys was a married man with a young family, which adds to the mystery of his mental state on the night of the crime.

HICKMAN, William Herbert ('The Fox')

Twenty-year-old clerk executed in 1928 for the murder of 12-year-old Marion Parker, daughter of a Los Angeles banker. Marion Parker was abducted from Mount Vernon School by

Hickman, who explained to her teacher that the child's father had met with an accident and she was wanted at home. By the following morning's post came a letter signed 'The Fox', saying Marion had been kidnapped and demanding £300 ransom money. The kidnapper wrote that he would phone arrangements that afternoon, and accordingly the demented Mr Parker waited at the chosen rendezvous, police concealed nearby. It was a futile vigil and next morning another letter came from 'The Fox': '. . . gave me your word of honour . . . not to tip the police . . . you lied . . . you are insane to ignore my terms.' A note in the child's writing was enclosed: 'Please, Daddy, I want to come home this morning. This is your last chance . . . come by yourself or you won't see me again.' A further meeting at Manhattan Place Car Park, Los Angeles, was arranged for that evening. The money was handed over to a softly spoken young man in an open car, who said he would leave Marion (dimly seen at his side) 'just down the street'. The father found his child dead; her hands and legs were hacked off, the body sadistically slashed, and wire bound tightly round the neck had been so placed as to prop open the child's eyelids. The missing limbs were found in Elysian Park, Los Angeles, and a laundry mark upon a towel wrapped over part of the remains led detectives to an apartment house, where they met, during their inquiries, a helpful, pleasant young lodger named Evans. Only after their departure did they realize that the shirt wrapped round the torso of Marion Parker bore the same initials as the one Evans wore when interviewed. Evans was William Herbert Hickman, who had recently been imprisoned for forgery while working in the same bank as Marion's father. He was known to blame Mr Parker for his prosecution, so a vengeance motive was established. Hickman fled, travelling the States of California, Oregon, and Washington before his capture. He admitted abducting the child, but denied the killing, blaming accomplices who were found to have no connexion with the crime. (Strange methods were employed to make Hickman talk: once a warder burst into his cell shouting, 'I've got a message for you from Marion!') Finally he confessed, stating: 'I always wanted to cut up a body, I used a pocketknife, then drained each piece and washed them in the bathtub . . . then I went out to a cinema . . . I didn't like the pictures, they were too sad and made me cry.' Found guilty of murder, he died on the scaffold at St Quentin Jail.

HOESS, Rudolf

Born 1900 in Baden-Baden. As a young child he had a great love of animals but was essentially a solitary boy, happiest when playing alone. He was brought up on strict militaristic lines. His father was a devout Catholic who firmly intended him for the priesthood and he was a devoutly religious boy with faith in God and seriousness in prayer. Obedience to the will of grown-ups and total acceptance of their word as right was impressed on him as the highest virtue, and although his father's Catholicism was antipathetic to the State, Herr Hoess insisted that State laws must be served unconditionally.

Rudolf's parents, though peacefully united, never displayed tenderness and he himself always fought shy of it, too. At 13 his religious faith underwent a severe crisis. His confessor betrayed a secret to his father and his faith in the priesthood was shattered. His father died before the 1914 War began and he longed to become a soldier. He served in Turkey and Palestine, fell in love with a nurse while in hospital and fell further away from the Church. He returned to a broken home, his mother having died, and instead of going to the intended theological seminary left, in anger with high-handed relatives, to enlist in a Freikorps or volunteer unit of former soldiers. These men refused to accept the Versailles Treaty and committed sabotage and murder against Ebert's government and Allied collaborators. In the Baltic States he participated in savage fighting and the massacre of civilians.

The Freikorps administered their own justice and as the result of a political murder Hoess received ten years' imprisonment. With his training for absolute obedience, his conscientiousness and sense of order, he did not find even Prussian prison discipline too difficult to endure. He had a breakdown, on the verge of madness, closely connected with the realization that he had forgotten how to pray and had lost his way to God. Sometimes he saw his dead parents and spoke with them. He slowly recovered, began reading a great deal, especially on racial research and ethnology, and was generally a model prisoner for which he received many rewards and promotions. After six years, in 1928 he was suddenly released due to a political amnesty.

He joined a back-to-the-land group of young people, married, and farmed. In 1932 he joined the Nazi Party. In 1933 Himmler, who inspected Hoess' troop of mounted SS on the Sallentin

Estate, was impressed by his bearing and urged him to join the concentration camp administration at Dachau. The prospect of reasonably rapid promotion, good wages, and being in uniform once again proved very tempting and the farming ceased. At Dachau he first learnt about 'the enemies of the State', the political prisoners and witnessed his first flogging at which he went hot and cold when the man began to scream. He was made a block leader against his will, though as a soldier he had to obey.

Eicke, his chief, was the organizer of the concentration camp system. His basic principles were hardness, the rooting out of all sympathy towards the prisoners and the engendering of intense hatred towards them. In this atmosphere Hoess carried out his duties to everyone's satisfaction. He masked whatever inner conflicts and diffident feelings of humanity that he had with coldness and stoniness, and in his autobiography says that at this point his *guilt* begins. He could not find the courage to give up the job, admit his weakness, his antipathy and break his vow to the Führer. He became reconciled, never daring to show other than indifference to the most dreadful forms of human suffering. He believed without reservation in the means and ends of the Party. He was posted to Sachsenhausen concentration camp where the conflict receded as he was no longer in such close contact with the prisoners.

On the outbreak of war he had to administer the execution of an SS man in conformity with the discipline of unbending severity and ever greater harshness. 'There is only one thing that is valid. Orders!' was Eicke's motto. About 1940 he was rapidly promoted and made Commandant of a concentration camp in process of being built at Auschwitz in Poland, a swampy, remote area. Himmler had ordered its enlargement and drainage. Hoess set to the task with his usual obedience, conscientiousness, and keenness to please his superiors. He was absorbed in it, living only for his 'work'. But he felt that everyone on the staff at Auschwitz was against him and preventing him from achieving his aims. He withdrew, trusted nobody, grew harder and more ruthless. Himmler intended the camp to hold 100,000 prisoners and enormous building tasks were undertaken.

Conditions soon reached the stage of open cannibalism, when Russian prisoners were killing and eating each other, but the work of building went on. In 1941 Himmler ordered him to supervise the installation and operation of gassing plants for the mass extermination of European Jewry. As a fanatical SS officer, he set to once more with zeal and thoroughness, sparing neither himself nor his staff. Himmler's orders were 'sacred', brooking neither argument nor interpretation and were ruthlessly carried out regardless of consequences. This apart, Hoess considered the plan thoroughly justified in its attempt to abolish Jewish 'supremacy'. He apparently never personally hated the Jews but as an automaton in the vast Nazi machinery he carried out his orders, stifling without much difficulty any conflicts or human feelings that interfered with the work. Above all, like any manager in modern technological society, he saw it as an interesting, complex, responsible, purposeful job of work needing the gifts of organization, attention to detail and that split personality which made it possible for the crematorium stoker to spend a happy Christmas dinner with his family before hurrying away for the evening shift. The fact that this particular industrial enterprise was the murder of millions of innocent human beings was one of indifference. The essential principles remained. Efficiency, economy, thoroughness, and authority.

Corpse production speeded up to thousands a week. Nursing mothers choked their babies so as not to go to the gas chambers with their children. Older babies were often thrown straight on the furnaces so as not to waste valuable gassing time. The hutments were knee high with corpses on whom were piled the dying, the half-dead, and the living who cried, 'Please won't they fetch us for the gas at last'.

As the tempo increased Hoess and his subordinates were tormented by secret doubts. But he forced himself to maintain utter impassivity in the face of unimaginable scenes, as the mothers filed into the gas chambers with the children and babies, sometimes convulsed with maniacal screams when they would be led away by the Special Detachment and shot in the neck, almost gently and courteously. He forced himself to watch and supervise every aspect. The gassing; the removal of hair and teeth by the Special Detachments who also worked with dumb indifference, shifting corpses with one hand whilst searching them for something to smoke or eat with the other; and the vast stinking pyres of burning corpses, with the clear knowledge that Hitler's orders could only be executed by *the stifling of all human emotions*. Eichmann, his superior and real originator of the gassings, was apparently unburdened by any inner conflicts whatsoever and even made Hoess feel that such human emotions were a *betrayal* of the Führer.

His wife and family, like those of any hard-working executive, lived extremely well, with their governess, pet animals and paddling pools not very far from the crematoria. But he learnt to disconnect them completely from his work. Eventually Auschwitz, which had become the greatest human graveyard in history, was divided up, and Hoess was promoted to a Head Office job. In 1945 with the news of Hitler's death amid the general chaos of the end, he and his wife decided to confirm this catastrophic finale of their world and the pointlessness of going on living, with poison. But they changed their minds for the sake of the children. He went into hiding as a farmworker and was arrested in 1946 by the British Field Security Police. Eventually he was taken to Cracow, tried, and hanged.

To the end he remained a convinced National Socialist, upset, not at the essential evil of National Socialism but at its failure to realize fully its ideals and the consequent disaster for the German people. For him the mass extermination of Jewry remained not wrong *in itself*, but wrong because it brought world hatred against Germany and thus served the Jewish cause. He claimed that he personally was never cruel or maltreated anyone and that his blood ran cold when he heard what was done in Auschwitz under his supervision. He declared that he was responsible, not because he *felt* responsible, but became the *camp regulations said* that he was responsible. Let the world regard him as a cruel sadist and mass murderer, in fact he too had a heart and was not evil but simply a cog in the Third Reich. Thus to the end he failed to recognize that his evil originated at just this point.

Before his death he wrote his autobiography. A significant document, much of which is taken up with the strangely toneless account of all the bureaucratic difficulties he faced in the achievement of his tasks and the fulfilling of his death quotas. He is still obsessed with what could have been done to make the whole business more efficient. Resentfully, yet with that curious grey timidity, he airs his grievances at the red tape, the continual interference, the backbiting and the jealousy. The *reality* of his 'work' from the fully human viewpoint barely seems to have penetrated his awareness. Even when he does use concepts like 'guilt' and 'inner conflict' one has the impression that for this man with his so-called 'religious' background, *they have no reality*.

He insisted to Gilbert, the American psychologist, at Nuremberg that he was entirely normal. 'I had nothing to say but *jawohl* — The thought of refusing an order just didn't enter one's head, regardless of what kind of order it was — Of course none of us cared for this work – but later on one became de-sensitized even in this cruel activity.' Gilbert found him 'apathetic, with cold eyes that gazed into space and not entirely of this world'. Even the idea of being hanged didn't bother him, very much. He characterized him as a 'robot murderer' and concluded that 'The gap between the detached and the inhuman – was filled by race ideologies, authoritarianism, militarism'.

J. G.

HOLMES, H. H. (alias of Hermann Webster Mudgett)
American swindler and multiple murderer.

Just as some cases seem to receive far more attention than they deserve – 'Jack the Ripper' is an example – so others remain curiously obscure and badly documented. The man who called himself H. H. Holmes may well be one of the most remarkable criminals in history, but for some reason very few students of criminology have heard his name.

Holmes' remarkable career of crime came to light through an accident. A Mr Perry, who ran a 'patent office', was found dead in his office, the evidence pointing to accidental death through a chemical explosion. An attorney named Jeptha D. Howe con-tacted an insurance company and told them that he believed Perry to be a man named Benjamin F. Pitezel, whom they had insured for $10,000. H. H. Holmes, as a friend of the dead man, went to Philadelphia to identify the remains, taking with him the dead man's daughter Alice, a girl of 15. The claim was allowed, and the insurance was paid to Pitezel's wife.

At this point, a convict named Hedgspeth wrote to the in-surance company warning them that the whole case was a trick. He claimed that he had met Holmes in the St Louis Jail two years earlier, and that Holmes had told him of a 'foolproof method' for defrauding the insurance companies. This con-sisted in getting Pitezel insured, and then obtaining a body similar to Pitezel and faking an explosion. Hedgspeth's part in the transaction was to recommend a crooked lawyer; he recom-mended Jeptha D. Howe. Now, it appeared, Holmes had failed to pay Hedgspeth the promised rake-off.

The insurance company preferred to disbelieve Hedgspeth's story, but their investigator pursued it, and soon began to un-earth evidence to indicate that the convict was telling the truth. A month later Holmes was traced to his father's house in Gilmanton, N.H., and arrested in Boston. He finally decided to 'confess' and declared that although it was true that he had swindled the insurance company, Pitezel had actually committed suicide.

Mrs Pitezel admitted that she was implicated in the fraud; she declared that after her husband's 'death' (she apparently believed he was alive somewhere) Holmes had taken away three of her children to stay with a widow lady at Ovington, Kentucky. She had not seen them since.

A detective named Geyer set out to retrace Holmes' movements with the three children. The search was successful; in Toronto, Geyer found the bodies of the two girls, and in Indianapolis the remains of the boy. Holmes was put on trial on October 28th, 1895, in Philadelphia.

A remarkable story slowly began to unfold itself to the investigators. Holmes had been born Hermann Webster Mudgett in Gilmanton, New Hampshire, on May 16th, 1860. His father was the postmaster. After graduation he became a schoolteacher, then studied medicine at Ann Abor, and obtained a degree at the age of 24. For a short time he practised medicine in New York.

At the age of 18, Mudgett had married Clara Lovering in Alton, New Hampshire, and had a son by her. Mudgett had deserted them in 1886. Changing his name he went to Chicago, where he began to court a girl named Myrta Belknapp. He married her bigamously in 1887. He then proceeded to swindle one of her well-to-do uncles, and a family quarrel resulted.

Holmes now embarked in earnest on his career of crime. He took a job in a drug store in Englewood, the southern suburb of Chicago; he was living in the northern suburb of Wilmette. The store was owned by a Mrs Holden. Then somehow, Mrs Holden disappeared, and Holmes was the owner of the store. In answer to inquiries, he said she was travelling in California. Holmes now took a flat in Englewood, where he began to have love affairs.

In 1890 a jeweller named Conner moved to Englewood with his wife Julia, their 8-year-old daughter Pearl, and his 18-year-old sister Gertie. Conner was invited to move into the drug store and set up a watch-repairing business. He accepted, and in no time Holmes had acquired two new mistresses. Later on, Conner packed up and left, and divorced his wife for infidelity.

Holmes' business was thriving, and he now bought a vacant lot across the street and proceeded to build a house on it. But the house was of unusual structure, and had some rooms that were intended for concealment; in fact, it was built like a medieval castle, with secret passages.

Julia Conner was a demanding women; she even objected to an apparently innocent affair between Holmes and a 16-year-old girl named Emily Van Tassell. One day, both Gertie Conner and Miss Van Tassell disappeared – like Mrs Holden. For a short time Julia had no rivals. An acquaintance of Holmes', to whom he had admitted getting Gertie pregnant, was later told that Gertie had died at her home in Iowa.

Holmes soon acquired a new blonde secretary. When Julia objected she disappeared, together with her daughter. The secretary's name was Emily Cigrand, and, after a few months as queen of the 'Castle', she too disappeared.

Towards the end of 1892 Holmes sold the drug store. Towards the beginning of 1893 he met another blonde, Minnie Williams, an heiress from Mississippi. Soon she was living with him in the 'Castle' as his wife. Six months later her sister Nannie was invited to come and stay in the 'Castle'. Minnie and Nannie disappeared, although Minnie was apparently killed many months after Nannie – in November 1893 – raising the interesting question of whether Minnie connived at her sister's murder.

In May 1893 the Chicago World's Fair had opened, and thousands of visitors required lodgings. Holmes' 'Castle' was packed every night. It is certain that he swindled some of his female guests, and it also seems probable that some of them 'disappeared'. Minnie's murder was apparently delayed until the end of the Exposition in October.

In November the 'Castle' caught fire and its roof burned; however, Minnie admitted that Holmes had set fire to it himself, so the insurance company declined to pay up. No doubt Minnie's indiscretion hastened her end.

Holmes had now become fascinated by another blonde, Georgiana Yoke, a respectable girl from Indiana, who declined to be seduced, but accepted marriage. Holmes 'married' her in mid-November 1893. Shortly after his marriage Holmes served his first term in jail for fraud; Georgiana bailed him out. During the next year Holmes appears to have been in partnership with Pitezel (who had come to Chicago from Kansas in 1888 with his family, and had been associated with Holmes in many shady deals since). Their association, disturbed by some quarrels, ended when Holmes murdered Pitezel, and then proceeded to kill his family, with the idea of collecting the insurance. Fortunately, he was arrested before he had time to kill Mrs Pitezel and the other children.

Police who examined the 'Castle' were astonished. There were peepholes into rooms, and concealed gas pipes controlled from the office, so that Holmes could fill any room with gas. (This feature anticipates Marcel Petiot's 'room of death'.) Some rooms were windowless, others padded with asbestos or lined with sheet iron. Two greased chutes connected the second and third floors with the basement, which contained a kiln large enough to cremate a corpse, and various surgical instruments.

One of the more startling features of the case is the number of people who had some insight into Holmes' shady existence, and yet who kept silent. A janitor admitted to seeing Julia Conner's body in the house. Charles Chopmen, a Chicago mechanic, came forward to say that he had been given the job of stripping the flesh from three bodies for Holmes. Holmes claimed that the bodies were obtained from medical school, and that the skeletons would be sold to medical students. Chopmen was paid $36 each for stripping the flesh. There were two women and one man; they may have been victims from the World Fair period. The man to whom Holmes had admitted his affair with Gertie Conner had accused him of killing her, but had not bothered to investigate.

On November 30th, 1895, Holmes was sentenced to death for the murder of Pitezel. An appeal was lodged, but failed. While in prison, Holmes wrote his memoirs for a newspaper, and described in detail twenty-seven murders. He later declared that the whole confession was a fake, designed to give the newspapers 'their money's worth'. He may also have hoped to persuade people that all the evidence against him was as valueless as his confession. (He declared also that he was suffering from some disease of the bones that had elongated his head and made him resemble the devil; this was also apparently a fabrication.)

Holmes was hanged on Thursday, May 7th, 1896. On the scaffold he declared his innocence of all the murders except those of Emily Cigrand and Julia Conner; but these, he stated, had died as a result of illegal operations.

Little is known of Holmes' character or of how he became a multiple murderer. Apparently there was a strong element of the actor in him. In some ways, he brings to mind Joseph Smith, the brides-in-the-bath murderer; both preyed on women, both were skilful confidence tricksters, both adopted the same pose of injured innocence after arrest. The great pity, though, is that America in 1894 possessed no psychiatrist like Professor Karl Berg, who examined Peter Kürten. It would be of absorbing interest to have some insight into the mind of a man like Holmes. It is just possible, of course, that Holmes was incapable of sincerity; the mentality of a confidence trickster, after all, may be radically different from that of a sadist. Like John George Haigh, the acid-bath murderer, he may have felt a compulsion to conceal himself from the world.

There is, perhaps, some interesting ground for study here. Haigh, Smith, Holmes, Rouse – these confidence tricksters-turned-murderers even show a curious resemblance in their physical types. All led double lives; all liked to simulate respectability. One day, some psychologist may discover something about the 'basic neurosis' of this type of criminal; it would be an interesting addition to our knowledge.

HOUSDEN, Nina

Twenty-eight-year-old Kentuckian, sentenced to life imprisonment in the House of Correction at Plymouth, Michigan, for husband-murder.

In 1947 Nina Housden and her husband, bus-driver Charles Housden, aged 29, lived in Highland Park, Michigan, near Detroit. Darkly beautiful, this woman suffered from an insatiable jealousy, continually accusing her husband of infidelity, although his diversions (bowling clubs, beer drinking) were innocuous, and his weekly wage packet of $65 hardly conducive to extra-marital relations. Made frantic by his wife's neurotic conduct, Charles Housden left her several times, being drawn back on each occasion by Nina's genuine remorse and seductive cajolery. Finally (after obtaining a court injunction forbidding her to phone him during working hours), the demented husband filed suit for divorce, despite protestations from his wife.

On December 18th, 1947, Nina Housden prevailed upon her estranged mate to meet her once more 'for old times' sake'. Taking him back to the Highland Park apartment, she plied him with drink and wifely lust until he collapsed, exhausted, on the bed. Mrs Housden then passed a length of clothes-line around her husband's neck, looped it, and strangled him; she slept all night beside the corpse. After breakfast Nina Housden rolled back the carpets, wadded the floor with newspapers, and in two lengthy sessions (with an interval for sleep) dismembered the man for whom she had held such a possessive love. Disposing of the bloodstained newspapers and a bloodstained dress in the apartment house stove, Nina Housden wrapped each hacked remain in gay Christmas paper, securing the bundles with blue ribbons; these bundles were piled up on the back seat of her Ford car, her intention being to drive back to her Home State and deposit Charles Housden's remains at some secluded spot in the Kentucky hills. During the journey the car broke down at Toledo, Ohio; told by a garage that it would take two days to repair, Nina Housden announced her intention of staying in the car for that period, rather than live at a hotel. When, on the second day, a disagreeable smell permeated both car and, eventually, garage, Mrs Housden explained that her back-seat bundles contained venison. By December 23rd the car was almost repaired, but as the car owner slept on the front seat (after a lunch of ham sandwiches and wine) an inquisitive garage hand investigated the odiferous packages in the back. Finding a decomposed leg in the first bundle, he and his colleagues called the police; questioned, Nina Housden readily admitted the killing, saying, 'Charles wasn't a bad sort. It was just that he ran around with other women.'

Found legally sane, Nina Housden was indicted on a charge of first-degree murder and found guilty.

HOWARD, Frances, Countess of Somerset (The Overbury Murder)

The murder of Sir Thomas Overbury in the Tower of London is one of the most famous crimes in English history.

King James the First, who succeeded Queen Elizabeth in 1603, was homosexual; he was also an extraordinary mixture of stupidity and sound common sense. He seems to have been a basically decent and affectionate man, who longed for emotional security. However, his physical traits cannot have been particularly agreeable to his favourites; his tongue was too large for his mouth, so that he spoke as if sucking a plum, and dribbled a great deal. His legs were so weak that he often had to lean on people's shoulders. He had a habit of slobbering affectionately on the cheeks of his favourites.

The chief of these favourites was a young Scot named Robert Carr, who had been a page, and had come to the king's attention in 1606 when he broke his leg at a tournament. Carr was tall, a blond young man, son of Sir Thomas Ker. By 1607 he was so much in favour that the king conferred on him the confiscated estate of Sir Walter Raleigh (who was in the Tower). Carr was James' pupil, confidant, and political adviser. (In 1610 he persuaded James to dissolve parliament; he was then 20 years of age.)

In 1601, some years before he met the king, Carr had become a close friend of Thomas Overbury, who was probably also homosexual. Overbury, eleven years older than Carr, was his opposite in most ways; Overbury was dark complexioned; he tended to be secretive and resentful; he was also clever. (His *Characters* take a very high place among English essays.) He became Carr's secretary, reading all the king's mail and secret dispatches. The situation cannot have been entirely to Overbury's liking; he and Carr had first become intimate when Carr was a pretty page boy, 11 years old; now Carr was the master. However, Overbury proved invaluable as Carr's secretary, and he was knighted in 1608. And when Carr fell in love with a teen-age beauty, Frances Howard, Overbury wrote his love letters.

Frances Howard, daughter of the Earl of Suffolk, was already married when she met Carr; she had been married in her early teens to the Earl of Essex, but the marriage had not yet been consummated. It never was. She came to Court as a girl of 15, in 1610; her beauty created a sensation (although a modern writer has pointed out that she had the face of a juvenile delinquent). Carr fell in love with her. James' eldest son, Prince Henry, also fell in love with her; but Henry was at loggerheads with his father, and when he died in 1612 (either of poison or typhoid) no one was surprised. Frances Howard lost her virginity to Carr. Shortly afterwards, her teen-age husband returned from abroad and insisted on taking his wife to their country home. Frances was agonized by the parting from her lover; she consulted a woman with the reputation of a witch – a Mrs Turner – about rendering her husband impotent by spells, and steadfastly refused to grant her husband any marital privileges. Although they slept naked in the same bed, they never became husband and wife. She bribed his servants to give the Earl various powders to render him impotent. She even consulted a woman called Cunning Mary about poisoning the Earl; Cunning Mary bilked her, but a prosecution against her was dropped when she threatened to tell about the poisoning plot.

In 1613, husband and wife spent part of their time at Court, and Carr began again to enjoy what the husband was denied.

James Camb

John George Haigh

Gaston Dominici

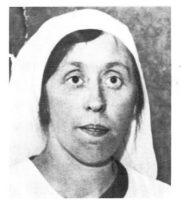

Nurse Dorothea Waddingham

Edith Thompson

Ruth Ellis

John Reginald Christie

Tony Mancini

Master Sergeant Marymont

Neville George Heath

Irma Grese

Leone Bouvier

Peter Kurten, the mass murderer
of Dusseldorf

Dr Buck Ruxton

LANDRU ('Bluebeard') with Mlle Marchadier

Jean Pierre Vacquier

Constance Kent

Brian Donald Hume

Peter Manuel

Henry Jacoby

Pauline Dubuisson

Sergeant Emmett-Dunne

Sidney Harry Fox

Adelaide Bartlett

Styllou Christofi

Guenther Podola

Alfred A. Rouse

Nathan Leopold and Richard Loeb

Ronald Light—at home after his acquittal in the
'Green Bicycle' Murder Case

Pauline Yvonne Parker, with head bowed, nine months before being accused of murdering her mother

Norman Thorne, photographed on his farm during investigations into the disappearance of Elsie Cameron

Dr Marcel Petiot

Yvonne Chevallier

Ronald Henry Marwood

Charley Peace

Daniel Raven

Elvira Dolores Barney

Her great-uncle, the Earl of Northampton, a Machiavellian figure, decided that the best thing would be for Frances to divorce her husband and marry Carr (who was now Duke of Somerset, lord treasurer, and a fabulously wealthy and powerful man). The king agreed; the wronged husband was persuaded to agree; he was even willing to declare that he was impotent with his wife. The Archbishop of Canterbury was reluctant to grant a divorce, but the king used all his influence.

The one man who did not agree was Sir Thomas Overbury. His objection was to cost him his life. It is difficult to imagine why Overbury became so hysterical about the prospect of Carr's marriage. He had written Carr's love letters and connived at the love affair, even if he disliked Frances. He had a sound sense of politics and knew how to further his own affairs. No doubt homosexual jealousy played its small part, but it hardly explains why he and Carr quarrelled bitterly about Frances. Finally, the king decided to get rid of Overbury, and offered him a diplomatic post either in Paris or Moscow. Overbury refused both, and was thrown into the Tower. Carr persuaded him to offer no resistance, assuring him that James' anger would soon pass, and that great advancement awaited Overbury. Carr was leading his friend into a trap.

The king certainly had no evil intentions towards Overbury; the thought of murder would have horrified him. But Frances Howard was determined that her enemy should die. One of her creatures, a rather stupid man called Sir Gervase Elwys, was made Governor of the Tower. This was at the instigation of the Machiavellian great-uncle, who also placed a friend of the 'witch', Mrs Turner, in charge of Overbury. Overbury was then slowly poisoned, over five months, by poisoned tarts and game. The poison was obtained from a Dr Franklin, a friend of Mrs Turner. Weston, Overbury's keeper, was in charge of the poisoning; at first, Sir Gervase Elwys had no idea of what was going on; but when he found out, he made no effort to interfere. (This later cost him his neck.) A young musician named Merston carried a pie to the Tower and slipped his finger under the crust to taste it; his nail fell off. He was one of many who had to be bribed to silence by the poisoners.

Finally, after long agony, Overbury died on September 15th, 1613. His parents had come from Warwickshire to intercede for him, but to no account. Overbury was quickly buried, and Frances was divorced from Essex and later married to Carr with enormous pomp. Francis Bacon was one of those who presided at the festivities, and Ben Jonson and Campion both provided masques.

But Carr's downfall was approaching. First, he discovered that Overbury had been a better royal secretary than he had realized. The king appointed a new secretary, but Carr disliked the man, and continually made a nuisance of himself. Carr also got into the habit of creating violent scenes with the king – failing to recognize that what the king wanted most was emotional security. He treated the king with continual rudeness and tried to domineer. Unfortunately, the king discovered a new favourite named Villiers, a young Cambridge student, and Carr's position became even shakier. He might easily have remained in power if he had been an astuter man, and had put himself out to soothe James, but he lacked tact.

Eighteen months after the marriage, a young man died in Flushing, and confessed before his death that he was the chemist's assistant who had administered the fatal dose of mercuric sublimate to Overbury. This statement was sent to the king, who ordered Sir Edward Coke to look into it. Sir Gervase Elwys was interrogated, and finally he, Mrs Turner, Weston (the gaoler), and Dr Franklin (supplier of the poison) were all put on trial and executed. This was in the autumn of 1615.

Carr and his wife were frantic, and Carr used his privy seal to break into a house and destroy some incriminating correspondence from Mrs Turner. However, more correspondence came to light; Sir Edward Coke placed Frances Howard and Carr under arrest. Carr was with the king at Royston when he was summoned by Sir Edward, and he declared he would not go. The king replied: 'Nay, for if Coke summons me, I must go.' He took an affectionate farewell of Carr and assured him he would be returning; but as Carr left, he was heard to say, 'I shall never see thy face again'.

In December 1615, Frances was delivered of a daughter, but the child was taken away from her in March of the following year. The trial finally opened on May 24th in Westminster Hall, and high prices had been paid for seats. Sir Francis Bacon prosecuted. The Countess pleaded guilty, and was condemned to death.

Carr was now told it was his turn to be tried, and he flew into a fury and shouted that the king would not dare to try him. He threatened to expose some secret in public. This may have been his homosexual relations with the king, or perhaps some knowledge of Prince Henry's death. The king was consulted that night, and was greatly upset; he finally sent word to Carr, promising that no death sentence would be carried out if Carr kept silence. Carr was tried the next day, with two men holding a cloak standing behind him to silence him quickly if he tried an outburst. Like his wife, he was sentenced to death.

The last stage of the tragedy is in some ways the most terrible. Husband and wife were confined in the Tower. (The Countess had pleaded that she should not be confined in the Bloody Tower, where Overbury had died – this overlooks the river – and her wish was granted.) Their love for one another had died completely. For six years they remained together in the Tower, and were then allowed to live in retirement – and disgrace – at their country home, Grays. They never spoke to one another. The life there seemed to poison the Countess's soul; she began to suffer from a disease of the womb – a cancer, perhaps – and her mind began to give way; she took a sort of pleasure in her misery and squalor. She died at the age of 39. Carr lived on, his only pleasure his daughter, who in due course married the Duke of Bedford. In later years, he went to see the king at Royston, and James broke down and cried on his shoulder.

From all accounts of her, Frances Howard seems to have been the same type of woman as Mme de Brinvilliers, of strong will and imperious temper; she was superstitious but completely irreligious; her only religion was the fulfilment of her own desires. It should be noted that Northampton, the Machiavellian great-uncle, died the year after the wedding (1614), so that he never knew of the complete collapse of all his designs for bringing power to the Howards.

HULTEN, Karl Gustav

Twenty-two-year-old Swedish-American (nickname Ricky) member of the war-time United States forces in Britain, convicted with Elizabeth Maud Jones of the murder of George Edward Heath, hire-car driver.

Hulten, a deserter from a paratroop regiment, met Elizabeth Jones (then known as Georgina Grayson) in a café on October 3rd, 1944; she lived in one room in King Street, Hammersmith, W6, and worked as a strip-tease artiste. The two formed an evil liaison; both were incorrigible 'romancers', Hulten liking to imagine himself as a gangster-type, Jones seeing herself as a gangster's 'moll'. Nightly they embarked on highway robbery schemes, travelling in a stolen army truck; they attacked pedestrians and cyclists, and one victim, a young woman, was hit repeatedly with an iron bar, nearly strangled by Hulten, and thrown into the River Thames. On October 7th, standing in Hammersmith Road, they hailed a hire-car, a Ford V8 saloon ('I knew the meaning,' said Elizabeth Jones afterwards, '. . . he wanted me to go with him to rob a taxi-driver'). The driver, George Heath, aged 34, agreed to take the couple to the end of King Street, Hammersmith, about a mile away; reaching this destination, Hulten directed Heath to drive on, afterwards asking him to stop at the beginning of the Great West Road. According to Elizabeth Jones:

'. . . I saw a flash and heard a bang. I was surprised that there was not a loud bang because Ricky had told me it would make a big noise . . .'

Jones then rifled the taxi-driver's pockets, taking out nineteen shillings, a silver pencil, and cigarette-case. Meanwhile 'the driver stopped breathing altogether'. They drove on to Staines, Middlesex, and dumped Heath's body in a ditch, where it was found the following morning. Jones and Hulten drove around in the Ford V8 all week-end, despite the fact that a description of the murder victim's car had been circulated. Hulten was arrested on October 10th as he climbed into the car, parked in Fulham Palace Road, Hammersmith; later that day his accomplice was arrested, chiefly as a result of an indiscreet remark to a policeman acquaintance, who had remarked about her pale appearance and received the reply, 'If you had seen someone do what I have seen done you wouldn't be able to sleep at night'. The two were charged with the murder of Heath, appearing at the Old Bailey before Mr Justice Charles on January 16th, 1945, the trial lasting six days. Both found guilty and sentenced to death, Hulten was subsequently hanged, but Jones reprieved; she was released in May 1954.

HUME, Brian Donald
Born 1919, illegitimate son of a schoolmistress, murdered Stanley Setty, October 1949, Arthur Maag, January 1959.

Spending his earliest years in a West Country institution, Hume was afterwards to claim that this experience gave him a 'chip on the shoulder'. Restored to but unloved by his mother at the age of 8 (she preferred to be known as his aunt), he left home at 14 and hitch-hiked to London where he became an apprentice

electrician, later embarking on a career of petty crime. Joining
the RAF on the outbreak of war in 1939, he contracted meningitis in 1940; found unfit for flying duties, he was posted to the
ground staff, being invalided from the service in 1941. Making a
remunerative living from various illegal rackets (i.e. selling
surgical spirit as 'Old English Gin') he also posed as Flying
Officer Don Hume after buying an RAF uniform for £5, and
acquired hundreds of pounds by cashing false cheques at RAF
stations throughout the country, as a result being sent to
Feltham Borstal. From 1942 he ran several successful enterprises, patenting among other things, the 'Little Atom Electric
Toaster'; setbacks occurred, and by 1948 Hume, now living
with his wife Cynthia at a seven-room two-storey maisonette in
Finchley Road, Golders Green, found himself short of money.
He met Stanley Setty, 46-year-old car dealer; the two formed a
money making if not friendly association, Hume selling cars
illegally acquired by Setty. Setty was a Jew, born Sulman Seti in
Baghdad, who had moved with his parents to England in 1907;
his business ventures, indulged from an early age, had not always
been successful (in 1928, after pleading guilty on twenty-three
counts to offences under the Debtors and Bankruptcy Acts he
served fifteen months' imprisonment) but by 1949 he was living
in sumptuous style with his sister and brother-in-law at a flat in
Maitland Court, Lancaster Gate. On the night of October 4th,
1949, Hume returned, after a drinking bout, to his Golders
Green maisonette; his wife and baby were out, but Setty was in
the drawing-room. There was a quarrel, chiefly concerning
Setty's rough treatment, a few days before, of Hume's mongrel
dog Tony. Hume attacked Setty with a German SS dagger: 'I
was wielding the dagger' he wrote in his subsequent confession
'just like our Stone Age ancestors did 20,000 years ago.' Setty
died from multiple stab wounds: 'I watched the life run from
him like water down a drain.' Hume deposited the body in the
coal-cupboard, then, after retrieving the car key from his
victim's jacket pocket, drove Setty's Citröen round to its usual
lock-up in Cambridge Terrace Mews. The next day, October
5th, he dismembered Setty's body in the breakfast-room with a
hacksaw, making three separate parcels of the legs, head, and
torso; he salvaged £100 from a bloodied £1,000 bundle, the
proceeds from a Setty car deal of the previous day. Taking care
to avoid both his wife and Mrs Ethel Stride the once-weekly
cleaner (due to appear at 2.30 pm) he deposited the head and
legs in a hired Singer car and drove to Elstree private airport,

where he had earlier booked a plane, an Auster, used before by Hume in smuggling ventures. Explaining that he intended going to Southend, Hume instead made for the English Channel, where he threw out the weighted pieces of body, together with the SS knife and the hacksaw and lino knife used in the dismembering. Forced to make a landing at Southend because of lack of petrol and bad weather, Hume hired a cab to take him back to London, paying the driver with one of his victim's £5 notes. The next-day he called in a decorator to paint out the bloodstains on the sitting-room floor, enlisting the man's help in carrying Setty's felt-wrapped torso to the car. ('It was so heavy that it slid and bumped down the stairs and made peculiar squishy gurgling noises.') Accompanied this time by his dog, and telling an inquirer at the airport that he was transporting fish, Hume again made for the Channel; the lead weights attached to the torso this time became dislodged, and the body floated, finally being washed up on to the Essex mudflats near Burnham-on-Crouch. It was found by Mr Sidney Tiffin, a local farmworker hunting wildfowl (who was able to claim the £1,000 offered by Setty's family for information leading to the car dealer's whereabouts), and identifiable through the fingerprints. One of the £5 notes used in Setty's last business transaction appeared in circulation, and was traced to a Southend car hire firm, one of whose drivers recalled driving a man from the airport at Southend to London; in this way Hume's journeying with bulky packages came to light, as did his association with Stanley Setty. A cloakroom ticket was found concealed at his maisonette which, when presented at nearby Golders Green Underground Station, led to the discovery, in the Left Luggage office, of the heavily bloodstained cabin trunk that had temporarily (and ineffectually, according to Hume) held the torso of Setty. Hume, taken into custody on October 27th, at first protested complete innocence, then invented a story concerning three hoodlums Mac, Greeny, and The Boy, who had persuaded him by means of money and menaces ('one of the men toyed with a gun as he spoke') to dispose of three parcels ('they could have contained "hot" printing plates for forged petrol coupons for all I knew'). He was sent for trial at Bow Street Magistrates Court on November 26th on the charge of murdering Stanley Setty. Pleading not guilty, Hume's trial began at the Old Bailey on January 18th, 1950, before Mr Justice Lewis (later, through illness, being replaced by Mr Justice Sellers); Mr Christmas Humphreys led for the Crown and Mr R. F. Levy, KC, for the

Defence. Various Crown witnesses spoke of events on October 5th. Mrs Stride, the cleaner, told how Hume had asked her to go out and buy another floorcloth as he had spoilt one by rubbing it on a stained carpet; she had neither seen nor heard anything unusual 'like the sawing up of bones'. Mrs Linda Hearnden, the manageress of a North London dyeing and cleaning firm, told how Hume had brought in a badly stained light-green carpet, with the request that it be dyed a darker shade. A Midland Bank accountant told how Hume had paid in £90, so clearing an overdraft of £78. A mechanic at a Golders Green garage told how Hume had come in about lunch-time and asked for a carving knife to be sharpened. An aircraft fitter at Elstree told how Hume had, on October 5th, placed two parcels in a plane, and Mr Joseph Staddon, an interior decorator, told how on October 6th he had helped Hume carry a parcel down the stairs of Hume's maisonette: 'It was about 2 feet 6 inches long ... very heavy. I could not lift it myself.' Mr Sidney Tiffin testified on the finding of the Setty torso on October 21st: 'I tied it to a stake which I drove into the mud, and went straight to the police.'

Hume persisted in his story of the three men who had utilized his flying ability to dispose of a corpse: questioned by Mr Humphreys about the signs of blood in the hall and sitting-room, Hume expressed bewilderment, saying it might have been caused by a visiting child.

Mr Humphreys: I suggest that you stabbed Setty in the sitting-room and that he died in the dining-room. . . .
Hume: Now you're romancing!
Mr Humphreys: And that you cut him up that night. . . .
Hume: Absolute boloney!

The jury failed to agree on a verdict; another jury was sworn and directed by the judge to return a verdict of not guilty on the murder charge. Facing a further indictment of being an accessory after the fact, Hume pleaded guilty and was sentenced to twelve years' imprisonment. Released on February 1st, 1958, after a period in Dartmoor (where, because of his knowledge in electronics he was affectionately nicknamed 'The Fuse' by his fellow-convicts), Hume was approached by the *Sunday Pictorial* and in May, under his new deed-poll name of Donald Brown, stayed at a Westcliff-on-Sea hotel, where he wrote out a series of articles entitled Confession, in which he admitted the killing of

Stanley Setty and the non-existence of Mac, Greeny, and The Boy. On May 25th, 1958, under the alias of John Stephen Bird (his plump, boyish features disguised by a centre parting, horn-rimmed spectacles, and moustache), Hume flew to Zürich, Switzerland, where he posed as a Canadian test-pilot, spending much of the £2,000 earned by his newspaper articles. For a period he visited America, where, his money running out, he first thought of robbing a bank. Returning at the end of June to Switzerland, he resolved to rob a London bank, deciding that the Midland Bank in Boston Manor Road, Brentford, would be his objective. At twelve noon on Saturday August 2nd, 1958, after taking two 'pep' pills and half a pint of bitter at the Globe public house in Brentford, he entered this bank brandishing a revolver and demanding money. He shot at and wounded a cashier, Mr Frank Lewis, and stole about £1,500, returning to Zürich the following day, where he continued to pay court to a Swiss girl, Trudi Sommer (his wife Cynthia having divorced him during his prison term). On November 12th he again raided the Brentford bank, critically shooting the branch manager and securing about £300 before racing out and catching a train at Kew Bridge Station for Waterloo, where he donned spectacles and became Canadian Mr Bird, journeying back to Zürich. A raincoat left on the train name-taped with one of Hume's known aliases, coupled with the bank staff's description of the persistent raider, convinced police that Hume was the Brentford raider. On January 30th, 1959, after breakfasting at the English church in Zürich on Communion bread and wine, 'Johnny Bird' went to the Gewerbe Bank, armed with a gun concealed in a cardboard box; he shot a cashier and managed to steal some loose coins before the alarm bell was set in motion. Running out of the bank, pursued by staff and passers-by, he shot at and killed 50-year-old taxi-driver, Arthur Maag, who threatened his escape; finally captured by the police, he pretended to be a Pole, an unsuccessful deception when a Polish interpreter was summoned. A Zürich psychiatrist, Dr Guggen-buhl-Craig, examined Hume in prison and pronounced him sane at the time of the Zürich bank robbery. While awaiting trial on the charge of murdering Maag, Hume wrote a sixty-thousand-word novel entitled *The Dead Stay Dumb*, a tale concerning gangsters and their 'molls'. Tried at Winterthur after being eight months in custody, he was found guilty as charged, and sentenced to hard labour for life.

J

JACCOUD, Pierre
Geneva's senior lawyer, chief of the Geneva Radical party, head of the Bar Association (his clients including Aly Khan and Sacha Guitry), tried in March 1960 for the murder of 68-year-old Charles Zumbach.

On May 1st, 1958, Zumbach was shot and stabbed in his home, the killer being interrupted by the return of Madame Zumbach (shot and injured), who described the assailant as being tall and dark. A month later (during which time he had journeyed to Stockholm to have his hair bleached) Maître Jaccoud was arrested on the charge of murdering Zumbach. Jaccoud's one-time mistress had formed a liaison with a young radio technician, André Zumbach; jealous, Jaccoud had sent his rival a series of hysterical anonymous letters. Guessing the writer's identity, André Zumbach threatened Jaccoud with exposure; intimidated and terrified by Zumbach's intention, Jaccoud determined to kill Zumbach and regain his letters. Going to Zumbach's house, he was surprised by Zumbach senior, whom he killed in a fit of panic. During police investigations five hundred letters (written over a period of ten years) from Jaccoud to his mistress were found; a Moroccan dagger bearing traces of blood and liver cells was at Jaccoud's home, as was an English raincoat, a missing button of which had been discovered at the scene of the murder.

Convicted of the crime, Jaccoud was sentenced to seven years' imprisonment, the sentence being eventually reduced to three years.

JACK THE RIPPER

In view of our complete ignorance of the identity of Jack the Ripper, it is strange that the case has continued to exercise such fascination for over half a century. Many people suppose that the Ripper crimes took place over many years and that his victims ran into dozens; whereas, in actual fact, the murders took place over a few months in 1888 and the victims were certainly not more than seven in number – quite possibly only four. The present writer has read an article in a spiritualist newspaper called *Two Worlds*, in which it is alleged that a medium, Mr Lees, helped to catch the Ripper; the article speaks

345

of the murders as extending over several years and running into hundreds! Similarly, an article in the surrealist magazine of the 1920's, *Minotaur*,[1] by Maurice Heine, speaks casually of 'the eleventh victim', and includes a dubious photograph of the 'eleventh victim'.

The many theories about the Ripper will be examined at the end of this article. The facts, briefly, are these: between August 31st, 1888, and November 8th, 1888, five murders took place within an area of half a mile in Whitechapel in the East End of London. All the women were mutilated with a knife and on several occasions some of the internal organs were taken away. After November 8th the murders ceased abruptly.

During the early part of 1888 there were two murders of women in Whitechapel that may possibly have been the work of the Ripper. The first was of an unfortunate woman named Emma Elizabeth Smith, aged 45, who was returning home in the early hours of the day following Easter Monday (April 3rd) when she was attacked. Twenty-four hours later she died in hospital of peritonitis, some sharp instrument like a spike having penetrated her abdomen. She claimed she was attacked by four men in Osborn Street at about four in the morning as she was returning home from a public house; they took her money (only a few coppers) and mistreated her. Her account of the four men seems circumstantial enough; she described one of them as being only 19.

The murder which is often regarded as the Ripper's first crime took place in Gunthorpe Street (then known as 'George Yard') in the early hours of the day following Bank Holiday Monday, August 7th. A prostitute named Martha Turner (or Tabram) was picked up by a soldier on Bank Holiday night and seen in The Angel and Crown drinking with him. Several hours later (at about 5 am) her body was found on the first landing of George Yard Buildings. She had been stabbed thirty-nine times; the murderer had used two weapons, one a bayonet or long-bladed knife, the other some kind of surgical instrument. He was also ambidextrous. The soldier who had been seen with her was traced, but had an alibi; all the soldiers in the Tower were paraded, but no arrest was made. It is impossible to state with any certainty whether this was the Ripper's first crime in

[1] Which can be examined, on application, at the Victoria and Albert Museum. The article is an imaginary dialogue between De Sade and Jack the Ripper.

Whitechapel, but most writers on the case are inclined to believe that it is the work of the Ripper. The present writer is inclined to doubt it.

At 2.30 am on Friday, August 31st, a woman friend saw a prostitute named Mary Anne Nicholls (known as 'Polly') at the corner of Osborn Street; she admitted to having had 'no luck'. Three-quarters of an hour later, her body was found by a carter named Cross on Bucks Row (now called Durward Street), lying in the entrance to the Old Stable Yard at the west end of the street. In the mortuary of the Old Montague Street Workhouse it was discovered that she had been disembowelled. Death was due to severing of the windpipe. She was identified by her husband, a printer's machinist, from whom she had been separated for seven years. She was 42 years of age, and known as a habitual drunk. When her husband saw the body, he was heard to say, 'I forgive you for everything now I see you like this.' It was revealed that she had been staying at a doss-house in Thrawl Street, where a bed could be had for fourpence a night. On the previous evening she had been turned away from the doss-house because she had no money. She commented, 'Don't worry, I'll soon get the money. Look what a fine bonnet I've got.'

A bruise on her face indicated that the murderer clamped his hand over her mouth before cutting her throat. A woman sleeping in a bedroom only a few yards from the murder heard no sound.

The next murder took place on September 8th. Annie Chapman, aged 47, was turned away from a lodging house in Dorset Street, having no money to pay for a bed. It seems probable that the murderer accosted Chapman outside the yard where the murder took place – at 29 Hanbury Street. She accompanied him down a passageway at the side of the house some time after 5 am. The body was found shortly after 6 am. The head had been almost severed from the body, and then tied in place with a handkerchief. The body was cut open, as in the case of Mary Nicholls, and the kidney and the ovaries had been removed. Two front teeth were missing (repeating a curious feature of the Nicholls murder) and two brass rings and some coppers were laid at her feet. In another corner of the yard was the torn corner of a bloodstained envelope, containing the crest of the Sussex Regiment. Under a tap was a leather apron. It seems possible that these last two items were intended to mislead the police. A soldier had been suspected in the Tabram case, and Whitechapel gossip named a man called 'Leather Apron' as the murderer. (He was actually a Polish Jew named Pizer, a shoe-maker, who was arrested and then released.) Again the murderer had carried out the crime with extreme coolness and had made no sound. There were sixteen people living at 29 Hanbury Street and a scream would have quickly brought help to the victim.

On September 28th a letter was sent to the Central News Agency signed 'Jack the Ripper' and theatening more murders. 'I am down on whores and shant quit ripping them till I do get buckled.' Whether or not it was by a practical joker, the name caught the public imagination when it first appeared in the newspapers (after September 30th).

The murders caused a universal panic. Meetings were held in the streets, criticizing the police and the Home Secretary. Bloodhounds were suggested, but they promptly lost themselves in Tooting. The newspapers of the time gave extremely full reports of the murders and inquests, and were tireless in offering theories.

A description of the murderer offered by someone who saw Annie Chapman talking to a man outside 29 Hanbury Street included a large moustache and a 'foreign appearance'.

On the morning of September 30th two murders were committed in Whitechapel. The first was of a Swedish woman called Elizabeth Stride. A hawker named Louis Deimschutz drove his horse and cart into the back-yard of the International Workers Educational Club in Berner Street. (A council school now stands on the site.) He saw a woman's body on the ground and rushed into the club to give the alarm. The woman's throat had been cut and she had been killed very recently – so recently that it is possible that 'Jack the Ripper' was interrupted and made his escape as Deimschutz entered the club. This was at 1 am.

At this time a 43-year-old prostitute named Catherine Eddowes was released from Bishopsgate Police Station, where she had been in charge for drunkenness. She was picked up by the Ripper and taken into a narrow alleyway that extends between Mitre Square and Duke Street, known as Church Passage (now St James' Passage). Police Constable Watkins passed through the passage on his beat at one-thirty. A quarter of an hour later he again passed through the square, and found the body of Catherine Eddowes in the corner of the square near Church Passage. Her face had been badly mutilated – perhaps to delay identification – and the body cut open in the usual way;

348

the left kidney and entrails had been removed and taken away. It was some time before she was identified, and in the meantime, one of the newspapers published a report that she was thought to be a certain 'Mary Anne Kelly'. This is a remarkable co-incidence, since the name of the final victim was Mary Jeanette Kelly.

A householder who lived in Berner Street (off the Commercial Road and the farthest afield of the Ripper's murders) testified that she saw a young man carrying a shiny black bag away from the scene of the crime. (Men carrying black bags were some-times attacked in the street in Whitechapel at this time, and the Ripper murders made this type of bag go quite conclusively out of fashion.)

After the murder the Central News Agency received another letter signed 'Jack the Ripper', regretting that he had been in-terrupted with his victims, and had not been able to send the ears to the police. (There had been an attempt to cut off the ear of Catherine Eddowes.) He also mentioned that 'number one squealed a bit', which is borne out by a witness in Berner Street who heard the cry. The letter was posted only a few hours after the murders, and was written in red ink.

The murders had caused unprecedented excitement, and bands of vigilantes patrolled the streets of Whitechapel at night. But as weeks passed without further crimes, the panic died down. (One theory suggests that the Ripper was incarcerated in a mental home during these weeks.) On November 9th the last of the murders took place at a house in Millers Court, which ran off Dorset Street (now Duval Street), probably between Dorset Street and White Row to the south. Mary Jeanette Kelly was younger than the other victims, but of the same class. She was 24. On the morning of November 9th at ten-forty-five a man knocked on the door of Mary Kelly to collect the rent. Getting no reply, he peered in at the broken window. What remained of Mary Kelly lay on the bed. The head had been almost severed from the body; the heart had been placed on the pillow. The entrails had been draped over a picture frame. The murderer had apparently worked by the light of a pile of rags, the ashes of which were burnt in the grate. Neighbours testified to hearing a cry of 'Murder' at about 3.30 am. The inquest revealed that no parts of the body had been taken away this time.

The panic caused by the murder led to the resignation of Sir Charles Warren, the unpopular Chief of Police.

There were three other crimes that some writers on the case

believe may have been committed by the Ripper. In June 1889, parts of a female body were found in the Thames. The head was not found, but a scar on the wrists enabled the police to identify the victim as Elizabeth Jackson, a prostitute who lived in a lodging house in Turks Row, Chelsea.

On July 17th the body of Alice McKenzie, known as 'Clay Pipe Alice', was found in Castle Alley, Whitechapel; her throat was cut and there were gashes across her abdomen. In his introduction to *The Trial of George Chapman*, H. L. Adam quotes the McKenzie case as one of the Ripper murders.[1]

Finally, on February 13th, 1891, the body of Frances Coles, a prostitute of about 25, was found under a railway arch at Swallow Gardens in Whitechapel; her throat had been cut and there were injuries to her abdomen. She was still alive when found, but died soon afterwards.

This last case has a curious pendant. Many years ago an article appeared in *Tit Bits* about General Booth, the founder of the Salvation Army, in which it was mentioned that Booth was certain that his secretary in 1891 was Jack the Ripper. The secretary, a young man, had been troubled by 'dreams of blood', and one day had told Booth, 'Carrotty Nell will be the next to go'. Carrotty Nell was the nickname of Frances Coles. After the murder of February 13th the secretary disappeared and was not seen again by Booth. It hardly seems likely that the secretary was Jack the Ripper, although he might well have been the murderer of Carrotty Nell; it is well known that the most appalling murder cases seem to provoke imitators. (See Elizabeth Smart, the Black Dahlia case, as a typical example.)

There have been many theories about the identity of Jack the Ripper, but unfortunately none of them is verifiable at this date. Leonard Matters, MP, suggested that the Ripper was a certain 'Doctor Stanley', a Harley Street surgeon whose only son died of syphilis contracted from Mary Kelly. He sought out Mary Kelly, killing the woman from whom he inquired, to prevent her being warned. 'Doctor Stanley' died many years later in Buenos Aires, and confessed his crime on his death-bed to a former pupil.

Although Matters offers all this as 'fact' he offers no evidence of any kind, and it seems almost certain that it is pure fiction.

A more ingenious theory was offered by a correspondent of the present writer. Neill Cream, the poisoner, who is reputed to

[1] As does William Roughead in the introduction to *The Trial of J. W. Laurie*.

have said on the gallows, 'I am Jack the . . .' before the trap fell, was in prison at Joliet in Canada in 1888, returning to England in 1891. At a certain point in his career, Cream was charged with bigamy; he claimed that he was in prison in Sydney, Australia, at the time. The governor of Sydney prison confirmed that a man of Cream's description had been in jail, and Cream was released.[1] But Cream was never in Australia. Is it possible that Cream had a double whom he had (perhaps) met in prison, and with whom he made an arrangement that they should alibi one another when necessary? Possibly, then, Cream's double was Jack the Ripper, and Cream was keeping to his part of the bargain – trying to provide his double with a final alibi – on the scaffold. The theory is amusing and ingenious, but has the disadvantage of being as unprovable as the Dr Stanley theory.

Equally ingenious is the theory of a man who signs his book *William Stewart, Artist*, who believed that Jack the Ripper was a woman. Stewart argues from a piece of evidence that was suppressed at the inquest – that Mary Kelly, the last victim, was pregnant. A pile of ashes was found in the grate at Millers Court, and Stewart surmises that these were the bloodstained clothes of 'Jill the Ripper'. The murderess then dressed herself in the spare clothes of her victim and walked out. Unfortunately for this theory, it is almost certain that Mary Kelly had no 'spare clothes', having pawned them all.

The most authoritative book written to date on the murders is *The Identity of Jack the Ripper* by Donald McCormick. After describing the murders with a great deal of attention to detail, Mr McCormick then offers his own theory, which is to the effect that the Ripper was a Russian named Pedachenko. William LeQueux, in his book *Things I Know*, stated that he had seen a manuscript called *Great Russian Criminals*, written by Rasputin and found in the cellar of his house after his death. In his manuscript, Rasputin claimed that Jack the Ripper was a Russian named Pedachenko, a doctor who worked in a maternity hospital at Tver. He was known to have homicidal tendencies, and was sent to England by the Tsarist police with the idea of embarrassing the British police. According to the 'Rasputin manuscript', he lived in Walworth and came into Whitechapel at night; he was aided in his murders by a friend named Levitski and a tailoress named Winberg. Mr McCormick claims to have seen an issue of the *Ochrana Gazette*, the journal of the Russian

[1] This story can be found in *The Life of Marshall Hall*, by Edward Marjoribanks.

secret police, which mentions Pedachenko's death (he is said to have died in an asylum after murdering another woman in St Petersburg in 1891), and states that he murdered five women in the East End in 1888. Mr McCormick produces more evidence to support his view than most of the theorists, but nothing quite conclusive. Among other things, he connects Pedachenko (or Konovalov – his real name) with George Chapman, the Polish barber, executed for poisoning his 'wives' in 1903; Chapman, curiously enough, had a barber's shop in the basement of George Yard Buildings at the time of the Tabram murder on August Bank Holiday.

There have been innumerable rumours about Jack the Ripper, one of which declares that he was the son of an aristocratic family who was caught and incarcerated in a private mental home near Ascot. Walter Sickert, the painter, is said to have taken a room in the East End, and to have been told by the landlady that she suspected her previous tenant of being Jack the Ripper; he had been an aristocratic young medical student who seemed to be in hiding from his family, and was subject to brainstorms. His parents had finally located him and had taken him to a mental home at Ascot. Sickert's landlady produced no evidence for her belief that the student was the murderer, only an 'intuition'.

Another frequently repeated story which has some connexion with the above is that the medium, Lees, helped to catch Jack the Ripper. In its most popular version, this story states that Lees had several 'visions' of the murders before they happened, and that one day, sitting on a bus travelling along the Bayswater Road, he saw a man he immediately knew to be 'Jack the Ripper' sitting opposite him. Lees followed the man to a house near Hyde Park, and discovered that it was owned by a wealthy physician. The matter was reported to the police, the wife of the physician was questioned, and admitted that she had her suspicions. The doctor was followed on one of his nocturnal rambles, arrested, and shut up in a private mental home to avoid scandal.

The weakness of the story lies in the certainty that the police would have taken pleasure in giving the widest publicity to the capture of Jack the Ripper. Perhaps it is to account for this discrepancy in the theory that the name of Queen Victoria is frequently brought into it. It is claimed that Mr Lees was twice interviewed by the Queen, who was greatly concerned about the Whitechapel murders. The story connected with Lees usually goes on to add either (a) that the doctor was the Queen's physician, or (b) that Jack the Ripper was some relative of the Royal Family.

There is, of course, no more evidence for this theory than for any other. But on the surface evidence, the two most plausible theories seem to be (a) that the Ripper was a young man – a medical student, perhaps, and (b) that he was a doctor of some kind, a 'toff' (as one witness described him) who wore a dark moustache and a watch-chain.

He was almost certainly a sadist of the same kind as Peter Kürten, and it seems likely that the abrupt termination of the murders may have been due either to his incarceration in a mental home or to his death. If Kürten had remained uncaught, the 'monster of Düsseldorf' might today exercise the same unhealthy fascination as 'Jack the Ripper' over the minds of students of crime. The Germans in particular seem to have found the Ripper a symbolic figure. (See, for example, Berg's *Lulu*.)

JACOBY, Henry
Youth of 18, executed for the murder of Lady White in 1922.

Jacoby, aged 18, was a pantry boy in the Spencer Hotel, Portman Street, London; he had been there for just three weeks, when, in the early hours of March 14th 1922, he thought he heard the whispering of men outside the basement where he slept. He called the night porter, and they made a search together, finding nothing. Back in bed – it was now about two in the morning – he began to daydream about wealth. And he was here, in a hotel full of rich people. . . . He finally decided to steal something from one of the rooms. In case he was interrupted, he took a hammer out of a tool bag some workmen had left in the basement. He tried the door of one room upstairs and found it locked. Another door – that of Lady White, 60-year-old widow of Sir Edward White, former chairman of the LCC – opened with a creak, and he went in and shone a torch around. As it fell on the sleeper in the second bed (it was a room with two single beds, one of them empty, of course) she woke up and screamed. Jacoby hit her several times with the hammer. Then, terrified with what he had done, he fled, washed the handle of the hammer and returned it to the tool bag, and went to bed. The body was discovered the next morning, and for several days, the police were baffled. Finally, Jacoby confessed – of his own accord – and was arrested. He was tried at the Old Bailey before Mr Justice McCardie on April 28th, 1922, Mr Percival Clarke prosecuting, and Mr Lucian defending. He was found guilty and sentenced to death, but there was considerable agitation for a reprieve. His ultimate execution caused much rancour, especially as Ronald True was reprieved at this time; people said that riches had procured favour. Jacoby met his end bravely. It is, in many ways, a pathetic case. Even an agitation to give him a Christian burial failed, and he is buried in Pentonville Prison under an inscription on the wall: H. J. 382.

JAMES, ROBERT (Rattlesnake Murderer)

Thirty-nine-year-old barber, charged with the murder of his wife in 1935. When Mary James (his fifth wife) was found dead in the lilypond at the James bungalow (named la Crescenta) near Los Angeles, it was thought she had committed suicide. The grief-stricken husband said so, and not until the police received an anonymous letter eight months later was the widower's anguish suspect. The letter (found afterwards to be from a woman friend of James with whom he had been boastfully indiscreet) claimed an immoral relationsip between James and his niece (a criminal offence in America) and alleged that Mary James had been deliberately killed. James was quickly brought to trial on an immoral conduct charge, found guilty and imprisoned. The body of his wife was exhumed, and the cause of death confirmed as drowning; but several punctures on the left foot were noticed and upon closer examination the leg was found to contain rattlesnake venom. Investigations into James' past revealed that his third wife had drowned in her bath, James collecting £5,000 insurance money. Police also learnt of a friend of James, 'Chuck' Hope, who had been seen frequently at la Crescenta around the time of the tragedy. Hope was proprietor of an eating house at Hermosa beach, and two G-men went to interview him, deciding that bluff was their best plan. Accordingly, when asked for their order, they replied 'Rattlesnakes', to the obvious consternation of 'Chuck'. They immediately inquired if he knew barber James, and soon the unhappy Hope was escorted to la Crescenta where his nerve broke; he told detectives the whole story, while seated glumly on the closed closet seat in the bathroom.

Soon after James' fifth marriage he had asked Hope to get him a couple of rattlesnakes; a friend of his wanted to kill his wife, he said, and 'Chuck' would receive a hundred dollars if he secured a 'hot' pair. The obliging Hope (he said afterwards that James had 'hypnotized' him) went the round of local rattlesnake vendors, but his purchases were puny specimens; James, getting progressively furious, would test their lethal efficacy on hordes of rabbits and chickens who seemed to thrive on rattlesnake bites. Eventually James told Hope to go to Snake Joe in Pasadena, a more reputable snake dealer, and soon two livelier snakes in a wooden box were delivered by 'Chuck' to la Crescenta. James tried them out on some chickens, who died. Delighted, he told Hope his real intention, saying he needed Hope's help to finish the job. ('I was helpless and couldn't resist the look in his eyes,' said 'Chuck'.) Mary James was placed, conscious, across the kitchen table, tied down with a clothes line and adhesive tape stretched across her mouth and eyes – under the impression, it was said, that she was to undergo an abortion. James then forced his wife's left foot into the box of snakes ('I saw at least one of them stick its fangs into her,' said 'Chuck') and then retired to the garage with Hope to eat sandwiches and drink rye. Still alive, however, upon their return, Mary James was dragged by her husband to the bathroom, where he drowned her in the bathtub.

Robert James, confronted in prison with this story, accused Hope of devising the whole scheme, but complicity between the two was proved, and they were handcuffed together when they heard the decision of the court of Los Angeles: sentence of death for James and life imprisonment for Hope.

JAPANESE WAR CRIMES

Though lacking the technological implementation of the Germans that resulted in the extermination of millions of human beings, the Japanese war crimes were unsurpassed in sheer horror, brutality, ferocity, and blood carnage. The path of the invading Japanese Army was one of humiliation, degradation, sadism, wholesale massacre, refined individual torture, rape, mutilation, and exploitation regardless of age or sex, POW or civilian. As with the Germans, there is an almost total absence of remorse, pity, or individual responsibility, and the note struck by the following diary extracts is a very rare one. 'I have already killed well over a hundred guerrillas. The innocence I possessed at the time of leaving the homeland has long since disappeared. Now I am a hardened sinner and my sword is always stained with blood. Although it is for my country's sake, it is sheer brutality. May God forgive us. May my mother forgive me.' A Petty Officer having difficulty in carrying out his part of a mass execution of prisoners on board ship recalls, 'Then, realizing that I was acting on orders from the Emperor of Japan, I closed my eyes, raised my sword and brought it down "whang" — His head was severed from his body. I had carried out Captain Saito's orders.'

As with the Germans, these war crimes were backed by a certain, and indeed very similar, ideology, and were quite purposefully planned by those at the top. During the 30's the Army gained totalitarian control of the nation. Its leaders were convinced of, and preparing for, Japan's divine mission to rule the world based on a 'national blood solidarity', focused on the Emperor. As with the Germans, preparations for a vast aggressive war in the East took place behind various diplomatic smoke-screens, hypocrisy, and ruthless treachery.

Methods used during the war in China which dragged on throughout the 30's were a foretaste of things to come. Said the Prime Minister in this connexion, 'As for those who fail to understand our intentions' (i.e. total domination), 'we have no other alternative but to exterminate them.' The climax was reached with the 'Rape of Nanking' in 1937. Within three days of its occupation by Japanese troops, 12,000 men, women, and children had been slaughtered. Rape was the order of the day. The gutters streamed with blood and the streets were strewn with mutilated corpses. Twenty thousand men were marched outside the city walls, machine-gunned and bayoneted. Another 30,000 who surrendered were lined up on the Yangtse and machine-gunned. The German Embassy actually characterized the Army as 'bestial'. Within six weeks 200,000 people were murdered, apart from mass looting and the firing of half the city. In the midst of it all General Matsui made his triumphal entry. At the War Crimes Trial his defence pleaded that illness prevented him from stopping this bestiality. He was sentenced to hang. Throughout the rest of the campaign Chinese prisoners were generally used for bayonet practice, machine-gun practice, and buried alive. Army officials only objected to letters and photographs sent home about the atrocities, not at all to the atrocities themselves. At Geneva the Japanese declared that this was no war in a 'legal' sense. The Chinese were simply bandits and the whole affair a 'punitive expedition'.

Regarding their treatment of POWs during the 1939–45 war,

the Japanese were still signatories to the Hague Convention of 1907, which quite unambiguously lays down a minimum of human decency to which such captured troops are entitled. Japanese Bushido principles consider surrender the depth of shame, and death for the Emperor the height of glory. Similarly, their captives who had surrendered and not died fighting deserved no respect, in fact, only disgust. Such deep-seated national-religious currents obviously proved far stronger than the Hague Convention, just as Germany's paganism proved far stronger than its Christianity, but of course, it cannot be used to justify a policy of savagery and brutality committed on defenceless, sick, starving, harried, living skeletons. Sounding exactly like Eicke's original concentration camp aims and methods, Tojo writes of 'the mistaken idea of humanitarianism ... towards prisoners of war'.

A common method of dealing with captured Allied aircrews was execution by the sword, demonstrated by the instructor in swordsmanship, after which the other officers tried their hand ' "It was difficult to cut today," one of them said. "In Hokiji's demonstration the neck was cut perfectly," said another.' At the trial of an officer in charge of such an action, he admitted everything and finally pleaded, 'It is your petitioner's humble view that a spirit of love of humanity as taught to us by Jesus Christ would give a deep, more lasting, stronger, and better influence upon the history of mankind than threats of rigorous and severe punishment.' Other airmen, in conformation with orders from the Army commander, were publicly paraded, insulted, and beaten by the townspeople, then covered with petrol and burned to death. Of another such mass execution, where the decapitated bodies were often used for bayonet practice, a soldier wrote, 'All is over. The head is dead white like a doll's. The savageness which I felt only a little while ago is gone and now I feel nothing but the true compassion of Japanese Bushido .... A senior corporal laughs loudly, "Well, he will enter into Nirvana now".' That *loud laugh* is most revealing and one wonders too about that 'true compassion'.

To construct the Burma–Siam railway the lives of 42,000 coolies and 16,000 POWs were sacrificed. The hellish conditions are reminiscent of Auschwitz and Belsen in their last stages. Thousands of living skeletons, putrefying with rampant tropical diseases and ulcers that stripped the flesh from knee to ankle, almost naked, sheltered from the monsoon rains by a layer of banana leaves and nothing else, were made to work or starve.

Work meant twelve to twenty hours every day. They had to salute every Japanese soldier at all times. The coolies, above all, were subject to terrible sadism and perverted tortures. At their trial those concerned spoke touchingly of how the 'Japanese troops participated in the joys and sorrows of the POWs and native labourers'.

For the Japanese absolutely nothing commanded any human respect or sanctity, neither hospital, school, nor church. Neither sick nor young. At the Alexandria Hospital in Singapore, every patient, nurse, doctor, and surgeon in the midst of an operation was bayoneted or raped and beheaded. This, in fact, was their normal procedure with hospitals. Ambulance convoys of wounded soldiers were covered with petrol and burnt to death.

Planned massacres of POWs in large groups were common. Declared one order, 'Whether they are destroyed individually or in groups – with mass bombing, gas, poison, drowning, decapitation – the object is to annihilate them all and leave no trace.' On the rotten transport hulks, thousands of such men were battened down for days without food or drink, weak with dysentery and diarrhoea. They died of suffocation and went insane. The mad screamed, while urine and even blood was drawn to slake thirst in a temperature of well over a hundred degrees. 'You are bred like rats and so can stay like rats', was the declared attitude. Sometimes they were left exposed on deck in the tropical sun, dying of thirst, while their guards bathed in drinking water. They arrived at their working destinations 'half-starved, half-demented wrecks of humanity, diseased and crawling with vermin'. On the death marches beatings and brutality were the norm. The Americans who surrendered at Bataan were given no food for the first five days of their march and were constantly bayoneted and kicked to death.

For the POW death was too often a merciful release. Kickings, beatings, and tortures went on ceaselessly. Camp Commandant Kurishima jokingly suggested that the bodies of dead prisoners be made into beefsteak in the kitchen. Yet not so jokingly, for in certain places it was actually done. This Kurishima was described by his victims as a split personality. 'An untamed and brutal savage – and in a much lesser degree a placid and harmless human being, possessing intelligence, strength of personality, and even generosity.' A whole gamut of tortures was practised for trivial offences, from the water torture to various forms of crucifixion. The infliction of humiliation was a keen enjoyment. At Kwarenko camp General Percival, among several

358

high-ranking officers, was severely beaten for a speck of dirt discovered under his finger-nail. At Macassar when food was found in the hospital dustbin, many of the staff, orderlies, and doctors were beaten senseless and given the water treatment. At Soengei Geru, in a barbed-wire cage six feet by four, erected on top of an ants' nest, nine men were confined, unable to move and compelled to stand to attention. Escapers from this camp were simply beheaded. Conditions in civilian internment camps were no different. Disease, exploitation, and living death in tens of thousands by the Knights of Bushido.

Evidence was given of vivisection on living victims. Of prisoners being dissected by doctors, and students, and having heart and liver removed while alive. A captured Japanese order reveals details regulating the obtaining, and eating, of the flesh of an American airman. An accused Japanese officer described how his general was annoyed at an evening party over the shortage of meat, and suggested getting some more by means of the impending execution of an American pilot. The 'meat' arrived promptly, and was duly cooked but apparently nobody 'relished the taste'. This was not an isolated incident. At another officer's party at which similar 'meat' was devoured, the admiral asked a major for a little liver from the next pending execution. There were many cases of Australian, American, and Japanese dead being cut up and eaten. The only counterorder issued was that which forbade the eating of their own dead. Otherwise they generally practised cannibalism from choice and obviously from a very atavistic and ritualistic compulsion.

Wholesale civilian massacres occurred throughout the war, and often entire tribal populations were, like the Suluks, almost completely exterminated. Thousands were systematically murdered, and their villages destroyed. At the very centre of it all was the Kempei Tai, the Japanese Gestapo, the professional torturers with an organized technique of terror and murder. Their actions, declared the War Crimes Prosecutor, 'plumb the very depths of human depravity and degradation. Horror, stark, and naked, permeates every corner of this case from beginning to end. I have searched diligently amongst a vast mass of evidence ... for some redeeming feature ... which would elevate the story from the level of pure horror and bestiality. I have failed.'

From 1946–8 twenty-eight major Japanese war criminals were tried and sentenced by the International Military Tribunal; seven were sentenced to hang, and nearly all the rest to life imprisonment. Other investigations and trials followed throughout the Far East. Several thousand more war criminals were tried in the following years. Pleaded Vice-Admiral Abe: 'Among hundreds and thousands of Japanese military men, has there ever been one person who thought that he could be charged with his own acts, which he has committed pursuant to an order? It is beyond the understanding of the Japanese that such things could be penalized.' This defence plea of 'superior orders', was put forward many times and though rarely successful, was accepted occasionally as a mitigating factor. The issue is generally conceived as establishing whether the order (which a soldier must obey) was known to the accused as being illegal, or as obviously outraging the general sentiments of humanity. If so, the plea must fail.

During the course of these trials, much knowledge was gained about the concepts, inner attitudes and values of the Japanese mind. At the very first War Crimes Trial in the Far East, which for political reasons was that of Captain Gozawa Sadaichi and nine of his subordinates, Gozawa frankly declared that had the position been reversed the captives would simply have been shot. All the accused were extremely favourably impressed by the conduct of their trials.

In particular it was realized that the fundamental 'principles' to which the Japanese looks for security and guidance in life situations, such as the precedence of the group; the superiority of man over woman; the importance of face saving and appearances, *do not include* such abstract ideas as justice and truth. Nevertheless, he exists through two poles of his being. One, dogmatic and rigid, based on the 'principles', and another, more private and human, which includes his own 'personal' truth. He resorts to the principles, the official maxims, when 'he is confronted with a problem which he cannot solve with the resources of his own personality'. This in fact creates a curious split and tension between two kinds of reality, especially exemplified in Army Regulations, without which 'the Japanese soldier would be helpless and lost'. Thus officers are always 'kind and benevolent', the soldier is always 'kind, honest, and chivalrous', and the Army is always 'just and benevolent'. The soldier knows otherwise, but appearances must be kept up. Thus venereal disease officially does not exist in the Army. Where it has to be diagnosed the treatment is itself a very severe form of punishment and deliberately painful.

In the Gozawa Trial there were many instances to illustrate the complexities of this double reality at work.

Relating to the slogans, 'Indians were not maltreated. Indians and Japanese were treated alike', Captain Ken was questioned:

Q. If there were bad Japanese who ill-treated Indians, you would not want them to go unpunished?

A. No. The only thing that in my Company there was not a single case in which Indians were ill-treated.

Q. You have already told us of the sugar incident. And there was the case where Sgt. T— was concerned. Those are both cases of Indians being maltreated?

A. That was the fault of the Indians. Indians were wrong.

Regarding the lack of conception of justice as we understand it, Capt. Gozawa was questioned:

Q. You are the man who claims to have had the power of awarding death sentence in April 1945?

A. Yes. I was given that power when there was anyone attempting to desert.

Q. And you gave that sentence of death to a man whom you had never seen after he had been accused?

A. I agreed with the opinion of Lt N—.

Q. You were satisfied to exercise that great power of having a man killed on the word of another man?

A. I had full confidence in all the platoon commanders, but especially this Lt N—.

Q. Do you still think that was right, Captain Gozawa?

A. Yes.

Q. So it would have been right for the President of this Court to condemn you to death on my word?

A. Yes. It would have been right.

Regarding the 'personal' truth, Sgt Jinichoro was questioned:

Q. Did you see Lt N— give any orders?

A. I do not remember.

Q. Surely you cannot forget that?

A. I was too busy with private work.

Q. If I was asking you questions in a little room and Lt N— was not there, do you think you would remember then?

A. Yes, I think I would remember.

At his trial Tojo, the Japanese war leader, claimed total disbelief of any inhumane acts as he had 'read about'. 'The character of the Japanese people is such that they believe that neither Heaven nor Earth would permit such things.' But the tribunal was quite clear that the atrocities 'were either secretly ordered or wilfully permitted' by all the Japanese leaders.

J. G.

K

KATYN WOOD Murders, The

Two weeks after Hitler's attack on Poland in September 1939, the Red Army advanced across its eastern frontiers. Polish officers and men who survived the assault were either murdered on the spot, imprisoned, or deported to Russia. Various promises of freedom to return home after the surrender of arms were made but these were apparently subterfuge by the Soviet military authorities to facilitate the rounding up of anti-Bolshevik elements.

Approximately 200,000 Polish prisoners were thus deported to Russia in the autumn and winter 1939–40. Fifteen thousand of them, including 9,000 officers, were assembled in three POW camps – Starobielsk, Kozielsk, and Ostashkov. In spring 1940 these three camps were disbanded and the men sent to secret destinations. Four hundred and fifty of them were sent to Moscow prisons and eventually freed, but the rest had simply disappeared.

Joseph Mackiewicz recalls how in Poland it was realized 'with anxiety and finally panic' that all communication from the three camps had ceased. After twelve months pestering of officials, one fearful relative learnt from the District Prosecutor in Ostashkov, 'The present whereabouts of your father are unknown.'

The 450 men sent to Moscow were considered potential Communist 'material', intended to go through thorough indoctrination. The idea of a Polish military group under the Soviet was born, for Germany might not always remain an ally. Beria and Merkulov, heads of the Security Police, broached this subject to three Polish colonels held in a Moscow prison. But when the question of captured Polish officers arose, who would form the core of any such Polish–Soviet army, Beria said awkwardly, 'No, not those. We made a big mistake concerning them. A grave mistake.'

In June 1941 Hitler attacked Russia. The Soviet Union became one of the Allies and the London Polish Government reached an agreement with her. This included the return of all POWs and deportees. It was carried out but Polish HQ in Russia soon realized that a great number of captured men were missing in the returns. About 15,000, including 8,000 officers. Soviet liaison officers answered their questions evasively. At first the Poles accepted their explanations in the context of Russia's tremendous war chaos and transport problems. After the passing of innumerable diplomatic notes, Vishinsky stated, 'I am convinced that these men have already been released. For me this problem simply does not exist.' Stalin queried the Polish ambassador innocently, 'Do you mean to say there are still Poles who have not been released?' The diplomatic questioning went on for months at highest level but the Soviet insisted on their ignorance, giving as the only possible explanations:

1. The return of the missing to Poland.
2. Their escape abroad.
3. Casualties occurring on the way to Polish recruiting centres.

By August 1942 the issue had led to a considerable deterioration in Russo-Polish relations.

However, at this very time when the Russians were maintaining their bland ignorance, some German-captured Poles now working for the Reich on the Russian front were having an important conversation with an old peasant, Partemon Kisielev, at Katyn near Smolensk, captured by the Germans in July 1941. As a result of this conversation Berlin broadcast the following in April 1943:

It is reported from Smolensk that the local population has indicated to the German authorities a place in which the Bolsheviks had perpetrated secretly mass executions and where the GPU had murdered 10,000 Polish officers. . . . A great pit was found, 28 metres long and 16 metres wide, filled with twelve layers of bodies of Polish officers . . . clad in full military uniform . . . all of them had wounds in the back of their heads caused by pistol shots.

Russia immediately countered the broadcast, from the Tass agency:

The Polish prisoners in question were interned in the vicinity of Smolensk . . . It was impossible to evacuate them at the time of the approach of the German troops. . . . If therefore they have been found murdered, it means that they have been murdered by the Germans . . .

The Allies accepted the Russian statement. The Poles would not and requested the International Red Cross to send a delegation to investigate. The Germans did the same, but the Russians refused their consent as a 'concerned party', without which the Red Cross would not proceed. *Pravda* then attacked General Sikorski the Polish head as a pro-Hitlerite. He was urged by the Allies to deny Russian responsibility for the murders but he refused. Russia severed diplomatic relations with Poland. The Allies were in difficulties for the abandonment of Poland's claim might shake the faith of those such as Yugoslavia, Greece, and Norway. The neutral Press was pro-Polish. But from a position of strength Russia organized a new Polish–Soviet army and insisted that no further talk on the subject was permissible among the Allies.

Meanwhile the Germans proceeded in their investigations, which had become intensive propaganda. With gruesome photos they showed the fate awaiting resistance to Bolshevism. They appointed an International Commission of Medical–Legal experts from European universities. This commission issued a communiqué which significantly left out the number of bodies, though from the start the Germans had claimed it as 10,000–12,000. A number approximating the missing Polish prisoners and which the Russians had never questioned. The communiqué insisted too that, 'the clotting together of the neighbouring bodies by dense putrefaction, and in particular the deformation due to pressure, point decisively to the fact that *this is the original grave*'.

The key question remained, *when* had it happened. For the answer must imply *who* had done it. The experts concluded the date as not later than spring 1940.

'If the Bolsheviks did it, why did they leave so many compromising documents and other objects upon their victims?'

'Because,' answered Colonel von Gersdorff, 'in 1940 they never believed that their enemies could occupy Smolensk . . . and dig up these bodies.'

The Germans kept silent on the *make* of the ammunition used. Soviet propaganda overlooked the German omission and also never raised the question. People from all over Europe were brought by the Germans to the graves, including British, American, and Polish officers.

Local inhabitants described the history of the place in Katyn Wood where the mass graves were sited. Since 1918 the Cheka had carried out executions there. In 1931 it had been fenced off, and in 1940 closely guarded. In spring 1940 transports had started arriving at the local station with Polish POWs. The place was covered with pine trees and nearby was a summer rest house for NKVD officials.

Joseph Mackiewicz, a journalist and writer, described the scene of the exhumations with:

> ... its ghastly, suffocating, cadaverous stink. ... The bodies were hauled out of the death pit and deposited in rows at the side. They were next taken, one by one, inspected and thoroughly searched. The uniforms were still in quite a good state ... All leather articles, including boots, looked at first sight as if they were made of rubber. As everything was soaked and glued with a most loathsome, stinking and gummy cadaverous liquid, it was impossible to unbutton the pockets or pull off the boots. ... Before me lay the opened pit, and at the bottom of it, layers and layers ... arms and legs entangled, everything pressed down as if by a roller. ... The pressed mass of bodies was glued with the cadaverous pulp as if soldered together. ... They had to wedge each body carefully and then tear it away from the others in order to drag it out.

Mackiewicz attempts to reconstruct the method of massacre:

> It is worse than the gas chambers. Here, to the contrary, every single man died slowly, each one waited for his turn to be dragged towards the death pit ... perhaps in the very eyes of the victim, the bodies of his comrades were arranged in the graves, in tight rows stamped down by the boots of the oppressors in order to make room for *him*. ... And then he in turn was shot in the back of his head which he was forced to bend ... Probably there were three assassins. Two of them held the victim by the arms, while the third fired the shot. ... The individual reactions and sufferings can sometimes be guessed from certain details – teeth knocked out by the butt-end of a rifle, or stabs from a four-sided Russian bayonet. Many had their hands tied with string, always with the same masterly knot. Some had their coats thrown over their heads and tied round the neck to form a bag which was filled with sawdust to silence the cries. ... Open mouths filled with sand ...

Among all the pitiful valuables, rotted and sticky, which were collected, it was the newspapers whose significance most impressed Mackiewicz.

> They pulled the crumpled newspapers out of the pockets, and when the first and second ... and the fifth ... and the

tenth . . . and every single one carried a date either of March or April 1940 . . . the tremendous importance of this dawned on me. . . . These newspapers could not possibly have remained in the pockets of the murdered men for a year and a half if, according to the Soviet version, they were still alive in August 1941.

After weeks of embarrassed investigation the Germans eventually revealed that the bullets were of *German* manufacture! They were marked 'Genschow' and it appeared that after the Treaty of Rapallo, 'the "Genschow" works supplied large amounts of ammunition to Soviet Russia . . . and also Poland . . . After the Russians had occupied half of Poland, great quantities of that very same ammunition fell into their hands. The German embarrassment and amazement was then also significant enough. If they were the murderers they would surely have used Russian ammunition or at least 'had a ready answer prepared beforehand'.

The final figure given was 4,143 bodies. All the diaries on them were dated from Kozielsk, so clearly the men from Ostashkov and Starobielsk were not murdered there. The Germans were afraid of undermining confidence by changing their original figure of 10,000–12,000, and so they left the figure of 4,143 an 'open' one, explaining that heat and flies rendered further investigation impossible. However, all the fragmentary evidence available points to a similar fate for the other missing prisoners.

After the Russians retook Smolensk, they issued a communiqué on Katyn in 1944. On the key question of the newspaper and diary dates it alleged that, '500 Russian prisoners . . . had been used to dig up the bodies, remove all documents dated later than April 1940, replace them by other papers dated April 1940, and then bury the bodies once more'. But Mackiewicz and others insist on the physical impossibility of doing this to a vast coagulated mass of corpses. *Even if* conceivable, 'surely such an operation would have left some trace on the bodies and their clothing. I . . . and several experts, are satisfied that no such traces were discernible.'

The Katyn Wood massacre was a consciously planned act of genocide based on a totalitarian ideology. The killers regarded this group of Polish officers as completely unredeemable 'material' from the 'educative' viewpoint. In exactly the same way the Nazis dealt with the Jews, the gypsies, and also the Poles. In fact, the Polish treatment of the Jews from the end of the nineteenth century was potentially of this order. On both Nazi and Bolshevik sides, however, conflicts of opinion sometimes occurred in the carrying out of their policies. For just as Beria, who was himself later to be fed into the same machine, regretted the 'grave mistake', so Himmler at Posen in 1943 recalled a similar 'mistake'. Referring to the initial deaths of Russian prisoners through the callous indifference of the advancing armies, he said, 'At that time we did not value the mass of humanity as we value it today, as raw material, as labour. What, after all, thinking in terms of generations, is not to be regretted, but is now deplorable by reason of the loss of labour, is that the prisoners died in tens and hundreds of thousands of exhaustion and hunger.'

J. G.

KENT, Constance
Sixteen-year-old daughter of Samuel Savile Kent, deputy inspector of factories (also reputed to be the illegitimate son of the Duke of Kent, father of Queen Victoria), who, in June 1860, murdered her half-brother, 4-year-old Francis Savile Kent.

In 1854 Mr Kent, a widower for fifteen months, married Miss Pratt, governess to his surviving younger children, Constance and William, aged 9. By 1860 the second Mrs Kent had three children of her own, of whom the eldest was Francis. In the morning of June 30th nursemaid Elizabeth Gough, who slept in the nursery with Francis, saw the child was missing from his cot; thinking Mrs Kent had taken the boy into her own room, Gough was not at first alarmed, and it was not until an hour later that it was realized the child was missing from the house. His body was found in a disused closet by the shrubbery, almost decapitated, with a deep wound in the left side. At the inquest the verdict of murder against 'some person or persons unknown' was returned. Gough was arrested, but, owing to a lack of evidence against her, released. Local police called in Scotland Yard, and Inspector Whicher took over the case; within a few days he arrested Constance Kent on a charge of murdering her half-brother. At the hearing before the magistrates it was learnt that one of Constance Kent's three nightdresses was missing. A basket of soiled linen had awaited the laundress on the Monday following the murder; a housemaid told Inspector Whicher that twice she had been sent off on some errand by Miss Constance, who (according to the inspector) would then have had the opportunity to take a nightdress from the laundry bag, so replacing her other heavily bloodstained nightdress, which, owing to its incriminating nature, had been destroyed. The laundress could be – and was – blamed for misplacing the garment. Two schoolfriends testified as to remarks made by Constance Kent about her unhappiness at home, but the evidence against the girl was inconclusive and she was released. Suspicion centred again on Elizabeth Gough, and she was re-arrested; it was hinted that the nursemaid and her employer were lovers and that, fearing exposure by a wakeful Francis, they resorted to murder. These charges failed, and shortly afterwards the Kent family moved to Wales, Constance choosing to go to a convent in France.

Years later, on April 27th, 1865, *The Times* printed the confession of Constance Kent, made on April 25th before the Bow Street magistrates; she had gone to court of her own volition, accompanied by the Rev. Mr Wagner, curate of a church at Brighton, where she had been living in a religious retreat for two years. The confession formed part of a letter to the Press from the doctor who tested her mental state:

> . . . a few days before the murder she obtained possession of a razor from a green case in her father's wardrobe. . . . She also secreted a candle with matches, placing them in a corner of the closet. . . . She took the child from his bed and carried him downstairs. . . . She says she thought the blood would never come . . . so she thrust the razor into its left side. . . . The light burnt out. . . . She secreted her [night] dress, eventually burnt it in her own bedroom and put the ashes into the kitchen grate. . . . As regards the motive . . . although she entertained a great regard for the present Mrs Kent, yet if any remark was at any time made which in her opinion was disparaging to any member of the first family she treasured it up and determined to revenge it. She had no ill-will against the little boy, except as one of the children of her stepmother. Although it became my duty to advise her counsel that she evinced no symptom of insanity at the time of my examination . . . I am of the opinion that, owing to the peculiarities of her constitution, it is probable that under prolonged solitary confinement she would become insane. . . .

Found guilty of the murder, Constance Kent was sentenced to death, but because of her youth the sentence was commuted to life imprisonment; she was released from prison in 1885, aged 41.

KINMAN, Donald
*Thirty-six-year-old vagrant and sexual psychopath, former resi-
dent of Phoenix, Arizona, admitting to the murders of nursing
orderlies Ferne Reed Wessel, 43, and Mary Louise Tardy, 28.*

Mrs Wessel, a woman of relaxed morals, was found sexually maltreated and manually strangled in a Los Angeles hotel bedroom
on Sixth Street on Easter Monday 1958. She had last been seen
the previous day, in a drunken state, being helped up to her room
(changed from a single to a double some little time earlier) by a
man whom hotel residents remembered being called 'Don', who
said he had come into Los Angeles that day by coach from
Phoenix, Arizona, and who had struck up an acquaintance with
Mrs Wessel at the bar. Fingerprints other than the victim's were
discovered in the bedroom, and these were filed; no further leads
to the killer's identity could be found.

Late in the afternoon of November 22nd, 1959, the decomposed nude body of Mrs Tardy was found in a trailer on Polk
Street, Sylmar, in the San Fernando valley; the trailer was owned
by Mr Chester Baker, who had been renting it for some time to
his roving stepson Donald Kinman, who had apparently decided to 'move on'. Mrs Tardy had been listed as missing the
previous Thursday (the time approximated for her death) when
she failed to return to her aunt's house. The night before,
November 18th, she had quarrelled with and left her boy friend
at Mahan's Grill, San Fernando, later being seen at the bar with
a stocky, curly-haired man, a description fitting Kinman. The
couple's movements were then traced to Flynn's Grill, where
they had stayed drinking before booking a taxi to the trailer's
address on Polk Street. Police were intrigued by similarities between the Wessel and Tardy killings: both had been strangled
and brutally violated after being partially suffocated by a pillow,
the clothing of both had been dumped on top of their bodies, and
both women had associated with a man known as Donald, or
Don, shortly before their deaths. Fingerprints taken in the Los
Angeles hotel room 19 months before tallied with prints taken
from the trailer, and bulletins concerning Kinman were immediately issued to police forces in the West. On December 2nd
Kinman gave himself up at the San Fernando police station on
MacNeil Street, and confessed readily to the murder of Mrs
Tardy: 'I don't know what came over me, but it just seemed like
something I had to do.' Asked why he had surrendered, Kinman
replied, 'My conscience has been bothering me.' After killing

369

Mrs Tardy he had gone to sleep by the corpse until late the following morning. Confronted with the evidence against him in the Wessel murder, Kinman admitted his guilt to the earlier crime. Asked by Captain Arthur Hertel of the Central Homicide Bureau as to what his fate should be, Donald Kinman replied: 'I guess I should get the gas chamber. I think I have it coming, don't you?'

KIRWAN, William Bourke (The Ireland's Eye Murder)

Kirwan was the first man to be convicted of murdering his wife by drowning.

William Bourke Kirwan was an artist who lived with his wife in Dublin; he was about 35. He had a mistress named Teresa Kenny who lived at Sandymount and who had borne him seven children.

In 1852 the Kirwans moved out to Howth, and their landlady noticed that they were quarrelsome for the first fortnight, although they seemed on better terms after that. On September 6th a fisherman named Nangle was hired to row the Kirwans out to Ireland's Eye, the island in Howth harbour, a favourite spot for picnickers. He was told to return for them at eight that evening. At about seven, fishermen heard screams coming from the island, but no one went to investigate. When Nangle returned at eight, Kirwan said he did not know where his wife was – he had been absorbed in his sketching. They went to look on the other side of the island, close to the 'Long Hole', and found the body of Mrs Kirwan, her bathing dress around her neck. The body was scratched and cut. A Coroner's court brought in a verdict of accidental death by drowning, but a month later, gossip led to the body being exhumed, and two doctors now declared that the cause of death was asphyxia, possibly by strangling. Kirwan was put on trial. He declared that he had not heard the screams at seven o'clock; he said that his wife was subject to epileptic fits (a fact he had not mentioned at the inquest). The jury found Kirwan guilty of murdering his wife by drowning, and Mr Justice Crampton passed the sentence. It was later commuted to penal servitude on Spike Island in Queenstown Harbour. When Kirwan was finally released, he joined Teresa Kenny in America.

On the evidence presented at the trial, Kirwan's guilt is by no means certain.

KISS, Bela
Hungarian amateur astrologer and mass-murderer, responsible for the deaths of twenty-four people, believed to have emigrated to America about 1926.

In February 1912, Bela Kiss, then aged 40, went to live in the Hungarian village of Czinkota, accompanied by his wife Maria, aged 25. Maria Kiss acquired a lover, Paul Bihari, and in December the inhabitants of Czinkota were informed, through the lamentations of Kiss, that Maria and Paul had gone away together. An elderly widow named Kalman became housekeeper to the forsaken spouse, and regarded the frequent arrival of women first with surprise, then understanding tolerance. Kiss started collecting enormous metal drums, filled (as he explained to village constable Trauber) with petrol, which would be in short supply during the approaching European war. Meanwhile Budapest police were searching for two widows, named Schmeidak and Varga, who had been missing for months. They were known to have visited the flat of a man named Hofmann, living near the Margaret Bridge in Budapest, who had also vanished. In November 1914, three months after war started, Bela Kiss (who had not shown military aspirations) was hastily conscripted from his Czinkota home and within a few hours was on his way to the Front; in May 1916 Constable Trauber received notice of his death in action. When, a month later, a party of soldiers entered Czinkota looking for petrol, Trauber remembered the metal drums Kiss had so prudently hoarded. Seven drums were found in the fallen warrior's house, each containing a garrotted naked woman preserved in alcohol. Letters were found in a bureau from numerous women in reply to newspaper advertisements inserted by Kiss, under the name of Hofmann, 'a lonely widower seeking female companionship'. When it was learnt that over twenty metal drums had been delivered to the Kiss residence, the surrounding countryside was searched and seventeen drums literally unearthed, all containing similarly preserved corpses, including those of Maria Kiss and her lover. The illicit couple were probably slaughtered in a fit of jealous rage, but subsequent victims had all parted with their savings to the homicidal Kiss. In 1919 the unlamented war casualty was seen crossing the Margaret Bridge, and it transpired that Kiss had exchanged identities with a fatality on the battlefield. In 1924 a deserter from the French Foreign Legion told the French Sûreté about a Légionnaire named Hofmann (answering to the physical description of Kiss) who would entertain the garrison with tales of garrotting; by the time the Hungarian police were informed, Hofmann had also deserted. In 1932 Detective Henry Oswald of New York's Homicide Squad (known as 'Camera Eye' to the Press) was certain he saw Kiss emerging from the Times Square subway station, but this killer has never been traced.

KLAUSS and DOELITZSCH
Found guilty of the murder of a rich merchant, Max Karam, in Alexandria, and sentenced to penal servitude for life.

Max Karam was murdered on the night of January 14th, 1922, when he was awakened by the noise of burglars, one of whom was trying to take the keys of his safe from under his pillow. One of them hit him several times with a jemmy while the other shot him through the head. Then, frightened by the noise, the burglars fled. (They had, in fact, no need to take fright, for the crime was not discovered until next day.)

The police suspected an 'inside job', since a hole had been drilled in the door near the bolt, and all wires had been severed. However, Sir Sidney Smith, then working for the Medico-Legal Department of the Egyptian police, pointed out that the facts indicated two professional burglars.

The dead man's widow now offered a reward of £2,000 for evidence leading to the conviction of the murderers, and on February 4th, 1923, a French prostitute named Henriette came forward; her protector had talked to a man who called himself 'Ferid Merkel' who admitted to committing the burglary, together with Herman Klauss, who used the name 'Klaus Chefer'. Klauss was traced to India, and the wrong man was actually brought all the way back to Egypt; however, the police who accompanied him recognized Klauss's photograph as that of a man who was put in prison in Calcutta for deserting ship. Merkel, whose real name was Fritz Doelitzsch, was arrested on board ship in Trieste. The two men tried to throw the blame on one another, but were sentenced to life imprisonment.

Here, the execution of justice came about by the combination of fortuitous circumstances: the widow's offer of a reward, and the inability of both men to keep silent about the crime. Klauss, like Doelitzsch, had spoken of the crime to casual associates who finally betrayed him.

KNOWLES, Dr Benjamin

Sentenced to death in 1929 for the murder of his wife, but later released. The 'murder' was almost certainly an accident. The worst that can be charged against Dr Knowles is habitual drunkenness and neglect.

Dr Knowles and his wife, a former music-hall singer, Madge Clifton, lived in a bungalow at Beckwail, Ashanti, West Africa, where Dr Knowles was the Medical Officer of Health. Knowles kept a loaded revolver by the bed because there had been some cases of housebreaking. The revolver – cocked – was placed on a chair, and Mrs Knowles sat on it. As she stood up it caught in the lace of her dress and shot her through the left buttock; the bullet emerged over the right hip. The trigger of the revolver was exceptionally light. Mrs Knowles was heard to say: 'My God, I'm shot,' and her husband replied, 'Show me, show me.' Two native boys on the verandah heard this and one of them ran to tell the District Commissioner. The latter hurried to the bungalow, but Dr Knowles seemed annoyed by his interference and sent him off, saying it was a minor domestic upset. The next day the District Commissioner mentioned the affair to a surgeon in Kumasi, a Dr Gush, who went out to the bungalow and insisted on examining Mrs Knowles. Her husband was drunk. Dr Gush ordered Mrs Knowles to dress, and took her to Kumasi hospital. She died on Monday October 22nd, 1928, but not before declaring emphatically that it had been an accident.

However, the police preferred to believe it was murder, and found two more bullet holes in the room to support this view – one in a table and one in a wardrobe. Although an acquaintance declared that the wardrobe hole had been there for a long time, Dr Knowles was tried for murder. There was no jury, and the Commissioner of Police prosecuted. Dr Knowles was sentenced to death. However, he appealed, and a year later the sentence was quashed. He died in London three years later, a broken man.

KRAMER, Josef

He was born in 1906 and joined the SS in 1932 in order to get a job. He was detailed for concentration-camp service, in which he remained till the German defeat. In 1936 he was at Dachau, in 1937 Sachsenhausen, in 1939 Mauthausen, promotions following regularly. In 1940 at Auschwitz as adjutant to Hoess, and 1941–4 Commandant at Natzweiler, where he supervised a hanging.

'I think his nationality was Russian. I cannot remember his name because he never appeared in my books. He was only delivered to be hanged.' By this time he had become an expert in gas chamber techniques and supervised the gassings of tens of thousands at Auschwitz before becoming Camp Commandant of Belsen, 1944–5.

He carried out his orders regardless of their content, primarily to keep his safe, comfortable job and not for ideological reasons. He was quite indifferent to the gigantic chaos of human suffering around him. Orders were orders, and he was without scruple or remorse of any kind. Even at the first moments of his arrest he showed not the slightest upset or concern over the inferno that was Belsen, slouching in his comfortable office armchair and tipping his cap back over his head.

Around him in a comparatively small, wired-off compound were found 40,000 living-dead; 'a dense mass of emaciated scarecrows, simply living skeletons, lying, sitting, shuffling about the place'. In huts made for 80, 600–1,000 victims were crammed. Thirteen thousand corpses were lying unburied, merely bones, yet it took four of the living-dead to carry each one of them. Typhus and dysentery were raging and the whole place was covered with excreta. Death had come from starvation, thirst, beating, and shooting. Within six weeks of the British arrival another 13,000 died. In Block 13 life averaged 13 days from arrival.

H. O. le Druillenec received half a litre of soup for his first four days and *nothing* for the last five, while working twelve hours a day dragging corpses. He described the last days at Belsen:

> Guards in the concentration camp in general are brutish, and the prisoners in time become brutish and such a thing as human kindness is quite unknown in such a place. I would like to try to make everyone realize what starvation, absolute starvation, no water at all for some six days, lack of sleep – for sleep near the burial pits was quite impossible – to be covered in lice and delousing oneself three or four times a day proving absolutely useless, is like. Then there is the fatalistic attitude between the prisoners towards what the end would certainly be – the crematorium or the pits. Add to this the foul stench and vileness of the place, the scenes which apparently horrified the whole world, which we saw day by day, the blows on the head, the hideous work, and in the last three days the Hungarian guards shooting at us just as if we were rabbits, from all

directions. If you can picture all this – you will get a remote inkling of what life was like at Belsen in those last three days.

Kramer was in complete charge of all this. The only drinking water available for these 40,000 was a small pond with corpses floating in it. In the nearby Panzer Training School there were 800 tons of food and a bakery for 60,000 loaves, but Kramer could not obtain any as he did not have the necessary special indents. Eventually cannibalism was rife. Corpses were seen with ears, liver, intestines, scrotum, or penis cut out by a knife.

Under his authority the guards carried rubber truncheons, whips, sticks, and revolvers. They beat people to death with their jackboots and iron bars for daring to get vegetable peelings from the swill bins. They beat people savagely and persistently, day in and day out, leaving them bleeding and dying for petty offences or for no offence at all: merely for the sake of beating and killing and their barbaric lust for bringing about pain and suffering. They compelled the prisoners to 'make sport', running round, falling down, getting up, running round, for an hour or more non-stop. They made them kneel for hours with stones in their hands. They pushed them on to electrified wires. *Appell*, or roll call, lasted up to six hours and for moving, one was hit on the head with a stick four feet long and an inch and a half thick.

Under cross-examination Kramer confessed belief in God and admitted gassing eighty prisoners to supply Dr Hoess of Strasbourg University with the bodies. He also stated that had he protested he would have been arrested, and frankly confessed that, rather than have that happen, he preferred to be a party to wholesale murder. He denied being present at gas selections and also most of the charges of ill-treatment at Belsen. For him not to execute a military order was quite out of the question. He was not concerned with the reasons for the imprisonment and murder of these victims but, 'Whether it was a political enemy or a Jew had nothing to do with me at all. I received the bodies, that was all.' *Bodies* is here the operative word, for Kramer certainly did not experience them as *human beings*. In evidence, Mrs Kramer said that her husband realized the wrong of what was being done, also denying that he had ever ill-treated anybody, emphasizing, in fact, that he had been taking care of them 'all the time, night and day'.

At his trial, evidence was given that he punished some Russian girls caught attempting to steal bread by making them kneel all day and depriving them of food. At gas chamber selections he beat people who cried, and kicked the children towards the lorries taking them to the gas chambers. He made dogs chase people into a fire and trained a gun on them lest they escaped the flames. He kicked a Russian prisoner to death in the snow. In the last days he stood at the kitchen windows with others shooting at groups of prisoners with Schmeisser guns.

His written statements about his concentration-camp life convey bland cynicism and impassive lying. He would like to give the impression that they were sanatoriums or rest centres and that under his authority absolutely nothing untoward happened. Only the odd, quite legal lashing or execution. Torture was simply unheard of. Otherwise, everyone had a 'natural' death, supervised by the doctor and communicated to the relatives.

In court, for the most part he simply denied all knowledge of gas chambers, whippings, cruelty, and mass executions, stating bluntly that it was 'untrue from beginning to end'. He insisted that he had done everything he could to remedy conditions at Belsen and found it 'very difficult to believe' that his staff were guilty of ill-treatment towards the prisoners. He was sentenced to death at the Belsen War Crimes Trial and hanged.

J. G.

KREUGER and VON ARBIN (The Swedish Dynamiters Case)

Sixten Flyborg, a wholesale tea merchant aged 26, soon after entering a taxi-cab at 3 am on March 31st, 1923, was blown to pieces in a violent explosion that wrecked the vehicle. Two months before, Flyborg had been the victim of a murderous attack upon answering his front door, but had proved reluctant to discuss the assault with police officers. The taxi-driver, who survived the blast, gave information that his fare had come from the house in the exclusive Kungsholmen district of Stockholm belonging to Eric Von Arbin, Swedish aristocrat and a partner of Flyborg in the tea business; by interviewing Von Arbin, who expressed grief and amazement, Flyborg's identity was established. Von Arbin said that Flyborg had spent a convivial evening with him and a mutual friend, Alexander Kreuger, aged 22; Flyborg had become hopelessly drunk, said Von Arbin, so a taxi was summoned and Flyborg helped into it only two minutes before the explosion.

The detonation had come from the back of the cab; remains of a leather strap were hanging from the grid that were identical with the strands tied to fragments of a wooden box lying within the blast area. Stromberg, the injured chauffeur, disclaimed all knowledge of the box, and revealed that after Von Arbin and Kreuger had hailed him, Kreuger had gone back into the house to fetch Flyborg – during which time Von Arbin had spent some time 'sauntering about' the back of the taxi.

Police discovered that the Von Arbin tea company was in financial difficulties, largely because of the dissolute living of all three men, and that Kreuger and Flyborg had each been jealous of the other's friendship with Von Arbin. Earlier in the year arson had been suspected when the tea company's premises were destroyed shortly after being insured for 30,000 kronor. When police found out that prior to the first attack on Flyborg his life had been insured by Von Arbin for 100,000 kronor (about £5,500), they questioned the two men more closely, even confronting them with the frightful remains of Flyborg. Kreuger joked throughout the inquisition, but Von Arbin collapsed and made a confession. He said that Kreuger had stolen twelve pounds of explosive (used in Sweden to blast out rock for house foundations) and, with a box and fuse attachment, had made the bomb that was placed on Stromberg's luggage-grid.

Their trial took place in Stockholm in 1926. Von Arbin gazed glumly ahead throughout the proceedings, but Kreuger, shorter and plumper than the tall aristocrat, displayed an exhibitionist's delight in everything, particularly the questions about his past. He talked of his visit to Hollywood, boasting of his friendships with film-actors Charlie Chaplin and Douglas Fairbanks; his marriage to Rumanian Princess Lucrezia Stazza the year before was mentioned and when asked why he deserted her Kreuger replied: 'One woman can only interest me for a short time.'

Found guilty of murder, they were sentenced to life imprisonment.

KÜRTEN, Peter
The Kürten case undoubtedly claims place with the unsolved Jack the Ripper murders as one of the most interesting series of crimes in the last century. This is not simply on account of the murders themselves, but because we know more about the mind of Kürten than of any other sadistic killer. This knowledge we owe almost entirely to the researches of Dr Karl Berg, who came to know Kürten well before his execution.

Kürten was born in Köln-Mulheim in 1883, the son of a moulder, a violent man, boastful and given to drunkenness. The family of thirteen were very poor, and lived for a time in a single room. The environment was heavily charged with sex. According to Kürten, all his sisters were oversexed, and one made sexual advances to him. Kürten was apparently not attracted by her, but he attempted incest with another sister – a sister whom his father attempted to rape, and on whose account the moulder served a term in prison. Kürten senior was in the habit of forcing his wife to have intercourse when he came home drunk, and Kürten frequently witnessed his mother being 'raped'. At the age of 8 he ran away from home for a short time, sleeping in furniture vans. He also admitted to Berg that his taste for sadism had first been awakened by a sadistic dog-catcher who lived in the same house, and who taught Kürten to masturbate the dogs. Kürten often watched him torturing the dogs.

Kürten was the third of thirteen children. His grandfather had served sentences for theft, and cases of delirium tremens, feeble-mindedness, and paralysis abound in his family connexions on his father's side. (His mother's side of the family were normal and hard-working people.)

When Kürten was 12, the family moved to Düsseldorf. But according to his own confession, he had already committed his first murder. At the age of 9, he pushed a boy off a raft on the banks of the Rhine, and when another boy dived in to help the first one, he managed to push him under the raft, so that both were drowned.

In his early teens he ran away from home again and lived as a vagabond and robber – attacking mostly girls and women. His adolescent sexuality was abnormal. He attempted intercourse with schoolgirls and with his sister, and masturbated excessively. From his thirteenth year onward he practised bestiality with sheep, pigs, and goats. He discovered that he received a powerful sexual sensation when having intercourse with a sheep in the Düsseldorf meadows and stabbing it simultaneously. He did this many times between his thirteenth and sixteenth years. At 16 he became an apprentice moulder, and received much ill-treatment; finally he stole money and ran away to Coblenz. There he lived with a prostitute who allowed him to ill-treat her. Finally, he was arrested for theft, and received the first of the seventeen sentences that were to take up twenty-seven years of his life. He was then 14. Released from prison two years later in 1899, he discovered that his mother was divorced from his father, and so decided to keep living a vagrant life. He lived with a prostitute of twice his age who enjoyed being maltreated, and this developed his propensities further.

In November 1899, according to Kürten's own account, he committed what he supposed to be his first adult murder: strangling a girl while having sexual intercourse with her, he thought she had died, and left her in the Grafenberger Wald. But no body was reported in that month, so it seems likely that the girl woke up and went home, saying nothing to anyone.

His first prison period, according to himself, made a real criminal of him; in the cells at the Berger Gate he met hardened criminals, and wanted to rival them. He had himself tattooed.

He served two brief sentences about 1900 for minor fraud, and then attempted to shoot a girl with a rifle, and was given two more years. Together with another sentence for theft, this brought his period in jail up to 1904. During this time, Kürten admitted, he used to dream of revenge, and found that his fantasies of killing excited him sexually. He deliberately committed minor infringements of prison regulations to get solitary confinement, so that he could indulge these fantasies freely. On his release he was called up as a conscript to Metz, but soon deserted. He also committed his first cases of arson, setting fire to barns and hayricks. The sight of fire caused him sexual excitement, and he also hoped that tramps might be sleeping in the hay. In 1905 he received seven years in jail for theft (he had been living with another woman who also lived by thieving). He served the term in Münster prison, and had an attack of 'prison psychosis', rolling himself in a bundle of silk and lying under the table, claiming to be a silkworm. He also claimed later that he was able to poison some prisoners in the prison hospital. He nursed fantasies of revenge on society, and dreamed of 'compensatory justice' – that is, that he could get his own back on his tormenters by tormenting someone who was completely innocent. This kind of illogicality is typical of murderers and psychopaths.

As soon as he was released from prison in 1912, he maltreated a servant girl during intercourse, and was soon back in prison for discharging fire-arms in a restaurant when he tried to accost a woman and was interrupted by the waiter. For this he received a year in jail.

On May 25th, 1913, he committed his first sexual murder. He had become a specialist in robbing business premises. He entered a pub in the Wolfstresse, Köln-Mulheim, on an evening when the family were out at a fair. In one of the bedrooms he found

13-year-old Christine Klein asleep. He strangled her, cut her throat with a penknife, and penetrated her sexual organs with his fingers. He dropped a handkerchief with his initials on it. But it happened that the child's father was called Peter Klein, and his brother Otto had quarrelled with him on the night of the murder and threatened to do something that Peter 'would remember all his life'. Otto Klein was arrested and tried, but released for lack of evidence. Public opinion was against him, and he was killed in the war, still under the shadow of the murder. Kürten later claimed that it was the memory of his sufferings in jail that prompted the murder. A few weeks after this crime, Kürten was again about to attack a sleeping girl when someone woke up and frightened him off. He also attacked an unknown man and an unknown woman with a hatchet, securing sexual orgasms by knocking them unconscious and seeing their blood. (Since the sadistic dog-catcher, blood had always been Kürten's major sexual stimulant.) He also burned another hay wagon, and attempted to strangle two women. Then, luckily, he spent the next eight years in prison.

In 1921 Kürten returned to Altenberg, declaring that he had been a prisoner of war in Russia. Here he met the woman who became his wife, at the home of his sister. She had had her own misfortunes; she had been engaged to a gardener for eight years and had been his mistress; then he refused to marry her and she shot him. For this she served a five-year jail sentence. When Kürten met her she was a raw-boned, broad-shouldered, prematurely aged woman. It is difficult to know why Kürten was attracted by her; perhaps because she seemed 'solid' and reliable or perhaps because she had suffered. Until the end of his life, ten years later, she continued to be the only human being for whom he felt normal feelings of affection and attachment. At first, she refused to marry him, but, when Kürten threatened to murder her, she consented. Then, for two years, he lived a fairly respectable life, working as a moulder in Altenberg, and becoming active in trade union circles and in a political club. But his sadistic activities persisted and he was twice charged with maltreating servant girls. In 1925 he returned to Düsseldorf, and was delighted that the sunset was blood-red on the evening of his return. Then began Düsseldorf's 'Reign of Terror'. But it began quietly enough. Like many maniacs of a similar type, Kürten began with a few widely spaced attacks; these became steadily more frequent and more violent, until, in the year 1929, they finally reached a climax. Between 1925 and 1928 Kürten admitted four cases of attempted strangulation of women, and seventeen cases of arson. On two occasions he set houses on fire.

The year 1929 began with six more cases of arson of barns and stacks. Then, on February 3rd, a Frau Kuhn was walking home late at night when she was suddenly attacked by a man with a knife. She received twenty-four stab wounds, and was in hospital for many months.

A few days later on February 13th, a 45-year-old mechanic named Scheer was found dead in the roadway in Flingern; he had been drunk when attacked, and had been stabbed twenty times.

On March 9th workmen discovered the body of 8-year-old Rose Ohliger lying behind a fence on a building site. She had been stabbed thirteen times; there had been some attempt at sexual assault, and an attempt to burn the body with paraffin.

The police were puzzled; it seemed impossible that a sex maniac should attack a man, woman, and child with the same ferocity. Yet all had been stabbed in the temples, which suggested the same man.

In April 1929 it seemed that the 'monster' had been caught. Following two more attacks on women, an idiot named Stausberg was arrested and confessed to the murders. He had a cleft palate and hare lip. The police were soon convinced that, although he was undoubtedly responsible for the latest attacks, he had not committed the murders. He was sent to a mental home.

For three months, Kürten satisfied himself with affairs with servant girls, whom he attempted to strangle 'playfully'. (All this emerged at the trial.) On July 30th a prostitute named Emma Gross was found strangled in her room, but it seems that Kürten was not responsible for this.

In August, Kürten strangled a girl he referred to as 'Anni', and pushed her body into the river; but the body was not recovered, so it is not certain whether this story was Kürten's invention. Also in late August, a young woman, Frau Mantel, was stabbed in the back as she walked in the western suburb of Lierenfeld, where a fair was being held. Her wound was not serious. In the same month a girl, Anna Goldhausen, and a man, Gustav Kornblum (who was sitting in the park), were stabbed in the back. In neither case were the injuries fatal. Then, on August 24th, a double murder horrified the city. The bodies of two children, 5-year-old Gertrude Hamacher and 14-year-old Louise Lenzen, were found on an allotment near their home.

Both had been strangled, and then had their throats cut. Neither had been raped.

The same Sunday afternoon, a servant girl named Gertrude Schulte was on her way to a fair at Neuss, and was spoken to by a man who called himself Fritz Baumgart. In a wood he attempted sexual intercourse, and the girl said, 'I'd rather die.' 'Baumgart' replied, 'Well die then,' and stabbed her several times. But she did not die, and was eventually able to give the police a description of her assailant.

This episode strengthened the police suspicion that there were two maniacs at work, since it seemed unlikely that the same man would kill two children on Saturday, and be out looking for further victims on Sunday.

In September, Kürten attacked three more girls and threw one of them into the river after his attempted strangulation. But these events caused little sensation in comparison with the next murder, which occurred in late September. Another servant girl, Ida Reuter, set out for her Sunday afternoon walk and never returned; the next day she was found in a field near the Rhine meadows. Her head had been battered with a heavy instrument (which turned out to be a hammer), and her handbag and knickers were missing; she was found in a position that indicated sexual assault.

The next case took place a few weeks later, in October. Again the victim was a servant girl, Elizabeth Dorrier. Again she was found (on October 12th) near the River Düssel at Grafenberg. Her death was also due to hammer blows on the head, and her hat and coat were missing.

On October 25th a Frau Meurer was accosted by a man in Flingern, who asked, 'Aren't you afraid to be out alone?' She woke up in hospital, her skin having been broken by a hammer, which had not, however, cracked the skull. Later the same evening, in the centre of the city, a Frau Wanders, who was seeking an escort, was accosted and knocked unconscious with a hammer, which had struck her four blows.

On November 7th a 5-year-old child, Gertrude Albermann, was missing from her home. Two days later her body was found near a factory yard, among nettles and brick rubble; she had been strangled and stabbed thirty-six times.

At this point Kürten imitated the 'Ripper's' tactics by sending a letter to a newspaper, stating where the body could be found, and mentioning the whereabouts of another body. (Kürten had a great admiration for the Ripper, and had studied the case carefully.) A spot in the meadows at Papendelle was mentioned. This led to the discovery of the body of Maria Hahn, who had been dead since August. Her body was dug up, after some days of searching, on November 14th, and was found to be completely naked. She had twenty stab wounds. Thousands of spectators streamed out to the spot where her body was found.

The murders were, of course, causing a panic in the Düsseldorf area that can only be compared to that caused by the Ripper in 1888 or by the Ratcliffe Highway murderer in 1811. Inspector Gennat, of the Berlin police, was assigned to the case. He had once had to follow up eight hundred clues to track down a murderer, and was noted for his thoroughness.

The German underworld was also greatly disturbed by the murders (as Fritz Lang showed in his film version of the crimes, *M*), and police raids made the criminals of the Rhine as anxious as the general public to see the murderer taken.

A tailor's dummy, dressed in Dorrier's clothes, was taken around the dance halls of Düsseldorf, in the hope that one of the dancers would recognize the clothes and remember the girl's companion on the day of her death.

But although no one knew it, the murders had come to an end, although the attacks would continue for six months more. There had been eight murders in ten months, and fourteen attacks.

In 1929, there were several attacks on girls walking alone, and Kürten also continued to playfully strangle his girl-friends, some of whom did not seem to object to the treatment. (Evidence of these girls figures largely in the trial.)

The episode that led to Kürten's arrest took place on May 14th, 1929. A servant girl named Maria Budlick – who according to Kürten, was ugly and bow-legged – came from Cologne to Düsseldorf looking for a job. The woman who was due to meet her at the station failed to appear, and she was picked up by a man who attempted to persuade her to go into a park. Remembering stories of the 'monster', she refused. He persisted, and while she was arguing with him, a pleasant, soft-spoken man came up and asked if he could be of assistance. The 'wolf' slunk away, and Maria Budlick willingly accepted her new friend's offer of some refreshment in his home at 71 Mettmännerstrasse. Here Kürten – the soft-spoken man – gave her a glass of milk and some bread and ham and offered to take her to a hostel. But instead, he took her out to the Grafenberger Wald, telling her the hostel was in the 'Wolf's Glen', and, as soon as they were alone, tried to have sexual intercourse with her standing up, at the same time seizing her throat. Then he released her, and asked if she remembered where he lived. She said no, so he left her alone.

Later, Maria Budlick wrote about her midnight adventure, in a half-joking vein, to a woman she had met on the train. The letter went to the wrong woman, since the name was mis-spelled, and the woman who opened it and read it handed it to the police. The police quickly got hold of Maria Budlick and she was able to take them to the Mettmännerstrasse. Unfortunately, she could not remember the house; but they went into a place she thought similar, and inquired from the landlady. The woman took her up to Kürten's room and showed it to her; she immediately recognized it. On the way downstairs, she met Kürten on his way up.

Kürten saw her too, and realized that he was close to arrest. It is difficult to know what he felt at this point. Even if the police convicted him of an attempted rape on Maria Budlick, this was no evidence that he was the 'monster'. Nevertheless, it would mean a further term in prison, and when the murders ceased in Düsseldorf, the police would have good reason for keeping Kürten under careful observation in the future. For some reason, Kürten decided to put an end to it all. In the early hours of the morning, his wife returned home from the restaurant where she worked. (Kürten usually met her outside, to protect her from the 'monster'. Her absence until the early hours of the morning had also given him his opportunity for his attacks.) Kürten confessed to her that he was 'in trouble again' and was wanted by the police for another attempt at rape. (She had saved him on an earlier occasion by persuading his victim to drop the case.) This time it would mean ten years in jail. Frau Kürten burst into tears – one of her chief fears was dying in a lonely and penniless old age. After a moment, Kürten told her the truth – that he was the 'monster', and that she could collect a reward by giving him up. For a long time she would not believe him, and he had to describe all his crimes in detail to convince her. They went out for a meal, and she was so upset that she could not finish her share; Kürten ate it up.

Finally, on May 24th, 1929, Frau Kürten told her story to the police. She had agreed to meet her husband near the Rochus Church later in the day. When Kürten arrived, a police officer with a loaded revolver met him; Kürten politely told him that he need not be afraid, and quietly accompanied him to the police station. The reign of terror was over.

In the fifteen months since the death of Rose Ohliger, thirteen thousand letters had poured in to the Düsseldorf police; nine thousand people had been interviewed and 2,650 clues followed up. In Germany, 900,000 people had been 'denounced' as the murderer, and all had been interviewed by the police. Tracking Kürten down must have cost many thousands of pounds. Of the 900,000, three charges were made against Kürten by people who had known his tendency to violence, including one girl who had been assaulted by him and thrown into the river; the police fined her for 'gross nonsense' and she only escaped the fine by an appeal.

On the other hand, it is not surprising that Kürten was not an obvious suspect. Even after his arrest, most of his neighbours and workmates considered that it was a mistake. He was known as a quiet, well-behaved man, a dandy in his dress, intelligent, and a good worker.

Kürten made a full confession of the murders, although he later withdrew it. Gertrude Schulte picked him out of a number of men paraded in front of her. Professor Berg was introduced to Kürten, and remarked that Kürten proved to be an intelligent truthful man, interested in his own case, and anxious to help the psychiatrist to understand the strange urges that had led to his crimes.

Some of the things Kürten revealed to Berg are terrifying. On one occasion when he could not find a victim in the Hofgarten, he seized a sleeping swan, cut off its head, and drank the blood. The swan was found the next morning. On another occasion, he saw a horse involved in a street accident, and had an orgasm. At first he tried to convince Berg that he killed for 'revenge on society', but was later frank in admitting the sexual origin of his crimes. The horror caused by his crimes gave him deep satisfaction. It was for this reason that he had gone back to the body of Rose Ohliger many hours after he had killed her, and poured paraffin on the body. Later still, he had lingered on the edge of the crowd, and had an orgasm provoked by the horror of the spectators.

The following is typical of Kürten's statements about his attacks:

In March 1930, I went out with my scissors. At the station a girl spoke to me. I took her to have a glass of beer, and we then walked towards the Grafenberg woods. She said her name was Irma. She was about 22. Near the middle of the woods, I seized her by the throat and I held on for a bit. She struggled violently, and screamed. I threw her down the ravine that runs down to the Wolf's Glen and went away.

385

Many young women gave evidence of similar experiences. One servant girl whom Kürten attempted to strangle complained that he was rough. He told her 'that was what love was'. She met him on several occasions after this! Another believed he was a single man and was going to marry her; one day she inquired at his home and was told he was married; this experience made her particularly bitter against Kürten. On another occasion, Kürten's wife caught him out with a woman and slapped her face. Kürten brushed her cheek with a rose and turned and walked off, leaving the two women together.

Kürten's wife never suspected his perversions; he had sexual intercourse with her periodically, but admitted that he had to imagine sadistic violence in order to go through with the love-making.

With respect to his crimes, Kürten's memory was of astonishing accuracy; seventeen years after the murder of Christine Klein, he was able to describe her bedroom in detail. On other points, his memory was average; it was obvious that he took such intense pleasure in his crimes that every detail remained in his mind. He admitted to dwelling on them afterwards and having sexual orgasms as he recalled their details. He also told Berg that he used to walk through the streets of Düsseldorf and day-dream of blowing up the whole city with dynamite. Hitler lost a talented lieutenant in Kürten, one who might have outshone Eichmann or Heydrich in mass murder.

The Hahn case revealed a curious aspect of Kürten's sadism – an element of necrophilia. The naked body had been sexually assaulted, both vaginally and anally; leaves and earthmould were found in the anus. Kürten admitted how, after killing her, he had buried her roughly. Later he decided to alter the location of her grave; he also had an idea that it would be exciting to crucify her body on two trees and leave it to be found. However, the body was too heavy; nevertheless, Kürten changed the location of the grave, and admitted to kissing and fondling the victim when he had dug her up. He returned often to the site of the grave and masturbated on it.

And yet one of Kürten's favourite dream fantasies was of saving Düsseldorf from the 'monster', and having torchlight processions in his honour. He would be nominated police commissioner for his service. (Perhaps Kürten had read the life of Vidocq.)

Kürten's trial opened on April 13th, 1931. In accordance with the German custom, it took place in front of three judges. Kürten's counsel was Dr Wehner, a young lawyer; the prosecution was led by the public prosecutor, Dr Jansen. Dr Jansen asked several times that the Press and public be excluded – no doubt because he wanted to reveal evidence that would leave no room for any but the death sentence – but his pleas were unsuccessful. Professor Berg gave evidence, describing Kürten as a 'king of sexual perverts' (a description that recalls Professor Wertham's description of Albert Fish). Professor Sioli gave psychiatric evidence for the prosecution, and Professor Rather for the defence. The defence was of insanity at the time of the murders. The case closed on April 23rd. Kürten's final remarks are of some interest: he declared that the real reason he had allowed his wife to give him up was that 'there comes a time in the life of every criminal when he can go no further'. He also added (what seems obvious from the evidence) that his victims made it very easy for him by allowing themselves to be accosted or by accosting him.

The jury was out for an hour and a half, and Kürten was sentenced to death nine times for murder.

For a while there seemed some hope that Kürten might not suffer the death penalty, which had not been carried out since a man named Böttcher had been executed in 1928 for the murder of a woman and a child in a wood near Berlin. It is indicative of the extreme liberalism in Germany in the early 1930's that there was something of a storm at the death penalty on Kürten, and the German Humanitarian League protested. Kürten appealed, but the appeal was rejected. Kürten himself was calm and well-behaved. He was bombarded with letters, love letters and letters describing sadistic punishments arriving in equal quantities. Many people asked for his autograph. (A girl who had been assaulted by Kürten when he was 16 described how he stood one day in front of the waxworks of murderers and burglars and said, 'One day I shall be as famous as they are.')

He was executed at six o'clock on the morning of July 2nd, 1931. He enjoyed his last meal – of Wiener schnitzel, chips, and white wine – so much that he asked for it again. He told Berg that his one hope was that he would hear the sound of his own blood running into the basket, which would give him intense pleasure. (He also admitted to wanting to throttle Berg's stenographer because of her slim, white throat.) He was guillotined, and seemed cheerful and unconcerned at the last.

L

LABBÉ, Denise
Twenty-nine-year-old French secretary, convicted in 1955 of the murder of her two-and-a-half-year-old daughter Catherine.

'Cathy' was the result of an affaire between Denise Labbé and a young doctor, who (like most of her lovers) departed her life as abruptly and with the same casualness as he had entered it; but Denise Labbé, for all her nymphomaniac tendencies, appeared a devoted mother. As she was working and therefore not able to tend Cathy herself, she boarded the child with a reliable foster-nurse, Madame Laurent, at Agly near Paris. At a May-day dance in 1954 at the Café Glacier by the square in front of Rennes Town Hall, Denise Labbé met cadet-officer Jacques Algarron, with whom she became infatuated; four years her junior, Algarron combined a startlingly handsome appearance with an exceptional brain. An expert mathematician, he also admired and subscribed to the works of German philosopher Nietzsche – in particular the theory of Übermensch, or 'superman', gradually evolving his own theory of a 'super couple' who would be bound together by a mutual disregard of (in their opinion) mundane values; in Denise Labbé, Algarron saw his prospective 'super-partner'. The resulting relationship bears a resemblance to the notorious liaison thirty years before in Chicago between two 'supermen' students (see LEOPOLD, Nathan). Algarron, more-over, demanded complete allegiance from his partner, whose in-fatuation was so extreme that her normal discernments were blunted and she submitted willingly to any indignity; this was propitious, not only consummating Algarron's notion of super-couple, but also his somewhat sadistic notions of sexual relations. (Denise Labbé spoke afterwards of a seaside visit, 'I was even very proud of showing my scars on the beach . . .') In a taxi, three months after their meeting, Algarron was to say:

'To form the ideal, the extraordinary couple, the only form of real cohabitation . . . a man and a woman must be capable of committing any act whatsoever for each other, even to the point of killing a taxi-driver.' On August 29th, 1954, Algarron asked Labbé if she would consider killing her child, Cathy, as proof of her absolute subservience, not only to him, but to his super-couple theory. Labbé answered that she would be prepared to do this, but her procrastination (whether through mother-love or cowardice) brought forth a series of ultimatums from Algarron, threatening to break off their affaire if she did not comply with this project; he also continued to send his fascinated (and, doubtless, uncomprehending) mistress long letters, nearly all of which were concerned with sexual symbolism:

... I think of you, and as I do a simple geometric line emerges before my window; it is a powerful tree shivering in a stormy sky. Very hard from the roots upwards which are plunged into the quivering matter of life itself, it rises as if drawn by the gulf of the heights, and shudders as the wind stirs the leaves along its backbone, in the same way that our eyelids turn blue as my fingernails mount the tender furrow of a woman's back from the dampness of her thighs to the diaphanous nape of neck. The green turns glaucous, the black pales with sap as the male erection of the tree trunk shrinks to the possession of a lightning streak of madness in the eyes of his lover. ...

... I expect from you more than the extraordinary and you know it. If your blood be as strong as mine, transporting you above yourself ... you will become the woman in the Couple I intend to create ...

By the end of September, frantic at the thought of losing Algarron (on the 21st he had written, 'I find a voluptuous sensation in abandoning a pretty quarry'), Labbé attempted to throw her small daughter out of a high window, finding herself unable, at the last minute, to commit the deed. A week later she threw Cathy into a canal, but, feeling remorse at once, caused the child to be rescued; the resolve to murder her daughter soon returned, however, and on September 30th she wrote in pessimistic vein to Algarron:

... Catherine never leaves her mother during the daytime and I can assure you that it is not going to be easy ... if it were not for our great love I would give up ... will my love for you be stronger than fear? Will the Devil triumph over God? My one great desire is rapidly to become your wife. ...

Algarron replied:

I can feel your isolation ... reply to me from the depths of your soul and read in my eyes strength and desire. The creation of our Couple will mark the apogee of my life to date ... you risk your heart Denise, and I doubtless risk my reason. But your intelligence and my heart cannot be kept out of the matter much longer.

On October 16th, Labbé made yet another abortive attempt at murdering Cathy, by throwing her into the river, which ran at the bottom of foster-mother Laurent's garden, but again the child was rescued, this time by neighbours who heard her cries. On October 19th, Labbé suffered a bad haemorrhage (the result of a bungled abortion) and was taken to hospital where she was visited by Algarron who said (according to her later testimony) that in order to continue their liaison it was essential the child Catherine should be murdered. On Monday November 8th, Labbé threw her daughter, head down, into a water-filled stone washing-basin; this time the intention was fulfilled, but when Algarron was told he remarked (again according to Labbé's testimony), 'I find it all very disappointing. It means nothing at all to me now!' Madame Laurent, meanwhile, was suspicious, remembering Cathy's recent mishaps, and investigations commenced; it was found that the child could not have accidentally fallen in the washing-basin because of a high spiked barrier. Labbé, uneasy, asked the advice of her brother-in-law, lawyer Jean Dusser, who advised her to go to the police admitting manslaughter; Labbé explained to the police that she had tried to save her daughter, but had been overcome by the vision of her lover's eyes, which had caused her to faint. The police were not impressed by this explanation and Denise Labbé was arrested on a charge of murder; two months later, on January 24th, 1955, she was also charged with the attempted murder of her daughter on the three previous occasions. Labbé's response now was to implicate her lover, telling the Examining Magistrate, M. Baer: 'I am the mistress of Jacques Algarron, Second Lieutenant in the School of Artillery at Châlons-sur-Marne. It was he who asked me to kill my child in order to prove my love for him . . .' Algarron was arrested, and when confronted with Labbé and her accusing cries in M. Baer's chambers replied: 'The girl is quite mad.' He was to repeat this assertion countless times in prison while awaiting trial, significantly indicating the photographs of his own two children (by former lovers) adorning his cell wall; but Denise Labbé persisted in her accusations of 'ritual murder', and wrote to foster-mother Laurent:

. . . Believe me, if Jacques had not ordered me to kill my daughter, the idea would never have entered my head. While he is denying everything now, there was a time when he was fixing the day and the hour when Cathy was to die. I have enough on my conscience with having murdered my daughter without having to invent such a story against Jacques if it were not true, believe me.

The trial of Labbé and Algarron commenced on May 30th, 1956, Maître Simon defending Denise Labbé, and Maître Floriot defending Algarron, with Judge Lecoq presiding over the court. Algarron now continued to ridicule Labbé's charges, and when questioned by the judge about his incriminating 'super-couple' letters replied: 'I did make some allusions . . . but whereas I remained in the abstract, she wanted to create something concrete.' Maître Floriot produced many of Algarron's former lovers in an attempt to refute the allegations of sadism thrown at his client, although one of them, downright Thérèse G., was hardly to produce the desired effect: '. . . one day he said to me that in love, two partners should make each other suffer mutually. "Excuse me, but I am normal," I told him, and he never mentioned the subject again.' Madame Laurent, the foster-mother, was not impressed by Algarron's protestations of innocence; in the witness-box she turned to him screaming 'Beast! Beast!' Denise Labbé having openly admitted her guilt, the Public Prosecutor, Advocate-General Francisque Gay, demanded for her the death sentence and penal servitude for life for Algarron. Out for three hours, the jury found Labbé guilty, but with extenuating circumstances, and Algarron guilty of having provoked the crime; they were sentenced to life penal servitude and twenty years' hard labour respectively. Even as she left the dock, Denise Labbé, with a depraved coquettishness, dropped her glove at the feet of her former lover.

LACENAIRE, Pierre François

Lacenaire is simultaneously one of the most interesting of men and the most commonplace of criminals. With Peter Kürten, he is one of the few men in criminal history who, in spite of their crimes, leave the reader feeling a certain sympathy. They have many points in common (although Lacenaire was no sadist), as will emerge in the following.

In 1834 there were about two hundred murders a year committed in Paris. (Less than in 1947, when there was an average of two a day.) One day the Commissionaire of Police was summoned to a room at 271 Rue St Martin, where an old lady and her son (an ex-convict and writer of begging letters) were living; they had not been seen for two days. Both were found dead, the widow stabbed and the man, Chardon, killed with a chopper.

They had been dead for two days, which placed the date of the crime as December 14th, 1834. The motive was obviously robbery.

On New Year's Eve, two weeks later, a bank messenger named Genevay called at 66 Rue Montorgueil to collect money from a M. Mahossier. In the room he was attacked by two men and stabbed in the back; but he managed to cry out, and the men fled, leaving him injured, but still in possession of eleven thousand francs.

Canler of the Sûreté was placed in charge of both cases. He made a routine check of all lodging houses and found that a M. Mahossier had stayed in one in Rue du Faubourg du Temple with a man named Fizellier. The description of Fizellier tallied with that of a man who had been arrested for theft a few days before, and sure enough, the man – whose name was François – admitted that he was 'Fizellier'. Canler further discovered that Mahossier also called himself Bâton, and that he frequented a café in the Rue Bondy. Bâton was duly arrested; but Canler soon discovered that he was not Mahossier. Yet it was possible that 'Mahossier' was a friend of Bâton who used his name. Bâton had a friend named Gaillard who corresponded to the description of Mahossier given by the bank messenger So the hunt for Gaillard was now on. He was traced to a lodging house in the Rue Marrivaux des Lombards; he had left, but had left papers behind – poems and inflammatory articles against the Government.

A prisoner named Avril promised to find Gaillard, but was unsuccessful. But François suddenly decided to admit that he was one of the murderers of the widow and her son. His accomplice had been Gaillard.

Avril put the police on to an aunt of Gaillard in the Rue Bar du Bec; she told them that her nephew was a bad lot and that his real name was Pierre François Lacenaire.

On February 2nd, Lacenaire got himself caught. The police in Beaune arrested a man who called himself Levi, and who was trying to negotiate a forged bill. Returned to Paris, Lacenaire admitted his identity, and when told of the betrayal of Avril and François, decided to revenge himself on them by revealing their part in the crimes. He and Avril had murdered the widow and her son, Lacenaire stabbing the widow with a shoemaker's awl; they took five hundred francs. And François had been the man who tried to strangle the bank messenger, while Lacenaire stabbed the man.

The three were tried on November 12th, 1835, at the Seine Assizes before M. Dupuy. By this time, Lacenaire was a famous man. Reporters and visitors thronged to the jail to see the man of letters turned criminal; his poems were read, his sayings and opinions repeated, his songs set to music. He was receiving the kind of attention that, had it come earlier, would have sweetened his character and prevented his becoming a murderer. He was suave and well-mannered; he became a close friend of Allard, Vidocq's successor as head of the Sûreté.

Lacenaire was determined that his two faithless accomplices should suffer, and he admitted everything coolly in order to implicate them. He succeeded; he and Avril were sentenced to death and François to penal servitude for life.

In jail, awaiting his execution, he wrote his memoirs (which Dostoievsky later printed in a magazine he edited, to increase circulation). They are a remarkable document, and tell us all we need to know of the man. Lacenaire was born in Lyon, the second child of a well-to-do merchant, in 1800. His elder brother was the favourite son; he developed a sense of injustice that soon expressed itself in thieving. One day his father pointed out the scaffold to him and told him he would end on it if he did not change his ways. Lacenaire was a lone wolf; a description in his memoirs is typical: 'All night I strode along the Quais. I lived ten years in an hour. I wanted to kill myself, and I sat on the parapet by the Pont des Arts, opposite the graves of those stupid heroes of July. . . . Henceforth my life was a drawn-out suicide; I belonged no longer to myself, but to cold steel. . . . Society will have my blood, but I, in my turn, shall have the blood of society.' He read Rousseau and became a revolutionary. But he had a resentment against life, not dissimilar to that felt by Edgar Edwards (see p. 26). Failures filled him with a desire to 'spite' life. (He did not believe in God, and so could not spite God.) This in turn was rationalized into a hatred of Society (as with Peter Kürten). It would have been useless to point out to him that 'Society' does not exist, and that even if it did, living the life of a criminal would not spite it.

Somewhat more rationally, he hated the complacent rich; but then, neither of the crimes for which he was hanged was committed against the rich.

A point came where he decided to be a criminal in the same way that another man might decide to devote his life to poetry. He observed his own lack of 'feeling' about life (again like Edgar Edwards and like Meursault in Camus' *l'Étranger*), that he had

killed two men in duels without the slightest feeling (did Dostoievsky borrow some of Stavrogin's character from Lacenaire?).
He was basically a poet and a metaphysician; he wanted a meaning in life. He surveyed life and found it inscrutable, revealing
no sign of an important destiny for himself. And he craved
revenge. But he lacked the discipline to carry out his ideal purpose; if he had possessed literary discipline he might have been
an earlier Lautreamont or Rimbaud; perhaps even a Swift or
Voltaire. He wanted to be a scourge of Society, its sternest critic.
In a sense, he was trying to put into effect the gospel of Shaw's
Undershaft, the armament manufacturer in *Major Barbara* who
said 'Thou shalt starve ere I starve,' and who then used every
means in his power to achieve success. (Having achieved it, he
became, as he pointed out, a sane and useful member of Society.)
But Lacenaire was too much driven by emotion to make a good
job of it, and finally brought himself to the guillotine.

LAFARGE, Marie

French *cause célèbre* which aroused an interest difficult to understand today. She was convicted of the murder of her husband by
arsenic on circumstantial evidence; but whether she was
guilty or not, it is almost certain that she would not have been
convicted on the same evidence in an English or American
court. (See Adelaide Bartlett, Annie Crawford, Madeleine
Smith.)

Marie Capelle seems to have been a most irritating young
woman, a sort of Madame Bovary, spoiled and petty, much given
to lying (which some modern apologists have called 'mytho-
mania') and thoroughly uncharitable in her judgement of friends,
as her memoirs reveal.

She was born in 1816, daughter of an officer who spoiled her.
When her father died in a hunting accident, her mother moved
to Paris, and Marie disliked living in a small flat. She was sent
away to school, but induced a nervous disease by fretting, and
was taken away. Her mother also died when Marie was in her
teens and she went to live with an aunt in Paris. Here she had a
certain social success and became an intimate of Marie de
Nicolaï, a young girl whose social standing was superior to Marie
Capelle's. An affaire involving a young man named Félix Clavé
and some love letters that passed between him and Marie de
Nicolaï show Marie Capelle in an unfavourable light as a born
deceiver and intriguer. Finally, when her friend married the

Vicomte de Léataud, some jewels disappeared, and Marie later came heavily under suspicion as a thief.

In 1829, when she was 25, she unexpectedly married a provincial ironmaster, Charles Lafarge, who had presented himself through a matrimonial agency in August. Marie disliked him, and apparently decided at an early date that she would remain a virgin. She was horrified to discover that he was a widower, but it was too late to withdraw from the marriage. However, she refused to allow her husband any intimacies, and strangely enough, he seems to have agreed that their love should be Platonic. On their arrival at his château at Le Glandier in Corrèze (which she disliked intensely because it was old and dilapidated) she wrote him a long letter explaining that she was in love with another man who wanted her to elope to Smyrna. It was almost certainly pure Bovary-ish invention. After a dramatic scene during which she threatened to kill herself, she graciously consented to remain with her husband. He decided to humour her, and hired six men to start making improvements in the house. On one occasion he broke into her bedroom, but only lay down on her bed to be sick.

In November 1839, Charles went to Paris to try to obtain a patent for an invention. The letters they exchanged are full of mystical language and protestations of love. A curious episode occurred while Charles was in Paris; Marie's mother-in-law said she looked pregnant, and Marie replied that, although she was a virgin, she suspected that she might be pregnant, 'through the grace of God', and proceeded to make arrangements for the baby's arrival.

Shortly before Christmas a case of cakes was sent to Charles in Paris. Marie apparently filled it with small cakes, after which it was screwed down; but when it arrived in Paris it contained one large cake and was nailed down. An associate of Charles, Dennis Barbier, whom Marie had antagonized, arrived in Paris just before the cake. When Charles ate some of the cake he was taken seriously ill, and finally returned to Le Glandier on January 3rd, 1840. Marie nursed him, but eventually he died. Shortly after his death, Marie was accused of poisoning him and arrested.

Until the *affaire Dreyfus*, few cases in France were to cause such popular controversy; France split into those who were pro-Marie and those who were anti. There were many curious features in the case. Immediately after her arrest, the husband of her old friend, Marie de Nicolaï, accused her of the theft of the jewels, and Marie Lafarge admitted that they were in her possession, but claimed that Marie de Nicolaï had given them to her to meet blackmailing demands by Félix Clavé. In fact, she produced several stories to account for her possession of them.

There seems to be no certainty that Charles was killed by poison. Admittedly, Marie had bought three lots of arsenic since her marriage, but then, Le Glandier was overrun by rats. And various experts on poisons failed to find arsenic in the body. One of them, the celebrated M. Orfila, declared that he found a small quantity, but not enough to kill a man.

Many people declared Marie Lafarge a saint, and there were many who vouched for her charm and fascination. Others saw her as a spoiled and pampered liar who may have killed her husband to avoid having sexual intercourse with him. (It has been plausibly suggested that this may be the solution of another famous poison mystery – the death of Charles Bravo.)

The case lasted through most of 1840, and Marie Lafarge was finally found guilty and sentenced to life imprisonment. Some evidence was given to indicate that she had put a 'white powder' into her husband's food.

She served most of her term at Montpellier, being allowed a servant in prison and the companionship of her cousin, Adèle. She wrote a book, *Hours in Prison*, a tragedy, *The Lost Woman*, and corresponded with Alexandre Dumas. In 1851 she was transferred to a maison de santé at Saint-Rémy; released by Napoleon III, she died at Ussat in the Pyrenees in 1852, still declaring her innocence.

LAMANA Kidnapping Case

On June 8th, 1907, 7-year-old Walter Lamana was lured away from outside his father's undertaking business at 624 St Philip Street, in the French quarter of New Orleans.

Two days later Peter Lamana received a ransom note demanding $6,000. The result was intense excitement and indignation throughout New Orleans, unprecedented since the murder of Police Chief Dave Hennessy by the Mafia, and the subsequent lynching of nine Italians accused of the crime. On June 12th, Italian citizens formed a committee pledged to the eradication of the Black Hand in New Orleans and finding the kidnapper of Walter Lamana. (The Black Hand was an Italian secret society, responsible, like the Mafia, for much labour racketeering and intimidation of Italian residents.) A mob formed which proceeded to search the neighbourhood of the kidnapping. This action brought one fact to light: two schoolboys declared that they had seen a man named Tony Costa going away with Walter Lamana.

On the Thursday following the kidnapping (which occurred on a Saturday) Peter Lamana received an anonymous letter advising the arrest of a barber named Morti, who seemed to be involved in the Black Hand. An Italian farmer named Campisciano was arrested; he had been seen riding on horseback near a wagon with black curtains. (Another small boy claimed he had seen Walter Lamana pushed into such a wagon.) On Friday June 14th, Tony Costa was finally arrested. Many other Italians were arrested, but released for lack of evidence.

An Italian merchant had received a threatening letter, which he claimed was written by a man named Tony Gendusa; the handwriting was very similar to that of the ransom note. A search for Tony Gendusa began, and his brother Frank was arrested.

Frank Gendusa was finally induced to admit that his brother Tony and a man named Leonardo Gebbia had been involved in the kidnapping of the child. Gebbia was arrested. Under third degree they admitted that the child had been taken to the farm of Ignazio Campisciano (who had been released by this time). Gebbia's sister Nicolina was also arrested. She was known as the sweetheart of a man named Luchesi, who was also implicated in the kidnapping.

Several men descended on Campisciano's farm, and he was seized, bound, and a rope looped around his neck as if in preparation for a lynching. After some 'persuasion', he led the posse to the body of Walter Lamana, who had, he claimed, been murdered on the Wednesday after the kidnapping by a man named Incaratero. Walter Lamana had been strangled and then killed with a hatchet or similar weapon. Mr and Mrs Campisciano were arrested. Maria Campisciano was allowed to take her son and a baby in arms to jail with her.

Now four men were still sought: Tony Gendusa, Incaratero, Luchesi, and a man named Stefan Monfre, whose name had been mentioned by Leon Gebbia. Six others were held: the Campiscianos, the Gebbias, Tony Costa, and Frank Gendusa. It seems reasonably certain that the two women were only accessories; Nicolina Gebbia claimed that she had been engaged to Frank Gendusa, but that her parents had thrown him out of the house (where he lodged) when they announced their engagement, and he had subsequently told her that he now intended to go to the bad, and would make money through a kidnapping. On the day after the kidnapping, he told her that the child was being held at the Campiscianos. At this point she might have saved the child's life by talking, and no doubt this weighed heavily with the jury, who eventually sentenced her to life imprisonment.

The Gebbias were tried after the other four. The first trial took place in Hahnville, and there were many attempts at mob violence (so that the State militia eventually had to be called in). The trial began on Monday, July 15th, five weeks after the kidnapping. It lasted for two days, and resulted in a verdict of 'guilty without capital punishment'. Frank Gendusa and the Campiscianos began life terms of hard labour, while Tony Costa died shortly after his arrival in Angola – either from natural causes or the third degrees he had endured. The verdict caused much indignation.

On November 12th the Gebbias were tried and sentenced to death by a jury who no doubt remembered the rage of the mob after the other four accused escaped with their lives. (Some members of the earlier jury had been forced to leave town.) This verdict is almost certainly unjust, since Leon Gebbia had no active part in the kidnapping, and his sister was only an accessory after the fact. Leon Gebbia was finally executed on Friday, July 16th, 1909. His sister was reprieved and sentenced to life imprisonment. Leon Gebbia was only 20.

It seems absurd that Gebbia should have been executed when the man who was obviously the villain of the piece – Ignazio Campisciano – should receive only life imprisonment. It seems certain that the kidnapping was not Campisciano's only venture into criminal enterprise; there were rumours of pedlars murdered on his lonely farm and hidden in the same swamp where Walter Lamana's body was found.

The Lamana case had at least one agreeable consequence for the Italian citizens of New Orleans: the power of the Black Hand was broken – temporarily, at any rate.

LAMSON, Dr George Henry
A morphia addict who poisoned his 18-year-old brother-in-law for gain, in 1881.

Lamson appears to have had an unfortunate career. He was born in 1850, became a doctor and served at the siege of Paris in 1871, and in 1876 and 1877 as a volunteer army surgeon in Serbia and Rumania. While serving in the Balkans he contracted the morphine habit. But even in Paris at the age of 21 he was regarded as a dangerous man in administering drugs. In 1876 he married a ward in Chancery, and gained possession of her small fortune, which he spent quickly. His brother-in-law died – there was some suggestion later that this was Lamson's first murder – and he benefited to the tune of £700. Lamson purchased a medical practice in Bournemouth, but like most of his ventures, it failed. He went to America in 1881, but came back as poor as ever.

In spite of his drug habit, he was an extremely pleasant-faced and sensitive-looking young man who inspired many people with a deep liking for him. But he soon passed from writing cheques on an overdrawn account to writing cheques on banks at which he had no account – always for small sums – and he began to wonder how he might best retrieve his fortunes. He had another brother-in-law, Percy John, who was 18 and lived in a private school, Blenheim House, in Wimbledon. Percy John suffered from curvature of the spine, and it seemed clear that he would not live for many more years. Lamson decided to expedite his death. This would mean that his wife would receive a half of the £3,000 that would otherwise become Percy John's property, when he came of age. Accordingly, Lamson bought a vegetable poison, aconitine, and tried it out on Percy John during the summer holidays at Shanklin on the Isle of Wight. He was seriously ill, but recovered. A second trip to America intervened between this and Lamson's second – and successful – attempt at murder.

On his return from the second American trip, Lamson was forced to pawn his watch and surgical instruments. (Presumably his wife and child were living with relations at this time.) On November 24th he managed to buy more aconitine from Messrs Allen and Hanbury. He then went to the Isle of Wight and cashed a dud cheque for £20, sending the man a telegram later explaining that a mistake had been made and asking him to delay cashing it. He decided that he would poison Percy John, then go to France, where he would receive the news of his brother-in-law's death with an appearance of shocked innocence. On December 2nd he went to Wimbledon, but for some reason put off the murder attempt to the next day. He sent a letter to Percy John saying he would be visiting him briefly before going to France, and followed it up with a call at the school at seven the next evening, December 3rd, 1881. Percy was carried up to the dining-room in his wheel-chair, and Lamson had a short conversation with him, during which he gave him a slice of cake. He cut this from an uncut cake, but probably had concealed aconitine in some of the raisins in it. There was also an odd little pantomime when he persuaded Percy John to swallow a capsule into which he had poured (in view of the headmaster) ordinary sugar supplied by the headmaster. Possibly this was intended to confuse the issue in the event of his being accused. He left at some time after seven-twenty, and Percy John was taken ill soon after, dying in agony four hours later.

Lamson was the obvious suspect, since the school doctors believed the boy had been killed by poison. In 1881 they had no chemical means of detecting aconitine, but the firm who had sold Lamson the poison saw the case in the newspaper and contacted the police.

Lamson now decided on a bold stroke – he returned to England on December 8th, and marched into Scotland Yard, explaining he had come to clear up the misunderstanding. He was promptly held in custody, and brought to trial on March 9th, 1882, at the Old Bailey before Mr Justice Hawkins. The Solicitor-General, Sir F. Herschel, led for the Crown, while Mr Montague Williams led for the defence. Lamson – a grave, pale, prepossessing young man with a Dickens beard and thin, intellectual face – pleaded not guilty. There was a great deal of wrangling about aconitine and its detection, but the facts were too black against Lamson, and he was convicted of murder. There were strenuous efforts made to save him, including attempts to have him declared insane, but after two stays of execution, he was hanged on April 28th, six weeks after the conviction. Being deprived of morphia in prison, he was prostrated most of the time. He confessed to the murder before his death, and wrote an incoherent, rambling document, also a confession. But on the day of execution he had to be carried to the scaffold half-unconscious, and begged the clergyman to recite an extra prayer. He denied his guilt in murdering his wife's other brother, Herbert John, right to the end.

LANDRU, Henri Désiré
French mass-murderer, executed in February 1922.

Landru was born in Paris in (or around) the year 1869, son of a fireman at the Vulcain Ironworks, who, from 1888 to 1910, worked for the firm of Masson. Landru was educated at the École des Frères, Rue de Bretonvillers, and was regarded as a clever boy. He was admitted sub-deacon at the religious establishment of St Louis en l'Isle. At the age of 16 he took a course at the School of Mechnical Engineering. He served his period as a conscript at St Quentin, and remained in the army for four years, during which time he rose to rank of sergeant. He seduced his cousin, a Mlle Remy, and she bore him a daughter in 1891. In 1893, he married her; this was while he was a quartermaster-sergeant in the 3rd regiment. In 1894, he returned to civilian life. He then entered the service of a firm where he had to pay a deposit; his employer disappeared to America with his deposit. It may have been this experience that made Landru decide to take his 'revenge' by a life of crime.

In 1900, Landru earned a sentence of two years for fraud; it seems that he tried to withdraw a deposit made at the Comptoir d'Escompte, using a false name; he was arrested, and tried (or pretended to try) to commit suicide in prison. This was the first of seven sentences. However, he continued to be married, and presented his wife with four children in all. In 1904 he was sentenced again to two years; in 1906, to a further thirteen months; in 1908, to three years. While in prison, he was summoned to Lille to be tried on another charge, and received another three years. It seemed that Landru had inserted a matrimonial advertisement in a Lille newspaper and made the acquaintance of a 40-year-old widow. He handed her his 'deeds', and she handed him a dowry of 15,000 francs, with which he made off. Mme Izoré would seem to have been his first female victim. Immediately before the 1914 War, the police were searching for Landru for various other offences, and in his absence he was sentenced to four years in prison and lifelong deportation to New Caledonia, the sentence to be put into effect when he could be arrested.

It may have been the war that decided Landru to start his career as a murderer. It may have also been the total absence of ties. His mother had died in 1910; his father, after staying with Landru's wife (in 1912) while Landru was in prison, committed suicide on August 28th in the Bois de Boulogne, shattered by his son's career of crime.

In 1914, Landru made the acquaintance of a widow, Mme Cuchet, age 39, who worked in a lingerie shop in the Rue Monsigny. She had a 16-year-old son. Landru was known to her as M. Diard, an engineer. She and Landru quarrelled, and Mme Cuchet begged her parents, sister, and brother-in-law to go with her to M. Diard's house, a villa near Chantilly, to help make things up. He was not in, but in a chest in the house the brother-in-law found many letters from women, and informed Mme

Cuchet that he was an impostor. She refused to listen, preferring to break off all relations with her family. She furnished a villa at Vernouillet, and went to live there with 'Diard' and her son André. Soon afterwards, the mother and son disappeared. This was in January 1915. In the previous June, Landru had opened an account of 5,000 francs at Chantilly; he later claimed that the money came from the 10,000 francs he had inherited from his father. Mme Cuchet's gold watch was given as a present to Landru's wife, who he continued to see.

Landru's next 'fiancée' was Mme Laborde-Line, a native of Buenos Aires, widow of a hotel-keeper. Landru met her at the beginning of June 1915. On June 21st, 1915, Mme Laborde-Line sold her furniture, telling the concierge she was going to live with her future husband at Vernouillet. She was seen at Vernouillet, gathering flowers. After June 26th, she was not seen again, but Landru sold her securities and parts of her furniture, and had the rest moved to his garage at Neuilly.

Landru's third victim was a widow, Mme Guillin, whose full name was Marie Angélique Désirée Pelletier, who lived in the Rue Crozatier, Paris. She was 51, and had turned a life annuity into cash for 22,000 francs. She met Landru through one of his marriage advertisements, and wrote to him on May 1st, 1915. She went out to visit Landru's villa at Vernouillet and returned to Paris delighted. On August 2nd she moved to Vernouillet, having given up her apartment in the Rue Crozatier and stored her furniture. On August 4th a removal van transferred all the furniture from Vernouillet to the garage at Neuilly. A few days later, Landru sold bonds belonging to Mme Guillin. In November and December of 1915 he committed various forgeries to get possession of 12,000 francs that Mme Guillin had in the Banque de France, using the name Georges Petit, and claiming to be her brother-in-law. He explained that she was paralysed and had placed her business affairs in his hands.

Now Landru took a villa at Gambais, a village south of Paris; it was called the Villa Ermitage, and was on the edge of the road, two or three hundred yards from other houses. He rented it from a M. Tric, giving himself the name of Dupont, an engineer of Rouen, and moved in during December 1915. His first victim there was a widow named Mme Héon, nine years Landru's senior, whose son had been killed in the war and whose daughter and best friend had died recently when Landru met her. In September 1915 Landru arranged for her furniture to be sold; she disappeared after December 8th. Three of her friends received postcards from Landru, saying that she could not write herself.

One of Landru's first acts in moving into the Villa Ermitage had been to buy a stove and a quantity of coal. It seems likely that Mme Héon disappeared into this stove.

Landru's next victim was, indirectly, the cause of his ultimate downfall. She was a 45-year-old widow, Mme Collomb, employed as a typist in the Rue Lafayette. She had a nest egg of 10,000 francs and lived with a man named Bernard, who either could nor or would not marry her. She saw Landru's advertisement on May 1st, 1915:

> Widower with two children, aged forty-three, with comfortable income, affectionate, serious, and moving in good society, desires to meet widow with a view to matrimony.

May 1st was the fatal day on which Mme Guillin was also writing to Landru. Mme Collomb replied to the advertisement, giving her age as 29, and soon 'M. Cuchet' (Landru this time adopted the name of his first victim) replied. Mme Collomb was captivated, but although she was only too eager to submit, she and Landru parted for a year – Landru having other fish to fry. When they met again, Cuchet took her to Gambais, and agreed reluctantly to meet her family, who all disliked him. In November 1916 Landru persuaded her to come and live with him in his flat in the Rue Châteaudun. On December 24th her sister came to visit Landru and his 'future wife' at Gambais. After Christmas Day Mme Collomb was seen no more. But a young soldier who claimed he was M. Cuchet's son paid a debt for her on January 29th and took flowers to her sister – flowers with a Nice railway label on them. After that, her family lost all trace of her. They wrote to the mayor at Gambais, asking his help. He put them in touch with the sister of a Mme Buisson, who had also disappeared after visiting the Villa Ermitage. The two families met and compared notes.

This, however, was to come later. Landru's next victim presents one of the most puzzling problems in the case; she was a poor, 19-year-old servant girl who was crying on a platform in the Métro when Landru asked her what was the matter. This was in January 1917. She had quarrelled with her mother, had no money, and would be out of work the next day. Landru offered her his room in the Rue de Mauberge. On March 11th, 1917, Andrée Babelay visited her mother to say she intended to get married. On March 29th they went out to Gambais; Landru took a return ticket for himself and a single for her. She was not seen after April 12th, although her papers were later found in Landru's possession. One can only assume that Landru started the liaison with his usual avidity for fresh sexual experience, and that when he tired of it he put an end to it in the usual way. The prosecution at his trial suggested that the girl had discovered something at the Villa Ermitage that made Landru decide to kill her.

The next victim was Mme Buisson, a widow with a small fortune of 10,000 francs, born in 1871. She also started corresponding with Landru in May 1915. She knew Landru for six months, then he disappeared for six months, telling her later that he had been to Tunis on business. In July 1917, at last freed from his other entanglements, Landru began to court her again. He made the acquaintance of her sister and mother, who knew him as Fremyet. Mme Buisson had a son, who finally left Paris. Landru now strove to isolate Mme Buisson from her family, particularly her sister, Mme Lacoste. He persuaded her to change her lodgings in April 1917. In June she ordered a wedding costume from her dressmaker. On August 19th Landru took a single and a return ticket to Garencières, near Gambais, and Mme Buisson was seen no more. September 1st was probably the date on which she was murdered. On September 1st Landru's cash also increased by 1,000 francs. Later that month Landru took care to settle her affairs, paying for the wedding dress, forging a letter to the concierge of her apartment in which he gave notice. The concierge doubted the signature and asked that Mme Buisson should call and confirm the notice; Landru called instead and explained that Mme Buisson had 'gone south'.

The eighth victim was a Mme Jaume, a religious woman, separated from her husband, who met Landru in the summer of 1917 through a matrimonial agent; she knew him as M. Guillet. In September she paid her first visit to Gambais. She left her house in the Rue de Lyanes on November 25th, 1917. Landru purchased a single and return ticket for Gambais. Landru's cash increased by 275 francs (the sum she had on her) and on November 30th he negotiated with the Banque Allaume for the remaining 1,400 francs she possessed.

The ninth victim was a pretty widow of easy morals, a Mme Pascal, 36 years old. Landru had started an affaire with her in October 1916 and she quickly became his mistress. She had very little money, and no doubt her case is similar to that of Andrée Babelay. She knew him as Forest. On April 5th, 1917, she went out to Gambais with Landru – on a single ticket. Her furniture was moved, with the help of Landru's son, and sold.

Landru's last known victim was a Mme Marchadier. She kept a small lodging house at 330 Rue St Jacques. In 1918, needing money, she corresponded with Landru, who called himself Guillet. She wanted to sell the house for 7,000 francs. Landru had no money at this time, and was forced to borrow money from his wife. He proposed marriage to Mme Marchadier and on January 1st, 1919, she wrote, 'I do not ask for anything better than to live in the country.' On January 9th she and Landru went to Gambais, where no doubt Landru's ardours persuaded her finally to live with him and sell her possessions. Landru was so short of money on this trip that he took single tickets out, and borrowed his return fare from a M. Vallet, a shoemaker. On returning to Paris, Mme Marchadier sold some of her furniture for 2,000 francs. Then, on the 13th, they returned to Gambais; a bus conductor who saw them travelling from Houdan to Gambais stated that Landru carried two bags of coal. Mme Marchadier's two dogs, of which she was very fond, came with them to Gambais. Mme Marchadier was not seen again.

The result of the meeting between the families of Mme Collomb and Mme Buisson was a police search of the Villa Ermitage, and finally a warrant for Landru's arrest. On April 11th, 1919, the day after the warrant was issued, Mme Buisson's sister, Mme Lacoste, was walking down the Rue de Rivoli when she saw Landru with a smart young woman on his arm. She followed him into a shop and heard him order a china dinner service to be sent to his address. She went to the police, who discovered from the shop that Landru was known as Lucien Guillet, an engineer, and that he lived at 76 Rue de Rochechouart. The girl accompanying him was Fernande Segret, 27 years old, an assistant in a furrier's shop. She had been picked up by Landru on a bus and was living with him as his mistress.

Landru was arrested at Rue de Rochechouart on April 12th, 1919. In his pocket was found a black covered loose-leaf notebook, which Landru tried to seize. It contained cryptic notes of all his eleven victims (including Mme Cuchet's son), and was the most important exhibit at the trial.

Landru was taken to Gambais, where a search of the garden revealed only the bodies of three dogs.

No sign of any of his victims was ever discovered. (This remains the most interesting aspect of the case – how did he dispose of the bodies with such thoroughness?) Landru was completely unco-operative. He claimed that the burden of proving him guilty rested on the prosecution, and refused to co-operate in any way in revealing the 'present whereabouts' of his victims, claiming that this was his own business. Many small bone splinters were found among the ashes at Gambais, but nothing that could be finally incriminating as a proof of murder. The clothes and papers of his victims were found in large quantities, however.

He was tried at Versailles Court from November 7th to 30th, 1921 (i.e. two and a half years after his arrest). Undoubtedly the French authorities encouraged the Press to give a great deal of space to the trial to distract attention from the Peace Conference, which was moving in a direction unfavourable to France.

Landru appeared to believe that he could not be convicted unless at least one body was found, and his defence consisted entirely of 'stone-walling'. The women had all been merely his business clients, and if he knew what had become of them, it was a secret between himself and them, which he would keep to himself. Possibly the jury took pleasure in sentencing him to death out of sheer exasperation with his stubbornness. Like another matrimonial killer, Max Gufler, he kept all his correspondences with women (169 in all) carefully filed. All were traced except the eleven victims mentioned in the notebook.

Witnesses were found who had smelt a putrid black smoke that poured from the chimney of the Villa Ermitage. One had seen Landru throw something into a pond by night; a youth spoke of fishing in this pond and drawing out a lump of putrid flesh.

The appearance of Fernande Segret in court caused something of a sensation, and the pretty girl told how she had met Landru on a bus in May 1917, how he had agreed to marry her and she had broken off with a fiancé of her own age, of how she had eventually agreed to live with him. At the time of his arrest the affair with Mlle Segret had been going on for two years, and he may have been in love with her. The whole of November 28th was occupied with Maître Godefroy's speech for the prosecution. The court was, as usual, packed to capacity, so that President Gilbert had to rebuke people who stood up for a better view of Landru, saying, 'You are not in a theatre.' The defence speech of Maître Moro-Giafferi lasted for two days and was of great brilliance, so that many people declared Landru could never be executed after it.

But the jury found him guilty, although they were persuaded by his advocate to sign a petition for clemency. In spite of this, Landru was guillotined on February 23rd, 1922.

Although he was undoubtedly a callous ruffian who deserved to be guillotined, Landru's downfall was not without its dignity. In court, his dry sense of humour frequently caused laughter, as when he remarked that most ladies reckon their age from confirmation, not from their birth. One day when a lady in the court could not find a seat, Landru rose to his feet and politely offered her his seat in the dock. At the end, he refused to be consoled by a priest, telling him to go and save his own soul. On the other hand, a reading of his trial (published in the *Famous Trials Series* by Geoffrey Bles) can hardly fail to cause irritation; even when the facts against him were overwhelming, he would continue to deny all knowledge with an infuriating persistence. When he was confronted by some fact that he could not explain, he would reply coldly that this was his secret and that French law allowed him the right to remain silent. He remained silent to the end.

LAURIE, John Watson (The Arran Murder)

A commonplace ruffian who murdered a fellow holiday-maker for money. On July 12th, 1889, Laurie became acquainted with his victim, a Brixton clerk named Edwin Robert Rose, when they were together on the steamer from Rothesay to Arran, which lies in the Clyde estuary – a well-known beauty spot. Laurie, who was 25, introduced himself as 'Annandale'. Later that day he called at a Mrs Walker's in the village of Invercloy and inquired for lodgings; she let an outside shed to him, which he said he would be occupying with a friend. Rose, who was a candid and open soul, made the acquaintance of two more men named Mickel and Thom, and introduced them to Annandale. On Monday July 15th, Mickel warned Rose about his companion, who had evidently made a bad impression on him; Rose had mentioned his intention of climbing Goatfell with Annandale, and Mickel told him on no account to do this. Rose seemed to agree, but when he had seen the two men off to Rothesay that afternoon, he forgot the warning and set out with Annandale for Goatfell. He never returned. The next morning Mrs Walker found her shed empty; her lodgers had apparently flown without paying rent.

But when the date of Rose's return to London came around – July 18th – his brother became anxious and the search began. But the body was not discovered until August 4th, when a search party found it in a place called Coire-na-fuhren (Gulley of fire), buried under some boulders; the pockets were empty and the face was badly battered. The body was carried nine miles to Corrie village. It was surmised that Rose had been pushed from a precipice above by his murderer, who had clambered down and finished him off with a rock.

The search for Annandale now began. It was found that a man corresponding to Annandale's description had rented a room in Rothesay, Port Bannatyne, on July 6th; he had gone to Arran on the 12th and reappeared at his lodgings on the 16th, Tuesday. On Friday, July 19th, he vanished without paying the £3 3s. 8d. rent due. Finally, this man was identified as John Watson Laurie, a pattern maker in the Atlas Locomotive Engine Works, Springburn, Glasgow, who was the black sheep of his family, and had been charged with theft earlier that year but, the money being made good by relatives, had escaped with an admonition. He was known to have gone from Glasgow to Rothesay on July 6th. A Glasgow acquaintance had seen Laurie in Rothesay, and later saw him with Rose. Later still, he saw Laurie back in Rothesay wearing a yachting cap which he remembered Rose wearing. This acquaintance, James Aitken, next saw Laurie in Hope Street, Glasgow, and asked him what he knew of the Arran mystery. (This was before the body was found.) Laurie 'hummed and hawed' and finally made off; Aitken went to the police.

In August Laurie wrote two letters to newspapers from Liverpool and Aberdeen, claiming that he had left Rose at the top of Goatfell with two men; he also declared that he was in Rothesay following a girl who had jilted him. (This appears to be true.) He said he intended to commit suicide.

Laurie was finally recognized at Ferniegair station, on the Glasgow line, on September 3rd, 1889; he was pursued into a wood by Constable Gordon, and some miners joined the chase. Laurie made a superficial razor cut on his throat before he was taken.

He was tried on Friday, November 8th, 1889, at the High Court of Justiciary, Edinburgh, before the Lord Justice Clerk, Lord Kingsburgh. Mr Stormonth Darling, the Solicitor-General led the prosecution; J. B. Balfour, afterwards Lord Kinross, led the defence.

Laurie claimed he had left Rose at six o'clock. He was seen by several persons with Rose, and, after six, alone. He was seen in the Corrie Hotel at ten o'clock, although Corrie is only a two hours' walk from Goatfell. Rose was last seen alive at about half past six, and at half past nine, a shepherd saw Laurie alone going in the direction of Corrie.

The defence case was that all Rose's injuries had been caused by a fall – an accidental fall – and that Laurie had then decided to rob and bury him.

There was one curious piece of evidence. The police at Corrie had buried Rose's boots in the sand, and later dug them up. Apparently this was because of a superstition that if this was done, Rose's ghost would not walk and disturb the living! (Apparently the police did not know about the ghost of Sergeant Davies, that was solemnly sworn to in the same High Court in 1754, and which had neither clothes nor boots!)

Laurie was found guilty and sentenced to death, but a considerable movement started to reprieve him. Finally, he was reprieved on grounds of insanity, and spent the remaining forty-one years of his life in Peterhead Prison. He became precentor in the prison chapel, and made one attempt to escape in 1893, being quickly recaptured. His only comment on the murder he had committed was, 'Rose hadn't very much, after all.' He died in Perth Prison in 1930, 69 years old.

LAX, Lorna (Murder of)

Lorna Lax, 12-year-old Californian, enthusiastic Girl Scout, was found stabbed, throttled by rope, and bludgeoned in secluded brushwood two hundred yards from her home in Kentfield, California (on the outskirts of San Francisco), two days after leaving a note:

> DEAR MOM, I'm MAd AT thE WOrld, SO ThErES only onE thing I know To do ANd that's To gET AWAY from thESE SEroundings SO I'm LEAVEINg. I'll Promise TO bE back SundAY Morning. I'M going To The city. your daughtEr. Lorna LAX.

As Lorna had behaved eccentrically on other occasions ('an unfortunate child, physically retarded, and emotionally troubled', said her parents) the letter did not cause concern until Monday, November 16th, 1959, when the girl had still not returned. That afternoon her body ('dead anytime between Saturday night and Sunday morning') was found by 13-year-old Norman Fortner; the murder spot, he explained afterwards, was a secret hideaway of Lorna's, where he and other chosen companions had frequently romped. There was no evidence of sexual violence, but the girl 'had been molested either before or after death'; it appeared that Lorna's hideaway was actually a 'sex-club' where she had charged local boys varying amounts (35 cents to one dollar) for 'initiation fees'. A school-friend of Lorna's gave the information that she had seen her at a college football game the previous Saturday, a few hours after she had written the departure note. On November 30th a purse found under the football field stand was handed in to the sheriff's office to be claimed. The owner, when contacted, said that certain contents were missing – two lipsticks, an eyebrow pencil, and a mirror; she was certain they had been in her purse at 8 pm on the night of the football game, and was able to identify cosmetics found by the body of Lorna Lax as her missing property. Questioning of sex-club initiates began anew, with emphasis laid on their Saturday afternoon activities. One youth, 15-year-old Clifford Fortner (the brother of the boy who had found the corpse), said he had been with Lorna Lax on the Saturday afternoon at sex-club headquarters.

Q. Did she have a purse with her?
A. Sure, she had a purse.
Q. Did you see what was in it?

The suspect listed the cosmetics found by the police that had not been in Lorna's possession until late on Saturday night, so incriminating himself. Confronted with the evidence, Fortner admitted going along to Lorna's hideaway on the Saturday evening, and making love to the girl before 'something came over me'. He battered her head with a torch, tried to strangle her with rope taken from a nearby swing, and, when these attempts proved unsuccessful, stabbed her several times in the abdomen with a steak knife before creeping back to his home. Under Californian law no one under 18 years can be executed, so Clifford Fortner will be held for an indeterminate period of detention.

LEOPOLD, Nathan

Nineteen-year-old amateur ornithologist and law student at Chicago University who, together with fellow student Richard Loeb, 18, was found guilty of the murder of 14-year-old Bobbie Franks.

Leopold and Loeb, considered intellectual prodigies by their friends and tutors, both came from wealthy German-Jewish homes and were accustomed to every kind of luxury. Each exercised an evil influence over the other, Leopold being infatuated by the charm of Loeb, Loeb being impressed by the intellect of Leopold, and both obsessed by the 'superman' philosophy of

Nietzsche, considering themselves beyond any observance of ethics or law. Bored, they carried out a series of petty thefts, then decided to carry out the 'perfect' murder.

On May 21st, 1924, in a hired car, they waylaid Bobbie Franks, a friend of Loeb's younger brother, outside his school in the Chicago suburb of South Side Kenwood, and invited him to take a ride. Probably flattered by their attention, the boy stepped into the vehicle; he was immediately gagged and his skull fractured four times with a heavy chisel. His body was taken to a culvert by the Pennsylvania railroad tracks and his head held under nearby swamp water to ensure death; the child's face was disfigured by hydrochloric acid and the corpse pushed into a drainpipe partially hidden by scrubs and weeds. The murderers then had a meal at a restaurant and returned to Leopold's home where they drank whisky, played cards, washed the hired car free of bloodstains and telephoned their victim's mother informing her that her son had been kidnapped and to expect ransom demands; the caller (who gave his name as Mr Johnson) said instructions would follow by post, and the police were not to be notified. Mr Franks did contact the police who had to tell him next day, May 22nd, that the body of a boy had been found; the father, already in receipt of a ransom note demanding $10,000 ('allow us to assure you that he is at present well and safe'), sent his brother-in-law round to the morgue and Bobbie Franks was identified despite the injuries and mutilations.

Leopold had dropped his spectacles by the culvert, and within eight days they were traced to him. He explained he often bird-watched in that area, and that he must have left them some time before the murder; it had rained incessantly days before that date, however, and the spectacles bore no weather marks. Asked about his activities on the afternoon of May 21st, Leopold said he had been out with 'Dickie' Loeb dating two girls 'Mae' and 'Edna', about whose present whereabouts he was vague. Two reporters on the *Chicago Daily News*, Al Goldstein and Jim Mulroy, checked specimens of Leopold's typing against that on the ransom note, and they matched; later the typewriter, an Underwood (stolen by the murderers the previous autumn from Loeb's old fraternity house at Ann Arbor), was dredged from a lagoon. Questioned for long periods by the police, Richard Loeb broke down first, and admitted the crime; Leopold's confession followed. Each accused the other of wielding the chisel.

Their trial, before Judge John R. Caverly, Chief Justice of the Criminal Court of Cook County, began in Chicago on July 21st,

1924; the defendants pleaded not guilty. Clarence Darrow, briefed by the murderers' parents for the defence, laid emphasis on his clients' abnormal mental states: Loeb was a schizophrenic and Leopold a paranoiac, neither therefore being responsible for their actions. Darrow's speech for the defence lasted two days; it was ponderous and emotional with Freudian undertones. To the agape courtroom he quoted from A. E. Housman's *Last Poems*:

> The night my father got me
> His mind was not on me;
> He did not plague his fancy
> to muse if I should be
> the son you see

and went on to more irrelevant whimsy: '... the mother who looks into the blue eyes of her little baby cannot help musing of the end of the child, whether it will be crowned with the greatest promises that mind can imagine – or whether he will meet death upon the scaffold...' Over-eloquent when describing (while deploring) his clients' possible summons to the scaffold, both Leopold and Loeb became hysterical. Darrow went on to say that Judge Caverly stood between the past and the future, between hate and love, and quoted the Persian poet, Omar Khayyam:

> So I be written in the Book of Love,
> I do not care about that Book above.
> Erase my name or write it as you will,
> So I be written in the Book of Love.

Despite the public clamour demanding the death sentence, the judge sentenced both to life imprisonment for the murder of Bobbie Franks, and to ninety-nine years' imprisonment for the boy's kidnapping. The murderers were removed to Joliet prison, where Loeb was killed in a prison brawl in 1936; Leopold was released on parole in 1958.

LEY and SMITH
Thomas Ley and John Lawrence Smith were charged together at the Old Bailey with the murder of John Mudie, a barman. A third man, John William Buckingham, turned King's evidence and was not charged.

The case is a curious one; Thomas Ley was certainly insane, and developed a strange obsession about Mudie; he then hired Smith

412

to murder him. But the obsession had no relation whatever to reality.

The career of Thomas Ley had been in many ways remarkable; in New South Wales he had once been the Hon. Thomas Ley, Minister for Justice, but a charge of bribery and two suspicious deaths – business associates of Ley who were in his way at the time of death – brought his political career to an end. Ley was a grossly fat man, whose fortune had been made by many dubiously legal activities. He returned to England in 1929.

A few weeks after he returned to England, Mrs Maggie Brook followed him; she was a widow of a Perth JP, and had been 40 when she met Ley in 1922. She became his mistress, and it was because of Ley's jealousy of her that the murder was committed.

Mrs Brook had a daughter, who married a man named Barron and went to live in Wimbledon. When the daughter was ill in hospital, Ley suggested to Mrs Brook that she should go and look after her son-in-law. This was in May 1946. On June 12th, 1946, at 10 pm, Ley telephoned Mrs Brook and accused her of having sexual relations with her son-in-law. (Mrs Brook was 66!) At two-thirty in the morning he arrived in a car and insisted that Mrs Brook return with him to his house in Knightsbridge Court.

There is no explaining Ley's strange jealousy obsession about Mrs Brook – they had ceased to have sexual intercourse ten years before. But there can be no doubt of his madness. He went to Mrs Brook's landlady in Wimbledon and declared that Mrs Brook had asked him to take her away because she was being pestered by the men in the house. He asked the names of the male lodgers, and Mrs Evans (the landlady) gave them. They included John Mudie, a 35-year-old barman and a decent young man who had only once ever spoken to Mrs Brook. Mrs Evans assured Ley that it was unlikely Mudie had slept with Mrs Brook. Later, Ley called again, saying he wanted to apologize to Mudie. Mrs Evans gave him Mudie's new address at Reigate, where he had become a barman.

Ley moved into a new property at 5 Beaufort Gardens. One day Mrs Brook's son-in-law received a phone call asking him to have tea with Mrs Brook at Beaufort Gardens. He was suspicious and checked with Mrs Brook, who knew nothing about the invitation. Barron was lucky, for Ley was waiting for him at Beaufort Gardens with hired thugs, who might very probably have killed him as Mudie was later killed.

After this failure Ley turned his attention to Mudie, and on

June 19th tried a curious trick to find out if Mudie was associating with Mrs Brook. He sent some cheques to Mrs Brook care of Mudie; Mrs Brook's counter-signature was needed on them. Naturally, Mudie had no idea where Mrs Brook was, and returned the cheques to the firm directed by Ley and Mrs Brook. Ley then had his solicitors write to Mudie demanding the return of the cheques, and finally went to see Mudie himself; Mudie satisfied Ley that the cheques had been returned and, after confirming this, Ley apologized. The reasons for his conduct are mysterious.

Ley now contacted John William Buckingham, a car-hirer, and invited Buckingham to a meeting. At this meeting, attended by Ley, Buckingham, and John Lawrence Smith, a joiner, Buckingham was told that Mudie was a blackmailer who must be decoyed to London and forced to sign a pledge not to bother Mrs Brook and her daughter again. A friend of Buckingham's, a Mrs Bruce, was also brought into the conspiracy. Her job was to go to the Reigate Hill Hotel and make Mudie's acquaintance. Smith hired a car, a Ford 8, number FGP 101, and on Wednesday, November 27th, 1946, drove down to a chalk pit situated on the Slines Road, leading from the main Croydon–Westerham road to Woldingham in Surrey. At about four-forty on this date, two labourers saw Smith standing on the edge of the chalk pit; when he saw them he ran away to the car, which was parked behind some trees, and drove off fast; they noticed the 101 in the number of the car, and also its make.

Mrs Bruce made Mudie's acquaintance according to plan, posing as a wealthy lady, and invited him to come and mix cocktails at a party to be given by her in London. Mudie accepted. On November 28th Mrs Bruce and Buckingham's son went to Reigate to pick up Mudie, and drove him to Beaufort Gardens, where Mrs Bruce let him in by a side door. She then closed the door and went off with Buckingham junior; this was the last she saw of Mudie. For this service she received £30. She had, of course, no idea that Mudie was to be murdered.

Inside the house, Smith and Buckingham pounced on Mudie and threw a blanket over his head, then tied him up with some clothes-line which Buckingham had bought. Buckingham was then given £200 – thirty of which were for Mrs Bruce – and told to go, and not to contact Ley again. (A few days later he was told that Mudie had signed the agreement, and had left the country with £500 given him by Ley.)

Now either Ley or Smith, or both, administered a brutal beating up to Mudie – probably Ley, in view of his motives. Then one of them strangled Mudie and the body was taken out to the chalk pit and dumped.

Two days later, on November 30th, the body was discovered by Mr Walter Coombs. A rope was tied around the throat, and there were signs of violent blows on the head, chest, and stomach. He was soon identified as Mudie, and among his possessions at the hotel were letters relating to his dealings with Ley. The police soon had Ley, Smith, and Buckingham under arrest and charged Ley and Smith with murder. Buckingham had gone to Scotland Yard of his own accord on December 14th, two weeks after discovery of the body, and made a statement.

Smith was an evasive witness who made a bad impression. He declared that he had left Mudie bound and gagged and alone in the house with Ley. He admitted his indifference to Mudie's fate, but claimed he did not believe Ley intended to murder him.

The trial opened on March 19th, 1947, at the Old Bailey before Lord Goddard, Lord Chief Justice. Mr Anthony Hawke and Mr Henry Elam prosecuted; Sir Walter Monckton led Ley's defence, and Mr Derek Curtis-Bennett defended Smith. Both pleaded not guilty, but Ley simply disclaimed all knowledge of Mudie. This was stupid, and it gave Ley's counsel an extremely difficult task.

An interesting witness for the defence was an ex-convict named Robert Cruikshank, who had been in Australia in 1929 (and so may have known Ley) and who was living in Switzerland at the time of the murder. But Cruikshank claimed that he had flown to England on the afternoon of the murder on some smuggling venture, and had a few hours to kill before flying back the same night. He decided to call on Ley, whom he claimed he did not know, hoping that Ley, as a rich Australian, might help him to get back to Australia. He also claimed that at 8 pm he found the house in darkness, and decided that it might be worth burgling. He let himself into the basement, and saw a man tied into a chair. His lighter failed at that moment, but he went to the man and pulled on the ropes. However, he abandoned any intention of freeing the man and made off. The whole point of Cruikshank's evidence seemed to be that he *might* have strangled the man by pulling on the ropes. Lord Goddard asked if he meant to confess to killing the man, and Cruikshank replied that it was only a possibility. In his summing up, Lord Goddard made no bones about the possibility that Cruikshank had been bribed to confuse the prosecution with a possibility that Mudie had died accidentally.

Both Ley and Smith were sentenced to death, but on May 5th, after an examination by three specialists, Ley was declared insane and moved to Broadmoor. A month later he died of a seizure. Since it would have been hardly fair to reprieve the master and not the man, Smith's sentence was also commuted to penal servitude for life.

LIGHTBOURNE, Wendell
Nineteen-year-old negro golf caddie, tried and convicted in Bermuda for the lust murder of London typist, Dorothy Rawlinson.

A multiple killer, Lightbourne's first victim was Bermuda widow, 72-year-old Gertrude Robinson, found raped and pummelled to death on the edge of her banana patch on March 7th, 1959. On May 9th, 59-year-old divorcée Dorothy Pearce who lived alone in a cottage on the south shore of Bermuda was found raped and beaten to death in her bedroom. The attack had been frenzied; the corpse bore teeth and scratch marks. Jewellery and money in the bedroom had not been taken, but fingerprints were found; checked, they did not tally with those of any known criminal or serviceman on the island. On May 14th a call for aid was made to Scotland Yard in London, and the Criminal Investigation Department sent two investigators to Bermuda, Detective Superintendent William Baker and Detective Sergeant John O'Connell. They decreed that all males in the south shore locality between the ages of 18 and 50 have their fingerprints taken, but this inquiry proved fruitless, no one was allowed to leave the island except with police approval, the ruling being extended to tourists and honeymoon couples. All investigations were futile, and after six weeks the Scotland Yard officers returned to London. On July 3rd, a 49-year-old woman, Rosaleen Kenny, was attacked in the murder locality; an intruder entered her home and attempted an assault as she lay in bed, but her screams arouse neighbours and the assailant ('dark-skinned, carrying a hoe') fled.

On Monday, September 28th, Dorothy Rawlinson, an English office worker who had arrived in Bermuda the previous May, was reported missing by her landlady, Mrs Anne Sayers: she had left her lodgings on the Sunday, intending to spend an afternoon on the beach. The weather was rough, owing to an impending hurricane and she had been unsuccessful in her quest for companions. Her motor-scooter was found, almost buried on the beach, and there were traces of blood on a rock; two hours later, Dorothy Rawlinson's clothes, systematically buried in the sand, were discovered, together with a handbag and her library book, Vicki Baum's *Mortgage on Life*. The day after, her body was found floating by a reef, mutilated by sharks but still bearing signs of a murderous, sadistic beating. A shopkeeper whose premises were near the beach remembered a negro coming into his shop the day of the killing; his manner was 'nervous' and his trousers wet as if they had been immersed in the sea: '. . . I assumed he'd been shell-fishing off-shore . . . his money was wet, too . . .' The negro was identified as Wendell Lightbourne of Spring Hill, Warwick, Bermuda, employed as a caddie at a golf club near the scene of the Rawlinson killing, which was half a mile from the Pearce cottage. Lightbourne said he had been fishing near the club on September 27th, and admitted he saw Dorothy Rawlinson sunbathing. Under questioning he broke down: 'I didn't hurt the girl . . . when I left her she wasn't dead.' Held on suspicion of murder, he was finally charged on October 31st with the murder of Dorothy Rawlinson. Sent for trial at Bermuda Supreme Court, he was found guilty and sentenced to death, the sentence being afterwards commuted to life imprisonment, to be served in England.

LOCK AH TAM
Murdered his family in a fit of insanity and was sentenced to death, although there can be hardly any doubt that he was, at the time, insane.

In 1895, Lock Ah Tam was a ship's steward, 23 years of age, in Liverpool; he decided to change his job to that of a clerk. He prospered and finally became rich and respectable. He married an Englishwoman, and had by her a son and two daughters. He was known as a generous, good tempered, and charitable man. His influence among his fellow countrymen was great; he was president of the largest Republican Society in China (supporting the cause of Sun Yat Sen), and the English representative of a kind of Chinese seaman's union based in Hong Kong. He represented three shipping lines in England. The English police often called on his help when it was a matter dealing with Tam's own countrymen. Tam had also set up a seamen's club in Liverpool, where he often played billiards.

It was here, shortly before the Chinese New Year, 1918, that

Tam was struck on the head with a billiard cue by a drunken Russian sailor. The blow seemed to have a strange effect on him; he became a morose, unpredictable man, often bursting into violence. (Many such cases can be cited; it would be interesting to know exactly what part of the brain is affected by blows on the head, for there are innumerable cases of murder in which the murderer ascribes his violence to head wounds.)[1] The effects on Tam were particularly bad when he had been drinking; on one occasion he broke up a party in a rage, throwing all the glasses into the fireplace, and actually foaming at the mouth.

Tam had formerly been known as an extremely gentle man; now he was feared as an unpredictable drunkard. (He insisted that he was never affected by drink because he always added a spoonful of salt to every glass of whisky.) He invested money and lost heavily (£10,000 in one venture) and was declared bankrupt in 1924.

On the last day of November 1925, Tam gave a party for his son's twentieth birthday. He drank a toast to his son, saying that he hoped Lock Ling would grow up as good a man as his father.

At about one in the morning, Tam flew into a rage about something, and shouted at his wife. His son hurried into the room and accused Tam of hitting his mother; Tam denied it, and orderd Lock Ling out of the room. The boy, followed by his mother and sisters, left Tam alone. Mrs Tam's companion, Margaret Sing, was then orderd to dress herself, which she did. When she returned to Tam's bedroom, he was holding a revolver. The son went off in search of a policeman; during his absence, Tam went to the scullery, where his wife and two daughters were sitting, and shot all three. He then phoned the police. The three women all died soon after.

The trial opened at Chester Assizes before Mr Justice Mackinnon on February 5th, 1926; Sir Ellis Griffith prosecuted and Sir Edward Marshall Hall defended. Hall claimed that Tam had been in a state of epileptic automatism when he committed the murders. This was not the first time he had made such a defence; a man named Henry Patrick had murdered his mistress with a Japanese dagger in a hotel, then openly confessed; the judge doubted whether he was epileptic, but Patrick fell down in a fit as the sentence was passed on him. He was sent to Broadmoor. Tam was less lucky; he was sentenced to death and executed.

[1] See also Goffler, Paul, Nelson, Christie.

At dusk on St Valentine's Day 1945 the body of Charles Walton, 74-year-old hedgecutter, was found under an oak tree on the slopes of Meon Hill, near Lower Quinton in Warwickshire. His own hayfork pinned him to the ground, having been driven in with such force that it penetrated the earth for six inches and required two policemen to pull it out. His hands and arms were lacerated, presumably in the fight for life, and the rough sign of a cross had been slashed on to his throat. The Warwickshire police called in Scotland Yard, and Chief Inspector Robert Fabian commenced investigations, but everywhere in Lower Quinton he found a reluctance to discuss the crime, although he heard rumours that this was an evil-eye killing. Some villagers referred darkly to bad crops 'despite the good weather', others mentioned a heifer that was found unaccountably dying in a ditch, while a few hinted that Charles Walton had held mystic communication with birds and animals. Then Fabian learnt that in 1875, in a nearby village, a similar murder had occurred, when a half-wit had killed one Ann Turner, believing her to be a witch. In one book (*Warwickshire*, by Clive Holland) was part of the murderer's confession: 'I pinned Ann Turner to the ground before slashing her throat with a billhook in the form of a cross.' In another book (*Folklore, Old Customs and Superstitions in Shakespeareland*, by J. Harvey Bloom, MA) there was actual mention of Charles Walton as a ploughboy of 15 seeing on nine successive occasions a phantom black dog that was supposed to presage death ('. . . the following day the lady's sister died'.) Chary of superstition, Fabian enlisted the help of the local RAF and RE: aerial photographs were taken of the murder site, and mine detectors scoured the field searching for Charles Walton's missing tin watch in the hope it might carry fingerprints; but nothing was discovered, and the crime remains unsolved. The American expert on primitive religions, Miss Margaret Mead, visited Lower Quinton in 1950, saying afterwards that she was 'almost satisfied' that the murder was a witchcraft killing.

LUARD Case, The

On August 24th, 1908, 58-year-old Caroline Mary Luard, personable wife of 70-year-old Major-General Charles Edward Luard, was found shot dead in a summer-house close to the Luards' rural residence, Ightham Knoll, near Sevenoaks in Kent.

The couple had left their house at two-thirty that afternoon. General Luard's destination was Godden Green golf links, three miles away, from which he wished to collect his golf clubs in preparation for a week-end visit. His wife parted from him after walking a short distance, her intention being to proceed to the 'Casa', an unoccupied woodland bungalow surrounded by bracken, from which there was a pleasing view of the country-side. Returning from the links, General Luard refused a lift from a car-owning friend, the Rev. R. B. Cotton. At home by four-thirty, the General entertained a Mrs Stuart to tea, expressing surprise that his wife had not returned. By early evening he went to the Casa, and found Mrs Luard prone on the verandah, two bullets in her head and four valuable rings missing from her left hand. (During the post-mortem it was established that the rings had been removed some time after the shooting.)

Police fixed the murder time: Mrs Annie Wickham, wife of a neighbour's coachman, had heard shots at three-fifteen, as had Daniel Kettle, a farm labourer. There was an absence of clues, although much talk of mysterious strangers seen in the vicinity – not unlikely, for hop-picking Eastenders were in Kent at this time enjoying their annual working holiday; nor had the General's wife any enemies. At the inquest General Luard was asked about fire-arms he kept at Ightham Knoll, and said he had not missed any revolver. The Rev. R. B. Cotton, questioned about his own mysterious stranger, mentioned a 'sandy-haired tramp' he had seen emerge from the woods about the time of the murder. A juryman was assured that no certified lunatic had a grudge against Mrs Luard. Upon the adjournment of this inquest, General Luard himself became chief suspect and received many abusive letters.

At the second inquest Mr Thomas Durrand, manager of a Sevenoaks brewery, spoke of seeing General Luard at three-twenty near Hall Farm, a quarter-hour's walk from the Casa. Ernest King, a labourer, testified that he saw General Luard walking towards Godden Green Golf Club at three-twenty-five, twenty minutes' walk from the Casa, and Harry Kent, steward of the golf club, said he had seen General Luard on the eighteenth green at three-thirty. All three witnesses spoke of the General's composure of manner. Servants at Ightham Knoll testified to the Luards' devotion, and General Luard himself, haggard and grief-stricken, presented a pitiful figure in the witness-box. This second inquest was adjourned, and General Luard, after putting up Ightham Knoll for sale, went to stay with his friend, Colonel

Ward, MP. One morning he walked out and threw himself under a train near the local junction at West Farleigh. He had left Ward a letter saying he could not stand the strain of being under suspicion. To another friend he left a note:

> I have gone to her I loved. Goodbye. Something has snapped.
>
> Luard.

The murder remains unsolved.[1]

LÜDKE, Bruno

German mass-murderer, whose crimes, committed during the Second World War, were hushed up by the Nazis. He was dispatched without a trial.

Lüdke was born in 1909; he was definitely mentally defective, in the same way as Earle Nelson. He began his murders at the age of 18. During the war he found it easy to kill. He was arrested for a sexual assault and sterilized by order of Himmler's SS. He was a petty thief (like Kürten) and a sadist who enjoyed torturing animals and (on one occasion) running down a woman with his horse-drawn delivery van. (He worked as a laundry roundsman.)

On January 29th, 1943, a 51-year-old woman, Frieda Rösner, was found strangled on the outskirts of a wood near Berlin where she had been collecting fuel. Kriminal Kommissar Franz, in charge of the case, examined all the known criminals in Köpenick, the nearby village. These included Lüdke, who lived at 32 Grüne Trift. When he was asked if he had known the murdered woman, Lüdke admitted that he had, and that he had last seen her in the woods. Asked if he had killed her, he sprang at his interrogator and had to be overpowered; he then admitted he was the murderer, and added that under Paragraph 51 (concerning mental defectives) he could not be indicted for the crime. Lüdke went on to confess to killing eighty-five women throughout Germany since 1928. His normal method was strangulation or stabbing with a knife, and although he stole their belongings, rape was the chief motive. Franz investigated the murders and after a year, reported that it seemed to be true that Lüdke was responsible for all the crimes he confessed to. But it is also true that local police chiefs blamed all their unsolved murders on Lüdke, the ideal scapegoat.

Lüdke believed that he could never be indicted because he

[1] See also Appendix 2.

was insane. In fact, the embarrassment of various police forces who had arrested innocent men for Lüdke's crimes led to the case being hushed up and treated as a State secret. Lüdke was sent to a hospital in Vienna where he was a guinea-pig for various experiments, and one of the injections killed him on April 8th, 1944.

LYONS, Lewis W.
Executed in New Orleans on March 24th, 1905, for the murder of the District Attorney, J. Ward Gurley.

Lyons developed a persecution mania, the result of a lifetime of various kinds of bad luck. Fifty-four years of age at the time of the murder, he had failed as a business man, and had been deserted by his wife. In 1895, he had been arrested for a theft of a diamond stickpin from a man named Carroll. He spent a night in jail and was allowed a $500 bail. Two weeks later, he was tried and discharged, Carroll now admitting that he had nothing to do with the theft of the pin. Infuriated by the injustice, Lyons sued Carroll and the two detectives who arrested him for $5,000 damages. Gurley represented him, together with an attorney named Mellen. They lost the case, and an appeal was also lost. Lyons now developed his persecution mania, spurred by the undoubted injustice, and eventually challenged Gurley to a duel. On July 20th, 1903, he arrived at Gurley's office with a pistol and his pockets stuffed with cyanide. He waited while a lady had a conference with the District Attorney, then went into his office, had an argument, and shot him dead. He then rushed into an adjoining office and shot himself through the head. His wound was not serious, however, and he recovered eventually.

The murder of the well-liked and mild District Attorney caused much popular outcry. The trial opened on November 11th, 1903, and Lyons apparently looked like a very old man, with one eye closed. He was found guilty after a trial of eight days. An appeal was lodged and he was re-tried on February 6th, 1904. Again he was found guilty.

At the time, New Orleans had an average of a murder every two days; it also boasted a sadistic hangman named Johnston, who enjoyed terrifying prisoners before their execution with grisly tales of executions that went wrong. Johnston, however, resigned just before Lyons' execution. The case seems almost certainly a miscarriage of justice.

M

MACKAY, George (alias John Williams). The shooting of
Inspector Walls
*Hanged early in 1913 for the murder of Inspector Arthur Walls,
Mackay has been described by Sir Patrick Hastings as a real-
life Raffles.*

On the evening of October 9th, 1912, a horse-cab called at the
house of Countess Flora Sztaray at 6 South Cliff Avenue, Eastbourne, to take her to dinner at the Burlington Hotel. The driver
thought he saw a man crouched on the portico over the front
door, and told the Countess as they drove to the hotel; she immediately went back to the house and phoned the police. At
seven-forty, Inspector Arthur Walls arrived at the house and
told the man, crouched in the shadows, to come down; the reply
was two shots, one of which killed the inspector.

The burglar – George Mackay – escaped back to his lodgings,
where he was living with a beautiful young girl named Florence
Seymour, who was expecting his child. Together, they buried
the revolver that had fired the shots, and a parcel containing
rope, on the beach. Mackay (who called himself Williams) wrote
to his brother in London, asking for money. His brother made
the mistake of showing the letter to a 'friend' of Mackay's,
Edgar Power, who was in love with Florence Seymour himself,
and probably saw in this an opportunity to get rid of her lover.
He went to Mackay's lodging at 4 Tideswell Road and gave him
money. 'Williams' used it to return to London. Power now went
to the police and told them the whole story; he and the police
concocted a plan to betray Mackay (who was known to everyone
as Williams). Power went to Florence Seymour and persuaded
her to take him to the buried revolver, saying that they must
change its location; the police were waiting for them, and they
frightened a confession out of the pregnant girl. Power then contacted Mackay and lured him into a police trap at Moorgate
Underground station. Mackay, who was the son of a Scottish
clergyman, refused to give his real name to the police, and was
tried under the name of Williams. (Even Sir Patrick Hastings,
who defended him, states in his memoirs that he does not know
Mackay's real name.) For some reason, Mackay's face was
covered with a veil in court, so that he became known as 'The
Hooded Man' in the Press. Mackay told Hastings that he was

not guilty, and that he would not try to avoid the death sentence by a plea of manslaughter.

His trial began at the Sussex Assizes in Lewes before Mr Justice Channel on December 12th, 1912. Sir Frederick Lowe prosecuted. In his summing up, the judge emphasized that there was no direct evidence that Mackay ('Williams') had fired the shot, but that his subsequent conduct was that of a guilty man. Williams' defence had been weak; it was claimed that the police had bullied the girl into incriminating her lover, and that the parcel of rope had been given him 'to dispose of' by a man named Freddy Mike.

Mackay was sentenced to death. He appealed, but the appeal was dismissed. There was also an attempt at a conspiracy to save Mackay; a man in Brixton prison declared that he was 'Freddy Mike', and that he could swear that the murder was committed by his twin brother who had now escaped to the Continent. The matter was debated in the House of Commons on January 23rd, 1913, but Mr McKenna, the Home Secretary, declared that he had investigated Freddy Mike's story and found it to be entirely untrue. Mackay was executed, having been allowed to kiss his new-born child. He gave the child a piece of prison bread, saying, 'Now no one can say your father never gave you anything.' Sir Patrick Hastings had had to arrange for the girl's confinement, since her notoriety made all hospitals refuse to take her in.

MAHON, Patrick Herbert
Thirty-three-year-old soda-fountain salesman, self-described 'Broth of a Bhoy', of Pagoda Avenue, Richmond, Surrey, convicted of the murder of 37-year-old Emily Beilby Kaye.

On May 1st, 1924, Mrs Patrick Mahon, suspicious of her husband's frequent absences from home, looked through his suit pockets; finding a Waterloo cloakroom ticket, she asked a friend to investigate. The friend (an ex-railway policeman), retrieving a Gladstone bag from the luggage office found the contents suspicious: heavily bloodstained apparel, a cook's knife, and a racquet case marked E.B.K. When Mahon claimed his Gladstone bag the following day he was apprehended by the police and taken to Kennington Road police station. He said that he had been carrying chunks of dog meat in the bag, but was told that it was human blood. He finally admitted that the initials on the racquet bag were those of his mistress, Emily Kaye, whose remains now lay in a bungalow (part of what had been a coast-guard station) on that desolate stretch of shingle known as the Crumbles, near Eastbourne, Sussex. He alleged that during the week-end of April 12–13th he had quarrelled violently with Emily Kaye, with whom he was staying at the Crumbles, and in a struggle she had fallen and hit her head on the coal scuttle, with fatal results; at the trial, pathologist Sir Bernard Spilsbury discounted the possibility of this.

Nothing recognizable as Emily Kaye remained at the bungalow. Saucepans filled with boiled human flesh, saucers and other receptables filled with solidified human fat, portions of unboiled flesh in a hat box, a fibre trunk and a biscuit-tin, a blood-drenched carpet, and a thousand minute fragments of bone retrieved from fireplaces and dustpans were found. All had been part of a female body, pregnant at the time of death: 'The organs were those of a healthy person,' stated Spilsbury. 'No disease was found to account for natural death. . . .' Mahon, who had a criminal record (he had been sentenced in 1916 to five years' jail for a hammer attack during a robbery), was tried at the County Hall at Lewes in July for the murder of Emily Kaye, Sir Henry Curtis Bennett, KC, prosecuted, Mr J. D. Cassells led for the defence and Mr Justice Avory presided. There was speculation as to the whereabouts of the victim's head, which was believed to have received a mortal blow from an axe (half broken) found in the bungalow. No trace of it was ever discovered. In Brixton Prison before the trial Mahon described how he had burnt the head on a stove in the middle of a thunderstorm; the intense heat caused the eyes to open, and appalled, Mahon had rushed from the house. (When asked about the head at his trial, Mahon was visibly disconcerted at rumbles of thunder outside.)

Emily Kaye, although aware that Mahon was married, had believed he intended to settle with her in South Africa and had given him most of her capital. Mahon became unnerved by this emotional entanglement; there was evidence that a saw and knife claimed to have been purchased on April 17th, after the killing, were bought on April 12th, shortly before he travelled down to meet Emily Kaye at the Crumbles.

Found guilty of murder, Patrick Mahon was executed on September 9th, 1924.

MAJOR, Ethel Lillie

Forty-two-year-old housewife of Kirkby-on-Main, Lincolnshire,
convicted of the murder of her husband, Arthur Major, aged 44.

In May 1934, the Majors were living at No. 2 Council Houses,
Kirkby-on-Main; Mrs Major and her son of 14 journeyed every
night to sleep at her gamekeeper father's house at Roughton
about a mile away. There had been incessant bickering between
the couple; according to Mrs Major her husband was a bully and
a drunkard, and had recently started a love affair with next-door-
neighbour Rose Kettleborough. (Letters were produced at the
trial purported to have passed between the lovers but there was
doubt as to their authenticity; Mrs Kettleborough denied an
intrigue with Mr Major and it is now widely believed that Mrs
Major wrote the letters herself.)

On May 24th, Arthur Major, after a short but agonizing illness, died; he had twitched violently and foamed at the mouth
before death, and a Dr Smith gave the cause of death as 'status
epilepticus'. The following day the local police received an
anonymous letter signed 'Fairplay': '. . . have you ever heard
of a wife poisoning her husband? Look further into the death of
Mr Major of Kirkby-on-Main. Why did he complain of his food
tasting nasty and throw it to a neighbour's dog, which has since
died? Ask the undertaker if he looked natural after death . . .'
Funeral arrangements were stopped, and the stomach organs of
both Arthur Major and the neighbour's dog were sent for
analysis to Dr Roche Lynch in London: 1·27 grains of strychnine were found in the man, and ·12 grains in the dog. (Another
neighbour, Mrs Elsie Roberts, spoke at the subsequent trial of
seeing Mrs Major give a plate of food to someone's pet dog in the
Majors' garden: 'Mrs Major watched the animal eat the food
then she tossed her head up, laughed loudly, and went in.')

Mrs Major, interviewed by police after the post-mortem,
mentioned strychnine poisoning before being told of the pathologist's finding. She went on to blame some corned beef for her
husband's death: 'I hate corned beef and think it is a waste of
money to buy such rubbish. I prefer a piece of fat bacon.' Mrs
Major's father, Tom Brown, had used strychnine in the course
of his work to destroy vermin, and kept a bottle of it in his
'poison box', which he always kept locked, carrying the key in
the pocket of his wide cloth belt. Later he admitted that there
was a duplicate key in existence: '. . . but I lost it years ago. I
never knew the going of it.' After being arrested on a charge of

murdering her husband, Mrs Major's belongings were examined, and in a shabby purse, together with a coin wrapped up in paper inscribed 'Mother's Penny', was found the missing duplicate key.

Mrs Major was tried at Lincoln Assizes before Mr Justice Charles, with Mr Norman Birkett, KC, as defending counsel; Mr Birkett called no evidence for the defence, and on November 2nd, 1934, the jury found Mrs Major guilty of murdering her husband, asking that a 'strong recommendation to mercy' be given. The Lord Chief Justice referred to this at the Court of Criminal Appeal, saying he found it delivered 'for some reason not stated'. The appeal was rejected, and Ethel Lillie Major was hanged at Hull on December 19th, 1934.

MALLOY, Michael (The Murder Trust Case)

Michael Malloy, durable alcoholic, murdered in 1932 by the 'Murder Trust', who inserted a rubber gas-pipe into his mouth when he was in, as usual, a drunken stupor. The Trust, whose offices were a speakeasy on Third Avenue, New York, consisted of speakeasy proprietor Tony Marino, Dan Kreisberg, bartender Joe Murphy, taxi-driver Harry Green, and undertaker Frank Pasque, who had secretly insured the fated Malloy for nearly $2,000. At first Malloy seemed indestructible, consuming with eagerness proffered pints of wood alcohol and tins of poisoned sardines, surviving with cheerfulness (and a mild head-cold) an enforced period of exposure in a sleet storm, although undertaker Frank Pasque, his convoy that night, contracted severe tonsillitis. Harry Green in his taxi even ran down the somniferous Malloy, placed in the road centre by Trust members, but after a short hospital session Malloy was back in the speakeasy 'dying for a drink'. Finally, the desperate Trust members (already by this time showing a loss on the project) resorted to the gas-pipe, but suspicious police eventually apprehended them and they were all tried and found guilty of Malloy's murder.

MANCINI, Tony (The Brighton Trunk Case)

Petty thief Tony Mancini (alias Hyman Gold, Jack Notyre) was tried at Lewes Assize Court in December 1934 for the murder of his mistress Violette Kaye (alias Joan Watson), vaudeville artiste turned prostitute, whose body was discovered in a trunk at Mancini's Brighton lodging. Mancini had previously shared a flat with Violette Kaye at 44 Park Crescent, Brighton, from which place she had, according to Mancini, 'blown' after a quarrel. Violette Kaye had met her death on or about May 10th, 1934, her body being stuffed into a trunk and eventually transported, with the rest of Mancini's belongings, to his new quarters at 52 Kemp Street, Brighton, where the police, curious about Violette Kaye's disappearance, made the gruesome discovery on July 15th that led to Mancini's arrest. (By a coincidence on June 17th a trunk, deposited ten days earlier at Brighton railway station, had been found to contain a woman's torso; identities of victim and murderer were never established.)

Violette Kaye's skull had been fractured, and the Crown (represented by Mr J. D. Cassels, KC, and Mr Quintin Hogg) alleged that a hammer head was left behind by Mancini at his Park Crescent lodging. Pleading not guilty, Mancini (who was charged under his real name of Cecil Lois England) claimed that he returned home from his work at the Skylark Café to find his mistress dead in their basement flat: '. . . she was on the bed . . . blood all over the sheets . . . I got frightened.' Mr Norman Birkett, appearing for the defence with Mr Eric Neve, questioned a police inspector about the steps leading down to the basement flat, eliciting the information that they were 'worn', 'steep', and 'narrow', and that the area floor had a 'hard stone surface'. Dr Roche Lynch the pathologist had found morphine in the corpse, but could not ascertain whether it was a fatal amount. In his examination of pathologist Sir Bernard Spilsbury, appearing for the prosecution, Birkett drew forth the admission that a skull fracture resulting from a fall was often indistinguishable from a fracture caused by a blow, and spoke of the possible consequences of a person 'slightly drunk, under the influence of a drug' falling down the Kemp Street basement steps. Mancini was asked by Birkett why he had not called the police upon finding Violette Kaye dead. 'The police? With my record?' replied Mancini.

In his final speech Birkett spoke of prostitutes' lives: '. . . the dangers to which they are constantly exposed'. He called upon the jury to 'Stand firm', and after two hours' deliberation they returned a verdict of not guilty.

MANNING, Frederick and Maria
Husband and wife, executed for the murder of Patrick O'Connor in 1849.

Mrs Manning, who was the moving force behind the crime, was born Maria de Roux; she was a Swiss lady's maid. She had two admirers: Patrick O'Connor, an Irishman of some means, whom she met on a Boulogne boat in 1846 when she was on her way to join her mistress, Lady Blantyre, on the Continent. The other was Frederick George Manning, a railway guard on the Great Western and a man of criminal tendencies. She finally decided to marry Manning, but kept up a friendship with O'Connor. They moved to Taunton and ran an inn called the White Hart; Manning continued to work for the railways, but he was dismissed when he seemed to be implicated in the theft of £4,000 worth of bullion. There was no evidence against him. But when a mail train was robbed a few months later he was arrested with two other men, and his confederates received fifteen years' transportation. The Mannings decided to return to London, and opened a beer shop in the Hackney Road.

O'Connor again became a frequent visitor, and one day Mrs Manning absconded with him. Manning traced them through the cab-man, and some kind of reconciliation took place. Soon the Mannings took apartments at Minver Place, Bermondsey. Here O'Connor continued to cuckold Frederick Manning.

The Mannings took in a medical student named Massey, and Massey was a little suspicious when Manning asked him questions about the effect of chloroform, and whether a man under narcotics could be induced to sign cheques. He was also asked about the effect of shooting someone with an air-gun. Then the Mannings decided that the medical student was *de trop*, and on July 28th, 1849, he left for other lodgings. The same day a crowbar and a quantity of quicklime were delivered to Minver Place. On August 8th Manning bought a shovel. Then on August 9th O'Connor was invited round for dinner. Mrs Manning shot him through the head. Manning confessed later: 'I found O'Connor moaning in the kitchen. I never liked him very much, and battered in his head with a ripping chisel.' O'Connor was then buried beneath the floor, and Mrs Manning called at his address, was admitted to his rooms by his landlady, and removed some money, bonds, and two gold watches. The next day she returned looking for foreign bonds. Manning was sent off to sell shares, and actually raised £110, although the second time he was sent, his nerve failed him, and he told his wife that he had not been able to find a market. Mrs Manning now decided that it was time to desert her unreliable confederate, and absconded while he was out of the house, leaving him without money. She left some luggage at London Bridge station, then travelled to Edinburgh from Euston. There she tried to sell some of the bonds. Manning remained in the murder house for two days, then lost his nerve and fled.

By now the police were suspicious; O'Connor's relatives were urging them to press inquiries. The empty house was searched; a constable noticed that two slabs in the back kitchen had been recently cemented, and levered them up; O'Connor's body was disclosed.

A hue and cry followed, it resulted in Maria Manning's arrest in Edinburgh within a few days. Manning had fled to the Channel Islands, but was recognized in Jersey. He moved to the small village of St Laurence, near St Helier, where his furtive conduct soon attracted attention; he was finally arrested there on August 21st. He immediately tried to throw the whole blame on his wife. The trial opened on October 25th, 1849, and neither of the prisoners would look at one another. Each tried to blame the other. The Attorney-General prosecuted. Mr Justice Cresswell sentenced them both to death.

The execution took place in front of Horsemonger Lane Jail. Charles Dickens, who was present, wrote to *The Times* denouncing the levity of the crowd. Mrs Manning wore black satin for her execution and caused black satin dresses to go out of fashion thereafter.

MANTON, Bertie (The Luton Murder Case)

On the morning of November 19th, 1943, several pedestrians noticed a bulky sack lying in a stream that ran by a public footpath on the outskirts of Luton. The footpath was used by hundreds of employees of a large motor works nearby. At 2.15 pm, two employees of the Luton Corporation, engaged in testing the water level, opened the sack and discovered the nude body of a youngish woman whose ankles were tied together, and her knees held against her stomach by a cord tied round the waist. Dr Keith Simpson, who examined the body, stated that it was of a woman of about 35; she had borne children, and was used to wearing false teeth, which had been removed before the body was found. Her face showed signs of a severe beating, and she was six months pregnant.

Identification proved to be a problem of some difficulty; even with the aid of Scotland Yard, the Luton police were baffled for three months. The face was 'restored' to some extent and photographs taken; these were displayed in certain public places and flashed on to cinema screens. The victim's 17-year-old daughter actually saw this many times but did not recognize it, while her two sons, aged 14 and 15, saw the photograph in shop windows. Their father had told them that his wife was visiting relatives, and they believed him.

Four hundred and four missing women were traced; two hundred and fifty lorry drivers who called at the Vauxhall motor works were interviewed.

The police decided that they should try to trace the woman's clothes; all clothes found on rubbish dumps or on waste ground were examined. This led finally to some result. On February 21st, 1944, pieces of a black coat were found; on one of them was a dyer's tag, which finally led the police to the house of Mrs Rene Manton of Regent Street, Luton. A photograph of Mrs Manton in the house soon convinced the police that the search was at an end. Mrs Manton had been missing since the previous November 18th.

Bert Manton, an employee of the National Fire Service, claimed that his wife was always associating with soldiers, and that she had gone off to her brother's in Grantham after their last quarrel in November. A midwife who was attending Mrs Manton had received a note signed apparently by the dead woman, saying that she had gone to Grantham. Mrs Manton's mother had received three letters since November, all posted in North London, with a Hampstead address; Hampstead was spelt 'Hamstead', and Manton spelled it this way when asked. Identification of Mrs Manton was soon established. Her dentist was able to give positions of roots of teeth left in her gums, and a fingerprint found on a pickle jar in the house corresponded to that of the dead woman.

Manton was arrested and charged with the murder. He soon admitted that he had killed his wife in a quarrel about associating with soldiers; he had struck her several times with a heavy stool 'and then had a blackout' and strangled her. (His admission to strangling was only made later at the trial, and discredited his story of blows struck in anger, since he had attempted strangulation first.) He had wrapped the body in sacks and hidden it in the cellar; then later wheeled it to the river on his bicycle and thrown it in under cover of the blackout.

Manton's relations with his wife had been bad for some time before the murder, and on one occasion she left him for four months. In spite of this, he was found guilty and sentenced to death.

MANUEL, Peter
Habitual criminal and multi-murderer.

On January 4th, 1956, a labourer walking over the golf course at East Kilbride, south of Glasgow, found the body of a young girl in a hollow. Her head had been split open; her clothing was disarranged; one stocking and her knickers were missing. She had not been raped. One of the photographs that appeared in the Press in connexion with the case was that of Peter Manuel; he was known to the police as a habitual criminal and had been interviewed.[1] The victim was identified as Anne Kneilands, aged 17.

In September 1956 there were three burglaries in Lanarkshire; one in Bothwell, and the other two in the district of High Burnside, close to East Kilbride. In two of the burglaries damage had been done to property, beds walked on with dirty boots, a mattress slashed, food eaten, and a few – but by no means all – valuables taken. The third of these cases involved three murders. This was in the house of William Watt, of 5 Fennbank Avenue; Watt himself was on a fishing holiday at Lochgilphead, but the cleaning woman who came on the morning of September 17th found Mrs Watt and her sister, Mrs Margaret Brown, dead in bed, shot through the head, and the 16-year-old daughter Vivienne also shot through the head and dying. The night clothes of the women had been disturbed, but again there was no rape. On September 27th William Watt was arrested; after sixty-seven days in Barlinnie Prison he was released on December 3rd, 1956.

Manuel was in Barlinnie Prison from October 2nd, 1956, until November 30th, 1957, and things remained quiet until he left the prison. On Christmas Day 1957 there was a case of housebreaking in Mount Vernon, when a camera and a pair of gloves were stolen. On December 28th, 1957, Isabelle Cooke, a schoolgirl of 17, left her home in Carrick Drive, Mount Vernon, to meet a boy-friend at a bus stop in Uddingston. She never

[1] Manuel apparently had scratches on his face after the murder.

arrived. Later, her almost naked body was found in a shallow grave near her home.

The last murders were again of a family of three. On Wednesday, January 6th, 1958, the foreman of a firm of civil engineers was sent to inquire why a Mr Peter James Smart had not arrived for work; Smart was a self-made business man of 45, who lived in Sheepburn Road, Uddingston. Finally, the house was broken into by the police, who found Mr and Mrs Smart dead in bed, shot through the head at close range, and their 11-year-old son Michael also shot through the head.

The police now heard of a young man who had been under suspicion in the Anne Kneilands case – Peter Manuel – who had apparently been spending money recklessly after January 1st, although he had been short of money before that. They went to the house of Samuel Manuel, at 32 Fourth Street, Birkenshaw (Peter Manuel's father). Here a search revealed a camera and a pair of gloves similar to those stolen on the Christmas Day burglary. On the evening of January 14th, 1958, Peter Manuel was charged with the Smart murders.

Manuel had been born in Manhattan, New York, in 1927. The family returned to Britain in 1932, and lived first in Motherwell, then in Coventry. Here Manuel was first put on probation for burglary (October 1939), and five weeks later was sent to an approved school for housebreaking. He escaped, committed more thefts, was returned to the approved school, and managed to keep up this pattern so that by 1942, when he was 15, he had been returned to the approved school eleven times. On one occasion he was guilty of an assault with a hammer as well as housebreaking. Just before Christmas 1942 he committed his first sexual offence, robbing and indecently assaulting the wife of a school employee. He was eventually caught and sent to borstal in March 1943. On his release in 1945 he rejoined his family in Scotland; they had moved back there in 1941 after being bombed out.

He moved to Blackpool and was acquitted on a charge of burglary in August 1945. Soon after his return to Scotland, in March 1946, he was sent to prison on fifteen charges of housebreaking. While he was serving this sentence he was convicted of rape and sentenced to eight years in jail. He was finally released from Peterhead Prison in the summer of 1953. He became engaged to a girl from Carluke, but the engagement was broken off after she received an anonymous letter detailing Manuel's past – the evidence points to Manuel as its author.

On the day that had been arranged for the wedding he appeared in Airdrie Sheriff Court, and successfully defended himself on a charge of indecent assault.

The Anne Kneilands murder, in January 1956, followed, and of the Watt family in September. On October 2nd, 1956, Manuel was sentenced to eighteen months' imprisonment for housebreaking at Hamilton; he was in Barlinnie Prison at the same time as William Watt.

He was released on November 30th, 1957, and on December 8th, Sydney Dunn, a Newcastle taxi-driver, was found shot through the head, with his throat cut, near his deserted taxi on the moors at Edmondbyers, County Durham. After Manuel's execution, a Coroner's inquest found that he had murdered Dunn. The murders of Isabelle Cooke and the Smarts followed on December 28th and January 1st, 1958. Before his execution Manuel confessed to three more murders: of Helen Carlin (Red Helen), a prostitute found strangled in Pimlico in September 1954, Anne Steele, a 55-year-old spinster found battered to death in Glasgow on January 11th, 1956 (seven Glasgow business men had offered a £900 reward for information leading to the murderer of Anne Kneilands or Anne Steele, although at that stage no one knew they were committed by the same man), and Ellen Petrie (English Nellie), who was stabbed in Glasgow in June 1956. It is also suggested, though without positive evidence, that Manuel tried several times to enter the London criminal world, but became known as a 'talker' and boaster, and always returned to Scotland.

On January 16th, 1958, Manuel signed a confession to the murders of Anne Kneilands, the Watt family, Isabelle Cooke, and the Smart family. (Later he claimed that the police had extorted the confession from him by threats involving his parents, and tried to withdraw it; it is true that, at this stage, his mother and father were also under arrest.) Manuel also led the police to a field near Baillieston Brickworks, where he unearthed a pair of woman's shoes, and also indicated where Isabelle Cooke's body was buried. The police eventually unearthed the body.

The trial opened on Monday, May 12th, 1958, before Lord Cameron. Mr Gordon Gillies, the Advocate-Depute, conducted the prosecution, assisted by Mr Ronald Sutherland (who had to take over the conduct of the case on the third morning, when Mr Gillies had a giddy spell), and Mr Victor Skae; the defence was conducted by Mr Harald Leslie, QC, and Mr Malcolm Morrison.

The trial provided several surprises. It appeared that Manuel had approached Lawrence Dowdall, the Glasgow solicitor, in October 1957 (although he must have written the letter from prison), offering information about the Watt murders (Dowdall was acting for Watt), and declared that he knew the man who had committed the murders. Later, Manuel met Watt himself and spun the same story about the murderer. His motive is obscure; it does not seem to have been money, but a strange desire to gain attention and keep in the limelight. One of the first surprises of the trial was Manuel's statement that Watt was the murderer of his own family. He also blamed one of the burglaries on a certain Charles Tallis and Mrs Mary Bowes. But the main surprise of the trial appeared on May 22nd, when Manuel dismissed his counsels and undertook his own defence.

Although the evidence ranged against him – including his own confession – made it obvious that only one verdict was possible, he tried hard to save himself, declaring that the police had forced the confessions from him by threats of involving his family in the murder charges. Some interesting aspects of the Glasgow underworld came to light when various witnesses spoke of the sale of guns, 'unloading' of stolen jewellery, etc. One witness told of how Manuel had tested out the gun that killed the Watts by shooting a cow through the nostril; the story is confirmed by a farmer.

There is no point in detailing Manuel's complicated – and frequently changing – stories. The trial lasted fourteen days and Manuel was found guilty on all charges except the Kneilands murder (where evidence was not strong enough to convict him), and sentenced to death. An appeal was dismissed and Manuel was executed on Friday, July 11th, 1958, at one minute past eight.

It is unfortunate that we have no details of 'case history' from the psychological point of view; but it seems reasonably certain that Manuel was a pathological criminal with a longing to be respected and feared; there also seems some evidence that he was an underwear fetishist, and that this was the motive in the murders of Anne Kneilands and Isabelle Cooke. He undoubtedly 'talked' his way to the gallows.

MAPLETON, Percy (alias Lefroy)

A mild-mannered young man with literary leanings, executed in 1881 for the brutal murder (by stabbing and shooting) of a fellow-passenger, Frederick Gold, in a London to Brighton train. Mapleton's profession was short-story writing; apparently not a remunerative one, since the motive for the killing was robbery. One of his final tales, published posthumously, concerns tragic music-hall comedian Joe and his faithless wife Nellie, who returns to him remorseful and 'dying of cold and want' on the anniversay of her shameless departure: ' "At last – Joe – darling husband – goodbye —" And with a sweet and happy smile . . . Nellie went down with the sun.'

MAREK, Martha (born Löwenstein)
Poisoner, executed in December 1938.

Martha Löwenstein, born about 1904, was a foundling who was adopted by a poor couple in Vienna; the father emigrated to America and was never heard of again; Martha, at the age of 15, took a job in a dress shop in the Kirtnerstrasse. This was in 1919. One day, a rich elderly gentleman spoke to her – Moritz Fritsch – and finally proposed that she should become his ward. He owned a large department store in Vienna. She was an exceptionally lovely girl who was fond of good clothes, and she accepted with pleasure. She became Fritsch's mistress, although it is not known whether she became the regular partner of his bedchamber or merely granted occasional favours. She was sent to a finishing school and to England and France for holidays. Finally, Fritsch became so fond of her that he altered his will, leaving her his fashionable house at Mödling. A year later – and about five years after Martha had become his ward – Fritsch died at the age of 74. Some of his relatives were enraged that he should leave the house and money to Martha, particularly his ex-wife, who wanted the body exhumed. However, she was over-ridden. A few months later, Martha married a young engineering student, Emil Marek, with whom she had been carrying on a secret affaire for some time before Fritsch's death.

Martha Marek was extravagant, and soon had no money and some debts. They then conceived an almost unbelievable scheme for making money. Marek would insure himself against accident for £10,000, and would then have a serious accident. At first, the insurance company refused to entertain the scheme, but on inquiry at the institute where he studied it was found that he was a decent and industrious young man, and that the Government was interested in an electrification scheme for the Burgenland which he had prepared. They decided to insure him after all; (they had no idea of the real state of his 'rich wife's' finances, of course). Then an amazing accident was staged; he was cutting down a tree with a sharp hatchet, and was found with his leg almost cut off. It had to be amputated just below the knee. But the doctor who examined the wound found that there were three distinct cuts on it, and the angle of the wound made it impossible that it had been self-inflicted. The police reached the conclusion that his wife had inflicted the wound with his agreement. They were charged with attempt to defraud. Frau Marek now approached a hospital orderly and bribed him to say that he had seen a doctor extending the area of the wound. She made a Press announcement to this effect and caused some stir. But the police finally got the orderly to admit he had been bribed. The couple were tried for attempt to defraud and the attempt to bribe the orderly; they were found guilty only on the second charge and sentenced to four months' imprisonment which they were held to have served already.

On the advice of the police, the insurance company dropped a hint that they might want to see Moritz Fritsch's body exhumed. The Mareks accepted a settlement of £3,000, which could hardly have covered the costs of the trial.

The next years brought several misfortunes to the couple; the house was sold, and they went to Algiers, where Emil tried to run a business; it failed and they found themselves destitute. They also had two children. They returned to Vienna, where Martha was, at one point, reduced to selling vegetables off a street barrow in the poor quarter.

In July 1932, Emil Marek died 'of tuberculosis'. The circumstances of his death – in a charity ward – were not suspicious. But a month later, their baby daughter also died. Even this aroused no suspicion.

Martha now became the companion of an aged relative, Frau Susanne Löwenstein, who lived in the Kuppelweisergasse; she was now just over 30, and still very beautiful. Soon, the aged relative died, with symptoms similar to those of Emil Marek – numbness in the legs and difficulty in swallowing. Frau Marek inherited her money. But she was an extravagant woman, and soon spent most of it. She let out some rooms to an insurance agent, Herr Neumann, and to a Frau Kittenberger. Soon Frau Kittenberger died, but Martha gained no particular advantage from this, for the old lady was insured for only £300.

Some time in 1937 Martha decided to try fraud again; she had her pictures removed at night by a small firm, who were sworn to secrecy, and then claimed they had all been stolen. The police managed to trace the removal firm, and so managed to save the insurance company the cost of the pictures.

Frau Kittenberger's son suspected that his mother had been poisoned, and the body was exhumed; sure enough, it was found that the old lady had been poisoned with a compound of thallium. The bodies of Emil Marek, Ingeborg Marek (their daughter), and Frau Löwenstein were all exhumed; all were found to have died of the same poison, which had been sold to Martha by a chemist in Florisdorf. Martha's son was traced; he was boarded out in Hitzing, and was seriously ill. His mother apparently visited him frequently and prepared his food. He was taken into hospital and his life finally saved.

With the advent of Hitler, the death sentence had been restored in Austria, and Martha Marek was beheaded on December 6th, 1938.

MARTIN, Marius (The Café Royal Murder)

Unpopular nightwatchman of London's Café Royal, Regent Street, found shot on either side of his face in the early hours of December 6th, 1894. A cellar-man named Delagneau found Martin's body in the passageway leading to the Glasshouse Street entrance. No one had forced an entry from outside, so it was evident that the murderer had hidden himself during the day, emerging when the coast was clear with the intention of killing Martin. Robbery was not the motive, as the money in Martin's coat pockets was untouched, and the safe (containing £450) untampered with. Hordes of café employees hated Martin, who had treated his fellow-workers with condescension and suspicion. As one voluble waiter put it: 'He send many people away while he is here. If he see a man go out with something under his arm he get that man away. The man say "Revenge" and he wait a long time, but he do it.'

An apprentice cook at the Café Royal had seen, the night before the murder, a short fat man 'waiting in one of the lavatories' who might well have been the assailant, as the light in this lavatory was found burning after the discovery of Martin's body. The 'short fat man' was never identified, however, and despite the interrogation of many grudge-bearing café scullions, the murder (committed during the period when Oscar Wilde and Shaw were Café Royal patrons) remains unsolved.

MARVIN, Ross (Murder of)

In 1909, during explorer Robert Peary's eighth and unsuccessful attempt to plant the 'Star Spangled Banner' at the North Pole, Professor Ross Marvin, aged 34 (formerly an instructor at Cornell University), who was. Peary's secretary and an Arctic explorer in his own right, met his death. This expedition was divided into seven parties, one of them being made up of Martin and two Eskimos, Kudlooktoo and Inukitsaq; Peary headed the main assault team, and it was agreed that all sections, upon reaching their objectives, should return to the expedition's ship, the *Roosevelt*, lying at anchor in Columbia Bay at Ellesmere Island, off the coast of Greenland. When the victorious Peary returned to the *Roosevelt*, he learnt with grief that his comrade, Ross Marvin, had been found drowned under a layer of thin ice by the two Eskimo escorts. 'It killed all the joy I had felt at the sight of the ship', wrote Peary afterwards in his memoirs. In 1926, six years after Peary's own death, Kudlooktoo and Inukitsaq remorsefully approached a Danish missionary, Jens Olsen, who had just started a programme of Arctic evangelism; they admitted to the shooting of Marvin, saying that his cruel and hysterical behaviour had proved he was 'ice-mad' and therefore a danger. Doubt at this story was felt, but the two Eskimos had confessed to murder in a land over which there was no legal control. It was impossible, because of this, to bring the two self-confessed killers to trial.

MARWOOD, Ronald Henry

Twenty-five-year-old scaffolder, indicted for the killing of a policeman and sentenced to death; this murder is chiefly notable for the melodramatic campaigning against capital punishment that ensued before, during, and after his execution at Pentonville Prison on May 8th, 1959. (The noise from sympathetic fellow prisoners on the eve of the hanging was so great that Marwood is reported to have requested, through a warder, that the racket be modified as he wished to have some peace and quiet.)

During a gang-scuffle outside Gray's Dance Academy in Seven Sisters' Road, Holloway, North London, on December 14th, 1958, 23-year-old policeman Raymond Henry Summers, while trying to intervene, was fatally stabbed in the back. Marwood was interviewed as a suspect by the police some days later but was released after saying he had not been near Seven Sisters'

439

Road at the time of the crime; wanted for further questioning, Marwood disappeared, even his young wife being apparently unaware of his whereabouts. On January 27th he surrendered by walking into Caledonian Road police station: 'I did stab the copper that night. I will never know why I did it.' (The earlier consumption of twenty ales had doubtless contributed to Marwood's reckless behaviour.)

Tried before Mr Justice Gorman at the Old Bailey in March 1959 (Mr Christmas Humphreys prosecuting and Mr Neil Lawson, QC, defending), the case against Marwood was a fairly straightforward one, in view of his earlier statement, although in court he now denied that he had held a knife when striking the policeman, asserting that police at Caledonian Road had 'put down things', despite his insistence that he had never possessed a knife. Mr Justice Gorman in his summing up reminded the jury that the killing of a police officer during the execution of his duty was a capital offence; they were not there to pass judgement on the social iniquities of a street brawl, but to concern themselves solely with the accused's guilt or innocence; with regard to the confession of January 27th, the judge stressed that such a statement must be voluntary, '. . . without any sort of inducement to make it by any promise or favour, or by menaces. . . .' After deliberating nearly three hours the jury found Marwood guilty.

Demonstrations against this conviction and the inevitable fate of Ronald Marwood were remarkable. It is uncertain whether the protests arose from a belief in Marwood's innocence or a desire to defame the police in general, whose reputation in certain (other than criminal) quarters is, unfortunately, not high. Marwood's alleged stabbing confession was bracketed by many citizens (not over-cynical, unthoughtful, or frivolous) with Derek Bentley's alleged shouted directive to his gun-wielding companion, Christopher Craig, in the Croydon police-shooting affray seven years before (see BENTLEY, Derek). That there is little doubt in this case of the convicted man's guilt makes the Peterloo-like scenes outside the prison on the morning of execution, and the cinema audiences catcalling the police during news-reel shots of those scenes, all the more regrettable.

MARYMONT, Marcus

Thirty-seven-year-old American Army sergeant stationed in England, found guilty by a United States General Court Martial in 1958 of the murder of his wife, Mary Helen.

At the court martial, held in Denham, Buckinghamshire, Marymont faced two charges; that of premeditated murder, and of having wrongful intercourse with Mrs Cynthia Taylor, an Englishwoman living in Maidenhead. He was found guilty of this latter charge also, and it was alleged by the prosecution that it was this extra-marital passion that prompted him to administer a fatal dose of arsenic to his wife. Marymont met Mrs Taylor (who was separated from her husband) at a Maidenhead club in July 1956, and in December of that year she became his mistress; during Christmas 1957 Marymont stayed with Cynthia Taylor, absenting himself from his three children and his wife – who, until she discovered an unposted letter from Marymont to his mistress in April 1958, was apparently unaware of her husband's love affair: '. . . our life was always a strain after that,' Marymont was to say in court, '. . . on various occasions my wife was crying. She appeared to be depressed, moody, and unhappy. This gave me a guilty feeling.' Mrs Marymont's ordeal was not wholly the mental one of extreme depression following the discovery of her partner's infidelity; gastric upsets commenced at roughly the same time, culminating in her admission ('just about dead' observed one doctor) to the American base hospital at Sculthorpe, Norfolk, on June 9th, 1958, where she died shortly afterwards. One doctor, obstetrician Albert Cook, advanced the theory at the time of Mrs Marymont's death that she might have been poisoned, but a fellow-physician joked that he must have read too many crime magazines; nevertheless, the bereaved sergeant showed a marked reluctance to his wife's corpse undergoing a post-mortem examination, explaining that his children did not like the idea of the body being cut up. Despite this family sensitivity, certain of Mrs Marymont's organs were removed and sent to Scotland Yard for analysis; not only was there a lethal dose of arsenic found in the liver, but arsenic in the hair indicated that Mrs Marymont had been dosed with the poison some weeks before her death. Many recollections pertaining to arsenic were to be forthcoming: Sergeant Marymont recalled that his wife had appeared unduly interested in some arsenical rat-poison he had purchased for his office, saying to him that they were themselves pestered with mice under the kitchen sink; 'I told her to use some if she wanted to,' said Marymont. A Mr Bernard Sampson, chemist, of High Street, Maidenhead, remembered Marymont as the man who had entered his pharmacy asking if arsenic was sold there: 'I said yes but we should want a permit. He said, "Oh, all right", and went out. . . .' Two cleaners at the Air Force Base, Sculthorpe, remembered Marymont as the man who, one evening, prowled around the chemical laboratory, expressing an interest in the arsenic containers: 'Don't they lock this stuff up? They ought to', Marymont had commented. Mrs Gertrude Marymont, mother of Sergeant Marymont, was flown from California to give evidence; she had received letters from her daughter-in-law, in which the latter's gastric illnesses were referred to, the younger woman writing that the medicine was worse than the disease. About her son, Mrs Marymont testified:

> He was always a good boy. We never had any trouble with him . . . he never stayed out late or anything like that. . . . In the war . . . he was sent to Alaska and won a medal for saving a man's life when a ship burned and sank. He swam under oil on the sea to rescue the man.

Found guilty of wife-murder, Marcus Marymont was condemned to life imprisonment, and is serving his sentence in America, at Leavenworth Prison, Kansas.

MASSET, Louise
Half-French piano and languages teacher, aged 33, executed at Newgate on January 9th, 1900, for the murder of her illegitimate 4-year-old son, Manfred Louis Masset.

Manfred was boarded out (for 37s. 6d. a month) at Clyde Road, Tottenham, cared for by a Miss Helen Gentle; Louise Masset lived with her married sister at 29 Bethune Road, Stoke Newington, where she fell in love with Mr Lucas, a 19-year-old medical student who lodged next door. For a period this love was reciprocated, even when the woman mentioned her child, but by autumn 1899 it is believed (in view of after events) that Lucas became less affectionate, no doubt exhausted by the double demands of examinations and passion. On October 16th Louise Masset wrote to Miss Gentle, saying that Manfred's father now wished the boy to be brought up in France; accordingly she collected Manfred on October 27th, telling Miss Gentle that their journey to France would start that very day from London Bridge station. Manfred, dressed in a white-braided blue suit and a blue cap with brass buttons, was last seen alive by the waiting-room attendant at London Bridge Station, who saw both mother and son walking towards the refreshment room. Three hours later the child's naked body was found in a lavatory at Dalston Junction Station; he had been suffocated, but had also sustained severe head injuries, apparently inflicted by a blood-stained chunk of stone nearby. On Sunday, October 29th, Manfred's clothes (identified from the newspaper description by Miss Gentle) were found in the waiting-room at Brighton station. Louise Masset, returning to London on the 30th from a Brighton week-end spent with her lover ('Miss Brooks and brother'), was arrested and charged with the murder of her son. The stone found in the lavatory at Dalston Junction exactly fitted a space in the back-garden rockery at Bethune Road, and at an identification parade the London Bridge waiting-room attendant picked out Louise Masset as the woman last seen with the child. The accused told how she met, by arrangement, two women at London Bridge station who had previously informed her of their intention to open a children's home at King's Road, Chelsea, and how, for a fee of £12 (paid in advance), they would accommodate Manfred for a year; that, said Louise Masset, was the last time she saw her child. At the trial the accused could give no satisfactory reply when asked by Sir Charles Matthews, prosecuting, why she had not obtained a receipt for the £12. (This King's Road kindergarten and its staff were never traced.) After the conviction a gathering of French governesses in London dispatched a petition begging mercy for their com-patriot to Queen Victoria; it made curious reference to the loss of life then being incurred by the Boer War: '. . . too much blood is flowing at this hour. Act so that a woman shall not contribute to swell this accursed torrent.' It is thought that Louise Masset so desperately hoped to regain and hold her lover's affection that she was even prepared to kill her own son, imagining that in some way he formed a barrier to the fulfilment of those hopes.

MATUSCHKA, Sylvestre
Certainly among the most remarkable of the post-1914 War mass-murderers, Matuschka was a man who could experience sexual excitement most deeply when he saw a train crashing, and con-sequently made an occupation of train wrecking.

Towards the end of 1931 the Vienna CID was looking into the past of 'Direktor Matuschka', who was suing the Hungarian

Railways as a victim of the Bia–Torbagy disaster, which occurred on Saturday, September 12th, 1931, when twenty-two people were killed in a train crash. Matuschka lived in Vienna at Hofgasse 9, and was Direktor of a 'housebuilding society'; he was married with one daughter. Matuschka's past proved to be so suspicious that Detective Inspector Peter Hain of Budapest was called in to help. He soon ascertained that Matuschka had been in the habit of purchasing explosives. In consequence, Matuschka was arrested and questioned; he finally confessed to being responsible not only for the Bia–Torbagy disaster, but also for the attempt to derail the Vienna–Passau train near Ansbach on New Year's Day 1931, and the derailing of the Vienna express near Berlin on August 8th, 1931, at Jueterborg. Sixteen passengers were injured.

Matuschka, who was the son of a slipper-maker, was born in the Hungarian village of Csantavér near Maria-Theresiopel, and he later served in the 6th Honved Regiment. He claimed that his peculiar perversion began when he was a boy, and a hypnotist at a fair suggested train disasters to him. During the 1914 War he served as a lieutenant in charge of a machine-gun company. In 1919 he married Irene Dér, daughter of one of his school-teachers. He made money through black-marketeering, and bought houses in Budapest, as well as becoming partner in a delicatessen business and a timber firm. In 1927 he was charged with swindling, but found not guilty. After this, he speculated in business and lost heavily. It may have been the strain of these losses that turned his mind to the idea of blowing up trains to obtain a sadistic pleasure. He prepared his attempts in great detail, before attempting to derail the Vienna–Passau express.

His first trial began on June 15th, 1932, in Austria. A mental expert called by the prosecution declared that Matuschka was amoralistic, a sadist, had a lust for power and for sensations, but was mentally well. During the trial, Matuschka seemed to be out to give an impression of insanity; he cried aloud, trembled, and prayed. He stated his profession as 'train wrecker, before that, business man'. The court could not reach an agreement, and further trials followed, during which Matuschka talked of a spirit called 'Leo' who ordered him to wreck trains. He was finally sentenced to death by hanging; a powerful factor in the final verdict was a map found in his home with the sites for further disaster. marked in red ink. He planned one a month, and the places included Amsterdam, Marseilles, Paris, and Ventimiglia. He was finally sentenced on November 20th, 1934.

MAYBRICK, Florence

Twenty-six-year-old American, convicted of the murder, in 1889, of her husband James Maybrick, aged 50, a Liverpool cotton broker.

Florence Maybrick, formerly Florence Chandler of Alabama, married in the USA in 1881. The Maybricks eventually settled at Battlecrease House, at Aigburth near Liverpool, where they lived in solid comfort, producing two children and employing several servants. Early in 1889, Mrs Maybrick took a lover, a Mr Brierly, with whom she spent three nights at a London hotel. It is uncertain whether Mr Maybrick realized that his wife was unfaithful, but that he suspected a liaison is certain: on Grand National day at Aintree he upbraided Brierly (whom the Maybricks had met accidentally) and upon the couple's return to Battlecrease House, Mrs Maybrick received a black eye. A month later, on April 27th, Mr Maybrick's health began to deteriorate. Always a hypochondriac, on this occasion he seemed genuinely ill, with fits of vomiting and diarrhoea and feelings of impending paralysis. No medicine proved efficacious, which was not surprising, since Maybrick had for years been stuffing himself with drugs and patent medicines, and was a constant consumer of strychnine and arsenic: 'I take this arsenic . . . because I find that it strengthens me. . . .' On May 11th, 1889, James Maybrick died, and almost immediately his wife came under suspicion of murder; Maybrick's relatives hovering around the sickbed said they had noticed dubious occurrences (such as the pouring of medicine from a small to a large bottle) and a family friend, a Mrs Briggs, had wired Maybrick's brother on May 8th: 'Come at once. Strange things going on here.' Alice Yapp, a servant, had that day seen flypapers (known to contain arsenic) soaking in a basin in her mistress' room, and although Mrs Maybrick afterwards explained that she had been extracting the arsenic for cosmetic purposes (see SMITH, Madeleine), considerable surmise arose when, after a post-mortem on May 13th, arsenic was found in the body of Mr Maybrick. Hyoscine, prussic acid, strychnine, and morphia were also discovered in the Maybrick stomach which for so long had been doused with palliatives and 'pick-me-ups', but on May 14th police marched into Florence Maybrick's bedroom and arrested her on a charge of murdering her husband.

('. . . I heard the tramp of many feet coming up the stairs . . . a crowd of men entered . . . "Mrs Maybrick, you are in custody on suspicion of causing the death of your late husband." I made no reply, and the crowd passed out.')

Sir Charles Russell was briefed for the defence of Mrs Maybrick, whose trial commenced at Liverpool on July 31st, 1889, under Mr Justice Fitzjames Stephen. The servant Yapp told how she had intercepted a letter from her mistress to Brierly, written three days before Maybrick's death. It contained phrases like 'he is sick unto death', 'I now know that he is perfectly ignorant of everything... even of the name of the street', and 'please don't leave England until I have seen you again'. The defence asserted that Maybrick, the durable drug-taker, had died a natural death.

Mrs Maybrick was found guilty of murder. Before the sentence of death she said: 'Although I have been found guilty, with the exception of my intimacy with Mr Brierly, I am not guilty of this crime'. Later, the sentence was commuted to life imprisonment, and Mrs Maybrick attained her freedom in 1904, after which she wrote a book entitled *My Fifteen Lost Years*.

McCLACHLAN, Jessie
Thirty-year-old domestic servant sentenced to death in September 1862 for the murder of 25-year-old domestic, Jessie McPherson.

On Monday, July 7th, 1862, Jessie McPherson's body was found in her basement bedroom at No. 17 Sandyford Place, Glasgow, a house owned by wealthy accountant Mr John Fleming and his family, who had been away for the week-end. Mr Fleming's father (who was to give his age variously as 78 and 87), who had remained over the week-end at Sandyford Place, remarked: 'She's been lying there all this time and me in the house!' The girl's body, nude, was battered and hacked by a meat-chopper or some similar instrument, the blows having been delivered, however, by someone having only a slight degree of strength; blood was everywhere in the basement (although efforts had recently been made to swab the basement kitchen, the floor being still damp) and two of old Fleming's shirts (kept in a basement wardrobe) were blood-bespattered. The old man said he had not seen the servant since Friday night, although at a later date when asked why he had himself opened the door on Saturday morning in response to the milkman's ring replied: 'On Saturday morning, ye ken, Jessie was deid, she couldna open the door when she was deid.' Silverware had been stolen, and it was found that Jessie McClachlan, a former servant in the Fleming

household and a friend of McPherson's, had pawned it for £6 15s.
at a shop in East Clyde Street, Glasgow, on Saturday. Jessie
McClachlan had been out on the Friday night, and it was established that when she returned home she had been wearing a dress
belonging to the dead woman. McClachlan said that the silverware had been brought round to her home on Friday evening:
'He said he was short of money and had to go to the Highlands
and didna like to lift money out of the bank.' The bloody im-
prints of a naked foot found on the victim's bedroom floor tallied
exactly with McClachlan's own footprint. McClachlan was
arrested and suspicion lifted from old Mr Fleming, who had, on
July 9th, actually been committed to prison; on September 17th,
1862, McClachlan appeared before Lord Deas in the Old Court,
Jail Square, Glasgow, Mr Gifford leading for the Crown and Mr
Rutherford Clark for the defence. Mr Fleming senior ('my
memory is not so fresh as that of a young man') said that he first
noticed McPherson's absence when she failed to bring him his
8 am porridge on the Saturday morning; asked why he had not
mentioned her disappearance to anyone he replied, 'I was expecting her every hour and every minute'. A neighbour, Elizabeth Brownlie, said she had heard the deceased refer to old
Fleming as 'that auld deevil'. A friend of McPherson's, Mrs
Mary Smith, said that on June 28th she met the girl in Sauchiehall Street, when McPherson had told her: 'I do not feel very
happy or comfortable with old Mr Fleming, for he is actually an
old wretch and an old devil.' A former servant to the Flemings,
a Mrs Martha McIntyre, described old Mr Fleming as being
obsessed by Jessie McPherson: 'He was always following and
inquiring after her.' Despite these insinuations against the old
man, the summing up of Lord Deas was unfavourable towards
the prisoner, and after retiring for only fifteen minutes the jury
returned a verdict of guilty. When asked if she had anything to
say why judgement should not be passed on her, Jessie McClachlan announced that she had prepared a statement she wished to
have read, then: '. . . I am as innocent as my child who is only 3
years of age at this date.' Mr Clark read the statement, in which
the convicted woman admitted visiting Jessie McPherson on
Friday night, July 4th: the two servants had consumed a gill and
a half of rum in front of the kitchen fire, aided by old Fleming,
who contributed half a bottle of whisky to the evening's enter-
ment. McClachlan (according to her statement) was then sent
out with fourteen pence to replenish the empty whisky bottle,
and returned to find Jessie McPherson lying moaning on the

floor, in a state of undress, bleeding from a head wound: 'I thought he had tried something wrong with her and she had been cut by falling.' Fleming was attempting to wash away the blood, and the pail containing water upset, drenching her (McClachlan's) gown, so that she had been obliged to borrow a garment belonging to the injured woman. Jessie McPherson revived for a spell, and told McClachlan that in her absence she had quarrelled with the old man about his persistent lechery, threatening to tell his family; she had flounced off to her room, 'to take off her stays and had her petticoats untied' when Fleming had entered and struck her heavily about the face with some instrument. Fleming had made McClachlan swear, on 'a big Bible with a black cover', that she would never talk about the night's happenings. McPherson's condition deteriorated, and while McClachlan was peering through the back windows of the house to see whether neighbours had been disturbed, old Mr Fleming went berserk, belaying the dying servant with a meat chopper; he then dragged the body to the basement bedroom, telling Jessie McClachlan that people would assume that burglars were responsible. Accordingly, he handed her a bundle of silverware from the sideboard, telling her she could pawn it. This statement Lord Deas described as 'a tissue of falsehoods', condemning the prisoner to die on October 11th: '. . . may God have mercy on your soul.' McClachlan screamed out: 'Mercy! Aye, He'll ha'e mercy, for I am innocent!'

There was much agitation demanding the reopening of the case, and public meetings were held in Edinburgh and Glasgow. On October 3rd the execution was postponed, and on October 13th a Crown Commissioner (Mr George Young, Sheriff of Haddington) appointed to review the case. It was found, among other things, that ten years before, old Mr Fleming had been chastised by his church for 'the sin of fornication with a servant Janet Dunsmore'. On October 24th a case report was submitted to the Home Secretary, as a result of which the sentence was commuted to penal servitude: 'The prisoner was an accidental and constrained witness of the murder and not an actor in it. She can never be hanged but as she concealed and adopted it she must be severely punished.' McClachlan served fifteen years of her sentence, and in 1884 went to America where she died in 1899.

No proceedings were ever taken against Fleming, although public feeling in Glasgow forced his family to take abode elsewhere.

McDONALD, Roland

Fifteen-year-old Amhurst, Maine, farm boy, sentenced to life imprisonment for the murder of 19-year-old village schoolteacher Louise Gerrish, found dead in a weedbed from shotgun wounds on 25th May, 1924, hours after she had left her farmhouse lodging to post a letter. A handbag under the body was empty, and as her châtelaine type watch, worn on a black and gold ribbon, was missing, it was assumed that robbery was the murder motive. Searching through her personal effects police found an ill-written message, scrawled on blue-line school paper:

'We wached you dance last night. Thanks for leving the window open. It was real good. We will be watching some more when you dance agin.'

Questioning two other girl teachers, police learnt that Louise Gerrish had enjoyed a maidenly 'pyjama party' in her bedroom four days before, when the three girls had cavorted to strains of the Charleston on the phonograph. Examination of scholars' handwriting revealed the unbidden watcher as a 16-year-old pupil, who named his fellow Peeping Toms as Roland McDonald and his 13-year-old brother Victor. Roland McDonald worked as a handy-boy around the farm where Louise Gerrish lived, and news that he had recently spent the inordinate sum of 50 cents on sweets increased police interest. The black and gold châtelaine ribbon of Louise Gerrish was found on the younger boy, who claimed he had received it from brother Roland. After interrogation, Roland McDonald admitted that he had followed Louise Gerrish out of the farmhouse and shot her as she walked through the woods to the post office at Amhurst. Asked why he shot the girl, the farmhand replied: 'Dunno.' Pronounced sane by a dozen psychiatrists, including two physicians sent by Harvard University, McDonald was convicted in October 1924 of the murder. Victor McDonald, aware of constant suspicion, shot himself two years later at the age of 15. Doubts arose as to the total guilt of Roland McDonald, and he himself, from his cell, in the penitentiary at Thomaston, Maine, began to protest his innocence. In April 1958 the authorities gave him a lie-detector test. Thinking that 30 years' assertion of innocence might counterfeit the delicate mechanism, Major Hennessey, the executive officer of Maine State police, was cautious in his questioning: 'Did you lie to the Parole Officer yesterday when you said you didn't kill Louise Gerrish?' 'No,' said McDonald, after a momentary hesitation. The detector graph needle rose rapidly, registering an apparent falsehood, ensuring that Roland McDonald would continue his prison sentence.

MENESCLOU

A youth of 19 or 20, mentally retarded, who murdered a child of 5. Details of the murder are not given in the account by Major Arthur Griffiths, who mentions merely that Menesclou was constantly in trouble at school, that he robbed his father and beat his mother, and that he spent three years in the navy. His crime, committed in 1880, was the murder of a 5-year-old girl – possibly for sexual motives. He lured her into his room with sweets and violets, and killed her. The body was concealed in his mattress overnight (he slept on it). The next day the police were summoned because a poisonous black smoke was belching from a chimney and the house was full of the smell of burning flesh. A workman went up a ladder on to the roof, and peered in the dormer window of Menesclou's garret; he saw Menesclou feeding his stove with pieces of meat. This turned out to be the child's body.

At his trial, he showed indifference. At one point, when public indignation caused a clamour in court, he screamed back: 'Well, you can do the same to me!'

MERRETT, John Donald (alias Ronald Chesney)

A study of this individual is perhaps the best possible argument for capital punishment. In fact, after committing his first murder, that of his mother, the charge was found not proven (a permissible verdict under Scottish law) and years later, after murdering his wife and his mother-in-law, Merrett (now known as Chesney) escaped the inevitable penalty by killing himself.

Merrett was born in 1908 at Levin, North Island, New Zealand, the only child of an electrical engineer immigrant and a North of England wine merchant's daughter with a penchant for inventing things (including a fireless cooker), who was to be deserted by her husband and return to England in 1924, where she and her gangling six-foot son lived outside Reading, 'Donnie' continuing his education at Malvern College. Academically bright (with a particular flair for languages), 'Donnie's' precocity was not, unfortunately, confined to lessons, and after an unsavoury episode involving a girl, Mrs Bertha Merrett moved, in 1925, to Edinburgh, where 'Donnie' was to attend the University under her surveillance. Mrs Merrett had a private income of £700 a year, and they eventually settled in furnished rooms in Buckingham Terrace. Ostensibly studying art, 'Donnie' spent all his waking hours at the Dunedin Palais de Danse studying the fox-trot in the company of dance-hostesses, his art being confined to the skilful forgery of his mother's signature on cheques, and by March 1926 he had drawn £458 from the unsuspecting woman's two bank accounts, although he was uncomfortably aware of recent correspondence from one bank querying the overdraft of one of their usually most astute and careful clients. At 9.40 am on the morning of March 17th, 1926, Mrs Bertha Merrett fell from her writing desk, bleeding profusely from a gunshot wound in her right ear. The daily maid, Mrs Henrietta Sutherland, told the summoned police a short while afterwards that she had actually seen her mistress, still holding a pistol, slip off the chair on to the floor, although she later altered this account, testifying that she had been engaged in lighting the kitchen fire when Donald Merrett came in, distraught, crying, 'Rita, my mother has shot herself'. The unconscious woman was transported to Edinburgh Royal Infirmary, her son (who accompanied the escort police) gloomily implying that financial embarrassment had been the reason for his mother's suicide attempt. Mrs Merrett, treated as a criminal because of her supposed attempt at self-destruction, was kept in the strictest custody, and, when she recovered consciousness, no one was allowed to discuss the nature of her injury. To a doctor Mrs Merrett said, 'I was sitting down writing letters and my son Donald was standing beside me, I said, "Go away, Donald, and don't annoy me", and the next thing I heard was a kind of explosion, and I do not remember anything more.' Donald Merrett was not a frequent hospital visitor, still spending most of his time at the Palais de Danse and still contriving to draw money by forgery from his mother's remaining bank account. On March 28th Mrs Merrett died, the post-mortem verdict being that her death was consistent with suicide. On March 30th, police found a bank pass-book, with cheques and counterfoils removed, in Donald Merrett's bedroom; this discovery started a line of inquiry in which signatures on cheques purportedly signed by Bertha Merrett were found to be clever forgeries, while Professor Harvey Littlejohn in Edinburgh carried out ballistic experiments on Donald Merrett's pistol ('for shooting rabbits'). Donald Merrett was, meanwhile, the responsibility of the Public Trustee, who, a trifle uneasy, it seems, about his troublesome charge (in July he had absconded to London with two girls, one of whom was under the age of 16), had had him medically examined, which brought forth the expert opinion: 'The lad is exceptionally well developed physically for his age and looks at least over twenty years. He talks intelgently and confidently, and is clear and lucid in his statements on general topics. He is sound in every bodily organ and mentally he is perfectly sane.' On November 29th, 1926, John Donald Merrett (whose temporary billet was now, inappropriately, Hughenden Vicarage, near High Wycombe, Bucks.) was arrested on a charge of murdering his mother, and a second charge of 'uttering as genuine' twenty-nine forged cheques upon his mother's account. Merrett was taken back to Edinburgh, where his trial commenced on February 1st, 1927, the accused pleading not guilty. Much of the evidence for the Crown was concerned with the bullet wound itself, and the absence of a surround of 'tattooing' or 'blackening' usually to be seen in cases of near discharge, that is, most suicides. Sir Bernard Spilsbury, appearing for the defence, thought however that the wound in question could be consistent with either suicide or accident, and it was largely through this expert's intervention that the jury, doubtless perplexed, gave the indeterminate Not Proven verdict, although unanimously finding Merrett guilty on the second charge.

Merrett served eight of his twelve-months' prison sentence, during which time he was often visited by an old friend of his mother, a Mrs Mary Bonnar, a genteel little eccentric who some time later was to grant herself the title 'Lady Menzies'. On his release, Merrett stayed with Mrs Bonnar at Hastings, where he soon acquired a rakish reputation. This did not deter Mrs Bonnar's daughter Vera, aged 17, who eloped with him to Scotland but who had to return to an irate mother one month later when her bridegroom was imprisoned for obtaining goods by false pretences. When Merrett was 21, he inherited £50,000 left in trust for him by his grandfather; he was persauded to make a marriage settlement of £8,400 on his bride, who was to receive the interest on this sum throughout her life, the capital reverting to Merrett in the event of her death. In the decade before the Second World War, Merrett (now using the name Ronald John Chesney) indulged in a life of crime; he had soon spent his inheritance, and so sought easy money by blackmail, fraud, thieving, and smuggling – this last occupation seeming particularly suitable, for with his gigantic stature, his beard and the one gold ear-ring he always wore Chesney resembled a *Boy's Own Paper* pirate. Even a war-time career in the RNVR was not to stop his illegal activities. There was a curious episode in an Italian prison camp when Chesney (captured at Benghazi) was recognized by one of his fellow prisoners as John Donald Merrett, an account of whose trial for matricide (one of the William Hodge trial series) was in the camp library; apparently Chesney laughingly refuted his resemblance to the published photographs, but nevertheless succeeded in destroying the book. Years later, Vera Chesney, instinctively terrified for her life, was to repeatedly take this same volume out of the local library, wondering, as she turned the pages, if her mother could possibly have been mistaken in her belief of her future son-in-law's innocence.

After the war Lady Menzies and Vera Chesney ran an old people's home in Montpelier Road, Ealing; Ronald Chesney lived mainly on black-market enterprises and with various mistresses, to one of whom (Gerda Schaller) he confessed to killing his mother. Inevitably Chesney began to muse on the possibility of acquiring the money he had settled on his wife years before. Visiting her on a lightning trip from Germany on February 3rd, 1954, he was especially amiable, bringing her a bottle of gin, a drink to which Vera Chesney had become addicted; he took her to the cinema, and hailed many of their mutual acquaintances around Ealing. Back in Germany, on February 10th, he donned horn-rimmed spectacles, brushed back his hair and slipped off his gold ear-ring (having earlier shaved off his beard), thus acquiring a superficial resemblance to Chelsea photographer Leslie Bernard Treville Chown, in whose name he had previously applied for, and secured, a British passport. That night he flew to England and plied his wife with more gin; having reduced her to a stupor, he dragged her to the bathroom and held her, head down, under a few inches of bathwater, with the obvious intention of making her death appear as a drunken misdemeanour. He was seen creeping from the house by Lady Menzies, a fateful meeting for her, the only witness to his presence in England that night; when police went to the house next day it was apparent that the bludgeoned and strangled old lady had put up a terrific struggle for her life. A heavily built man had been seen in the vicinity on the night of the crime, a description fitting Vera Chesney's husband, about whom the police were curious, particularly when realizing that Ronald Chesney and the one-time suspected murderer John Donald Merrett were the same person. A notice asking about the whereabouts of Merrett, alias Chesney, was printed in the *Police Gazette*, and the International Crime Police Commission in Paris was alerted. On February 16th the body of Ronald Chesney was found, shot dead in a wood near Cologne. His arms bore bruises and scratches and pink fibres identical with those from Lady Menzies' scarf were found on his clothing, as were her dog's hairs and traces of recently removed blood (not Chesney's own) on his trouser leg; under his mother-in-law's nails were fragments of skin obviously wrested from Chesney's arms during the death-struggle, and on the old lady's cardigan were dark hairs, similar to Chesney's. At an Ealing inquest on the two women the jury decided that Ronald John Chesney was responsible for both deaths.

MERRIFIELD, Louisa
Forty-six-year-old domestic worker, found guilty (after a trial lasting eleven days) of murdering 79-year-old widow Sarah Ann Ricketts.

On March 12, 1953, Mrs Merrifield, with her lately acquired third husband, 74-year-old Alfred Edward Merrifield, took a position as housekeeper to Mrs Ricketts, who lived in a bungalow (Homestead), in Devonshire Road, Blackpool. Mrs Merrifield had applied for the job in response to a newspaper advertisement, and apparently Mrs Ricketts was so impressed by the Merrifields' zeal in executing their household duties that by March 31st she had altered her will in their favour. On Saturday, April 11th Mrs Merrifield met an acquaintance, Mrs Brewer, and said: 'We are landed. We went living with an old lady and she died and left me a bungalow worth £4,000.' On Tuesday, April 14th Mrs Ricketts died, although she had been in reasonably good health when examined by a Dr Wood the previous day. Mrs Merrifield described afterwards how she had found her mistress on the floor of the bedroom at 3.15 am: 'I picked her up and put her into bed. She said she was thankful to me. Those were the last words she spoke.' Mrs Merrfield unsuccessfully requested an undertaker to cremate her employer's body 'at once', but a post-mortem was performed (at about the same time Mrs Merrifield was making arrangements to have a Salvation Army band play 'Abide With Me' outside the bungalow)

454

and the cause of death found to be yellow phosphorus, a poisonous substance found in some types of rat poison. Mrs Merrifield was known to have purchased one such brand of rat poison, and (although a tin was never found in or about the bungalow premises) a teaspoon coated with a gritty, sweetish substance was taken from Mrs Merrifield's handbag. A forensic expert at the subsequent murder trial at Manchester Assizes said that such a residue would form if the spoon had been used to mix phosphorus with rum; although there was no chemical evidence of phosphorus Mrs Merrifield had admitted offering 'a few spots of rum' to Mrs Ricketts on the night of April 13th, and now the jury were invited by the prosecution to sniff at an eggcupful of this spirit containing rat poison. Professor J. B. Webster, director of Birmingham's forensic laboratory, called by the defence (led by Mr J. di V. Nahum), maintained that Mrs Ricketts had died from natural causes, namely, cirrhosis of the liver.

The Crown (led by Sir Lionel Heald) were curious to learn why Mrs Merrifield had not called in a doctor until 2 pm, when Mrs Ricketts was already dead:

Did it not occur to you to do anything for her at that [*sic*] time?

Well, it was not such a nice time in the morning to go out on the streets and call a doctor.

... there is another explanation why you did nothing – that is, you saw the old lady was going, and wanted her to go?

Mrs Merrifield's appeal against the verdict was dismissed, and she was executed on September 18th, 1953. The jury had failed to agree in the case of the seemingly bewildered, newly wed Mr Merrifield, who had also been charged with murder. Mr Justice Glyn-Jones ordered a retrial at the following Assizes, but in the meantime the Attorney-General issued a fiat of *nolle prosequi* (unwilling to prosecute) and Mr Merrifield, on receipt of this document by the Governor of Strangeways Jail, was immediately released.

MEXICO

Country which has the highest murder rate in the world; only malaria and heart disease cause more deaths.

M'GUIGAN, John (Murder Trial)

Twenty-four-year-old Irish vagrant, charged in August 1935 with the murder of 17-year-old Danny Kerrigan.

The victim had been 'walking out' on the evening of August 12th with his fiancée, 17-year-old Marjory Fenwick, in a rural spot, Cuddies Strip, on the outskirts of Perth, in Scotland, when he had been shot at and fatally wounded by an unknown assailant who leapt out from some bushes. According to the girl's testimony, the killer then tore off her clothes and raped her. Most of her clothes (including shoes and stockings) were never found, and there was disbelief cast on her story about the sexual assault; although in obvious distress and not *virgo intacta* when examined at 1.30 am on August 13th, her claim of chastity prior to the murder date was doubted. Her wrists, however, had been tied with a handkerchief stolen from a nearby house, and another blue handkerchief was found by the murder-spot; living in a tent near the scene of the murder was John M'Guigan, and the blue handkerchief was proved to belong to him. On August 28th Marjory Fenwick picked M'Guigan out as her assailant at a police identity parade, and he was accordingly sent for trial in Edinburgh on November 25th, 1935. The indictment included burglary (of the handkerchief used to tie the girl's wrists), the murder of Danny Kerrigan, and the assault on Marjory Fenwick: 'You did pull off her clothing, tie her hands, lie on top of her and did ravish her.'

Two men gave evidence that they had seen M'Guigan walking from Cuddies Strip on the evening of the killing. A ploughman, who knew M'Guigan owned a gun, spoke of the accused's fear that the police would associate him with the crime. One, Mr Gow, gave evidence of M'Guigan's 'Peeping Tom' propensities; he had seen a man 'with something cocked up at his eye' (later proved to be a telescope stolen by M'Guigan) spying on a couple near Cuddies Strip, and identified M'Guigan as this rustic prowler.

The summing up (by the Lord Justice Clerk) went against the prisoner: '. . . . don't forget that the man who was capable of shooting Kerrigan dead in the presence of that young girl when they were sweethearting together was a man capable of any crime.'

The jury found M'Guigan guilty on the housebreaking charge, guilty of rape; and on the murder charge brought in the (Scottish) verdict of Not Proven. The jury was thanked by the Lord Justice Clerk for their 'discriminating' verdict.

M'Guigan was sentenced to penal servitude for ten years.

MILLER, Adrian

Twenty-nine-year-old earnest-mannered, bespectacled engineering student, convicted of the murder of 17-year-old commercial student Alice May Girton, found suffocated and raped in the bed-sitting-room she rented in a house on Lafayette Street, Fort Wayne, Indiana. She was found by her landlady at 9.30 am on October 13th, 1938, and the police pathologist estimated that death had occurred from seven to eight hours previously. Miss Girton had received a visit from her fiancé that night, and one of her fellow-lodgers, Adrian Miller ('I hardly know Miss Girton at all'), told detectives how he had seen a man leave the victim's apartment 'stealthily' about 2.40 am. Interviewed, the fiancé denied any knowledge of the crime, he admitted to a police record for larceny some years before, and was held on the technical charge of vagrancy pending further inquiries. Within a few minutes of this interrogation, Detective Captain John Taylor, in charge of the case, received a lengthy typewritten letter from lodger Miller:

> I have been wishing I could help you solve the mystery. I think the keynote is a psychological study of the characters involved . . .

He spoke of the murdered girl's introspective personality, the result of a polio-withered left hand, and how she yearned for the social life, although warned by Miller himself of the danger of knowing men 'with few moral scruples'. Miller elaborated on his former statement, now naming the fiancé as the man he had seen leaving Alice Girton's room, and how he had heard someone falling in the room seconds before this surreptitious departure. Miller's letter was soon followed by Miller himself, eagerly asking if the girl's fiancé had been arrested, and proffering more theories on the psychology of both the murdered and the murderer. Confronted with the fiancé, he positively, if uneasily (in view of the other's wrath), identified him as the man he had seen leaving the murder room at 2.40 am. Police by now suspected Miller's unrestrained sleuthing and his exhaustive knowledge concerning the slain girl, of whom he had, hours earlier, disclaimed knowledge. Captain Taylor, with two other detectives, crept into the engineering student's room as he slept; shaking him into semi-consciousness, Taylor asked Miller if he had gone to Miss Girton's room immediately after her fiancé left, and received a revealing reply from the sleepy and now incriminated Miller, 'No, it was later'. Subsequently he admitted to the killing.

> . . . she seemed fond of me. But she kept seeing this other man . . . when he was in the room with her, I knew he must be making love to her. I couldn't stand it. Then about midnight I heard him leave . . . I knocked on Alice May's door . . . I seized her by the shoulders and shook her. And then her robe fell away and I saw her in just her pyjamas. I guess I went crazy then. . . .

Throughout the case Miller denied raping his victim; at his trial the jury found him guilty of murder in the first degree, and he was sentenced to death, several attempts being made by his lawyers to stave off this penalty. Miller himself wrote another lengthy letter, this time to the Governor of Indiana State Prison, stating that the study of mathematics and chemistry would make a life sentence tolerable, and that: '. . . by living I might still do much good'. To a deputy warden who suggested he might better study the Bible instead of a text on calculus, Miller replied, 'All the universe operates on a system of perfect mathematics, and perhaps I shall be nearer to God in this book than by reading the Bible'. Miller was electrocuted on August 16th, 1939.

MILLS, Leonard Herbert
Nineteen-year-old clerk of Mansfield Street, Nottingham, charged with the murder of 48-year-old Mabel Tattershaw.

On August 9th, 1951, crime reporter Norman Rae of the Sunday newspaper *News of the World* received a telephone message from a Nottingham call-box: 'I've just found a woman's body. It looks like murder.' The newspaper at once contacted Nottingham police, who traced the caller, Leonard Mills; he led police to the body of a strangled woman, Mrs Tattershaw, in a rural spot near Sherwood Vale, saying he had met a 'sinister, limping man' in the vicinity. In an article, 'How I Met Murder', Mills described for *News of the World* readers how he had found the body while searching for a quiet spot where he could write a sonnet. After finding the corpse he sat down and read Shelley's 'Ode to Death'.

On August 25th at Nottingham Magistrates' Court, Mills was

charged with the murder of Mrs Tattershaw. Reporter Rae told of frequent meetings with the accused, when Mills would elaborate on his original story, concerned always with the financial worth of his information. On August 24th, Mills met Rae at a hotel and wrote out a statement on hotel notepaper which Rae submitted to the police. In the statement Mills wrote how the possibility of committing a perfect murder had always intrigued him. Seated next to insignificant housewife Mabel Tattershaw (a complete stranger) at Nottingham's Roxy Cinema on August 2nd, he believed he had found the perfect 'murderee' and made friendly overtures, arranging to meet her the following day. On the evening of August 3rd Mills took Mrs Tattershaw for a walk and they sat down in the place Mills had selected for his macabre experiment: '. . . I had not interfered with her, nor did I . . . I put on a pair of gloves . . . knelt with my knees on her shoulders. The coats were placed on her so that she would not clutch, nor gather any thread within her finger nails . . .' Then: '. . . no motive, no clue. Why, if I had not reported finding the body I should not have been connected with the crime in any manner whatsoever. I am quite proud of my achievement.'

Professor J. M. Webster, pathologist, said that the victim had been struck, probably by fists, both before and after the strangulation. Evidence was given that hairs from Mills' head were found on Mrs Tattershaw's dress, and fibres under her nails came from his blue suit. Tried at Nottingham Assizes in November 1950, Mills was found guilty of the murder of Mabel Tattershaw and sentenced to death.

MILSOM and FOWLER (The Muswell Hill Murder)

Henry Smith, a retired engineer approaching 80, lived on his own at Muswell Lodge, a large house in its own grounds at Tetherdown, Muswell Hill, North London. The gardener, Webber, had rigged booby traps, guns that fired when a wire was disturbed, and this had discouraged one burglar.

On the morning of February 14th, 1896, Mr Smith was found dead in the kitchen at Muswell Lodge, with signs of a long struggle; his death was due to head wounds and he was tied with strips of cloth, which had been cut by two penknives, lying on either side of the body. The safe in his bedroom stood open. Jemmy marks were found on the drawing-room and scullery windows, but it had been the kitchen window that had finally admitted the burglars.

Two men had been seen in the area in the days previous to the murder, and suspicion came to rest on a couple named Albert Milsom and Henry Fowler, who lived in Kentish Town. Milsom was a small, shifty crook; his partner was an immense ex-convict, out on licence. A ten-pound note taken from Mr Smith's house was finally traced back to Fowler. A detective who had been observing the two before the murder also noted that they disappeared from their haunts immediately afterwards.

There was only one clue at Muswell Lodge: a child's toy lantern, found near the body. Fifteen-year-old Henry Miller, Milsom's brother-in-law, virtually condemned the two men to death when he declared: 'That's mine', and proceeded to explain various marks on the toy that made him so sure.

The manhunt now began, a postmark on a letter affording the first clue. Milsom and Fowler moved swiftly around the country, from place to place, spending money, changing their names periodically. They had joined a travelling show, in which the proprietor had allowed them to buy partnership. Finally, after a search that led from Liverpool to Manchester, Cardiff, back to London (where Milsom's family succeeded in joining him) then to Swindon and Bath, they were caught towards dusk on Sunday, April 12th, 1896, in a shop at Monmouth Street, Bath. Milsom came quietly enough, but Fowler fought violently and had to be subdued with blows on the head from a revolver. The next day Fowler denied all knowledge of the crime, declaring that his resistance had been due to his notion that the detectives wanted him for breaking his parole; when it was pointed out that his violence was greater than such a fear warranted, he replied sullenly: 'I was in beer.'

Milsom soon cracked and admitted the crime, giving circumstantial details; he declared, however, that he had been outside when Fowler had killed the old man (who had been awakened by the noise of their entry). They appeared at Highgate Police Court, and were sent for trial to the Old Bailey, where Mr Justice Hawkins presided. Evidence against them was overwhelming; two women had seen them lurking near Muswell Lodge two days before the murder; Milsom had been able to indicate the exact whereabouts of the burgling tools which they buried in the grounds of the house. The evidence of the women disposed of Milsom's declaration that he knew nothing of the contemplated crime until Fowler called on him the evening before the murder. Fowler seemed dominated by an urge to make sure that Milsom hanged too, and declared that the murder was committed by Milsom. In his summing up, Mr Justice Hawkins dwelt on the evidence of the two penknives and the obvious deduction that both men had helped to bind the old man (who was already dead when he was tied). When the jury retired, the two men were left in the dock, and Fowler made a determined and almost successful attempt to strangle his partner; it took twelve minutes to overpower him.

Both were sentenced to death; they were hanged together with a man named Seaman who had committed a double murder in Whitechapel.

MONEY, Sophia, and Robert (The Merstham Tunnel Mystery)

The death of Mary Sophia Money is still an unsolved mystery. She was an attractive young girl who earned her own living and lived away from home. She lived at 245 Lavender Hill, Clapham, and apparently had no men friends. On Sunday, September 24th, 1905, she told a Miss Hone, another employee of the dairymen for whom she worked, that she was going out for 'a little walk'. She called in a sweet shop at about seven in the evening and said she was going to Victoria. At eleven o'clock that night her body was found in the Merstham Tunnel, near Merstham, on the Brighton line. She was badly disfigured by the train, and had apparently been pushed, or had fallen out, in the tunnel. The guard of a train that left London Bridge at nine-thirty-three for Brighton said he had noticed a man and a woman (who corresponded to Miss Money's description) at East Croydon; they had seemed furtive. And a signalman at Purley Oaks said he had seen a couple struggling in a carriage as the train passed; the man seemed to be trying to force the girl on to a seat. The supposition would seem to be that the girl left home to meet a man friend, who persuaded her to come for a run to Victoria. At Victoria he may have offered to take her home, and got her on to the Brighton train, either with the intention of getting her to spend a night with him in Brighton, or of raping her on the train. A struggle followed, she was hurt, and thrown out of the carriage.

Her brother, Robert Henry Money, a dairy farmer, was a shifty character who lived a double life. He had affairs with two sisters, and had two children by one of them and one by the other (whom he married). In 1912 he took both women to Eastbourne, unknown to one another, and shot the whole party of five. One of the women escaped, wounded; Money then shot himself and set fire to the house with petrol, leaving a suicide note signed 'Mackie'. It has been suggested that he murdered his sister. This is remotely probable.

MONSON, A. J. (The Ardlamount Mystery)
Acquitted of the murder of his pupil, Cecil Hambrough, by a Scottish verdict of not proven, Monson had insured his pupil's life (in his wife's favour) for £20,000.

The case is famous for its complexity; but an account of the lengthy and mostly crooked financial dealings that preceded it is not necessary to understand it. Briefly, its history is as follows:

The victim's father, Major Hambrough, was a man in his forties and he owned the Ardlamount Estates, situated in the Isle of Wight and other parts of the British Isles, which were worth £135,000. The estates were entailed, and the major received an income of £4,000 a year from them. When his son Cecil – who was 18 – came of age, the estates could be sold by mutual consent of father and son. But the major was a rather stupid and vague man, who got himself heavily into debt, and mortgaged his life interest in the estates for £37,000, which he quickly spent. There was danger of his going bankrupt, and he approached a man named Tottenham, a moneylender, who took charge of his affairs, but also introduced the major to Monson. The immediate aim was to buy back the life interest and remortgage it to another company, who would pay more than £37,000 and demand a lower rate of interest than £2,000 a year. (This was the sum the major should have paid to the company to whom he mortgaged his shares. It sounds as if he had a very bad deal. The company who had lent him the £37,000 on security of the life interest had foreclosed, leaving him penniless.)

Monson was an army tutor, a man of great strength of character and restless mind. Monson proposed to the major that he should undertake the care and tuition of Cecil Hambrough until Cecil entered the army, and the major was happy to agree.

Tottenham's scheme for re-floating the major's finances was to surrender the major's insurance policies, worth £8,000, and use the money to start negotiations for buying back the life interest. However, the major had to be insured to safeguard the interest of any other mortgagee, and, as he was a sick man, the problems of re-insuring him were so immense that Tottenham's schemes were held up. Monson decided to take things out of

Tottenham's hands and to re-purchase the life interest himself by financial juggling. Unfortunately, some of the early stages of his financial juggling caused him to lose the major's trust completely. This was in 1892. But Monson still had Cecil living with him, and was determined to keep his grip on the youth. Cecil seems to have been completely in Monson's hands, and at one stage promised to invest £100,000 in exchange for £300 down and £5 a week for a year!

Monson had apparently determined to swindle the none-too-honest Mr Tottenham, and at one point told him that the agents of the estate had agreed to accept £48,000 for it, and a deposit of £250 – an absurdly small sum. He added in the same letter that he had told Cecil that the price was £50,000 – £1,000 for each of them when they came to share out the spoils! At one point, Cecil allowed Monson to sue him for his keep and tuition fees (he was living with the Monsons), and the judgement against Cecil – for £800 – was promptly sold to Tottenham for £250 ready cash. Tottenham was plainly banking on Cecil's expectations.

The major had by now placed his affairs in the hands of an honest lawyer named Prince, so that Prince and Monson were now rivals for the estate, trying to persaude the insurance company who held the life interest to re-sell it.

Perhaps with the idea of getting into possession of his future property, the Monson family (Monson, his wife and children), plus Cecil Hambrough, moved up to Ardlamount in Argyllshire, north of the Clyde. Monson secured a lease on the house for £900 a year, the first instalment to be due in August 1893. He now tried hard to insure Cecil's life, and after some initial difficulty (he tried to insure it for £50,000, but had no convincing reason to offer) he managed to insure it for £20,000, paying as a premium £250 that the gullible Tottenham had advanced as the deposit on the estate. Cecil was promptly persuaded to assign these policies to Mrs Monson, who was declared to be lending him £20,000 for the purchase of the major's life interest. (Actually, the Monsons were penniless.) This assignment was illegal, as Cecil was under age, but perhaps Monson hoped the insurance company would pay up – in the event of Cecil's untimely death.

In August 1893 occurred the tragedy for which Monson was tried. On August 8th Monson went to Glasgow, and returned with a mysterious man whom he introduced as Scott, who was to inspect the boilers of a yacht Cecil wanted to buy. The next day, he went out boating, and when out alone with Cecil the boat overturned. Monson and Cecil came in very wet, and Monson declared that Cecil had struggled to a rock (he could not swim) while Monson had gone back to shore and rescued him in another boat. Later, Monson was to be charged with attempting to murder Cecil by drowning.

The next day Mrs Monson left early to shop in Glasgow, and Monson, Scott, and Cecil went out shooting. They were seen to enter a wood; shots were heard, and Monson and Scott returned to the house saying that there had been an accident and Cecil was dead. Cecil, he said, had shot himself with the gun he was carrying, while he and Scott had been walking in front. Cecil's body was carried to the house.

At this stage, no one even suspected murder. Indeed, it would not have been suspected at all if Monson had not tried to claim the insurance. But the insurance company were suspicious, matters were re-examined, and Monson was arrested a fortnight after the death, on August 29th. There was an attempt to find Scott, but he seemed to have vanished completely. Later, when the trial opened, 'Scott' was declared to be outlawed – it being assumed that he had disappeared to escape standing trial for murder with Monson.

Monson was tried at the High Court of Justiciary at Edinburgh, before Sir John Hay Athole Macdonald; Alexander Asher led for the Crown, and Mr Comrie Thompson for the defence. He was charged with attempted murder (the boat episode) and the murder of Cecil Hambrough. The case lasted for ten days and was of enormous complexity, because of the financial dealings involved. The defence was able to claim that it was in Monson's interests to keep Cecil alive, and that he would not benefit in any way by his death; Monson, they said, did not expect that the insurance company would pay up.

The Crown had prepared its case extremely badly. Its theory was that Cecil had been shot through the head by Monson as he walked along the dyke (not in the ditch, where Monson claimed he had shot himself, but on top of the dyke); Monson had used a 12-bore shotgun, and a tree in direct line with Cecil's head was scarred with pellets. The defence produced a man from India who had shot himself in the way Monson claimed Cecil had shot himself.

The judge's charge to the jury was favourable to Monson, and the jury found the case Not Proven.

MOONLIGHT MURDERER, The (Texarkana, Texas, 1946)
Typical of a certain kind of unsolved murder case, this one emphasizes the difficulty encountered by the police when it is a question of the maniac-type sexual killer.

On the night of February 20th, 1946, a young couple were seated in their car near Texarkana, Texas, listening to the radio, when the door was swung open, and the man was struck on the head with a revolver. The girl was also knocked unconscious as she attempted to run away, and was raped. It was daylight when the man regained consciousness, carried his fiancée to the car, and drove to the nearest house for assistance. Six men were arrested almost immediately, following the description given of the attacker by the young couple, and tyre-tracks were noticed close to the spot where the assault had taken place. However, no positive evidence could be obtained, and the men were released. Towns within two hunded miles of the Texas–Arkansas border were alerted to be on the lookout for the criminal.

A month later, on March 24th, Richard Griffin and Polly Anne Moore, a 24-year-old salesman and his 19-year-old girlfriend, parked their car only a mile away from the spot where the previous couple had been assaulted. Griffin was shot through the head, the girl was shot twice, mutilated with a sharp knife, and sexually assaulted. Evidence showed that Griffin had been murdered two hours or so before the girl. Tyre-prints near the murder site were identical with those found near the scene of the previous assault. The bullets came from a ·32 revolver.

On both occasions a bright full moon had simplified the sex-maniac's search for victims.

Again, many suspects were arrested and released.

On April 13th a 15-year-old girl, Betty Jo Booker, had been playing a saxophone at a local dance. She left the dance after midnight with her boy-friend, 17-year-old Paul Martin. The next morning, both bodies were found a mile away from the car. The youth had been shot in the back three times. The girl had evidently been dragged away from the car, and was shot and mutilated about four hours after the death of her boy-friend. She had been tortured for some time before she was killed; she was also raped.

Scores of suspects were interviewed, and all available police in Texas and Arkansas were used on the case, without result. The newspapers headlined the unknown killer, and a 'reign of terror' began in the area of the murders.

On May 3rd, 1946, again on the night of a full moon, a wealthy farmer, Virgil Starks, was shot as he sat reading a newspaper at ten-thirty. His wife, rushing into the room, was also shot. She managed to run to the house of a neighbour, A. V. Prater, and gave the alarm. This crime had occurred within the state of Arkansas.

Evidence showed that the murderer had killed Virgil Starks with a ·22 rifle, and had entered the house immediately after Mrs Starks ran for help. His intention was probably to assault the housewife in his usual manner; the familiar tyre-tracks were found near the house. Mrs Starks recovered from her wounds a few weeks later.

Measures for discovering the criminal were on the enormous scale that is usual in such cases. Hundreds of men were interviewed in towns for a hundred miles around. All military personnel were investigated. A detective with a dummy dressed like a woman sat in a car for night after night in the murder area, but the murderer ignored the bait.

After the murder of Virgil Starks, the crimes stopped. In 1954 a man confessed to being the killer, but careful investigation revealed that this was impossible.

There seems one likely explanation of the sudden cessation of the murders. A few days after the death of Virgil Starks, a man committed suicide by leaping under a train near Texarkana. His description fitted that of the murderer; he was obviously not the hobo type; but he was unknown in the vicinity. His identity was never established. But at the same time that he committed suicide a small car was found burning in a heavily wooded area near the site of the murders. It was definitely a case of deliberate arson, but the tyres had been destroyed, and the ground was too hard to show tracks. It seems remotely possible that the murderer was a Jekyll and Hyde character who was affected by the full moon, and who may have committed suicide in a fit of remorse.

MOREY, PELL, and ROYAL (The Michigan Murder Trio)
Nineteen-year-old Bill Morey, 18-year-old Max Pell, and 17-year-old David Royal, convicted of the murder of nurse Pauline Campbell, aged 34.

In the early morning of September 16th, 1951, Pauline Campbell was found with brutal head wounds outside a nurses' hostel in Washington Heights, a quiet residential street in Ann Arbor,

Michigan; she was removed to nearby St Joseph's Hospital (where she had been working seventeen minutes before), but died soon afterwards. Her skull was lacerated twice, and either wound would have proved fatal; there was no evidence of sexual assault, but her black calf handbag was missing. There had been several robbery assaults on nurses in the vicinity, one having occurred the previous Tuesday night, September 11th; the victim then had heard her assailant call out, 'Goodbye, Bob', a few seconds before being struck down by a heavy implement. There were no clues as to the killer's identity. Pauline Campbell's fiancé, a nursing orderly whom she had known for fourteen years, could give no help, apart from a résumé of the girl's character: 'Pauline was an old-fashioned girl, you don't see them like her any more . . . she certainly wouldn't have paid the least attention to any man trying to pick her up.' He himself was able to provide a satisfactory alibi.

All male institutions were checked, including the Veterans' Rehabilitation Center for maladjusted servicemen, but no 'leads' were found. Local citizens began to agitate for better street lighting in the murder area, and hospitals, suspecting a killer with an anti-nurse fixation, provided escorts for their nurses going to and from their work. Police Chief Enkeman consulted psychologist Richard T. Nordlund of Jackson Prison as to the probable type of killer. Nordlund was uncertain as to whether the killer was a maniac: '. . . more likely . . . a young man, or one of a group of young men . . . roaming the hospital territory because young women are always about.' Eventually Enkemann joined Mayor William E. Brown in offering a reward of $500 'for information leading to the arrest and conviction of the murderer of Pauline Campbell'. A 19-year-old student at Michigan Normal College came forward ('my father said it was my duty to go to the police') with news of the past activities of three of his friends, Morey, Pell, and Royal, who had boasted to him of attacking and injuring a nurse the previous week. Morey, a freshman at Michigan Normal College, Pell, a garage hand, and construction worker Royal were taciturn when questioned about the killing, and refused to submit to lie-detector tests. When Enkemann, however, threatened to 'take apart' Max Pell's car in a search for clues, Pell roared protestingly ('don't touch my car') and confessed to the murder:

We did it, all right . . . we drove around looking for a nurse we could knock off for her money . . . Bill grabbed the mallet

. . . I was driving as slowly and quietly as I could . . . They wanted to lift her into the car, but I stopped them right then. . . . I didn't want blood in my car. They'd got her head inside and I saw it would mess up my upholstery . . . so we left her. . . .

Morey's confession followed, together with an example of his own astuteness during the attack of September 11th: 'I yelled out, "Goodnight, Bob", figuring that if there was trouble they'd look for someone named Bob. Darn clever of me, wasn't it?'

On November 13th, 1951, Morey and Pell were found guilty of first-degree murder, and eventually sentenced to life imprisonment; Royal, the youngest, stood a separate trial and was sentenced to from twenty-two years' to life imprisonment.

MORGAN, Samuel
Twenty-eight-year-old soldier whose guilt in a murder case was proved conclusively by scientific evidence.

Late on the night of November 2nd, 1940, 15-year-old Mary Hagan was found raped and strangled in a cement blockhouse (an anti-invasion structure); she had been missing from her home in Waterloo Road, Liverpool, since 6.40 pm, when she left to buy an evening paper. Dr J. B. Firth, Director of the North Western Forensic Laboratory, called to the murder scene, removed samples of soil from the floor of the blockhouse, also a small piece of wet, muddy material found near the body. The victim's shoes were fairly muddy (as was natural on a wet night), but gave no indication that Mary Hagan's body had been dragged along the ground; the girl had either been carried or lured to the blockhouse by the lust-murderer. There was an indeterminate thumbprint in dried blood on the left side of the neck, which would seem to have come from someone with an injured bleeding thumb. The material found in the blockhouse, when cleaned of mud, appeared to have been in use as a bandage, consisting of three layers; the outer, longer strip was brown, and resembled a field dressing of the type issued to soldiers. The inner bandages were impregnated with ointment, which was analysed as a zinc and acriflavine compound, acriflavine being at that time a substance not in general use by the public, although used in Service and Civil Defence dressings. Through routine police inquiries a soldier suspect, Samuel Morgan, was detained on November

15th; he bore on his right thumb a circular wound some days old. His sister said he had cut it on barbed wire a fortnight before, and she had bound it for him with one of his army-issue dressings, a small length of which, being left over, he had told her to keep. It was noticed that both the blockhouse bandage and the bandage produced by Morgan's sister had a double row of stitching holes by the selvedge, the natural edge of the material; the factory producing this type of field dressing was visited, it being noted that it was unusual for the selvedge to have more than one row of holes. The warp and weft of the two bandage exhibits were examined and found to be identical, and marked similarity in their torn ends indicated that they had been rent apart. Samples of mud from the blockhouse and dirt from Morgan's uniform were observed microscopically, and 'marked agreement' noted. A witness testified that on the murder night Morgan had rushed into a public house in a distraught fashion. Blood was on his cap, and his thumb was bleeding profusely; the witness had bound up the thumb with a field dressing produced by Morgan. Found guilty of the murder of Mary Hagan and his subsequent appeal rejected, Morgan was hanged at Walton Prison on April 4th, 1941.

MORNARD, Jacques (alias Frank Jacson), Trotsky Assassin

In the afternoon of August 20th, 1940, exiled Russian Communist leader Leon Trotsky received a visit from a man known to him as Frank Jacson, 26, journalist, whose mistress, Sylvia Ageloff, was a devoted supporter of Trotsky's political creed. Few people gained admittance to the Mexican fortress (a villa in Coyoacan, a suburb of Mexico City), where the 61-year-old revolutionary lived, still regarded as a deviationist and potential menace by Russian dictator Stalin and his satellites. An abortive attempt on Trotsky's life had been made on May 24th, when twenty men, disguised as policemen, had gained admittance to the villa (through the gullibility or possible collusion of secretary Robert Sheldon Hart, a 23-year-old American, found days afterwards shot dead in a bed of quicklime), had machine-gunned Trotsky's bedroom and thrown incendiary bombs as their target and his wife Natalia cowered under the bed. Four days after this incident Frank Jacson paid the first of many visits, and on this hot August day Natalia Trotsky expressed amazement that her guest should be carrying a raincoat. Left alone with Trotsky (Jacson said he wished to consult him concerning an article draft) the younger man produced from the raincoat pockets a fourteen-inch dagger, a ·45 automatic pistol, and an ice pick, which he rammed into Trotsky's head. Jacson, bludgeoned by guards summoned by Trotsky's screams ('Who made you do it? The Soviet Secret Police?'), was taken into custody muttering, 'They've got something on me. They are keeping my mother as a prisoner.' Trotsky died next day, his brain ($3\frac{1}{2}$ lb in weight) having been pierced to a depth of three inches. In Jacson's pocket was a letter expressing disillusionment with Trotsky, who, he said, was only motivated by the desire for personal revenge and who had instructed him to assassinate Stalin. He was sentenced to Mexico's ultimate penalty, twenty years' imprisonment; he proved a model prisoner, teaching illiterates to read, setting up a prison electrical repair shop (employing twenty-six men), and even taking a beautiful Mexican woman Roquelia Mendoza, as his common-law wife, a practice permissible in Mexico prisons.

This assassin's true identity remains in doubt. He had been introduced to Sylvia Ageloff in Paris in 1938 as Jacques Mornard, a Belgian reporter; he joined her afterwards in New York as Frank Jacson, explaining that he had used a forged passport in order to avoid the Belgian call-up. Jacson-Mornard himself said he was Jacques Vandendreschd, born in Teheran, son of that country's Belgian ambassador, but this story was found to be false. As he could speak a Barcelona dialect, one investigator looked up Madrid police fingerprint files on Civil War political prisoners, and found that Jacson-Mornard's prints tallied with those of anti-Franco fighter Ramon Mercades del Rio, born 1914, whose mother had been a member of the Barcelona Communist Party and later an agent of the Russian Secret Police, fleeing to Moscow with some of her children in 1937 after Spanish forces were routed.

On his release from jail on May 6th, 1960, Jacson-Mornard had a passport issued to him by Czecho-Slovakia, and was last seen in Havana.

MORRISON, Steinie
Russian-Jewish immigrant (he always referred to himelf as Australian), age about 30, convicted in 1911 of the murder of Russian-born Leon Beron.

At 8 am on January 1st, 1911, a policeman discovered the body of a middle-aged man among some thorn bushes on Clapham

Common; death was due to heavy head blows (the skull being fractured), and three deep stabs had been inflicted on the body. A curious feature was that after death the face had been systematically slashed many times, each mark bearing a vague resemblance to the letter 'S'; the meaning behind these mutilations has never been satisfactorily explained, although many excitedly believed them to signify 'spic', the Russian word for spy, or 'spiccan', a Polish word with the same meaning. (During his summing up at the subsequent trial Mr Justice Darling rather crossly imputed, looking at photographs of the corpse, that anyone who could see the letter S in those scratches must have better eyes or a more vivid imagination than he himself could lay claim to possess.) No valuables of any kind were found upon the body, which was soon identified as that of 48-year-old widower Leon Beron, who lived with his brother in a three-shilling-a-week room in Jubilee Street, Mile End Road, Stepney, since 1894. He had an income of £25 a year from some East End property, which had caused him to be known, somewhat grandiloquently, as 'the landlord'. Of miserly instincts, he was known to carry a sum of not less than twenty sovereigns in a washleather purse, which was always tied to his waistcoat pocket by a safety-pin; he also sported a large gold watch on a chain, from which dangled a five-pound piece, of the type struck for Queen Victoria's first Jubilee in 1883. Most of Beron's time had been spent at the Jewish-type Warsaw Restaurant in Osborn Street, Whitechapel Road, whose zealous patrons (mostly émigrés) would spend literally every hour of their waking day there, using the premises more as a convivial centre of debate and nostalgic chat than as an eating house. (For eighteen pence Mr Alexander Snelwar, the proprietor, would provide lunch, dinner, and liquid refreshment.) For the past two months Beron's constant companion at this establishment had been tall, good-looking Steinie Morrison, whose natural charm and good manners belied the fact of his habitual criminality. After Beron's death he was not seen at the Warsaw Restaurant; it was learnt that he left his lodgings in Newark Street (telling his landlady, Mrs Zimmerman, that he was going to Paris) and lived for a week with a prostitute, Florrie Dellow, at 116 York Road, Lambeth. The police, naturally curious, began a search for him, finally apprehending Steinie at Cohen's Restaurant, Newark Street, at 10 am, Sunday, January 8th, just as he was about to start his breakfast. Ostensibly conducted to nearby Leman Street Police Station because, as a ticket-of-leave convict, he had failed to notify his change of address, Steinie Morrison blundered by saying: 'You have accused me of a serious crime; you have accused me of murder.' Inspector Wensley, in charge of the case, was to deny accusing the suspect of the killing at this stage, although Police Constable Greaves later testified that Steinie had indeed been cautioned; doubt, however, was cast on this constable's testimony because some months before he had brought a false charge against a fellow-constable. Florrie Dellow's room was searched and in the lining of a black 'billycock' hat police found a cloakroom ticket issued at St Mary's Station, Whitechapel, which was redeemed for a paper parcel containing a loaded revolver and forty-four cartridges; the cloakroom clerk identified Steinie Morrison as the man who, under the name of Banman, had deposited the parcel on the morning of January 1st. Steinie's little arsenal, although having no bearing on the case, did little to establish him as a creature opposed to violence. Two people now came forward to identify Steinie as Beron's companion during those hours immediately before the murder: Mrs Deitch, a gasfitter's wife, said she had seen the suspect with Beron in Commercial Road, Stepney, between 1.30 and 2 am on New Year's morning, and a taxi-cab driver, Alfred Castlin, identified Steinie as one of two men he had driven at 3.30 am from the cab-rank by Kennington Church to Finsbury Gate. One hansom-cab driver, Edward Hayman, later (on January 17th, a week after Steinie Morrison's arrest, and in response to a police-bill) identified the prisoner as one of two men he had driven from the East End to Clapham Common 'about two o'clock in the morning', and another hansom driver, Andrew Stephens, identified Steinie as the man he had driven alone, back from the north-east corner of Clapham Common to Kennington Church.

The trial of Steinie Morrison began at the Old Bailey before Mr Justice Darling, on March 6th, 1911; Mr Richard Muir led for the Crown, and Mr Edward Abinger for the defence. The evidence against the prisoner was circumstantial but considerable, and there must have been little doubt as to the ultimate verdict. The proceedings were noteworthy because of the volatile personalities of many of the witnesses (mostly aliens) who were not in the least intimidated by the trappings of the courtroom and the questioning of counsel. Steinie himself insisted on standing proudly hand on hip, throughout the nine-day trial, despite an indication from the judge that he could sit. The atmosphere was to be set by the victim's brother, Solomon Beron (a sevenpence-a-night lodger at Rowton House), who was so infuriated by what he considered the effrontery of Abinger's questions:

Q. Did anybody help the deceased man with his rent?
A. You go and ask him. I cannot tell you. If you ask me silly questions I will give you no answer

that he went, literally, raving mad and had to be conducted from the Old Bailey to a lunatic asylum. Joe Mintz, a waiter at the Warsaw, who had noticed Steinie carrying a long, heavy implement ('a flute', said Steinie) the night before the murder:

Abinger. Have you ever tried to hang yourself?
A. That has nothing to do with the case.

Sixteen-year-old Janie Brodski, who claimed (somewhat irrelevantly, in view of the estimated murder-time) that Steinie had spent the early evening of December 31st at the Shoreditch Empire (one of the turns was Harry Champion singing 'Ginger, You're Barmy'), and whose antipathy towards the police had caused her to omit this piece of evidence during previous interviews:

Q. Did you ever, at any of these interviews, tell the police you had seen Morrison in the Shoreditch Empire on New Year's Eve?
A. No.
Q. Why not?
A. Because I was angry at the time and would not answer any questions.
Q. What were you angry about?
A. The people in the street were talking of policemen coming to my door. I asked them several times not to, but they went on doing it.

Mrs Deitch, the gasfitter's wife:

Q. What is your husband? (Abinger)
A. He is a gasfitter.
Q. And what are you?
A. What am I? I am a woman, of course.
Q. I can see that, but what is your occupation?
A. That is a fine question to ask me. I am at home in the house, looking after my children.

Abinger pressed on, hinting that Mrs Deitch let part of her house to a prostitute, Lizzie Holmes, receiving payment on a percentage basis:

Q. Where did you get that fur from?
A. That is my business.
Q. Tell us, please.
A. Why should I tell you? You insulted me last time, but you will not insult me today. You asked me last time where I got my fur from. My husband bought it, what he worked for. I do not ask you where your wife got her fur from.

(The following day five highly questionable female lodgers from the Deitch home were brought into court, much to the fury of this lady.) Because of defence imputations against the good characters of Crown witnesses Deitch and Mintz, the judge ruled that the usual privileged position held by an accused person should in this case be forfeit, and Steinie therefore underwent cross-examination about his past; his numerous housebreaking exploits and prison sentences became known, and his reputation as a felon established.

After the judge had sentenced Steinie Morrison to death, with the customary plea for the Lord to have mercy on the prisoner's soul, Steinie howled out that he declined such mercy: '. . . I do not believe there is a God in heaven either.' His sentence commuted to life penal servitude, Steinie Morrison eventually died at Parkhurst Prison on January 24th, 1921, after fasting to death in a fit of pique.

(See also entry under 'Sidney Street'.)

MÜLLER, Franz

The first train murderer. Müller, a tailor, murdered Thomas Briggs in a train between Bow and Hackney Wick on July 9th, 1864. He threw the body out on to the line. (Briggs was actually not dead, and died shortly after he was found without recovering consciousness.) The motive was robbery, but Müller was in such a hurry that he left £5 in his victim's pocket, and snatched only his gold watch. He also made the mistake of taking the wrong hat away with him. Dick Tanner, one of the founder members of the London detective force, set about patiently checking with London jewellers, and eventually located the missing watch-chain. The jeweller, a man named Death, of Cheapside, was able to describe his customer – a foreigner, probably German. Newspaper publicity brought a man named Jonathan Matthews, who thought he recognized the description of the hat found in the railway carriage in which Briggs had been beaten to death; he had bought two of them, he said, one for himself and one for Franz Müller, a tailor. The police called at Müller's address, but he had left. Tanner traced another acquaintance of the missing man who had received a letter which indicated he was on his way to America. Tanner discovered that Müller had embarked on the SS *Victoria* for New York. So he hurried to forestall the fugitive, travelling on a faster ship, the *City of Manchester*. Müller was arrested, and found to have in his possession the missing watch. Brigg's hat was also found.

Müller was sentenced to death. He maintained his innocence until the end, but confessed a few minutes before the trap fell.

MURPHY, Charles
Remarkable desperado, whose career of crime ended in early 1932, when a judge in Seattle sentenced him to seventy-five years in jail.

Born in Massachusetts in 1887, Murphy ran away from home at 16 to avoid a charge of breaking and entering. He enlisted in the Australian Army in 1915, when it was discovered that he had given a false name and that he had deserted his wife and two children in Australia. Stationed on the Suez Canal, Murphy proceeded to assault a number of French girls. Luckily for him, he was wounded and sent to a hospital in London before the charges caught up with him. In 1918, just before an order for his arrest reached London, he fled to America, taking with him a well-to-do woman who was serving as a volunteer nurse. In New York, he deserted her. Two years later, in Stockton, California, he bigamously married a local girl. However, his real wife addressed a letter to him there which fell into the hands of his new wife, and she went out to fetch the police. When she returned, Murphy – now alias Dalton – had disappeared again. In 1921, he turned up in Woodland, Cowlitz County, Washington, and was hired as a farmhand by Mike Whelan, an ageing recluse who kept large sums of money in the farmhouse. Six weeks later, he murdered Whelan and left with the money. The next important event in Murphy's career was the murder of yet another 'wife' in February 1930. His name now changed to

475

Lindsay, he was living in Seattle, manager of a hotel. He and his 'wife' had adopted a girl named Verna, and a friend of Verna's moved into the house with them. Lindsay promptly seduced the friend; his wife made a scene, and was killed with a hammer and buried in the back garden. His 'daughter's' teen-age friend then became his mistress for several weeks, until Lindsay declared that they would all three go to Hollywood, where he knew a film producer who could get the girls into films. Lindsay abandoned his teen-age mistress in a restaurant, and drove off with his foster daughter. The tearful girl returned to her father – an unemployed labourer – and told her story; this led eventually to the discovery of Mrs Lindsay's body in the back garden, and an alarm for Lindsay. The foster daughter was finally traced in Oakland, Cal., where Lindsay had abandoned her. In the following month, he changed his name to Simpson and took another job in Napa, Cal. The 18-year-old daughter of a neighbouring farmer attracted him. On a fake story of a 'scholarship' which he had arranged for her at the University of Southern California, he abducted her, spent a few nights in hotels with her, and vanished again.

He was caught in Los Angeles, recognized by the son of a restaurant owner from a police-circulated handbill. To make sure of his identification, the youth showed Murphy the photograph of a naked woman, and took the photo – with fingerprints – to the police.

When arrested, Murphy alleged that he murdered 'Mrs Lindsay' in self-defence, since she had attacked him with a bread knife; however, since bloodstains had been found in the bedroom, proving she had been murdered while asleep in bed, his story was not accepted.

Murphy appears to be a straightforward case of a criminal obsessed by women, who, under different circumstances, might have been merely a Casanova. With the exception of the murder of Mike Whelan, all his crimes are connected with his insatiable appetite for girls.

N

NELSON, Earle ('The Gorilla Murderer')

Moronic American sex killer. Born on May 12th, 1897. Nine months after his birth, his 20-year-old mother died of venereal disease contracted from the father. A photograph of Nelson at

3 shows a loose-mouthed, degenerate infant with a vacant expression. Up to the age of 10 he was 'quiet and morbid'. Then he was knocked down by a street car which caused a hole in his temple and rendered him unconscious for six days with concussion of the brain. After this, he suffered periodically from pains in the head and dizziness. Towards the end of his life, the pains were so violent he was unable to stand on his feet.

An aunt, Mrs Lilian Fabian, brought him up. She told the court that Nelson had a habit of walking on his hands or picking up heavy chairs with his teeth. He was apparently much given to talking 'smut'.

On May 21st, 1918, he was charged with an assault on a child in a basement to which he had gone to get tools. ('That was another habit of his, to go into basements.') During the hearing, it was revealed that he had been called up for service but discharged as insane by the Naval Hospital Board. Nelson was committed to an asylum.

During the next six months he made three escapes. After the last getaway in December 1918, he was not recaptured for two and a half years. He married in 1919. Reconfined, he escaped again in November 1923.

From then until 1926, little is known of his movements, or whether he committed any murders. But between February 1926 and his capture, he committed twenty-two murders.

In San Francisco, in late February 1926, the strangled and outraged body of Miss Clara Newman was discovered by her nephew in an attic lavatory. The 60-year-old woman had displayed a 'Rooms to let' notice in her window.

On March 2nd, Mrs Laura E. Beale of San José, also aged 60, was found under precisely similar circumstances. Newspapermen christened the unknown killer, 'the Dark Strangler'.

On June 10th, in San Francisco again, 63-year-old Mrs Lilian St Mary was strangled, raped, and thrust under a bed. Fourteen days later, in Santa Barbara, Mrs George Russell was discovered in the same condition. Two months later, Mrs Mary Nesbit, of Oakland, California, was strangled and raped.

In October 1926, came three murders in three days, October 19th, 20th and 21st, at Portland, Oregon.

The police here showed some slackness. On the 19th, Mrs Beata Withers, a pretty 35-year-old divorcée, was discovered by her 15-year-old son stuffed into a trunk. The police attributed the death to suicide. The next day, 59-year-old Mrs Virginia Grant was strangled and left hidden behind the furnace of a house she had advertised to let. This time, the police attributed the death to natural causes. Some jewellery and a coat were missing.

On October 21st, Mrs Mable Fluke was found strangled in the attic of a house she advertised to let. A scarf was tightly knotted round her throat. The police decided that this was probably murder.

Nelson now returned to San Francisco, and on November 18th, strangled and raped 56-year-old Mrs William Edmunds. Six days later, he killed Mrs Florence Monks in Seattle, his tenth victim. He now returned to Oregon City and strangled Mrs Blanche Myers, aged 48. Mrs Myers, who advertised a 'Room to let', was found under a bed.

The police decided to try tracing the jewellery that the 'Dark Strangler' frequently stole. Three old ladies who ran a South Portland lodging house took some jewllery to the police, explaining that it had been sold to them by a young man who had taken a room with them, leaving on the day Mrs Myers was murdered. He had stayed for five days. The jewellery proved to be that taken from Mrs Monks. A reward of $2,500 was offered by the Portland police.

Nelson now went inland, to Council Bluffs, Iowa, where 49-year-old Mrs John E. Beard was strangled and raped two days before Christmas.

Nelson now moved on to Kansas City, where he killed Mrs Bonnie Pace, who was only 23. And then, two days after Christmas, he strangled Mrs Germania Harpin, aged 28, and throttled her 8-month-old baby with a piece of rag.

Four months now elapsed before the 'Gorilla murderer' (as he had been dubbed by the Press) made the headlines again. On April 27th, 1927, 60-year-old Mrs Mary McConnell was strangled in Philadelphia.

Nelson now proceeded to murder with terrifying frequency. On May 30th, in Buffalo, Mrs Jenny Randolph, aged 35, was the victim. Two days later, at Detroit, it was a double murder; Mrs Minnie May, aged 53, and her tenant, Mrs Atorthy, were strangled in a lodging house. Two days later, 27-year-old Mrs Mary Sietsema was raped and strangled in Chicago.

Nelson now crossed into Canada – his major mistake.

Nelson arrived in Winnipeg by road, hitch-hiking, on June 8th. He sold all his clothes, and changed them for a suit in which he would not be identified. He then took a room with Mrs Catherine Hill, 133 Smith Street, paying a dollar deposit and claiming that he was working for a builder at St Boniface across the river. He wanted a quiet room because 'he was a religious man of high ideals'. Mrs Hill was favourably impressed by him, although she noticed that he disliked looking her in the face. Her description makes it apparent that Nelson was not obviously insane or moronic, and that he laid claim to some interest in religion.

The same day, Nelson murdered the daughter of a couple who lived at Mrs Hill's, 14-year-old Lola Cowan. The circumstances of the murder were apparently so horrifying that they were not made public. The child was not discovered until four days later, when someone happened to look under the bed in an unoccupied room.

At 6 o'clock on the evening of Thursday, June 9th, William Patterson returned to his home at 100 Riverton Avenue to find his wife missing. At 10 o'clock, when he had put the two children to bed, he phoned the police, but they had no report of an accident. He now discovered that the lock of his suitcase had been forced and $7 stolen. He decided to pray, and fell on his knees beside the bed. He then noticed the body of his wife under the bed; she had been battered with a hammer and raped. The time of death was estimated at 11 that morning.

Nelson apparently went to a second-hand clothing shop, where he sold the clothes stolen from the Pattersons' house, and then went for a shave, where the barber noticed blood on his hair. In a street car, he fell into conversation with a man named Hofer, who was a Hutterite from the colony at Pigeon Lake. Nelson apparently seemed extremely interested in the sect, and entered into a lengthy discussion on religion, during which he stated that he was a good Catholic, but that he sometimes drank too much. On the outskirts of the city, he hitched a lift with a man named Hugh Elder, with whom he discussed a sect called Mennonites.

On Saturday, June 11th, he engaged a room in Regina. The landlady was alone with him in the room for a time, but apparently Nelson was not in the mood for murder. In the evening, he accosted a little girl on Twelfth Avenue; his landlady, Mrs Rowe, interfered and got the girl away.

He changed hats, and the proprietor was suspicious and questioned him; this seems to have frightened him, for he left Winnipeg in a hurry, leaving behind the clothes he had bought.

A man named Isadore Silverman gave him a lift, and they became so friendly that they stayed at the same hotel that night, and again, the following night, actually shared a room. They separated at Boissevain.

Here, his career of murder ended. In the post office at Wakopa, he was recognized by Leslie Morgan, who telephoned the police. Nelson was arrested on the road between Wakopa and Bannerman. He was lodged in jail at Killarney, but succeeded in escaping that night by picking a lock with a nail file. The whole district was mobilized, and a panic started; but after stealing some clothes, Nelson was re-caught, after barely twelve hours of freedom.

He was tried at Winnipeg on November 1st, 1927, on a charge of murdering Mrs Patterson. The trial lasted four days. Nelson was well dressed, and seemed completely calm and at ease. Only two defence witnesses were called: his aunt and his wife, whom he had married in early August, 1919. She and Nelson had lived together for only six months. Nelson was insanely jealous, and apparently showed no moral responsibility of any kind, although he once gave his blood for a transfusion to his wife when she was in hospital. (She was later a hospital matron.)

The defence of insanity was not greatly helped by the evidence of Nelson's aunt and wife, although their testimony gave abundant proof of abnormality. Nelson developed persecution manias very easily. When his wife was in hospital, he would stay for long after the visiting time, alleging that she was having affairs with the doctors. He bought a rosary, and told his wife that his face was like Christ. He often seemed to forget what he was doing and would stare blankly into space. On one occasion, he came to a boy's school where she was working, wearing evening dress, to ask her if she was coming to a dance; since it was midday, his wife found the suggestion peculiar.

He was found guilty and hanged at Winnipeg on January 13th, 1928.

There is strong presumptive evidence that the twenty-two murders mentioned above do not complete the list of Nelson's victims; for example, he may well have been guilty of a triple murder that occurred in Newark, NJ, in 1926, when Mrs Rose Valentine and Mrs Margaret Stanton were strangled and Mrs Laura Tidor, who came to their assistance, was shot.

Photographs of Nelson show an ape-like face with receding forehead, projecting lips, and strangely expressionless eyes.[1]

[1] For the above account I am indebted to L. C. Douthwaite's *Mass Murder*, John Long, 1928.

NEU, Kenneth

Executed in 1935 for the murder of Sheffield Clark. The case excited an extraordinary amount of attention at the time because of the romantic good looks of the accused.

The murder was one of those absurd affairs that seem to point either to the irresponsibility or to the insanity of the accused. Neu was a handsome, plausible young man with an engaging smile and a way of talking that was largely derived from the cinema and popular songs; he was 25. In New York on September 2nd, 1933, he was picked up by a man named Lawrence Shead, who claimed to be a theatre owner from New Jersey. Neu had been trying to get a job as a singer in night-clubs, and Shead offered him a job. However, it transpired that Shead's attentions were inspired by his homosexual inclinations, and Neu ended by smashing his skull with an electric iron and leaving with Shead's clothes and some money. He went to New Orleans, where he quickly seduced a waitress named Eunice Hotter, and after spending three nights with her, rashly undertook to 'show her the bright lights' of New York. He had no money, but opened a conversation with a 63-year-old business man, Sheffield Clark, in the lobby of the Jung Hotel. Late that night, he called on Clark in his room and tried to blackmail him, saying that he would accuse Clark of making homosexual advances. When Clark reached for the telephone, Neu killed him with a black-jack. He then left the hotel by the lift, and got Clark's car from the car park (telling the attendant he was Clark's son).

Neu then motored with Eunice Hotter towards New York. He took off the number plate and substituted a chalked board reading 'New Car in Transit'. In New Jersey, police stopped the car and asked what the sign meant. Neu, Eunice Hotter, and a hitch-hiker were kept in jail overnight. Then it was noticed that Neu's description tallied with that of the man who had been seen with Lawrence Shead just before his death. Neu admitted the murder quite frankly, and went on to describe his murder of Clark. Finally, he was sent to New Orleans for trial, since the police feared that Shead's alleged homosexuality might prejudice a jury in Neu's favour.

It soon appeared that Neu had been married once, and had been a soldier, sailor, and night-club singer. He had been born in Savannah, Georgia, and had been in the Georgia State Mental Home. His main interest in life was women. He claimed that his discharge from the army was due to an affair with the colonel's wife, although his discharge papers stated he was a psychotic. In New Orleans he had stayed at the DeSoto Hotel, where he had told employees that he was an aviation instructor working for the Chinese Army.

The trial opened on December 12th, 1933. His attorney, Clarence Dowling, tried to get him adjudged insane, but after a thirty-three-day examination by State psychiatrists, this plea was disallowed. The defence was of insanity. Neu appeared to be extremely cheerful, no doubt glad of the attention, and sang on his way to and from the court; he even executed some dance steps. A Dr Unworth testified that Neu suffered from cerebro-syphilis and that he believed his brain was already deteriorating. In spite of this, he was found guilty. An appeal was lodged. In prison Neu was visited by Sisters of Mercy and a young woman who apparently fell in love with him. He referred to her as 'my mystery woman' and the newspapers made much of the affaire, which Neu claimed was 'on a high spiritual plane'. He wrote a song called 'I'm as fit as a fiddle and ready to hang', and sang and tap-danced in his cell. Towards the end some newspapers became less than flattering about his affaire. He was converted to the Roman Catholic faith, and many women's clubs continued to appeal for his life right to the end. The mystery woman, Aline Hull, 25, committed suicide in 1950.

NODDER, Frederick (alias Hudson)
Forty-four-year-old motor engineer found guilty on November 23rd, 1937, of the murder of 10-year-old Mona Lilian Tinsley.

At 4 pm on January 5th, 1937, Mona Tinsley came out of the Wesleyan School, Guidhall Street, Newark, a town in the English Midlands; she never returned to her home at No. 11 Thoresby Avenue, about twenty minutes' walk away, and at 9.30 pm her father informed the police. A search that night proved fruitless, but the following day three people gave information: a 11-year-old boy said he had seen Mona Tinsley with a man near the bus station, a woman had seen her near the Retford bus stop in Newark (Retford being a town some twenty miles from Newark), and another woman, Mrs Annie Hird, said she had seen an ex-lodger of the Tinsleys' loitering near the child's school the day before – '. . . looking to see if he could see any-one'. The Tinsleys' lodger (who had left after three weeks in October 1955 because of non-payment of rent) was Frederick Nodder, known to Mr and Mrs Tinsley as Frederick Hudson, and to the Tinsley children as 'Uncle Fred'; he had been introduced to the Tinsleys by Mr and Mrs Grimes, Mrs Tinsley's sister and brother-in-law, who lived at 9 Neil Road, Sheffield. Accordingly, on the evening of January 6th police interviewed Nodder at his semi-detached house, Peacehaven, in the village of Hayton, three and a half miles from Retford. The Chief Constable of Newark, Mr Harry Barnes, was told by Nodder that he knew nothing of the whereabouts of Mona Tinsley, 'a niece of a friend of mine in Sheffield'. Nevertheless, Chief Constable Barnes took Nodder into custody on a charge of non-payment of an affiliation order (bastardy warrant), while the search for Mona Tinsley continued. Childish writing, later identified as Mona Tinsley's, was found on a piece of paper in Nodder's house; the charwoman of a house nearby had noticed, at noon on January 6th, a small girl standing at the back door of Peacehaven while Nodder was digging in the garden. On January 7th at an identification parade, Nodder was picked out as the man who had accompanied Mona Tinsley on the afternoon of January 5th. A bus conductor recalled Nodder as the man travelling with a small girl that afternoon on his Retford-bound bus; the man had requested a return ticket for himself, but a single ticket for his companion. On January 9th Nodder made a statement to the police in which he admitted seeing Mona Tinsley on January 5th as she came out of school; the child, he said, had asked after her aunt, Mrs Grimes, and expressed a desire to see her new baby cousin, Peter. '. . . She particularly asked me if I would take her to see Auntie . . . she said she wanted to come with me, and foolishly I agreed, repenting my action as soon as we started off. . . .' Nodder said that the child remained at Peacehaven that night; the following day he sent her off alone to her aunt's house at Sheffield, a bus journey of one and a half hours. On January 10th Nodder was charged with abducting Mona Tinsley, and tried at the Warwick Winter Assizes, Victoria Courts, Birmingham, March 9th and 10th, 1937. Found guilty, he was sentenced to seven years' penal servitude. Passing sentence, Mr Justice Swift observed to the prisoner: 'What you did with that little girl, what became of her, only you know. It may be that time will reveal the dreadful secret which you carry in your breast.'

On June 6th, 1937, Mona Tinsley's body was recovered from the River Idle,[1] a tributary of which, Bolham Shuttle, was 1·9

---

[1] The medium, Estelle Roberts, is said to have accurately predicted the whereabouts of the child's body.

miles from Nodder's house. The child had been dead before immersion in water, and there was the mark of a ligature around the neck; Dr James Mathewson Webster, pathologist, who examined the remains, concluded that death had been caused through asphyxia due to strangulation. On July 29th, Nodder was charged with the murder of Mona Tinsley, and his trial opened on November 2nd at the Nottingham Assizes, Shire Hall, Nottingham, before Mr Justice Macnaghten. Counsel were the same as at Nodder's previous trial for abduction; Mr Norman Birkett, KC, and Mr R. E. A. Elwes acting for the Crown, and Mr Maurice Healy, KC, and Mr N. F. M. Robinson for the defence. Nodder, as before, pleaded not guilty. The defence theorized that Mona Tinsley had met a murderous stranger on her lone journey to Sheffield, but on November 23rd the jury returned a verdict of guilty in less than an hour, and Frederick Nodder was sentenced to death. He was executed on December 30th at Lincoln Prison.

NOURRIC Family, The
Convicted in 1928 of the murder of a French bank messenger.

Since the days of Lacenaire, bank messengers have been re-garded as fair game by the French criminal fraternity. One of the most notorious cases, perhaps, is the murder of the mes-senger of the Societé Générale by the Bonnot Gang in December 1911; when waylaid in the Rue Ordener, he was carrying half a million francs (£25,000).

On February 28th, 1927, Leon Després, the messenger of a suburban Paris bank, failed to return at his usual time – six in the evening. The police were finally able to make out a list of thirty-five places at which the messenger was due to call. It was finally established that he had called at twenty places. The twenty-first was unknown, but he had certainly not called on any other customer after number twenty-one. The police made a careful check on the district – a slum area – that lay between the address of the twentieth and twenty-second customer, and finally discovered that a family named Nourric in the Rue de la Fosse Moreau had been called upon by the messenger. Després had not been seen leaving the house, but two hours later, at dusk, Nourric (who was a paviour by trade) and his brother-in-law, Duquenne, had been seen to push a handcart with bicycle wheels, loaded with some large object covered with sacking, to-wards the Boulevard de Nueilly-sur-Marne and the River Marne.

Meanwhile, the bank manager, who had found the address of the twenty-first customer, called on the Nourrics, who told him that the messenger had indeed called, and had left with some money. The police afraid the Nourrics would bolt, called on them to question them, and then arrested them. It was soon established that the family – Nourric and his wife and the brother-in-law – had been borrowing money prior to February 28th, although when the police called they were eating a large meal with several bottles of wine. The next day they were arrested on suspicion.

As the Marne was in flood, it seemed that the chances of the body being discovered were small; but on April 13th, 1927, a bargeman on the river near the Quai de Bercy noticed a large package being carried downstream; he pulled it in with a boat-hook, and found a man's body sewed into a parcel of canvas with electric flex and wire. Papers identified him as the missing Després. Death was due to blows on the head with a heavy instrument.

In their cell, the Nourrics admitted the murder to some police spies disguised as prisoners. A search of their house brought to light lengths of cord identical to that which trussed the body, and the other half of an underskirt which had been bound around the head of the corpse.

Bloodstains were also found on the handcart. This evidence finally condemned the Nourrics, in spite of their steadfast denials. They were tried in March 1928 and found guilty. Nourric, who had struck the blows, was sentenced to life imprisonment; his wife and brother-in-law received twenty years each.

The case is mainly of interest as a piece of skilful police routine investigation, and condemnation depending upon circumstantial evidence that nevertheless left no possible doubt of their guilt.

O

O'BANION, Dion
Thirty-two-year-old Irish hoodlum, ex-altar boy at the Holy Name Cathedral, controller of an illicit liquor racket in Chicago during the early days of American Prohibition, and a suspected instigator of several gang killings, murdered in 1924.

Dion (or Dean, Deanie, or 'Gimpy') O'Banion graduated through petty crime (he was, among other things, a paid muscleman and safe-blower) to become a tradesman in illegally brewed alcohol even before July 16th, 1920, when all intoxicating drink was outlawed in the United States with the passing of the Eighteenth Amendment – better known as Prohibition. When the so-called 'dry' era started, O'Banion and his henchmen (including the infamous 'Bugs' Moran – see CAPONE, Al) concerned themselves with supplying Chicago's North Side with 'bootleg hootch', occasionally encroaching on the South Side, much to the hardly contained fury of Johnny Torrio (see COLOSIMO, Jim) who, with his young henchman Al Capone, considered himself as the sole pleasure-promoter for the South Side territory, controlling, apart from drink supplies, all the gambling dens, drugstores and brothels. O'Banion, either through genuine religious scruple or some strong Freudian kink that overcame even his overriding business acumen, eschewed the idea of controlling houses of prostitution, but nevertheless became rich in his self-appointed role as Bacchanalian envoy to the Chicago North Side, living sumptuously down Pine Grove Avenue with his wife, Viola, and indulging in philanthropic-style outings to Chicago's slum areas as well as frequent visits to Mass. Much of O'Banion's time during the day was spent tending blooms at William F. Schofield's flower-shop down North State Street, in which he held half-shares, and it was rumoured that for a modest extra fee O'Banion would not only supply the funeral floral tribute, but also the corpse.

O'Banion, like so many of his countrymen, was both wily and quarrelsome, living in an atmosphere of feuds. Torrio's attitude towards him hardly mellowed when, after being persuaded to buy O'Banion's half-million dollar interest in the Sieben brewery ('I intend setting up away from Chicago,' Deanie had said) he found himself arrested too shortly afterwards during a police raid on that brewery; from that time on, angry mutterings of 'double cross' were heard on the South Side whenever the Irishman's name was mentioned. Again, he quarrelled bitterly with two Sicilian ruffians, the Genna Brothers, Mike and Angelo (The Terrible Gennas), who operated the hootch syndicate on Chicago's West Side (and who, incidentally, paid hush-money to over 400 policemen, including five police captains), by accusing them of unfairly selling their tenement-brewed liquor – made from corn sugar – at cut-price rates, three dollars a gallon as opposed to the O'Banion brew at six dollars a gallon. When reminded that the Terrible Gennas were not noted for their amiability of temperament, O'Banion said, 'Aw, to Hell with them Sicilians,' a tactless remark, when one considers the murderous principles of the Mafia, or Unione Siciliano, the secret society first imported into America about 1899, to which most lawless Sicilian immigrants held allegiance. (Al Capone, although of Neapolitan stock, was to become one of this society's most notorious members.) Nor was the ebullient Celt popular with the Chicago police; apart from the obvious reasons, he had unwittingly embarrassed them by attending, as Guest of Honour (along with his henchmen, including Hymie Weiss, later to be his successor, and Three-Gun Alterie) a banquet which leading police personalities also attended in surprising, though apparent, ignorance of its adulatory character.

When Michael Merlo, the first president of the Unione Siciliano, died on November 8th, 1924, O'Banion must have anticipated brisk trade in his flower-shop; Torrio, for example, ordered a tribute costing $10,000, while Capone selected a more diminutive but still lavish display at $8,000. It is known that a certain party ordered a memorial spray on November 9th, to be collected at noon the following day, but only the porter at O'Banion's flower-shop was witness to the carnage which followed at noon on November 10th when the Irishman interrupted his bloom-arranging to greet his expected customers -- who apparently were known to him, although unknown to the porter (a fact for which that individual, on afterthought, must have been thankful). O'Banion was shot six times at close range through the head and torso, and died instantly. The assassins were never found, although Messrs Torrio, Capone, and the Genna Brothers (to mention but a few) were closely questioned by the police, then allowed to go; all these suspects subsequently sent floral tributes to O'Banion's funeral. Three-Gun Alterie, grief-stricken at the death of his chief, challenged the killers to a duel 'at State and Madison Street at any time, including high noon'; the offer was never taken up. Al Capone, after the sanctities of the funeral rites, could not resist a final epitaph on O'Banion: 'His head got away from his hat.'

O'BRIEN (alias Count de Lacy)
Irish adventurer, who, posing as a rich Polish count, was accepted into Tsarist society shortly after leaving Ireland for Vilna in 1905 and led a life of fraud and deception before his arrest in 1911, for the murder in St Petersburg (now Leningrad) of his brother-in-law, Captain Buturlin.

The family of wealthy General Buturlin, living in Vilna, were charmed by 'Count de Lacy' and gratified when he married the

487

graceless Buturlin daughter, not realizing the attractions, to de Lacy, of a large marriage dowry. Life in Vilna palled for O'Brien, and the 'Count and Countess' moved to the more ostentatious social round of St Petersburg, where de Lacy became a favourite at Court. Soon in need of more money, the bogus count tried selling land (over which he claimed ownership) to a gullible Polish merchant; but the transaction proved slow, and O'Brien considered a more drastic measure – the extermination of his in-laws, his aim being to inherit, through his wife, the vast Buturlin fortunes. He bribed seedy grey-beard Dr Panchenko, who worked at the Laboratory of Plague Cultures, obtaining from him two tubes of cholera endotoxin, which he spread lavishly on slices of bread and butter before graciously offering it to his brother-in-law, Captain Buturlin, who was on a visit to St Petersburg. The captain survived, the enraged de Lacy learning afterwards that his brother-in-law had been inoculated against the cholera that was epidemic at that time in St Petersburg.

Desperate, de Lacy decided that, under pretext of having further cholera inoculations, Captain Buturlin would be injected with diphtheria bacteria. Accordingly, he arranged an inoculation session at Dr Panchenko's, but whereas he and his wife received harmless injections, his brother-in-law's treatment this time proved lethal. General Buturlin demanded a postmortem, and to the relief of de Lacy and Panchenko it was reported that the young captain had died of blood-poisoning. Madame Muravieva, Panchenko's mistress, was suspicious about the affair, having noted de Lacy's frequent visits and overheard several dubious remarks ('. . . make sure of it . . . give him two phials full . . .'), and she voiced her suspicions to another admirer, who went at once to the Chief of Police. Panchenko, on this slender evidence, was charged with the murder of Captain Buturlin; unnerved, the hapless doctor blurted out the truth. In January 1911 their trial commenced in a courtroom crowded with agape aristocrats, the defence of O'Brien, alias Count de Lacy, being paid for by an erstwhile victim, his father-in-law General Buturlin. Panchenko admitted guilt and de Lacy pleaded not guilty. Both were convicted, de Lacy being sent to prison for life and Panchenko for fifteen years. O'Brien's wife, the 'countess', was mentally deranged by the tragedy and died within the year.

Kitty Ogilvy was born Katherine Nairn, the daughter of Sir Thomas Nairn of Dunsinnan. In 1765, when she was 19, she suddenly declared that she would marry Thomas Ogilvy of Eastmiln (in Forfar) a man who seemed to her family in every way ineligible. He was 40, he was not rich, and lived in a shabby four-roomed house in Eastmiln, with three members of his family – a cousin, Anne Clark, his younger brother Patrick, and his mother – and three female servants. Nevertheless, Kitty Nairn married him – for love, apparently – and moved into a house that now held eight people. There was also a profligate youngest brother, Alexander, studying medicine. The mother and cousin did not take to Kitty, and made her life difficult. Anne Clark had been a prostitute, then Alexander's mistress, and had been sent by him to effect a reconcilation with his family – apparently his debauches had caused him to lose favour. Possibly Anne Clark hoped that in some way Alexander might succeed to the 'estates'.

Patrick Ogilvy, the brother, was a lieutenant, and he and Kitty soon became fond of one another, going around hand-in-hand and showing their affection quite openly. It is probable that the relation was as innocent as that between Pelléas and Mélisande. But Anne Clark began to spread stories that the two were lovers, and on one occasion, Ogilivy's mother even sneaked upstairs to listen outside a bedroom door. In May, four months after the marriage, Ogilivy ordered his brother out of the house, but later changed his mind. At about this time, Kitty wrote a letter to Patrick, and in the course of it reminded him of something she had asked him to do for her. She later declared that she had asked Patrick to bring her laudanum (for sleeplessness) and an aperient (for constipation). But what Patrick did was to purchase laudanum and arsenic in Brechin. The poison and the drug were delivered to Kitty by a brother-in-law, Andrew Stewart, to whom she confessed that her marriage was unhappy and she wished her husband dead. Stewart suspected he had brought poison and told the mother so; they talked of taking the poison out of Kitty's drawer. But nothing was done, and the next day Thomas Ogilvy was ill; Kitty took him a bowl of tea, which made him more ill. He now believed he had been poisoned by his wife, and said, 'My death lies at her door.' At midnight on June 6th, four months after his marriage, he died. The funeral was about to proceed normally when Alexander arrived and ordered that it should be stopped because his brother had been murdered. Kitty and Patrick were arrested and charged with incest and murder. The jury – in Edinburgh – sat continuously for thirty-three hours, and returned verdicts of guilty. Patrick was executed in September. Katherine was pregnant, and so the date of her execution was postponed until Monday, March 17th, 1766. Fortunately, she managed to escape – in the garb of a midwife – from the Tolbooth Prison, and left in a coach and four for Berwick, now wearing an officer's uniform. It was a Scots Sabbath, so pursuit was delayed, and she escaped to London, where she hired a Gravesend sailing boat at Billingsgate, and was taken to Calais for eight and a half guineas; she also paid a further four guineas for the boatman to wait four days for her return; but she did not return. It is not known what happened to her; various stories have it that she went to America and married, that she married a Dutchman, and that she died in a convent at Lille in an odour of sanctity. Alexander broke his neck in Edinburgh after being sentenced to seven years' transportation. It is still not unlikely that it was he, with the aid of Anne Clark, who engineered the death of Thomas Ogilvy.

OGORZOV, Paul

The 'S Bahn murderer', a railway worker and Nazi party member, who murdered women on the train or near the railway line in 1939, 1940, and 1941. He was a sadist who killed for sexual satisfaction, usually raping the victim. He used a piece of lead cable as a cosh, and enjoyed the fear of his victims.

Ogorzov was 28 when his trial began on July 24th, 1941. It lasted one day only, the Nazis being anxious to hush it up since he was a party member. He was found guilty of eight murders of women, mostly near Rummelsburg, on the Berlin line. He was executed two days after his trial. No medical report was offered, and details of the murders are not available.

ONUFREJCZYC, Michial (Pronounced Ono-free-shic)

Sentenced to death for the murder of his partner, Stanislaw Sykut, in 1955, but granted reprieve because the body of his partner was not discovered.

Onufrejczyc had been a soldier in the Polish Army and had served in the 1914 War, being wounded twice; in the Second

World War, he also served with conspicuous gallantry, winning nine medals. At the end of the war he settled in England, and bought a small farm at Cwm Du, near Llandilo in Carmarthenshire, South Wales; it was called Cefn Hendre.

The farm drifted towards bankruptcy. Onufrejczyc took a partner, Stanislaw Sykut, who paid £600 for a half-share. Sykut was an old army comrade; he was 57, a year younger than Onufrejczyc. The partnership began in March 1953. But it did nothing to improve the financial affairs of the farm, and Onufrejczyc, who was a violent and impatient man, was accused on May 18th of causing physical harm to his partner. To Police Sergeant Phillips, Onufrejczyc said: 'Very sorry, sir. Partner no work. Me no hit partner again.'

On November 14th, 1953, Sykut's notice to end the partnership expired. But he stayed on at the farm. He was last seen by the village blacksmith on December 14th. After that date his mail remained uncollected at the post office. Sergeant Phillips (who had found the bodies of John and Phoebe Harries a month before, and thus helped to hang Ronald Harries) went out to the farm during a routine check on alien registration, and found thousands of small blood spots all over the kitchen wall. Sykut's razor and various other belongings were found in the house. Onufrejczyc claimed that his partner had left the farm without notice on the morning of December 18th, and tried to persaude the blacksmith that it was on the 17th (not the 14th) that he had last seen Sykut alive.

The surrounding countryside was searched over an area of forty miles, but the body was not discovered. In the meantime, Onufrejczyc was not arrested. He tried various subterfuges to establish evidence that his partner had been alive after December 14th.

Nearly a year later, the body still being undiscovered, the police decided to arrest him. On September 14th, 1954, he appeared before a special court of five magistrates in Llandilo. The hearing lasted three weeks, and he was sent to the Swansea Assizes.

Onufrejczyc now claimed that the bloodstains on the kitchen wall came from Sykut cutting his finger on the hay machine. (He had previously claimed they came from dead rabbits, but analysis had established they were human. Onufrejczyc refused to have his own blood tested to verify if the stains could be from himself.) Mrs Stanislava Pokora, a 'pen friend' of Onufrejczyc, told how she had accused Onufrejczyc of murdering his partner; he had started to sob, and told her a cloak and dagger story of how Sykut had been taken away by men from the Polish Embassy.

He appeared before Mr Justice Oliver in November 1954; he was defended by Mr Elwyn Jones. He was found guilty on circumstantial evidence and sentenced to death. An appeal was dismissed on January 10th, 1955. On January 23rd the Home Secretary, Mr Chuter Ede, granted a reprieve, commuting the death sentence to penal servitude for life. There can be no doubt that he was bearing in mind the Timothy Evans case, and Christie's later confession to the murder of Mrs Evans.

[At the time of writing (1960) the body has still not been found.]

OWEN, John (or Jones)

Wolverhampton-born tramp 'between 35 and 40 years' [police report], who in May 1870 murdered an entire family in Denham Village, Middlesex. Owen had received casual work from village blacksmith Emmanuel Marshall the previous March, but harboured an insane grudge against his temporary employer, believing his wages to have been inadequate. His wrath did not, in time, diminish, but culminated one night in the desire for revenge; this he effected by breaking into the isolated premises and, wielding the blacksmith's own sledgehammer, breaking the skulls of the blacksmith, the blacksmith's wife and and mother, his sister and three of his children (two of the children were staying elsewhere). There were no signs of resistance, and it is popularly (if erroneously) supposed that the revengeful Owen secreted himself behind the kitchen door in the middle of the night, neatly felling each member of the Marshall clan as they entered to investigate the nocturnal noises. The slaughter complete, Owen stole the blacksmith's best suit and boots, and, after deliberately smashing a framed portrait of that unfortunate man, departed. He was actually seen leaving the house by an old lady, and informed her that he was Marshall's brother; later she furnished the description of Owen that was instrumental in securing his arrest.[1] His spirited remarks when captured are worthy of record: passing through Slough railway station under escort he made an obscene gesture at the lynch-minded mob, and expressed a desire to be in their midst armed with the sledgehammer; just before his inevitable execution he remarked to the waiting journalists, 'My friends I am

[1] By Superintendent Dunham. See Augustus Payne.

about to suffer for the death of – let me see! what was the name?
– oh, Emmanuel Marshall – but, my friends, I am innocent!'

P

PACE, Beatrice Annie
Small-statured, pretty widow aged 36, widow of Harry Pace,
quarry-man and sheep-breeder, for whose murder she was tried
at Gloucester Assizes in 1928.

The Paces had lived, since their marriage in 1917, at Fetterhill
Farm, Coleford, a remote spot in the Gloucestershire hills. It
appeared afterwards that Mrs Pace's life had been one of misery;
her husband was not only erratic-tempered and violent, but
obsessed to an abnormal extent with the welfare of his 100 sheep.
Frequently beaten by her husband, on one occasion Mrs Pace's
pet dog was thrown repeatedly against a wall until it died
because Harry Pace, having found one of his flock killed on the
railway line, went berserkly violent in his grief. In July 1927
Pace became ill with severe stomach pains and partial paralysis
of the limbs. He was removed to Gloucester Infirmary, where
arsenical poisoning was diagnosed – it must have been caused,
said the somewhat puzzled doctors, through contact with sheep-
dip containing this poison. (Pace's constant query throughout
this illness: 'How are my sheep?') He was discharged from hospital in October 1927, although still requiring medical attention;
a young miner friend came in daily to massage his legs. On
Christmas Day, however, a surge of renewed health inspired
Pace to indulge in some old tyrannies; he attacked his wife with
firetongs, smashed the fender and threatened to cut everyone's
throat. On December 27th the stomachic pains returned, more
violently; on January 10th, 1928, after much agony in his hillside
cottage, Harry Pace died. Five days later, as the funeral cortège
was about to leave the cottage, police intervened by order of the
Coroner, Mr Maurice Carter, whose action was instigated by
Mr Elton Pace, the dead man's brother, who suspected foul play;
he had mentioned to the police, among other things, how his
mother (during Harry's convalescence) had tasted her son's bed-
side glass of water and found it 'salty and nasty'; and how, at
the beginning of his brother's mysterious illness the previous
July, he, Elton, had discovered his sister-in-law stretched across
her husband's sickbed 'a-bellocking' in by no means unhappy
tones, 'Ah, Harry, you be a-dying!'

The inquest began at an inn near the Paces' cottage on January 16th, when it transpired that Harry Pace's organs contained 9·42 grains of arsenic; Home Office pathologist Sir William Willcox believed Pace to have suffered from arsenical poisoning since July. The inquiry moved to Coleford, and was repeatedly adjourned and readjourned until the following May, when the Coroner's jury returned the verdict: 'We find that Harry Pace met his death by arsenical poisoning administered by some person other than himself.' The Coroner (who was to be much criticized for his action) directed that if the case was to go further a suspect must be named; accordingly, the foreman of the jury eventually announced 'We find that Harry Pace met his death by arsenical poisoning administered by Beatrice Annie Pace.'

Beatrice Pace's trial began on July 2nd before Mr Justice Horridge, with the defendant pleading not guilty. Mr Norman Birkett appeared for the defence, with Solicitor-General Sir Frank Boyd Merriman prosecuting. Birkett inquired of Leslie Pace, the victim's 10-year-old son, 'Did your Dad wear a rather large moustache?' – making the point later that sheep-breeders have been known to poison themselves accidentally by getting their moustaches contaminated with sheep-dip. Harry Pace himself had expressed the opinion that his illness was due to contact with sheep-dip; Sir William Willcox, however, reiterated that this means could not account for the amount of arsenic found in the body. Mrs Pace, in an earlier statement to the police, had expressed a conviction that her husband had killed himself and now Mr Birkett elicited from Harry Pace's mother, Mrs Elizabeth Porter, the fact that another son of hers had committed suicide. Elton Pace remained adamant in his conviction of Mrs Pace's guilt; asked about her reaction at Harry Pace's death, he banged with his fists on the witness-stand, yelling: 'She was as unconcerned as this here box.'

After five days, just before Beatrice Pace was due to give evidence, Norman Birkett submitted to the judge that, in his opinion, there was no case to go before the jury, and that the trial should be stopped. The judge concurred: 'I am inclined to agree with Mr Birkett. . . .' The crowd waiting outside the Assizes appeared overjoyed at the turn of events, and concerned itself with the immediate prospect of lynching the now unpopular Elton Pace, who received their jeers and threats, so we are told, with commendable calm and contempt.

PAGE, Vera, Case

An unsolved murder of 1931; the body of 11-year-old Vera Page (reported missing two days before) was found in the morning of December 16th slumped across the tradesman's entrance of a house in Addison Road, Kensington, London. She had been raped and strangled and her face and clothing were be-spattered by soot, coal-dust, and candle-grease; in the folds of her coat sleeve was an adult-size fingerstall containing lint, which smelt of ammonia. As decomposition was fairly advanced and her clothing dry, although rain had fallen the previous night, it was thought that the killing had occurred elsewhere many days earlier, and that until being transferred to Addison Road the body had been concealed in a warm, dry place. At the Coroner's inquest a Mr Percy Orlando Rush was in an unen-viable position with much circumstantial evidence against him. Rush had worn a fingerstall similar to the one found on the body, ammonia was used at his work (a laundry), burnt-out candles were found at his home, coal-dust and soot found on his clothing, and he had no satisfactory alibi covering the period when Vera Page was abducted. During Rush's inquisition by Coroner Ingleby Oddie, a woman stood up and shouted, 'That man is telling lies, sir.' The jury found the evidence against Rush insufficient, and returned an open verdict of murder by some person or persons unknown.

PALMER, Inez
Twenty-three-year-old West Virginian, found guilty in 1927 of murdering her lover's step-mother and sentenced to life imprison-ment. (Released in 1938, she died three years later.)

Forty-two-year-old Sarah Stout was found by her husband, 67-year-old William, dead on the kitchen floor of their farm-house in the Axtel Ridge section of Vinton County, southern Ohio. Death was due to strangulation, caused by prolonged pressure of a small 'half-moon' shaped object on the windpipe; these half-moon dents were seen elsewhere on the corpse, which was also partially burnt, having first been soaked in kerosene. Mrs Maude Collins, the sheriff, noticed tiny semi-circular im-pressions in the ground outside the farm-house; she supposed these indentations to come from a walking-stick, possibly the murder-weapon.

Arthur Stout, 32-year-old step-son of the deceased, who

worked as a farmer nearby, said he had not visited his father's house that day, November 17th, 1926; but a new clock key, found near the body, was traced to a jeweller, Jacob Hauser, who said he had delivered it to Arthur Stout, whom he had finally located at the elder Stout's farm-house in the afternoon of November 17th. Then it was revealed that Sarah Stout, three weeks before, had tried to have her step-son arrested on a charge of threatening her life. Arthur Stout was arrested; while his son was being handcuffed, father Stout yelled: 'You are making a mistake, Sheriff Collins . . . what a fool you are not to recognize the real killer!' More information was not forthcoming from the old man.

Arthur Stout's attractive so-called housekeeper visited him regularly in jail; during one visit she showed Sheriff Collins a note purported to have been written by William Stout: 'I can't stand it any longer . . . I can't testify against my own son when I done it myself . . . I am going away and I want to leave all my property to him for what I've made him suffer – both farms and everything.'

Dissatisfied as to the genuineness of the note, Sheriff Collins commenced searching for clues to the whereabouts of William Stout; his murdered body was recovered from a well on his farm-land. Inez Palmer was asked for a specimen of her handwriting; refusing to give it, Sheriff Collins voiced her suspicions to the silent and stubborn housekeeper. These suspicions changed to certainty when it was discovered that the heel-impressions from Inez Palmer's high-heeled shoes matched the 'walking-stick' indentations and the marks on Sarah Stout's throat. Confronted with this fact, Inez Palmer confessed to both killings, Sarah Stout had attacked her morals: '. . . I flew into a rage . . . knocked her to the floor . . . jammed one spike-heeled shoe into her throat until she ceased to struggle . . . Pop knew I done it . . . I conceived the plan to do away with him . . . that way I could get Arthur back and we would have everything the old man left.'

Information reached Sheriff Collins that in October 1926 Arthur Stout had offered the 18-year-old brother of Inez $50 to kill Sarah Stout; because of this, Arthur Stout was accused of being an accessory both before and after the fact of the actual killings. Like her, he was sentenced to life imprisonment, dying in the penitentiary at Columbus, Ohio, in 1941.

PALMER, William
Mass-poisoner

Palmer was born at Rugeley, Staffs, in 1824, son of a saw-mill proprietor. Both sides of his family had a history of moral degeneracy and drunkenness. When Palmer was 13, his father died. The will settled £70,000 on the eldest son, Joseph; Joseph settled ten per cent of this on William. At the age of 21 he inherited about £9,000.

Palmer left school at 17 and was apprenticed to a firm of Liverpool druggists. In Liverpool, he quickly became acquainted with all kinds of crooks associated with racing. Soon, he left the firm under a cloud, having stolen money from letters addressed to the firm.

Palmer now became apprenticed to Dr Edward Tylecote of Hayward, Cheshire. During these five years, he had fourteen illegitimate children, and ran a private practice in abortion. On leaving Dr Tylecote, Palmer took a job in the Stafford Infirmary. Here he became acquainted with a man named Abbey, whom he poisoned one day with strychnine in a glass of brandy simply to see how the poison worked. No suspicion was aroused by Abbey's death.

His next victim appears to have been one of his illegitimate children by a woman called Jane Mumford; the child died after a visit to its father. At the age of 22, Palmer went to London, where he finally gained his doctor's diploma, and was able to return to Rugeley and put up a plate outside his door. Here he had only one rival practitioner, an octogenarian named Bamford. Soon, Palmer decided to poison one of his creditors, a man named Bladon. Bladon was invited to stay at Palmer's house, and was duly poisoned. Dr Bamford was called, and helped tend the dying Bladon. Mrs Bladon arrived, but was hardly allowed to catch a glimpse of her husband before he died. Bladon's friends urged her to go to the police, but she had conceived a liking for Palmer, and refused to do so.

The next victim was another creditor, named Bly. Palmer owed him £800. The dying man managed to tell his wife of the debt before he died, but when she asked Palmer for it, he replied that Bly had owed him the £800, and that he would be obliged if the widow would produce the money.

Palmer now decided to extend operations to his family; he started with an uncle, 'Beau' Bentley, another drunken profligate. Palmer proposed a brandy drinking match; the result was the same as in the case of Abbey; Uncle Bentley died within three days.

His next attempt was a failure. He invited to his house the wife of another Uncle Bentley, who soon felt indisposed. Palmer made her up some pills which he urged her to take before going to bed that night. But she felt better, and decided not to take them. Palmer seemed offended the next morning, and made her promise to take one that night. Not wishing to offend her relative, she threw the pills out of the window on to a chicken run. The next day, several chickens were found dead.

No precise account of Palmer's murders exists, but it seems probable that he murdered four of his children by his wife; these four died in convulsions in their early infancy. L. C. Douthwaite claims that Palmer also murdered several of his illegitimate children. It is almost certain that he caused the death of his mother-in-law, who died two weeks after coming to stay with him.

Palmer was married to the illegitimate daughter of a colonel in the Indian Army, whom he seems to have chosen for the large dowry she brought him. At all events, he decided to get rid of her too. His favourite mare, Nettle, had lost the Oaks of 1853, and Palmer had backed her for £10,000. He insured his wife's life for £13,000, and then waited until the autumn; but by then, his creditors were clamorous, and Annie Palmer's life ended in September. Palmer put up an admirable show as a bereaved husband, and got two octogenarian doctors to sign the death certificate ('English cholera'), including the complaisant Dr Bamford.

The insurance was paid, after much hesitation, but even £13,000 was not enough to stem the rising tide of debt. Since the insurance companies had been so obliging in the matter of his wife, he decided to insure the life of his brother, a drunkard named Walter, for no less than £82,000. Then Walter was invited to stay with his brother. For five months, Palmer plied Walter with drink, hoping that he might die legitimately of alcohol poisoning; but Walter was inured to this form of poison. Finally, Walter succumbed after a drinking bout. But the insurance companies were suspicious, and refused to pay up. Palmer became desperate. He tried to insure an illiterate racing friend, George Bates, for £25,000. But the companies were suspicious, and their detectives reported unfavourably on the transaction. They also saw the boots, a youth named Myatt, at the hotel where Walter had died, and the boots declared that he had seen

Palmer pour something into Walter's drink. On hearing about this, Palmer hurried around to the hotel, and actually induced Myatt to have a drink with him. For several days after this, Myatt was prostrated with appalling gastric pains, which finally cleared up.

Now Palmer planned what was to be his final murder. He had a young friend named Cook, who, like himself, was heavily in debt. Cook's only asset – he had gambled away all his others – was a mare named Polestar, which was engaged in the second race at Shrewsbury on Tuesday, November 13th, 1855. Cook betted heavily on Polestar. On the Tuesday, he and Palmer attended the race, and Polestar won. This was Cook's bad luck. He and Palmer celebrated victory with a dinner at the Raven Hotel in Shrewsbury. The next day, Palmer and Cook returned to the hotel and had more drink. In the evening, they were joined by a couple of racing men named Herring and Fisher. While these two were present, Cook drank a glass of brandy and leapt to his feet with the words: 'Good God, there's something in that that burns my throat.' Palmer seized the glass, saying 'Nonsense', and drained the remaining half-inch from it. That night, Cook was very ill, but recovered sufficiently the next day to lend Palmer money, which Palmer immediately lost by backing a loser.

Palmer and Cook now returned to Rugeley, where Cook put up at the Talbot Arms. The next morning, after a cup of coffee taken in Palmer's presence, Cook became very ill. He spent several days in bed, getting steadily worse. However, on the Monday, Palmer went to London to collect Cook's winnings, and when he returned, Cook had managed to get up and dress. Dr Bamford had left him some pills. Palmer now bought some strychnine and prussic acid, and continued to dose Cook who, incredible as it seems, did not realize he was being poisoned. Palmer now tried forging a cheque with Cook's signature, for £350, but the forgery was so clumsy that the bank refused payment.

That Monday evening, November 19th, 1855, Palmer took more pills to Cook; when the patient had taken them, his body became so convulsed that his head touched his heels, and he died a few minutes later. Palmer now forged a document showing that £4,000 had been negotiated for his benefit by Cook.

Cook's step-father became suspicious and demanded an autopsy. Palmer was arrested on a money-lender's writ, and the bodies of Mrs Palmer and his brother were exhumed.

The circumstances of the autopsy are unbelievable. Not only was Palmer allowed to be present, but he was almost allowed to escape with Cook's stomach in a jar! Palmer then tried to bribe the driver taking the jar to London to break it. He also managed to get hold of the letter containing the results of the analysis, and wrote to the Coroner, enclosing a present of game, and pointing out that the analyst had stated that no strychnine was found in the body.

Because of the violence of local feeling, Palmer was tried in London at the Old Bailey. Lord Campbell presided; the Attorney General, Sir Alexander Compton, prosecuted; Sergeant Shee defended. No strychnine had been found in the stomach of Cook, owing perhaps to its contents having been spilt when it was thrown into the jar, but circumstantial evidence was damning, and Palmer was convicted and sentenced to death. He was executed at Stafford.

PARKER, Pauline Yvonne
Sixteen-year-old schoolgirl, found guilty with Juliet Hulme (aged 15) of the murder of her mother, Mrs Honora Mary Parker (also known as Mrs Rieper) at Canterbury, New Zealand.

In the afternoon of June 23rd, 1954, the two girls ran into a tea-shop near a park, saying that the mother of one of them had been seriously hurt; the body of Mrs Parker was found lying across a path in the park, her head brutally lacerated. The girls (who seemed hysterical) maintained that the older woman had accidentally slipped and banged her head '. . . (it) . . . kept bumping and banging' – but this tale was so patently untrue that the two girls were questioned more closely. Detective Brown, interrogating Pauline Parker, told her she was under suspicion, then:

'Who assaulted your mother?'
'I did.'
'Why?'
'. . . I won't answer that question.'
'When did you make up your mind to kill your mother?'
'A few days ago.'

For some time the relationship between the two girls had shown Lesbian tendencies, and both sets of parents sought to end the friendship; Mrs Parker's natural concern was judged annoyingly insistent by her daughter, and led to sinister philosophies in the girl's diary:

February 13th. Why could not mother die? Dozens of people, thousands of people, are dying every day. So why not mother, and father too?

June 20th. We discussed our plans for moidering mother and made them a little clearer. I want it to appear either a natural or an accidental death.

On the morning of the day of the crime, the diary entry read:

. . . I felt very excited and the night before Christmassy last night. I did not have pleasant dreams, though.

A brick wrapped up in a stocking was the murder weapon, and was actually found alongside the corpse. A pathologist found that death was due to a fractured skull, and there were forty-five injuries in all; the throat was bruised, as was one finger – probably the result of attempting to ward off blows. (Juliet Hulme, after her arrest, said she had not been really sure whether murder was contemplated: '. . . after the first blow was struck I knew it would be necessary for us to kill her.')

At their trial in Christchurch both girls appeared unrepentant. Details were given of their strange relationship. They had written letters to each other, each assuming bizarre identities: Juliet had been, among other things, Charles II, 'Emperor' of Borovvia, and the 'Emperor's' mistress Deborah; Pauline had chosen to be Lancelot Trelawney, a Cornish soldier of fortune. They believed themselves to be geniuses: 'I am apart from the law', Juliet Hulme had said. They continued erotic experiments: '. . . we enacted how the saints would make love in bed', Pauline Parker had written in the diary.

There was controversy as to their sanity, but the jury returned a verdict of guilty. Owing to their youth, they were not hanged, but sentenced to be detained 'until Her Majesty's Pleasure be made known'. Both were released in 1958.

PARSONS, Rachel (Murder of)

Seventy-one-year-old wealthy eccentric, battered to death in her home, Branches Park, near Newmarket, by one of her servants, 26-six-year-old stableman Dennis James Pratt. An irascible woman, Rachel Parsons was a recluse who lavished her affection on her racehorses, overfeeding them while keeping her staff ('thieves and scum') underpaid. 'She was very bad-tempered,' said Leo Grimes, a former stableman, 'although she could be a lady when she liked.' A Miss Hilda Pink, who had been employed by the victim for three turbulent months, was to write to the court, saying she was not surprised at the murderous assault: '. . . she paid me weekly, but there was a tussle each time.' Mr Charles Bell, a former trainer of horses for Miss Parsons, said: 'She was a very difficult employer . . . it was impossible to please her. . . . I think she called me everything in the dictionary.' On July 1st, 1956, Dennis Pratt called on Miss Parsons to claim his holiday money: '. . . she told me to get out and that I was not going to get the money . . . she came for me and hit me on the head with her handbag. She was in a horrible mood . . . I told her to stop and hit her with an iron bar. I do not remember how many times I struck her . . .' After the killing Pratt stole Miss Parsons' binoculars ('I wanted to help my wife and sell them'), and it was when police questioned him over the selling of these that Pratt confessed to the crime.

At Pratt's trial, presided over by Mr Justice Diplock, the jury decided that the accused had acted under great provocation, and the murder charge was reduced to one of manslaughter. Pratt was sentenced to ten years' imprisonment.

PATRICK, Albert T.
A wily forger of extraordinary cunning, tried in 1900 for the murder of William Rice; although he was sentenced to life imprisonment, he was finally pardoned and released.

William Rice was a rich old man who owned oil wells in Texas; he was in his eighties when he met the man who was to become his secretary and confidential valet, Charles Jones. This was in 1897. In November 1899, Albert T. Patrick, a scoundrelly lawyer, appeared at the Rice flat in Madison Avenue and tried to bribe Jones to furnish evidence that his employer's residence in Texas was not established, which would affect Rice's claim to his late wife's estate. Jones refused. But Patrick called again; Jones was a weak man, easily dominated, and allowed himself to be persuaded by Patrick to forge Rice's signature to a letter about the lawsuit in Texas. Patrick soon learned from Jones that Rice had left all his money to the William Rice Institute in Houston. He persuaded Jones that this was completely unfair, and then produced a second will, leaving half the estate to Patrick and a large part to Jones; the remainder to Rice's heirs. When Jones asked about destroying the original will, Patrick pointed out that it would be better to leave it for the heirs to see; they might then feel less inclined to raise objections to the new will.

But soon Patrick had a still better idea – a new will leaving all the estate to himself. Again Jones was induced to forge it (in June 1899), Patrick explaining that it would look less suspicious if nothing was left to Jones, and that he would see that Jones gained substantially by it all. Patrick also made Jones write to him a series of letters, all signed by 'Rice', building up a background of good fellowship between Rice and the lawyer, and discussing many intimate details of his finances with him. Carbons of these letters were inserted in Rice's files.

Three Rice cheques were now intercepted, and forged cheques sent off to the payees by Jones. This was to test Patrick's forgery of the signature. In case the bank detected it, Rice would reply that he himself had signed the cheques. The cheques passed through without trouble.

However, Patrick made one serious slip in the matter of forging Rice's signature. He used a signature of Rice and traced over the top of it. But he used the same signature each time instead of using several different samples. No one ever writes his signature *exactly* the same twice, and this was later to be one of the weak links in Patrick's schemes.

About this time – mid-1900 – Rice had a slight attack of indigestion; a doctor was called (recommended by Patrick) and supplied pills that cured the complaint. Patrick bought mercury pills and substituted them for the original ones; next time Rice had indigestion, it grew rapidly worse. Patrick now forged a cremation order, in case the body had to be cremated quickly to hide traces of poison.

On September 16th, 1900, while the old man was ill, a telegram came advising him of a fire at one of his oil plants in Texas and asking permission to rebuild. Rice sent a telegram giving permission; this would have drained the New York account, in which Patrick had such an interest, so the telegram was intercepted by Jones.

However, the old man now began to recover, so Patrick decided he must die. He told Jones that he would have to chloroform him. Jones refused, but was finally bullied and cajoled by Patrick into agreeing. So, when Rice was asleep, he saturated a sponge in chloroform and placed it in a towel over the old man's mouth. At this moment, the doorbell rang; two old ladies of Rice's acquaintance were calling. Jones let it ring, and the old ladies went away very puzzled, since they could hear someone moving about in the flat.

Rice died as a result of the chloroform; Jones opened the

windows and let out the smell, then called a doctor, who un-hesitatingly ascribed cause of death to heart disease. Rice, after all, was 84.

Patrick now proceeded with his plan. He sent telegrams to all Texas relatives of Mr Rice informing them of the death and stating that the funeral would be at 10 am the next day. One of them wired for them to hold up the funeral until he came, but Patrick had the forged cremation order, and ignored the tele-gram. Here came hitch number one: it was impossible to cre-mate Rice immediately; at least twenty-four hours of notice were needed.

On September 24th, 1900, a friend of Patrick, David Short, presented a cheque for $25,000 at the Swenson Bank; it was made out to Abert T. Patrick and endorsed Albert T. Patrick. The clerk pointed out the inconsistency, and Short left the bank, returning with the cheque correctly endorsed. However, his manner was nervous, and Eric Swenson, one of the bank's partners, phoned Rice's flat. Jones told him that the cheque was in order. The clerk decided to call and see Mr Rice; Jones answered the door and admitted that Rice was dead. Payment of the cheque was now refused, even though Patrick appeared personally and demanded immediate payment. The elderly lady callers had by now informed the police of their suspicions. Several cheques made out to Patrick by Rice were examined and the signatures were found to be absolutely identical, pointing to forgery. Jones and Patrick were arrested.

Even in jail Patrick showed his amazing hold over Jones. They were lodged in cells next to one another, and Patrick managed to pass a penknife to Jones, telling him to kill himself and that he would 'follow'. (How he was supposed to get the knife back is anyone's guess.) Gurgling noises drew the attention of a police-man to Jones' cell, and he was found lying in a pool of blood with a gashed throat. However, he recovered.

Rice's body was examined, and chloroform found in the lungs. When Jones recovered enough to talk, he made a full statement, implicating Patrick.

Having turned State's evidence, Jones was released and Patrick was tried alone. His defence was ingenious; he wanted to know what proof there was that Rice had been murdered, claim-ing that the chloroform found in the lungs was actually em-balming fluid. But Jones' statement condemned him.

Patrick was sentenced to death. There was a great deal of popular sympathy for him – for some reason, the general public seems to feel no great hatred for men charged with murder for swindling purposes – perhaps even a sporting admiration. In any case, Patrick's sentence was commuted to life imprisonment, but he was finally pardoned and released. No doubt this may also have been due to a feeling that he had made a very sporting effort to enlarge his fortune and failed through sheer bad luck.

It is unfortunate that full details of Patrick's life are not available; a photograph at the time of the trial shows a bald-headed man in his fifties with steel-rimmed glasses, the picture of a respectable lawyer, but there seems little doubt that the Rice case was the climax of a lifetime of fraud, and possibly (since he was released) not its conclusion!

PAUL, Sidney George
A pathetic murder case in which a neurotic man killed his wife because he was in debt and feared that his wife would suffer.

Paul seems to have been an unlucky man. An orphan at 10, he was wounded in the 1914 War, and later attacked by natives in the Belgian Congo and sustained head injuries. He married a young Belgian nurse, who accompanied him to the Congo. Back in England, a sack-manufacturing business failed, and he finally lost his employment as a salesman in 1938. They had four children and his wife was expecting a fifth. He continued to go out every day, not telling his wife that he had no job. He borrowed £150 from his sister, and a cheque he made out to her to repay some of it was returned marked RD. His wife found out, and repaid some of the money from her own money. They were living in Rosebery Vale, Ruislip.

On Saturday, October 3rd, 1938, Paul murdered his wife with a hatchet, and then inflicted wounds on himself with a razor, and ran outside, shouting for help and claiming he had fought with a burglar who had attacked his wife. He handed a policeman a button which he said he had torn from the murderer's coat. A doctor who examined him realized that the wounds on his head had not been inflicted with a hatchet, and were probably self-inflicted. Moreover, the button, which had a length of thread adhering, was found to match four other buttons in a drawer; one had an identical piece of thread on it.

He was tried at the Old Bailey before Mr Justice Asquith; there was much sympathy for him, and even the prosecuting counsel, Mr G. B. McClure, suggesting to the jury that it was a 'merciful' murder, caused by an anxiety neurosis. Mr Easter-wood defended.

Although sentenced to death, the Home Secretary commuted the sentence to penal servitude. Paul continued to maintain his his innocence.

PAYNE, Augustus
The accused in a still unsolved Victorian murder case.

Hezekiah Reville was a butcher in Slough; in 1881 he was about 40, married to a woman of 35, with two assistants, Philip Glass and 'Gus' Alfred Payne. Reville disliked Payne, who was about 17; he thought he was dishonest and lazy; however, Mrs Reville does not seem to have had the same feelings.

On Monday, April 11th, 1881, Anne Reville was murdered by blows of a chopper, struck from behind. Glass and Reville had both left the shop, and Payne had been alone with the murdered woman for five minutes before he, too, he claimed, went home. A few minutes later she was found, sitting in full view of the street in the lighted shop, quite dead. Payne was the obvious suspect, and was accordingly arrested. Reville had an alibi; he had been on his way to the pub, but at the actual moment his wife must have been murdered, he was (so he claimed) outside a tobacconist's shop waiting for a friend, who was a very long time getting served. This has led some writers to suggest that Reville murdered his wife, hurrying back from outside the shop. There are a few points to support this idea and which suggest that Reville wanted to incriminate Payne. Reville claimed that his wife and the apprentice were on bad terms, but other witnesses denied this. He claimed that he had handed money to his wife before leaving the shop, and that this money was stolen (providing a motive for Payne). But Payne had neither money nor bloodstains on him when he was questioned a few minutes after the murder; moreover, Reville – rather strangely – did not mention the missing money until some time after the murder, which suggests that it was an afterthought.

There was also found by the body a written note – an obvious forgery – that purported to come from an enraged customer named Collins, who said that the butcher would not sell him any more bad meat. As an attempt to throw the police off the scent, it was singularly inane. But Reville said he saw Payne writing a note as he went out of the shop. Surely the assistant would not have used his master's time – and under his master's nose – to write the note; if Reville had asked him what he was doing, it would not have been easy to fabricate a convincing excuse.

Reville obviously wanted to throw suspicion on Payne, and did everything in his power to do so. The investigation was in the hands of Superintendent Dunham, a popular man in the area since he had gone into an inn in Reading and arrested a desperate character named Owen who had murdered the village blacksmith and his wife, his three children, and his mother. (This took place in Denham in 1870.) Dunham arrested Payne, who was tried at Aylesbury on Thursday, April 28th. Payne's manner was completely impassive throughout his trial, as it had been all along. (He had not even showed surprise when told that Mrs Reville had been murdered.) The jury was out for half an hour, and acquitted him.

All the theories as to who committed the murder are pointless since there is obviously a great deal that we do not know. Payne apparently had no motive for killing Mrs Reville (who, in spite of her husband's disapproval, used to give Payne a penny for beer money every evening). But he *may* have had a motive. So may Reville himself. Payne's completely cold demeanour throughout the proceedings is against him; but it is no crime to be unable to feel. The day before the murder there was what looked like a deliberate attempt by Reville to provide Payne with a motive; he complained about Payne's honesty to Glass and his mother, and asked Glass to speak to Payne about this. But Glass did not do so, and so Payne had no known cause of resentment against the Revilles at the time of the murder.

PEACE, Charley

Gargoyle-faced 'old-lag' burglar and murderer, born about 1832 in Angel Court, Sheffield. He was also a violinist, a reciter of monologues, a sanctimonious humbug, an animal lover, an ardent pacifist, woodweaver, and picture framer. In 1877, during a quarrel, he shot dead his next-door neighbour Mr Dyson (with whose wife he had been associating) in the yard adjoining their homes at Banner Cross Terrace, Sheffield, from then on being known as the Banner Cross Murderer. He sought refuge in London, where he lived at Evelina Road, Peckham, his legal wife occupying the basement and 'Mr and Mrs Thompson' (Charley Peace and one Susan Grey – 'a dreadful woman for drink and snuff') residing in the upper regions. He disguised himself by walnut-staining his face, dyeing his hair black and donning spectacles. The Thompsons regularly attended church and held musical soirées, during which Charley would entertain the guests with violin virtuosity and recitations – doubtless including in his repertoire the elegy he wrote, when hearing in prison of the death of his infant son John Charles:

> Farewell my dear son, by us all beloved
> Thou art gone to dwell in the mansions above
> In the bosom of Jesus who sits on the throne
> Thou art anxiously waiting for us to come home. . . .

By night he would bundle his burglaring tools into the violin case, harness his pony, Tommy, into the trap, and (not forgetting his revolver) would set out on a housebreaking expedition. After two years' professional success in South London, he was caught in a Blackheath garden by PC Robinson (whom he shot in the arm) and his true identity was established. He was transported up north to be tried at Leeds Assizes for Dyson's murder, on the way attempting to escape out of the train window. Convicted of the crime, he confessed to another killing, years before, in Manchester. He was calm during his pre-execution breakfast, delivering a little homily to the warders on a Christian state of grace, but a flash of the true rascally Charley came when he glowered down at his plate to observe: 'This is bloody rotten bacon.'

PELIZZIONI, Serafino
The main interest in this case is that the accused was tried twice for the same murder, and another man was convicted for it while he was actually in the death cell.

The murder itself was a commonplace pub brawl that occurred at the Golden Anchor, a pub on the corner of Great Saffron Hill (which runs parallel to Hatton Garden) and Castle Street, London, EC1. In this area, bounded by the Grays Inn Road, Holborn, and Farringdon Road, lived an Italian colony. Sometime around Christmas 1865, the landlord of the Golden Anchor, an ex-policeman named Shaw, offended the Italian colony by throwing out one of their number and shouting some insult about an Englishman being worth any three Italians. On Boxing Day, a picture-frame maker named Gregorio Mogni, a man of 40, came in and slapped the landlord's face. Trouble was averted, but the Italian faction were rude to the potboy, Rebbeck, when he went through their room. On returning to the next room where a group of Englishmen were gathered, Rebbeck warned them that the Italians were looking for trouble and carried knives. Rebbeck was pushed through the window into the yard, where he gathered many staves, with which the Englishmen armed themselves; they then shouted a challenge to the Italians to come in if they dared. A moment later the Italians took up the challenge; a brief fight ensued, and when the room cleared again, it was found that two Englishmen were seriously stabbed and an Italian was being held by the others. Rebbeck had a stab in the right lung, from which he recovered only after a long and serious illness; a man named Michael Harrington had been stabbed in the stomach, and the knife had been twisted, pulling out several feet of intestines; he died in hospital that night, refusing to sign a form implicating his opponent because he said he forgave him.

The man who was caught was an Italian named Pelizzioni. No knife had been found on him or near him (except a small penknife) and his story was that, far from being one of the attackers, he had been called as a peacemaker from the Three Tuns public house in Cross Street, and had gone into the room to stop a brawl. He was a man of some standing in the Italian community, and later in court made the impression of a serious and decent man. However, the Englishmen were (understandably) determined that someone should suffer for what, at that time, looked like two deaths (hope had been abandoned for Rebbeck), and declared that only one Italian had burst into the room, the others being beaten off outside, and that consequently Pelizzioni must be the murderer.

Pelizzioni was tried at the Old Bailey before Baron Martin (who had tried George Townley) on February 3rd; he was found guilty and sentenced to death.

Now a new turn came in the case. Gregorio Mogni had fled to Birmingham; a certain Mr Negretti went after him, found him in a carpenter's shop at Edgbaston, and asked him angrily if he was aware that his cousin (Pelizzioni) was about to suffer for his (Mogni's) crime. Mogni admitted that he was the one with the knife, and returned to London, where he gave himself up at King's Cross Police Station. The police evidently felt that this was a manoeuvre to save Pelizzioni by confusing the issue, and refused to prosecute Mogni – especially as Mogni refused actually to say that he had done the stabbing of Harrington. Accordingly, Mogni was privately prosecuted; he pleaded self-defence, and was eventually sentenced to five years' penal servitude for the manslaughter of Harrington. It was now plainly impossible to execute Pelizzioni, who was first granted a stay of execution, and then retried at the Old Bailey on April 13th before Mr Justice Montague and Baron Channell; after three days he was finally found not guilty and released.

Shortly after this, the Golden Anchor lost its licence.

PERRY, Arthur
Case of wife murder in New York in 1937, where the man who was finally convicted 'rigged' evidence to point to the guilt of another man.

On the morning of June 2nd, 1937, the body of Mrs Phennie Perry, aged 20, was found in a pathway leading to the Log Island Railway, near Beaver Road, in the Jamaican section of Queens County. She had been killed by blows from a piece of concrete which lay nearby, and her baby girl was unhurt beside the body. It looked like a case of murder by a sex maniac. When the body was moved, a bloodstained shoe (with a hole in its sole) an electric iron and some papers belonging to Ulysses Palm, 153rd Street, Jamaica, was found underneath it.

A night watchman, a dipsomaniac, had heard screams at 10.30 the previous evening, and had called the police; two impatient policemen in a patrol car had seen that he was drunk and had gone off without investigating.

It was soon discovered that the dead woman lived in the flat above the Palms. In Palm's flat was found the other shoe of the pair, a bloodstained and torn shirt (of which a strip was found under the body), and papers that showed Ulysses Palm to be a Deacon of the Amity Baptist Church. The dead woman's husband, Arthur Perry, who was 22, worked for a steel construction corporation.

Both Perry and Palm were taken in for questioning. Perry declared that his wife had gone away the previous afternoon to spend the week-end with her sister. But he had seen her later in the evening, after a Bingo game, and she had told him that Palm had tried to break into her bedroom that morning. Perry had then gone to see Palm and had threatened him; Palm denied everything and told Perry to bring his wife. There had also been a matter of a highly suggestive letter that Palm was alleged to have written to Mrs Perry, in the course of which she was told that if she showed it to her husband he would kill her.

This letter was produced, but a writing expert later declared positively that it was not written by Palm; he could not state definitely, however, that it was written by Perry.

Palm appeared to be totally innocent; he was a 39-year-old married man, who had a perfect alibi for the murder. He had worked until 10.10 pm on the evening of the murder, and this was vouched for by several people. It took him an hour to get home from Flushing by trolley bus, a distance of ten miles.

There were obvious discrepancies here. Perry claimed he had quarrelled with Palm at 9.50 and then left to go to his sister's house, but the quarrel must have occurred later, since Palm was not home until 11.15. And an usher in the Plaza theatre, where Mrs Perry played Bingo, said that she saw Perry leave the theatre at about ten o'clock with a woman and baby.

Examination of the shirt showed that the 'tear' had been started with a cut with a knife or scissors.

Perry's clothes were examined. The shoe found under the body was Palm's; Palm said he had given the pair to Perry, and Perry admitted this, but claimed he had returned them. The hole in the sole of the shoe was surrounded by bloodstains. Perry's sock had a bloodstained sole in the same position. The notepaper the letter was written on was like that found in Perry's apartment, but unlike that found in Palm's. Experts who examined the letter later in the case declared that certain formations proved it to be written by Perry. A detective who was put in jail with Perry, posing as a wanted murderer, claimed that Perry admitted to murdering his wife, but said that he loved her and he had no idea why he did it.

Perry was tried on September 23rd, 1937, and found guilty; the Court of Appeal reversed the conviction. But a second trial, on November 14th, 1938, sustained the original verdict, and Perry was electrocuted on August 3rd, 1939. Although no motive for the murder was established (except minor quarrels between husband and wife) it was obviously premeditated.

PETIOT, Dr Marcel
Guillotined in May 1946 for the murder of twenty-seven people. He admitted to killing sixty-three people in his house at 21 Rue Lesueur, near the Etoile.

Petiot made a fortune from his victims by posing as a member of the French Resistance, and offering to help them escape from France. They were told to report to his surgery at Rue Lesueur after dark, bringing all their belongings. There they were given an injection by Petiot – against malaria or any other disease that Petiot claimed was common in the country to which they would escape. They were then led into a small, triangular room with walls of rough cement and asked to wait; Petiot then went out and watched his victims' death agonies through a small trap-door in the wall. This was the method, and for many years it was foolproof.

Petiot was born in Auxerre in 1897, son of a minor postal official. Apparently he showed criminal tendencies at school, stealing from classmates. He began his real criminal career by robbing letter-boxes. In 1917 he was conscripted into the army and stole drugs from a casualty clearing station and sold them at black-market prices to morphia addicts in Dijon. In some curious way Petiot managed to get himself discharged from the army with a pension and free treatment for psychoneurosis. He qualified as a doctor in 1921. There can be no doubt of his remarkable mental abilities, for he spent part of his years of study in an asylum, and part with his mother, who later declared that she never saw him study.

He practised medicine in Villeneuve, and in 1928 became mayor. While still a bachelor he employed an unusually attractive housekeeper. She became noticeably pregnant, and then disappeared. She was never seen alive again.

Petiot married and had one son. Even as mayor he seems to have retained his tendency for petty crime, and was in trouble with the police for robbing his electric light meter. He was also convicted of thefts from a municipal store, and sent to prison; this appears to be the reason that he ceased to be mayor in 1930. Nevertheless, he was well liked by his fellow-townsmen.

It was also in 1930 that one of his patients, Madame Debauve, was robbed and killed. Gossip named Petiot as her killer, but his chief accuser, whom he was treating for rheumatism, died suddenly, and the gossip ceased. Petiot signed the death certificate. Another woman, who accused him of encouraging her daughter's drug addiction – which he was supposed to be curing – also disappeared. In 1945 inquiry was made into these two deaths, but it was found that his police dossier had disappeared from Villeneuve.

In Paris he was convicted of theft of a book from a shop, but finally discharged on condition he submit to psychiatric treatment.

At the beginning of World War II he was convicted of drug

trafficking and was stated to be an addict himself; but he managed to escape with a £10 fine.

It seems probable that Petiot acquired the house in the Rue Lesueur with the express purpose of murder. A builder made certain alterations to it, completing them in September 1941; they included the triangular death room, which was window-less. A wall was increased in height to prevent neighbours from being able to see into the courtyard. The upper part of the house was not used; Petiot had a flat and small consulting-room at 66 Rue Caumartin.

A detailed list of Petiot's victims is not yet published,[1] but it seems reasonably certain that the first was a Polish furrier named Joachim Gusbinov, a neighbour of Petiot's in the Rue Caumartin. He sold his fur business and withdrew two million francs from his bank. Then, in January 1942, he called on Petiot at Rue Lesueur, and was never seen again. Another early victim was a colleague of Petiot's, Dr Paul Braunberger; there was also a whole family, the Knellers. Petiot's method seemed to be to employ four men who lounged around cafés and bars and found men and women who wanted to escape abroad. These men had no idea of the ultimate fate of Petiot's customers.

The murders continued throughout 1942, until May 1943. Then, it appeared, Petiot was arrested by the Gestapo under suspicion of helping saboteurs to escape from France. His arrest was preceded by a curious incident; the Gestapo blackmailed a Jew into calling on Petiot to inquire about escaping. The Jew disappeared, and the Germans assumed that he had taken advantage of Petiot's escape facilities. Petiot was held until December 1943, when he was released. It seems possible that the Gestapo discovered that he was part of a murder machine, and decided that he could be regarded as an ally of Germany. Petiot continued his career of murdering Jews and Frenchmen who wanted to escape.

On Saturday, March 11th, 1944, Petiot's neighbour in the Rue Lesueur, M. Jacques Marcais, was sickened by the greasy black smoke that poured from his neighbour's house, and complained to the police. Two policemen called, and found a card pinned to the door that directed inquiries to Rue Caumartin. They telephoned Petiot, who replied that he would be over immedi-ately. But in the meantime the smoke from the chimney so en-raged the police sergeant that he called the fire brigade. The

[1] At the time of writing, full details of Petiot's life and crimes are not available to the authors; it is hoped to remedy this in a future edition.

chimney was on fire. The firemen forced an entry, and found the offending stove in the cellar. They also found the remains of twenty-seven bodies lying around the cellar, most of them partly dismembered. As the police crowded through the house, Petiot entered and calmly walked around; he identified himself unhesitatingly as the owner of the house. When the police sergeant told him he would have to arrest him, Petiot took him aside and informed him that what he had discovered was the execution chamber of the French Resistance; the bodies were those of pro-Nazis and collaborators. The sergeant let him go. Petiot returned to the Rue Caumartin, packed some suitcases, and fled with his wife Georgette and 17-year-old son.[1] The police carried their investigations to Auxerre and the radio shop of Petiot's brother, where it was soon established that Petiot had spent a night on leaving Paris. Petiot's wife was also found in Auxerre, but appeared to be ignorant of her husband's grisly trade.

In June 1944 came D-day, and on August 24th Paris fell. Petiot had disappeared. The newspapers devoted a great deal of space to him, and there were many conflicting reports – of his body being recovered from two different rivers, of his being a doctor in a German concentration camp, etc. Some people believed what his wife Georgette had suggested that Petiot was working for the Resistance. But many newspapers stated their belief that he had actually been working for the Gestapo.

In October, Petiot made the mistake that led to his arrest: he wrote to the paper *Résistance* declaring that he had been 'framed' by the Gestapo, who had made his house a dumping ground for corpses while he was in prison. He stated that the Gestapo's method in making such a fuss about the murders was to distract attention from Russian victories. The writer stated that he was still an officer in the Resistance. The handwriting of the letter was checked against that of all officers who were enrolled in the Free French forces in Paris. Finally, it was found that it corresponded exactly with that of Captain Henri Valéry, serving at Reuilly; he had been a member of the Free French forces for exactly six weeks. 'Valéry' was arrested on November 2nd, 1944, as he left the Métro station at St Mandé Tourelle in the eastern outskirts of Paris. It turned out that he had been hiding in a flat in the Rue Faubourg St Denis, and had grown a beard. Because

[1] Police in France are not allowed to make forced entry into private premises during the night; this gave Petiot an extra twelve hours in which to escape.

of a habit of standing at the open window with a hairy, bare chest, he became known locally as 'Tarzan', and a complaint was made to the police! The man who had been sheltering him was a housepainter, Georges Redoute, who knew Petiot, and whom Petiot had told that his home had been destroyed in an air raid and his wife killed. In view of the immense publicity that followed, it is hard to see how Redoute continued to believe this during the seven months Petiot stayed.

Petiot was interrogated at the Quai des Orfèvres. It was discovered that he had entered the army on September 27th, and was given the task of making prisoners talk. His secretary, 25-year-old Mlle Cécile Dylma, described him as a gentle man who had some curious sadistic traits.

Petiot declared that the twenty-seven bodies found in his cellar were mostly of German soldiers. He admitted that he had killed sixty-three people, but declared he had been working for the Resistance, and had also helped many patriotic Frenchmen to escape. He named several famous Resistance leaders as his colleagues; unfortunately, they were all dead.

His trial opened after seventeen months of investigation, on March 18th, 1946, and lasted for three weeks. It took place at the Seine Assize Court. M. Pierre Duval was the Public Prosecutor, while a brilliant lawyer, René Floriot, defended. The long, sad procession of relatives of the victims threaded through the courtroom. A Resistance officer was called to prove that Petiot was completely ignorant of many matters in which he claimed inside knowledge. On the fifth day of the trial the entire court went to Rue Lesueur and looked at the murder room, and at the hole through which Petiot had inserted the periscope to watch his victims die, at the cellar on the other side of the courtyard which Petiot had filled with lime 'for whitewashing'. At 9.30 pm on April 4th, 1946, the jury of seven members and three judges retired; at midnight, they were back, with a verdict of guilty for twenty-four of the twenty-seven murders. It was a scene of some excitement, and Judge Leser could not make himself heard; when Petiot finally made out the verdict, he shouted and fought with his guards.

His appeal was rejected, and he was guillotined on the morning of May 26th, 1946. It is estimated that his profits from murder ran into six figures. (From the Kneller family alone he made £15,000.) Petiot was in every way a 'killer for profit'.

PIPER, Thomas

Twenty-six-year-old Nova Scotian, convicted in March 1876 of the murder of 5-year-old Mabel Young.

One afternoon in May 1875, soon after a Sunday School session at the Warren Avenue Baptist Church of Boston, pupil Mabel Young disappeared. Taken to the Sabbath school by an aunt, Miss Augusta Hobbs, who had that day given her niece a book of moral tales called *Apples of Gold*, the child had last been seen in the church vestibule. The alarm was given by Miss Hobbs at 4.15 pm, and the Sunday School staff and pupils began a search for the missing child. A teacher, Miss Hattie Morrison, noticed (as she stood out in the street calling the child's name) great consternation among the church belfry pigeons; they were swooping and squawking, apparently disturbed. Groaning was then heard from the belfry, and Miss Morrison informed the church librarian, Mr Walter Sawyer, who approached the bell tower to investigate. Finding the sexton unco-operative ('I've lost the tower keys'), he forced the lock with a pair of pincers and rushed up the tower stairs. On the upper deck of the belfry he found Mabel Young; although her eyes were staring and she wailed periodically, the child was unconscious. Her skull had been shattered, and she survived for only twenty-four hours; the weapon used, a bloodstained cricket bat, was found under a loose board in the belfry. But for the noisy pigeons, her body might have lain unnoticed. The sexton, Thomas Piper, was held on suspicion of murder, it then being discovered that he had a year previously been charged with the similar murder of a young girl, but released owing to lack of evidence. The keys of the belfry were found in Piper's pocket; two people said how they had noticed a man leaping the twelve feet from the lowest belfry window to the ground, presumably to avoid openly meeting the tower-bound church librarian and Miss Morrison. Piper was tried twice; he pleaded not guilty and, as the evidence against him was largely circumstantial, the first jury failed to agree. The defence counsel theorized that the child had wandered up to the belfry tower alone, and was stunned by the upper deck trap-door, which accidentally fell on top of her. Piper struck a more realistic note by remembering a group of unidentified and antagonistic small boys who had been loitering around the Sunday School that day. Found guilty at his second trial, Piper afterwards made a confession, in which he also admitted the previous killing, when 7-year-old Bridget Landregan had been battered to death with a club. Piper was hanged in May 1876, in the rotunda of the prison, with hundreds of spectators on the floor and in the galleries.

PLEIL, Rudolf

German sex murderer who committed suicide in his cell in February 1958. Pleil was a habitual criminal, a burglar among other things, who began by attacking women in order to rob them. (He always robbed his female victims as well as raping them.) Since 1945 he reckoned to have killed fifty women. He was a small, fat man with a friendly face (although he had a receding forehead which produced an ape-like effect).

Pleil, like Kürten, enjoyed murder, and referred to himself boastfully as 'der beste Totmacher' (the best death-maker). Full details of his crimes are unfortunately not available at the time of writing. Like Kürten, he used many weapons for his murders – stones, knives, hatchets, and hammers to kill and mutilate his victims. When in prison he often wrote to the authorities, offering to reveal the whereabouts of another murder; in this way he would get an 'airing' to the town where he had buried one of his victims. On one occasion, he wrote to the mayor of a town offering his services as hangman, and telling him that if he wanted to study his qualifications, he shoud look in the well at the end of the town; a strangled body was discovered in this well. Pleil was a vain man who took pleasure in the horror he aroused and described himself as 'quite a lad'. He is quoted as saying: 'Every man has his passion. Some prefer whist, I prefer killing people.'

PODOLA, Guenther Fritz Erwin
Thirty-year-old German, found guilty at the Old Bailey in September 1959 of the murder of Detective-Sergeant Raymond Purdy.

On the afternoon of July 13th, 1959, 30-year-old Mrs Verne Schiffman, an American model living in Roland Gardens, South Kensington, received a telephone call from a 'Mr Fisher', who had earlier threatened blackmail. Acting on police advice, Mrs Schiffman prolonged the conversation while the call was traced (South Kensington Underground Station, KNIghtsbridge 2355), and police sent from Chelsea Police Station to intercept the blackmailer. Two detective-sergeants, John Sandford and

Raymond Purdy, approached the call-box ('OK, lad, we are police officers') and took hold of a man, who, however, twisted free and was chased into a block of flats, 105 Onslow Square. Recaptured in the hall, the man sat on a window-ledge guarded by Purdy while Sandford tried, without success, to locate the housekeeper. Purdy momentarily turned his head in Sandford's direction and his captive shot him dead with a black automatic pistol, escaping a second later. In less than twenty-four hours (by his fingerprints on the window-ledge, his pocketbook found in Purdy's pocket, and by various contacts) the wanted assassin was identified as Guenther Podola, a German national recently expelled from Canada who had arrived in England from Düsseldorf the previous May. From the day of the killing to Thursday July 16th, Podola lived in a state of siege in Room 15 of the Claremont House Hotel, 95 Queens Gate, Kensington, half a mile away from Chelsea Police Station; the hotel did not provide food, and Podola spent his time smoking and listening to news bulletins concerning the murder on his portable radio. During the Thursday afternoon police called at the hotel and asked to see Mr Paul Camay, the name Podola was using. Receiving no response from within Room 15 to the cry, 'Police! Open this door!' and hearing a click similar to the cocking of a gun, Police-Sergeant Chambers charged the door and Podola was knocked down by the joint impact of police officer (weighing $16\frac{1}{2}$ stone) and door, landing with his head in the fireplace, although still continuing to struggle with Chambers, Inspector Vibart, and Detective Morrissey. Presently, Podola, who had somehow sustained a severe blow above his left eye, appeared to relapse into unconsciousness, reviving only to be overcome by spells of violent shivering and twitching. Podola was removed to Chelsea Police Station, and from thence to St Stephen's Hospital, Fulham, for treatment. On July 20th he was charged at West London Magistrates' Court ('his legs shaking and wobbling') with the murder of Sergeant Purdy, afterwards being taken to Brixton Remand Prison.

Podola's trial began at the Old Bailey on September 10th, and lasted eleven days. He was defended by Mr Frederick Lawton, QC, the Recorder of Cambridge, the Crown Prosecutor being Mr Maxwell Turner, Senior Treasury Counsel at the Central Criminal Court and Recorder of Hastings. Mr Lawton informed the court that Podola had lost his memory for all events in his life up to July 17th; the Crown asserted that the amnesia was feigned, and that even if it was genuine there could be no question of the prisoner being unfit to plead. The jury had to decide first on the preliminary issue of Podola's mental condition.

Dr Colin Edwards, neurologist, who had examined Podola on July 21st and September 10th, was called by the defence; the thought that Podola might be feigning had, said Dr Edwards, entered his mind – 'but I felt I had to dismiss it'. Three other doctors gave evidence for the defence, agreeing with Dr Edwards' contention. For the Crown, Dr Denis Leigh (who had examined Podola on ten occasions) gave his opinion that Podola was feigning amnesia: Dr Francis Frisby, who had first examined Podola on July 20th, also thought Podola had been malingering. Asked by Mr Lawton whether Podola had successfully deceived the four defence doctors Dr Frisby replied. 'That is true'. On September 21st the defence called yet another physician, Dr David Stafford Clark, who had not examined Podola but who had had considerable experience of amnesia cases. He sought to refute the theory that victims of amnesia necessarily lost acquired skills (Podola in the witness-box had admitted knowledge of chess, pontoon, and the French language). On September 23rd the jury retired to consider the question (as informed them by Mr Justice Edmund Davies), 'Is the defendant now suffering from a genuine loss of memory covering at least all the events with which he was concerned between July 1st, 1959, and the time of his arrest on July 16th, 1959?' After three hours the jury returned: Podola, they thought, was not suffering from genuine loss of memory. Now facing the capital charge of murder, Podola pleaded not guilty; this trial commenced on September 24th, after a new jury had been sworn. Found guilty on September 26th, Podola was refused a certificate for appeal to the House of Lords by the Attorney-General, and was subsequently hanged on November 5th, 1959.

POMMERENKE, Heinrich

Twenty-three-year-old German sex murderer, sentenced to six times life imprisonment in 1960. Pommerenke is typical of the straightforward sex maniac, driven by a violent sexual appetite and a tendency to introversion that made it difficult to satisfy. Although he boasted that he had seduced his first girl when he was 10, Pommerenke admitted that women ignored him (he was a small youth with a girlish, almost pretty face). He was born in Mecklenburg in the village of Bentwich near Rostock. At 15 he waited for girls outside the local dance hall and tried to knock them down and rape them. According to his own account, his first murder occurred after he had seen a Hollywood epic called *The Ten Commandments*, and was disgusted by the scene of women dancing around the Golden Calf. He decided that women are the root of all the world's trouble and that they ought to be taught a lesson. He murdered a woman in a park immediately after the film. Yet he declared that he never intended to kill – only to render the woman incapable of fighting back (kampfunfähig) while he raped her. When finally arrested, he was charged with ten murders with rape and twenty cases of rape, as well as with thirty-five other crimes, including burglary. One of his victims, Klimek Dagmar, aged 21, was pushed from a train; Pommerenke then jumped off the train and stabbed her to death. A week later, on June 8th, 1959, he throttled 16-year-old Rita Waltersbacher. At his trial he said he wanted to kill seven women, counting seven a lucky number. Sex films made him feel so tense inside that, 'I had to do something to a woman'. He was sentenced on October 22nd, 1960, his sentence amounting to 140 years in jail.

POOK Case, The

Victorian *cause célèbre*. On the morning of April 26th, 1871, shortly after 4 am, PC Donald Gunn discovered in Kidbrooke Lane, Eltham, the body of a 17-year-old maidservant, Jane Clouson. The girl was still alive when the constable found her, but died shortly afterwards in hospital from head injuries, caused apparently by blows from a hammer. The weapon was found near the scene of the crime. Jane Clouson was in the early stages of pregnancy.

It transpired that the girl had worked for the family of Ebenezer Pook, a Greenwich printer, until twelve days before her death, when she was dismissed for her intimacy with the younger son, Edmund, a youth of 20.

The police found bloodstains on the clothes of Edmund Pook. He had been out on the evening of the murder, and claimed he had been to Lewisham; he could produce no one to support his alibi. On the evening of her murder, Jane Clouson had told her landlady that she was going to meet Edmund; and Jane's cousin, Charlotte Trott, told the Press that Jane had told her that she intended going away with Edmund, who would eventually marry her. The Press also published the statement that witnesses would be produced who would declare that Edmund had been seen with Jane on the evening of the murder, and had been seen running away from Kidbrooke Lane covered in mud after the murder. A shopkeeper was found who identified Edmund as the man who had bought the hammer with which Jane Clouson was murdered, from him.

A Greenwich solicitor named Henry Pook – no relation of the accused – volunteered to defend him. His methods of defence were so violent and emotional that he got himself into serious trouble with the police in the course of the trial.

The evidence against Pook seemed overwhelming: the blood on his clothes and his hat, witnesses who declared they had seen him near the site of the murder, a Mrs Plane who testified that Pook had come into her shop to clean mud off his clothes late on the evening of the murder, the motive – Jane Clouson's pregnancy – purchase of the murder weapon. The defence alleged that Edmund Pook had spent the evening in Lewisham, keeping watch on the house of a girl with whom he was associating, that he suffered from epileptic fits and nose bleeding, which could account for the stains on his clothes, and that a cut on his wrist accounted for some of the bloodstains. Any amorous association with Jane Clouson was denied outright.

The trial opened on July 12th, 1871, with Mr Huddleston, QC, defending, and Sir John Coleridge prosecuting. Chief Justice Bovill summed up in Pook's favour three days later (July 15th), pointing out that most of the evidence was circumstantial, and that some of the witnesses had been demonstrably inaccurate. Pook was acquitted. But his reception in Greenwich was unfriendly, and it was evident that most people believed in his guilt.

The solicitor, Henry Pook, who had throughout the case shown a carping and violent spirit, now involved himself in court actions to finally clear the name of his client. A 'Pook Defence Fund' was started. The author of a pamphlet called *The Eltham Tragedy Reviewed* (which assumed Pook's guilt) was prosecuted. Henry Pook replied to the police charge that he used insulting and indecent language towards them with counter-charges of insulting behaviour from the police. Finally, Pook won his battle – it became dangerous to openly accuse his client of the murder. But public opinion continued to be against Edmund Pook.

The accounts of the inquest, the murder trial and the subsequent legal actions are exceptionally confusing; this enormous confusion almost certainly saved Pook from the gallows.

PRINCE, Albert

French *cause célèbre*, almost certainly suicide, although the Right Wing Press declared it was murder by freemasons to prevent exposure of Government corruption. His death was preceded by the Stavisky scandal; Stavisky was a Russian adventurer who had succeeded in making a fortune by various immense frauds, and who handled the municipal finances of Bayonne. In 1933 the precarious nature of these finances finally became obvious when Stavisky could not borrow more money to repay his creditors, and there was an attempt to arrest Stavisky near Chamonix, in France, during which Stavisky either shot himself or was shot. The newspapers declared he had been shot to avoid scandal. His friends were all influential men in the Government.

Albert Prince, the famous Councillor of the Court of Appeal, was one of those to be 'investigated' by the police, and on the day he was due to be interviewed, he went to Dijon, and was later found – in small pieces – on the railway line near Dijon, having been run over by four trains.

On the morning of February 20th, 1934, Mme Prince had received a phone call that purported to come from a Dr Ehrlinger in Dijon, saying that M. Prince's mother was dangerously ill, and asking that M. Prince should come immediately. A phone number was given, which later turned out to be false. Mme Prince thought the voice on the phone sounded very close – much closer than Dijon.

However, M. Prince went to Dijon, but once there, made no attempt to contact his mother (who was perfectly well). Instead he went to a hotel, and later went to a prostitute's room, where he merely sat on the bed. She was apparently the last person to see him alive. It seems likely that M. Prince staged his own suicide, making it look like murder to spare his relatives (good Catholics) the shame of a suicide in the family. But there are still Frenchmen who believe Prince was murdered to avert scandal.

PRITCHARD, Dr Edward William
Sentenced to death for poisoning his wife in 1865.

Pritchard was born in 1825, son of a captain in the Royal Navy. When he was 21 he was commissioned as an assistant surgeon in the Royal Navy, and served until he was 26. At Portsmouth he met a pretty Scottish girl, whom he married. She was Mary Jane Taylor, and the husband and wife moved to Hunmanby, near Filey in Yorkshire. They had five children. Pritchard soon became known as a habitual liar and boaster in Hunmanby, and his frequent amours did much to ruin his reputation as a responsible medical man. He was a freemason, and used his membership of that body for self-advertisement. In 1858 Hunmanby became too hot to hold him and he sold his practice. For a year he travelled abroad as a medical attendant to a gentleman, and then started to practise in Glasgow. Here he soon made himself as unpopular as he had been in Yorkshire. His vanity seems to have been overwhelming, like his mendacity. He would lecture on his travels, and distribute photographs of himself to anyone who showed any tendency to admiration. He even gave one to a stranger he encountered on a train. He claimed to be a friend of Garibaldi (who had never heard of him), and when he applied for the Andersonian chair of Surgery, he submitted as testimonials the names of many eminent English doctors, who had certainly never heard of him. (He did not get the appointment.) He manufactured evidence for his friendship with Garibaldi by presenting himself with a walking-stick engraved, 'from his friend General Garibaldi'.

On May 5th, 1863, his failing professional reputation was further damaged when a servant girl mysteriously died in a fire at his home at 11 Berkely Terrace, Glasgow. A verdict of death by misadventure was returned; but the girl had made no attempt to leave her bed, so it seems probable that she was unconscious when the fire started; moreover, Mrs Pritchard was absent from home that night.

Pritchard pressed a claim against a suspicious insurance company and won it.

In 1864 Pritchard moved to Sauchiehall Street, where he bought a house with money supplied by his wife's mother, Mrs Taylor. There, in the same year, his wife caught him kissing a 15-year-old servant girl, Mary M'Cleod, whom he had seduced. (She became pregnant, but allowed Pritchard to perform an abortion.)

In November 1864 Mrs Pritchard fell ill, and went to stay with her family in Edinburgh, where she got better. On returning to Glasgow, she became ill again and took to her bed, where she stayed until her death in March 1865. On December 8th Pritchard bought an ounce of Fleming's Tincture of Aconite, and made three similar purchases during the next three months.

A Dr Gairdner was summoned, and was so suspicious of her symptoms that he suggested to Mrs Taylor's son (also a doctor) that Mrs Pritchard should be removed from the house. Pritchard claimed that she was too ill to move, so Mrs Taylor, who was a healthy and powerful woman, although 70 years old, moved in to nurse her daughter. On the day of her arrival, she ate some tapioca (who was later found to contain antimony) and promptly fell ill. She finally died during the night of February 24th. A Dr Patterson who called suspected that she was under the influence of some powerful narcotic, and refused to give a death certificate, which Pritchard finally supplied himself, stating cause of death as apoplexy. On the week of March 13th Pritchard decided to finish poisoning his wife, which he did to such good effect that she finally died on the night of March 17th. But a cook and housemaid who had tasted some of the food eaten by Mrs Pritchard became ill, and there was considerable suspicion of the doctor. He certified the cause of death as gastric fever, and took the body to Edinburgh to be buried. On his return he was arrested on suspicion of murder. Someone had written an anonymous letter to the police (probably Dr Patterson, although he denied it). The bodies of Mrs Taylor and Mrs Pritchard were examined and both found to contain antimony and aconite. (Pritchard had declared that Mrs Taylor's death may have been caused by an overdose of a medicine containing opium.)

The trial opened at the High Court of Justiciary, Edinburgh, in July 1865, before the Lord Justice Clerk (Right Hon John Inglis). Prosecuting were Lord Ardmillan and Lord Jerviswoode, the Solicitor-General Mr Gifford, and Mr Crichton. Defending were Mr Rutherford Clerk, Mr Watson, and Mr Brand. It was noted that the organs of both victims were impregnated with antimony, although there was no trace of it in the stomachs, pointing to poisoning over a period. During the trial, Dr Patterson showed himself extremely hostile to the prisoner. The defence tried to blame Mary M'Cleod for the poisoning, a suggestion which the judge dismissed in his summing-up. The jury found Pritchard guilty after an hour's deliberation. In prison he applied himself to his devotions, and confessed to the murders, attempting, in one confession, to implicate Mary M'Cleod, although he later admitted that he alone was responsible for the murders.

His execution in Jail Square, near Hutcheson Bridge, was attended by a record crowd of 100,000.

The motive of the murders is obscure, although Pritchard

must surely have been a man who felt the ground slipping away from underneath him as his lies and attempts to gain admirers brought only dislike and pity, and might have decided that he needed to make a completely fresh start. He was certainly slightly insane, and his hypocrisy sometimes savours of total self-delusion; for example, when his wife's death was announced, he cried: 'Come back, my dear Mary Jane. Don't leave your dear Edward.' When the coffin was about to be taken to the station, Pritchard kissed his wife's lips repeatedly, muttering words of love.

R

RAIS, Gilles de (or Retz)

Gilles de Rais, Marshal of France who fought beside Joan of Arc, was charged with witchcraft, and with the sadistic murder of many children. There are some modern commentators who believe that the whole affair was trumped up by the Church, who wanted possession of his lands.

Rais was born in 1404, and in 1420 he married a wealthy heiress, Catherine de Thouars, and so became one of the richest men in Europe. He was known as Blue-beard because of his glossy blue-black beard, and played an honourable part in the fight against the English. After the coronation of Charles VII he retired to his estates at Machecoul, Malemort, La Suze, Champtocé, and Tiffauges. He lived with immense extravagance, a bodyguard of two hundred knights, a private chapel, and one of the finest manuscript libraries in Europe. Soon his large expenditures led him to sell land, and his heirs obtained an injunction from King Charles to prevent him selling more. This order was ignored in Brittany, where Bishop Malestroit and Duke John V were eager to acquire his lands. Rais turned to alchemy to mend his fortunes, seeking the philosopher's stone that would turn all base metals to gold. Gilles de Sillé, a priest, conducted more-or-less scientific researches into the problem; when he failed, Rais became a prey to a series of charlatans, ending, in 1439, with a defrocked priest, Francesco Prelati of Florence. It was probably Prelati who turned Gilles from the scientific pursuit of the philosopher's stone to black magic and invocation of the Devil, using the blood of young children. Gilles (if he was guilty) probably discovered that he enjoyed inflicting pain on children.

Gilles' downfall began with a minor misdemeanour. He sold

Malemort to the Treasurer of Brittany, Geoffroi le Ferron, and refused admission to Geoffroi's brother, Jean le Ferron, whom he beat and imprisoned. Jean le Ferron was a priest, and Bishop Malestroit seized on this pretext to try to have Gilles declared a heretic. (This would mean that Gilles' lands would go to the Bishop.) He was tried on September 28th, 1440, and his accusers were so certain of finding him guilty that some of his lands were actually disposed of before the trial began. He was charged with his abuse of a priest, with conjuring demons, and with sexual perversion involving children. Gilles laughed at these charges and declared them too silly to deny. One of the charges declared that 'spurning the natural way of copulation', Gilles had committed sodomy with young boys and girls, and his victims were sometimes alive, sometimes dead, and sometimes even in their death throes when these perversions were committed.

After preliminary hearings beginning on September 28th, the formal trial opened on October 15th, 1440. It was alleged that dismembered bodies of about fifty children were found in a tower at Machecoul. Rais was tortured on October 19th, as were his servants and four alleged accomplices. One servant declared that Gilles rubbed his sexual member against the thighs or bellies of children, and, having experienced a discharge, then took pleasure in seeing their heads cut off or in doing this himself. It was alleged that he took great pleasure in watching the death throes of children, sometimes sitting on their chests while they were dying, and on one occasion, torturing and killing one child in front of his brother before doing the same to the other child.

Torture had less effect on Gilles than the threat of excommunication; but this latter threat made him break down completely and 'confess everything'. On October 26th, 1440, he was strangled (and his body partly burned) together with two of his associates. He begged the parents of the murdered children for forgiveness, and all sobbed with him. The Church seized his lands and property.

RANSOM, Mrs Florence Iris Ouida
An attractive red-headed woman who, in July 1940, murdered her lover's wife, daughter, and their maid.

The lover, Lawrence Fisher, had been on distant terms with his wife for some years. They had lived in Twickenham with two daughters and had become estranged; they had both taken lovers who had visited the house; Fisher's mistress was Mrs Ransom. Later, Fisher had moved to a farm at Piddington, Oxfordshire, taking Mrs Ransom, who had installed her mother as housekeeper and her brother Fred as cow-man. (Fisher was unaware of the relationship.) Mrs Dorothy Fisher and her 19-year-old daughter Freda moved to a cottage at Matfield, near Tonbridge, where a maid, Charlotte Saunders (aged 48), looked after them.

On July 9th, 1940, Mrs Ransom took her brother's shotgun (which he had taught her to use) and went to Matfield. She carried the shotgun wrapped in brown paper. There, she in some way induced the wife and daughter to go with her into the orchard, and shot them both down; she fired more shots into them as they lay dying. The maid hurried out, and was also shot. Mrs Ransom then journeyed back to Bicester; she did not notice that she had dropped one of her white leather gloves in the orchard.

Chief Inspector Peter Beveridge of the CID was in charge of the case, and soon found many witnesses who had seen Mrs Ransom near Matfield on July 9th. Mrs Ransom was duly arrested and tried for the triple murder; she strenuously denied it, and denied even that the housekeeper and cow-man were related to her. She was sentenced to death, but reprieved and sent to Broadmoor (although insanity had been no part of her defence).

RATTENBURY, Alma
Tried at the Old Bailey in 1935, with her lover, George Percy Stoner, for the murder of her husband.

The Rattenburys had come to England from Canada in 1928. They bought a house at Manor Road, Bournemouth, named Villa Madeira, and lived amicably together. Francis Rattenbury, who at 63 was twenty-five years his wife's senior, lived in semi-retirement from his profession as an architect. His attractive wife (who at one time had written song lyrics for a living) tended the house and garden and her two sons, one from a previous marriage and one born of the present union in 1929; she tended her husband with loving kindness and humoured his moods which were frequently influenced by vast intakes of whisky. Mrs Rattenbury's life would have bored many less sensitive and artistic women into taking a lover, although her behaviour has

since been excused by many as the result of nymphomania, itself
a symptom of incipient tuberculosis. Mrs Rattenbury employed
a companion-help, Miss Irene Riggs, whose devotion to her
mistress was almost as great as her devotion to Roman Catholicism and who, commendably, was to remain devoted throughout
a period when her religious code of ethics must have been sorely
tried by happenings at Villa Madeira. In September 1934, Alma
Rattenbury advertised in the local paper for 'a daily willing lad,
14–18, for housework'. This brought George Stoner into the
household; at 19 he was a year ahead of the specified age-limit, a
bulky, unprepossessing youth ('always weak at school', said his
father) who soon shared Irene Riggs' devotion for Mrs Rattenbury. Nor was this unreciprocated; Stoner eventually 'boarded
in' at Villa Madeira, but long before this he and Alma Rattenbury were lovers, enjoying a relationship which, however wrong
morally, seems to have sprung from a genuine and loyal affection
between the two, despite the fact that Mrs Rattenbury was twice
the age of Stoner. It is generally supposed (and alleged by his
wife) that Mr Rattenbury was 'un mari complaisant', and that,
providing he was well supplied with alcohol, he remained reasonably content. Once, under the pretext of going to Town for a
surgical operation, Mrs Rattenbury took Stoner up to London
where they stayed from March 19th to 22nd, 1935, at the Kensington Palace Hotel (Mr Justice Humphreys was afterwards to
hint darkly at the 'orgies' performed within these august precincts on that occasion), Mrs Rattenbury spending money at
Harrods on new clothes for the young man, evidently deriving
much pleasure from being a female counterpart of Professor
Henry Higgins. Not surprisingly, Stoner's was an extreme
passion, and when, upon returning to Bournemouth after this
Kensington idyll, he learned that Alma Rattenbury was to take
her husband over to see a friend at Bridport the following day,
Monday, March 25th, and that she would be obliged to share,
for once, the connubial bed, Stoner's jealous fury was unbridled.
On the Sunday evening he savagely attacked Francis Rattenbury about the head with a mallet as the older man lay resting
on his bed; it would seem to have been a premeditated attack as
Stoner had borrowed the mallet from his grandmother a few
hours before. Dr O'Donnel, the Rattenbury's doctor, summoned on the phone by Irene Riggs ('Mr Rattenbury has been
injured') in his turn summoned the police, who were greeted by
Mrs Rattenbury in a state of drunken hysteria insisting that
she had killed her husband who, she maintained, had lived too

long. The scene was a macabre one: blood splashings, the radio-gram on full blast, Mrs Rattenbury wildly confessing and kissing policemen, laughing and crying alternately and once – when she trod on her husband's dental plate that had somehow landed on the carpet – screaming with horror. She was given sedatives, but on the following morning again asserted that she had been responsible for the attack on Mr Rattenbury, who now lay critically ill in nearby Strathallan Nursing Home. Upon being escorted by police out of the house she passed by Stoner and Irene Riggs, when Stoner made the observation, 'You have got yourself into this mess through talking too much.' Mrs Ratten-bury was in Holloway when her husband died from his injuries on March 28th; on this day Stoner admitted to the killing, say-ing, 'Do you know Mrs Rattenbury had nothing to do with this? When I did the job, I believed he was asleep. I hit him and then came upstairs and told Mrs Rattenbury.'

Alma Rattenbury and George Stoner faced a joint trial on a charge of murdering Francis Rattenbury; the proceedings took place at the Old Bailey, May 27th–31st, 1935 (local feeling being a deterrent to holding the trial at Winchester Assizes), and were presided over by Mr Justice Humphreys. Mr R. P. Croom-Johnson appeared for the Crown, Mr T. J. O'Connor was counsel for Mrs Rattenbury, and Mr J. D. Casswell for Stoner. The prosecution sought to prove that the murder was the result of a plot between the two accused, but the jury found Mrs Rattenbury not guilty and she was discharged; the verdict on George Stoner was a foregone conclusion, and he was con-demned to death, a sentence afterwards commuted to life imprisonment. Mrs Rattenbury never knew of her lover's final fate; three days after her acquittal she fatally stabbed herself six times, dying at the side of a stream in Christchurch, near Bournemouth.

RAVEN, Daniel

An apparently motiveless murder of 1949. Daniel Raven, a Jew aged 23, was a successful advertising agent living at Edgware-bury Lane, Edgware, Middlesex; on October 6th his wife gave birth to their first child, a son. On October 10th his wealthy parents-in-law Mr and Mrs Leopold Goodman joined him during visiting hour at the Muswell Hill maternity home, leaving the building at 8.55 pm (shortly before Daniel Raven) and arriving home at Ashcombe Gardens, Edgware (only

500 yards from their daughter's home), presumably about 9.30 pm. At 10 pm a relative, Mr Frederick Fraiman, visited the Goodmans' house, rang the doorbell and got no reply; curious enough to clamber through a window to investigate (the Goodmans were evidently no gadabouts) he found the bodies of Mr and Mrs Goodman in the blood-streaked dining-room. Seven savage blows had been inflicted on Mrs Goodman's head, twice as many on her husband's. (Later it was found that the weapon was a television aerial base.) Police were summoned, and investigations commenced under Detective Inspector J. Diller. There were no signs of robbery (nor any signs of a 'break-in'), indeed piles of paper money lay everywhere (including that cache under the mattress, beloved to householders and so familiar to the housebreaker) which made Diller suspect a motive other than theft. He instinctively mistrusted Daniel Raven who, when called to his in-laws' house, sat shaking on the stairs crying: 'Why did they tell me to go? Why didn't they let me stop?' Raven maintained he had brought the old couple back from the nursing home, and that they had insisted on his returning home, despite the fact that they had recently had burglars. A police officer, previously dispatched by Diller on an information canvass of other Goodman relatives, now returned with the news that earlier in the evening Daniel Raven had worn a dark suit, not the pale grey suiting worn by the crouching figure on the stairs; moreover, Diller noted, Raven's shirt looked fresh, as if newly put on. Accompanying detectives to Edgware Police Station, Raven, when requested, reluctantly handed over his house keys, proffering the information that he had just had a bath. Diller, entering Raven's house, was aware of great heat; with presence of mind he swiftly retrieved from a roaring boiler the partially burnt remains of a dark-coloured suit which, when analysed, was found to be saturated with blood belonging to the Goodmans' blood group. A pair of Raven's shoes, newly washed and discovered hidden in the garage, also showed signs of blood from this group; even the upholstery in Daniel Raven's car was smeared with blood. Raven admitted ownership of the dark suit ('how the blood got on it I don't know') which, he asserted, he had left discarded on the bathroom floor an hour or so before; no traces, however, of a recent bath were found.

Charged with the murder of Leopold Goodman, Daniel Raven protested his innocence, declaring that his father-in-law had made many enemies by indulging in illegal business transactions. An interesting note is that while awaiting his trial

(February 1950) at Brixton Prison, Raven became very friendly with another prisoner also waiting trial on a murder charge, Brian Donald Hume, who later was to achieve so much notoriety as a double murderer. No plea of insanity was put forward at Raven's trial, the defence contending that the murder had been committed by some other person. Found guilty, Raven was subsequently hanged.

READ, James Canham
Sentenced to death in 1894 for the murder of his mistress, Florence Dennis.

Read was a book-keeper at the Royal Albert Docks, with a wife and seven children and an income of £156 a year. He lived in Jamaica Road, Stepney. He was an attractive man, and found his respectable life boring, so he enlivened it by having love affairs. In about 1889 he met a Mrs Ayriss, with whom he had a liaison. They made contact by writing to post offices. Then, one day in 1892, he met Mrs Ayriss walking with her 18-year-old sister, Florence Dennis. The two were instantly attracted. Read finished his liaison with Mrs Ayriss and concentrated his attention on her sister, who soon became his mistress. Florence Dennis was not his only complication at this time; he had installed another mistress in a cottage in Mitcham, where he visited her at week-ends; she thought he was a commercial traveller.

In June 1894, Florence discovered she was pregnant, and had to tell her parents about the affair with Read. She wrote him a brief note on June 19th, 1894, and the coldness of its wording indicates that the strain of becoming a mother had made her feel less affectionate towards Read; it begins, 'Dear Sir', and simply asks him what arrangements he intends to make. She had gone to stay with her sister at Southend. Read delayed her for a few weeks, and then finally asked her to meet him near Prittlewell (a village in the Southend area). She left home on a Sunday evening in late June, and was never seen alive again. But Read was seen with her in the Prittlewell area, and later was seen there alone by an old lady who later identified him.

Mrs Ayriss was worried by her sister's absence and sent Read a telegram asking where she was. Read sent a feeble reply stating that he had not seen 'the young person' for eighteen months. But he felt discovery drawing near, and stole some money from his firm to make his escape. He hastened to his mistress in Rose Cottage, Mitcham.

Florence Dennis' body had been found by a farm boy, and Mrs Ayriss' inquiries soon put the police on Read's trail. Read's mistress accompanied him into Croydon, where he bought a light suit of clothes. He then stayed in the cottage, wearing only his new suit, and growing a beard. The police searched unsuccessfully at his Jamaica Road home for the revolver that killed Florence Dennis and for any clue to Read's whereabouts. But Read finally gave himself away, with the usual carelessness of murderers; a letter card he sent to his brother finally led the police to him at Mitcham.

He was tried at Chelmsford Assizes in November, with Mr Frank Lockwood, QC, prosecuting, and Mr Cock, QC, defending; the trial took place before Baron Pollock. The inquest on the dead girl had already returned a verdict of murder against him.

The evidence was damning – mainly of intrigue, posting letters to strange post offices and clandestine meetings. Read's family admitted that he had a revolver of the type used in the murder, although the weapon was not found. Read was sentenced to death and hanged.

RENCZI, Vera[1]

Twentieth-century Rumanian murderess who murdered her two husbands, her son, and thirty-two lovers, and kept their bodies in zinc coffins in the basement. She could not bear to think of the lovers going to other women.

Vera Renczi was born in Bucharest of rich parents. When she was 10, the family went to live in Berkerekul. Vera already showed signs of nymphomania and intense possessiveness towards her lovers, as well as a violent and imperious temper. When she was 15 she was discovered at midnight in the dormitory of a boys' school. She eloped several times with lovers, but always returned home when she grew tired of them. Then she fell in love with a wealthy business man, many years her senior, and married him. They had a baby son. Then, one day, Vera announced that her husband had deserted her without warning. For a year she lived quietly, then suddenly began to frequent night cafés. Finally, she declared that she had heard

[1] It is to be regretted that the editors have been unable to obtain any dates relating to this case; they hope to remedy this in a future edition. The present account has been condensed from Bernard O'Donnell's book *The World's Worst Women*.

that her husband had been killed in a car accident, and married again, this time a handsome young man. Her new husband was unfaithful, and four months after her marriage, he also went 'on a long journey'. A year later, she announced that he had written to say he was leaving her for ever.

Her lovers continued to come and go with regularity, but the last – the thirty-second – was missed by his young wife, and the police searched Vera's house, and discovered the thirty-five zinc coffins in the basement, including that of her son. (Like Jeanne Weber, she had acquired a taste for killing, and was unable to stop.) She admitted poisoning her lovers with arsenic, sometimes over a 'last supper'. Her son, she said, had threatened to expose her. She used to sit among her coffins in an armchair in the evenings.

She died in prison, after being given a life sentence.

ROBINSON, Henrietta (The 'Veiled Murderess')
Twenty-six-year-old supposed descendant of King George III, found guilty of the murders of Timothy Lanagan and Catherine Lubee.

Mrs Robinson, in 1853 a resident of Troy, New York, lived across the road from Irish grocer Lanagan, his wife, and sister-in-law Catherine; she was an erratic customer, her attendance at the Lanagan grocery governed by her temper. (Once Mrs Lanagan had been obliged to eject pistol-wielding Mrs Robinson from a Lanagan social evening when that lady took exception to a remark from a gentleman guest.) At 6 am one morning in May 1853, after a period of strained relationship, Mrs Robinson called at the Lanagan shop and purchased 'a quart of strong beer and a pound of soda crackers'. At 8 am Mrs Robinson's gardener called with the request of a loan to Mrs Robinson of two dollars; apparently there was some delay in the transaction, for Mrs Robinson soon followed her gardener, complaining that she was being forced to wait. At 1 pm Mrs Robinson called again on the Lanagans, and was invited to lunch; she insisted on treating the family to beer, to which she added (as an 'improvement') powdered sugar. Mr Lanagan and Catherine Lubee partook of the brew, two hours later being stricken with violent vomiting and diarrhoea; they both died in agony the next day. Arsenic was found in their bodies, and also under a carpet in Mrs Robinson's house. Arrested on the murder charge, she unsuccessfully feigned insanity in court, although in addressing her counsel after his plea she is said to have remarked: 'An able speech, Mr Townsend, but you might have said all that was necessary in fifteen minutes. The idea of my insanity is absurd.' The prisoner invariably appeared at her trial with blue veiling swathed around her face, which earned her the epithet the 'Veiled Murderess'. The jury found her guilty as charged, and Henrietta Robinson was sentenced to death; the sentence was commuted to one of life imprisonment and Mrs Robinson was sent to Sing Sing. In 1874 she was transferred to the Matteawan State Asylum, where she died in 1905.

ROBINSON, John (The Trunk Murderer)

At midday on Friday, May 6th, 1927, a man deposited a large trunk at Charing Cross Station. By the following Monday it smelt so oddly that it was opened. Inside were several paper parcels, the first of which proved to contain a woman's head. Some clothing found in the trunk bore a laundry mark, and through this the dead woman was identified as Mrs Minni Bonati, the estranged wife of an Italian waiter who had been leading a loose existence in the West End for some time.

For many weeks the police were baffled, although the man who sold the trunk came forward and described his customer as a well-dressed and well-spoken man who looked as if he might have served in India. The clue that led to this man being traced was a glass-cloth that had obviously been removed from a snack bar or restaurant. This was finally traced to a refreshment room near Rochester Row, and a barmaid told the police of a regular customer who had ceased to come in since the time of the murder – a man named John Robinson who had an estate office in Rochester Row opposite the police station. Robinson was finally located (he had left the office) at the Elephant and Castle. At first he denied all knowledge of the murder, but later decided to confess. He claimed that Mrs Bonati had accosted him and gone up to his office with him, where she had become abusive and demanded money; he had hit her and she had fallen and knocked her head on a chair, killing herself. Robinson had then panicked and decided to dismember the body and conceal it in the trunk. He did this the next day.

He was tried at the Old Bailey and found guilty; he was executed on August 27th, 1927 at Pentonville. The crime appears to be motiveless; but it was undoubtedly his dismemberment of the body which – as in Norman Thorne's case – led to the death sentence.

ROBSART, Amy

Married at the Court of Edward VI, June 4th, 1550, to Robert Dudley, future Earl of Leicester, she being then 18 years old, he one year older. (The adolescent king wrote in his diary: 'Sir Robert Dudley, third son to the Earl of Warwick, married today Sir John Robsart's daughter, after which marriage there were certain gentlemen that did strive who could first take away a goose's head which was hung alive between two great posts.') Eight years later (November 17th, 1558) Queen Elizabeth I came to the throne; she was to show great interest in handsome Robert Dudley, making him Master of the Horse and a Knight of the Garter. One Spanish envoy to the Court, Quadra, wrote in a letter: 'Lord Robert is the worst young fellow I have ever encountered. He is heartless, spiritless, treacherous, and violent. Every day he presumes more and more, and it is now said that he means to divorce his wife.' (One Anne Dowe of Brentford was tried and sent to prison for saying that Queen Elizabeth had had a child by Lord Robert Dudley.) In 1560 the Dudleys moved to Cumnor Place, a country house in Oxfordshire. On September 4th the Queen told a foreign envoy that Lady Dudley was dying, although it was afterwards learnt that she was in excellent health. On September 8th Amy Robsart was found dead, her skull fractured, at the foot of the great staircase at Cumnor Place; it was at first assumed that she had accidentally slipped, but later the rumours grew that she had been murdered. Robert Dudley had been at Court at the time of his wife's death, but many believe that Anthony Forster, Dudley's Comptroller of the Household at Cumnor, together with Mrs Oddingsells, Forster's mistress, had connived at Dudley's instigation to murder Amy Robsart. Appleyard, Dudley's brother-in-law, said years afterwards that at the inquest he had 'covered her death for Leicester's sake'. (After the inquest and throughout his life, Appleyard was loaded with favours by both Leicester and Queen Elizabeth.) Contrary to expectation by some, Robert Dudley, although undoubtedly Elizabeth's lover, never became Prince Consort. In 1584 a Jesuit priest, Father Parsons, wrote a book called *Leicester Commonwealth*, an indictment of Leicester's doings: on the title page was a text from Job – 'The Heavens shall reveal his inquity, and the earth shall rise up against him',

535

and in the book Leicester was described as 'full of hypocrisy, treachery, cowardice and whatnot', and reference was made to his complicity in the killing of his wife years before.

Sir Walter Scott romanticized the event in his book *Kenilworth*; an opera has been written around Amy Robsart's story, and in many countries she is considered a tragic, ill-used heroine.

ROHDE, Dr Werner, and the Natzweiler Trial

When confronted by the sheer magnitude of the murders and atrocities committed at such camps at Auschwitz, Belsen, and Majdanek the imagination grows bewildered, as though floundering out of its depth in some quite strange land. It continually asks the question, 'Did this *really* happen?' In this 'really' is manifested the struggle of consciousness to relate itself to a quite new realm of human possibility, which at first takes on the aspect of a waking dream. Similarly, when the first news of the gassings reached the outside world it was simply not believed. Hannah Arendt asserts that the men responsible staked on this very fact, that ordinary people simply cannot believe what is possible for man.

As the counterpart of the imagination's dilemma, those who survived all feel profoundly that no words have or are yet capable of describing their essential experience. David Rousset insists that there is an *unbridgeable* gap separating those who went through the camps from the rest of humanity. The Natzweiler trial is important because its scale is 'normal' enough for the mind to be able to focus sharply, and at very close quarters on the Nazi way without completely losing its grip. The exact details of the incident concerned can never be known because the nine accused lied, evaded, distorted, and covered up for each other in the attempt to save themselves, but the basic facts are certain enough.

Among the 300 concentration camps of Nazi Europe, Natzweiler, with its 3,000 men, was the group HQ of 20 sub-camps. The whole group held 28,000 prisoners of whom eventually 6,000 died from ill-treatment. Even before the murders charged at the trial, 90 Jews had been gassed together under the authority of Josef Kramer, in order to provide material for Professor Hirt's Anatomy Department at Strasbourg University. Even after it, 150 Frenchmen were executed on the night of September 2nd, 1944. At the time of the murders charged it was under the command of Hartjenstein, who had come from Auschwitz to be interchanged with Josef Kramer.

On the afternoon of July 6th, 1944, two officials of the Karlsruhe Gestapo handed over four women to camp commandant Hartjenstein for execution. Three of the women – Denise Borrell, Vera Leigh, and Diana Rowden – were English members of the Special Operations Executive, parachuted into France in order to help the Resistance and carry on underground warfare against the Germans. They had all been denounced in 1943, arrested as political prisoners and sent to Karlsruhe Jail. This was a prison for civilian women and they were detained there in 'protective custody'. The Berlin Gestapo ordered the Karlsruhe Gestapo to arrange for an execution in a convenient concentration camp, which they did, knowing full well that the four women concerned were neither under sentence of death nor had they been legally proceeded against.

Normally, orders for the executions of 'regular inhabitants' were sent from Berlin via the camp Political Department to the Adjutant's office. The whims of these minions of death were conveyed by secret teleprinter with the specifications as to hanging or shooting. Normally, after an execution a report was sent to the next of kin that the internee had been shot while trying to escape. Sometimes a prisoner would enter accompanied by a special note, 'I have asked through the RSHA (i.e. Berlin HQ) for "special treatment" for X'. But in this instance no note and no orders were ever received. In fact, the Political Department were specifically instructed that no files were to be made for these women.

One or two prisoners had seen the women arriving 'looking pale and tired', and during the course of the afternoon had even managed to make contact with them for a few minutes. Rumours quickly spread round the camp that they were to be executed that evening. When camp officials ordered all prisoners to be in their huts by 8 pm and not dare show their faces near the blacked-out windows, it was clear that something sinister was happening.

Amid the solemn panoply of the Nazi death gang the murder ritual was carried out. In the darkness there assembled and walked towards the crematorium those always present on such occasions, which took place three times a week. SS Dr Rohde, the new camp doctor, with SS Dr Plaza, the old doctor who was still his superior; Hartjenstein, the Commandant; Wochner, head of the Political Department; Meier, chief of the guards; Berg, the crematorium stoker; and Straub, the executioner and crematorium chief. Without any explanation the women were brought from the camp prison where they had been waiting, into the crematorium. On the left was Straub's office, then the chamber where the baskets of ashes were kept, then a room with eight beds, the dissecting room, the doctor's office, the lavatories, the morgue, and, of course, the execution chamber, with its four large ceiling hooks next to the oven.

On this occasion Berg, the stoker, a habitual criminal with twenty-two sentences, who had spent the entire years from 1932 onwards in prison camps and concentration camps, received unusual orders from his chief, Straub. This man, he testified, told him at six o'clock 'to have the oven heated to its maximum by nine-thirty and then to disappear. He told me also that the doctor was going to come down and give some injections.' At nine-thirty Straub and Dr Rohde came in and chased him out of the furnace room. He returned to his own room, pretending to be asleep, though he managed with others to observe what was happening.

Meanwhile, medical orderly Bruttel had been phoned by Dr Plaza to bring phenol and a syringe to the crematorium. He 'got the impression that the doctors did not wish to carry the necessary instruments themselves to the place of execution and that they felt that they would gain more courage and confidence by the presence of quite a number of people for an act which was evidently highly distasteful to them'.

Dr Plaza and Otto, the acting adjutant, had gone to Dr Rohde. They told him that four French spies were to be hanged and suggested a painless killing by injection. In court he stated that he refused. 'I was astonished that this task was to be given to me – because as a physician I had the task of saving life.' An hour later they asked him again and he refused. 'Otto ordered me to do it and explained that this was a military duty.' Plaza, who was also his superior, added, 'We have to do this'. Rohde continued, 'I was annoyed that this task had been put on to me as a doctor, and yet on the other hand as a subordinate I had to obey the order given me by my superiors. My only solace was that I could save these women from being hanged, and this was the most humane way – to put them to sleep in a painless fashion. . . . According to German military law a subordinate is not allowed to countermand or question orders given by a superior or to avoid carrying out the order.' Dr Plaza filled the syringe and Dr Rohde gave the first injection. However, he was so 'upset', 'nervous', and 'shaky' that Dr Plaza had to give the three other injections himself.

He emphasized, 'I could only think I was doing a humane kindness and helping as a medical man. For me it was the heaviest task I ever had to do in my life and it needed my maximum strength of mind. . . . I could not withdraw from this business. . . . Orders were given by superiors and had to be followed, otherwise one would have brought oneself, and perhaps one's family, into great danger, because at that time there was already in force the law of punishment of families.' In the morgue, 'three of the women were already undressed and the fourth woman was being undressed by an SS corporal. . . . As apparently rigor mortis had already set in he was unable to take off the pullover which the woman was wearing, so he had tried to tear it open. I then yelled at him and told him that the bodies would have to be undressed in a decent manner.' When challenged on his concern with 'humane kindness' as to whether he had ensured that the dose was a fatal one, he evaded the issue; 'I did not think much about it. I tried to dismiss this incident from my mind as quickly as I could. I never talked to anybody after this incident happened.' In spite of his personal friendship with the Commandant as his family doctor, he never protested to him about being compelled to do this work unwillingly because, 'I had no right to — I was not yet in office.'

Lieutenant-Commander O'Leary described how he had seen 'flames coming out of the chimney of the crematorium', and how Berg explained next morning to him, 'that each time the door of the oven was opened the flames came out of the chimney and that meant a body had been put in the crematorium'.[1] Schultz of the Political Department was told by Straub how, 'The women were told to undress in front of the doctor. They refused. Then it was said that they were going to be inoculated and they asked why, and then it was said that it was against typhus and then they laid bare their arms and were inoculated.' Straub also showed him scratches on his face, 'There, you can see how she scratched me – look how she defended herself'. Bruttel, the medical orderly, managed to stop outside in the passage while it was all being done, 'because I did not want to

---

[1] Marcel Rausch, a prisoner, heard screams between nine and ten. 'I now suppose that the women, still unconscious from the injection but alive when put in the oven, must have recovered consciousness and screamed.'

have anything to do with it, and it was clear to me that nobody could ask me to do such a thing seeing that I was a First Aid man'. But the next day he asked Dr Plaza, 'in a humble way as I was his subordinate, how he could ask us First Aid men to be present at such a thing', and he replied, 'I would rather have too many than one too few'.

The evasive attitude of all the accused came out most clearly in the attempt to prove that Straub was not only camp cremator but also camp executioner. He himself, who had done a lot of cremating at Auschwitz, told how he received extra sausage and drink for his work but completely denied executing anybody. His frightened underling Berg, whose original deposition had testified to his once having cremated eighty women simultaneously, told of him like this:

Q. Who was the executioner?
A. I have got to get this clear.
Q. Was there an executioner or not?
A. Yes there was an executioner.
Q. Well, who was it?
A. A prisoner was detailed to do the job, but Straub was responsible as far as the crematorium was concerned.
Q. Who actually carried out the hanging – was it you or Straub?
A. It was not me.
Q. Was it Straub?
A. Yes, it was Straub.

Meier, the guard commander, answered like this:

Q. For all executions who was in charge – who was the official camp executioner?
A. That I do not know. I once watched a public execution through hanging and Kramer was in charge.
Q. Who actually prepared the noose and the drop?
A. As far as I know, at this execution the prisoners erected the gallows.
Q. Where was Straub?
A. Straub was also present.
Q. Was not Straub in charge of all executions?
A. I cannot say how much he would have been responsible for in this respect.

The defence put forward the decisive question as being: Was the order to kill these women *unlawful*? Respecting which, 'the

British Manual of Military Law says that a soldier is not obliged to examine *carefully* as to whether an order is lawful or not. . . . In German law . . . the soldier . . . has to be *quite positive* that it was unlawful.' The unlawfulness of the order would depend on whether a trial had been carried out and it was up to the prosecution to prove to the contrary. In war it was not uncommon for sentences to be passed without the presence of the accused. The Geneva Convention nowhere explains how a sentence should be passed in such an instance, and in this respect, 'We all know that the Nazi régime went its own peculiar way'. Nor does International Law denote the manner of execution. The court should consider 'if the manner in which the ordered execution was carried out was humane'.

Six of the accused claimed that they were not even present at the murders. In his deposition, Hartjenstein, the Commandant, denied absolutely any knowledge of the whole affair, adding that he could give no explanation for such ignorance, except that 'it may have been deliberately kept from me by my staff'. Wochner stated, 'I was very much against all brutal actions. . . . I just got to know that the execution had taken place.' Orderly Bruttel declared, 'As a soldier I had to carry out orders given me by my superior officer, but I must admit that I was not entirely for blind obedience. As a medical orderly I have never done anything contrary to the honour of the Red Cross.' Straub declared that 'he had never harmed anyone in the camp . . . and that finally he knew that God would protect the innocent'.

In final pleas the defence spoke of Straub as 'a good and orderly man'; of Wochner as having a 'clean record' and a 'clean life'; of Hartjenstein as 'generally popular and that he had a good education'; of Berg for whom 'non-compliance with an order given by an SS man would be punished with death'; of Bruttel, 'he took no part in other executions . . . he showed human sympathies'; of Dr Rohde as acting 'without reasoning . . . through serious illness . . . he was certainly not an Anti-Christ'. About whom Professor Verse said, 'He was a good student in the best meaning of the word', and Professor Paulsen said, 'He was a human being, a doctor and a soldier'.

Understanding of Dr Rohde's evidence must be helped by the knowledge that he and Straub too 'had also been at Auschwitz where they had been responsible for countless atrocities'. What in fact his real attitude was at the moment of administering the phenol can never be known. It may have been pleasure, the indifference of habit, or the assumption that the victim was not really human, so common to the Nazi master-race exponents. However, the implications of the *defence on which he relied* are clear enough and they point to a man who was certainly aware of moral issues and who was by no means totally devoid of a moral consciousness. The consciousness, that is, which normally presents itself when the cold-blooded killing of another defenceless, unknown human being is contemplated. Indeed, the secrecy surrounding the murders, including the confinement order for the camp which had never been given till then, and the suicide of adjutant Ganninger a few days before the trial opened, points to the awareness of moral issues by others concerned as well. It contrasts with the actions of the Japanese Kempei Tai, who tortured people to death quite openly and unceremoniously in the middle of Singapore so that their screams were heard day and night for streets around.

As Rohde was concerned in 'countless atrocities' at Auschwitz, he belonged to that group of Nazi doctors like Mengele and Klein and dozens of others who headed the gas chamber selections and carried out the dreadful 'medical' experiments. When *these* deeds were performed there can in essence be no question of a moral conflict or a moral consciousness. These men were then acting neither as doctors nor soldiers, but as creatures possessed by an *amoral* madness, which saw one part of mankind as brutal all-powerful masters and the rest as *Dreck*, lower than animals. As with Rohde, these men spanned the scale from a certain moral consciousness to amorality. They had faithfully followed their master, who had made it his declared aim to rid men 'of a chimera called conscience and morality and from the demands of a freedom and personal independence which only a very few can bear'.

The defence that Rohde relied on was that his duties as a soldier were higher than, and came before, his duties as a doctor. Which means, in fact, that his duties to, and fear of, the group (i.e. as a soldier) came before his duties to humanity, the fundamental reality of human existence (i.e. as a doctor). The prosecution insisted that *this was precisely the crux*. Not only was it *no defence*, but it was, in fact, the very reason for the accused being in court, for the existence of the court and for the war. 'If, over the last few years, a few people in Germany had had the strength and the will to assert their power, to refuse to obey the order of criminals, would not that have ended the whole of this system and brought about a similar system to our own?' It is no answer to say, 'I obeyed an order which was obviously one that

542

should never have been given'. In effect this was where the crime, the murder, the guilt really began. For the accused *had himself* put the group duties first. With his own freedom he had done this and here was the guilt in the failing of his primary responsibility. Responsibility to the moral consciousness.

In his penetrating work on menticide and mental seduction, Joost Merloo describes these 'highly learned and polished Nazi doctors who started their professional life with the Hippocratic oath, promising to be the helping healer of man, but who later in cold blood inflicted the most horrible tortures on their concentration camp victims. They had lost their personal standards and ethics completely and justified all their crimes through the Führer's will.' Theirs was 'that poisonous feeling of power that drags them farther and farther away from every human feeling; their victims become people without human identity, merely speaking masks and egoless robots'. And of course in this descent down the abyss the 'masters' themselves have quite lost their human identity in the process. They too become masks with no real human centre whatsoever.

On the crucial question the prosecution insisted that the evidence overwhelmingly pointed to no trial having taken place, as normal law understands it, with the accused being present. Lieutenant-Commander O'Leary said that no Special Service Officers were ever known to have been given a trial. Whereas the Hague Regulations demand for spies that, 'once they have been reduced into captivity – trial is in every case indispensable'. In fact the Judge Advocate went further and in referring to Hague Rule 162, 'persons sent in balloons for the purpose of . . . maintaining communications are not as such liable to be treated as spies', disclosed the uncertainty as to whether they were in fact spies. Even more so then was a proper trial necessary. Above all does International Law utterly forbid summary execution. There were no death warrants and no death certificates. The crux remained, 'whether, if anyone gives an order, emanating even from the highest authority, which obviously cannot be legal, you are going to obey it or not'. Wochner's defence counsel had unknowingly but quite clearly revealed the truth. 'The entire execution took place without any form at all. If formalities had been followed we would not be standing here today.'

Finally, regarding Dr Rohde the Judge Advocate emphasized, 'There is nobody more independent of military discipline than the medical officer. Apart from the actual disobedience (which

543

in this case was anyway concerned with *unlawful* orders) – there are a thousand and one ways of escaping a duty of this kind. He would only have had to say, "I have lost my dope" or "broken my needle" or something of that kind. He never asked for the warrant of execution – or anything like that – things that you would have thought would at once have leapt to the mind of an educated man who wished to escape a duty of this kind.'

Dr Rohde was sentenced to hang; Hartjenstein to life; Straub to thirteen years; Wochner to ten years; Berg to five years; and Bruttel to four years. After this trial Hartjenstein, Wochner, Berg, and Straub were tried for other war crimes and sentenced to death.

J. G.

ROUSE, Alfred Arthur

Commercial traveller, born Herne Hill, London, 1894, convicted in 1931 of the murder of a hitch-hiker whose identity is unknown.

Educated at a council school (Eton and Cambridge, according to Rouse's later boasts) the son of a small-time actress (a beautiful, scintillating Society woman, said Rouse) who was separated from her husband, Rouse was injured in the head during the First World War at Givenchy in May 1915. An operation was performed in the left temporal region of the head, and it has frequently been suggested that this effected a mental change in Rouse, making him sexually licentious (he neither smoked nor drank) and generally irresponsible. Married to Lily May Watkins in 1914, by 1930 he and his wife lived in Buxted Road, Finchley, North London; Rouse was a popular member of local clubs, and at parties his renderings of such ditties as 'Trumpeter, What Are You Sounding Now?' and the 'Cobbler's Song' from *Chu Chin Chow* were much approved. By his own efforts he had got a job as representative of a brace and garter firm, which brought him £500 a year (at that time a sizeable income) and travelled the country in a Morris Minor saloon car, number MU 1468. His wife had not borne him children, which was a matter of regret for Rouse, who seems to have been genuinely fond of them. These paternal aspirations, however, were most adequately fulfilled; his illegitimate children were legion, and maintenance orders were regularly presented at Buxted Road. His wife knew of some of Rouse's affaires (he is said to have seduced over eighty women during his commercial travels) and indeed looked after young Arthur, aged 5, the child of domestic

544

servant Helen Campbell, whom Rouse had bigamously married in 1924. By October 1930, the durability of both Lily May Rouse and her husband's financial state was declining, and there was talk between them of a separation. Rouse's current crisis was an ex-nurse, Ivy Muriel Jenkins, then expecting his child at her parents' home in Gelliager, Glamorganshire, who had been led to believe that a palatial house awaited her at Kingston-on-Thames, Surrey.

At 2 am on November 6th, 1930, two young men, William Bailey and Alfred Brown, were returning from a Bonfire Night dance to their homes in Hardingstone Village near Northampton; walking down Hardingstone Lane, a turning just off the main Northampton to London road, they saw a bright glow by the hedgerow about 50 yards ahead. A man (whom they later identified as Rouse) climbed out of a ditch on the opposite side of the lane, saying, as he passed them: 'It looks as if someone has had a bonfire.' On closer scrutiny, Bailey and Brown discovered a blazing car, with flames leaping to a height of fifteen feet. Police were summoned, and when the fire subsided a charred body was seen sprawled across the two front seats, it being then assumed that an accident had occurred. A description of the individual seen climbing out of the ditch was issued (fortunately for the course of justice it had been a clear moon-lit night) in case this man could be of help during the forthcoming insurance company inquiries. The ownership of the car was traced, through the unburnt registration plates, to Alfred Arthur Rouse, and his wife was contacted at Finchley on the afternoon of November 6th; she said she had last seen her husband, briefly, at 1 am that morning, although in fact Rouse was to testify that he had visited her from 6.20 am to 7.20 am. Mrs Rouse's mistaking the time seems fairly feasible on a dark winter's morning; certainly Mrs Rouse, knowing the time of the supposed accident, travelled that day to Northampton, where, shown pieces of clothing retrieved from the car, said they looked like her husband's. (She was not shown the corpse, which was unrecognizable.) Mrs Rouse was not at any time called upon to give evidence and throughout the case, and since, achieved an almost saint-like reputation for her long-suffering. Meanwhile (as was later established) Rouse was on his way to Gelligaer, where Ivy Jenkins, the birth imminent, lay critically ill. This visit would imply either a curious loyalty, or stupidity, on Rouse's part, in view of the generally accepted theory that his intention was to 'bury' his identity and start life afresh under

545

another name. Upon his arrival Ivy Jenkins' father showed him a picture of his burnt-out car, which was in the evening paper, and one can imagine how heartfelt was Rouse's dismayed comment: 'I did not think there would be much fuss in the papers about the thing.' More details were in the morning papers: a description of the man seen clambering out of the ditch who (as the police had already noted) tallied with a description of the car's owner whose name was now published. Rouse hurriedly boarded a coach for London, where the police, alerted, apprehended Rouse at 9.20 pm on November 7th by the Hammersmith Bus Terminus and asked him to make a statement. ('... I am glad it is over, I have had no sleep.') Rouse, taken to Hammersmith Police Station, said that late on the evening of November 5th, he had picked up a hitch-hiker on the Great North Road, 'just this side of St Albans'. Eventually Rouse had stopped the car, and instructed his passenger to refill the petrol tank while he himself walked over to a field in order to relieve himself; soon he was aware that his car, fifty yards or so away, was on fire: '... I saw the man was inside and I tried to open the door, but could not, as the car was then a mass of flames ... I did not know what to do ... I saw the two men ... I lost my head ... really don't know what I have done since.' Rouse said there had been talk of a 'smoke' shortly before he left the car, as if imputing carelessness over a match to his unfortunate passenger, although this hardly explained the presence of the body inside the car instead of outside, by the petrol tank. Although by now charged with murder, Rouse had provided a possible explanation of the disaster, but on Saturday, November 8th, the prisoner (now under detention at Angel Lane Police Station at Northampton) became remarkably indiscreet about his amatory complications; this statement was quoted during the Police Court proceedings, and, widely published by the Press, did much harm to Rouse's defence, although Mr Norman Birkett, KC, prosecution counsel at the trial, chose to leave out all reference to Rouse's 'harem'.

The trial, at Northampton Assizes, began on January 26th, 1931, under Mr Justice Talbot. From the start Rouse's boastful personality and his verbal pretentiousness ('In the course of my travels it was my custom to use a motor-car as my method of transport') created animosity, although many were appalled at Rouse's obvious mental incapacity: when asked the date of his war wound he dithered, 'A few months after I joined up. I joined on August 8th, I think it was, and I was wounded on April 15th. I believe it was February. May 25th I think it was.'

Sir Bernard Spilsbury, pathologist, who had examined the corpse, gave damning evidence when he spoke of finding a petrol-soaked scrap of material in the fork of the left leg; Sir Bernard also averred, from the position of the body, that the victim had been conscious before the start of the fire. Rouse's own callousness while under questioning from Norman Birkett did much to condemn him. Birkett, suggesting that Rouse had thrown his unconscious victim, face down, across the front seats of the car prior to firing the car, brought forth an indignant bleat from the accused:

Most decidedly not. I should not throw a man. If I did a thing like that I should not throw him forwards. I should think where I put him, I imagine.

Q. You would imagine what?
A. Hardly that I should throw him down like nothing. That is absurd.
Q. If you rendered him unconscious, would you have a delicacy about his posture?
A. No, but I think if I had been going to do as you suggest I should do a little more than that.
Q. Would you?
A. I think I have a little more brains than that.

Found guilty on January 31st, Rouse had his appeal rejected on March 4th and was executed on March 10th. On March 11th the *Daily Sketch* published his confession in which he admitted strangling his companion, then: 'I got out of my car . . . and made a trail of petrol to the car . . . I also poured petrol over the man and loosened the petrol union joint and took the top off the carburettor . . . I ran to the beginning of the petrol trail and put a match to it.'

This has become one of the celebrated cases of the century, fascinating even those not usually interested in crime. There is a feeling that the nature of Rouse's war wound caused his moral ineptitude. As Mrs Rouse wrote after the trial to Helen Campbell (with whom she was on surprisingly friendly terms): '. . . myself I cannot but grieve to think it was only through his head-wounds that made him a sex-maniac and even the doctors during the case said to me, "can a leopard change his spots?" . . .' How mistaken Mrs Rouse was, however, when, in another letter to Miss Campbell, she wrote: '. . . still, soon everything will be ended to do with this awful case. Even Madame Tussaud's have an effigy. . . .'

ROWLAND, Walter Graham
Thirty-five-year-old labourer, the first man ever to occupy the condemned cell at Strangeways Jail twice over.

In October 1946 two children returning from Mass stumbled across the body of a woman on a bomb-site near Deansgate, Manchester; she was identified as a prostitute, Olive Balchin, and she had been battered about the head, presumably by a bloodied leather-beater's hammer lying nearby. The hammer would seem to be a recent purchase, its brown wrapping-paper also near the corpse. A waitress had seen Olive Balchin with a man the night before her body was found, but it was not until police had worked on the case for a week that they learnt of a lodger in a hostel whose unsociability by day and solitary wanderings by night had attracted attention. Accosted in his cubicle by detectives, this man, Walter Rowland, said straight-away, 'You don't want me for the murder of that woman, do you?' After this injudicious outburst Rowland relapsed into silence, eventually admitting that he knew Olive Balchin – 'Lil' he called her – but denying a knowledge of how she met her end. His clothes were examined, and substances in the trouser turn-ups corresponded with oil, brick-dust, and weed-stuffs found on the bomb-site; two hairs removed from a jacket were identical with hairs on the victim's head. Rowland was also identified as the purchaser of the hammer. A bloodstain on one of Rowland's shoes was of Olive Balchin's blood group. Protesting his inno-cence, Walter Rowland faced trial for the murder of Olive Balchin, was found guilty and held at Strangeways Jail, where years before he had been imprisoned following his conviction (and eventual reprieve) for the murder of his young daughter.

On January 22nd, 1947, three weeks before Rowland's appeal to the Court of Criminal Appeal, a prisoner in Walton Jail, Liverpool, confessed to the murder of Olive Balchin in a state-ment to the prison governor. Mr J. C. Jolly, KC, and Super-intendent Tom Barratt of the Metropolitan Police were ap-pointed to inquire into this confession; the prisoner, David John Ware, aged 38, was driven around Manchester recounting his actions on the day of the murder. Ware's trouser turn-ups, however, unlike Rowland's, were free of any bomb-site matter, and his description of the killing ('blood shot up in a thin spray') was at variance with the pathologist's report; moreover, no trace of blood was found on Ware's clothing. Eventually, on February 22nd, Ware made another statement repudiating his confession:

> ... had nothing whatever to do with the murder. I made these statements out of swank more than anything, but I had a feeling all along that I wouldn't get very far with them ... I also thought I was putting myself in the position of a hero. I wanted to see myself in the headlines. In the past I wanted to be hung. ...

Rowland, who for a time must have thought he had a good chance of cheating the gallows yet again, was hanged at Strangeways on February 27th, 1947, threatening that his ghost would for ever haunt those detectives who, he maintained, had caused his wrongful arrest.

RULOFF, Edward
Born in New Brunswick, 1819, he tempered a certain academic brilliance with habitual criminality, involving murder, robbery, and the receiving of stolen goods.

Becoming a schoolteacher in his twenties, he taught at Dryden, New York, marrying Harriet Schutt, one of his pupils. In time, Harriet, with their only child, Dottie, was to unaccountably disappear from the Ruloff home at Lansing; suspicion was attached (not unnaturally, it seemed) to Ruloff himself, who had recently sought aid in hoisting a heavy box on to a wagon, although hours later he was seen alighting from the same wagon and carrying that same large box, this time alone and with apparent ease. In the absence of a corpse, Ruloff was charged with the abduction of Harriet, found guilty and served a sentence of ten years; due for release, proceedings were started to indict Ruloff for the murder of his daughter Dottie, despite legal objections from that learned gentleman, who pertinently pointed out the need for a 'corpus delicti'. Unnerved, however, by the apparent singlemindedness of the authorities, Ruloff broke out of the jailhouse (with the aid of the jailer's son) shortly before his objections to the proposed trial were to be heard by the Court of Appeals. Always obsessed by learning, he made his way to Allegheny College in Meadville, Pennsylvania, where he impressed the President and Fellows so much (he had mastered the classics during his prison term) that they referred him to a college in the south which had a vacancy for a languages master;

needing cash for the journey, Ruloff robbed a jeweller, was captured, recognized, and again thrust into jail to await the decision of the Court of Appeals regarding daughter Dottie. The court decided that it was by no means certain Dottie was dead, whereupon (regardless of callous demands from a posse of Ruloff's ex-neighbours outside the courtroom, calling for his immediate extinction) Ruloff was released. For the next ten years he pursued a varied career; prison sentences (for robbery and receiving) alternating with periods of bizarre scholarship: Ruloff inventing a universal language, Ruloff studying philology, law, conchology, geography, and Ancient Greek lore. He eventually, in 1870, studied the best method of breaking into a shop at Binghamton, Broome County, New York, and robbing the safe. This he perpetrated with two other scoundrels, but they were interrupted in this infamous activity by two of the shop clerks living on the premises, one of whom, a Mr Merrick, was fatally shot in the resulting scuffle. During the escape, Ruloff's companions were accidentally drowned, but Ruloff was to be identified as one of the robbers because a shoe left behind at the scene of the murder showed signs of having belonged to someone without a great toe, a disability Ruloff suffered through an attack of frostbite. The surviving clerk, also, was adamant that Ruloff was one of the assailants, and when, during the trial, Ruloff attempted to utilize his law-learning by a relentless cross-examination of this witness, persisting in a query concerning the visibility in the shop, he drew forth a reply which by its truthful *naïveté* was convincing and therefore damning to the questioner: 'Why, you know how dark it was! You were there!'

Found guilty of this murder, Edward Ruloff was hanged, despite the outraged sentiments of capital punishment opponents, who thought that an impressive intellect in a murderer (Ruloff's brain, when examined after the execution, weighed 10 oz. above the average) was an additional reason for avoiding the death penalty.

RUMBOLD, Freda

Forty-three-year-old housewife, convicted at Bristol Assizes in November 1956 of the murder of her husband. On August 25th, 1956, timber contractor Albert Rumbold was found, shot through the head, in bed; he had been dead for three days. On the bedroom door was a notice, 'Please do not enter', and a towel doused in eau-de-Cologne and Dettol was pressed against the bottom of the door. Mrs Rumbold's sister, who had inquired about her brother-in-law's whereabouts (and who eventually sent for the police), was told that Albert Rumbold had been accidentally shot during a marital scuffle: 'He slipped off the bed,' said Mrs Rumbold, 'I pulled him up, tidied him, and left him.' She asserted that her husband had threatened to shoot both her and his young daughter. Dr C. E. M. Ware, pathologist, was to tell the court at Mrs Rumbold's trial that he believed Albert Rumbold to have been asleep when the fatal shot was fired, and the Director of the Forensic Science Laboratory at Bristol said that the gun, a 12-bore shotgun, could not have been fired without considerable pressure on the trigger. There was evidence that Mrs Rumbold had purchased this gun in Yeovil 'for pigeon shooting': she had afterwards asked friends to buy her cartridges in Taunton for an acquaintance who was going deer shooting in Scotland. At the trial Mrs Rumbold's mother spoke of her son-in-law's sexual eccentricities: '. . . he was a very odd person, particularly at the time of the full moon . . .' Mrs Rumbold herself said: '. . . I used to spend nights in my daughter's bed . . . and on the landing.' The accused admitted that she had forged her husband's signature to obtain loans from the bank. Mr G. D. Roberts, prosecuting, asked if she had not hated her husband, fully intending to get rid of him when she had forged these documents; this Mrs Rumbold denied.

Found guilty of murder, Freda Rumbold was reprieved.

RUSSELL, George
Housebreaker and habitual criminal, executed at Oxford Prison on December 2nd, 1948. The case is interesting mainly because of the careful investigation of Chief Superintendent Frederick Cherrill of Scotland Yard which led to tracing the murderer.

Mrs Freeman Lee was an old lady of 96 who lived alone in a seventeen-room house in Maidenhead. When she had come to live in Ray Park Avenue, in 1908 with her husband and son, she had been a wealthy woman who gave many parties. The son was killed in the war and the husband died later, and Mrs Lee became a recluse. Her money was gone; she lived on a small grant from a Benevolent Society, although she was generally supposed in the neighbourhood to be rich.

On June 1st, 1948, the milkman wondered that her milk had been untouched for two days, and told the police. Later, her body was discovered doubled up in a trunk in the hall. She had been battered and tied up, and had suffocated to death in the trunk. There were no clues of any kind; she lived in one room, and the rest of the house was full of mouldering clothes and furniture. But Cherrill noticed a small square box among the bedclothes, and found its lid on the floor. There were only two fragmentary fingerprints on it, but they were enough to identify the housebreaker as George Russell, an inefficient little 'screwsman' who was not usually given to violence. Russell was arrested at a tramps' hostel in St Albans five days later, and admitted that he had been at Wynford, Mrs Lee's house, to look at some gardening she wanted doing; the garden had been in such bad condition that he decided against it; later, someone in a café told him Mrs Lee was very rich. However, he sang hymns in the street at Staines and made enough money to go on to Brighton. But he added that he would not dream of killing an old lady for money she didn't actually possess; a statement that gave him away, since he knew nothing of Mrs Lee's poverty. The fingerprint evidence led to his conviction.

RUXTON, Dr Buck
Parsee, born 1899, Bachelor of Medicine of Bombay and London Universities (real name Bikhtyar Rustomji Ratanji Hakim), convicted at Manchester Assizes on March 13th, 1936, of the murder of his Scots mistress, Isabella Van Ess (formerly the wife of a Dutchman), known as Isabella Ruxton.

In 1930, with their first child (two more were subsequently born), the Ruxtons went to live at 2 Dalton Square, Lancaster, where the doctor had acquired a practice. Both were quick-tempered and there was much quarrelling due to Ruxton's suspicions of infidelity; twice Mrs Ruxton sought police protection. During his trial Ruxton said of their relationship: 'We were the kind of people who could not live with each other and could not live without each other.' Their last known disagreement was on September 7th, 1935, when Ruxton accused Mrs Ruxton of having an affair with a young Lancaster Town Hall clerk, with whose family Mrs Ruxton had just spent a holiday in Edinburgh. (It was stated later that there was no truth in the doctor's allegations.) On September 14th, 1935, Isabella Ruxton drove alone in the doctor's Hillman Minx car to Blackpool to meet her two sisters and to view the annual Blackpool Illuminations; she left her sisters at 11.30 pm, the last time she was seen alive. At 6.30 am on Sunday, September 15th, Mrs Agnes Oxley, the

Ruxtons' charlady, who customarily arrived every day at Dalton Square around 7.15 am, received a visit from the doctor, who told her not to bother coming in that day: 'Mrs Ruxton and Mary (the Ruxtons' nursemaid) have gone away on a holiday to Edinburgh . . . but come as usual tomorrow.' During that morning tradespeople and one patient were to call at 2 Dalton Square. All were told through the partially opened door that Mrs Ruxton and the maid Mary Rogerson were in Scotland; the patient who had called about a minor surgical operation was told to come instead the following day: '. . . we are busy taking the carpets up ready for the decorators . . . look at my hands, how dirty they are.' At 11.30 am Ruxton took his three children to a friend's house, requesting her to look after them during his wife's absence; it was noticed that Ruxton's right hand was bandaged, and he explained he had cut it that morning with a tin-opener. Later he called at the Rogersons' house, leaving a message that their daughter had accompanied Mrs Ruxton to Scotland for a week or two. Some time on the Sunday afternoon he requested a patient of his, Mrs Hampshire, to come to Dalton Square to scrub down the staircase 'ready for the decorators coming in the morning'. Mrs Hampshire noticed the bath was a 'dirty yellow . . . I gave the bath a good scrub with hot water and Vim, I could not get the stains off.' Ruxton gave Mrs Hampshire one of his suits ('badly stained, but he said it was a good suit and I could have it cleaned') and some rolled-up carpets. The following day Ruxton tried to take back the suit: '. . . he said it was very undignified for a man to wear another man's suit. . . .' When Mrs Hampshire attempted cleaning the carpets by throwing on buckets of water, 'the colour of the water that came off was like blood'. On September 16th Ruxton hired an Austin car and on September 17th was involved in a slight collision with a cyclist at Kendal, in the Lake District; a policeman investigating the accident was told by Ruxton that he was returning from a business trip in Carlisle. Up to September 20th two other charwomen, Mrs Smith and Mrs Curwen, found a great many bloodstains about the house, together with an unpleasant smell; Mrs Curwen was sent out for eau-de-Cologne and a syringe, and Ruxton sprayed the house. On September 29th, 1935, the dismembered remains of two bodies were found in a ravine near Moffat, Scotland. At first it was thought one of the bodies was that of a man, and Dr Ruxton, after reading out a *Daily Express* account of the 'Ravine Murder' to Mrs Oxley, remarked: 'So you see . . . it is not our two.' ('I replied that I hoped not.') By now rumours were circulating about the missing women. Ruxton went around muttering that the two had been deceiving him and that Mary Rogerson had connived at his Bella's marital misdemeanours; he hinted Mary was pregnant (later proved false) and her disappearance a timely one. On October 9th, Mary Rogerson's mother informed the Lancaster Police her daughter was missing, and the following day Ruxton made a statement to the police: 'I would like discreet inquiries made by the police with a view to finding my wife. . . .' A 'slip' copy (i.e. one of a limited number containing local news for a certain area) of the *Sunday Graphic* was found wrapped round one of the remains. The district in this case was Lancaster and Morecambe, which resulted in the Chief Constable of Dumfries, Scotland, contacting the Lancaster Borough Police. A blouse and a pair of child's rompers also found with the body parts were identified as coming from the Ruxton household. The Press speculated on a possible connexion between the missing Lancaster women and the Moffat remains, and Ruxton protested to the Chief Constable of Lancaster: 'This publicity is ruining my practice!' On October 13th, Buck Ruxton was charged with the murder of Mary Rogerson; on November 5th he was charged with the murder of Isabella Ruxton. His trial for the murder of Isabella Ruxton started on March 2nd, 1936. Counsel for the Crown were Mr J. C. Jackson, KC, Mr Maxwell Fyfe, KC, and Mr Hartley Shawcross; with Mr Norman Birkett, KC, and Mr Philip Kershaw as counsel for the defence.

The remains found comprised two skulls, two trunks, seventeen parts of limbs, and forty-three portions of soft tissue. They had been examined by pathologists, including Professor John Glaister, Professor of Forensic Medicine at Glasgow University; Professor Sydney Smith, Professor of Forensic Medicine at Edinburgh University; and Professor J. C. Brash, Professor of Anatomy at Edinburgh University, who undertook the task of reconstructing the bodies. All identifying characteristics had been removed from both bodies. Mary Rogerson was known to have had a squint in one eye, and the eyes from Body No. 1 (that of the younger woman) had been removed; Mrs Ruxton's legs had been the same width from the knees down to the ankles, and the legs belonging to Body No. 2 had had the soft tissues sliced. Life-size photographs of the assumed victims' heads were superimposed over pictures of the skull remains, and found to match. There was evidence of throttling in Body No. 2, and both bodies had been dismembered and drained of blood soon after death.

Buck Ruxton pleaded not guilty to the charge of murdering Isabella Ruxton, and to the inference that he also killed the only witness of his crime, Mary Rogerson, replied in court: 'That is absolute bunkum, with a capital B, if I may say it.' In a previous lengthy statement entitled 'My Movements' (referred to during the trial), Ruxton maintained that Mrs Ruxton had left with Mary Rogerson to go to Edinburgh on September 15th, leaving about 9.30 am ('. . . she shouted, "Toodleoo, Pa, there is a cup of tea on the hall table for you . . ." ') and that he had seen neither of them since. (Also described in 'My Movements' was a car trip to Gretna Green on September 29th, an excursion Ruxton arranged for his children and two spinster patients: '. . . I joked, "I say, it is rather tempting for me to go to Gretna with two single women".') Ruxton appealed unsuccessfully against the verdict on April 27th, and was hanged at Strangeways Jail, Manchester, on May 21st, 1936.

S

SACCO and VANZETTI
Nicola Sacco, born 1891, and Bartolomeo Vanzetti, born 1888, both Italian, sentenced to death for the murders of Frederick A. Parmenter and Alessandro Berardelli.

The victims, employees of the Slater and Morrill Shoe Factory, were on April 15th, 1920, transferring $16,000 from one factory to another along a street in South Braintree, Massachusetts, when they were fired at and killed by two men, who snatched the metal money boxes and made off in a car. Police believed this car was a Buick, stolen the previous November; an Italian named Boda had been seen driving a car similar to this Buick, together with two friends, Sacco and Vanzetti. All three were questioned, Boda being allowed to go (he left almost immediately for Italy); Sacco and Vanzetti had been armed with revolvers when apprehended, and they were detained at the police station charged with possessing firearms without a permit. They were questioned about another hold-up in the vicinity the previous December; Sacco, shoemaker, was able to produce an alibi, but Vanzetti, fish peddler, was charged with this robbery and, despite the fact that thirty witnesses testified to his being miles away at the time of the crime, he was convicted by Judge

Webster Thayer and sentenced to fifteen years' imprisonment. Both men were charged with the Braintree murders, their trial commencing on May 31st, 1921. Many thought the men were being victimized because of their Radical sympathies. When arrested, Sacco was found in possession of a pamphlet, announcing a political meeting to be held the following week:

> Fellow workers, you have fought all the wars. You have worked for all the capitalists . . . have you harvested the fruit of your labours? . . . have you found a piece of land where you can live like a human being and die like a human being? On these questions, on this argument, and on this theme the struggle for existence, Bartolomeo Vanzetti will speak. Admission free. Freedom of discussion to all. Take the ladies with you.

But many were convinced the men were rogues. Both were armed when arrested, Sacco carrying a loaded ·32 Colt pistol (said afterwards by a firearms expert to be the murder gun) and Vanzetti having a ·38 Harrington and Richardson revolver. Both denied knowing Boda, although they had been seen with him, and when asked by the police why he carried a revolver, Sacco feebly replied, 'To protect myself. Lots of bad men.' Both had fled to Mexico during the Great War to avoid the call-up, and their political sentiments aroused much wrath. Found guilty of murder on circumstantial evidence, a series of appeals for a new trial were launched, the hearing of which was to last six years.

Judge Thayer himself was alleged to have referred to the defendants (within the precincts of his golf club) as 'dagos' and 'sons of bitches' and was overheard to remark to a companion, 'Did you see what I did to those anarchistic bastards?' William G. Thompson, for the defence, said, 'I have known Judge Thayer all my life. He is a narrow-minded man; he is an unintelligent man; he is carried away by his fear of the Reds. . . .'

Finally an appeal for a new hearing was taken to the Supreme Judicial Court of Massachusetts in January 1926, the dispute being mainly a legal one, i.e., that the case five years before had been unfairly presented to the jury; this appeal was rejected. On April 9th, 1927, the two men were sentenced to death before Judge Thayer. When asked if he had anything to say, Sacco replied in halting English: 'I never knew, never heard, even read in history anything so cruel as this court . . . after seven years prosecuting they still consider us guilty . . . I know the sentence will be between two classes, the oppressed class and the rich class . . .' Vanzetti likewise replied: 'I am not only innocent of these two crimes, but I never commit a crime in my life I have never steal and I have never kill . . . I would not wish to a dog or to a snake – I would not wish any of them what I have had to suffer for things that I am not guilty of. I am suffering because I am a radical . . . I am so convinced to be right that if you could execute me two times and if I could be reborn two other times I would live again to do what I have done already. . . .'

Despite urgent world-wide pleas for clemency coming from people including George Bernard Shaw, Einstein, John Galsworthy, and H. G. Wells, Sacco and Vanzetti were electrocuted on August 23rd, 1927.

SAFFRAN, Fritz, and KIPNIK, Erich

Two men accused of a murder in many ways similar to that of Rouse, and Tetzner. Saffran was the young and popular manager of a large furniture store, Platz & Co., in Rastenburg. Although, in 1930, the store seemed to be doing extremely well (in spite of the depression), it was actually all but bankrupt; Saffran had been selling large quantities of furniture on hire-purchase agreements, and his customers were not paying. He tried various extreme measures – borrowing money at high rates of interest – and finally resorted to fraud. One day he read in the newspapers about the burning car murder of Kurt Tetzner, and decided that this might be his way out of the difficulty. Saffran was a married man (he had married the daughter of the firm's owner), but he had been having an affair with Ella Augustin, who was a clerk in charge of accounts at the store. Most of the employees believed it was a one-sided affair – for Ella was known to be in love with Saffran – but the girl had actually been his mistress for some time. She was not pretty, but was known as a rebellious woman, of strong character.

The third accomplice was Erich Kipnik, the chief clerk. He was persuaded to help Saffran in the plan to save the store. They would kill a man and burn his body in the store, so that it would be thought that the dead man was Saffran.

The three formed a 'murder camp' in the Nikolai Forest. Ella would stay behind; the two men would rove the countryside in their cars, looking for victims. On one occasion, all three went out together. They picked up a man near the village of

Sorquitten and Kipnik started to batter his head with a life preserver; Ella became hysterical, and they let the man go. On another occasion, they picked up a man who told them he had six children; they let him go, out of pity. (At least, so Saffran claimed at the trial.) On September 12th, 1930, near Luisenhof, they met a pedestrian, 25-year-old Friedrich Dahl, who had been out of work for some time. What happened next is obscure (for the men tried to throw the blame on one another at the trial). But either Saffran shot the man, or Kipnik knocked him unconscious. They then concealed the body for two days, and on September 15th, took it into the store late at night, soaked the place in twenty-five gallons of petrol, and set it on fire. An immense explosion shook the building. Thirty people were still at work on other floors, but they somehow all managed to escape. Kipnik then rushed out of the flames, declaring that Saffran was dead; they had seen flames in the store, he claimed, and Saffran had rushed in to rescue the books. The body was discovered later in the burnt-out building. There was no suspicion whatever of foul play, although Saffran had insured his life for £7,000.

Ella Augustin and Kipnik played their parts well. But two days after the fire, a chauffeur was asked by Ella to drive her sick mother to Königsberg. The driver – a man named Reck – called at the house at three in the morning, and was surprised to see Saffran, who climbed into the car. Reck drove Saffran as far as the village of Gerdauen, then refused to go farther; Saffran got out and walked. The chauffeur did not notify the police, but he talked about it to acquaintances. (He was later charged as an accomplice, but this seems unlikely.) A hunt began for Saffran and Ella was arrested. Saffran was staying with a poor carpenter, a relative of Ella's, in Berlin; he decided to steal the carpenter's papers and escape to Hamburg, where he could take a boat to Brazil. He went to a station outside Berlin, Spandau, but had the incredibly bad luck to be recognized by an old army acquaintance, who notified the police. Saffran was drinking coffee in the waiting-room in Wittemberg – where he was changing trains – when he was arrested.

The corpse found in the burnt store was examined, and doctors discovered it had lain in the earth for several days before being burnt. No missing bodies could be traced in the cemeteries, but a picture of the teeth published in a dental journal produced a dentist who identified them as belonging to Dahl.

The three conspirators were tried at Bartenstein, East Prussia, on March 23rd, 1931. Kipnik and Saffran tried to throw blame on one another. When the wife of the victim appeared in court, both men vied with one another in shouting pleas for forgiveness across the court. The prosecutor snapped, 'Stop this play acting!' Ella Augustin declared that Kipnik was the murderer, while Kipnik shouted that he was fundamentally a decent man, and that Saffran had ruined his life.

Although both were condemned to death, this was later commuted to life imprisonment. Ella Augustin was sentenced to five years in prison.

SALEM MURDER CASE OF 1830

Habitual criminal Richard Crowninshield, aged 28, of Essex County, Massachusetts, was hired by brothers Joseph and Francis Knapp to kill their 82-year-old uncle, Captain Joseph White, from whom they mistakenly believed they would inherit money. In the night of April 6th, 1830, as he slept in his opulent house on Essex Street, Salem, Massachusetts, Captain White was bludgeoned and stabbed to death. Despite the Committee of Vigilance, formed after the murder by the horrified citizens of Salem, two months passed without a clue to the murderer's identity. Then an imprisoned pickpocket in New Bedford Jail testified 'in chains' before the Grand Jury that the Salem killer was a one-time associate of his, Richard Crowninshield, who, as a result of this disclosure, was thrown into the prison at Salem. Later, Captain Joseph Knapp, the father of Joseph and Francis, accidentally opened a blackmailing letter intended for his namesake, son Joseph. The writer, one Grant, hinted at the recipient's knowledge of some dark deed and demanded $1,000. Foolishly, Joseph Knapp junior advised his father to show the letter to the Committee of Vigilance. They justified their existence by finding out that Grant was an ex-convict (real name Palmer) who, when questioned, revealed the Knapp brothers' part in the murder plot.

Crowninshield, realizing the game was up, promptly hanged himself in his prison cell with two handkerchiefs.

The most eminent lawyer of the day, Daniel Webster, was called in to aid the prosecution; the Massachusetts law of the day ruled that an accessory to a murder would not be tried until the actual murderer was convicted, and with Crowninshield's suicide the State foresaw complications.

Francis Knapp was tried first, the jury failing to agree on a verdict; but after the second trial he was convicted of murder. Joseph Knapp, tried a month later, was also found guilty of murder. During both trials Webster's eloquence was noteworthy.

On the Victim: 'A healthful old man to whom sleep was sweet, the first sound slumbers of the night held him in their strong embrace.'

On the Murderer: 'With noiseless foot he paces the lonely hall half lighted by the moon; he winds up the ascent of the stairs . . . beholds his victim before him . . . the moon resting on the grey locks of his aged victim shows him where to strike. . . .'

On the Murder: '. . . He plies his dagger, though it is obvious that life has been destroyed by the blow of the bludgeon.'

On the guilty soul: 'A culture is devouring it . . . it can ask no sympathy from Heaven or earth. . . .'

Both brothers Knapp were publicly hanged.

SANGRET, August (The Wigwam-girl Murder)
French-Canadian soldier, convicted on March 2nd, 1943, of the murder the previous summer of Joan Pearle Wolfe, with whom he had been living in a crudely constructed 'wigwam' on a heath near Godalming, Surrey.

On October 7th, 1942, the remains of a female, badly decomposed, were found buried in the heather on Hankley Common. One limb had been gnawed by rodents, and the body was little more than a receptacle for maggots; Dr Keith Simpson, pathologist, had it removed to Guys Hospital (where he lectured in forensic medicine) and it was placed in a tank of carbolic. It was estimated that death had occurred five weeks previously. Police searching Hankley Common found a pair of shoes buried in the heather, and a canvas bag containing a rosary and a bar of soap; a massive birch branch with human hairs adhering to it, was discovered pushed into the heather, and the hairs were identical to those on the scalp of the corpse. Shortly afterwards a national registration card bearing the name Joan Pearle Wolfe was found on the heath, and a letter demanding marriage of the recipient, since the writer was pregnant. Surrey police informed Chief Inspector E. Greeno of Scotland Yard (in charge of the case) that Joan Wolfe was a vagrant type who had been 'living rough', with a soldier from a nearby Canadian army camp. The soldier, rugged French-Canadian August Sangret, had con-

structed a primitive abode of birchwood and heather clumps
where he and Joan Wolfe had lived throughout the spring and
summer of 1942. Sangret was interviewed by Inspector Greeno,
who made no mention of the found remains; the soldier admitted his relationship with Joan Wolfe, but said she had failed
to keep an appointment with him on September 14th. Sangret
mentioned a knife of his, left sticking in a tree close to the rural
'wigwam', which had been stolen around the time of the girl's
disappearance; Greeno had just learnt that the victim had been
stabbed viciously with a knife, but this information had not been
released to the Press. Sangret's kit was examined and faded
bloodstains on a blanket corresponded to the approximate
positions of a head, hand, and arm of a person the size of the
murder victim. A knife fitting the stab wounds was found
obstructing a drain in a washhouse used by Sangret's unit, and
Inspector Greeno remembered that during his first interrogation
of the suspect, the French–Canadian had suddenly asked permission 'to visit a latrine' which was attached to this washhouse.
Sangret, arrested, was tried for the murder of Joan Wolfe before
Mr Justice Macnaghten at Kingston Assizes; after six days, on
March 2nd, 1943, he was found guilty, and executed at Wandsworth on April 2nd.

SEDDON, Frederick

*Forty-year-old insurance agent of Tollington Park, North
London, accused with his wife in 1912 of the murder of their
lodger, Miss Eliza Barrow, by the administration of arsenic.*

Ambitious, money-loving, Seddon had many interests – freemasonry, lay-preaching, but his favourite occupation was to pore
over the latest Wills column in the daily newspaper, although it
would upset him to learn of any rich person dying intestate,
their money going to the Crown: 'All that money wasted –
thrown into the gutter – it is criminal.' He met his match in
miserly Miss Barrow, an elderly slut, who came to lodge with the
Seddons in 1910, bringing with her a cash box containing £200
in gold. Impressed by Seddon's astuteness in money matters
she sold over £1,600 of shares and purchased from Seddon an
annuity which brought her in an income of £3 5s. a week. Bad-
tempered, dirty, and friendless, she died in her upstairs room in
September 1911 from (according to the medical certificate)
epidemic diarrhoea. Seddon arranged a pauper's funeral for
her, haggling the cost with the undertaker, and claiming

commission on the coffin sale, although, unaccountably, he had
memorial cards printed – which were never sent out:

> A dear one is missing and with us no more
> That voice so much loved we hear not again
> Yet we think of you now the same as of yore
> And know you are free from trouble and pain . . .

Had such a card been sent out to Miss Barrow's relations their
suspicions might never have materialized; but they heard accidentally of her death some days after her burial, and when Seddon, questioned about her property, was insulting and evasive,
they communicated with the police and the body was exhumed.
By a grim coincidence, Seddon's business interests took him to
St Mary's Hospital, Paddington (where Miss Barrow's body
was taken), and he was actually shown over the pathologist's
laboratory at the time the remains were being examined. A
large amount of arsenic was found in the body, and Seddon was
charged with the murder of Miss Eliza Barrow, greeting the
accusation with the remark, 'Scandalous! It is the first of our
family that has ever been charged with such a crime.' (Mrs
Seddon was charged a month later, but at the trial was acquitted.) Mr Marshall Hall was briefed to defend Seddon, but,
for once, had no faith in the innocence of his client: 'It is the
blackest case I have ever been in.' Evidence was given that
Seddon's young daughter Maggie had been sent to buy flypapers (known to contain arsenic) shortly before Miss Barrow's
final illness, but it was Seddon's own callous attitude that
helped to convict him. Questioned about the £200 in gold that
he was said to have counted out an hour or so after Miss Barrow's death, he roared out: 'It is a scandalous suggestion – I
would have had all day to count the money.' The jury came to
the conclusion that Miss Barrow's meagre store of wealth had
tempted Seddon to kill, and he was found guilty of murder.
Mr Justice Bucknill, a fellow mason, had great emotional
difficulty in pronouncing sentence of death, but the only feeling
Seddon ever showed about the whole business was when, after
the appeal had been dismissed, he heard with disgust of the
poor price his property had brought: 'That's finished it.'

SEEFELD, Adolf
German homosexual mass murderer.

Seefeld, who was 65 when he was executed in 1936, was a tramp and travelling watchmaker. Little is known of his psychology, as the Nazis had no interest in such matters. He was first charged with the murder of a young boy in 1908, but the charge could not be proved. However, he spent twenty-three years in jail for sexual offences against young boys before his final arrest.

Seefeld was thought by many gullible country people to be a witch who could put spells on cattle and pigs. He usually slept in the open, even in winter. On one occasion he travelled with a young boy for three months, but the boy was not murdered. When he was confined in a mental home near Potsdam, he refused to speak a word for two years. He was a student of the Bible and could quote it at length.

Seefeld killed by using a poison he concocted from wild plants and fungi. The boys were all found in an attitude of repose, with no sign of sexual assault. (He confessed to twelve murders in all.) Among the victims were: Kurz Gnirk, aged 11, killed on April 16th, 1933; Ernest Tesdorf, aged 10 (November 2nd, 1933); Wolfgang Metzdorf, aged 7 (November 7th, 1933); Alfred Praetorius, aged 10 (November 22nd, 1933); Hans Korn, aged 11 (January 16th, 1934); Edgar Diettrich and Arthur Dinn, found together in a forest at Neu Ruppin on October 16th, 1934 (they were aged 6 and 4 respectively), two boys called Thomas and Neumann, found on February 16th, 1934; and a boy called Zimmermann, murdered on February 23rd, 1935. It can be seen that, as in the case of Kürten and many other sexual murderers, the intervals between the murders decreased towards the end, and there are even two murders on the same day.

Seefeld was arrested after the murder of Zimmermann, and was tried in February 1936. There was no attempt to psychoanalyse him, but the trial was full of moral comments on his wickedness. He was executed on May 23rd, 1936.

SEYMOUR, Henry Daniel
Habitual criminal and housebreaker, sentenced to death for the murder of Mrs Annie Louisa Kempson at Oxford in 1931.

Born about 1879, son of an English doctor, he was first arrested in Johannesburg when he was 20. Thereafter, his career was studded with arrests and periods in jail. One of his schemes was to rob the jewel room of the British Museum; he had facsimile keys made of the jewel cases; his confederates were afraid of the police activity that would follow such a *coup*, and backed out, so that he was forced to drop the idea. Another of his schemes was to rob a burial ground of wealthy Chinamen to find jade; this also came to nothing.

Mrs Kempson, aged 58, lived alone in a semi-detached house in St Clements Street, Oxford. On August Bank Holiday Monday, 1931, she was found dead in her ransacked house, beaten about the head and stabbed in the neck; death had occurred at least twenty-four hours before. From the unwashed breakfast things and the fact that tomatoes Mrs Kempson was known to have eaten the previous Friday evening were undigested in her stomach it was thought that the murder was committed shortly after breakfast on Saturday. A man had been seen at the Kempson front door early on Saturday morning, and further inquiries revealed the man to be ex-convict Henry Seymour, then resident in Oxford and working as a vacuum-cleaner salesman, who had recently sold one of these cleaners to Mrs Kempson. Missing from his home, he was discovered to have stayed a day before the murder at an Aylesbury hotel, leaving without paying the bill. A Mrs Andrews of Oxford, a former customer of Seymour's, then came forward to say that he had come to her with a hard-luck story and she had lent him 4s. 6d. Seymour's next movements were traced to an ironmonger's shop, where he bought a hammer and chisel; Mrs Andrews gave him a bed for the Friday night and he left this benefactor's house on the Saturday morning with only sixpence left. At noon Seymour was seen in an Oxford public house drinking heavily. By late afternoon he returned to the Aylesbury hotel, but had insufficient money to pay the full bill, so the management retained his suitcase. Police in pursuit of the suspect examined the contents of the case and discovered a hammer and chisel, both scraped and washed clean; minute fragments of paper were scattered over the bottom of the case, which, when sprinkled with drops of water, unfolded to reveal the maker's name and were identifiable as the tools sold to Seymour the previous Friday. The hammer was too small to have caused Mrs Kempson's head injuries, but pathologist Sir Bernard Spilsbury, acting on the theory that the hammer head had been covered with layers of cloth, discovered under the microscope infinitesimal scraps of material. A blotter in the hotel room held up to the mirror disclosed a Brighton address;

here Seymour was apprehended. It was a widow's house, and the salesman, having purchased another chisel, had bored two spy-holes in the floor of his bedroom (situated above that of his landlady) so he could keep watch on the widow to ascertain where she kept her money and valuables. When arrested, it was discovered that he had assaulted a woman in Devonshire in the previous year, and had been ordered to pay her £10 compensation. He had attacked Mrs Kempson to obtain the £10, and wished to avoid any further attention from the police in case they knew about money he had embezzled from a firm for which he had been working. His guilt was easily proved and he was executed.

SEZNEC, Guillaume

The affair of Guillaume Seznec is one of the worst blots on the history of the French police – a history that is very often as discreditable as that of the American police in the Prohibition era. The main 'villain' in this matter was Pierre Bony, who later became a collaborator during the war, and was largely responsible for the crime wave in France in 1946 by his policy of protecting the gangsters. Bony was later shot by a firing squad.

Guillaume Seznec was the owner of a sawmill, but he was also known to be mixed up in several shady deals. He had no criminal record, however. Early in May 1923 he was approached by Pierre Quemeneur, owner of a timber business, who had been offered a deal in American Army surplus Cadillac cars, which he intended to sell to the Soviet Republic. Quemeneur needed ready cash, and he approached Seznec, an old war comrade. Seznec offered to buy Quemeneur's villa, the manor of Traou-Nez-en-Plourivo, near Brest, on the coast. On May 23rd, 1923, Seznec and Quemeneur met in the Hôtel des Voyageurs at Brest, and a waiter saw Seznec pay over a large sum in gold – $4,000. Quemeneur handed over the title-deeds of the manor.

The next day the two men set out for Paris in a Cadillac to meet a dealer named 'Charlie'. The car broke down repeatedly. At Houdan they dined at the Plat d'Étain restaurant, and left, with Quemeneur at the wheel. The police later claimed that this was the last time that anyone but the murderer saw Quemeneur alive. An hour later, a mason at Gambais saw Seznec, alone, repairing the car yet again by the roadside. Seznec said later that Quemeneur had gone on to Paris from the Houdan Station.

He spent the night in the car and returned home to his sawmill at Morlaix.

A week later, on June 4th, Quemeneur's sister went to Seznec's mill to ask him if he knew where her brother was; he said no. Another week passed, and on June 12th, Quemeneur was reported as missing to the Paris police. The next day his sister received a telegram: 'Will be back in a few days,' signed 'Quemeneur'.

Seznec was arrested and charged with the murder of Quemeneur. And Inspector Pierre Bony, then a young man, set out for Normandy to 'crack' the case. He was a self-educated man, son of poor parents in Auvergne, and driven by consuming ambition. He was attached to the Sûreté.

Bony immediately declared that he had found Quemeneur's briefcase in the left-luggage at Le Havre; it contained the contract for the sale of the manor. Bony declared that this contract had been typed out after the murder by Seznec, who had also forged Quemeneur's signature. All that was necessary, Bony said, was to find the typewriter. The police had already searched Seznec's sawmill three times with no success. Then a policeman was seen to carry a large, wrapped object into the mill, and a few hours later, Bony announced triumphantly that he had found the typewriter. He was photographed holding it, and reporters noticed that it looked completely dust-free, 'as if it had just been unwrapped'.

A Breton tram conductor named Le Her came forward and claimed that he had talked to Quemeneur on a tram on May 26th – two days after the alleged murder. He had sworn in the Breton dialect; a fellow passenger had laughed, and they had chatted for a long time in the Breton dialect. However, Bony declared that Le Her was a bad character who had no doubt been bribed. It is strange to record that Le Her later married Seznec's daughter Jeanne, who was one day to assert that her husband had murdered Quemeneur.

More interesting was the testimony of five sailors who had been at sea on the night of May 27th to 28th and had seen, in the clear moonlight, a man shoot another man on the lawns of the Quemeneurs' manor. Bony studied this testament carefully, and then 'mislaid' it; the magistrate who had taken the deposition of the sailors tried to establish Seznec's innocence after the trial, but systematic police opposition drove him finally into a private mental home.

The case, then, was that Seznec had murdered Quemeneur on

the Housan road and buried his body, then gone back to Havre, where, on June 13th, he had bought a typewriter and forged the contract. The woman in the shop (oddly enough, a friend of the Commissioner of Police) identified a photograph of Seznec as the man who had bought the typewriter later discovered in the mill.

The case opened on October 24th, 1924, at the Finistère Assizes, in the Palais de Justice at Quimper; Seznec's advocate was Maître Moro-Giafferi, who defended Landru. Because of Bony's evidence, Seznec was found guilty and sentenced to penal servitude for life in French Guiana. Twenty years later, in July 1947, Seznec returned to France to live with his daughter, who had spent her life trying to clear her father's name. He was 71 years old. Jeanne was married to Le Her, who beat her constantly. One day, as her husband was about to beat her again, she shot him with his own revolver. She was acquitted of manslaughter. Her father died on February 13th, 1954. Jeanne Seznec declared that the man who had murdered Quemeneur was her own husband, Le Her. Whether this is true or not, it seems certain that Seznec was not guilty; before he was executed in the Mont Valérien fortress, Bony admitted to 'framing' Seznec.

SHELLEY and NEWMAN ('Moosh' and 'Tiggy')
Executed on August 5th, 1931, for the murder of a fellow down-and-out, known as 'Pigsticker'.

In the area enclosed by the Watford and Barnet by-passes was a wild area of woodland and bushes. A great many tramps and itinerant navvies lived there in makeshift huts. Half a mile away was a rubbish dump used by the LMS Railways, known as Scratchwood Sidings. It was in this huge pile of smouldering rubbish that a navvy named McGlade noticed a human arm protruding. The police were called, and the body of a man was pulled out of the rubbish. Sir Bernard Spilsbury put the death at three or four days before the discovery (June 1st, 1931), and cause of death as a blow on the left temple with a heavy object.

The vital clue was finally supplied by a navvy named Armstrong, who had shared a hut with two men known as 'Moosh' and 'Tiggy' for a night. The real names of Moosh and Tiggy were William Shelley and Oliver Newman, aged 57 and 61 respectively; they had constructed their hut in the middle of the wilderness, and worked at navvying nearby. They were feared locally as tough and touchy characters. On the previous Saturday, Armstrong had been half-asleep on the floor of their hut when he heard a quarrel outside, and saw Moosh and Tiggy beating a man with iron bars. They carried the body away in a sack, slinging it over a pole. Armstrong gave no indication that he had seen this, but he told the police when they questioned him.

The dead man was soon identified by a mate as a navvy known as 'Pigsticker', noted for his dishonest habits.

The police arrested Moosh and Tiggy, waiting around their shack all night (the men kept three savage dogs, and were expected to resist arrest). However, they 'came quietly', and admitted killing 'Pigsticker' quite cheerfully. He had been in the habit of stealing from them, and on the night in question, they had missed some bacon and bread, and had beat him up. When they realized they had killed him, they buried his body in the heap of smouldering rubbish.

A touch of comedy was introduced into the Old Bailey (where the trial took place over two days before Mr Justice Swift). The defence counsel asked whether there was a clock in the hut; Armstrong, in the witness-box, replied, 'No, but there was, and here it is', and produced an alarm clock. Moosh cried out indignantly: 'Gor blimey, Tiggy, he's pinched our alarm clock.'

They were sentenced to death and executed on August 5th, 1931. Moosh made the curious remark that the death sentence was twenty years late. But a case such as this illustrated the barbarity of the death sentence, for the murder was hardly premeditated.

Armstrong's part, although that of a good citizen, no doubt, is hardly admirable; his way of repaying their hospitality cannot be considered generous. Moreover, since he stole the alarm clock, it is conceivable that 'Pigsticker' (whose real name was Herbert Ayres) may not have been guilty of the theft of the bacon and bread on the fatal night; if this is so, then Moosh and Tiggy killed the wrong man!

SHEWARD, William

Unsuccessful tailor, living in St Martins-at-Palace, Norwich, who in 1851, during a drunken quarrel, stabbed to death (with a pair of tailoring shears) his querulous wife Martha, who at 56 was considerably older than her husband. For days after he worked at disposing the body: '. . . the house began to smell . . .

I made a fire . . . and commenced to mutilate the body . . . the head I had put in a saucepan and put on the fire to keep the stench away. I then broke it up and distributed it about Thorpe . . .' (a part of Norwich) '. . . came home . . . emptied the pan in the cockey in Bishopsgate Street, with the entrails, etc., putting the hands and feet in the same saucepan, in the hope they might boil to pieces . . . the long hair I cut into small pieces, and they blew away as I walked along.' Some parts of the body were found, but thought to be the remains of a young girl; no one associated them with the missing Mrs Sheward, who had frequently threatened to leave her husband. In 1862 William Sheward married again, becoming the landlord of the Key and Castle Sun at Norwich in 1868 after an unsuccessful attempt at being a pawnbroker. Since murdering his first wife, however, he had been dogged by remorse; on January 1st, 1869, during a visit to London, his memories of Martha Sheward made more poignant by alcohol, he walked into the station of P Division (Walworth) of the Metropolitan Police and confessed the crime of twenty years before. 'Some of the body,' he said, 'is still preserved in spirits of wine at the Guildhall in Norwich.' These pickled remains, recovered, were confirmed as being those of a woman in her fifties. When sober, Sheward tried to retract his admissions, but was eventually found guilty of murder at Norfolk Assizes, and hanged on April 20th, 1869, inside Norwich Castle.

SIDNEY STREET (The Siege of)

A group of foreign anarchists, mostly Russians, planned a jewel robbery in December 1910, as a result of which three policemen lost their lives, and the famous 'Siege' took place a few weeks later – in January 1911 – when two of the gang were trapped at 100 Sidney Street, off the Mile End Road, East London.

The jewel robbery may have been one of a series, for there had been a great many robberies by forcing entry through a wall or ceiling during the preceding year. The anarchists, men who had been deported from Russia by the Tsarist police, wanted money to continue disseminating their propaganda.

The gang consisted of at least eleven men and three women; all were members of an anarchist club in Jubilee Street, and were led by George Gardstein, a man with many aliases, a Lett who had been expelled from Russia. Other members included Fritz Svaars, Karl Hoffmann, Josef Solokov, Jacob Peters, and 'Peter the Painter', a mysterious figure whose name may have been Peter Piatkov or Straume. Some writers have suggested that he was a Tsarist agent whose business was to provoke the anarchists to acts of violence that would cause them to be deported.

The gang rented numbers 9 and 11 Exchange Buildings, a cul-de-sac that ran parallel with Houndsditch. They then proceeded to bore through the wall connecting No. 11 with the jeweller's shop of H. S. Harris at 119 Houndsditch. This was on the evening of Saturday, December 16th, 1910, a windy night. The noise of hammering was heard by the man who lived next door to the jeweller's; he called a policeman, who knocked on the door of 11 Exchange Buildings.

A foreigner opened the door and the policeman, PC Piper, inquired for 'the missus'. Told she was out, he replied he would call later. He then summoned several other policemen – amounting in all to seven uniformed officers and two in plain clothes – and they knocked again at No. 11. The door was opened again, and a police sergeant was admitted. Then the shooting began, in which one policeman was killed outright, while two were fatally injured. The other four uniformed police received wounds. But the leader of the gang, Gardstein, was also shot accidentally by one of his own men. The anarchists at No. 9 (two doors away – No. 10 was empty) heard the firing and made their escape. The anarchists from No. 11 supported their dying comrade through the deserted streets at midnight (the inclement weather kept the inhabitants of Whitechapel indoors) to a house at 59 Grove Street, where he was attended by two women associates of the gang – Sara Trassjonsky, 'Peter the Painter's' mistress, and Luba Milstein, Fritz Svaars' mistress. A doctor was called, but Gardstein died in the night, and the police were notified the next day. Sara Trassjonsky was arrested. The police found a great deal of burglars' kit abandoned in Exchange Buildings. Some of it had been manufactured by Gardstein in the laboratory of Malatesta, the anarchist who was also a member of the Jubilee Street club.

A nation-wide man-hunt led to the arrests of several of the gang – Dubov, Jacob Peters, Fedorov, Rosen, and Hoffmann, and the three women (who included Nina Vassileva, who was Gardstein's mistress and may have been present at the shooting). But at a later trial, all these were acquitted. (Nina Vassileva was sentenced to two years in jail but the sentence was quashed.)

On January 2nd the police received information that two of the gang – Svaars and a man named Josef – were in the second-floor room of Mrs Betsy Gershon, an associate of the anarchists, at 100 Sidney Street. Mrs Gershon was actually a prisoner, for the men had taken off her skirt and shoes to prevent her from leaving. The police quietly surrounded the house and evacuated it in the early hours of January 3rd, 1911; they sent the landlady, Mrs Fleishman, up to get Mrs Gershon with a request to go and fetch a doctor. The fugitives lay low when the landlady knocked and allowed their prisoner to go. At dawn (about seven-thirty) the police threw gravel at the windows of No. 100. The men immediately opened fire. Sergeant Leeson was seriously wounded (but not fatally). The Scots Guards were sent to Sidney Street from the Tower, and Mr Winston Churchill (the Home Secretary) arrived to watch the fun. The firing went on all morning. At one o'clock, the house burst into flames. The police refused to allow firemen to approach, and the anarchists died in the fire. (One of them had been shot in the head.) Several firemen were injured, one fatally, when part of the building collapsed.

None of the other anarchists was arrested, and those who had been arrested earlier were ultimately acquitted. Sara Trassjonsky went insane and died in Colney Hatch Asylum soon after. Some writers have suggested that this case and the Steinie Morrison case are connected (Leon Beron was murdered on December 31st, 1910), and that Beron was killed by the anarchists. (He had two S's slashed on his face when his body was found.) This has never been proved, but is maintained convincingly by James E. Holroyd in his book *The Gaslight Murders*. Peter the Painter is said to have died in Australia; Sergeant Leeson (who was shot in the Siege) saw him in Sydney some years later; Leeson also says that Peter the Painter's brother informed him that Peter had died in America in 1914.

SILVERA, Vincent
Executed in Kingston, Jamaica, on February 16th, 1953, for the murder of his wife.

The main interest of the case lies in the scientific work used to convict the murderer. Silvera was born in 1914, and was a butcher by trade. His wife, Martha Silvera, had once been very beautiful; she was a mixture of Chinese, Indian, and negro. She had had two children before her marriage to Silvera in 1942. In 1950, Silvera began an affair with a younger woman, Princess Campbell, and began to quarrel with his wife, who, on one occasion, went to live with her mother in St Elizabeth

On June 15th, 1952, Martha disappeared, and Silvera told various stories to her friends to account for her absence. He even wrote a letter to a friend of his wife's, signing it with his wife's name. The friend failed to recognize the writing and handed it to the police.

On June 19th a headless body was found on the cliffs near Anchovy; some clothes were recovered from the sea a few miles away, in Bryan's Bay. On the 29th the police received the forged letter from Martha Silvera's friend, and Silvera was arrested on the 30th. He claimed that Martha had left for Lacovia, St Elizabeth, where her father was ill. This was easily proved to be false. Police found photographs of the missing woman in the house; they were enlarged and superimposed on photos of the corpse; they fitted exactly. (The same method had been used in the Ruxton case.) A dressmaker identified some of the clothing taken from the sea as being Martha Silvera's. The left hand of the corpse had a mole on the palm, between the index finger and the thumb; so had the missing woman. (So, oddly enough, had her two sons.) The quality and distribution of pubic hair indicated that the corpse, like the missing woman, had a mixture of Chinese, negro, and Indian blood. The head (which was never found) had been severed by someone skilled in dissection; and Silvera was a butcher.

Silvera's trial lasted seventeen days; he refused to give evidence and called no defence witnesses. He was found guilty and sentenced to death.

SIMECECK, James
Twenty-five-year-old farmer, living near Ellsworth, Wisconsin, murdered 28-year-old Mrs Verna Petan and her three children, George 10, Neil 6, and Sylvia 3.

On a late afternoon in January 1942, lumberjack Joe Holcomb saw a neighbour's farm-house in flames; he managed to recover three bodies before the roof fell in. All had died before the fire started: the children's throats were slashed, and Verna Petan had been sexually maltreated, stabbed, and shot. (The body of George Petan was discovered later in the house debris.) Time of death was estimated at around 4.15 pm. Suspicion fell on a tramp who had pestered farmers' wives for food and who admitted being on the highway near the Petan smallholding on the afternoon of the murder. The tramp had served a jail sentence for rape, and had violated his parole; he asserted his innocence:

'I'm not guilty! Playing a little rough with a girl who had been leading you on anyhow is one thing, but the cold-blooded murder of a young mother and three kids – that's different.' An Elmwood, Wisconsin, doctor cleared the tramp of suspicion by saying that he had given him a lift in his car that afternoon, and they had driven past the Petan house: 'I remember he was with me when I noticed a car in Verna's driveway . . . a dark-coloured sedan, kind of old.'

A woman came forward the day following the murders to say she had noticed a neighbour the previous afternoon driving in the direction of the Petan farm: '. . . it was young Jimmy Simececk, a good friend of the Petan family, and usually when he drove to town he would stop to see if Verna needed anything from the stores. You see, the Petans didn't have a car.' Simececk admitted he was at the Petan house the day before, to inquire if he could pick up any groceries while in town: 'But Verna said she was pretty well stocked up, and would wait until my next visit.' Blood found on Simececk's shirt was analysed and found to be animal blood. Lumberjack Holcomb, questioned further about his grim findings, suddenly recalled that in the blazing kitchen he had seen a box of groceries on a chair: '. . . like they had just been brought from the store and hadn't been put away yet.'

Simececk's house was examined, and a shirt and pants found in a closet were heavily stained with human blood; a ·32 calibre revolver (a test bullet from which matched the bullet in Verna Petan's body) and a hunting knife were found hidden in the attic; coarse blond hairs caught in Mrs Petan's wedding ring matched Simececk's hair. Simececk admitted his guilt: 'I'd had an urge to make love to her, but when she started screaming I shot her and stabbed her. Her screams brought the children from outdoors. . . .'

Found legally sane, James Simececk was brought to trial in March 1942; he was found guilty on four separate counts of murder, and sentenced to four terms of life imprisonment.

SLATER, Oscar (born Leschziner)

A German-Jew, born 1873, convicted in May 1909 of the murder, the previous December, of 83-year-old Marion Gilchrist in her luxurious first-floor flat at 15 Queen's Terrace, Glasgow. On the day of the murder 21-year-old Helen Lambie, Miss Gilchrist's maid, had been sent out by her mistress to buy an evening paper. On returning from this errand the maid was approached by Mr Arthur Adams who occupied the groundfloor flat; he had, he said, heard strange violent noises coming from Miss Gilchrist's flat – his ceiling, he claimed, had been 'like to crack'. When they entered the Gilchrist flat a man came out of the spare bedroom and sped past them 'like greased lightning'. Seconds later 14-year-old Mary Barrowman was almost knocked down in the street outside by this fleeing intruder. Marion Gilchrist's body was found in the dining-room, her head crushed by sixty ferocious blows. The old lady possessed much jewellery, but only one piece was missing – a crescent-shaped diamond brooch. The police had little information to go on, the three witnesses to the intruder giving only vague (and differing) descriptions of the man. Then the police were told by cycle dealer Allan M'Lean that a man called Slater had been trying to pawn a diamond crescent-shaped brooch in a Glasgow club. Police called at Slater's flat in St George's Road, but found that Slater with his prostitute mistress had left for New York in the liner *Lusitania*. It transpired that Slater had pawned a crescent-shaped brooch on November 18th, but three weeks before the killing, nor had it been Miss Gilchrist's brooch; this should have absolved Slater from any complicity in the crime, but the Glasgow police (who had been criticized by the populace for their failure to arrest anyone for the murder) pursued Slater to America, from which country he was extradited in February 1909. Helen Lambie, Arthur Adams, and Mary Barrowman had previously been transported under police escort to New York, where they had all (notwithstanding their conflicting descriptions of the intruder) identified Oscar Slater as the intruder. Unfortunately for Slater, his character was bad; he had, for example, lived off the earnings of prostitutes, and had found gambling more remunerative than honest employment. But this did not make him a murderer, and his subsequent trial in May 1909 for the murder of Marion Gilchrist is one of the most disgraceful episodes in the annals of British justice. During the proceedings, held at the High Court of Justiciary in Edinburgh, the Lord Advocate, Mr Alexander Ure, KC, met with no opposition from defending counsel when he attacked Slater's mode of life, adding: 'I say without hesitation that the man in the dock is capable of having committed this dastardly outrage.' Key witnesses Lambie, Barrowman, and Adams repeated their assertions that Slater resembled the intruder, although Barrowman admitted that she had been shown photographs of Slater before her identification of him in New York, and Adams (who was shortsighted) was clearly unhappy when giving a cautious opinion that the prisoner 'closely resembled' the man seen emerging from the Gilchrist flat. Helen Lambie, who had previously said that she did not see the intruder's face, now claimed to have seen him side-face and said he was clean-shaven, although there was evidence that Slater, on the day of the murder, had worn a moustache.

A jury of fifteen returned a majority verdict of guilty; Slater (who had not been called to give evidence on his own behalf) cried out, 'I know nothing about the affair. You are convicting an innocent man!' Due to hang on May 27th, Slater was reprieved, and commenced life imprisonment.

Through the years many individuals protested at what they considered the wrongful conviction of Slater – Conan Doyle, Edgar Wallace, and Marshall Hall among them. Eventually, nineteen years after his trial, Oscar Slater was vindicated on appeal; he was released and given £6,000 as some compensation for his terrible ordeal. It is perhaps, irrelevant, but still curious to note that Slater never showed any gratitude towards his benefactors; indeed, he seemed almost to resent Conan Doyle, who by most accounts fully reciprocated this dislike. Slater married in 1937 and lived in Ayr, Scotland, until his death in February 1948.

SMALL, Frederick L.

Resolute wife killer, who chloroformed, battered, strangled, and shot his wife to death before burning the corpse in his home by Lake Ossipee, near Boston in Massachusetts, USA. One night in 1916, residents of Mountainview, a holiday spot by the shores of Ossipee, noticed the Small bungalow aflame. Afterwards the remains of Mrs Arlene Small were found in the cellar, lying in a pool of water which had helped to preserve her corpse from the blaze; the body had evidently slipped through a weak spot on the living-room floor into the cellar below. (It transpired that Frederick Small had plastered this inadequate part of cellar ceiling himself, having expressed dissatisfaction with the local builder.) The violent and multiple nature of Mrs Small's death established, it was also apparent that she had died hours before the fire started. Frederick Small, summoned from Boston to where he had departed the previous afternoon, expressed horror at the killing ('My chum, my pet – who could have done this wicked thing?') and hinted that a lumberjack from nearby woodland might be responsible. But the bullet that had shot Mrs

Small came from her husband's ·38 revolver, and the rope still intact around her neck came from his boat. Revelations about Small's past cruelty to Arlene, and the fact that only a short time before he had insured her life for £5,000 made police suspicious. Discovery, in the burned-out bungalow, of an empty five-gallon kerosene tin together with cog wheels, springs, and an alarm-clock attachment increased this suspicion, and the Press hummed with rumours of an 'arson machine' whose lethal properties could be timed. Thus, it was argued, the bungalow could have been set ablaze at the moment Frederick Small was in Boston watching the film, *Where are my Children?* The defence tried to quash this theory when Small was brought to trial for the murder of his wife at Carroll County Courthouse, Ossipee, producing a university professor who ridiculed the idea. The prosecution's reply was to bring into court a mechanic who contrived on the spot an 'arson machine' from apparatus identical to that salvaged from the fire. Small was found guilty and sentenced to death.

SMETHURST, Dr Thomas
A puzzling Victorian murder case. Smethurst was accused of the murder of his mistress, Isabella Bankes, by poison, and he had some motive since she had willed £1,750 to him. On the other hand, he was a well-to-do man, and the motive seems inadequate.

Smethurst was living in a Bayswater boarding house with his wife, who was twenty years his senior, when he met Miss Bankes in October 1858; she also came to live in the house. She was 43. She soon became Smethurst's mistress. The landlady smelt scandal and asked her to leave. She did, but Smethurst left with her and married her bigamously in Battersea Parish Church; they then lived as man and wife in Old Palace Gardens, Richmond; this was in December. Miss Bankes became ill in March 1859, with much vomiting and other symptoms of poisoning. The two doctors Smethurst called in diagnosed poisoning. (They did not know that she was also pregnant, and that this might account partly for her vomiting.) Three doctors went to a local magistrate to report the poisoning when they learned that Smethurst would benefit by her will, and Smethurst was arrested; he was released, however, because of Miss Bankes' illness. But she died the next day, May 3rd, 1859, and Smethurst was arrested again. However, no poison was found in the body, and Smethurst's finances were in a healthy state, so that the money could hardly have been the motive. His defence alleged that Miss Bankes' illness was dysentery, aggravated by pregnancy sickness (she was seven weeks pregnant). Smethurst was found guilty, but a controversy arose, and Sir Benjamin Brodie, a great physician, examined the case at the request of the Home Secretary; on his recommendation, Smethurst was released. He received a year in prison for bigamy, and when he came out, was successful in obtaining Miss Bankes' estate. He was 56 years old at the time of his release.

SMITH, George Joseph (The 'Brides in the Bath' Murderer)

George Joseph Smith is one of the most powerful arguments against judicial savagery in criminal history. He was born in Bow in 1872, and when he was only 9 years old he was sentenced to eight years in a reformatory. This undoubtedly had the effect of making him a ruthless enemy of society. Anyone who has visited a Borstal institution today, and can envisage how much more horrible they must have been in 1880, may have more sympathy for George Smith than for the judge who condemned him.

In 1896 he was sentenced to a year in jail for receiving stolen goods – the actual thief was a servant girl who stole under his direction. He was released in 1897, at the age of 25, and a year later married Caroline Thornhill in Leicester, where he had become a baker and confectioner. He used the name George Oliver Love. Two years later they separated, and his wife went to Canada. But in her two years with him she had also become a criminal; under her husband's influence, she became a maidservant in London and pilfered from her employers. When finally arrested, she gave Smith away and he again was condemned to two years in jail for receiving stolen goods – the maximum sentence. While his wife had been living with him, Smith had 'married' a middle-aged London boarding-house keeper and, one assumes, made money out of her. When he was released from prison in October 1902, he went back to the lady and spent all the money he could get from her; then he left her.

During the next six years he perfected his method of 'marriage swindler'. It is not known how many women he 'married' and left (the women were diffident in coming forward), but the technique was probably always the same: once the woman was 'married' and had trusted her husband with her money, he went out on some pretext – to buy a paper – and vanished.

In 1908 he met and 'married' the woman for whom he seems to have felt genuine affection. He had set up in Bristol as an antique dealer; Edith Mabel Pegler answered his advertisement for a housekeeper, and on July 30th, 1908, Smith married her at Bristol under his own name. Miss Pegler seems to have had no suspicion of her husband's real trade; he explained his absences by telling her that he had to travel around buying antiques.

In August 1910, Smith was travelling in Clifton (Bristol) when he met Bessie Constance Annie Munday, a woman of 31 and possessor of £2,500. Smith called himself Henry Williams. The courtship was swift; before the end of August they were 'married' at Weymouth Registry Office. Miss Munday was Smith's second 'wife' since his marriage to Edith Pegler; the first was a lady whom he had deserted in the National Gallery after stealing her money (£350) and selling her clothes. As a result of this previous swindle, Miss Pegler had been established in a house at Southend.

Smith soon discovered that Miss Munday's capital was firmly tied up. He managed to get possession of a mere £135, and deserted her, leaving a letter telling her that she was to tell her relatives that the money had been left in a bag on the beach and stolen.

For the next two years, Smith seems to have lived quietly with Miss Pegler at Bristol, Southend, Walthamstow, and London, ending in Bristol again. In March 1912, Miss Munday was living at Weston-super-Mare. She met Smith in the street and was instantly reconciled to him. Again, Smith tried to get possession of her property, without success. So he tried another method. They made wills in one another's favour, and then Smith bought a zinc bath for £1 17s. 6d. On July 13th, 1912, Miss Munday was found drowned in this bath in their house in the High Street, Herne Bay. Smith obtained her property, and rejoined Miss Pegler at Margate. He explained his affluence by saying he had had a profitable business trip to Canada.

Smith now bought seven houses in Bristol for £2,180.

His next victim was a healthy professional nurse named Alice Burnham, whom he met at Southsea. She was the daughter of a coal merchant. Smith obtained her ready cash – £100 – and insured her life for £500. They were married on Ocober 31st, 1913, and on December 12th, 1913, she was drowned in her bath in a house in Regents Road, Blackpool. Again a verdict of death by misadventure was returned, and Smith made £600 by her death. His landlady was so disgusted by Smith's callous attitude to his dead wife that she refused to let him sleep in the house.

Smith's reply to her reproaches was, 'When they're dead, they're dead.'

There followed another quiet year with Miss Pegler. Then, in September 1914, he repeated his old trick of 'marry and run', marrying Alice Reavil, a domestic servant in Bournemouth, and absconding with £100 or so and her clothes and jewellery. Then, in December 1914, he met his last victim, Margaret Elizabeth Lofty, lady's companion and clergyman's daughter, who was suffering from a broken heart when Smith met her. This was soon cured and she married him on December 17th, 1914. The marriage took place at Bath – perhaps a saturnine joke on Smith's part – and he gave his name as Lloyd. They moved to Bismarck Road, Highgate, and she made a will leaving all her property to John Lloyd. The day after they moved in, the land-lady heard sounds of a struggle in the bathroom and hands slap-ping the side of the bath. A few minutes later, she heard the organ pealing in the sitting-room – John Lloyd was playing. Water began to leak through the ceiling, and soon Lloyd ap-peared at the front door, saying, '*I have bought some tomatoes for Mrs Lloyd's supper.*' This was a part of Smith's ritual; before Miss Munday's body was found, he was out buying fish; with Miss Burnham, it was eggs.

Miss Lofty was found drowned in her bath, and the verdict, as usual, was 'misadventure'.

The death was reported in the papers, and a relative of Miss Burnham saw it, and was struck by the similarity in the two cases; he reported it to the Aylesbury police; another was his landlord at Blackpool, Mr Crossley, who had been so horrified by Smith's callousness about Alice Burnham's death. He wrote to Scotland Yard. The Yard immediately followed up the trail, and warned Smith's solicitor in Shepherd's Bush not to pay over the insurance money for Miss Lofty's death. Finally, in January 1915, Smith was arrested on a charge of causing a false entry to be made on a marriage certificate. As evidence against him accumulated, the charge was altered to murder.

Smith's trial began on June 22nd, 1915, and lasted for nine days. It took place before Mr Justice Scrutton at the Old Bailey, Sir Archibald Bodkin prosecuting and Sir Edward Marshall Hall defending. The jury were out for twenty-three minutes and returned a verdict of guilty. Smith protested his innocence to the end, but was executed – in a state of collapse – on August 13th, 1915.

Typical of Smith's calculating callousness as an incident in connexion with his purchase of the bath in which Miss Munday was drowned; the shop asked £2 for it, but Smith beat them down by half a crown!

An example of the legends inspired by murderers is a story heard by the present writer in Leicester. A baker living in Wharf Street, Leicester, some time at the beginning of the Second World War, told the father of the present writer that he was convinced there was a body buried under his baking oven, since it had sunk several times in a few years, and he had to keep putting wedges underneath it. He claimed that the baker's shop had been occupied by Smith, and that there was a local story that Smith had killed an old man 'for his money' and buried him there. The baker added that he did not want to call in the police because they would interrupt business by removing his oven and digging up his kitchen.

It is possible, of course, that there may be one of Smith's victims buried under the oven in Wharf Street. But it should also be remembered that Smith was a baker in Leicester (his address does not seem to be available) when he was only 26, some years before he began his career of murder. Admittedly, he returned in 1902 (when he was 30) searching for his wife; but no 'old man' is mentioned in the somewhat fragmentary accounts that exist of Smith's career.

SMITH, Joe (The William Bissett Murder)
Straightforward case of murder for robbery, of interest only because, in spite of its obvious nature, the police had to do much patient investigation before the murderer could be brought to trial.

William Bissett was a well-to-do old man, 71 years of age, who lived in Church Street, Slough. On December 19th, 1947, he was reported missing to the Bucks. Constabulary. He was known to carry too much money on him. It was soon discovered that he had last been seen on the previous day, at about ten-thirty, talking to a gipsy named Joe Smith in the Cock Inn. He had pulled out a large bundle of notes to pay for a drink. He had left the Inn with Smith and not been seen again.

Smith at first declared that Bissett had walked on home after they parted; later, he admitted to hitting the old man, and later still, to robbing him of £35 and a gold watch and chain. In the gipsy camp was found a pair of bloodstained trousers, soaked with water to the knees, and digging revealed a sack with the old man's clothes in it. In a nearby stream was found the body, bruises on the face, and with the neck broken. It might be assumed that the police had an 'open and shut' case against the gipsy, but there were probems. Although Bissett had been dead some sixty hours when found, he had been in the water for only twenty-four hours. Yet there was water and sand in the lungs. The defence might easily claim that Bissett had not been badly injured, but had staggered to the stream and met his death by drowning. Painstaking police investigation finally revealed that Bissett had been carried to the gipsy encampment across the stream, while still alive. The stream was swollen in December, and he had been allowed to fall in and had swallowed water. His body had then been hidden in the gipsy camp for a day, and finally taken to the stream. Smith had almost certainly had accomplices, but these were never discovered, although two gipsies finally admitted that Smith had awakened them and tried to sell a gold watch; he had also burned a £5 note.

Smith was found guilty and sentenced to death.

SMITH, Madeleine
Twenty-one-year-old architect's daughter, who in 1857 was tried for the murder of her lover, 30-year-old clerk Émile L'Angelier.

Madeleine Smith lived with her prosperous family at 7 Blythswood Square, Glasgow. In 1855, she met L'Angelier, a Frenchman who earned £100 a year in the office of Huggins and Company, seed merchants. '. . . I often wish you were near us,' wrote Madeleine in the early stages of their acquaintance, 'one enjoys walking with a pleasant companion, and where could we find one equal to yourself?' The two became lovers, and Madeleine's letters more passionate, each one signed 'Mimi', L'Angelier's pet name for his mistress: '. . . I must now conclude with a fond embrace and a dear, sweet kiss. I wish it was to be given, not sent. Kindest, warmest love to you, my husband dear. Love again from thy very fond, thy loving and ever devoted . . .' Madeleine's father forbade the association, but they continued to meet clandestinely: in Madeleine's basement bedroom, in a wood near the Smiths' country residence and at the home of a mutual friend. A coolness in Madeleine's ardour, both in person and on paper, coincided with rumours of her impending marriage to Mr William Minnoch, a Glasgow merchant. Soon Madeleine was writing to request the return of her letters, adding a postscript: 'I did once love you fondly, but for some time back I have lost much of that.' Panic-stricken when L'Angelier showed a sinister tendency to keep the incriminating mail ('hate me, despise me – but do not expose me!'), Madeleine inexplicably resumed her passionate wiles, and was presently arranging further meetings with the French clerk. Two such appointments were kept, both in the basement of the Blythswood Square house, each time Madeleine offering L'Angelier a cup of cocoa. After the first meeting L'Angelier was ill; after the second, on March 23rd, 1857, he collapsed and died upon returning to his lodgings. Dr Penny, Professor of Chemistry in the Andersonian College, Glasgow, examined the body, and found one-fifth of an ounce of arsenic in the stomach. Madeleine's letters were discovered and on March 31st she was arrested on a charge of murdering L'Angelier, her trial opening on Tuesday, June 30th, at the Edinburgh High Court of Justiciary.

There was evidence Madeleine had attempted to buy prussic acid earlier that year, but the servant dispatched on this peculiar quest had returned empty-handed, saying the chemist required a doctor's prescription. Madeleine then became obsessed by a desire to kill rats, although neither of the Smith residences was known to be pestered by vermin. Three separate purchases of rat-poison were made, all containing arsenic mixed (as the law regulating poisons required) with soot or indigo, neither of which substances were found in L'Angelier's body. Madeleine herself, apparently forgetting the rats, said she had used the arsenic as a cosmetic (applied externally this was a Victorian method of beautifying the skin) but as soot and indigo could hardly be termed cosmetic, this statement implies that Madeleine found some way of extracting the poison. The defence asserted the probability of suicide; Dr Christison, toxicologist, said that the amount of arsenic actually swallowed by L'Angelier was likely to have been double the amount found in the stomach, and suicides generally took enormous doses of poison. It was implied that it was impossible for L'Angelier to have partaken unknowingly of the arsenic in a cup of cocoa. The jury's verdict was the Scottish one of not proven, and Madeleine Smith was freed.

Years later, after two marriages (first to a man named Hora, then to artist George Wardle) she settled in London, mixing with so-called 'Bohemian' types. It is said she once served a meal to George Bernard Shaw, and that George du Maurier (unaware of her identity) declared at a Hora soirée: 'Madeleine Smith's beauty shouldn't have saved her from the scaffold.' She died in America in 1928.

SNYDER, Ruth

An intense Norwegian of 32, living in Prohibition-time New York, who preferred the attentions of corset-salesman Judd Gray to those of her husband Albert, art-editor of a boating magazine. On several occasions she tried to kill Albert – by gas, drugs, and suffocation, but he only remonstrated mildly with his wife, urging a course of Christian Science as a means of curbing her violence. Then Judd ('Lover Boy') handed Ruth ('Momsie') one of his traveller's samples, with three objects concealed within the pink folds – a heavy sash-weight, some picture wire, and a bottle of chloroform. They clumsily staged a break-in at the Snyder residence, hoping that lawless intruders would be blamed for the murder of Albert Snyder. But the tale had inconsistencies and soon Mrs Snyder and Mr Judd, each accusing the other of striking the fatal blows, were standing trial before such fashionable court witnesses as Peggy Hopkins Joyce, D. W. Griffith, and Aimee Semple Macpherson. Small, bespectacled Judd seemed of weaker stuff than Ruth, labelled 'Granite Woman' by reporters. Both were electrocuted in January 1928. A reporter at Mrs Snyder's execution concealed a minute camera on his leg, thus recording for posterity a blurred vision of the 'Granite Woman's' last seconds.

STACEY, William

Twenty-four-year-old killer of Darlynne Todd on November 22nd, 1954, in Chicago. Darlynne Todd, a 16-year-old house-wife, was found bludgeoned, choked, and stabbed to death in the Wilson Avenue flat in which she lived with her husband and baby. She was clad only in panties, but had not been sexually assaulted. In the room was found the appointment card of a photographic agency. The young photographer, William Stacey, finally confessed to the murder. He had gone to the apartment at ten-thirty, several hours after Darlynne Todd's husband had gone to work, to photograph the baby. Mrs Todd was dressed only in a bathrobe and panties. When she had bent over the cot, the robe had fallen open. Stacey assaulted her with the intention of raping her, but ended by knocking her unconscious with a baseball bat which he always carried in his equipment bag (as 'a divider for supplies') and stabbing her eight times.

Stacey alleged – and there is no reason to doubt him – that he considered himself a religious and church-going young man. The obvious comment on the case is that this seems to have been his hard luck as well as Mrs Todd's. Most young men, finding an attractive 16-year-old girl half-naked, several hours after her husband has gone to work and she is expecting a photographer, would have considered it an invitation to love-making. When the bathrobe fell open, the result was not a simple desire for sex, but a sense of self-division that produced violence.

The interest of the case – otherwise commonplace enough – lies in the clarity with which the motives can be seen, and on the light it sheds indirectly on the problem of sexual violence. The sexual stimulation is abundantly present (as see also the case of the murder of Panta Lou Liles by Charles Floyd). Brought into contact with an attitude of similar casualness, no conflict results. But mixed with religious taboos, it produces an explosion out of all proportion to its cause.

STANSFIELD, Philip
Convicted of the murder of his father in 1687.

Philip Stansfield was the eldest son of Sir James Stansfield of New Milns (now Amisfield). He was a heavy drinker, and his father, finally exasperated by his profligacy, cut him out of his will and conferred the estate on his youngest son. But he felt some apprehension about Philip, and tried to avoid him. There is a story that Philip had one day thrown a stone at a street preacher, who had remarked that he did not know who threw the stone, but that whoever it was, he would have a larger crowd at his death than the crowd who were listening to the sermon.

On the evening of the tragedy, November 21st, 1687, Sir James apparently stayed out late to avoid his son, who was at home, and returned with a clergyman, a Mr John Bell. Bell subsequently proved to be worse than useless. In the middle of the night he heard noises and some cries, but 'supposed they were evil spirits' and bolted his door. He was either a coward or a simpleton. The next morning, Philip apparently came and asked him where his father was; Bell said he didn't know; Philip said he had been seeking him on the 'banks of the water'. The body was then found to be floating on a pond in the garden. Bell retired to his room trembling, and later opined that it was murder committed by evil spirits.

Philip had the body buried quickly, refusing permission for it to be examined, but the authorities decided to exhume it. It was then found that Sir James had been strangled, not drowned. Philip was asked to help replace the body in the coffin, and, as he touched it, it bled. (The indictment had the phrase that this had happened 'according to God's usual method for discovering a murder'.) Philip was alarmed and fled from the room.

Two children were subsequently discovered who revealed that there had been accomplices in the crime. Philip had spent the evening in the cottage of an outside servant, James Thompson, and had complained that his father had treated him badly; he proposed that Thompson and a woman of ill-repute named Janet Johnston should help him to murder the old man. The three then went out; when they returned, Thompson remarked: 'The deed is done.' The boy, who was in bed, heard them say that Philip had kept guard outside the room while the old man was killed.

At the trial, Sir George Mackenzie, who was known as 'the bloodthirsty advocate', spoke at length, and in conclusion asked that the jurors themselves should be put on trial if they failed to return a verdict of guilty. Philip was condemned to death, and sentenced to have his tongue cut out for urging two servants to curse the King and himself cursing his father. His lands and goods were confiscated.

When he was being hanged, the knot slipped and he fell on his knees on the platform; the hangman had to strangle him. His contemporaries regarded this as another sure sign of his guilt – that he had met the same fate as his father. Someone, who may have wanted to prove this further, took down his body – which had been hung in chains – and dropped it into a ditch of stagnant water.

STARR, Belle
Perhaps, with 'Calamity Jane', the most celebrated female out-law of the Wild West.

She was born as Myra Belle Shirley Starr on February 5th, 1848, in a log cabin somewhere on the Missouri frontier. Her father, John Starr, is said to have been of aristocratic Virginian descent, and had 800 acres of land ten miles north-west of Carthage, Missouri. When Belle was 8 she became a member of the Carthage Female Academy.

The Kansas–Missouri border war ruined her father's tavern business, and he moved to Scyene, Texas.

Cole Younger, the famous outlaw, met Belle Starr in Texas shortly after he had broken with a half of the gang of bank robbers led by himself and Jesse James. Younger was in Texas with Jesse James at the time he met Belle, and he is generally supposed to be the father of her daughter Pearl.

Her next lover was a train robber, Jim Reed. He and Belle fled to California to escape the law, and she presented Reed with a son, Edward. In 1869, Belle, Reed, and two other outlaws tortured an old Indian in North Canadian River country until he told them the hiding place of $30,000 in gold. She returned to Texas and played the bandit queen for all she was worth, wearing a velvet gown, riding-boots, and six-shooters.

In 1874 Reed was killed by a member of his gang; Belle left Scyene and became leader of a gang of horse thieves in the Indian-held section of Oklahoma. In 1876 she took an Indian called Blue Duck as a lover, and then Sam Starr, a Cherokee. Belle was now 28. She and Sam Starr settled near Briartown, north of the Canadian River. Belle named the place Youngers Bend. The Starr clan was led by 'Uncle Tom', who had burned a whole family to death in 1843. Jesse James once paid a visit to Belle at Youngers Bend.

In 1883 Belle's newspaper renown began when she was tried as leader of a gang of horse thieves by 'Hanging Judge' Parker in the Federal Court of West Arkansas. She was found guilty and sentenced to six months in jail; Sam got a year. They served the time at Detroit and returned to Youngers Bend. In 1885, Sam took a vacation in the hills (perhaps with the law on his trail) and Belle took as a lover another wanted killer, John Middleton. But Middleton was ambushed and killed, and Sam reappeared, to take up his old trade of horse stealing. In 1886 they were again charged with horse stealing, but the case was dismissed for lack of evidence, and Belle gained more publicity. At Christmas Sam was shot by a dying Indian deputy whom he had shot in a drunken brawl; Belle then took 'Jim July', a Creek Indian, as a lover. Jim was wanted on a larceny charge, and Belle persuaded him to give himself up as she was convinced there was no evidence; she rode to Fort Smith with him in January 1889. On the way home she was ambushed and murdered, probably by a neighbour, a wanted man who suspected that Belle intended to betray him. She was buried on February 3rd, 1889, in front of the cabin at Youngers Bend; on her grave were the highly inappropriate words:

Shed not for her the bitter tear
Nor give the heart to vain regret,
'Tis but the basket that lies here
The gems that filled it sparkles yet.

Although Belle Starr was never accused of murder, she certainly took part in many killings. With 'Ma Barker' she is among America's most vicious criminal women.

The legend that describes her as beautiful is untrue; she was hatchet-faced and of 'tough' appearance.

STAUNTON, Louis
Tried at the Old Bailey, with brother Patrick Staunton, Patrick's wife Elizabeth, and Alice Rhodes, in September 1877 for the murder of Louis' wife, 36-year-old Harriet.

In 1875, auctioneer's clerk Louis Staunton, then aged 24, married; wife Harriet, ten years older, was unattractive and mentally deficient, but the inheritor of £3,000. The first months of married life were spent in Loughborough Park Road, Brixton, where Harriet's uneasy mother paid them one visit, lasting ten minutes. ('Louis, Mama is here,' called Harriet, opening the door. Upon being asked how she was, Harriet replied, 'Middling well, Mama.') The following day Harriet's mother received letters from Louis and Harriet, both informing her that it would be better if she did not call again.

In the spring of 1876 Harriet gave birth to a boy; during the summer she was moved to Patrick's cottage near Cudham, in a remote part of Kent, where Louis gave his brother £1 a week (from Harriet's own money) for looking after her. In November, Louis moved to a farm-house nearby, where he lived with Elizabeth Staunton's younger sister, Alice Rhodes. (Both Elizabeth and Alice were distantly related to Harriet.) In February 1877 Harriet's mother accidentally met Alice Rhodes at London Bridge; suspicious when she noticed Rhodes wearing one of Harriet's brooches, she received evasive replies when she asked about her daughter's welfare and whereabouts. Nevertheless, she traced Louis Staunton's farm-house abode, and on March 5th called on him, only to receive abuse and have the door slammed in her face. On April 8th, Patrick and Elizabeth Staunton deposited Harriet's child at a London hospital ('its mother neglected it') where, within a few hours, it was to die from starvation. On April 12th, Louis and Elizabeth Staunton obtained lodgings at 34 Forbes Road, Penge, in South-east London, 'for a sick lady'; here, at dusk, they brought Harriet (although none of her clothes), where she died the next day. A surgeon, Mr Dean Longrigg, gave, at first, the cause of death as 'cerebral disease and apoplexy'. A customer at the local post office, by coincidence a brother-in-law of Harriet's, overheard someone inquiring about the registering of a death; hearing that the home address of the deceased was Cudham, and remembering his mother-in-law's abortive visit there and her concern about her daughter, the man informed the police and a line of inquiry was started which was to end in the arrest, on a murder charge, of the three Stauntons and Alice Rhodes.

At the inquest on Harriet Staunton it had been stated that there was not an ounce of fat on the body, which was in a filthy condition, dirt-caked and verminous. Pathologists examining the remains decided that the cause of death was neglect and starvation; Mr Longrigg, who was present at the post-mortem, held this opinion, and at the trial was questioned by Mr (afterwards Sir) Edward Clarke, defending Patrick Staunton, who suggested that Harriet's death might have been caused by tuberculosis, phthisis, diabetes, or Addison's disease. Tubercles had been found on the brain, but had (according to Mr Longrigg) no bearing on the death: '. . . the amount of tubercle was very, very slight.' Dr J. S. Bristowe, an expert on morbid anatomy, who had read the pathologists' reports on Harriet's death, appeared for the defence; he believed she might have died from tuberculosis, as did another pathologist, Dr Payne, who had also read the medical depositions on the condition of the corpse. He was questioned by the Attorney-General, Sir John Holker:

What, in your opinion, caused the emaciation? – I cannot attribute it to anything without knowing more of the case.
Is it consistent with starvation? – Yes, it may be.
Is it consistent with tuberculosis? – Yes, it is consistent with tuberculosis.

Mr Justice Hawkins, who had showed intolerance of conflicting medical opinions, summed up heavily against the prisoners, and on September 26th, 1877, they were found guilty and sentenced to death. Agitation followed in medical quarters, many doctors believing that Drs Bristowe and Payne were correct in their assumptions. Seven hundred doctors, headed by Sir William Jenner, signed a petition of protest and sent it to the Home Secretary. On October all four prisoners were reprieved; Alice Rhodes was released, the others served varying terms of imprisonment.

STRATTON Brothers, The (The First British Fingerprint Murder)

On a rainy Monday morning in March 1905, an elderly couple named Farrow were found battered in a chandler's shop in Deptford High Street. The husband was dead, and his wife died three days later in hospital. The motive had obviously been robbery, and two black masks, made of silk stockings, were found in the shop. A right thumbprint was found on the tray of the cashbox, which did not correspond to either of the victims or a policeman who admitted touching the tray. The robbery had obviously been committed under the delusion that the Farrows kept a large sum of money on the premises. Actually, they were only employees of the shop, and had only a few pounds in the cash-box.

Scotland Yard was called in. Chief Inspector Fox assumed that the men must be locals, since they had been afraid of identification; this was made even more certain when it was found that the masks were made from a pair of Mrs Farrow's stockings, indicating that the murderers were afraid she might recover and recognize them.

A careful police check on all known criminals in Deptford finally led suspicion to fall on two young hooligans who had already served several terms for housebreaking, Albert and Alfred Stratton. Alfred was the elder of the two, and a detective who knew his mistress got her into conversation when he noticed her with a black eye; she was finally persuaded to admit that Alfred and Albert had been out of all night on the night of the murder. Later he had destroyed a coat he wore that night.

On the Sunday after the murder, a police officer heard that Alfred was in a certain public house. With some courage he went in alone (the place was full of prostitutes, seamen, and petty criminals) and told Alfred to come outside, where he arrested him for murder. Albert was later located in a lodging house in Stepney. The thumbprint on the tray was found to have eleven points of resemblance to Alfred's right thumbprint.

The police had considerable corroborative evidence of the guilt of the Strattons, but the thumbprint was an important part of the evidence. Mr Justice Channell, in his summing up, was cautious about the thumbprint evidence, being of the old school, but admitted the extraordinary resemblance. The Strattons were found guilty and sentenced to death.

SYKES, Troisville
Killer of the New Orleans famous brothel madame, Kate Town-
send, on Saturday, November 3rd, 1883, in Basin Street.

Kate Townsend had been Sykes' mistress for some twenty-five
years when she was murdered. He had met her when they stayed
in the same house in Canal Street; later, when Kate moved into
the Basin Street house – the most expensive brothel on Basin
Street – he moved with her. She was a powerful woman, who
weighed more than twenty stones at the time of her death.
Apparently, she was in the habit of beating Sykes, and had been
in an ugly mood and under the influence of drink for many days
before the murder. Sykes was apparently a presentable man who
spoke and dressed like a gentleman. On the morning of the
quarrel, Kate Townsend apparently summoned Sykes to her
room and called him names. Sykes then alleged that she attacked
him with a pair of shears and a bowie knife. Sykes received a deep
slash on one of his thighs and some scratches. He claimed that
'everything went blank' until he found himself bending over
Kate's body, holding the bowie knife.

His trial began on January 29th, 1884. Since he was known to
be of an exceedingly mild and even cowardly disposition, while
his victim was noted for her strength and violence, he was found
not guilty and acquitted. Kate Townsend's estate went to him (it
amounted to almost $100,000), but legal complications arose,
and four years later he was granted only $340 under the law of
concubinage. Only $34,000 went to the State, the remainder
having been absorbed by lawyers' fees.

Accounts of the murder and trial make interesting reading today, because of the insight they give into New Orleans at the end
of the nineteenth century, in the days before the town became
famous for its jazz. The brothel quarter was eventually closed
down before the Great War.[1]

T

TARNOVSKA, Marie
Tried in 1910 for conspiring to murder an unwanted lover and
sentenced to eight years in prison.

Marie Tarnovska was born O'Rourk, daughter of an Irish Count
living in Russia. (An ancestor had been one of Peter the Great's

[1] See *Murder in New Orleans* by Robert Tallant, Wm. Kimber.

mercenaries.) Her mother was Russian. At the age of 12, she was sent to an exclusive school for the daughters of noblemen in Kiev. At thirteen she was already beautiful and mature. At the age of 16, she persuaded a lover, Count Tarnovskiy, to elope with her and marry her, after which they returned to Kiev and became favourites in polite society. However, Count Tarnovskiy (as Marie's father had warned her) soon returned to his old libertinism, and Marie finally took his brother Pietro as a lover. However, she decided to end the liaison and sent Pietro off; he committed suicide. Shortly afterwards, a wealthy financier also committed suicide when she transferred her favours to an officer of the Imperial Guard, Alexis Bozevski.

Bozevski was an ardent and violent lover; finally, Marie decided to get rid of him. She allowed him into her bedroom one night and received him in her nightgown (which was diaphanous). When her husband entered, she proceeded to struggle and pretend that Bozevski was assaulting her. Count Tarnovskiy shot the startled lover, who died soon after, attended by Marie (who no doubt explained that she had been forced to pretend his caresses were unwelcome to save her good name). Marie now exerted herself to get her husband sent to Siberia, purchasing the loyalty of a lawyer named Prulikov in the usual way. Prulikov failed; the husband learned the truth of the 'attempted rape' and left his wife penniless. Marie immediately persuaded Prulikov to leave his wife and three children and to travel with her all over Europe and North Africa. (Her own two children were in the custody of their father.) Prulikov tried to leave his mistress and return to his wife at Marseilles, but left the train at the next station and returned to her.

There is undoubtedly a touch of Manon Lescaut about Marie. Back in Russia, she immediately took another lover, Count Paul Karmarovski, a colonel who had just returned from the Russo–Japanese war. Prulikov, who had embezzled a great deal of money for his mistress, was sent packing until he should be of further use.

Karmarovski made the mistake of telling Marie that one of his best friends, Dr Nicholas Naumov, was a woman-hater. Marie regarded this as a challenge, and soon had Naumov so completely in her power that he fired a bullet through his hand and allowed her to tattoo him with a dagger (she sterilized the wounds with eau-de-Cologne).

The triangle was now complete. Marie decided that she wanted to be rid of both Karmarovski and Naumov. She evolved the neat plan of persuading both Naumov and Prulikov to kill Karmarovski. When Prulikov discovered that he was a supernumerary, she told him to wait at the hotel with detectives and arrest Naumov as soon as he had killed Karmarovski. She completed her persuasion of Naumov with a 'night of love'. Marie also had the idea of persuading Karmarovski to insure himself in her favour for £20,000.

All went according to plan; Karmarovski was shot by Naumov, and Naumov was arrested by detectives who were waiting with Prulikov downstairs. However, Marie's part in the conspiracy soon came to light, and, after a spectacular trial in Venice, she was sentenced to eight years in prison, Prulikov to ten years, and Naumov to three years. Marie served two years and was released in ill-health in 1912; she died in the early 1920s.

TAWELL, John
Crippen was the first murderer to be arrested through the agency of the wireless telegraph, but the first murderer to be arrested through a telegram was a Quaker named John Tawell. It was in 1845.

Tawell had had a remarkable career; at the age of 20 he had been charged with forgery, had narrowly escaped the death penalty, and been transported to Sydney. There he served his time and set up in business as a chemist. He became a very rich man, dabbling in other things besides drugs and medicines; for example, he cornered the market in whalebone (for use in combs, brushes, etc.).

Finally, he returned to England a respectable man, always dressed as a Quaker, known for his gifts to charity. He bought a house in Berkhamsted, seduced a pretty servant girl called Sarah Hadler, and installed her as his mistress in the Paddington area. She called herself Mrs Hart. After a time she bore Tawell a second child. Tawell, meanwhile, had married (although his first wife died after a few years).

His first attempt to murder her was apparently made in September 1843, when she became ill after drinking some stout he had brought for her. By now she was living at Salt Hill, near Slough.

On January 1st, 1845, he called on her again and sent her out for stout. Later, between six and seven, a neighbour heard stifled screams and saw Tawell emerging from the cottage. He ignored her when she spoke and hurried off. She found Sarah Hadler writhing on the floor; a few minutes later she died. A post-mortem revealed that she had been poisoned by prussic acid.

Meanwhile, a telegram had been sent from Slough to Paddington, describing Tawell's dress and saying he was suspected of murder. He was followed by the police to his lodgings, and the next morning they questioned him. He said he had not left town the previous day, and was arrested.

A chemist of Bishopsgate came forward and identified Tawell as the man who had bought prussic acid from him on the morning of the murder.

Tawell's defence claimed that Sarah Hadler had died from the cyanide contained in apple pips; a large basket of apples was found in the room. But it was pointed out that the cyanide can only be obtained by crushing and distilling apple pips. (The defence was conducted by Fitzroy Kelly, later Baron Kelly, who thereafter became known as Apple-pip Kelly.)

It was a cruel and stupid murder, for the dead woman was completely devoted to Tawell, and had no intention of spoiling his prospect of a second marriage. Tawell confessed later to the murder (he claimed earlier that she had committed suicide in front of him), and gave as his only motive that he was afraid his adultery would become known to his wife. But it is also known that he had become financially embarrassed at the time of the murder, and wanted to cease paying Sarah Hadler her pound a week.

He was convicted on March 14th, 1845, and hanged two weeks later.

TAYLOR, Edwina, Case

On August 31st, 1957, 4-year-old Edwina Taylor was reported missing; she lived with her parents and younger brother Marc in Tudor Road, Upper Norwood, London, and the search that followed was one of the biggest ever organized by the Metropolitan Police. On September 5th her body was found on a heap of coal in the disused basement of a house in St Aubyn's Road, Upper Norwood; Dr Camps, pathologist, stated that the cause of death was brain fracture and strangulation.

The tenant of the ground-floor flat was missing. He was Derrick Edwardson, aged 31, against whom there had been eight convictions – including one for indecently assaulting a girl of five and one for uttering a writing threatening to murder, when he described how he intended to entice a child into his flat where

593

he would rape and kill her. Edwardson's locker at the Acton factory where he worked was opened, and inside was a pair of overalls containing a note:

I killed four-year-old Edwina Taylor. I enticed her to my flat and strangled her with the intention of raping her after death. But I realised that I had killed someone that somebody must have loved and I felt ashamed of myself. I threw her body into the coal cellar, it is still there now as far as I know. I cannot get the smell of her decaying body out of my system. I will surrender tonite. I did not interfere with her.

Edwardson's photograph was circulated to every police station, and was flashed on television screens, but he was not found until on September 9th, after spending the day at the nearby Odeon cinema watching *St Joan* and *Son of an Outlaw*, he gave himself up at Wealdstone, Middlesex, police station. The forensic evidence again Edwardson was damning. Bloodstains of Edwina's group were found in Edwardson's kitchen and on his clothing; hairs from his dog were found on her sandals and cardigan and green wool fibres from the child's coat were found in his trouser turn-ups.

Edwardson was tried at the Old Bailey on October 25th. He pleaded guilty and was sentenced to life imprisonment. After Edwardson's conviction the father of Edwina Taylor wrote to the Home Secretary requesting legislation for the stricter control of known sexual degenerates.

TAYLOR, Louisa Jane
Thirty-seven-year-old widow, a milliner by trade, found guilty in 1882 of the murder by poisoning of her landlady.

In August 1882, soon after her husband's death, Louisa Taylor visited one of the deceased man's friends, 85-year-old William Tregillis, who, with his aged wife, rented two small rooms in the upper part of 3 Naylor's Cottages, Plumstead. Mrs Taylor duly became the Tregillis' lodger, sleeping with Mrs Tregillis in the 'back', while Mr Tregillis pursued solitary slumber in the 'front'. During September, Mrs Tregillis went into a bodily decline; daily she shivered and vomited, while her teeth (according to her husband at the subsequent trial) went 'as black as coal'. A Dr Smith, summoned, diagnosed ague, but asked Mrs Taylor to bring him a specimen of the vomit, a task that lady persistently eschewed on account of (as she later explained) its disgusting nature. Mr Tregillis himself was mentally unalert (he had spent some time in a lunatic asylum), although perturbed by his wife's illness, but even he was suspicious when Mrs Taylor suggested an elopement, regardless of the ailing wife. ('I said, "My wife is not dead. How could I expect to live with you? I would not come unless I married you." ') Mrs Taylor's proposal was strange, considering her relationship with Edward Martin, a watercress vendor, a man much nearer Mrs Taylor's own age. Mr Tregillis was even more amazed when told by Mrs Taylor that she had left him £500 in her will, a copy of which she gave to Tregillis after showing him a curious and brief missive stuck inside an OHMS envelope: 'Madam, you have had £500 left you and can draw it any day.' Regardless of this imminent wealth, Mrs Taylor purloined £10 pension back-pay just after Tregillis had drawn it, under the pretext that his wife wished to see it and have it safe under her pillow. Aroused to wrath at last (Mrs Ellis, the woman on the ground floor, spoke of seeing Mrs Taylor handling the money), the old man consulted the police and Louisa Taylor was charged with the theft on October 6th. Intrigued by the sudden transition of Mrs Taylor from obliging sick-nurse to villainness, Dr Smith brooded on the vast amounts of sugar-of-lead she had been obtaining from him, ostensibly for a skin complaint; with growing dismay he recalled the symptoms of Mrs Tregillis, particularly the discoloured teeth and gums, a sure sign of lead poisoning. On October 9th he asked a police surgeon to examine Mrs Tregillis, who was obviously dying, and had his worst thoughts confirmed; in accordance with the custom of the time, a legal inquiry was held in the victim's room, with the mortally ill woman giving evidence against Mrs Taylor (now in custody) in front of the local magistrates. Mrs Tregillis pointed the accusing finger – literally – at her lodger, recalling how her health had only begun to deteriorate when the younger woman entered the household, and how she had once seen Mrs Taylor pouring some white powder into her medicine bottle. Mrs Tregillis died on October 23rd. At the inquest the doddering Mr Tregillis spoke of the lodger: 'I believe she wanted to get my pension and put me into a lunatic asylum after my wife was gone.' Martin, the watercress man, who on one occasion had called at Dr Smith's for sugar-of-lead for Mrs Taylor now, unhappily and with obvious untruth, denied ever having done this. In December Louisa Taylor was brought to the Old Bailey to face trial on a charge of murdering Mrs Tregillis; the judge was Mr Justice Stephen, who, years later, was to preside over the famous Maybrick poison case. Found guilty, she was executed on January 2nd, 1883. Louisa Taylor's motive for murder is obscure; a young and not unattractive woman, one feels she could have secured bigger game than the wretched Tregillis couple without resorting to murder (the old man's pension was, in any case, less than the amount she received regularly on account of the deceased Mr Taylor) – unless, of course, Mrs Taylor had begun to feel a lust to poison for the sheer pleasure of doing so.

TETZNER, Kurt Erich

A German murderer whose methods were remarkably similar to Alfred Rouse's (although he committed his burning-car murder a year before Rouse; German law took so long to try him that Rouse had been executed by that time!)

Tetzner appears to have been in every way a ruthless criminal. A few months before his burnt-out car was found, he had dissuaded his mother-in-law from having an operation for cancer; he had then insured her life for ten thousand marks (£500) and persuaded her to undergo the operation after all. She died three days after it and Tetzner collected the insurance. The ease with which he got the money apparently inspired him to try Rouse's methods. He discussed the question with his wife, and when she suggested that he dig up a dead body from the cemetery and put it in his car, he pooh-poohed the idea, saying, 'There must be blood around.' He tried advertising for a travelling companion, but a young man who applied obviously felt there was something wrong and changed his mind. One day Tetzner almost succeeded; he gave a lift to a mechanic named Alois Ortner (who later gave evidence at the trial), persuaded the man to look under the car for an oil leak, and attacked him with a hammer. Ortner fought back and Tetzner drove off; a few moments later, Ortner collapsed unconscious. The police at Ingolstadt would not believe his story, and suspected him of an attempt to rob a passing motorist.

On the night of November 25th, 1929, Tetzner gave a lift to a travelling journeyman, 21 years of age. The youth was thinly clad and complained of cold. Tetzner wrapped an overcoat round him pinioning his arms, and strangled him with a rope. Outside Ettershausen, in Bavaria, he crashed the car into a tree and set it alight. Tetzner's wife was sent for and identified the body as that of her husband, who was insured for £7,250. But the insurance company were suspicious, and watched the 'widow's' movements; she had no telephone in her own flat, but she was called to a neighbour's flat twice to answer telephone calls from a Herr Stranelli in Strasbourg. Stranelli was arrested by the French police and found to be Tetzner. He confessed to the murder, but after five months in jail, changed his mind and said that he had knocked a man down and killed him, and had decided to take advantage of the accidental death to defraud the insurance companies. Doctors who gave evidence at the trial – which took place in Ratisbon – agreed that there were injuries to the body that supported his story. But Tetzner's story of his murder plot was against him. He even admitted in court that he had thought of throwing pepper into a man's eyes and burning him alive while he was helpless. He was sentenced to death, and executed at Regensburg on May 2nd, 1931. Before his execution he had told the true story of the murder.

Although there can be no doubt that he deserved his fate, it is hard not to feel that it was his own fault that he was caught, and, having been arrested, that it was his own fault that he was condemned. If he had thought of the story about the accidental death to begin with, and kept quiet about his earlier attempts at murder, he might have escaped the final penalty.

THOMAS, Donald George (The Murder of PC Edgar)
Army deserter, found guilty of the murder of PC Edgar in 1948; the death penalty was suspended at the time, so he was sentenced to life imprisonment – one of the few examples in English law when a man who has killed a policeman has escaped with his life. (See Browne and Kennedy, Marwood, Bentley, Mackay.)

PC Nathaniel Edgar, aged 33, a married man with two children, was patrolling the Southgate area of North London on February 13th, 1948, keeping a careful watch out for burglars, since there had been many recent cases in the Highgate and Southgate area. Shortly after eight in the evening, a woman out walking with her brother heard three shots on Wades Hill, and saw a man running along Broadfields Avenue. She found PC Edgar lying in the garage entrance at 112 Wades Hill, bleeding freely. The constable had taken the name and identity number of his assailant before he was shot; as a consequence, the man was soon identified as an army deserter. An appeal for his whereabouts was broadcast, and a Mr Winkless of Camberwell told the police that his wife had deserted him to live with Thomas. A photograph of

Mrs Winkless was published in the Press, and it brought immediate results; on the morning it was published (February 17th, 1948), a landlady in Clapham, Mrs Smeed, contacted the police and said she thought the woman was living in her top flat with a man. Police arrived; the woman took Thomas's breakfast in as usual, and the police burst in and succeeded in overpowering Thomas before he could fire a Luger that he kept under the pillow.

Thomas was 23 at the time of his arrest; he had been born in Edmonton and had been among the most intelligent boys in the school, as well as captain of the cricket eleven. However, after his call-up in 1945, he became a deserter, and spent 160 days in detention. He had also served periods on probation and at an approved school, which seems to have had the effect of increasing his criminal tendencies.

THOMPSON, Edith

Convicted of incitement to murder in 1922, she was hauled in a drugged stupor to the gallows at Holloway the following year, at the age of 28; Frederick Bywaters, her lover (a PO liner steward and eight years her junior), tried with her, was convicted of the murder of Edith Thompson's husband. He disclaimed to the end any suggestion that she knew of his intention to kill. As the Thompsons walked towards their Ilford home after an evening at the Criterion Theatre in London, Bywaters sprang out and fatally stabbed Percy Thompson; Edith Thompson was heard to cry, 'Don't, oh don't!' Nevertheless, she was charged with murder conspiracy, soliciting murder, administering poison with intent to murder and administering a destructive thing with the same intent. Letters to Bywaters had been found, full of, among other things, innuendoes concerning her own attempts at murdering Percy Thompson; she described how she put a ground electric-light bulb in his porridge ('I used a lot, big pieces too'), but pathologist Bernard Spilsbury discounted the probability of this at the trial, after a post-mortem of the body. It was clear that Mrs Thompson lived largely in her imagination, but Mr Justice Shearman was horrified both by the letters and the adulterous association; his summing up was damning, and therefore the verdict of 'guilty' unsurprising, although many were shocked when the verdict on Mrs Thompson was upheld in the Court of Criminal Appeal. For three decades she has excited sympathy. The literary worth of her letters has been exaggerated, rambling, and gossipy, they do not qualify as 'love letters of the age' or 'beautifully scribed gems'. ('. . . darling your old pal is getting quite a sport. On Saturday I was first in the Egg and Spoon race and first in the 100-yard Flat race and third in the 50-yards last race. . . .') Many books and plays have been based on the crime and the events leading up to it, the most famous being a novel by F. Tennyson Jesse, *A Pin to see the Peep Show*.

THORNE, Norman
Twenty-four-year-old unsuccessful poultry farmer, Band of Hope speaker, Sunday School teacher, boys' club enthusiast, convicted of the murder of 23-year-old Elsie Cameron.

On December 5th, 1924, Kensal Green, London typist, Elsie Cameron, set out for Crowborough, Sussex, to visit Norman Thorne at his smallholding; bespectacled, insipid, fragile, yet she clung vigorously to the idea of marriage with Thorne, whose earlier amorous inclinations showed signs of waning. On December 10th her father wired Thorne for news of his daughter, and heard by return: 'Not here . . . can't understand.' Two farmworkers had, in fact, seen Elsie Cameron, attaché case in hand, walking towards Thorne's farm on the evening of the 5th, but the missing girl's fiancé, simulating distress to neighbours, local police, and journalists alike, insisted they were mistaken. Thorne appeared to welcome police inquiries – 'I want to help all I can' – and eagerly showed them around his poultry farm and the broken-down shack where he lived; he asked one Press photographer to photograph him feeding chickens at a particular spot, which later turned out to be Elsie Cameron's burial site. A female neighbour of Thorne's, who unaccountably had not been aware of the commotion, finally came forward a month after Elsie Cameron's disappearance to say she had seen the missing girl walking through the gate of Thorne's farm on December 5th; as a result of this information Crowborough police on January 11th called in Scotland Yard. Digging up the poultry farm began in earnest, and on January 15th Elsie Cameron's corpse, with head and legs severed, was found.

Thorne now said that Elsie Cameron had indeed arrived at his farm on December 5th. There had been a quarrel about a friendship with another girl and he had stormed out of the hut; on his return, at 11.30 pm he found Elsie Cameron had hanged herself with the clothes-line, and was dangling from a beam. He panicked, 'I got my hacksaw . . . sawed off her legs and head by the glow of the fire. . . .' In the morning he buried the remains in one of his chicken runs: 'It is the Leghorn chicken run, the first pen from the gate.'

At his trial for murder at Lewes (before Mr Justice Finlay, prosecution led by Sir Henry Curtis-Bennett, KC, accused defended by Mr J. D. Cassels, KC) there was controversy between pathologist Sir Bernard Spilsbury, who had examined the remains on January 17th, and Dr Robert Brontë, pathologist called by the defence, who inspected the remains a month after Spilsbury's post-mortem. Spilsbury had found signs of injuries to 'the head, face, elbow, legs, and feet, which together were amply sufficient to account for death from shock . . .', but no evidence of hanging. (Nor had the police found any trace of rope-markings on the wooden beam.) Spilsbury refuted Brontë's suggestion that the 'creases' or 'grooves' found on the victim's neck were attributable to hanging, saying they were natural marks to be found on most female necks.

Thorne was found guilty, and when the case was taken to the Court of Criminal Appeal application was made for the medical evidence to be reviewed by a Commissioner appointed by the Court. This application was rejected, as was the appeal, and Thorne was ultimately hanged.

It was certainly Thorne's stubbornness in insisting on the suicide defence that hanged him. He might well have pleaded manslaughter, of quarrelling with Elsie Cameron and killing her in a fit of temper (which is very probably what happened). Elsie Cameron was known to be a thoroughly neurotic and unstable girl, who had been a shorthand typist, but was unemployed for six or seven months preceding her death because of her neurotic condition. In the first six months of 1924, she had been constantly under medical supervision for neurasthenia and loss of energy. Once, on a visit to Thorne's parents, she had been hysterical and 'difficult'. Her unstable mental condition also manifested itself in a periodic conviction of her pregnancy – she had told Thorne she was pregnant just before arriving at the farm although examination of the corpse showed this to be untrue. (She arrived without even a change of underwear, but with a baby dress!) If Thorne had had the sense to go for medical aid immediately after her death, instead of sawing up her body by candlelight (a certain way of prejudicing a jury) he might have escaped with a short term in jail.

His case exemplifies what may be regarded as the lesson of all murder: that murder is never 'justified', no matter what pressures are brought to bear on the murderer. There is always a simpler way out.

THURTELL, John.

The murder of William Weare by John Thurtell (who acted in conspiracy with Joseph Hunt and William Probert) excited unusual attention at the time, and has remained one of the 'notable crimes' of the nineteenth century. It is hard to understand why; the victim, like the three conspirators, was a scoundrel. It was a 'gang murder' like any in Chicago in the 1920s. All four men were 'sportsmen', gamesters, and, when opportunity arose, swindlers.

Some time in September 1823, Weare played Thurtell a game of billiards and won a considerable sum of money – probably by cheating. Thurtell decided to kill him. So Weare was invited for a week-end's shooting at a cottage belonging to Probert between Elstree and St Albans. On the morning of Saturday, October 25th, 1823, Thurtell and Hunt bought a pair of pistols from a pawnbroker in Marylebone. In the afternoon they set out in two gigs, Thurtell and Weare in one and Hunt (an effeminate man and a professional singer) and Probert in the other. Arriving near the cottage, which was in Gills Hill Lane, three miles from Elstree on the way to Aldenham, Thurtell produced a pistol and fired straight in Weare's face. The bullet glanced off his cheek-bone, and Weare jumped out of the gig, shouting with fear and offering to give Thurtell his money back if he would spare his life. Thurtell ran after him, wrestled with him, and managed to cut his throat with a penknife. The blood spurted into Thurtell's mouth, choking him. To finish his victim off, he jammed the pistol at his head with such force that it penetrated the skull and dug into Weare's brains, filling the barrel with blood and tissue. Five minutes later, he met Hunt and Probert in the lane, and went and had supper at Probert's cottage with Probert's wife (who was old and ugly, but had brought Probert a large dowry) and his one-eyed sister-in-law, Miss Noyes. He presented the watch-chain off Weare's watch to Mrs Probert. At midnight the men dragged the body into the pond in Probert's garden. (Later, morbid curiosity seekers denuded the garden of every single leaf in an effort to get a keepsake of the crime.) The next morning, Thurtell and Hunt went out into the lane to recover the pistol and penknife, which Thurtell had mislaid. They found two labourers at work in the lane, and the men watched with curiosity as the two suspicious-looking characters searched the ground among the weeds. Thurtell and Hunt looked in the wrong place; when they were gone, the labourers came across the pistol and bloody penknife lying on top of the dyke. They told a county magistrate, and the murder hunt began. In the meantime, the murderers took Weare's body out of the pond and dumped it in another pond some distance away. Two Bow Street Runners were put on to the case; they questioned Probert, who immediately offered to turn King's evidence (beating Hunt to it!), and Hunt lost no time in showing them where the body was. Thurtell and Hunt were arrested; the case caught the public imagination, and a dramatized version of Mr Weare's murder was played to crowded houses at the Surrey Theatre. As a result of this, the trial was delayed until January 6th, 1824. In accordance with the custom of that time, the accused men had to defend themselves. Hunt was in such a state of terror that he wrote out his speech and had it read for him. It was mostly a whine that he had been promised immunity if he co-operated with the law. (His plea to turn King's evidence was rejected.) Thurtell, an enormous, imposing figure of a man, made a long speech. Some writers on the case describe this speech as rambling and boring, and say that there was a hum of conversation in court as he reached the peroration; others say it is one of the most remarkable pieces of eloquence in nineteenth-century murder trials, that it was finished in a deathly silence, and that everyone, even the prosecuting counsel, was deeply moved. The speech is partly a sentimental appeal, explaining that he was the son of 'unaffectedly pious' parents and was his mother's favourite child, that he had been led astray by bad companions into gaming, etc., but that he was a man of honour and incapable of murder. The murderer, he said, was Probert. He ended by begging the jury not to upset his parents by having him hanged.

However, he was hanged, two days after the trial, with a record crowd to watch. Among the crowd were ballad hawkers, selling the poem with the famous stanza:

> They cut his throat from ear to ear
> His head they battered in.
> His name was Mr William Weare
> He lived in Lyons Inn.

The poem is inaccurate, since Thurtell alone was the murderer.

He met his death nonchalantly, and a few hours before his execution asked to read a newspaper account of 'the big fight' that had taken place the day before. He was immensely popular with the warders in the prison, and many eminent people said it was a pity to hang such a man. (George Borrow later said the same.)

Hunt's sentence was commuted to transportation to Botany Bay, where he lived to an old age.

TIERNEY, Nora Patricia
Twenty-nine-year-old Irishwoman, found guilty of the murder of 3-year-old Marion Ward.

In August 1949, the body of Marion Ward was found in a ruined house on a bomb-site in St Johns Wood, London; her head was battered with nine hammer blows, but there was no evidence of sexual assault. (Near by was a mummified body of a merchant seaman, but it was soon established that there was no connexion between the two corpses.) Marion had been left by her mother a few hours earlier, playing with Stephenie Tierney, 6-year-old child of next-door-neighbour Nora Tierney. Police interrogated Mrs Tierney, who soon confessed to the killing: 'I don't know why I did it.' Shortly afterwards she insisted that her husband, James Tierney, was the killer, saying that she had heard Marion screaming and had seen her husband attacking the child with a hammer; afterwards, said Mrs Tierney, he had wiped his finger-prints off the hammer with a damp cloth. ('Will you say you did it?' said my husband – 'they won't hang women but they hang men.') Mrs Tierney's fingernails were examined, and fibres of cloth from Marion Ward's cardigan discovered; a footprint near the murder-spot corresponded to Mrs Tierney's right shoe; James Tierney was found to have been elsewhere at the time of the murder. Nora Tierney was arrested on a charge of murdering the child, and tried eventually at the Old Bailey. Found guilty, she smiled and said, 'Thank you' to Mr Justice Hilbery, when he pronounced the death sentence. Her appeal failed, but with the execution date already fixed she submitted to a medical exam-ination; found insane, she was committed to Broadmoor Criminal Lunatic Asylum.

TOPLIS, Percy
Robber and murderer, whose case is of interest mainly because of the nation-wide manhunt that took place in Britain after his murder of a taxi-driver in 1920.

Toplis had behind him a career of petty crime and rebellion against authority, in 1920. Early in that year he was in the army and stationed at Bulford Camp, near Salisbury. He was frequently in trouble with authority, and he decided to desert. On April 25th, 1920, the body of a taxi-driver, George Spicer, was found near Andover; he had been shot in the back of the head with a revolver. His taxi, a grey Darracq, was missing. A soldier who had been in Southampton on the 24th told of being hailed by Toplis, who had boasted about carrying a revolver.

A friend of Toplis named Fallows had also disappeared from the camp; a man dressed as a sergeant-major had walked into the cookhouse and asked him to come out with him. A few days later, Toplis and Fallows were seen in the grey Darracq in Swansea by a policeman. Then, unexpectedly, Fallows returned to the camp, and told of how Toplis had asked him to come and help sell a car; he swore that he had no knowledge that the car belonged to the murdered man; the magistrate believed him and discharged him.

Now the manhunt was on for Toplis, who lived by robbing motorists and burgling houses; he went from Wales to London, where he had his moustache shaved off. (He then regretted it, and asked the barber where he could buy a false moustache like his own!) He went to Tilbury, and worked as a painter on a boat to Dundee. From there he went to Aberdeen, then tramped to the village of Tomintoul, said to be the highest in the British Isles. Here he did odd jobs for farmers, and lived in a lonely hut. When the local constable went to investigate him, with two other men, he shot two of them down and rode off on a bicycle.

In mid-May he was still on the run, doubling about Scotland; then he made for Carlisle. It was in June that a Constable Fulton, returning home from work, saw him lying by the roadside, asleep, in an RAF uniform. The constable spoke to him, and said jokingly: 'You might be that fellow Toplis.' Toplis agreed, laughingly, and the constable went on home. There he read the police description of Toplis, and set out after him on a bicycle. He found Toplis in a wood, but when Toplis threatened him with a revolver, he wisely decided to go home and summon help. He then hurried to Penrith, where a squad of police marksmen joined him; they all crowded into a big car, and set out looking for Toplis. They soon passed a man in a brown suit carrying a parcel, and Fulton recognized his man. The car stopped; Toplis pulled out his gun and fired, but missed; a moment later he lay dead, riddled with police bullets.

TORRIO, Johnny (see Colosimo, Jim)

Neapolitan hoodlum who took over control of much of Chicago's 'vice-empire' in 1920 at the age of 34, shortly before Prohibition. Although never indicted for murder, any study of Chicago's gang-killings during the 1920s is incomplete without reference to Torrio. He it was who brought the tough young Alphonse Capone from New York to Chicago to act as his bodyguard when his chief, 'Big Jim' Colosimo, was murdered in May 1920; Torrio himself was suspected of this killing, and was to be questioned closely when his North Side rival was slain four years later (see O'BANION, Dion). An attempt was made on Torrio's own life on January 24th, 1925, when he was shot down outside his Clyde Avenue apartment in Chicago after a shopping expedition; Torrio refused to name the would-be assassins ('I won't rap any of them'), believed to have been vengeance-bent associates of O'Banion led by O'Banion's successor, Hymie Weiss (afterwards shot down himself, probably by Capone's gang). After his near-murder Torrio lost the zest for controlling Chicago's world of corruption, and abdicated in favour of his chief lieutenant, Al Capone: 'It's all yours, Al.' He departed for his native Italy, but returned to America a decade or so later. Torrio was eventually deported by the United States authorities to Italy in 1956.

TOWNLEY, George
Victorian cause célèbre. Townley pleaded insanity after stabbing to death the girl who had jilted him, 'Bessie' Caroline Goodwin.

Townley was the son of a merchant and was born in 1838; he met Bessie Goodwin when she was 16, in 1857. They became engaged two years later. Her father was a well-to-do civil engineer. Townley became a clerk in a mercantile firm, and it was perhaps for this reason that Bessie's family told her to terminate the engagement; Townley's prospects were possibly not as great as they had supposed. Bessie was sent to be housekeeper to an 82-year-old relative, Captain Goodwin, at Wigwell Hall, near Wirksworth, Derbyshire.

The affaire seems to have dragged on, nevertheless, and three years later, in 1862, they became engaged again. But a young clergyman (whose name was kept out of the trial) came to stay at the Hall, and apparently Bessie's relatives regarded him as a better match for her. Bessie wrote on August 12th, 1863, asking Townley to release her. On Friday, August 21st, he went to a clergyman who lived near Bessie and asked for information about the young clergyman at the Hall. That evening he called at the Hall and spent some time with Bessie; evidently he made a last-minute attempt to persuade her to marry him. At about half past seven he cut her throat with a knife he had bought especially for the purpose. The aged relative, instead of getting excited, told Townley to come in and have a cup of tea.

The trial took place at Derby on December 11th, before Baron Martin, and the prisoner was sentenced to death, the judge breaking down and sobbing as he spoke the sentence. However, doctors examined Townley for insanity, and he was finally 'respited'. This caused much public clamour. Less than two years after the murder, Townley committed suicide in Pentonville prison by diving over a staircase on to a stone floor; he died on February 12th, 1865.

TROPPMANN, Jean Baptiste
Killer of a family of eight people.

Troppmann was born in 1849 in Alsace; his father was a mechanic who remained poor, in spite of a flair for invention. His poverty embittered him. Jean was a mother's favourite, and grew up a homosexual. He inherited from his father enormous hands (so it seems possible that the surname of the family was derived from this characteristic – 'too much hand'). He was beaten regularly by his father, and his mother's favouritism drew on him the spite of his brothers and sisters. He grew up a habitual liar.

At school his moroseness made him the natural target for all the bullies; but he soon showed a formidable, mad-dog frenzy when attacked that made them leave him alone after a while. He started a course of rigorous athletic training and soon developed remarkable strength of body.

On leaving school at 14, he went to work in his father's workshop. Here at first he was also bullied and sneered at. His chief tormentor was his brother Edward. The persecution came to an end when one day Jean smashed Edward's face in with a hammer without warning.

He gained a temporary popularity by saving the life of a fellow workman by his alertness and physical strength. His sexual inversion may have kept him aloof. At all events, his one deep love in his life was his mother. His favourite book was Eugene Sue's absurd concoction of horror and mystification, *The Wandering Jew*.

He began studying chemistry in secret. (There was no reason to study it in secret, but this was typical of Troppmann's nature.) Also, prompted perhaps by Eugene Sue, he studied poisons, and developed one which he considered completely undetectable.

In December 1868, Troppmann senior sold some machines to a Paris factory, and sent Jean to help instal them. People who knew him then testify that the problem of becoming rich obsessed him.

Five months after installing the Paris machinery (when he lived at Pantin) he moved to Roubaix to instal more. Here he met Jean Kinck, a fellow Alsatian, and Troppmann's victim-to-be. Kinck was a successful business man who enjoyed boasting about his money. To him, Troppmann proposed various schemes for making money, hoping to be able to abscond to America with Kinck's money. Kinck made inquiries, and turned down the ideas. Now Troppmann produced an even more fantastic story, declaring that he had stumbled on deposits of precious metals in the mountains of the Upper Rhine. (At his trial, Troppmann claimed that he had actually told Kinck about a press for coining false money in an abandoned château at Herrenfluch, Alsace, which Kinck could take over for 5,000 francs, but this was probably to discredit Kinck and to lessen his own guilt.) This time Kinck was taken in, and set out with some ready money and a couple of blank cheques to meet Troppmann at Bollwiller, in Alsace. Here, he was poisoned over a meal, and his body buried under a heap of stones in a moat between Guebwiller and Bollwiller. Troppmann walked to his home at Cernay, and dropped a hundred franc note in his mother's lap, saying, 'Take it, there's something for you to live on.' On the evening of August 26th, 1869, the day after the murder, Troppmann wrote to Madame Kinck, saying that her husband had hurt his hand and so could not write, and asking her to cash a cheque for 5,500 francs. She did this, and Troppmann presented himself at the Guebwiller Post Office to collect the money, claiming to be Jean Kinck. But the postmaster refused to hand over the money, demanding identification. Troppmann forged an authorization from Kinck, but still the postmaster refused to hand over the money. The caution of the postmaster sealed the fate of the Kinck family; for with his money, Troppmann intended to bolt to America. Even so, he tried another method of getting the money, and went to

Roubaix, where he persuaded the Kinck family that he was about to make them millionaires, and got Mme Kinck to send the boy Gustave to Guebwiller to collect the money. However, there were further misunderstandings, due to Mme Kinck's illiteracy, and the boy failed to obtain it. The boy came to Paris, where he was met by Jean Baptiste, who made him write to his mother telling her to bring the whole family to Paris. Then Gustave was stabbed to death in the open countryside and buried on Pantin Common; the immense savagery of the murder suggests that Troppmann was a sadist, or that there was some other sexual motive.

Mme Kinck was on the point of childbirth, but she set out with her five children for Paris; Jean was late meeting the train; he had been digging their grave out at Pantin. Mme Kinck inquired at the Hôtel de Fer du Nord, and was relieved to hear that Jean Kinck was really staying there. (It was Troppmann's pseudonym.) They returned to the station to wait for him. Troppmann turned up late, and they all took a cab to Pantin, where her husband, Troppmann claimed, was staying.

On some excuse, Troppmann stopped the cab on a lonely part of the road, and persuaded Mme Kinck to alight with the two youngest children, leaving the other three in the cab. Twenty minutes later, he returned and took the other three, paying off the cab.

The next morning – Monday, September 20th, 1869, a labourer named Langlois noticed pools of blood on the road across Pantin Common. He fetched help, and they dug at the spot where the earth had been newly turned. There they found the Kinck family. All had been murdered with a ferocity that again suggests the sadist. The 2-year-old girl had been disembowelled, and the rest of the family were hacked with a spade. The grave also contained marbles, coins, sausages, bits of bread, and a doll.

The coat of the boy Émile had the name of its maker inside – a man in Roubaix – and the family was soon identified. The discovery caused a nation-wide sensation, crowds flocked to Pantin; special trains were run and sweet hawkers sold refreshments. Newspapers were full of the affair, and one even suggested that the Government had arranged the murders to distract attention from the grave international crisis (which flared into war a year later). The same suggestion was repeated in 1921 – with more justification – at the trial of Landru.

Jean Baptiste fled to Havre with the intention of escaping to

America. Here, in a bar, he was spotted as a suspicious character by a gendarme, who suspected that he might be a harbour sneak-thief. He claimed he had no papers (his only papers were in the name of Kinck, which was now known all over France), and the gendarme took him to the station for questioning. *En route*, Troppmann ran away and jumped into the harbour. He was fished out, and searched. The Kinck papers on him made the police realize what a catch they had made.

He was then taken back to Paris, where huge crowds waited at the Gare St Lazare. He identified the bodies in the morgue, and declared that Kinck had murdered his family (with the help of Gustave) when he had found his wife in bed with a lover. (This seems unlikely, considering her condition.) When shown Gustave's hacked body, he exclaimed: 'The swine – he's killed his son as well!' However, Kinck's body was discovered on November 24th, and his last defence disintegrated.

In prison he rambled on about making money, and seems to have considered having his photograph taken and sold. He commented, 'My name is known throughout France . . .'

The trial opened on December 28th, 1869. The defence claimed that such a crime would have been too much for one man, and insisted that he had three accomplices; but circumstantial evidence was against him. He was condemned to die on January 19th, 1870.

On the day before his execution, a huge crowd collected. He was executed in the early hours of the morning, with the moon still in the sky. He fought like a madman on the scaffold, locking his feet on the steps of the ladder, and managed to bite the executioner before the knife fell; at the last moment, he tried to twist his head clear of the falling blade.

It should be mentioned that Troppmann's first murder occurred at Roubaix, where he got into a brawl and threw a man into the canal; the man drowned in the shallow mud.

TRUE, Ronald
An unfortunate case where abnormality led eventually to insanity and murder. True was sentenced to death for the murder of a prostitute, Olive Young, but reprieved and sent to Broadmoor.

True's mother was 16 and his father 17 when he was born in 1891. When he was 11, his mother married a wealthy man. Ronald was a habitual liar and was cruel to his pets. He was at Bedford Grammar School until he was 18. It was at some time in his early teens that his mother lay dangerously ill, and when an aunt told Ronald that she might die, he commented: 'If she does, I'll give you her two best rings.'

At 18 his family sent him to New Zealand to learn farming, but he was back again within a year. The same thing happened when he was sent to the Argentine. He joined the Canadian Mounted Police but was soon thrown out. In Mexico, he probably acquired his taste for morphia.

In August 1914 he was in Shanghai. He returned to England and joined the Royal Flying Corps. On his first solo flight at Farnborough he crashed and sustained head injuries. After this he became more abnormal than ever. He was generally regarded as an eccentric. In 1916 he crashed again, and a little later had sudden pains in his right hip while in a theatre. In hospital his drug addiction was realized when small doses of morphia had no effect. The pain was probably syphilis, from which True believed himself cured. After this period in hospital he had a nervous breakdown and was invalided out of the service. He worked as a test pilot at Yeovil but soon lost the job and went to New York. This was in June 1917. Here he became a social lion with his stories of shooting down German planes. A young actress, Frances Roberts, fell in love with him and married him. True obtained a job as an instructor at the Mineola Flying School, and when it was transferred to Houston, he went with it; however, his impostures were soon discovered and he was dismissed. He drifted to Mexico, then to Cuba, then finally back to England – to mother – sick and penniless, with a wife who was expecting a baby. But he was as much a nuisance at home as usual, and his family found him a job on the Gold Coast, with the Taquah Mining Company; his wife went with him. But his strange conduct and wild lies soon got him dismissed, and he was back in England again. His family decided to make him an allowance and let him alone. This was the final push; True became a hopeless drug addict, had several 'cures', and became steadily more abnormal. He began to hate his wife, and developed a fantasy of another Ronald True who was his implacable enemy. He was released from a nursing-home run by Dr Parham in 1920 and lived with his wife for nearly a year in Portsmouth. Then he went to London, claiming he had a job. Alarmed by a suicide letter, his wife went to look for him and found him a physical wreck in a Soho dive. He went into a London nursing-home, but was so violent that he needed two male nurses. After this, he went to stay with an aunt, Mrs Angus, in Folkestone; his wife was on tour, and his aunt looked after the child, a boy. True's irregular life alarmed her, but soon he developed a tendency to brood for hours. His affection for his son turned to suspicious hostility, and the child was kept out of his way. Mrs Angus told his parents he should be certified, but before this could happen, he told her he was going to Bedford, and went to London. His wife followed him but he told her he had left her for good. He prowled London's night haunts with a loaded revolver, looking for the other Ronald True.

In London in early 1922 he met a Mr James Armstrong, and the two became very friendly. True told Armstrong he was flying valuable cargoes to the Continent, and Armstrong had no suspicion that his wealthy and agreeable companion was a dangerous lunatic.

True spent a great deal of money in London, and when it was gone, lived by passing dud cheques, bilking hotels, and possibly by robbery (on February 28th he pawned a lady's gold watch and some jewellery). He robbed Armstrong's mother of her purse, and also robbed Olive Young, a call girl he had met in the West End, of a £5 note. He formed a violent attachment to a Mrs Wilson, told her that he was hunting another Ronald True, a dangerous criminal, and threatened to shoot her if she danced with other men. He told her that Scotland Yard had given him permission to carry the loaded revolver to protect him from the other Ronald True. Luckily for her, True stopped contacting her.

Just before the murder, True met a Mr and Mrs Sach, whom he had known at Mineola, and told them about the other Ronald True; he even pointed out a man at the Palais de Danse, Hammersmith, as his criminal 'double'. He told them that another enemy of his lived in a basement flat in Fulham, and that he intended to go and shoot it out with him.

He had moved out of the Victoria Hotel in Northumberland Avenue without paying his bill, and crossed the road to the Grand Hotel. There he had ordered a hired car, and managed to use it for several days without paying a penny.

Olive Young, whose real name was Gertrude Yates, lived at 13A Finborough Road, Fulham, in the basement flat. On Sunday, March 5th, 1922, at 11 pm, there was a ring at her doorbell and True – whom she had been avoiding since the theft of the £5 – appeared. He spent the night with her, and she must have been unaware of his homicidal intentions, for she was unalarmed when, at seven the next morning, he woke her up with a cup of tea. As she sat up, he hit her on the head with a rolling-pin, and then hit her four more tremendous blows. When he had had his own tea and biscuits, he dragged her into the bathroom. At 9 am, the charlady, Mrs Emily Steel, called, and True came out of the bedroom, looking bright and cheerful; she recognized him and said, 'Good morning, Major True.' She helped him on with his overcoat, accepted a half-crown tip, and True went out, saying that Olive Young was still asleep and that he would send a car for her at midday. Within a few minutes, Mrs Steel discovered the body and informed the police. They remembered that True's wife had appealed for help when he was hunting his 'double' with a loaded revolver; they had put her in touch with a private detective, who had been keeping an eye on True.

True had spent a normal day, pawning Olive Young's jewels for £25, and going to Croydon for tea. In the evening the chauffeur of the hired car drove him to the Hammersmith Palace of Varieties. On returning to the garage, the chauffeur found the police waiting; he went back with them to the Hammersmith Palace, where True was quietly arrested in a box he was sharing with Armstrong.

He was lodged in Brixton Prison Hospital and kept under observation by Dr East and Dr Young. He made a violent attack on a fellow prisoner, whom he accused of stealing his food, and somehow slipped into the ward where Henry Jacoby, the murderer of Lady White, was in custody; he slapped the youth on the back and shouted gleefully: 'Here's another for the murderer's club. Only those who kill outright accepted.'

Dr East decided he was suffering from congenital mental disorder, aggravated by drug-taking. Dr Smith and Dr Studdart, psychiatrists for the defence, agreed. True came up for trial on May 1st, 1922, at the Central Criminal Court before Mr Justice McCardie; Sir Richard Muir prosecuted, and decided to rely on cross-examination and the McNaghten rules rather than trying to find another doctor who would declare True sane. His instinct proved right, for True was found guilty and sentenced to death on May 5th, 1922. However, the Home Secretary, Mr Shortt, intervened, and had True re-examined by three more medical men, Sir Maurice Craig, Dr Dyer, and Sir John Baker; they declared emphatically that True was insane. The Home Secretary thereupon granted a respite of execution, and True was sent to Broadmoor. The decision caused an uproar – especially since an appeal had been dismissed by the Lord Chief Justice. The 'True scandal' became a political issue, and it looked as if Mr

Shortt would have to resign; however, he made a sharp and lucid speech in the House, stating the law, and was cheered as he sat down.

However, it has been suggested that True's reprieve led to the death of Edith Thompson, who might have been reprieved but for the uproar caused by True's escape from the hangman, and the Home Secretary's fear of jeopardizing his position.

True spent a happy twenty-eight years in Broadmoor, popular with his fellow patients, taking an active part in the social life, and died at the age of 61, in 1951.

TURNER, Joyce

A capable and attractive 28-year-old mother of six, founder and head-nannie of the Hanover Kiddies' Nursery in Columbia, South Carolina, who became so aggravated by the loafings of her husband, part-time bartender Alonzo ('a lazy good for nothing bum') that she planned his murder, enlisting the eager aid of next-door neighbour Mrs Audrey Noakes and waitress friend Clestell Gay, a plump divorcée. Late one night in June 1956, fortified by cups of coffee from the Noakes' kitchen and despite a fit of dithering ('Are you going to do it or not?' asked Clestell), Joyce Turner shot her husband while he lay, as usual, asleep in bed, afterwards telling the police about a white-faced housebreaker, a tale which was supported by Mrs Noakes' account of a tall, thin stranger who had fled across her back-yard after the killing. While Alonzo was being deposited inside Paschals' Funeral Home, Mrs Turner told of his cardsharping and philandering with other men's wives, hinting that many would rejoice over his untimely end. Police followed these leads, but no evidence was found of idle Alonzo's wild life, and when sale of the murder weapon (a ·22 calibre gun) was traced to Mrs Turner's chum, Clestell, the truth came out. The three women were tried separately and each sentenced to life imprisonment, Mrs Turner remaining unrepentant: 'He always wanted to die in bed, I merely arranged it, that's all.'

TWITCHELL, George S., Jun.
Forty-two-year-old Philadelphian, convicted in 1869 of the murder of his mother-in-law, Mrs Hill.

The Twitchell maidservant, Sarah Campbell, returned from the Sunday service one evening in November 1868, and encountered her master, Mr George Twitchell, in the hall, clad in dressing-gown, making inquiring remarks as to the whereabouts of his wife's mother, a permanent resident in the Twitchell house-hold. Mrs Hill was found dead in the back-yard; the body had multiple injuries, particularly about the head. A neighbour, Mr W. N. G. Morrell, on hearing the commotion, dashed into the house to hear weeping Mrs Twitchell declaiming: 'Mother fell out of the second storey window!' Morrell, finding blood on the stairs, landing, and second storey windowsill, replied to the Twitchells: 'One of you two has committed this murder.' He then summoned the police, who escorted the Twitchells to a waiting barouche. During the jail-bound journey Mrs Twitchell was hysterical, begging her now silent husband to clear her of guilt and insisting that a homicidal and knowledgeable burglar was the culprit: 'Mother always carried from two thousand to three thousand dollars in her bosom.' It was found that the im-pecunious Twitchells would profit from the old lady's death; neighbours testified that the three savage Twitchell dogs had remained silent throughout the supposed raid. The Twitchells were charged with the murder of Mrs Hill, and granted separate trials. George Twitchell, pleading not guilty, was, after a two-week trial, found guilty and sentenced to death, whereupon he made a confession stating that his wife had, that night, killed her mother.

> . . . I was roused by her repeated calls . . . I found her much excited, saying, 'I have had a quarrel with mother and killed her.' We threw the body of Mrs Hill out of the window to make it look as if she fell out . . . I now make these disclosures that I may have peace with God. . . .

An unknown person delivered prussic acid to George Twitchell in his cell, and he committed suicide. Mrs Twitchell's trial was postponed indefinitely, and she was subsequently released.

V

VACHER, Joseph

French Ripper type of murderer who found his victims in the south-east country regions around Belley, from 1894 to 1897. Born in 1869, his temper was always erratic, but not until his conscription in 1890 did he show violent tendencies. Then, as an act of despair because his promotion to full Corporal had not materialized, he cut his throat with a razor. (Upon show of such military zeal his promotion came through shortly afterwards.) Soon Corporal Vacher began to eye the throats of his comrades and mutter about 'flowing blood', so he was removed to an infirmary. During a sick-leave he met Mlle Louise B. of Baume-des-Dames, who did not spurn him with the usual speed of her sex (Vacher was no Adonis, and had homosexual tendencies) but in a jealous fit he injured her with three bullets, finally firing the pistol into his own face. The right eye was damaged, and one side of his face partially paralysed. Committed by the court to the Asylum of Saint-Ylle (where his raving bemused even the most beserk of his fellow lunatics), he was transferred, in 1893, to the Asylum of Saint-Robert, from where he was discharged 'cured' on April 1st, 1894. He moved out with a large sack containing a set of maps, an umbrella, a cudgel (on which were carved the words, 'Mary of Lourdes; Who does good, finds good'), an accordion, a pair of scissors – and a set of knives. Six weeks later a 21-year-old factory girl, Eugénie Delhomme, was knifed, disembowelled, and raped on a quiet country road near Vienne; she was the first of fourteen people to be murdered by 'the Ripper of the South East'. The victims were mostly young farmworkers of both sexes; all were mutilated and raped after death, some bearing teeth marks. A blackbearded vagrant type had been noticed around the area, with a scarred face and a raw, suppurating eye, and soon the police linked the identities of the former lunatic and the man wanted for murder. Vacher's last murder attempt came on August 4th, 1897, when, in the Bois des Pelleries, he pounced on a woman gathering pine cones; not only was she of Amazonian proportions with a voice to match, but her husband and children were at hand, and, hearing her roars for help, dashed to the rescue. With the aid of nearby peasants Vacher was hustled along to the local inn, where he played cheerful tunes on his accordion until the police arrived and identified him. He was, in time, charged at Tournon with the murder of a shepherd boy, Victor Portalier. There was much controversy over Vacher's sanity, Vacher himself maintaining that his madness was caused by a bite from a rabid dog many years before. The jury found him guilty of murder, and on December 31st, 1897, he was executed.

VACQUIER, Jean Pierre

A small, talkative, dandyish French inventor in his forties sentenced to death at Guildford Assizes in July 1924, for the murder by poisoning of Alfred Jones, landlord of the Blue Anchor Hotel at Byfleet in Surrey. Mrs Jones, taking a lone holiday (from the cares of bankruptcy) in Biarritz the previous year, had met Vacquier at her hotel, where he was employed to maintain the residents' latest novelty, a wireless set. A passionate relationship followed, although neither spoke the other's language. Vacquier, complete with a French–English dictionary, followed his beloved back to England, where he hoped to sell the patent rights of his newly invented sausage-machine. Subsidized by Mrs Jones, he lived for six weeks at the Blue Anchor Hotel. One morning, Alfred Jones, who had been drinking heavily, died in agony after drinking a remedial dose of salts which were found to contain strychnine. Both lovers were questioned and Press photographs taken of the vain Vacquier, who delighted in posing. One of these photographs was seen by a chemist who recognized the man who had purchased strychnine some weeks before and Vacquier was arrested. Constant yells and gesticulating from Vacquier (who had to have an interpreter) made a diverting trial, but the evidence against him was overwhelming. He was hanged at Wandsworth Prison on August 12th, 1924.

VAN BUUREN, Clarence G.

South African sex murderer. The main interest of the case lies in the use of a medium, Nelson Palmer, to help discover the body. The case has, therefore, something in common with the Nodder case, where Estelle Roberts is said to have accurately foretold that the body of Mona Tinsley would be found in the river.

Myrna Joy Aken failed to return home on October 2nd, 1956, and a search was instituted in Durban, SA. A friend reported that she had seen the girl entering a light-coloured Ford Anglia. The car was finally traced to a radio shop, where the owner admitted that it had been used by one of his salesmen, Clarence Van Buuren, who had returned it on the day after the murder and subsequently disappeared.

Eight days after her disappearance, the medium, Nelson Palmer, went into a trance and told the girl's brother that her body would be found in a culvert sixty miles south of the city. He accompanied the party to the spot, a mile and a half to the north of the village of Umtwalumi, where, as he had predicted, the naked body was found in a culvert. She had been shot to death and raped. (A few weeks later, Palmer repeated his feat of locating a dead body – this time, a doctor who had committed suicide.) Nine days after the murder, Van Buuren was arrested near Pinetown. He was in possession of a revolver of the same type that killed Joy Aken.

Van Buuren had a considerable police record, including theft, forgery, passing bad cheques, and escaping from custody. He had been married three times – his first two wives having left him on learning of his record. Buuren claimed to the end that he was innocent, and that he had 'disappeared' because he had been seen last in the girl's company and was afraid he would be suspected. Before his execution, he repeated his declarations of innocence, and declared that he hoped the real murderer would suffer for ever from a bad conscience.

VOIRBO
French radical and political fire-eater, who murdered an old man, Désiré Bodasse, to get the money to enable him to marry (for the second time – he was already married at the time).

Voirbo was the illegitimate son of an executioner's assistant, who, according to legend, told Voirbo, 'You shall die by my hand.' Voirbo was a tailor by trade, and was married to a woman named Helen, who apparently had some criminal leanings which landed her in jail. While she was confined there, Voirbo became attached to a young girl, Adélia Rémondé, who was a nun, or about to become one; she had forgone her vows for Voirbo's sake. She had a fortune of fifteen thousand francs (which would have gone to the Church if she had become a nun – a disaster in the eyes of the anti-clerical Voirbo).

Désiré Bodasse was a 72-year-old roué who, for some reason, enjoyed the company of the saturnine Voirbo. But he refused to lend him ten thousand francs to enable him to marry his nun, and Voirbo decided to kill him. He came to this decision on December 13th, 1868, and implemented it the next day, luring the old beau up to his room in the Rue Mazarine by saying that Adélia and her cousin were there; he killed the old man with a blow from a flat iron. He then dismembered the body and poured molten lead into the ears, after which he threw the head into the Seine off the Concorde Bridge. Other small pieces of the body he threw quite openly into the Seine from a basket. He emptied the entrails down the lavatory. There remained two legs and some clothes, as well as a watch. He hid the legs in a trunk, and went with Bodasse's clothes up to the old man's room in the Rue Dauphine, where he lit a candle and kept it burning, to give neighbours the impression that the old man was still at home and well; he also kept the cuckoo clock wound. He sewed the legs into bags of black glazed calico (an absurd mistake) and decided to drop them into a well behind Lampon's Eating House in the Rue Princesse. On his way there, on the night of December 22nd, he had a very close shave; two policemen, on the lookout for burglars, stopped him, and proposed to take him to the station. He had taken the precaution of carrying a large basket of food, and declared that he had just come from Langres; the parcels, he said, contained hams. The police let him go, and he dropped the legs into the well on a piece of twine. He then left his old lodgings, took a house in the Rue Lamartine, and in January 1869, married his nun.

The legs were found by the owner of the restaurant on January 26th, and Gustave Macé was placed in charge of the case. He had a fairly simple task. The tailored sewing of the parcel was the clue, and Macé supposed he had to search for a tailor who knew the eating-house. Witnesses told of seeing Voirbo and Bodasse together; Macé examined Bodasse's room, and found the clock ticking; the landlord said Bodasse had been in the evening before. But in the back of Bodasse's watch, Macé found the numbers of some of his bonds, and soon discovered that Voirbo had paid his rent with one of them before he left his old lodging. Voirbo was interrogated, and then followed; Macé saw him stir up a mob at a political meeting where one old man preached free love. But Macé had a final inspiration; he suspected that, no matter how well Voirbo had cleaned the room in the Rue Mazarine, blood would have collected under some of the tiles; he proved to be right. Voirbo broke down and confessed. He managed to make a last dash for liberty, but was soon caught. He evaded justice, however; someone smuggled a razor into the jail in a loaf and he cut his throat.

The day after his arrest he had intended to sail for America.

VOISON, Louis

Forty-two-year-old burly red-faced Frenchman convicted of the murder of Émilienne Gérard. On November 2nd, 1917, the torso and arms of a woman wrapped up in a meat sack and sheet were found by a roadsweeper in Regent Square, Bloomsbury, London; the legs were in a nearby paper parcel. A piece of brown paper on which were scrawled the words, 'Blodie Belgiam', was with the remains, and a laundry mark on the sheet traced the probable victim – Émilienne Gérard, a Frenchwoman aged 32, living at 50 Munster Square, near Regent's Park, who had been missing since the night of October 31st. An IOU for £50, signed Louis Voison, was found at her apartment, and a portrait of Voison, apparently her lover, gazed down from the mantelpiece. Police questioned Voison, a butcher living in the basement of 101 Charlotte Street, in the Soho district of London. When first approached Voison was sitting with another compatriot woman friend, Berthe Roche, in his kitchen; he said he had last seen Mme Gérard on the afternoon of October 31st, when she asked him to tend her cat as she was going to France for a few days. Chief Inspector Wensley, in charge of the case, asked Voison to write 'Bloody Belgium', and five times the butcher painstakingly wrote 'Blodie Belgiam'. In Voison's cellar, enclosed in a cask and covered with powdered alum, were the head and hands of Émilienne Gérard. Charged with the murder of his mistress, Voison responded with a Gallic shrug and complete denial, saying that on November 1st he had visited Munster Square and found the head and hands of Mme Gérard on a table, and the whole flat blood-bespattered; he had attempted to clean the place up and had panicked, thinking, he said, that a 'trap' was laid for him. Berthe Roche, charged with him, screamed protestingly, but there was evidence that she had been at the Charlotte Street basement (which resembled a charnel house) ever since the night of October 31st. The back room of the basement was obviously the scene of the crime, with human blood everywhere; even Voison's pony-trap in the outside stable was bloodstained, and it was assumed the butcher had used this transport to convey the remains to Regent Square, a mile away. (The 'Blodie Belgiam' missive, intended by Voison as a 'red herring', had served only to incriminate him.)

Pathologist Bernard Spilsbury found that the victim's head had been savagely battered by a dozen blows, which, although vicious, had not fractured the skull, and it was his opinion that Roche had struck these blows, probably in a jealous frenzy at her rival's intrusion. There were also signs of strangulation, and the limbs had been severed with a butcher's knife by someone experienced in the craft of butchery.

In January 1918 Louis Voison and Berthe Roche appeared at

the Old Bailey, although Roche was remanded, to be charged as
accessory after the fact at the next sessions. Voison pleaded not
guilty, repeating his story of having found the Gérard remains at
the Munster Square apartment. All court procedure had to be
translated into French for him, but the judge rendered the death
sentence in the defendant's own language. The eventual appeal
was dismissed and Voison was hanged.

Berthe Roche was sentenced to seven years' penal servitude,
but after two years she went insane and died.

W

WADDINGHAM, Dorothea Nancy
*Thirty-six-year-old ex-factory hand, one-time ward orderly at
Burton-on-Trent workhouse, petty criminal (charged and convicted in the past for a series of thefts and frauds), found guilty in
1936 of the murder of 50-year-old Miss Ada Baguley.*

In 1935, Dorothea Waddingham (she used her maiden name,
but she was the widow of a Thomas Willoughby Leech, by whom
she had several children), together with her lover, 39-year-old
Ronald Joseph Sullivan, ran a nursing home at 32 Devon Drive,
Nottingham; called 'Nurse', she had no medical qualifications
but was capable enough to minister to the needs of aged creatures not requiring complicated treatment. Little is known of
Sullivan; he won the Military Medal for gallantry during the
1914–18 War and now flitted genially enough around the Devon
Drive establishment doing most of the rough chores, being
chiefly remarkable for his having (apparently) fallen in love with
someone so physically unattractive as Dorothea Waddingham,
with her protruding teeth and vacuous expression. Authority in
the shape of the County Nursing Association endorsed the
labours of Waddingham and Sullivan by, early in January 1935,
asking them to take in a Mrs Baguley, 89, and her middle-aged
daughter Ada, suffering respectively from senility and disseminated sclerosis, 'creeping paralysis'. On January 12th the Baguleys moved into the home and, after a trial stay of three weeks,
pronounced themselves well satisfied with the arrangement. The
now overworked nursing couple, however, heaving about the
helpless and obese (17 stone) Ada, while attending to her wants,
were not so satisfied, particularly since the Baguley payment was
only £3 a week. Nurse Waddingham was heard to remark that
the Baguleys would have to pay five guineas a week each for

similar treatment in hospital: '. . . and that is really the proper place for them.' On May 4th, Ada Baguley, despite dissuasion from her uneasy solicitor, made a new will, leaving her property (she owned a small business) and money (about £1,500) to Nurse Waddingham in return for life-long treatment for her mother and herself. On May 12th, Mrs Baguley died; her health had seemed to deteriorate from May 6th, Royal Silver Jubilee Day, when the Devon Drive inmates had enjoyed a celebration tea-time treat of tinned salmon. On September 10th, Ada Baguley, seated in the garden with a novelette, received what was to be her last visitor, a Mrs Briggs, whom she greeted cheerfully and from whom she accepted a gift of chocolates; a few hours later, at 2 am, Miss Baguley relapsed into a coma and was soon dead, an event which, although surprising her doctor (who had expected a more protracted demise in view of his patient's complaint), did not deter him from furnishing a death certificate giving cerebral haemorrhage due to weakness of the heart arteries as the cause of death. As Miss Baguley had undoubtedly, during her lifetime. been an advocate of cremation, Nurse Waddingham now set about, with some zest, to comply with the dead woman's wishes. An extraordinary letter, expediently dated August 29th, 1935, was produced, purporting to have been signed by Ada Baguley (although written by Sullivan), addressed to her own doctor, and now sent off to the Nottingham Medical Officer of Health, whose consent to the cremation was required. The letter expressed a desire for cremation 'for health's sake. And it is my wish to remain with Nurse and my last wish is my relatives shall not know of my death.' Understandably suspicious, the Medical Officer, Dr Cyril Banks, ordered a post-mortem on Ada Baguley, and over three grains of morphine were discovered in the corpse; an examination of Mrs Baguley's remains was now deemed necessary, and it was found that her death also had been expedited by morphine, 'a quantity in excess of a medicinal dose'.

Jointly charged with the murder of Ada Baguley, Waddingham and Sullivan faced trial on February 24th at Nottingham Assizes before Mr Justice Goddard, afterwards the Lord Chief Justice, who soon ruled that as there was insufficient evidence against Sullivan he should be immediately discharged. The prosecution, headed by Mr Norman Birkett, KC, alleged that Ada Baguley had been poisoned by surplus morphine tablets prescribed for another patient. (Neither of the Baguleys had even been prescribed morphine.) Waddingham mentioned tablets given her for Miss Baguley's use by that lady's physician, Dr

621

H. H. Manfield: 'I took them to be half-grain morphia tablets because some were given to me when I had pneumonia.' Dr Manfield denied this story: 'I never prescribed them. I never gave them.' The jury added an inexplicable recommendation for mercy, but Dorothea Waddingham was hanged on April 16th, 1936, shortly after writing a letter to Sullivan requesting him not to worry nor to be afraid for her.

WAGNER, Louis
Fisherman by trade, born 1845 in Uckermunde, North Prussia, and convicted of double murder twenty-eight years later.

In the 1860s, Wagner (described as strongly built, ruddy-faced, and handsome – 'all the girls were after him') emigrated to America, where he settled in the town of Portsmouth, on the Atlantic coast of New Hampshire. In 1871 he was employed by a Norwegian, John Hontvet, who owned a fishing-schooner, the *Clara Bella*; during this period Wagner lodged with the Hontvet family, who owned a two-storeyed timber dwelling on the island of Smutty Nose, one of a cluster of sparsely inhabited islands known as The Shoals, about ten miles off the mainland. With Hontvet and his wife Maren lived brother Matthew Hontvet and his 38-year-old spinster sister Karen Christiensen, and young brother Ivan Christiensen with his wife Anethe. These were the only people living on Smutty Nose, and by account were a congenial lot, Wagner himself testifying that while suffering a bout of rheumatism during his sojourn as lodger the womenfolk in particular had been 'most kind'. In 1872 Wagner found other employment on the schooner *Addison Gilbert*, remaining on good terms with the Hontvets although preferring to live on the mainland at Portsmouth; in December of that year, however, the *Addison Gilbert* was wrecked and Wagner rendered jobless and, apparently, desperately in need of money. It is difficult to ascertain whether honest employment was then unobtainable (although one can hardly imagine so), but some quirk prompted Wagner to remark several times: 'I am bound to have money . . . even if I have to do murder for it.' An ex-shipmate, James Lee, was informed by Wagner: '. . . if I could get a boat and row to The Shoals I could get money enough.' By March 1873 Wagner owed his landlady, Mrs Johnson of 25 Water Street, Portsmouth, three weeks' rental of $15.

During the evening of March 5th ('the snow lay thick and white upon the land in the moonlight', records one chronicler),

Portsmouth fisherman James Burke discovered that his rowboat had been stolen. At seven-thirty on the morning of March 6th, some fisherfolk named Ingerbredsen living on the island of Appledore, a short channel-distance away from Smutty Nose, were astonished to see Maren Hontvet, garbed in only a blood-stained nightshift, screaming across to them from the Malaga Rocks, that part of Smutty Nose nearest the Ingerbredsen dwelling. Taken over by boat to Appledore, the distraught woman told how she and her two female relatives (their menfolk out on a protracted fishing excursion) had been attacked in the night by a thieving intruder whom Anethe (to their misfortune) had shrilly identified as 'Louis', the former lodger. Karen Christiensen and Anethe had been axed to death, but Maren had clambered through a window and fled for concealment to a re-mote cove on Smutty Nose, thinking, rightly, that Wagner with his knowledge of the premises would surely find her if she ran to one of the outbuildings. (Wagner's footprints in the snow were to be traced next day, traversing all sheds in the smallholding.) Anethe was the first to die, then Karen, whose death-screams had been heard by the frantic Maren when slithering through the snow to safety. It was found that Wagner had consumed a hearty meal before rowing back to the mainland after the futile search for Maren; the handle of the teapot was red with blood from his fingers. His haul, however (the real purpose of the excursion), was but $20, filched from various pocketbooks in the house.

The journey back to the mainland must have taxed him physi-cally – bloodblisters and severe chafing marked his hands from the rowing – and mentally – for he must have realized the inevita-bility of arrest. When that came, he protested innocence, al-though upon his return to Water Street in the early hours he had remarked to his landlady's daughter: 'I have got myself into trouble' – which was, in the circumstances, something of an understatement. Arrested in Boston on March 6th (and almost lynched there by an infuriated mob), he faced trial on June 9th, 1873, for the murder of Anethe Christiensen. His many alibis proved false and he was found guilty on June 18th of murder in the first degree, being eventually hanged on June 25th, 1875, still asserting in a strong German accent his innocence and a belief in God's 'holy Wort and His commandments'.

WAINEWRIGHT, Thomas Griffiths

Wainewright might be regarded as the English Lacenaire: an intelligent man who turned murderer for gain. Admittedly, Lacenaire was in most ways a stronger and more worthwhile character: but they have one important thing in common: there was a fatal flaw in the character that dictated the easy way out in times of difficulty.

Wainewright was born in 1794, and his mother died in giving birth to him (she was 21). When his father died, his grandfather, the editor of *The Monthly Review*, became his guardian, and Wainewright went to live at Linden House at Turnham Green. (These were the days when Turnham Green was a small village outside London, not simply a spot on the Old Bath Road.)

At 18 he entered the army as a guardsman, but soon tired of this. He was a dandy of the Oscar Wilde type, and remarked that no artist should serve as a soldier unless permitted to design his own uniform. On leaving the army he turned to literature and painting, and soon achieved some success; he became a friend of Charles Lamb, Macready (the actor), Hazlitt, Wordsworth, and Forster (the biographer of Dickens). William Blake admired one of his paintings. He wrote art criticism (and Oscar Wilde quotes long and typical extracts in his essay *Pen, Pencil and Poison*) and entertained lavishly. He married Frances Ward, and began to find himself pressed for money. He asked his trustees for permission to sell his stock; they refused. He forged their signatures (four of them) and presented the forged document at the Bank of England. The bank handed over more than £2,000 without blinking.

Wainewright soon spent this, and decided to poison his grandfather. So in 1829 he and his wife got themselves invited to Linden House, Wainewright procured strychnine, and soon the old gentleman died of 'a fit'. No one suspected, and Wainewright inherited a considerable fortune as well as Linden House. But his creditors absorbed most of the fortune. The upkeep of the house was enormous. Worse still, his mother-in-law, Mrs Abercrombie, asked if she could come and live with him, bringing her two daughters by her second marriage. Wainewright was far too vain a man to admit his real financial state; he let them move in, and then set about poisoning Mrs Abercrombie. She died in August 1830, thus reducing the burden. But her death brought no money to Wainewright, and he brooded on how to use his poison to improve his finances. Finally, he decided to insure

624

Helen Abercrombie, his pretty 20-year-old sister-in-law, and then kill her. He insured her life for £18,000 with various companies, and then got Madeleine, the sister who held the interest in the policies, to assign two of them to him. On December 12th, 1830, Wainewright and his wife and child moved up to Conduit Street with the two sisters. By December 20th, Helen was dead. Wainewright instructed Madeleine to demand the money, but the insurance companies were suspicious. Wainewright sued, but the case took five years to be decided, and finally decision was given against Wainewright. In the meantime, pressed by his debtors, he disappeared to Boulogne, where he poisoned the father of a young girl whom he was trying to seduce, after insuring his life for £3,000. Wainewright gained no advantage by this murder; he had simply become a habitual poisoner.

In 1831 he returned to England secretly, but was recognized in a hotel in Covent Garden by a Bow Street Runner. By now he was known universally as 'Wainewright the poisoner'. However, he was tried only for forgery and sentenced to transportation for life. He died in Hobart, Tasmania, in 1852, at the age of 58, a vain and garrulous man who never ceased to boast of his past acquaintance with the great. He declared he had poisoned Helen because her thick ankles offended him.

WAINWRIGHT, Henry

One of the most brutal crimes of the late nineteenth century – and one of the most pathetic, from the victim's point of view – was the murder of Harriet Lane by her lover, Henry Wainwright.

Wainwright's father, a brushmaker in the East End of London, had died in 1864, leaving a fortune of £11,000 among his five children. Henry had been married since 1862. He had a brushmaker's shop in the Whitechapel Road, next to the Pavilion Theatre, and a house in Tredegar Square. He was an extremely popular man, who had given readings from Dickens, Barham, and Hood at Christ Church Institute and lectured on 'The Wit of Sidney Smith' at the Leeds Mechanics Institute. He enjoyed reciting 'The Dream of Eugene Aram'.

In 1871, he met Harriet Lane, a pretty milliner's apprentice, at Broxbourne Gardens, a popular pleasure resort in the 1870s. She was the 20-year-old daughter of a gas manager at Waltham Abbey and was well educated. She soon became Wainwright's mistress. Wainwright set her up in a house at St Peter's Street, Mile End, and on August 22nd, 1872, a daughter was born to her. In December 1873, another girl was born. A notice that appeared in the *Waltham Abbey Weekly* declared that she had married a 'Percy King' of Chelsea. King was, of course, Wainwright.

Harriet had only one friend and confidante, Ellen Wilmore, another milliner, whom she told that Wainwright treated her like a lady. He paid her £5 a week and gave her many presents and dresses.

Soon, his double life led to difficulties. His brother William dissolved their partnership, and an attempt to run the business with a new partner soon made debts of over £3,000. Harriet's allowance was cut, and she became quarrelsome, as well as showing an alarming tendency to drink. Wainwright decided that the only answer was to kill her. He enlisted the help of his brother, Thomas Wainwright, and they started calling on Harriet together, Thomas being introduced as 'Edward Frieake' (who was actually an auctioneer friend of Wainwright's in the City). Harriet supposed that the intention was to transfer her to 'Frieake' and was not averse to the exchange.

Wainwright actually tried the simple way out of the difficulty one day in August 1874. In the presence of Harriet and his assistant Rogers, he wrote to Mrs Wainwright confessing his misdemeanours and saying that he would never see her again. But Rogers destroyed the letter, under the impression that he was doing his employer a good turn.

In early September, Harriet got very drunk one night outside her lodgings, and a crowd collected around the Wainwright brothers. As a result of this scene, she was given notice to quit the rooms where she lived with Ellen Wilmore. Evidently the subject of her transfer from Wainwright to Frieake had been broached that evening. A few days later, Harriet became excited and happy; the transfer had been completed, and she was going to live with Frieake. On September 11th, 1874, she spent a long time on her appearance, and finally left to join Frieake. It was the last time she was seen alive by Ellen Wilmore. Three weeks later, Miss Wilmore received a letter saying that Frieake had promised to marry her on condition that she stopped communicating with her old acquaintances, and that they were about to embark for the Continent. Telegrams signed 'Frieake' to Miss Wilmore and Wainwright confirmed this. Then no more was heard. Miss Wilmore was suspicious, and communicated her suspicions to Harriet's sister, Mrs Taylor. A private detective was engaged, but he discovered little more than that Wainwright's auctioneer friend Frieake was not the same man who had 'married' Harriet. Harriet's father called on Wainwright and begged him to say where Harriet was, whether alive or dead. Wainwright assured him he did not know.

Wainwright had a paint room next to his shop, part of a warehouse. Soon, a sickening smell from this paint room set his tenants complaining. Nothing was done, and the tenants – his assistant Rogers and his wife – left the rooms above the warehouse.

In June 1875, Wainwright was declared a bankrupt, and his warehouse passed into the possession of a Mr Behrend. Wainwright decided it was time to move Harriet's body to new premises in the borough. On September 11th, 1875 – one year after the murder – the remains were dug up, and wrapped in American cloth. And now came the incredibly stupid mistake that cost Wainwright his life. He called in a youth named Stokes and asked him to keep an eye on the parcels while he fetched a cab. Wainwright should have sent Stokes for the cab. Because while he was away, Stokes looked into one of the parcels, and a severed human hand fell out. Wainwright returned, took the parcels, and got into his cab. Stokes began to run after it, and tried telling two policemen to stop it. They laughed at him.

Meanwhile, Wainwright saw a ballet-dancer friend called Alice Day, and offered her a ride in his cab. He wanted a witness, no doubt, to his complete nonchalance on the drive. Meanwhile, Stokes had found two policemen who *would* believe him, and as Wainwright got out at an ironmonger's shop (perhaps to buy a spade) a policeman accosted him and asked to look into the parcels. Wainwright tried offering them £50 each, without success. The human remains were discovered. He was charged with the murder of Harriet Lane on September 21st, 1875.

Both Henry and his brother Thomas were tried at the Old Bailey on November 27th, 1875. Circumstantial evidence against him was damning. Harriet Lane had been shot twice in the head and her throat cut. Henry was executed at Newgate on December 21st, 1875; his brother received 7 years in jail as an accessory after the fact.

WAITE, Dr Arthur W.

There is a certain amount of comedy in the remarkable murder case of Arthur Waite, arrested in 1916 for the murder of his in-laws.

Waite was apparently a most engaging young man, with easy and charming manners. He had known Clara Peck, the daughter of a rich man of Rapid Falls, Michigan, since they were children. He had an unfortunate career of theft and petty crime until, in September 1915, he married Clara Peck, and decided to kill her parents and anyone else in the family whose demise would make him richer. He is a remarkable case of a totally amoral man. He began by trying to poison his wife's aunt, who had done a great deal for him; he tried arsenic, ground glass, and various germs of typhoid and pneumonia which he obtained from hospitals. When there was no noticeable effect, he invited Clara's mother to stay with them. She very quickly succumbed, and was quickly cremated. ('Her last wish,' Waite explained.) Mr Peck, shattered by his wife's unexpected death, came to stay with his son-in-law at their home in Riverside Drive, New York. He soon felt ill. Waite tried administering germs to him, damping the sheets of his bed to give him pneumonia, and taking him rides in the car after the seat had been wet. He also released tubes of chlorine in Mr Peck's bedroom, hearing that chlorine lowered the resistance to germs. Finally, tiring of all this, he poisoned him with arsenic. The body was embalmed and sent back to Rapid Falls. But Mr Peck's son Percy, who had always disliked Waite, had the embalmed body examined for poison, and arsenic was discovered. Waite phoned his 'dear friend' Catherine Peck (whom he had tried to poison) and asked her advice about killing himself; she managed to dissuade him, and the next day he was arrested. The newspapers soon discovered many details of his past that were unknown to his wife: how he had been saved from jail several times by his parents, how he had been thrown out of college for theft, how he had finally obtained his doctor's degree by cribbing, and forging credentials. He had spent six years in South Africa, where he had tried hard to marry an heiress; he had been asked to resign shortly before his contract expired, and had returned to the United States with a suspiciously large sum of money (considering his salary).

Waite tried hard to clear himself; he tried to bribe a negro servant with $1,000 to say that she had not seen him putting white powder into Mr Peck's food. He tried to bribe the embalmer with $9,000 to say that the embalming fluid had contained arsenic. The embalmer accepted the money, but the police caught up with him.

Waite finally decided to try a defence of complete moral imbecility; he cheerfully admitted his attempt to poison Catherine Peck, and added that his wife would have been, 'the next to go' because, 'she was not my equal in anything, and . . . I mean to get a more beautiful wife'. He also declared that he was a split personality, and that the half of him that drove him to murder was an Ancient Egyptian who could remember Cleopatra, the Nile, and 'the voluptuous pyramids'.

Experts were produced to prove that a man who killed so cheerfully could not be sane, but a jury found him guilty. He was executed in late May 1917, reading Keats and the Bible right to the end. (He was also fond of Ibsen, Poe, and Maeterlinck.) An autopsy revealed that he had slight meningitis on one side of the brain, and that his heart was abnormally large.

WALDER, Arnold

Twenty-two-year-old chemist's assistant, who clubbed to death chemist Pierre Legrange and maidservant Zélie Gaillot at the shop premises in the Place Beauvau, Paris. Slight, spry Walder, born of poor parentage at Einsiedeln, in Switzerland, was always an enterprising individual; twelve years of age when his father died, leaving behind a penniless widow and five children, young Arnold straightaway stole a handcart, placed his long-suffering mother in the shafts and, drawn this fashion, travelled with his younger brothers and sisters to Havre, collecting money *en route* by performing harmonica solos. The eldest Walder soon left his family, and sought a living in Paris, becoming by turns a hotel-boy, a barber, a traveller for a wine firm, a weaver, a navvy, and eventually an assistant in Legrange's pharmacy. A lover of dandyish clothes and women, Walder gained extra much-needed money by pilfering bottles of perfume from the pharmacy and selling them at half-price; when he decided that America was indeed, for him, the land of opportunity, he pondered on how best to secure the passage-money. On Sunday October 5th, 1879, only Legrange, his servant Zélie Gaillot, and Walder were left on the premises (which also served as living quarters for the Legrange family). From 12 to 4 pm Legrange and his two helpers were frequently seen. From 4 to 8 pm (when the shop closed) only Walder was noticed, beaming genially behind the counter, and dashing to and fro after the required potions and prescriptions; this was because his employer and the servant lay dead in the cellar (whence they had gone to unpack a crate of mineral waters) – their skulls battered, presumably by a bloodstained pestle which lay nearby. The discovery was made the following day by Émanuel Fleuty, an odd-job boy, and from the start the identity of the murderer was obvious; Walder was missing (it was learnt later that he had caught a night train to Havre) and a heavily bloodstained shirt initialled 'AW' was found in Legrange's room, which had been completely routed for valuables. Walder's haul was a curious one: 1,500 francs, a gold watch, a pearl tie-pin, a revolver, some scent bottles, a chest of poisons, and three flannel vests.

A photograph of the wanted man (given by one of his mistresses) was issued immediately by the police and circulated throughout France, Europe, and America, together with a comprehensive description of Walder, which mentioned not only his height (5 ft. 6 in.), his drooping eyelids, his sparse 'horse-shoe' beard, and his enormous feet, but also the woman's garnet ring he always wore, his cuff-links with the animal's head motif, his initialled lace handkerchiefs, his elegant black-twill frockcoat faced with cotton-silk, and his cigarette-case shaped like a hunter's horn. Mme Legrange, meanwhile, had received a note in Walder's handwriting shortly after the murders: 'Your husband and the girl resisted me and I was forced to kill them. I now regret what I have done, and I offer, if ever I make my fortune, to repair the wrong I have committed. But for life there is no compensation.' The postmark of this letter was Havre, but although all boats, hotels, and houses in that town were searched, Walder was not found; in fact, directly after posting this letter he had made his way back to Paris, stayed there overnight at the Hôtel Bony (as A. Walter, 32, commercial traveller), before departing the next day to Evreux, where he entered the local chemist's and tried (unsuccessfully) to sell two bottles of his murdered master's geranium perfume. From now on Walder (his American project apparently discarded) devoted his attentions to communicating with the police by means of dramatic messages placed in bottles, an activity which earned him, throughout France, the nickname Bottle-imp.

Message No. 1 was fished up from the Seine at Mantel and read:

I have committed suicide. Better that, than the terror of the guillotine.

Message No. 2, fished out of a canal near Versoul:

I am going to drown myself in order to escape the guillotine.

Message No. 3, from a bottle found on the shore near Lillebonne:

Whosoever finds this bottle will know that Walder threw himself into the river from the bridge of Saint-Pieres.

By the time the fourth bottle-message was picked up at Palavas ('Monsieur or Madame, Unable to endure my remorse I have put an end to my existence'), it must have been obvious to anyone that the elusive, teasing Walder, so far from being a suicide, was very much alive, and keeping remorse at a minimum.

He was never captured; every year, on the anniversary of the crime, he would send a 'card of leave-taking' to the furious Paris Commissaire of Police:

Walder the Proteus
Ex-assistant in the Pharmacy of the Late Legrange:
P.P.C.
No. 0 Scamper Street,
Paris.

WALLACE, William Herbert
Fifty-two-year-old myopic-looking Prudential Company insurance agent, sentenced to death at St George's Hall, Liverpool, on April 25th, 1931, for wife-murder; conviction later quashed by the Court of Criminal Appeal.

Frail, music-loving Mrs Julia Wallace, aged 50, was found murdered at her home, 29 Wolverton Street, Liverpool, on January 20th, 1931. The previous evening a telephone message had been left for Wallace by 'R. M. Qualtrough' at the insurance agent's chess club, which conducted its sessions in a city café. Mr Qualtrough requested Mr Wallace to call by his home at 25 Menlove Gardens East the following night as he had 'something in the nature of his (Wallace's) business' to discuss. Wallace, given the message on his arrival at the club, expressed ignorance over the identity of Mr Qualtrough and of the whereabouts of Menlove Gardens East. Later it was established that the telephone call had come from Anfield 1672, which was a booth near Wolverton Street. Wallace left his home (he said at 6.50 pm) in the early evening of the 20th; certainly at 7.10 pm he was seen boarding a tramcar at Smithdown Junction, some distance from Wolverton Street, so it is assumed he left his home not later than 7 pm. His destination was the Menlove Gardens area of Liverpool, and for the next hour he was to inquire of various people the proximity of Menlove Gardens East. Those questioned included Thomas Philips, a tram conductor; 'a lady . . . out of a house' (never traced); Sidney Green, a clerk; a Mrs Katie Mather living at 25 Menlove Gardens West ('I saw a tall, slight man standing at my door'); and a policeman, PC James Sargent. When speaking to the latter, Wallace drew attention to the time ('it is just a quarter to eight') before walking away. None of these people knew of a Menlove Gardens East, although some were aware of Menlove Gardens North, South, and West. At 8.45 pm Wallace returned to Wolverton Street, and had difficulty opening both the front and back doors. He enlisted the aid of his next-door neighbours, Mr and Mrs Johnston ('the doors are locked against me'), and this time the back door opened without undue pressure: 'There was no violence in the action of opening the door,' said Mr Johnston at Wallace's trial. The Johnstons entered the house with Wallace, and Julia Wallace was found in the front sitting-room; walls, furniture, and carpet were all drenched with blood and Mrs Wallace was lying on a rug in front of the unlit gas fire. Her head had been brutally battered; brains and blood oozed out of a gaping temple wound. Underneath the body was a partially burnt macintosh coat, and Mrs Wallace's skirt was charred down one side as if, when falling down, she had brushed against the lighted gas fire. Mrs Johnston knelt down, distressed, crying, 'Oh, you poor darling!' but Wallace's behaviour throughout was calm: 'He was very quiet,' said Mr Johnston, 'he didn't shout or anything.' Wallace informed the Johnstons that 'about £4' was missing from the house, then Mr Johnston went for the police. Mrs Johnston recalled accompanying Wallace to the murder-room again: 'They have finished her,' said Wallace, 'look at the brains.'

On February 2nd, Wallace was charged with the murder of his wife. 'What can I say in answer to such a charge, of which I am absolutely innocent?' he said. Wallace's trial commenced on April 22nd, 1931. Counsel for the Crown was Mr E. G. Hemmerde, and for the defence Mr Roland Oliver: Mr Justice Wright presided. Alan Close, a 14-year-old boy who helped his father on a milk round, stated that he had seen Mrs Wallace alive at 6.30 pm on the day of the murder: 'I remember the time because when I passed Holy Trinity Church it was twenty-five minutes past six, and it takes me five minutes to get to Mrs Wallace's.' This testimony clashed with that of the pathologist, Professor John MacFall, who had started an examination of the corpse at ten minutes after ten, and from the state of *rigor mortis* judged that death had taken place at least four hours before.

'If,' said Mr Oliver, questioning the pathologist, 'if she was alive at half past six, your opinion is wrong' – to which MacFall reluctantly assented.

Assuming Alan Close's evidence and that of Thomas Philips to be correct, then Wallace, if guilty of wife-murder, had accomplished the act in, roughly, twenty minutes. No trace of blood was found on Wallace's person or under his fingernails, and a popular theory is that before killing Mrs Wallace he stripped himself naked, so that by having a quick post-murder bath he could rid himself of any incriminating gore. Another theory is that the naked, murder-bent Wallace had donned the macintosh (found under Mrs Wallace) to shield himself from the spurts of blood, and that afterwards he attempted to burn it. It is interesting to note, in view of these theories, that no damp towels were found in the house, and the only blood other than that in the front sitting-room was a minute clot in the lavatory pan. The murder-weapon was never found, but, again, assuming Wallace's guilt, it would have been reasonably simple to dispose of it during the lengthy quest for Menlove Gardens East.

The viciousness of the crime was referred to: the skull was completely shattered. 'This,' Professor MacFall observed, 'was not an ordinary case of assault or serious injury. It was a case of frenzy.' Roland Oliver questioned the pathologist further: 'The fact that a man has been sane for fifty-two years, and has been sane while in custody for the last three months, would rather tend to prove that he has always been sane, would it not?'

'No, not necessarily.'

'Not necessarily?'

'No; we know very little about the private lives of people or their thoughts.'

The summing up by the judge was favourable to Wallace: the 'loops and doubts' of circumstantial evidence was referred to, and surprise was felt when, after an hour's absence, the jury returned a verdict of guilty. (Wallace himself had been confident of acquittal, as he stepped back into the dock to hear the verdict: '. . . again I saw myself looking for the exit from the dock into the well of the Court, and thinking that I would take a taxi from the rank outside the building. . . .')

Wallace appealed against the verdict, and after two days' deliberation (May 18th and 19th) the Court of Criminal Appeal quashed the verdict and Wallace was freed. He died of a liver complaint on February 26th, 1933, shortly after retiring to the country. To the end he maintained knowledge of the murderer's identity, and wrote articles for the Press to this effect: 'Now let me say this . . . I know the murderer. . . . In the porch of the front door of this lonely house of mine I have fitted an electric switch and lamp . . . to safeguard my life. The position of the switch is known only to myself and before I open my door I touch it, so that the house, outside and inside, and every recess where an assailant may be lurking, are lit up. The figure which one day I fully expect to see crouching and ready to strike will be that of the man who murdered my wife.'

Recent students of the case, including Richard Whittington-Egan, have become convinced that Wallace was innocent, and that the murderer was a business associate of his whose motive was robbery. The man in question was alive until recent years, and became extremely violent when Mr Whittington-Egan and other investigators tried to get him to talk about it.

WARDER, Dr
A mysterious case of suspected wife murder; however, Warder took his own life before he could be brought to trial. Even so, it is doubtful if he would have been found guilty.

Warder's three wives all died under suspicious circumstances. He was an expert on poisons, and was called in that capacity to given evidence at Palmer's trial in 1856. He was first married in 1863, and after a separation, his wife rejoined him in Devonshire, where she died soon afterwards. Two years later, he married again, and his wife, whose life was insured, died eight months after the wedding. In 1866, he moved to Brighton, where he married the sister of a doctor, Miss Ethel Branwell; she was 36 and he 46. Soon after the marriage she fell ill with pains in her bladder, and a Dr Taafe prescribed opium and henbane. This improved her, but she continued to be ill, and finally died. Dr Taafe asked for a post-mortem, and some of her organs were sent to the famous pathologist – the Spilsbury of his time – Alfred Swayne Taylor. Taylor could detect no poison, but said that the symptoms of death were consistent with the occasional administering of doses of aconite. But before the inquest jury returned a verdict, Dr Warder committed suicide with prussic acid. The inquest decided that Mrs Warder died of aconite administered with malice aforethought by her husband. However, there is no proof of this. But it may well be that, as an expert on poisons, Warder was well qualified to kill his wives without leaving a trace. No motive has ever been suggested except (possibly) insanity.

WATSON, The Rev. John Selby
This is certainly one of the most pathetic of Victorian murder cases.

Watson led a completely blameless life as a well-known Victorian Headmaster, scholar, and translator, until he killed his wife in a fit of rage in 1871. He was born in 1804 at Crayford in Kent; his parents were poor, but a grandfather educated him, and he finally took his degree at Trinity College, Dublin, at the age of 34. He was known as an excellent classical scholar. Here he met a girl, Anne Armstrong, and they became engaged. But it was twenty years before they could get married, for Watson had no money. He went into the Church and was ordained Deacon by the Bishop of Ely in 1839. He became a curate at Langport, Somerset, until he was 37, then decided to become a schoolteacher. In 1844, the governors of Stockwell Grammar School in London advertised for a headmaster, and Watson obtained the post. It was extremely badly paid; the headmaster was to receive £300 a year and an extra four guineas for each boy attending the school above the number of seventy. However, it meant that Watson could marry Anne Armstrong, which he did when he was 41, at St Mark's, Dublin, in January 1845.

In 1848 Bohn's Classical Library – then just beginning – published a number of his translations of Xenophon, Cicero, and Lucretius. Some were later reprinted in Everyman's Library. Watson also wrote a life of Bishop Warburton, a life of Porson, a book of religious meditations on Samson, Solomon, and Job, and a most amusing book on the *Reasoning Power in Animals*. But he made little money, although the school flourished and he was a popular headmaster.

In 1870, the governors of the school committed an act of unparalleled shabbiness; they decided to dismiss Watson – now 64 years of age – without a pension. The school had been declining for a few years, as Watson's powers – weakened by constant overwork to make a poor living – began to fail. On September 30th, 1870, he was dismissed. At Christmas, they cut down their establishment to one servant, and warned their landlady – who charged them over a pound a week for their house, a high rent for those days – that they would have to find cheaper premises. Watson worked at an immense History of the Popes up to the Reformation, and submitted it to Longman's; but he became – naturally – terribly depressed. There is also reason to believe that his wife was often bitter and quarrelsome, possibly taunting Watson with impotence (since she had always wanted children). In September 1871, he went to Chelsfield, Kent, for a day to help the rector, whose curate was absent; the Rev. Ffolliott Baugh later testified that he seemed in a completely dazed and listless condition, and made no conversation whatever.

On Sunday, October 8th, 1871, the couple went to church in the morning and were visited in the afternoon in their house at 28 St Martin's Road by the ex-housekeeper of the school and her husband; Watson did not seem pleased to see them, but was frigidly polite. They were the last – apart from Watson – to see Mrs Watson alive. At nine in the evening, Ellen Pyne, the servant girl, returned from her half-day and was told that her mistress was away overnight. Two days later, when Mrs Watson had still not returned, Watson tried to poison himself with cyanide. The girl found him and summoned a doctor. He had left a note saying that he had killed his wife in a fit of rage. They found his wife in a small bedroom; she had died from head wounds, which had been inflicted by an old pistol that was later found in a drawer.

Watson recovered, and was tried at the Old Bailey on January 10th, 1872, before Mr Justice Byles. The Hon. George Denman, who prosecuted, was extremely sympathetic towards the prisoner. The defence, led by Sergeant Parry, pleaded that Watson had been temporarily insane.

Watson was found guilty, but the jury recommended mercy, and he was eventually reprieved. He died twelve years later, in 1884 (July 6th), at Parkhurst Prison, an old man of 80.

He must be the only murderer whose death was advertised in *The Times*. It is also worth recording that *The Times* published a curious correspondence after the trial on the subject of Watson's Latinity. Watson had left a paper in Latin which contained the sentence, *Saepe olim amanti amare semper nocuit*, and there was some disagreement about its meaning; translations ranged from 'Often to one who loved a long time ago, has to love perseveringly proved detrimental' (from a member of the Athenaeum), to 'Many men have found that it is a great mistake to be true to the object of a boyish passion' (a more likely translation in view of the nature of the case).

It seems a pity that there was no radical left-wing newspaper to declare openly that the men who were really guilty of the crime were the Board of Governors of Stockwell School; it is only to be hoped that the wide publicity received by the case caused them some embarrassment – although this may be doubted.

Neither was it ever ascertained what Mrs Watson said that provoked her husband to go to the bedroom, fetch a pistol, and deal his wife eight shattering blows on the head. A passage in Watson's book on Porson tells how the wife of a Dr Parr insulted Porson, and goes on to say that undisciplined women think it is their right to say what they like to men, certain that no gentleman will chastise them as they deserve; the passage bears a certain stamp of personal bitterness.

WEBER, Jeanne

One of the few known cases in criminal history of a sadistic female killer of children. Her story would make a sensational film in the manner of early Hitchcock, for it is full of strange, melodramatic touches.

Jeanne Weber's case history is, unfortunately, not available. In 1905, she was a married woman living in the Passage Goutte d'Or in Paris. Two of her children had died, and only a third, 7-year-old Marcel, was still alive. She drank too much, which neighbours attributed to sorrow at the death of her children.

On March 2nd, 1905, her sister-in-law went to the local laundry (a description of one can be found in Zola's *L'Assommoir*), and left Jeanne Weber in charge of her 18-month-old girl, Georgette. A few minutes later a neighbour rushed into the laundry to tell her that Georgette was ill. Jeanne Weber told the mother that Georgette had suddenly gone blue in the face and begun to choke. However, the child seemed to recover, and the mother returned to the laundry. Three hours later she returned to find the baby dead, with blue marks on its throat. A doctor declared the cause of death to be convulsions.

On March 11th, the sister-in-law and her husband again left Jeanne Weber in charge of one of their children, this time Suzanne, aged 2. They returned in time to find Suzanne dying of 'convulsions'; the child died minutes after their arrival.

The stupidity of the parents would seem to be incredible, for, on March 25th, Jeanne Weber was again entrusted with the care of their third child, Germaine, aged 7 months. The child was heard to scream out, and neighbours found her choking. There were red marks on her throat. Jeanne Weber left the flat, but returned next day to inquire after the child – now in good health. Again the mother went out, leaving Jeanne Weber in charge of the child; when she returned, it was dead. A doctor certified the cause of death as diphtheria.

Three days later, Jeanne Weber's own child, Marcel, died in the same way – it was actually on the day of his cousin's funeral. Still no one suspected his mother.

On April 5th, 1905, Jeanne Weber invited her two sisters-in-law to dinner; one of them brought her 10-year-old son, Maurice. Jeanne Weber persuaded them to go out shopping, leaving the boy in her charge. When they returned, Maurice was suffering from a convulsion, with foam-flecked lips. The child's mother accused Jeanne Weber of strangling him, and she denied it indignantly. The boy recovered, but the House Surgeon of the Hôpital Bretonneau noted the signs of strangulation on his throat, and the mother charged Jeanne Weber. She was arrested and tried. The official pathologist, Dr Thoinot, declared that he could find no evidence that the children had been strangled, and when Jeanne Weber was tried before the jury of the Seine on January 29th, 1906, the pathologist's negative report led to her acquittal.

Jeanne Weber returned home. Her husband had left her, certain of her guilt, and the neighbours made her feel her unpopularity. She disappeared for fifteen months, during which time she may have lived by prostitution.

On April 16th, 1907, she killed again. A. M. Bavouzet had taken her as his mistress about a month before. He lived in the village of Chambon, near Villedieu on the River Indre. His son Auguste died of 'convulsions' and was found with the characteristic black marks round his throat. Although there was some suspicion, a burial permit was granted. But the 12-year-old daughter of M. Bavouzet happened to be looking through some two-year-old numbers of the *Petit Parisien* when she found Jeanne Weber's photograph looking at her. Jeanne Weber was soon arrested and charged again with murder. The body of the boy Auguste was again examined and this time a verdict of death by strangulation was returned. However, Dr Thoinot was again called in, pooh-poohed the idea of strangulation, and declared that death was due to intermittent fever. A controversy arose, more experts were called in, and they all agreed with Thoinot. Jeanne Weber was acquitted a second time. Public opinion had swung in her favour, and she was brought back to Paris in triumph, an unfortunate woman dogged by ill-luck.

Soon she found employment in a sanatorium, run by one of her sympathizers. Here she was actually caught squeezing the throat of a little boy as he lay struggling in bed. He was in a dangerous condition, but recovered. Jeanne Weber was told to leave the sanatorium and allowed to go free.

In Paris, she confessed to the chief of the Sureté, M. Hamard, that she had murdered her nieces. He decided she was insane, and had her sent to an asylum at Nanterre. She walked out one day and went to live with a sympathizer named Joly at Lay-St-Remy, near Toul. But M. Joly soon tired of her, and she became a prostitute among the thousands of railway workers in Toul, eventually living with a man called Bouchery. Finally, she moved with him into an inn run by a couple named Poirot, where she worked as a domestic. The Poirots had two children, and one day Jeanne Weber asked if the boy could share her bed, since her husband was inclined to beat her when he came home, but would not do so with a child present. The Poirots agreed. At ten in the evening, strange noises were heard coming from her room. Knocking produced no response, so M. Poirot forced the door. They found Jeanne Weber in a state of maniacal excitement; the bed was bloodstained, and the child dead. This time, she had been unable to restrain the excitement that her strangling produced, and had killed the child with violence and then continued to tear at the body. M. Poirot struggled with her and held her until the police arrived. It was soon established that she was Jeanne Weber. However, she was now obviously insane, and was interned at the asylum at Mareville, where she died soon afterwards while attempting to strangle herself.

WEBSTER, John White

Fifty-seven-year-old professor (Master of Arts and Doctor of Medicine at Harvard, a member of the American Academy of Arts and Sciences, member of the London Geological Society, etc.), convicted of the murder of fellow academist, Dr Parkman.

The victim (who held, like Webster, a position at Boston's Medical College) was last seen alive on November 23rd, 1849. His family, residing at No. 8 Walnut Street, became alarmed when Dr Parkman failed to return to lunch. For days empty buildings were searched and the river dredged in a search for the doctor. On November 25th, an uneasy Professor Webster called at Walnut Street and revealed that Dr Parkman had called on him to collect the repayment of a loan; the doctor, according to the professor, had left brandishing $483, which lent conviction to the theory that the missing man had been waylaid by a thief and murdered. A porter, Littlefield, felt that Professor Webster knew of the doctor's whereabouts, and, with hammers and chisels (with his wife keeping guard), broke through to a vault below the professor's apartment: 'I held my light forward ... the first thing I saw was the pelvis of a man and two parts of a leg. I knew it was no place for these things.' The professor, informed of the porter's find, explained: 'That villain! I am a ruined man!' When taken into custody for the murder of Dr Parkman he made an abortive attempt at suicide by swallowing strychnine, although insisting he knew nothing about the remains. Fragments of false teeth, identified as those belonging to Dr Parkman had been found in Professor Webster's furnace, but the professor continued to disclaim all knowledge of the dismembered corpse. The professor was tried before Chief Justice Shaw. So many Bostonians wished to see the trial that a shift system of seating in the public gallery was arranged thus permitting a change of spectators every ten minutes; it was estimated that sixty thousand people witnessed parts of the trial, which lasted eleven days. Found guilty, Professor Webster still maintained his innocence: '. . . to Him who seeth in secret, and before Whom I may ere long be called to appear, would I appeal for the truth of what I now declare . . . that I am wholly innocent of this charge. . . .' Later he confessed to the crime; there had been a violent quarrel concerning Dr Parkman's loan and Professor Webster's continued inability to repay:

> . . . I felt nothing but the sting of his words . . . in my fury I seized whatever thing was handiest – it was a stick of wood – and dealt him a blow . . . he did not move . . . he was absolutely dead. I took off the clothes and began putting them into the fire . . . my next move was to get the body into the sink . . . there it was entirely dismembered. The only instrument was the knife . . . which I kept for cutting corks. While dismembering the body a stream of water was running through the sink, carrying off the blood in a pipe that passed through the lower laboratory. There must have been a leak in the pipe, for the ceiling below was stained immediately round it.

Despite this claim that the killing blow had been struck in momentary anger, so appealing for a new verdict of manslaughter, Professor Webster was hanged in August 1850.

WEBSTER, Kate
Thirty-year-old Irishwoman from Killane, County Wexford, who in 1870 was convicted of the murder of her employer, Julia Thomas, in Richmond, Surrey.

A convicted thief and prostitute, Webster obtained employment in January 1879 as housekeeper to Mrs Thomas, an elderly widow who lived alone at 2 Vine Cottages, Park Road, Richmond; Webster, however, spending much of her time at the local hostelry. On Sunday, March 2nd, after Mrs Thomas had returned from church, a quarrel broke out between mistress and servant; Webster attacked Mrs Thomas with an axe, hacking her to death. On the floor of the scullery she dismembered her late employer; pausing for a brief visit to a public house, she returned to the house and boiled the remains in the large kitchen copper, tying some of them up into packages, others being stuffed on to the fire. During the days following, Webster sold much of Mrs Thomas' property, including her false teeth, for which she obtained six shillings. (Legend has it that the local publican was persuaded by Webster into purchasing two jars of 'best dripping'.) She enlisted the aid of a man friend in dropping a large boxful of remains over Richmond Bridge, Mrs Thomas' head having been thrown over Hammersmith Bridge by Webster some hours earlier. It was arranged that John Church, landlord of the Rising Sun Hotel in Rose Gardens, Hammersmith, should purchase the furniture at No. 2 Vine Cottages; it was an amicable agreement, with Church living at the Richmond house for a few days with the furniture-selling 'Mrs Thomas'. A Miss Ives, who had let No. 2 to Mrs Thomas, and who lived next door, became suspicious when she saw the furniture being loaded into a removal van; during her questioning of the bewildered Church, Kate Webster fled the district, incidentally taking £18 of Church's money. Church made a statement to Richmond police; eventually a Scotland Yard detective found the ex-housekeeper in her home village of Killane, wearing Mrs Thomas' clothes and jewellery. Charged with the murder of her mistress and theft, Kate Webster screamed denials, accusing other people, including John Church. Her trial began on July 2nd, 1879, concluding on July 10th;

found guilty of murder, she was hanged on July 29th, having confessed her crime the night before to the prison chaplain.

WHITEWAY, Alfred Charles

Twenty-two-year-old lust-killer (hobby knife-throwing), hanged at Wandsworth Prison on December 22nd, 1953, for the murder of Barbara Songhurst, aged 18, by the Thames towpath at Teddington, Middlesex.

On Sunday May 31st, 1953, Barbara Songhurst, with her friend Christine Reed, aged 16, set out after lunch to go cycling. The following day the body of Barbara was found in shallow water off Ham Fields, near Richmond, Surrey; she had been stabbed and raped before being thrown into the river. Search was intensified for the missing girl-friend, Christine Reed, and on June 6th her body was found in the River Thames at Richmond; her skull was twice fractured and she was stabbed in the back and chest, having been raped after death. (In view of the ferocity and nature of these attacks, the police realized the man they wanted was the worst and most dangerous type of sexual maniac, and on June 8th, Assistant Commissioner Ronald Howe of Scotland Yard was to issue a direct appeal to the public for aid in finding the killer.)

Three youths who set up camp on the river bank were the last people to see the girls alive; they had chatted and indulged in 'skylarking' with them during that Sunday evening, until the girls, gathering up their belongings and cycles, remarked they must return home. Campers farther down the bank said they heard screams about 11 pm and someone reported seeing a man riding a woman's cycle along the towpath about 11.20 pm. (Christine's cycle was recovered from the river the day after the murders, but Barbara's was never found.)

Chief Inspector Hannam of Scotland Yard and his helpers spent a month dragging the river and examining statements in an effort to find clues to the killer's identity. The familiar theories about 'moon killers' were brought forward, and one Sunday newspaper offered £1,000 for any information leading to the arrest and conviction of the murderer.

Alfred Whiteway, a labourer with past convictions for thieving, was under detention by the police at the end of June for having assaulted two people, one a girl of 14 whom he had attacked with a chopper and raped in Oxshott Woods, Surrey, on May 24th. He claimed he was with his 19-year-old wife (from whom he lived apart owing to housing difficulties) until 11.30 pm when he cycled to his parents' home at 24 Sydney Road, Teddington. He said he knew Barbara Songhurst as she had lived in Sydney Road 9 years before: 'I knew Barbara then when she was about six but I've not seen her since.' (Statement made at Richmond Police Station on June 29th.) At New Scotland Yard on July 30th he made two statements, and in the final one he confessed to the murders: 'It's all up. You know bloody well I done it, eh! I'm mental. . . .'

Whiteway was charged on August 20th with the murders. When cautioned he said: 'I deny the charges.' The trial opened at the Old Bailey on October 26th, 1953.

There was a distressing diversion when a police constable was questioned. On June 17th, Whiteway was apprehended on Oxshott Heath and was driven to Kingston Police Station in a police car. The following day the constable had found an axe under the rear seat of the car, where Whiteway had been sitting. Stupidly he took the axe home and used it for chopping wood. On July 15th, realizing its import, he handed it to a fellow constable. The prosecution alleged that this axe, exhibit 15, was the one used to inflict the injuries during the towpath killings; it fitted exactly into a wound in Christine Reed's skull. (Questioned, Ivy Elizabeth Whiteway, the defendant's sister, aged 15, said it was similar to one at her home that had been missing for six weeks.) The wretched constable paid for his momentary folly, and collapsed in the witness-box during his interrogation by Mr Peter Rawlinson, Defence Counsel. The prosecution, led by Mr Christmas Humphreys, mentioned Whiteway's 'remarkable' collection of knives, including a Gurkha's kukri knife, which the police alleged Whiteway admitted using in the murder attacks. A month before the murders he had been seen by schoolmaster Roy Tarp hurling knives (including the kukri knife) at trees by the river bank. One of Whiteway's shoes, worn on May 21st, showed a strong blood reaction, and there had been an effort to clean it. The prosecution alleged that Whiteway killed the girls because he realized that Barbara Songhurst could identify him.

Mr Justice Hilbery, in his summing up referred to '. . . these two light-hearted people in the springtime of their lives . . . little thought that a foul death awaited them, as they went farther along the towpath . . .' He was scornful of the suggestion that the police had written the Whiteway confession: 'Look at the statement. . . . Do you think that an experienced novelist, a writer of fiction could have done much better than that? It is said to have been done by a police officer.' The jury was out for forty-seven minutes, finding Whiteway guilty of murder.

Whiteway appealed against his conviction and sentence of death, but Lord Chief Justice Goddard dismissed the appeal saying: 'This case is one of the most brutal and horrifying that has ever been before this court and any other court for years.'

WILLIAMS, John (The Ratcliffe Highway Murders)

Red-haired Irish labourer, believed to be in his twenties, who murdered two entire families in London's East End in the early part of the nineteenth century; Thomas de Quincey devotes much writing to this individual in his appendix to the treatise, On Murder, Considered as one of the Fine Arts.

Towards midnight on Saturday December 7th, 1811, 18-year-old Margaret Jewell, servant to the young Marr family (Timothy Marr ran a hosier's business in the Ratcliffe Highway), was sent out to purchase oysters for supper; diligent but unlucky in her quest at such a late hour, she returned to the Marr establishment at 1 am to find the door locked and the house silent and dark. De Quincey, in his account, describes masterfully the girl's increasing sensation of horror and foreboding, particularly when recalling the sinister stranger she had seen prowling round the house earlier in the evening, and goes on (doubtless with dramatic licence) to relate how stealthy footsteps were heard from within the building, and how the hysterical servant's screams attracted passers-by and neighbours, so leading, within a few minutes, to the finding of the Marr family (Timothy, wife Cecilia, and young baby) together with their 13-year-old apprentice John Goen, all with their skulls smashed and throats cut; nothing had been taken from the premises. The whole of London, in fact, was appalled by the senseless slaughter, and when another family was murdered, obviously by the same hand, on December 19th, there was panic. Now the victims were an elderly publican Mr Williamson, his wife Catherine, and their maidservant, 50-year-old Bridget Harrington; the killer slipped into the inn, the King's Arms, 81 New Gravel Lane, shortly after closing time on 11 pm; Mr Williamson invariably left the front door open to 'oblige' the nocturnal imbiber. The Williamsons' lodger, 26-year-old John Turner, alone in his bedroom, and disturbed by unfamiliar sounds, crept downstairs and, himself unseen, saw a stranger, 'in creaking shoes', bending over one of the corpses; terrified but resolved to remain alive, he returned to his room and effected an escape by knotting his bedclothes together into a 'rope' by which he escaped through the window, dropping on to the local nightwatchman, George Fox, who immediately broke into the public house and found the corpses. Even greater ferocity had been employed during the second series of murders; Bridget Harrington was almost decapitated, and Mr Williamson (who had evidently put up a struggle for life) savagely hacked in every limb. The couple's grandchild, 14-year-old Kitty Stillwell, had escaped the massacre, the killer apparently having been disturbed by the inquiring watchman. A sailor's maul was discovered by one of the bodies; it bore the initials 'JP' and was found to belong to a Swedish sailor, John Petersen, who, being then on the high seas, had a perfect alibi; he lodged when in London, with a Mrs Vermiloe, and it was a fellow-lodger, John Williams, whom the police now suspected. Little is known of his interrogation (at Shadwell Police Office) save that he refused to answer several questions, although admitting that he spent much time at Williamson's tavern. He had been seen walking towards the King's Arms late on the evening of the murders, and had returned to his lodging in the early hours of the morning with a bloodied shirt – the result, Williams explained, of a card-game brawl. Arrested and taken to New Prison at Coldbath Fields, he committed suicide on December 28th by hanging himself from a wall-rail in his cell. He was accorded a suicide's burial being transported by cart on the morning of December 31st through East End crowds to the cross-roads by Cannon Street and New Road (near present-day Cable Street) where he was buried in quicklime and a stake driven through his heart. (Cross-roads were traditionally selected for suicides so as to confuse their restless souls' sense of direction; one assumed that in Williams' case the stake – reminiscent of Hall Caine – was an added measure taken by uneasy citizens to ensure his 'staying put'.) De Quincey, in 1854, described Williams as a grotesquely fey, thin, albino-faced creature, but in fact a contemporary print (drawn during the burial procession) shows a stocky, muscular, plebeian labourer-type spreadeagled in death upon a slanting shaft of wood.

The evidence against Williams was circumstantial; the killings terminated, however, upon his death. Popular with women, he had confided to a barmaid friend shortly after the Marr murders: 'I am unhappy, and can't remain easy.' A syphilitic, it has also been suggested that he killed out of a grudge towards humanity.

WOOD, Robert (The Camden Town Murder)
The Camden Town Murder is the first case in which a man accused of murder, availing himself of the right to give evidence on his own behalf (Criminal Evidence Act 1898) has been found not guilty.

On the morning of September 12th, 1907, Phyllis Dimmock, a prostitute, of 29 St Paul's Road, Camden Town, was found with her throat cut by the man who was living with her as her husband. His name was Bert Shaw, and he worked all night as a railway worker. He believed that his 'wife', with whom he had recently set up home, had abandoned her old trade. Her death soon revealed that this was wishful thinking.

Phyllis Dimmock's body was found in the bed; the room had been ransacked, and an album of picture postcards lay on the floor.

Her favourite public house was known to be the Rising Sun in Camden Town, and police there gained information that led them to trace Robert Percival Roberts, a ship's cook who had slept with Phyllis for three nights before the murder. Roberts had a sound alibi, but he was able to give the police a lead. Phyllis had shown him a postcard signed 'Alice' which asked her to keep an assignation in the Rising Sun, and a letter signed 'Bert'. Phyllis Dimmock was apparently out to convince Roberts that she had a valid reason for not allowing him to spend that night with her.

The postcard was eventually found by Bert Shaw, and it was printed in the *News of the World*, with a caption: 'Can you recognize this writing?' As a result of this, an artist's model named Ruby Young, who lived in the Earls Court Road, recognized the handwriting as that of her lover, an artist named Robert Wood. Wood called on her before she could post a letter to the *News of the World*, and told her a convincing story to explain his involvement with the murdered girl. He had met her casually in a Camden Town public house, he said, and had bought her a drink. Phyllis told him she liked postcards, and he offered to let her select one from a batch he happened to have in his pocket, which he had bought in Bruges. She asked him to write 'something nice on it', and he scrawled the appointment at the Rising Sun for Monday. She asked him to sign it 'Alice', and he had

646

gone off with the card, promising to post it to her. He had met her by chance in the street the next day, and she had reminded him of his promise. He had bought her a drink again on Monday evening, but had not seen her after that.

Wood must have been a good talker, because Ruby Young believed his exceedingly implausible story, and agreed not to claim the £100 reward. The foreman at the factory where Wood worked also recognized the card, but was taken in by the story and agreed to keep quiet.

Ruby Young was sincere in her agreement not to betray her lover (although their relation was apparently cooling off), but she could not resist telling a friend 'in absolute confidence'. The friend repeated it to a journalist friend; the delighted journalist terrified Ruby into repeating it to him, and sent for the police. Wood was arrested as he left the offices of the London Sand Blast Glass Works in Grays Inn Road, where he worked, on October 4th, 1907.

The next day he was identified by several women as a man who had been friendly with Phyllis Dimmock for over a year; a car-man, MacCowan, also declared that he had seen Wood leaving 29 St Paul's Road, at 4.45 on the morning of the murder. Wood tried out a fake alibi which he had arranged with Ruby Young, but she had already told the police the truth.

The case for the prosecution depended on circumstantial evidence. This consisted mainly of the postcard, and of a burnt fragment of a letter which Phyllis Dimmock had also shown to Roberts, making an appointment at the Eagle on Wednesday, the evening of the murder, and signed 'Bert'. The handwriting, the prosecution claimed, was identical on both.

The trial took place at the Old Bailey on December 12th, 1907, before Mr Justice Grantham, with Sir Charles Mathews for the Crown and Mr Marshall Hall defending. There was a great deal against Wood, pointing to premeditation to murder. He had a peculiar walk, with a jerk of the shoulders, and Cowan had recognized this. Phyllis Dimmock had kept her hair in curlers on the evening of the murder, which showed she was not expecting to look for clients. Many people had seen Wood with her in the Eagle public house, but it could be presumed that Wood's intention in using the Eagle for their assignation was to avoid recognition, since the pub was unfamiliar to him. These included Wood's friend Lambert, who had met Wood in the Eagle (opposite Camden Town Station) on the evening of the murder with a young woman in curling pins, and had later been cautioned by Wood not to mention the girl if the police asked questions. Sir Charles pointed to the frantic search of the apartment for the incriminating postcard, and the attempt to simulate robbery by taking some jewellery – an attempt that failed because two gold rings had been left untouched.

Marshall Hall succeeded in throwing a great deal of doubt on MacCowan's evidence, and declared that the character of many of the Crown witnesses – brothel keepers, gin-sodden sluts, etc., indicated the weakness of the Crown's case. He argued that there was no credible motive for Wood committing the crime, and that none of the stolen articles was ever traced to Wood. The weapon was never found. But Wood had no blood on his clothes, which would be unusual if he had killed Phyllis Dimmock.

The final witness for the defence was Wood himself, a handsome and quiet-spoken young man, who made an excellent impression in contrast to most of the Crown witnesses. It was obvious that public opinion was strongly on his side. (Wood's father and brother had already testified that he returned home at 11.30 on the evening of the murder.) The judge's final direction to the jury was obviously taken by the audience in court to be an instruction to acquit the accused, and there were cheers. The jury returned after seventeen minutes to declare the prisoner not guilty. There were cheers and demonstrations.

The unfortunate Ruby Young was extremely unpopular and had to be smuggled away from the Old Bailey in a charlady's uniform; the angry mob might easily have killed her. It is doubtful if she intended to betray Wood.

Wood later changed his name, and lapsed into oblivion.

The trial excited immense popular interest which is hardly comprehensible in retrospect. Sickert painted several pictures of the Camden Town Murder. It seems very probable that Wood was, in fact, not guilty, and that Phyllis Dimmock was murdered by a 'client' after Wood's departure.

WREN Case, The
Murder in a sweet-shop, memorable only for the durability of the victim.

At 6 o'clock on September 20th, 1930, a small girl was sent by her mother to buy blancmange powder at Miss Wren's sweet-shop in Ramsgate. Finding the shop door locked, the child looked through the glass panel and saw Miss Wren, aged 82, sitting in her back parlour. Miss Wren came and opened the door; the old woman's face was a mask of blood and her gait unsteady, but she asked the child what she wanted and proceeded to place various types of blancmange powder on the counter. The child ran home and described Miss Wren's condition; the old woman was taken to hospital. She had eight wounds and bruises on her face and seven severe lacerations and punctures on top of the head; there were also traces of strangling. No money was missing from the shop.

At first Miss Wren offered the dubious explanation that she had tripped over the fire tongs; then, as her delirium increased, she muttered about a man 'with a red face', who had attacked her with the fire tongs. Towards the end she uttered Biblical-sounding phrases like: '. . . he must fear his sins. . . .'

Miss Wren lived with her terrible injuries until September 25th. Her murder remains unsolved.

Y

YOUNGBLOOD, Param
A deaf-and-dumb youth, who murdered and raped 7-year-old Margie Jones in Georgia in 1958.

Youngblood had been convicted of attacking two teen-age girls in Little Rock, Arkansas, on August 21st, 1951; he had stabbed one and shot the other. He was sentenced to fifteen years in prison, but was paroled after five. (The girls both recovered.) On his release, he lived in Toomsboro, Georgia, with his mother, and travelled around as a pencil salesman. In Kentucky, he met Mrs Jane Harrison, who had six grandchildren, three of of whom were deaf mutes; Youngblood became a close friend of the family. In August 1958, Mrs Harrison came to Tooms-boro to visit the Youngblood mother and son. On August 16th, Youngblood took four of the children to the cinema. Afterwards, he drove the car two miles into Washington County, amd made three of them get out and walk; they were Jo Ann and Paul Lee Cox, aged 3 and 6, and Anna Mae Blair, aged 11. Youngblood drove with 7-year-old Margie Jones. The children walked to a farm, where the farmer raised the alarm.

Youngblood was now on the run. He tried to force a youth to change cars, but the youth drove away, followed by bullets; Youngblood then held up a family in their station wagon and drove away in it. A day later, the child's body was found; she had been shot twice.

Youngblood was seen by a policeman driving out of Macon, and police set up a roadblock near Rutland, Houston County. As the Buick station wagon speeded towards the police cars, bullets began to fly, and Youngblood shot himself through the head as he braked to a stop. He was dead when the police got to the car.

APPENDIX

Discarded fragment from *The Outsider* by Colin Wilson

The Faust Outsider

Speaking of Netchaev, Stavrogin tells Shatov: 'He's got the idea I could play the part of a leader of the Revolution because of my "unusual aptitude for crime".'

And Shatov, provoked, asks: 'Is it true that in Petersburg you belonged to a secret society given up to bestial sexuality? Is it true that the Marquis de Sade could have taken lessons from you? Is it true that you seduced and debauched children?'

But Stavrogin is not one of those who are 'possessed by devils' – for all that this is true. *He would like to be possessed*: all his crime is an attempt to be possessed. He envies Netchaev and his revolutionaries because they *are* possessed – and he despises them because they are little enough to be possessed by such rubbish.

Yet the Outsider's 'extraordinary aptitude for crime' springs out of this desire to be possessed. At the end of a 'lukewarm day', Steppenwolf records: 'A wild longing for strong emotions and sensations burns in me, a rage against this toneless . . . sterilized life. I have a mad impulse to break something to bits . . . to commit outrageous follies. . . .'

It is not far from this to Stavrogin's criminal perversions. Steppenwolf is a German; his temper is humanitarian and rational. Stavrogin is a Russian; he is not afraid of extremes. Steppenwolf also has the 'unusual aptitude for crime' – in embryo. If he had the courage to seize the essence of Blake's maxim; 'rather murder an infant in its cradle than nurse unsatisfied desire', he would have become a very dangerous man to Society. Fortunately for Society, there is always something of the Hamlet about the Outsider; he is not usually a man of action. If Barbusse's Outsider had followed his impulse he would have stalked around Paris at night, intent on rape; *that* would have been the logical outcome of his desire for the anonymity of 'all women'. The Outsider has a morbid horror of the rational mechanism of Society – for his deepest impulse is to feel *freedom of choice*. That is why he can never subscribe to a social ideology; it is also the reason why 'the banal ritual' of ordinary pleasure fails to satisfy him. He must feel himself the chooser. It is only one step from the Barbusse Outsider to the criminal Outsider. And the criminal Outsider is possessed – or wants to be possessed – by crime, for he prefers to be the slave of a diabolical impulse rather than be the slave of the Government or the everyday routine treadmill. The most superficial knowledge of criminology will tell us how much more dangerous are the 'possessed' criminals than the men who commit crimes for gain.

In fact, at the risk of digressing, let us compare a few instances of well-known crimes of violence. Take, for example, these cases: Burke and Hare, the Edinburgh body-snatchers, or Williams, the Ratcliffe Highway murderer; and contrast with them the unknown criminal known as 'Jack the Ripper' – or the Düsseldorf sadist, Peter Kürten. In the first two cases, the criminals were no more than glorified footpads. Burke and Hare found that the Edinburgh School of Medicine paid well for bodies to dissect; so they helped to meet the demand by picking up a steady stream of down and outs, making them drunk and them scientifically murdering them in the Edinburgh backstreets. These men killed like animals: they were themselves 'victims' of the economic law of supply and demand. The lack of horror occasioned by their crimes can be gauged by a popular lyric about them, that ended:

> Burke's the murderer, Hare's the thief,
> And Knox the boy who buys the beef.

Williams' Ratcliffe Highway murders were the subject of an essay by Thomas de Quincey, in which he tried hard to paint Williams as a demoniacal 'cold monster' – and failed completely to do so because even De Quincey's magnificent language could not hide the fact that Williams was merely a drunken butcher. Williams killed two families with a mallet – seven people in all – yet he was so stupid that the police had no difficulty in finding him. Within six weeks of his first murder, he was buried beneath a cross-road in London's East End. We feel no more *horror* about these crimes than about watching a lion eating raw meat at the Zoo. They are symptoms of social evil as much as of human corruption.

Compare these criminals with 'Jack the Ripper'; whose six crimes are the most appalling in British criminal history, whose 'reign of terror' in Whitechapel lasted for four months, and then, after a murder of unparalleled brutality, stopped suddenly. His identity is unknown to this day. Nothing is known of him except what these six murders tell us; the victims were always women – so they can be categorized as 'Lustmord'.[1] They were all committed with a knife, and usually some of the victim's internal organs were taken away by the murderer. These are the only facts known, but it is possible to hazard some interesting guesses on the strength of what is known of the Düsseldorf murders of 1929. For Kürten's case is one of the best documented records of criminal mania that we possess.

Kürten committed his first murder when he was 19 (in 1899), and after a final attack of homicidal mania that lasted through most of 1929, he gave himself up to the police. He was a sadist; inflicting pain gave him pleasure. He killed men, women, and children, using various weapons – a hammer, a hatchet, knives, scissors – always with the same purpose – to *stimulate a faculty that could not be stimulated otherwise*. Kürten admitted to the psychologist who examined him (Professor Berg) that the pleasure he derived from returning to the scene of his murders the next morning and seeing the horror of the crowd, was almost as great as his pleasure in committing the murder itself. He also admitted to indulging in fantasies of destroying a whole city with dynamite, and of committing some act that would horrify all the world. (We can imagine his delight if he had been alive to witness Belsen and Hiroshima.)

Yet Professor Berg insists on Kürten's intelligence, his gentleness in everyday matters. In the same way, all the doctors who examined him were struck by his *honesty*. Kürten's case makes an absorbing study for readers who are interested in what St Augustine calls, 'the abyss of human nature'.

Thus we may say that both Jack the Ripper and Kürten were men who succeeded in being 'possessed by crime' – or by neurosis if you prefer it. If the term 'neurosis' is used, it must be realized that the crime is *not* the neurosis, but the *escape from it*.

In Stavrogin, we have the case of a man who did not succeed in being possessed by crime. And the difference between success and failure is, on the whole, the difference between the 'Insider' and the 'Outsider'. Stavrogin could never murder as Kürten murdered, because, as he says, his desires are not strong enough. This is a common characteristic of the Outsider, who is 'never himself in what he does', and, consequently, never does anything that corresponds with his deepest instincts.

[1] Literally joy-murder, i.e. sex crimes.

MEMORANDUM ON THE QUESTION OF CAPITAL PUNISHMENT
SUBMITTED TO THE GOWERS COMMITTEE

This subject has intered me for many years, particularly since the trial of Rex *v* Dickman at the Newcastle Summer Assizes in July 1910, who was tried for the murder of a man named Nesbit in a train. Dickman was executed for what was an atrocious crime on August 10th, 1910, his appeal to the Court of Criminal Appeal being dismissed on July 22nd, 1910. The case has always troubled me and converted me into an opponent of capital punishment. I attended the trial as the acting official shorthand-writer under the Criminal Appeal Act. I took a different view to the jury; I thought the case was not conclusively made out against the accused. Singularly enough, in view of the nature of crime, five of the jurymen signed the petition for reprieve, which could only be based upon the notion that the evidence was not sufficient against the accused.

It may be asked, why raise the question now? I am doing so partly because of Viscount Templewood's evidence when he was reported as saying there was a possibility of innocent men being executed: partly because of the evidence of Viscount Buckmaster before the Barr Committee on Capital Punishment; but mainly because of the remarkable and disturbing matters concerning the Dickman case which have come to my knowledge over the intervening years, which I will now relate.

The Dickman case is the subject of a book by Sir S. Rowan-Hamilton, which was published in 1914, based on the transcripts of the shorthand notes of the trial and certain other material. I did not read this book till August 1939, when, owing to certain passages in the book, I wrote a letter to Sir S. Rowan-Hamilton, who had been Chief Justice of Bermuda, who replied in a letter dated October 26th, 1939:

> The Cottage,
> Craijavak,
> Co. Down.

Sir,

Your interesting letter of the 24th August only reached me today. Of course, I was not present at the incident you referred to in the Judge's Chambers, but Lowenthal was a fierce prosecutor. All the same Dickman was justly (convicted?), and it may interest you to know that he was with little doubt the murderer of Mrs Luard, for he had forged a cheque she had sent him in response to an advertisement in *The Times* (I believe) asking for help; she discovered it and wrote to him and met him outside the General's and her house and her body was found there. He was absent from Newcastle those exact days. Tindal Atkinson knew of this, but not being absolutely certain refused to cross-examine Dickman on it. I have seen replicas of cheques. They were shown me by the Public Prosecutor: also see the note on the first page of the preface. He was, I believe, mixed up in that case, but I have forgotten the details.

Yours very truly,
S. Rowan-Hamilton, Kt.

In 1938 there was published a book entitled *Great Unsolved Crimes*, by various authors. In that book there is an article by ex-Superintendent Percy Savage (who was in charge of the investigations), entitled 'The Fish Ponds Wood Mystery', which deals with the murder of Mrs Luard, wife of Major-General Luard, who committed suicide shortly afterwards by putting himself on the railway line. In that article the following passage appears: 'It remains an unsolved mystery. All our work was in vain. The murderer was never caught, as not a scrap of evidence was forthcoming on which we could justify an arrest, and, to this day, I frankly admit that I have no idea who the criminal was.' This book first came to my notice in February 1949, whereupon I wrote to Sir Rowan-Hamilton, reminding him of the previous letters, and asking for his observations on this statement of the officer who had conducted the inquries into the Luard case. On February 22nd, 1949, I received the following reply from Sir S. Rowan-Hamilton:

Lisieux,
Sandycove Road,
Dunloaoghaire,
Co. Dublin.
22nd February, 1949.

Dear Sir,

Thank you for your letter. Superintendent Savage was certainly not at Counsel's conference and so doubtless knew nothing of what passed between them. I am keeping your note as you are interested in the case and will send you later a note on the Luard case.

Yours truly,
S. Rowan-Hamilton, Kt.

I replied, pointing out what a disturbing state of facts was revealed, as it was within my knowledge that Lord Coleridge, who tried Dickman, Lord Alverstone, Mr Justice A. T. Lawrence, and Mr Justice Phillimore, who constituted the Court of Criminal Appeal, were friends of Major-General and Mrs Luard. (Lord Alverstone made a public statement denouncing in strong language the conduct of certain people who had written anonymous letters to Major-General Luard hinting that he had murdered his wife.) I did not receive any reply to this letter, nor the promised note on the Luard case.

Mr Winston Churchill, who was the Home Secretary who rejected all representations on behalf of Dickman, was also a friend of Major-General Luard.

So one has the astonishing state of things disclosed that Dickman was tried for the murder of Nesbit by judges who already had formed the view that he was guilty of the murder of the wife of a friend of theirs. If Superintendent Savage is to be believed, this was an entirely mistaken view.

I was surprised at the time of the trial at the venom which was displayed towards the prisoner by those in charge of the case. When I was called in to Lord Coleridge's room to read my note before the verdict was given on the point of the non-calling of Mrs Dickman as a witness, I was amazed to find in the judge's room Mr Lowenthal, Junior Counsel for the Crown, the police officers in charge of the case, and the solicitor for the prosecution. When I mentioned this in a subsequent interview with Lord Alverstone, he said I must not refer to the matter in view of my official position.

I did my best at the time within the limits possible. I went to Mr Burns, the only Cabinet Minister I knew well, and told him my views on the case and the incident in the judge's room; which I also told to Mr Gardiner, the Editor of *The Daily News*, who said he could not refer to that, though he permitted me to write in his room a last-day appeal for a reprieve, which appeared in *The Daily News*. Mr John Burns told me afterwards that he had conveyed my representations to Mr Churchill, but without avail.

C. H. Norman,
27 November, 1950

SELECT BIBLIOGRAPHY

BARKER, Dudley, *Lord Darling's Famous Cases*. Hutchinson, 1936.

BERG, Dr Karl, *The Sadist*. (Peter Kürten.) Heinemann.

BIRKENHEAD, Earl of (F. E. Smith), *Famous Trials*. Hutchinson. *More Famous Trials*. Hutchinson.

BOWKER, A. E., *A Lifetime with the Law*. W. H. Allen, 1961.

BRICE, A. H. M., *Look Upon the Prisoner*. Hutchinson.

BROWNE, Douglas G. *and* BROCK, Alan, *Fingerprints*. Harrap, 1953.

BROWNE, Douglas G. *and* TULLET, E. V., *Bernard Spilsbury, His Life and Cases*. Harrap, 1951.

CAMPS, Dr Francis E., *Medical and Scientific Investigations in the Christie Case*. Medical Publications Ltd. 1953.

COHEN, Louis H., *Murder, Madness and the Law*. World Publishing Company, New York, 1952.

DILNOT, George, *Celebrated Crimes*. Stanley Paul & Co. 1925.

DOUTHWAITE, L. C., *Mass Murder*. John Long, 1928.

FAMOUS TRIALS SERIES edited by George Dilnot. Geoffrey Bles. Including volumes on Landru, Green Bicycle Case, Patrick Mahon, Maria Marten Case, Constance Kent, Professor Webster, etc.

FURNEAUX, Rupert, *The Medical Murderer*. Elek, 1957. *Famous Criminal Cases* (6 volumes). Odhams. *Crime Documentary* (2 volumes).

GIONO, Jean, *The Dominici Affair*. Museum Press, 1956.

GLAISTER, J., *Medical Jurisprudence and Toxicology*. Livingstone, 1953. *Medico-Legal Aspects of the Ruxton Case*. Edinburgh, 1937.

GODWIN, George, *Crime and Social Action*. Watts & Co., 1956. *Peter Kürten, a Study in Sadism*. Heinemann, 1945.

GRIBBLE, Leonard, *Famous Manhunts, a Century of Crime*. John Long, 1953.

GRIFFITHS, Major Arthur, *Mysteries of Police and Crime* (3 volumes). Cassell, 1898.

HAYWARD, Arthur L., *Lives of the Most Remarkable Criminals Who Have Been Condemned and Executed . . .—From Papers Published 1735*. Routledge, 1927.

HIRSCHFELD, Magnus, *Sexual Anomalies and Perversions*. London Encyclopaedic Press, 1938.

HOLYROYD, James Edward, *The Gaslight Murders*. Allen & Unwin, 1960.

HUMPHREYS, Christmas, *Seven Murderers*, Heinemann, 1931.

HUSON, Richard, *Sixty Famous Trials*. Daily Express Publication, 1938.

HYDE, H. Montgomery, *Sir Patrick Hastings, His Life and Cases*. Heinemann, 1960.

IRVING, H. B., *A Book of Remarkable Criminals*. Cassell, 1918.

JENKINS, Elizabeth, *Six Criminal Women*. Sampson Low Marston & Co., 1949. Pan Books, 1958.

KENNEDY, Ludovic, *Ten Rillington Place: Christie and Evans*. Gollancz, 1961.

KING, Veronica and Paul, *Problems of Modern American Crime*. Heath Cranton Ltd., 1924.

KINGSTON, Charles, *Remarkable Rogues . . . Some Notable Criminals of Europe and America*. John Lane, 1921.

LABORDE, Jean, *Amour, Que de Crimes . . .* (Pauline Buisson, etc.). Gallimard, 1954.

LEFEBURE, Molly, *Evidence for the Crown*. Heinemann, 1955.

LEOPOLD, Nathan, *Life Plus Ninety-Nine Years*. Gollancz, 1958.

McCORMICK, Donald, *The Identity of Jack the Ripper*. Jarrolds, 1959.

MACKIEWICZ, Joseph, *The Katyn Wood Murders*. Hollis and Carter, 1951.

MATTERS, Leonard, *Jack the Ripper*. W. H. Allen, 1950. (Pinnacle Book.)

MAYHEW, Henry, London's Underworld; Extracts from Mayhew's *London Labour and the London Poor*. Edited by Peter Quennell. Spring Books, 1951.

NOTABLE BRITISH TRIALS SERIES edited by Harry Hodge. William Hodge. London.

PARTRIDGE, Ralph, *Broadmoor; a History of Criminal Lunacy and its Problems*. Chatto and Windus, 1953.

PEARCE, Charles E., *Unsolved Murder Mysteries*. Stanley Paul, 1924.

PELHAM, Camden, *Chronicles of Crime, or the New Newgate Calendar*. 2 volumes. Reeves and Turner, 1886.

PENGUIN FAMOUS TRIALS SERIES edited by Harry Hodge. Penguin Books.

PLAYFAIR, Giles *and* SINGTON, Derrick, *The Offenders: Society and the Atrocious Crime*. Secker & Warburg, 1957.

RUSSELL, Lord, *The Scourge of the Swastika*. Cassell. *The Knights of Bushido*. Cassel, 1958.

SCOTT, Sir Harold, *Scotland Yard*. André Deutsch, 1954.

SIMPSON, Dr Keith, *Forensic Medicine*. Arnold, 1947.

SMITH-HUGHES, Jack. *Nine Verdicts on Violence*. Cassell, 1956. *Six Ventures in Villainy*. Cassell, 1955. *Unfair Comment Upon Some Victorian Murder Trials*. Cassell, 1951.

SMITH, Sir Sydney, *Mostly Murder*. Autobiography. Harrap, 1959.

SONDERN, Frederic, *Brotherhood of Evil: the Mafia*. Gollancz, 1959.

STEAD, Philip John, editor. *Memoirs of Lacenaire*. Staples Press, 1952.

STEKEL, Dr Wilhelm, *Sexual Aberrations*. 2 volumes. Vision Press, 1953.

SVENSSON, Arne *and* WENDEL, Otto, *Crime Detection*. Cleaver-Hume Press. London, 1955.

TALLANT, Robert, *Murder in New Orleans*. William Kimber, 1953.

TRAINI, Robert, *Murder for Sex, and Cases of Manslaughter Under the New Act*. William Kimber, 1960.

WAGNER, Margaret Seaton, *The Monster of Düsseldorf: the Life and Trial of Peter Kürten*. Faber & Faber, 1932.

WAR CRIMES TRIALS SERIES edited by Sir David Maxwell Fyfe, 1948.

WEBB, Duncan, *Deadline for Crime*. Muller, 1955.

WILKINS, Albert, editor, *Inside the French Courts*. Hutchinson.

WILSON, John Gray, *The Trial of Peter Manuel*. Secker & Warburg, 1959.

659

CLASSIFIED INDEX

665

GENERAL INDEX